I PROTEST
Selected Disquisitions of E. W. Scripps

E. W. Scripps, in preferred garb, with "Miramar" in background

I PROTEST

SELECTED DISQUISITIONS OF

E. W. SCRIPPS

EDITED AND WITH A
BIOGRAPHICAL INTRODUCTION
BY OLIVER KNIGHT

MADISON, MILWAUKEE, AND
LONDON
THE UNIVERSITY OF WISCONSIN
PRESS, 1966

Published by
The University of Wisconsin Press
Madison, Milwaukee, and London
P.O. Box 1379
Madison, Wisconsin 53701
Copyright © 1966 by the
Regents of
the University of Wisconsin
Printed in
the United States of America
by North Central Publishing Co.,
St. Paul, Minnesota
Library of Congress Catalog Card
Number 66-11806

For Margaret C. Hawkins

Preface

This book resulted from a chance encounter. At the annual meeting of the Association for Education in Journalism, at Pennslyvania State University in 1960, Professor John Stempel, chairman of the department of journalism in Indiana University, where I was then teaching, told me the research director of Scripps-Howard Newspapers was looking for a historian with a newspaper background who might be interested in editing the papers of E. W. Scripps. Professor Stempel had given him my name, and then urged me to see him. More curious than interested at that point, I stepped into the next room and met the research director, Dr. John Scott Davenport, who explained that Scripps had written a number of disquisitions, and invited me to the firm's Cincinnati office to examine them.

A short time later, I visited Cincinnati and met Charles E. Scripps, Scripps' grandson and now chairman of the board, who suggested that I take copies of the disquisitions home with me, read them, and appraise their publishable worth. After reading twelve bound volumes of carbon copies of Scripps' disquisitions, short stories, and plays, I felt certain that some disquisitions should be published. Curiosity had turned into intense interest.

Charles Scripps and I then entered into a contract by which he paid all expenses of research and writing, but which guaranteed my scholarly independence in doing the job as I saw fit. Throughout the association I have become ever more appreciative of Mr. Scripps' awareness of the historical worth of these papers and of his research-oriented attitude.

In the first assessment of the project, I saw the book as a collection of documents presenting the thinking of one man who had been in a position to exercise considerable influence. As such, it ordinarily would have called for only a minimum of biographical and historical background. But research in Scripps' personal papers made it clear that the biographies of Scripps had been inadequate, and that something more had to be done if a reader were to be able to place the disquisitions in perspective.

Three biographers have written of Scripps. The first, Gilson Gardner, had been Washington correspondent for the Scripps newspapers and a Scripps intimate. His book *Lusty Scripps* made limited use of Scripps' papers, and emphasized the bizarre as much as anything else. The second, Negley D. Cochran, had been a Scripps editor and also an intimate. His book *E. W. Scripps* lacks balance and research. The third, Charles McCabe, was then married to a Scripps granddaughter. The book that he edited, *Damned Old Crank; A Self-Portrait of E. W. Scripps Drawn from His Unpublished Writings*, is both unfair and superficial.

The resulting problem became nettlesome. Obviously, more biographical treatment was called for. Yet the presentation of a document collection forbade the full development of a critical biography. The question, then, was: How much biography and within what limits?

The answer seemed to lie in concentrating on the formative elements in Scripps' career, those personality characteristics that projected into his thinking and writing, and those documents that illuminated the disquisitions. In short, the biographical introduction attempts to focus upon only those aspects of Scripps' life which would make the disquisitions more understandable.

To make the demarcation clearer, for those few who might be interested, a full biography of Scripps or a history of the Scripps newspapers would cause an author perforce to comb the newspapers to determine whether they adhered to or deviated from Scripps' stated principles. I considered such an evaluation as beyond the scope of the work in hand, particularly since the secondary sources in journalism history have united in describing Scripps newspapers in terms that agreed with Scripps' avowals of purpose. Similarly, a full evaluation of Scripps' life and work would call for presentation of both sides of the family quarrel that broke out at the time of World War I, particularly the clash between Scripps and his eldest son. But, within the scope of this book, it is considered sufficient merely to note that Scripps did face a challenge to his familial authority and to present his points of view theretoward, again as a means of making clearer his general attitudes as reflected in the disquisitions. Regrettably, this approach biases the account in Scripps' favor, but physical limitations precluded an analysis of so complex a situation.

The bulk of the basic research into the life and characteristics of E. W. Scripps was done at his home, "Miramar," north of San Diego, during the summer of 1961. Historical research, while a happy calling under any circumstances, would be happier still if it all could be done in the atmosphere that Mrs. Margaret C. Hawkins provided through her hospitality at "Miramar"; Mrs. Hawkins was the widow of Scripps' son, Robert P. Through the weeks of research, she never failed to give generously of her time in discussing her recollections of Scripps and in arranging for me to meet and talk with individuals who provided information not to be found in documents. Through her thoughtfulness, I worked in the adobe-walled suite that had been Scripps' own. Miss Eloyse A. Johnson, secretary of the Ellen B. Scripps Foundation, guided me through the mass of materials in the "Miramar" files, pointing out collections that might have been overlooked otherwise.

Interviews with several persons who knew Scripps well also broadened my understanding of Scripps. Scripps' one surviving child, Mrs. Nackey Scripps Meanley, whose ranch adjoins "Miramar," answered questions freely and candidly, besides making available some of the letters received from her father. Also in California, I had the assistance of E. F. Elfstrom and Jerry Clemans, who served as Scripps' secretaries during the declining years when Scripps lived most of the time aboard his yacht. Later, Roy W. Howard, now dead, devoted an entire day in his New York office to answering questions about Scripps; Howard had been with the Scripps organization since 1905, first building the United Press from a fledgling into a global news service before being handpicked by Scripps to help guide the destiny of a new combination — Scripps-Howard — shortly after World War I.

At "Miramar" I concentrated on family correspondence, especially that which was the most vital to an understanding of Scripps — the voluminous correspondence between him and his sister Ellen. His letters to her stood in lieu of a diary from 1880 until his death, and her letters to him analyzed his character and personality as no other source does.

Because time prevented their examination at "Miramar," the 60 Letterbooks of Scripps' general correspondence — books in which carbon copies were pasted — were microfilmed. The resulting 30 reels, representing about 37,500 pages, were examined in Madison during the fall and winter of 1961–62. Later, Scripps' private files and other documents in the Cincinnati office of the E. W. Scripps Trust were consulted through the assistance of Robert F. Winkler, secretary-treasurer of the Trust.

Throughout the research, Dr. Davenport — who is now executive assistant to Mr. Scripps — remained the central point of contact. Without his enthusiastic support of the project and his never-failing assistance in clearing the way to essential document collections, this book would never have come into being.

When the time came to prepare the disquisitions for publication, I used photographic reproductions of the original disquisitions, which are in the

Cincinnati office. Each was chosen on the basis of the idea presented, and the cogency, clarity, and literary artistry (if any) with which it was presented. Division of the disquisitions into subject areas is purely my responsibility. The originals are bound chronologically, which makes it difficult to grasp Scripps' thinking on any one subject, because he discussed one subject today, another the next time.

When the manuscript was completed, it was read in whole or in part by Professors Ralph Nafziger, Scott Cutlip, and Jack Barbash of the University of Wisconsin; Vernon Carstensen, then at Wisconsin but now at the University of Washington; and Edwin Emery, University of Minnesota. To each of them I hereby express my gratitude, and, in that banal academic expression, absolve them from all blame for the book's shortcomings. The meticulous editing of Mrs. Margaret Hickey made the book better than the manuscript had been.

In conclusion, as a relativist I must confess to certain biases. A newspaperman before I became a historian, I cannot help sympathizing with Scripps' ideals of journalism. Furthermore, I came to like E. W. Scripps — at a distance, for Scripps would seem to have been an abrasive personality who would have been utterly impossible in daily contact, yet one who can evoke empathy when his intimate papers are read more than a generation after his death.

OLIVER KNIGHT

August, 1965

Contents

REFORM

POLITICS

FOREIGN AFFAIRS

AMERICAN BUSINESS AND LABOR

Illustrations

ABOUT THE DISQUISITIONS

You are about to meet a vigorous American thinker who emerges from obscurity for the first time in these pages. In meeting him you also will encounter him: a crusty individualist rebelling against custom, mediocrity, and the status quo; or a jeering misanthrope; or a great idealist; he can sometimes be read in a number of ways.

Although E. W. Scripps was known as the little-known publisher whose chain of small evening newspapers fought for reform and the common man, only a few of his contemporaries had the opportunity to recognize him as an important thinker in their time. A complex man of many contradictions, Scripps stood in shadows of his own making. But the fact that his seclusion hid him from public view as a thinker does not mean that his rebellion, protest, and creative thought were wasted on solitude. On the contrary, as a direct actionist he brought his influence to bear without projecting his name and personality into unwanted prominence.

A forceful intellect harnessed to explosive energy made Scripps a questing thinker throughout his life. An insatiable hunger for knowledge made him a scholar of greater calibre than many who devote their lives to scholarship. These qualities he combined in the disquisitions which have remained private documents until now, except for the publication of a scattered few which have done justice neither to the man nor to the body of thought contained in them. Regarding himself as an anthropologist and sociologist as well as journalist, practical economist, political thinker, iconoclast, and reformer, he seemingly paled at no topic.

Before encountering him, however, you must heed a word of caution: Some of these selected disquisitions may not necessarily reflect Scripps' personal conclusions, beliefs, or even inclinations. The principal reason for this seeming paradox is that Scripps was an "experimental" thinker. He would take an idea just because it was an idea and develop it, simply to see where it would lead. Sometimes the result was startling, as in "Belligerent Rights in Class Warfare." Or he would react against a book that presented only one point of view — his own, if you please — and deliberately construct the opposite. Sometimes he stood at the bar as the devil's advocate, presenting the contrary of what he believed or wanted to believe. But the products of advocate and devil's advocate, of experiment and conviction, were all mixed in his files without any guide whatsoever as to which was which.

One might assume that Scripps' other personal papers (his correspondence and memoranda) would flux the genuine from the hypothetical and the whimsical. Unfortunately for the assumption, Scripps wrote letters the same way he wrote disquisitions — throwing out ideas to stimulate the thinking of lieutenants, friends, and correspondents. No letter could be considered as authoritative unless he signed it personally. He signed precious few. He left no clear-cut articles of faith, no comprehensive statement of "This I Believe."

Still another complication arises from Scripps' moodiness. A man who swung rapidly between elation and depression, he expressed himself convincingly in whatever mood. Contradictions result because, as he put it, "My convictions, if such, vary with the condition of my liver." [1]

The possibility that one disquisition might be inconclusive or non-representative can also be seen in any series of disquisitions in which he grappled with the same general subject. An example is the series, written over a period of several years, in which he wrestled with the problem of environment versus heredity as the determinant of character and achievement. Eugenics troubled him similarly. Even more clearly do disquisitions on socialism illustrate the point. For many years before World War I, Scripps sympathized with socialism in theory only, discussed it on several occasions, and even conceded that it might be the way of the future, but personally he could never accept or endorse socialism. As an autocrat with a towering sense of individualism, he could not reconcile collectivism with his moral principles and naturalistic conception of the universe. He approached such bothersome subjects from various angles in different disquisitions.

The warning against automatic acceptance of any given disquisition as being representative of Scripps' convictions must not be carried so far as to rob the disquisitions of their vitality and individualism. Nor must it obscure the fact that Scripps presented conclusions based on his own accumulated knowledge most of the time, and sometimes expressed private opinions that were not meant to be recognized by others.

---

[1] "What's the Use?" May 23, 1909, E. W. Scripps Writings, 2:164, hereafter referred to as EWS Writings. Page numbers are from the original set of volumes.

Most of the disquisitions here presented probably do reflect Scripps' attitudes, except where noted, but some may not. Even this reservation is necessary, because allowance must be made for Scripps' cultivated inconsistency, his maxim that thinking is the hardest work a man can do and that most men fail because they do not do enough of it, and his determined effort to excite people to their utmost mental effort regardless of his personal views on a given subject.

However, it would be in keeping with the spirit of Scripps to ask: "What difference does it make whether they portray one man's personal opinions? The important consideration is the merit of thought as thought and the possible good an idea might bring to humanity even if it harmed him who brought it forth."

Because the disquisitions were not written for publication, Scripps did not have to place his name and reputation behind every one. The result is that the disquisitions represent his bold, independent, and unadorned thinking.

In a sense, the writing of the disquisitions represents the realization of a youthful dream. Coming from an Illinois farm family where books were as important as chores, Scripps early developed a lifelong habit of constant, extensive, perhaps compulsive reading. From early years he substituted independent, eclectic reading for the formal education for which he nourished outspoken contempt.

The childhood reading, plus the tradition of a literary family, led to boyhood dreams of a literary career. But circumstances deflected him into the newspaper business from which he never was able — and probably did not really want — to cut loose. Preoccupation with the building of a newspaper group, now known as Scripps-Howard, kept him from writing during the active years of his business life, but did not diminish his reading or stifle his far-ranging mind.

Finally, when he did retire in 1908 (retirement always was a relative term with him), he released part of his pent-up ambition and part of his demanding energy in writing the disquisitions, on which he set great personal store. He did not start from scratch, for he had looked upon himself as a thinker and philosopher from early manhood. Continuing but possibly intensifying his earlier habits, he came to conclude ruefully that he was about the only man he knew who really had time to sit on a hill and read and think.

He made a hardpan estate north of San Diego the hub of his universe through discourse with carefully chosen visitors and through an almost incredible diet of books and magazines. The resultant intellectual stimulation, plus the long-stored facts of his almost total recall memory, produced about 500 disquisitions. All but 11 were written between retirement in 1908 and death in 1926. Only a handful of persons ever saw even some of the disquisitions, and none but his personal staff saw all of them. His devoted sister, Ellen Browning Scripps, received a copy of almost every disquisition, but some he withheld even from her.

Despite the great pains he took to shut himself off from public view, a few contemporaries knew of and respected his power of thought and his burning desire to right the social and economic ills of America in the late nineteenth and early twentieth centuries. The few kindred souls who sought him out, or were sought out, had the good fortune to read one or more of the disquisitions. An even smaller number had the opportunity to discuss specific disquisitions with him.

Sometimes he pulled out a recent disquisition and read it to a visitor to illuminate some point in their conversation, as he did with Lincoln Steffens and Clarence Darrow on one occasion. When he wrote one he thought might be good, he mailed copies of it to writers he respected, the economist Scott Nearing was one, and asked for their criticism. Mostly, however, the disquisitions remained in his files.

During his eighteen years as literary gentleman in chambers, he gave various reasons for writing the disquisitions — for the education of his children because he wanted them to become original thinkers, for the benefit of his grandchildren, to help clarify his thinking, for amusement, as a diary. Yet he could concede that "I have still secretly hugged the hope that I was really a philospher and an original genius who would possibly, and even probably, produce at least some matter which would be of great value to the public, if ever submitted to." [2]

He also linked his purpose to his position as head of his newspapers — what he called the Scripps institution or the Concern. Upon retiring in 1908 he relinquished only business control to his eldest son, James G., retaining personal editorial control until 1911. In the latter year he wrote: "Of late years instead of personally controlling, directing, and teaching my sons and my other lieutenants, I have resorted to the practice of writing certain disquisitions . . . causing these to circulate in the way of carbon copies among those who must be kept informed not only of my opinion but my resolution. . . ." [3]

In addition, he once said, "One thing is certain, that not until I formulate in writing the results of any of my thinking do they become enduring elements in my mind." [4]

[2] "Esau's Birthright, The Mess of Pottage," Feb. 16, 1910, EWS Writings, 3:80.

[3] E. W. Scripps to C. D. Willard, Apr. 29, 1911, EWS Writings, 3:368. Hereafter, letters from E. W. Scripps will be cited as from EWS.

[4] Unsent letter from EWS to Gilson Gardner, Aug. 6, 1916. See Bibliography.

Looking back in 1922, he recognized that the disquisitions might influence posthumous opinions of him: "yet of all the things I have ever written, I believe [that] in these disquisitions I have expressed myself most frankly on such subjects as I have written of." [5]

During the last months of life another purpose appears to have crept in. He seemed to have sought desperately to sum up his views and find the meaning of life as he had lived it.

Given Scripps' inconsistency and volatility, one could infer that each of the assigned reasons should be read as the reason of the moment, were it not for the fact that Scripps' will left all the disquisitions in trust for his grandchildren until the youngest reached the age of twenty-one. That fact alone indicates that his pre-eminent purpose was to benefit first his children and then their children. Parenthetically, that view illustrates two of Scripps' stronger personal characteristics — Scripps the patriarch and Scripps the teacher. His other purposes, while consistent with his nature, thus devolve into minor and even temporary positions.

Quite aside from purpose, one motivation appears to be constant throughout his years of production. It is this: "My temperament seems to demand some sort of creative or constructive work, and writing seems to at least partially satisfy this craving." [6]

Yet there seems to be a purpose or motive left unsaid anywhere in Scripps' papers. Various qualities of his character seem to reflect an effort to break through the barriers of the unknown and arrive at Meaning: his crackling vitality of thought; his fascination with man; his ability to synthesize; his impatience with ordinary thought patterns within carefully marked-off disciplines; his frustrating attempts to reconcile idealism with harsh realism; his efforts to substitute common-sense naturalism for the artificial strictures of custom and religion; his once-excited effort to stimulate "an entire new system of investigations of sociology, economics, and psychology, and to at least make a start in a new way, considering the effects of environment." [7]

Scripps' earliest and clearest statement of purpose is contained in the following excerpt from "Has a Man a Right to Live?" dated December 10, 1908. Incidentally, this discussion of the disquisitions bears no recognizable relation to the central idea of the disquisition — characteristically so, for many disquisitions were of similar conglomerate construction. He wrote:

Some of my friends and visitors have been reading some of my essays. Some of them have been very complimentary in their expressions. They naturally would

[5] EWS to Gilson Gardner, Sept. 9, 1922, EWS Writings, 10:153.
[6] EWS to Ellen Browning Scripps, Apr. 16, 1925. Hereafter, letters between Scripps and Miss Scripps will be cited as EWS to EBS, and vice versa.
[7] EWS to EBS, Apr. 25, 1918.

be: in the first place, they are my guests; in the second place, many of them are beholden to me for employment and business opportunities.

Some of these men have even gone so far as to urge me to publish, or permit to be published, some of my disquisitions or at least to allow them to be used by other men than myself for the purpose of being furbished up and put in more practical shape for publication.

At times I feel a little conceited, and then I think that some day I will reread the essays and edit them or rewrite them for publication. I am sure that some of them furnish very acceptable reading matter to larger or smaller numbers of people.

Why should they not do so? They have one characteristic — that is to say, some of them have the characteristic — of being perfectly frank. They are expressions of my own actual thoughts — some of them are. Some of them are mere whimsical fancies: a development of some bizarre idea. But even when they are the latter, they still have the quality of what might be called a confession of my own fundamental, moral principles.

Now, for a good part of my life I have been a writer for the public, and during all my life I have spent a great deal of my time in reading what other people have written.

Now, I know that no man who writes for the public ever thinks of (he never dares) being perfectly candid. Every writer knows that he is a hypocrite, and every writer knows that every reader of his knows that he is a hypocrite, in that he expresses on many subjects convictions and opinions which he does not hold.

.   .   .   .

If there is any real merit in my disquisitions, I am certain of one thing and that is that nearly all of the merit would disappear — that is to say, would not have come into existence — had I been writing for publication.

As a matter of fact, I did not begin this particular series of papers with any idea that they would be read by anyone; and it was only because it did not occur to me that my secretary would ever think of showing them that I did not prohibit their exposure. However, I took no exception to his course, but was rather amused and interested, and, truth to say, somewhat flattered by the idea that I had been "discovered," even by a few of my intimate partisans. In fact, I found that I had been writing for a public, little as it was. One very natural and marked effect of this has been that I find that I am not so candid now as I have been sometimes in the past.

It is true that from the beginning the character of my papers has been largely affected because there was at least one reader, namely, the stenographer, and still more largely affected by the fact that I had not only no objections to but rather a desire for the reading of some of my essays by my own sons. In a way, I have sometimes regarded these essays in the nature of private lectures to my children. I have always felt like turning myself inside out to the boys. I suppose that every normal parent has more or less of this propensity to nourish its offspring at no matter how great a personal sacrifice.

Pepys could never have written the diary that he did write except in the form and manner that he did write.

. . . .

Pepys might well have thought (I do not myself know whether he provided or intended to provide for any future translation and publication) that the chances were a million to one that those things which he wrote would be known to no one but himself.

I presume that ordinarily but very few men would concur in this idea. "Why," most people would ask, "would a man take the trouble to write to no one but himself?" I believe I know why, and I believe that there are and have been a great many other men who know why, he should have done this very thing.

Men think to themselves long and hardly [*sic*], and they think much of many things which they do not intend to ever communicate to human beings. A number of men even commune with themselves by word of mouth. They take pleasure in putting into words, and hearing those words speaking, their inward thoughts, and such men are generally covered with confusion and filled with mortification if perchance their words have been heard by even those near to them in affinity.

I know for myself that I have long, perhaps all my life, indulged in writing for no purpose of publication or giving information of any kind to others, but for the sole purpose of enjoying the exercise of formulating my own thoughts; and also for the profit that I derive from the fact of having so formulated my thoughts, since this practice assists memory.

Were I on a desert island, hopeless of rescue, profoundly convinced that no other living person would ever discover my hiding place or any relics of myself, and had I writing facilities, I am sure that no small part of my recreation would consist of writing things for no reader.

Two points in Scripps' exposition require emphasis. First, he had been writing for himself alone, he thought, and it was the secretary, not Scripps, who first called the attention of others to the writings. At the time, the secretary was Harry Schmetzstorff, who later changed his name to Smithton. Second, Scripps referred to his writings interchangeably as essays and disquisitions. Later he came gradually to refer to them almost invariably as disquisitions.

Adoption of the word "disquisition" indicates the seriousness with which Scripps approached the work. Many years later Smithton said "disquisition" was chosen carefully from different available words.[8] Clearly, then, Scripps intended rigorous examination following serious investigation, as contrasted with what might be considered the somewhat lighter nature of an essay. It is equally clear that the disquisitions do not always live up to the designation.

His 500 disquisitions deal, among other things, with religion, social con-

[8] Harry L. Smithton, "Notes."

science, riches, coming revolution, principles of journalism, eugenics, heredity, morality, national wealth, political bosses, a coming war with Japan,
political reforms, temperance versus alcoholism, biology from a philosophical point of view, population problems, international affairs, women, Utopia, sex, character analyses of relatives and associates, man and nature, gold
supplies, child labor, snobs, astronomy, minimum wage, education, agriculture, rattlesnakes. Naturally such an outpouring is of uneven quality. On
some subjects he could be reckoned an expert. On others, such as science,
where institutions of his founding or encouragement were greater contributions than his thought, he did not presume to be more than a dilettante.

The disquisitions indicate that his thinking revolved to a large extent
within a circle — albeit a large circle of social justice, economics, politics,
international affairs, and journalism — and that he missed much of what
went on in the world in spite of his wide reading. Like most people, he just
did not keep abreast of everything. For instance, he happened to be in
Chicago in 1914, on his first trip east of the Rockies in many years, and was
shocked at the change that had come about in women's fashions.

Another facet of the disquisitions illustrates an important personal
characteristic. Although concerned above all with man, his concern was with
man in the abstract. Devoted to the interests of the common man, he wanted
nothing to do with the common man personally. In fact, he was fond of
quoting an unnamed author who had said he would die for the common man
but not live with him. Not even in his personal relations could Scripps come
down to the plane of little things that give life its effervescence. He was almost pure intellect, and could not characteristically write with deep warmth.

His egocentrism likewise shows through in this description of the disquisitions:

> Having acquired the habit by long practice of writing, my retirement from
> active journalism did not relieve me from the necessity of expressing myself. I
> soon enough found that I could enjoy myself even more by speaking to no audi-
> ence than I ever enjoyed myself while talking to the million. This was because I
> have felt perfectly free to say anything I damn please, to write things that might
> cause me to be tarred and feathered or even hung if what I wrote appeared in
> the public press.[9]

Scripps' methods were as individualistic as everything else about him. Apparently the idea for a disquisition could come from anywhere — from observations past and present, reflections, something read, something heard
in conversation, reminiscence. Then he turned it over in his mind for days

---

[9] EWS to Frederic C. Howe, Apr. 1, 1919.

and maybe weeks. On two occasions, in 1910 and 1922, he said he did not attempt to develop a disquisition until the idea had occupied his mind for some time. Apparently, then, that aspect remained constant. Also, it appears that he developed the idea through reason alone, without bothering to test a thesis through research.

When ready to proceed, he called in his secretary, almost always a man, and began dictating. Most often, a disquisition took the ordinary form, but sometimes he made disquisitions of his regular correspondence. As he dictated, he was a completely free agent, knowing he wrote for no man's eye during his lifetime. "I do not have to be conventional," he said. "I do not have to be correct, even, for I do not have to fear the criticism of any man; and, better still, I do not have to express myself in such a way as to be comprehensible to a composite audience. I am not driven to modify my words so as not to give offense to one class or so as to attract the attention of another." [10]

When he was through, he was through. Rarely did he trouble to edit the disquisitions or even to review them after transcription. One after another bears the notation, "Not Reviewed by EWS after Dictation." Only those he regarded as having particular importance received a second look — those pertaining to control of his newspapers, for example.

Because he did not call for the disquisitions again for editing and polishing, the shorthand notes might long repose on the secretary's table before being transcribed. Consequently, error of undeterminable proportion may be inherent in many of them, through stenographic error. Except where Scripps edited the disquisitions, the stenographic errors are still there, compounded by instances where Scripps may not have expressed himself accurately.

Several aspects of Scripps' character account for his negligence in this regard, if so it can be called. First, he was a creator, an idea man. Detesting detail, he galloped from concept to concept, leaving routine and administration to carefully chosen lieutenants. Another factor is best presented in his words:

After I have dictated a disquisition, I experience a feeling of spiritual exhaustion, an exhaustion so great that it makes even a casual revision of same for the purpose of eliminating stenographic errors a painful process. I have never, I think, reread, except for revision purposes, any of my disquisitions. I have trusted the documents to the care of the chance occupant of the secretary's office. [Scripps had twenty-seven secretaries between 1908 and 1926, all but four of them men.] I am so constructed constitutionally that I have as much or more

[10] Unsent letter from EWS to William S. U'Ren, Dec. 21, 1914.

aversion to the inspection of the excreta of my brain as I have to inspecting my physical excrement.[11]

When the secretary typed the disquisitions, he made a varying number of carbons. Ordinarily, one copy always went to Ellen B. Scripps and, for many years, a copy went regularly to Robert F. Paine, an editorial chief of various titles who refused to stop working even in retirement. Otherwise, the number of carbons depended upon how extensive a circulation Scripps intended for the disquisition.

Through dictation Scripps encased the disquisitions in the brittle English of speech. Given to intricate thought patterns, he wound up some sentences beyond the capability of a Philadelphia lawyer, and left them that way. He simply did not possess the temperament of a stylist, nor would he labor over form and design.

That he was aware of his waterlogged style is shown in the following letter to his former partner, Milton A. McRae; it must be read with the understanding that Scripps could, and often did, excuse himself through rationalization:

I read over again last night your speech to the Detroit boys about "climbing the hill on the road to success." I did so for the purpose of making a sort of mental comparison between your composition and my own. [McRae was an articulate man who loved the limelight as much as Scripps detested it.]

Of course I know that there is, and ought to be, considerable difference in the composition of speeches and essays. Still, he who speaks lucidly is apt to write lucidly, while he who in writing uses complex and involved sentences is sure to use similar language in speaking. I would consider it the greatest boon if I were able to express the things that I think in language as plain and intelligent as that which you use.

I think there is a marked difference between us two in one respect. You want to get an idea into your hearer's mind as quickly as possible, and to spare your hearer all mental labor in grasping your theories and effects. On the other hand, I experience a sort of devilish pleasure in clothing my ideas in words that will mystify the indolent-minded, or excite the greatest possible amount of mental energy on the part of the one who really wants to understand.

In fact, by instinct, I am esoteric. Notwithstanding this certain kind of pleasure I enjoy in formulating involved sentences, I regret it, since even if I do make my readers work to understand me, I must do a whole lot of unnecessary work in setting them the task.

If I were a writer for the public, if I desired to gain their money, or fame from

[11] EWS to J. C. Harper, longtime counsel for the Scripps-McRae League, Aug. 29, 1916.

the public, I would have long before this labored hard to forego my own style and to learn your style, or a style similar to your own. . . .[12]

His admission of being esoteric by instinct may help explain the convoluted structure of some disquisitions, as may this cryptic remark: "forget it not, I am by profession at least a despiser of logic." [13] One author came to the rather startling conclusion that Scripps sought nothing less than to discover a new way of thinking.[14] However, nothing in substantiation of that conclusion has been found in 50,000 or more pages of Scripps' personal papers. Still, the "despiser of logic" may have to be regarded as an inferential key to the conglomerate construction. Possibly a more reasonable explanation is that the conglomeration results from a stream of consciousness as Scripps sought to say as much as possible in one sitting. That Scripps often "warmed up" in conversation for minutes and sometimes hours before getting to the point tends to reinforce this explanation.

While he secretly hoped he might be discovered as an "original genius," he sometimes was startled to discover that he was not always original. There were times, he remarked, when he found to his "surprise and humiliation" that someone else had presented the same or similar views months, years, or even centuries before.[15]

With two exceptions, Scripps adamantly refused to let his disquisitions be published in full or in part. However, the issuance of some to his chief editorial lieutenants at least implies that they could be used for guidance or as raw material for editorials. To maintain his position he had to resist the sometimes insistent demands of intellectual leaders who became enthusiastic about the worth of certain disquisitions. For instance, Steffens became so eager to have "Arithmetic and Humanity" appear in print that he telegraphed for permission to publish it after he had received a copy for comment. That is the disquisition filled with the poignancy of a father's thoughts who, waiting for his favorite son to die, turns his thoughts away from self and toward humanity as a whole.

Only two definitely are known to have been published during Scripps' lifetime. The first was "America First," written in 1915 as he contemplated the effects of war on America. What he called a "garbled" version was distributed by his own Newspaper Enterprise Association. The full text appeared in *Harper's Weekly*,[16] which ceased publication the next month, as

---

[12] EWS to Milton A. McRae, Jan. 6, 1917.
[13] "A Blind Leader of the Blind," July 20, 1921, EWS Writings, 9:201.
[14] Charles R. McCabe (ed.), *Damned Old Crank* (New York, 1951), p. viii.
[15] "Esau's Birthright, The Mess of Pottage," Feb. 16, 1910, EWS Writings, 3:80.
[16] *Harper's Weekly*, Apr. 8, 1916, pp. 373–74.

Scripps wryly remarked. The by-line read, "By a Famous American Editor." But Scripps' name was attached to the second one published, "Letter to the Editor of the *New Statesman*," which Scripps thought would be too long for that British journal. When the *New Statesman* published it [17] in the correspondence section it bore the title, "The Future of British Industry," and appeared above Scripps' name. An editor's note identified Scripps as the newspaper publisher who also was controlling owner of the United Press. On learning indirectly that the letter had been published, Scripps was as elated as a high-school boy who gets his first story in the hometown weekly, although he had not yet seen the issue containing his letter.

Despite his refusal to let the disquisitions be published during his lifetime, he anticipated eventual publication, even though he vacillated about it. In a moment of melancholia he could doubt that anything he had ever written would be of value to anyone except perhaps a curious grandchild.[18] At another point, he could say to Darrow that as a journalist he would not print "such stuff" because it would not pay to print it. Rather, he said: "If I were a great thinker and really knew that my thoughts were of the greatest value, I think that I would not make haste to publish by means of the printed page. I think that I would choose rather to lend my thoughts to the very few prophets who were my contemporaries." [19] That consideration may have actuated his periodic distribution of copies to leading thinkers with a request for their criticism.

For the most part, though, the evidence indicates that he did hope or expect they would be published after his death. A few of his comments in this regard also might bear upon his purposes in writing the disquisitions:

I have a suspicion that there are a number, at least a few, of my disquisitions that are worth careful preservation. I think that it is possible that, if I should have what is called a literary executor, some of these disquisitions could be assembled and edited and published, and that the publication of them would be a more or less valuable contribution to American letters.[20]

After comparing American with European scientists and economists to the disadvantage of the Americans as writers, he wrote his sister:

I am rather inclined to deduce from all this that my own disquisitions, just because of their flabbiness and their flimsiness and their journalisticness, might meet with some public favor if they were published. It is the likeness of these American writers to my own writings that causes my disapproval of them.[21]

[17] *New Statesman*, Nov. 4, 1916, pp. 107–9.
[18] EWS to EBS, Dec. 19, 1923.
[19] EWS to Clarence Darrow, Apr. 11, 1914.
[20] EWS to J. C. Harper, Aug. 29, 1916.
[21] EWS to EBS, June 23, 1922.

On another occasion he placed a recent group of disquisitions with all the others, "unprinted, and probably to be unprinted, at least until after my death." [22]

In 1922 he made his one and only effort to bring his papers together for publication. To his long-respected Washington correspondent, Gilson Gardner, he entrusted the editing of the disquisitions, along with two major documents — the "Autobiography" and "A Statement History of the Concern," which was a financial record of his newspapers. He expected Gardner to edit the disquisitions only in the sense of correcting obvious stenographic errors, knowing they had been mishandled by the ever-changing stream of secretaries, both in transcription and in preservation. But Gardner failed to satisfy Scripps on this one occasion, distorting the autobiography into a whitewash that aroused Scripps to wrath. Accordingly, Scripps directed in 1925 that all the papers be withdrawn from Gardner.

Retaining his faith in their publishable worth, he insisted that some might be valuable contributions "to a certain sort of literature."

"But," he added, "I think it is quite improbable that any capable and intelligent man would consent to labor through the great quantity of chaff in order to find the few grains that would be worth noticing." [23] He may have been right about that. At any rate, nothing more was done during the remaining six months of his life, and upon his death the disquisitions were frozen in the E. W. Scripps Trust until the youngest grandchild should reach age twenty-one, which event occurred in 1951.

The disquisitions were then to have become the property of his one remaining son, Robert P. But by that time Robert P. was dead, and the disquisitions passed to Robert P.'s estate, ultimately being transferred to his son, Charles E. Scripps. In the meantime, the disquisitions had been bound into four sets of twelve volumes each for distribution within the family.

For those presented here, evidence sometimes was available to indicate whether a given disquisition did or did not reflect Scripps' view; in such cases, that has been noted for the reader's convenience. Because so many disquisitions were not reviewed by Scripps after dictation, the positive rather than the negative has been shown — that is, those that were reviewed are so indicated, and the absence of comment means that a disquisition was not reviewed. Because the disquisitions were dictated and seldom revised, they do not represent the manual production of E. W. Scripps; therefore, they have been edited for mechanical style uniformity.

The disquisitions here presented come from the E. W. Scripps Writings, except where otherwise noted.

[22] EWS to EBS, June 13, 1925.
[23] EWS to Robert P. Scripps and Harry L. Smithton, Sept. 17, 1925.

ABOUT E. W. SCRIPPS

Right the Wrong
Smite the Strong
Whatever is, is Wrong

Loudly the voice of protest boomed from E. W. Scripps and echoed through more newspapers than any other man had ever controlled. He protested directly through his penny papers during the years of early struggle through the mid-1880's. But he left the writing to others in the years of ascendancy thereafter: as he built the first horizontal combination of newspapers, wire service, and syndicate; endowed his papers with social conscience; dedicated them to the common man's fight for social and economic justice; put the soul of a newspaper above the profits; and made protest the spirit of the Scripps papers.

BOYHOOD

Scripps' protest came from a rebelliousness that was stamped into him as the youngest in a family of thirteen children, growing up on the farm in Schuyler County, Illinois, where he was born on June 18, 1854. In another sense, he was the youngest in three families, for his father had children by each of three wives, resulting in loyalties and jealousies that produced much turbulence among the surviving offspring, notwithstanding the remarkably strong family bonds that held them together.

His father, James Mogg Scripps, had failed as a bookbinder in London before emigrating to America in 1844, a widower with six children. He came to America to take up a farm that his father, William Armiger Scripps, a London newspaper publisher, had bought near Rushville, Illinois, where other Scrippses had settled. William Armiger Scripps remained in England. En route to Illinois, James Mogg stopped off in Cleveland where he married his third wife, Julia Osborn, a thirty-year-old school teacher. Afraid of the raw farm, the city-bred James Mogg tried his hand at several other trades, failing in each, before the farm-bred Julia took the situation in hand. Under her lead the farm gave the enlarging family a fairly comfortable living.

19

His parents named him Edward Willis, but his middle name has been mis-spelled consistently as Wyllis. Various family records show both spellings, but he spelled it Willis on the only occasion on record on which he wrote his name in full — a will signed in 1906. Ordinarily, he signed his name as E. W. Scripps or Edward W. Scripps.

If Scripps was not an unwanted child, he thought he was, which may explain his ever-warring compulsions to win recognition on the one hand and crawl into a hole on the other. He once said he was born "of an acci-dent, the last expiring flame of passion burned to ashes in the aged bodies of my parents." [1] His mother was forty, his father fifty-two at the time of his birth. His being unwanted explains, perhaps, why his mother whipped him so often without any just cause that he could see, held that he was naturally wicked and bound for hell, and caused the other family members to regard him as the one most likely to disgrace them all. She filled his young life with traumatic experiences, and he probably did the same for her. With his sensi-tive, imaginative, brooding, individualistic nature, he so differed from all her other kin that she simply could not conceive that such a thing as he could be in existence — or so he interpreted it. He regarded his mother with bitterness until he was a grown man, [2] and never with real affection in any of his writings.

For mothering he turned to his half sister Ellen Browning Scripps, eighteen years his senior, a short, ill-proportioned, and homely woman whose sweet-ness, common sense, and serene assurance made her a family mainstay. El-len B. took young Eddie as her special charge. So dear became each to the other that the relationship virtually was that of mother and son, and they came to regard themselves as the two halves of a single identity. She molded his foremost characteristics — individualism, independent thought, idealism, and integrity. The family traits of strong-willed individualism and withdrawal may have predisposed him somewhat, but he and she were identical in nature and outlook, up to the point at which temperament set his turbulence apart from her placidity. While both found much with which to argue in the world, they responded differently. His rancor contrasted with her acceptance. To his "whatever is, is wrong" she counterpoised, "whatever is, is right." Where he rebelled, she said, "I accept." It was at that point that they complemented one another to form a spiritual and in-tellectual union.

Otherwise, her article of faith that every man should be himself was his. Her resentment at being forced to do anything was his. Her sense of re-

---

[1] E. W. Scripps to James E. Scripps, Apr. 20, 1889, hereafter cited as EWS to JES and vice versa.
[2] E. W. Scripps, "Autobiography," pp. 26–36.

sponsibility to the less fortunate members of the family was his; her disregard for money as such, his; her dislike for publicity, his; her freedom from the constraint of religious dogma, his; her wide range of intellectual interests, his; her unitary concept of the universe, his; her sense of personal responsibility, his; her love of solitude, his. So, too, their sense of justice. In fact, she was recognized as the mother of the "soul" of the E. W. Scripps newspapers that fought for the common man.

Throughout his adult life she almost invariably wrote an inspiring, encouraging, and ambition-prodding letter on his birthday, the general nature of which suggests that she may have filled the boy's head with the assurance that he was cut out for a grand role in life.

Ellen B. introduced the boy to the world of books in which he lived almost as much as in the world of man. Because English bookbinders kept one or more copies of each book bound, James Mogg Scripps had brought a handsome library to the Illinois farm. On long winter evenings the family gathered beside the fireplace and listened as Ellen B. read in her precise English accent.

With such encouragement he learned to read for himself before he was four or five. From then on a book was his constant companion, whether reading in bed with a snip of candle for light or during long hours on a fence rail. Being read to remained part of his daily routine as a grown man, especially as an aging man whose eyesight was so weakened that he seldom could read for himself.

He also had a champion in his half brother George H., who returned from the Civil War a cripple; the family had lost another son in the war. Fifteen years older than Scripps, George H. took up a farm near their father's when he came back from the war. Against the family predictions that Ed would become the black sheep, George H. insisted that he would turn out all right. Though sometimes sorely provoked at Scripps when they became associated in the newspaper business, the salt-tongued old bachelor saw to it that nothing bad ever happened to his younger brother.

Scripps also felt a close attachment for his two full sisters Annie [Julia Anne] and Virginia. The former, his senior by seven years, he made a confidant. The latter, but two years older than he, was as rambunctious as he. Plain and fancy profanity came to mark her forthright speech, and other family members either gave in or ducked her. But he seems not to have felt close to his full brother Fred.

The only happiness in his boyhood came from books, solitude, and Sister Ellen. Of the childhood joys drawn from shared pleasures with other children, he knew little or nothing, because playmates bored him with chatter or angered him with criticism. Growing up on the family farm, he was an ugly kid and an odd kid. His mop of seldom-trimmed red hair earned the derisive nickname of Turkey Egg, and a cast in his right eye created an ominous appearance of which he did not become aware for many years. He did not fit in with ordinary people thinking ordinary thoughts, for the ordinary insulted the quick intelligence, and conceit, of the child before he was old enough to know why. A creative flair and an indestructible shell of individualism made him refuse to accept anyone's rut. As a consequence, his family regarded him as troublesome and his teachers fought with him. Unable to do anything the way other people did it, he established rapport with hardly anyone. The lack of companionship drove him in upon himself, incubating a lifelong loneliness.

So awkward that he was the last one called when other boys chose sides, he rarely even played ball as a child nor could he stand up to another boy in a fight after he suffered rheumatism in his early teens. In addition, he was sickly throughout childhood and remained sickly (real and imagined) in spite of a robust appearance through life. As a boy he thought it unfair that he should be ill more than his brothers and sisters. All of which helped produce his rebellion.

> I was not happy. And as I recognized no God to complain to, and as I hadn't learned now to use the word "nature" as I use it now, I was constantly at a loss for an object to rail at. My general attitude was that of rebellion against everything.[3]

Loving nature, he found his moments of greatest exaltation during nature's most violent moods—thunderstorms and tornadoes. Although he loved the growing things, he detested the wearisome prairie and niggardly streams which denied his soul the beauty he craved. Nonetheless, being alone "in vacant places was for me to be in paradise as compared with being in the company of other human beings." [4] By trying to escape the tormenting presence of people, he early embedded escapism as an abiding characteristic. Escape meant solitude, solitude meant the chance to do exactly what he pleased, usually reading and daydreaming, and that meant happiness.

He also found some reassurance by holding himself superior to those about him, refusing to recognize anyone as his equal. He held them in disdain and felt they regarded him with contempt, which only gratified his vanity. Superciliously, he took the view that the respect of the people around him could be obtained only by one of their own kind, which he refused to be.[5]

To call him maladjusted and have done with it is to dismiss the significant.

[3] *Ibid.*, p. 42.
[4] *Ibid.*, p. 64.
[5] *Ibid.*, p. 62.

Man and boy, he knew the loneliness of the exceptional individual who finds congenial company but rarely and of the supreme egotist who seldom has patience for anyone else. Even the quicker-than-average man was too pedestrian for one of Scripps' intelligence, seriousness, depth, grasp, and conceit. Just as no playmate wore well with the boy, few men wore well with the man.

That Eddie Scripps was a contrary little monster is shown in the reverse of his sad and vainglorious recollections of childhood. Quick to storm, quick to tears, quick to sulk, quick to nurse imagined grievances, he was a wayward and strong-willed child. A glimpse of this is caught in a letter from his mother, after he had left home, who surmised that he would be happier back on the farm, "if you could have your own way and do just as you had a mind to. . . ." [6]

Because schoolteachers were imposed on him, he went around them, determined to get knowledge his way, not theirs. His way was to read whole books of his choosing, theirs to chop a small book into so many lessons. Consequently, he did not learn his lessons, failed in recitation, did not learn the multiplication table beyond seven. Some of his difficulty was due to a lack of verbal memory, although he otherwise had almost total recall of what he wanted to remember and the way he wanted to remember it. All along he knew himself to be the ablest pupil in school, even though the record showed him the poorest, a conclusion he reached in observing that his teachers gave him more attention and argued with him more than with other children.

In my case I made up my mind that the cause of all my trouble was that I had an original way of doing everything. I was just as successful in acquiring knowledge as I was unsuccessful in imitating other people's methods. My teachers gave me credit for what I did and were much interested in me, but they scolded me and marked me down because they would not or could not understand my way of doing things.[7]

Scripps left school when he was about fifteen, because his father had fallen into a lingering last illness, and young Scripps had to take over the farm, the four other sons being gone. Two abiding characteristics came to the fore when he assumed this responsibility — the ability to recognize and seize opportunity, and to get others to work for him. Both characteristics emerged in the same incident. Hiring Rushville boys of his own age to work in the fields, he saw an opportunity to get them to vie with each other. He paced off an equal number of rows for each boy to hoe and turned the work into a race with himself as referee. That got the work done and still let him do what

[6] E. W. Scripps, "History of the Scripps League," p. 13.
[7] E. W. Scripps to his son James G. Scripps, Dec. 14, 1900, hereafter cited as EWS to JGS and vice versa.

he wanted to do: sit in a fence corner and read.[8] Through his later business career Scripps had the same quickness to recognize opportunity and turn it to advantage. He also held firm to the rule that he would never do anything he could get someone else to do as well or better than he could.

Advancing toward manhood while his father lay dying, Scripps turned his thoughts to what he wanted to make of his life, reaching his year of decision in 1872. Constant reading through most of his eighteen years had seeded daydreams of a literary career,[9] but family example awakened an ambition to become a newspaperman. His grandfather, William Armiger Scripps, had been the first journalist in the family, editing the *True Briton* and publishing the London *Daily Sun*. A cousin, John Locke Scripps, helped found the Chicago *Tribune*. Other cousins established papers in Schuyler County.

Entry into journalism seemed almost assured because his half brother James E. was editor of the Detroit *Tribune*, but James E. dashed young Scripps' hopes. James E. wanted nothing to do with his sickly, self-centered, contentious half brother. He did not want him on the *Tribune*, and he most certainly did not want to look out for him in Detroit.

With the family avenue to journalism abruptly closed, his dying father became preoccupied with finding a place for Ed whom he regarded as the brightest but least promising of all the children. The father suggested clerking in a store, but Scripps scorned "trade" as though he were a young English aristocrat rather than the son of an Illinois farmer. At length, the father arranged for him to become a schoolteacher, and persuaded him to take the Newberry school a few miles from Rushville.

Scripps rode over to Newberry with a friend, Hiram Shields, the only boyhood friend remembered by name in Scripps' writings. Scripps made final arrangements with a school director who let him know that a nearby group of tough-looking boys would be his pupils. On the way home Scripps asked Shields what he thought the chances would be in case of a fight.

"Golly, Ed," Hiram said, "I know you can lick any one of them, maybe any two, but, darn it, if the whole crowd get on you, you are gone." [10]

A sudden opportunity to go to Detroit saved him from the onerous test by which many young schoolmasters were tried. After learning of the Detroit opportunity he withdrew gracefully and his sister Virginia took the school in his stead. He confessed candidly in later years that he did not know whether fear of those boys or the lure of journalism sent him to Detroit.[11]

[8] EWS, "Autobiography," p. 72 f.
[9] *Ibid.*, p. 55.
[10] EWS, "History of the Scripps League," p. 7.
[11] *Ibid.*

EARLY NEWSPAPER CAREER

Apparently the opportunity to go to Detroit in the fall of 1872 arose when his father and James E. agreed to advance several hundred dollars each to help a young English cousin open a drugstore in Detroit, arranging for Scripps to learn the drug trade with him. Scripps, however, told conflicting stories of how it came about. Scoffing at the absurdity of becoming a drug clerk, Scripps nonetheless seized the chance to go to Detroit, determining to get a place on the *Tribune* and filling his head with dreams of what he would accomplish as a newspaperman. At the same time, Scripps recognized he was ill-fitted for journalism. In a day when newspapermen wrote copy in longhand, he could write neither legibly nor in a straight line. Nor could he spell. Regarding a newspaper apprenticeship as the best corrective for his faults, he kept his sights fixed on the *Tribune*.

To ready himself for the trip, he called at a relative's store in Rushville where his teen-age cousin John S. Sweeney sold him a suit for fourteen dollars. He and Sweeney had played, quarreled, and hoed corn together, and were to quarrel, fight, and manage newspapers together. Scripps sewed into his vest eighty dollars that he had saved from selling firewood, produce, and coal strip-mined from the farm. He regarded the small hoard as a final reserve that would keep him from being absolutely dependent on anyone, and started the habit of always having a small "go to hell" fund beyond the reach of anyone else.

Packing his meager effects in an oilcloth traveling bag, he donned his father's overcoat, pocketed a railroad pass issued to the Detroit *Tribune*, boarded the train in Rushville on November 2, 1872, and headed north — a clumsy, six-foot, red-haired, thin-bearded country bumpkin off to whip the world. On the way he stopped in Chicago to visit an uncle, his first visit to a large city. Shocked and terrified, Scripps detested cities the rest of his life. While in Chicago he got caught in the rain, and his new suit shrank. The trousers crawled up his legs and the coat could not be buttoned. He did not forget that John Sweeney had sold it to him.

No one met him when his train pulled into the Michigan Central depot in Detroit on November 4. Trudging through slush and a falling wet snow, he made his way to the *Tribune* office, guided by a map drawn by his older brother Fred, who had worked in Detroit briefly before returning to the farm. At the *Tribune* block, he carefully counted off the confusingly similar doors and windows which Fred had marked exactly on the map.

At last he entered the precincts of the Detroit *Tribune* and once again was in the midst of Scrippses, but not in a warm family bosom. James E. was president of the company that owned the *Tribune* and another half brother, William A., was foreman of the job shop. On entering, Scripps first encountered his cousin, George C. Scripps, who had left Rushville the year before as green then as Scripps was now, but who had blossomed as a counting-room clerk. William A., known as Will, came in and introduced Scripps to other employees in the office. James E. gave him only a curt nod and cold greeting. Will took him to breakfast in a restaurant.

A gulf of age and personality separated Scripps from his half brothers. Not only were he and James E. virtual strangers because of the nineteen years difference in age, but they were strong and opposite personalities whose antipathy always remained near the surface. Though older, Will's weaker personality laid him vulnerable to Scripps' persuasiveness. Knowing that James E. would not have him on the paper for a moment but that Will often managed to have his way too, Scripps played Will against James E. to get what he wanted — a job on the *Tribune*.

When Will took him to breakfast, Scripps played his ace. After all, the English cousin, Ernest Saunders, was not ready to open the drugstore, and Scripps needed something to do in the meantime. When they returned to the office, Scripps was installed as office boy in the counting room.

A few weeks after Scripps went to work, the *Tribune* went through an upheaval that placed his older brothers in a separate business. Because the paper had started losing money, the minor stockholders combined to force the resignation of James E. as president and editor. As a good businessman as well as editor, James E. had given much attention to the paper's job-printing office, a usually profitable appendage of most newspapers of the time. Taking advantage of the other officers' ignorance of the financial importance of the job office, James E. traded his and Will's stock in the company for all the job business, including equipment. James E. and Will then formed a partnership to run a job-printing plant in the *Tribune* building, taking with them the only profitable part of the *Tribune*'s business.[12]

Scripps went to work for his brothers as office boy, and continued to manipulate them by periodically quitting and going off alone, forcing them to look him up and humor him. In that way he progressed from job to job in the printing shop, learning to set type and kick a job press.

Finally Saunders opened his drugstore in the spring of 1873 and Scripps went to work for him. Here Scripps' autobiographical testimony conflicts with a letter written at the time. His recollection was that he went into the drugstore as a concession to his father and brothers, but in the spring of 1873 he wrote that he was going to work for Saunders to escape his brothers' care and control.[13] However, the drugstore interlude lasted only a few days.

[12] *Ibid.*, pp. 9–10.
[13] EWS to EBS, Mar. 30, 1873.

Saunders had Scripps help mix some ersatz liquors, adding various flavors and colorings to alcohol, branding the various bottles port, sherry, bourbon, and what not. When a customer slid the first dime across the counter for a glass of wine, Scripps saw himself as nothing but a rum seller. Then a teetotaler, he quit the business.[14]

Going off independently, he teamed up with a mechanic named Lynch who made window blinds of wooden slats. Scripps saw a means of exploiting Lynch's casual business into a profitable industry by painting signs and advertising on the blinds. Busily engaged in stenciling blinds one day, he suddenly heard the jangle of James E.'s key chain behind him. James E. laughed at him, browbeat Lynch for hiring a minor, and took Scripps back to the print shop.[15]

The landmark date in the establishment of Scripps newspapers occurred a short time after Scripps returned to the job shop — Easter Sunday, 1873. Scripps and James E. were walking home from services at St. John's Episcopal Church when a policeman informed them the *Tribune* building had burned during the night. Hurrying to the building, they saw that only the four walls remained. Their apparent disaster turned into a fortune, however. James E. and Will settled with an insurance company for about $20,000, the most money they had ever had. Besides, they were able to recondition practically all the presses. Scripps saw an opportunity for himself in the puddled lead that once had been type and realized $1,000 through salvage — his first real money, and possibly a Scrippsian hyperbole.

Their father died a few weeks later, forcing a new center of union on the family. When the sons and daughters gathered in the Rushville home after the funeral, all were at loose ends. James E. was having to plan his future anew. Will was unsettled. Ellen B., who had left a job as an editor on the Detroit *Tribune* to come home and nurse her father, was adrift. George H. was tired of farming and wanted to sell out. Fred likewise wanted to get away from the family farm which he had taken over when Scripps left. Virginia was at liberty, and Annie was ill. The eldest sister, Elizabeth, was a widow with two children. Young Scripps still had one consuming ambition and one only — to be a newspaperman.[16]

But James E. was nursing a dream — a new kind of a newspaper, small, cheap, condensed. He had told Scripps about it many years before, in a conversation so rare that the boy remembered it vividly. Then thirteen or fourteen years old, Scripps was reading Peter Parley's tales in the boys' bed-

14 EWS, "Autobiography," p. 91.
15 *Ibid.*, pp. 95–99; EWS, "History of the Scripps League," pp. 11–13.
16 EWS, "History of the Scripps League," p. 20.

room when he heard the jangle of James E.'s key chain behind him. Taking the book from the lad, James E. had squatted down and begun to talk. That in itself was enough to impress the incident upon the boy's mind, for his brother seldom spoke to him during visits home. Musing, almost as if talking to himself, James E. had told the attentive youngster that he wanted to adapt to journalism the Peter Parley idea of condensing long stories to their essentials. Most newspapers then were the large "blanket sheets," containing long stories set in small type. If he got the chance, James E. would publish a small daily paper in large type, condensing into quickly read form all the news and even the short fiction that appeared in the larger papers. James E. had taken as his model Samuel Bowles III, who made the Springfield (Mass.) *Republican* a trailblazer in condensation.[17]

With the family taking a new direction in 1873, James E. decided to make his dream a reality. He and Will agreed to separate, James E. taking his half of the insurance money for his dream newspaper and Will his half for a new printing shop with the latest equipment. Scripps aligned with James E. Within a few months Ellen B. and George H. had also both cast their lot with James E. Ellen B. took a place as an editor. George H. sold his farm and put his money with his brother. The others gradually became charges on them during the years that followed.

Scripps eagerly took part while James E. spent the summer preparing for the advent of the paper that he was to call the Detroit *Evening News*. Knowing Scripps wanted to be a reporter, James E. told him he planned an economical paper, using what he called "cheap boys." By this he meant Scripps and other youngsters who would earn their living as carrier boys and learn to be reporters on their own time. Scripps objected, but James E. bluntly told him he was so uneducated and crude that he would never become a writer, much less an editor.

James E. planned a two-cent paper, in contrast to the five-cent blanket sheets, thus bringing to the West the same concept with which penny papers first competed with established New York papers in the 1830's. By developing a route of one hundred subscribers and buying his papers for one cent each, Scripps would, James E. figured, earn four dollars a week, which would pay his board and allow him to devote the rest of his time to learning journalism. Despite his first distaste for carrying papers, Scripps swung into the job with a flourish. Going full-throttle as he always did, he developed more than his allotted one route, hired boys to carry the papers for him, and became so preoccupied with circulation that he lost thought, for a time, of becoming a reporter.[18]

[17] EWS, "Autobiography," pp. 103, 106.
[18] *Ibid.*, pp. 110–13.

Meantime, James E. drew on his extensive background for a breakthrough in western journalism. Contrary to usual publishing practice but not without precedent, he farmed out the various functions. He contracted with William H. Brearley, who was to lead in founding the American Newspaper Publishers Association many years later, to be advertising manager. Brearley, whom James E. first had hired as advertising manager for the *Tribune*, opened his own office, receiving 25 per cent of gross advertising receipts and taking all risk of collections and slow payments. The composing-department contract went to a man named Hart who was to meet his own payroll. The paper was to be printed by the Detroit *Free Press*. James E. hired a Vermont Yankee, C. A. Worthington, to look after delivery and sale of papers to newsboys.[19] For editorial talent James E. turned to Michigan newspapermen who had won prizes for the best local papers; James E. had offered these awards, when editing the *Tribune*, as a means of developing goodwill. He formed a staff of F. H. Burgess as managing editor, Ellen B. as exchange editor, and Gil Osmun, R. B. Ross, a man named Barron, and another named Swan.[20]

Finally the great day came. The Detroit *Evening News* slowly emerged from the press of the *Free Press* on August 23, 1873. Businessmen hooted. Here was a dinky four-page paper, six columns to the page, each page about eighteen inches long. Other Detroit publishers united in predicting failure — a favorite pastime of his contemporaries — and businessmen thought James E. crazy. So perilous appeared the prospects that James E. could get credit from no one — bankers, paper dealers, type manufacturers, merchants. He had to husband his small capital carefully, paying cash for everything.

However, circumstances made the experimental paper popular immediately. Within a matter of weeks after the first issue, the country plunged into the paralyzing depression of 1873, but the depression helped the paper instead of choking it to death. Where other papers sold for 25 and 30 cents a week, the *News* sold for 10 cents. James E. also happened to tap the same new market, created by increasing literacy, that had made the New York penny papers successful. The older Detroit papers had been established during a time of more limited literacy, directing their appeal to the genteel and educated. During the intervening years population had grown to 80,000 and literacy had increased in Detroit, making the workingman a market for a newspaper he could afford.

The Scrippses scrimped and worked hard, gambling to establish themselves with a new type of journalistic product that represented their im-

[19] EWS, "History of the Scripps League," pp. 27–28.
[20] *Ibid.*

mediate economic survival. Scripps and Ellen B. lived with James E. and his family. Each day they reached the office by 7 A.M., taking lunches with them, and worked until 5 or 6 P.M. After supper James E. and Ellen B. prepared copy for the next day, and James E. kept his own books as part of his regular night work.

Strictest economy became the watchword. Every piece of copy paper was used twice. Reporters used one side of a sheet today and the other side tomorrow, the first having been marked through after the type had been set. James E. customarily wrote on the inside of a flattened envelope.

When George H. sold his farm and came to the *News* as business manager a few months later, he established a new means of economizing. Assisted by cousin John Sweeney (who had sold Scripps the suit that shrank) as clerk, George H. discounted the printers' "strings" himself. In the days of hand-set type, printers were paid by piecework, each printer pasting up proofs of the type he had set and turning in his "string" at the end of the week. Being a footloose and bottle-loving breed, however, printers often had immediate and urgent need of cash during the week. Some papers permitted office speculators to cash the midweek strings at a discount, but George H. ruled that if any discounting were done, he would do it in the business office. By thus discounting strings in the front office before payday, he shaved as much as 5 per cent from the cost of setting type.

James E. soon consolidated all operations in one place. Buying a lot on which there was a dwelling which he converted into offices, he built a shell of a building and he installed a second-hand press.

In the meantime, Scripps had thrown himself into the circulation work, making success of the *News* a matter of personal and family pride as he expanded his routes and acquired others until he had two thousand subscribers as a separate sub-business of his own. Within a few months Scripps' income from his city routes rose to fifty dollars a week, making him the highest-paid member of the staff, and James E. assigned him to building an equally substantial country circulation. At the time, newspapers relied on a hit-or-miss system of newsstand and annual mail subscription for distributing their papers outside the city of publication. In establishing an area circulation for the *News*, Scripps claimed later, he pioneered out-of-town home delivery that became standard with American dailies.[21] Systematically he followed transportation routes, first working all towns along one railroad and then all along the next, establishing one or more routes in each. He discovered that his routes remained stable if he chose a certain type of youngster as carrier, preferably a ten- or twelve-year-old son of a widow who had the sympathy of the community. From this he learned that

[21] EWS to EBS, May 26, 1891.

more than half his success depended upon the right person for the job.[22] Living on his income from the city routes, he left his earnings from country circulation with James E., thereby becoming a creditor and eventually a stockholder.

When James E. recalled him from the country sometime late in 1874, Scripps once again started moving toward his delayed objective — a job in the editorial department. With free time and plenty of money, he loafed around the city room, buying drinks and cigars for the reporters (although he did not yet drink), and learning as much from them as he could as he prepared to begin a reportorial career by working for nothing. In customary fashion, James E. ridiculed Scripps' editorial pretensions. In the presence of Ellen B., George H., Annie, and James E.'s wife, he had Scripps write something. Then, for the benefit of all concerned, he laughed uproariously at the spelling and grammar, brutally trying to crush Scripps' ambitions.[23] Parenthetically, James E. put on exactly the same show to ridicule Scripps' full sister Virginia.[24] Indignant at having been subjected to such an ordeal, Scripps announced that he intended to become a newspaperman in spite of his brother, if not on the *News* then on some other paper. Protesting that it would be disloyal to work on any other paper, James E. did not persist in his refusal, but maintained that Scripps would succeed only in making a poor newspaperman out of a good businessman.

Scripps applied to City Editor Michael J. Dee for a job. Possibly obeying instructions from James E., Dee refused. Undaunted, Scripps bought a cheap pine table and chair, and moved them into the city room where he began to practice rewriting stories from other papers. He also told Dee that he was ready to do anything that needed doing — getting a story, running errands, running copy, anything. With cigars, whiskey, and flattery, he forced his free services on the Irish city editor. Running errands, he met many people, opened doors with his name, and was on the alert for news.

But when he turned in a story it was terrible. To begin with, he still could not spell. His lines angled downward across the page so badly that he hardly reached the middle of the page on the left before he ran off the bottom corner of the page on the right. On more than one occasion, Dee crumpled the copy with a curse, "declaring that he and the printers had better use of their time than deciphering my scrall [*sic*]." [25]

In time he won through sheer persistence. Because the other reporters grumbled at coming in early to rewrite local stories from the morning papers (James E.'s policy was that his paper, though condensed, should

[22] EWS, "Autobiography," p. 121.
[23] EWS, "History of the Scripps League," pp. 33–34.
[24] Eliza Virginia Scripps to Ellen B. Scripps, July 25, 1900.
[25] EWS to his daughter Nackey Scripps, Jan. 14, 1915.

contain every story found in any other), Scripps drifted into the assignment. His first break came one morning when R. B. Ross, a big Scotsman who particularly hated to get up early, came in late for his turn at early rewrite. Scripps had already clipped and rewritten the local stories. When Dee arrived, Ross persuaded him that young Scripps could do the work as well as anyone else. Thereafter, the other reporters habitually came in late for rewrite, and Scripps gradually became the early rewrite man. He began reaching the office earlier than ususal, and virtually made himself assistant city editor. This freed Dee for what he liked and did best — writing. Scripps also went to night school briefly.

Scripps consumed a year in the gradual process of working his way into the heart of the paper, all the while without a cent of pay. He knew that his brother was aware of his work, for James E. marked the paper daily. At the end of the year, sometime in 1875, Scripps went to his brother, claimed he had finished his apprenticeship, and announced himself ready for business.

James E. wrote a check for $520, whereupon Scripps baldly laid out a whole new scheme that would take him to his heart's desire. Claiming that Burgess as managing editor wrote such poor editorials that the local staff was ashamed of the paper, he suggested that Dee, an able writer, should be made editor at his city editor's salary of $30.00 a week. That, of course, would leave the position of city editor vacant. But then the *News* had a perfectly good replacement readily available for the city editor's job and at $15.00 a week — one Edward Willis Scripps.

With James E.'s consent, Scripps became city editor of the *News* in 1875, at age twenty-one, and Dee got his promotion. That called for a celebration. Scripps had taken his first drink upon reaching twenty-one, but this time he did more than take a drink. He got drunk for the first time in his life, so drunk that the others had to put him to bed.[26]

Already a lively paper, the *News* became, as Scripps told it, a rip-snorting newspaper with an enterprising staff. As city editor, Scripps gave his city staff of three to five reporters as little government as possible. On the contrary, he urged them "to raise as much hell as possible." [27] After becoming city editor, Scripps wrote little for the *News*, except during the legislative session of 1877 when he acted as Lansing correspondent.

Under his guidance and through the energy of Dee and Ross, Scripps said, the *News* developed what he called "personal journalism." Journalism historians usually identify personal journalism as the equating of a paper with its editor, as Greeley and the New York *Tribune*, but Scripps defined

[26] EWS, "Autobiography," pp. 130–31.
[27] *Ibid.*, pp. 169–74.

it as exposing by name supposedly respectable persons who were found to be behaving otherwise. He also claimed that the Detroit *Evening News* introduced personal journalism as exposé.[28] His claims and interpretations open an area of investigation for historians.

When the exposés produced libel suits, James E. escaped personal liability by incorporating the paper as the Detroit Evening News Association in 1877. Incorporated for $50,000 with $30,000 actually subscribed, the association had 50 shares, confined to the family. James E. took 30 shares; George H., 16; Ellen B., 2; Scripps and John Sweeney, 1 each.[29]

Scripps' lone share resulted from his having left his country circulation earnings with James E. It was that $600 investment, the value of a $1,000 share on a three-fifths subscription, that laid the foundation of his later fortune and the extensive E. W. Scripps newspaper properties, making him worth, according to one estimate, $40,000,000 at the time of his death in 1926. For it was that stock which he used as collateral in borrowing money from other members of the family to start later papers and using stock from the later papers as collateral in turn.

During the first five years in Detroit, Scripps matured and changed considerably. For several months he remained the roughly dressed, careless country boy, but with the first flush of prosperity from his city routes he bought better clothes, started wearing a silk top hat, and moved to a hotel. To make himself more acceptable to young ladies, he took dancing lessons. Through hard work that brought rewards, he suppressed some of the inner conflicts that had tortured him. The sulking subsided, but he continued to insist upon having his own way and doing things in his own way.

He also had acquired the habit that was to ruin his health — constant and heavy drinking. Although he waited until he was twenty-one to taste liquor, he developed the taste with a flourish, moderation never his in anything. He scarcely could have avoided learning to drink, because drinking was expected of newspapermen in the 1870's. His city editor carefully instructed him in the fine art of remaining bibulous but not soused, with the intention of getting a news source drunk enough to tell the truth.[30]

EUROPEAN INTERLUDE

Scripps had become a quite different young man by 1878 when he made his first trip to Europe. The fairly innocent country boy of 1872 had turned into a city slicker of garish taste, dressing as a dandy, smoking cigars constantly, drinking heavily, and having a way with women. He had carried all to excess during the winter of 1877–78 when serving as the *News'* cor-

[28] *Ibid.*, pp. 177–79.
[29] *Ibid.*, pp. 156–57.
[30] "Temperance, Prohibition and the Alcohol Habit," EWS Writings, 1:333–34.

respondent in Lansing. A reaction habit developed that was to add to the misery of his internal seething for the next few years: he hated himself for being unable to withstand temptations of the flesh and became even more irascible and nervous, his letters and recollections showing strong guilt feelings.

The chance to go to Europe came in the spring of 1878 when George H. met with a misadventure with a woman, and chose to become inaccessible for a time. Collection of an inheritance in England provided an opportune excuse for going abroad. George H. proposed to pay all expenses if Scripps would go with him.

The trip became an early turning point in Scripps' life, for he then carefully considered his future route through life. Thinking and reading, he pondered the specific goal he should seek, the attitude he should take toward society and its conventions, and the means by which he should achieve fame. As an outgrowth of his deliberations he made four important decisions in Europe: (1) that he would become rich; (2) that he would rise above the common herd; (3) that environment and circumstance, not heredity, determined success; and (4) that he would begin his independence with a paper in Cleveland.

His first decisive experience came one night in London. Walking on his favorite promenade, Brook Street, he stopped to watch guests entering a mansion. As he observed the livery of footmen and the finery of arriving guests, the young American became dissatisfied with his own dress — a loud plaid suit, silk hat, diamond stud, yellow dogskin gloves. What he saw perplexed him. The men and women alighting from the carriages and treading a velvet carpet spread across the sidewalk impressed him as being insignificant in face and form. On the other hand, the servants were fine-formed young men, their appearance as gentlemen belied only by their Cockney accent and foul jests. Walking the streets until well past midnight, he tried to think through the meaning of the contrast. He decided that heredity could not possibly have anything to do with determining the superiority or inferiority of the two groups he had observed, and concluded that their relative positions resulted from environment and the accident of birth. Discarding his former conviction of real equality among men, bred in him by the idealism of agrarian democracy, he decided that two classes of men occupied the world — the slave and the slave driver. If he had to be one or the other, he determined to become a master of men.

His conclusion meant an agonizing compromise. From some time early in boyhood, circumstances had caused him to become a revolutionist with the blasphemous prayer: "God damn the rich and God help the poor." But he also saw that, for himself as an individual, he had to be either a "slave" or a "slave driver," as he put it. His determination to become one of the masters of society did not really blot out his earlier dedication. For he became both rich and radical. In other words, he preserved his basic conviction with regard to society as a whole, but in grasping the power of wealth for himself he made use of that which he condemned.

A related experience confirmed his decision to rise above the herd. Already something of a misanthrope, he was walking toward the city one evening when he met the rush-hour tide of humanity head on. Fighting his way against the crowd over London Bridge, he became nauseated by so much nameless humanity, ugliness, misery, hopelessness, and dull blankness. Depressed and almost hysterical, he halted in the middle of the bridge and turned toward the Thames, closing from view the press of humans. Into his mind floated the conception that only chance had kept him from being one of them, that one person alone meant nothing among millions of human beings who, in the mass, could be swept from the world in an instant of death and their going not be noted. What, then, was he that he was different from them? At the moment, nothing. Ultimately he made his way to the end of the bridge and leaped into a hansom cab. "And on that homeward drive, more than ever was I resolved to dissociate myself from the crowd; to climb up and out and over it, no matter by what means, even though crime itself and the worst of crime should form the rungs of the ladder which I felt I must climb, if I were not to become a suicide." [31]

James E. became impatient with his brothers, idling away their time and money on European frivolity. Possessed of Puritan righteousness, he sought to shame them home and back to work. "You have already delayed laying the foundation stone for your fortune too long and not another month should be wasted," he warned Scripps.[32]

James E. also tested on them his plan for a "cordon" of newspapers in the Midwest — then still known as the West — beginning in Cleveland.[33] Scripps and George H. responded favorably, answering almost immediately from Paris. With that approval, James E. then advanced more definite plans for the Cleveland paper. George H. would have charge of business management, Scripps would be city editor, and Burgess the editor.[34] James E. suggested Scripps follow the model of the Chicago *Daily News* but improve upon it in both style and content.[35]

The very night before James E. had written that letter in Detroit, young Scripps had observed his twenty-fourth birthday in Rome, undergoing

---

[31] EWS, "Autobiography," pp. 199–212.
[32] James E. Scripps to George H. Scripps, May 19, 1878; JES to EWS, July 29, 1878.
[33] James E. Scripps to George H. Scripps, May 19, 1878.
[34] James E. Scripps to George H. Scripps, June 12, 1878.
[35] JES to EWS, June 19, 1878.

something of a religious experience. After receiving news of his brother's planned expansion while in France, he had begun to dream about it and embroider the scheme with his own designs. In Rome he chose to be alone on his birthday. Spending a good part of the day in old churches, he said, "my exultation took almost religious form." [36] After dinner alone, he strolled aimlessly in the moonlight until he saw before him the shadowy form of the Colosseum.

Having just read the *Decline and Fall of the Roman Empire* whose author, Gibbon, had seen the concept of what became his classic work during a night of meditation in the Colosseum, Scripps made his way to near the middle of the floor of what he said was the Colosseum but may have been the Forum. Climbing up on the capitol of a broken column, he stretched out and lay there for hours, smoking cigar after cigar, dreaming dream after dream of emperors, generals, adventurers, and E. W. Scripps. Knowing that he was about to embark on a great adventure himself, which of all the great men of Rome should he emulate? Oddly, for one so impulsive and impatient, he fixed on Fabius, the general whose delaying tactics made his name synonymous with cautious waiting. "The world belongs to him who waits if he doesn't wait too long, if he waits only long enough for his opportunity and then is quick to seize it," said Scripps.[37] Recognizing the incongruity of starting a career of mutiny by waiting, he added:

But from that day to this [1915] I have been ruled very largely by the resolution I made that night in the Coliseum [*sic*] at Rome. Let the other fellow have all the glory; let him occupy the place in the limelight; for me I only care for the power. I do not care for the use of the power until it is necessary or useful to me to use the power. It was to wait and wait patiently for the opportune moment and then act promptly.

As I dreamed, I poetized my Brook Street philosophy and my London Bridge sensation, and deepened and strengthened my resolve to be one of the great men of the world. I proposed no greater career for myself than that of a journalist; but as a journalist I saw, or thought I saw, that I could apply and make use of the story of the Roman Empire. I decided that I would establish a little kingdom such as Rome was in its prehistoric beginning. I decided that I would extend this kingdom of mine, which would consist of my first newspaper, to another and then another newspaper, and I determined so long as I lived to go on extending my kingdom into perhaps an empire of journalism.[38]

Whether directly traceable to that night in Rome, one of Scripps' favorite injunctions to his sons and lieutenants many years later was: Make haste slowly.

[36] EWS, "Autobiography," pp. 223–26.
[37] *Ibid.*
[38] *Ibid.*

Having resolved to found his own newspaper empire, Scripps wrote to James E. and proposed that he become No. 1 man of the new Cleveland paper. Obviously taken aback by the brashness of the suggestion, James E. would not hear of it and told Scripps bluntly that he considered his editorial experience "altogether too limited." James E.'s letter also implied that he might have been at his wit's end trying to place the unstable younger brother happily. Referring to the latter's Lansing experience, he said he would not permit him to go to Washington at all as correspondent for the *News*, as Scripps had also suggested. He would, however, be glad to make room for him in Detroit, but Scripps had said he wanted to leave Detroit. For that reason, James E. said, he had suggested Cleveland. Assuring Scripps that he had not thought of placing him in a subordinate capacity exactly, he had seen it possible to propose him as head of one of two coordinate departments. However, he was willing to let George H. decide whether Scripps should be editor.[39]

James E. also lectured him severely for his weaknesses. Scripps was energetic and skilled as a writer but next to useless as an editor. Someone else had to get his copy in shape for the printers, and this affected the young man's market value. Maintaining that the ability to edit was more important than the ability to write elegantly, James E. said: "It [journalism] is essentially a careful, plodding, painstaking profession and with your disposition and idiosyncrasies can be acquired only by a vast amount of self control and mental discipline, which I fear you will never incline to." [40]

FOUNDING OF CLEVELAND PRESS

When Scripps and George H. returned from Europe in the early fall of 1878, the Scrippses immediately executed the plan for the Cleveland *Penny Press*, forerunner of the present Cleveland *Press*.

Scripps collided with James E. at once. James E. would not have anything to do with the new paper if Scripps were to be the editor. Instead, he held to his original plan — George H. as business manager and Burgess to be transferred from the Detroit *Evening News* and made managing editor in Cleveland. Scripps bulldozed his way with an ultimatum, as he often did, threatening to find other financial support and start the paper himself if James E. refused to acknowledge him as editor. However, the ultimatum was largely bluff, for he knew George H. would support him in a showdown and that James E. would give in. He was right on both counts. George H. threw the balance toward Scripps by deciding to remain in Detroit, forcing James E. to accept an entirely new combination, because they had to have a family member in Cleveland.

[39] JES to EWS, July 29, 1878.
[40] *Ibid.*

The organization finally agreed upon sent Scripps to Cleveland as editor, with cousin John Sweeney, transferred from Detroit, as business manager. Forming the firm of Scripps and Sweeney, each young man put up his one share of *News* stock as collateral for a 20 per cent interest in the *Penny Press*. Furnishing the $10,000 capital, James E. and George H. each held 30 per cent.

The agreement gave Scripps his first newspaper at age twenty-four, and he seized absolute control. Having elbowed Burgess aside to get the editor's chair, he now butted Sweeney to one side by placing the composing room under the editor. He knew the composing room was the strategic pivot in the ceaseless conflict between editorial and advertising departments. By placing it under his thumb, he gained final authority over the content of the paper. During the years in which he built his own chain of papers, he maintained that same arrangement as an inviolate rule: Scripps editors had command of the composing department, and they were to run the paper; the business manager was simply to sell the paper and advertising space.

The two young men spent several weeks in preparing for publication. They rented a three-story building adjoining the Theater Comique, a degraded variety house, and installed a second-hand, four-cylinder Hoe rotary press that had been used to print the Chicago *Tribune* and a New York paper. By that time, they had spent $6,000, leaving but $4,000 to carry them until the paper started making money. The margin proved insufficient, causing them to borrow $2,500, which placed the initial cost of the Cleveland *Press* at $12,500.

Sweeney went after advertising like a truculent bear after honey, but competition among the larger papers had cut advertising rates to about half what the space was worth, just to fill the space,[41] forcing Scripps and Sweeney to make a profit from newspaper sales alone in the beginning. Whereas the older papers employed their own carriers, the *Penny Press* was to be sold directly to newsboys at one-half cent per copy. The boys were to be independent businessmen, doubling their money on the papers they sold. Scripps and Sweeney thus would have to show a profit or at least break even on an income of one-half cent per copy. Toward this end they had an advantage in modeling after the economically operated Detroit *Evening News*. Using the same principle of condensation that had made the *News* successful and profitable, they intended to make the four pages of the *Penny Press* quickly read and full of information.

Scripps organized the editorial department on a grander scale than James

[41] Cleveland *Penny Press*, Mar. 19, 1881.

E. had envisioned, although it was modest enough — himself at the head at $12 a week, two desk men at $15 and $16 a week, and three cub reporters at $6 a week. For one of the desk jobs he imported Henry Little from Detroit, one of the numerous relatives who worked in the Scripps enterprises. In all, the *Press* employed thirty persons, including carriers.

When the shoestring preparations cleared the way for publication of their first number on Saturday, November 2, 1878, Scripps suddenly confronted a new test. Never had he gotten out a paper, either as editor or managing editor, and he still lacked the editing know-how of which James E. had complained. Furthermore, he had been so busy with mechanical details that he had given no thought to the content of the first issue. On the Friday night before the appearance of the first issue he went to the office to begin preparing copy, knowing that at last E. W. Scripps had a newspaper of his own, a captain feeling his own quarterdeck under his feet for the first time. Upon his performance would depend the fate of his Brook Street resolution. Slave or slave driver? The hour had come.

Buck fever paralyzed him. He could think of nothing to write. Sweat moistened his red whiskers, oozed onto his broad brow, clammily held his shirt to his thick shoulders. The sweat came, on a cold night in an unheated office, but copy, no. He got up and left. Disregarding the showdown, he went home and slept soundly.

He was back at the office by seven the next morning, swinging into the new schedule, producing a newspaper under deadline pressure. When the first issue came from the press that day it contained twelve and one-half columns of editorial matter, of which Scripps personally had written more than half.

Cleveland's first penny paper was printed on one sheet of paper folded in the center to make four pages, each measuring 10 by 16 inches. Rough and imperfect, the first *Penny Press* showed Scripps' editorial haste. But with his first issue, he set a pattern that was to continue for some years. What the newsmen of the time called "matter" consisted mostly of short (one-line to two-inch) stories, items, comments, whatever one might call them, and a few longer "articles" about various incidents. On the front page of the first issue Scripps said the *Penny Press* was politically independent. He then conformed to a journalistic trend of the time in which some other newspapers ceased being partisan organs.

Just as the *News* had caught the crest of change in Detroit, so the *Penny Press* rode a flood tide to success. "I have often wondered what would have happened to me had I made my first newspaper venture in some sleepy, slow-growing town instead of starting in Cleveland just when that city, by reason of newly acquired oil and iron interests, was beginning to hum." [42]

Cleveland was just recovering from the 1873 panic when Scripps set up shop in a city then emerging as an industrial complex. He arrived near the end of a decade in which population had increased roughly 70 per cent, going from 92,828 in 1870 to 160,146 in 1880. Indeed, a new industrial age had dawned in Cleveland during the seventies, particularly with the consolidation of Rockefeller's refineries in the Standard Oil Company and the introduction of acid open-hearth steelmaking by Charles Otis in an area already producing steel. Besides the basic oil, iron ore, coal, and meat-packing, city factories absorbed the rising tide of European immigrants, putting them to work at making hard goods.[43]

But it was to the brawn, not the brains, of the booming industrial city that Scripps directed the appeal of his newspaper. Here the Brook Street compromise first came into direct play — he was out to make money for E. W. Scripps and there it stopped. Riches for himself did not mean courting the rich for a place among them. Rather, the fiery rebellion of his "God damn the rich" placed Scripps on the side of the workingmen, who were beginning to renew their fight for better treatment.

With these men Scripps cast his lot, guided by emotion and instinct instead of any intellectual conviction. Always he placed his little paper on the side of the striker, organized labor, and the underdog generally. However, he had no axe to grind for them. His job was to report the news. As a consequence he adopted and adhered to the policy that the *Penny Press* would print the news, no matter whose name was involved. Whereas the older papers, as he saw it, had ingratiated themselves with the powers of wealth and politics,[44] Scripps found profit, pleasure, and honor in siding with the working people. He solidified his position along that line, and continued it through the remainder of his working life,[45] although it was James E. who first identified the workingman as the primary market for Scripps newspapers. Those who did not like what Scripps was doing called his paper the "Penny Puke" and the "Frankfort Street Handbill."

At least one competitor watched the *Penny Press* carefully and with some apprehension — Edwin Cowles, who owned the morning *Leader* and the *Evening News*. At two cents a copy, the *News* was the only Cleveland paper selling for less than a nickel when Scripps came to town. When Cowles came into his office each evening he called for "that little penny paper" at

[42] EWS to JGS, Aug. 10, 1909.
[43] William G. Rose, *Cleveland; The Making of a City* (Cleveland, 1950), p. 361 f.
[44] Charles E. Kennedy, *Fifty Years of Cleveland . . . 1875–1925* (Cleveland, 1925), p. 20.
[45] EWS to H. N. Rickey, Aug. 12, 1903.

once, studied it carefully, calculated how long it would last, and chuckled. After a year he stopped chuckling.[46]

A bitter rivalry developed between Scripps and Cowles who, in the manner of the time, made contemptuous and defamatory statements about one another's newspapers. Scripps came to call the *Leader* the "olecoles organ," without benefit of quotation marks.

In 1915 Scripps assessed his early Cleveland experiences as follows:

The Cleveland Press has been one amongst a very small number of American newspapers that have been equally successful as journals leading public opinion in their communities and as profit-paying properties.

. . . .

Almost by accident, it secured for its first editor a man who had a genius for the calling, hardly suspected by himself, and not at all recognized by others. (Difficult as it may be for me to tell the truth, the whole truth, and nothing but the truth in my autobiography, as a rule, it is easy enough to be frank sometimes.)

. . . .

That which distinguished the Press from its contemporaries in those days was the fact that the Press suppressed nothing but published nothing to gain the favor and approval of those people in the community who flattered themselves that they were the better classes.

The Press was not given to publishing scandalous gossip. I do not recall that anything salacious, so-called, was ever printed, except in cases of court procedure where an accurate report was required of delicate, or indelicate, subjects.

. . . .

When I took my seat as editor of the Press it was with the resolve that I would always keep in view the women folks, and that, so far as it was possible in carrying out my thoroughgoing system of journalism, I would avoid making any woman cry.

. . . .

[One incident where a story brought tears to a woman's eyes made Scripps feel like abandoning journalism:] I was feeling that I was a sort of public executioner — something even as bad as a hangman — and that I could not be an honest journalist without causing innumerable women to weep.

The Press, I have said, aimed to tell the truth without fear or favor, in the days when most newspapers suppressed more news than they published, and anyone with a pull could boss the editor. But there was another way in which I was determined to carry my democratic experiment still further. The Press definitely took the side of the working people. It made strong efforts toward developing trade unionism in Cleveland. Naturally my whole policy was regarded in those days as revolutionary.

. . . .

I had the people, the common people, of the town with me; but against me was the respectability, or the alleged respectability of the city.

[46] Kennedy, *Fifty Years of Cleveland*, p. 20.

.   .   .   .

I was a willful, headstrong, and determined young man. It was not in me to conceive failure possible. I would have what I wanted and would get what I wanted in the way that I wanted it. I was engaged in founding a newspaper. My whole mind and will was concentrated on this one thing. There was only one thing worthwhile avoiding, and that was failure. I think that had there been 999 chances out of 1,000 of losing my life by proceeding along the course that I had determined on, and only one chance for living and succeeding, I would not have hesitated.

I must confess something more; I believe that if it had been necessary for me to break every statute of the state in order to accomplish the end I had in view, those laws would have been in great danger of being broken.

.   .   .   .

So far as I can remember, I was only chockfull of opinions and ideas that were more the result of emotional activities than reasoning, and, having a newspaper under my control, I just turned myself loose on the public.[47]

In general, the files of the *Penny Press* substantiate Scripps' recollections of news treatment. For instance, he wrote autobiographically that the *Press* alone of Cleveland papers had accurately reported as suicide the death of Leonard Case, the millionaire philanthropist whose legacy established the Case School of Applied Science.[48] While not quite that blunt, the *Press* story did, however, leave the impression that Case took his own life, saying Case died with his head and a saucer of chloroform under a blanket; friends said he used chloroform to relieve asthma; he had been sickly all his life.[49] Salacious or no, the *Press* seems to have reported every suit involving bastardy that reached Cleveland courts, succinctly recounting the details of seduction. Curt, sometimes flippant, irreverent, and saucy writing turned one- and two-paragraph stories into gems of completeness, and blunt stories told readers what happened in court and on police calls.

Scripps and Sweeney treated advertisers contemptuously, but soon made a profit from advertising through some rule of perversity in human nature. Hating men in power and detesting merchants as tradesmen, Scripps thumbed his nose at advertisers. When given the chance he would prefer a story that hurt a merchant over one that did not. Sweeney was just as independent with advertisers as Scripps was, but merchants bought space even though they knew he charged twice for some of the space; that is, he charged both advertisers for the cutoff rule separating two advertisements in the same column.[50]

The money came in so slowly at first, however, that James E. and George

[47] EWS, "Autobiography," pp. 250–66.
[48] *Ibid.*, p. 253.
[49] Cleveland *Penny Press*, Jan. 6, 1880.
[50] EWS, "Autobiography," pp. 267–74.

H. almost deposed Scripps. A few months after the paper started, and when the borrowed $2,500 had been spent, James E. and George H. descended upon Cleveland without notice, threatening to kill the paper unless Scripps and Sweeney ran it on receipts alone and not on any more borrowed money. Under duress, Scripps and Sweeney agreed to run the paper on $400 a week. By the end of 1879, after little more than a year of operation, the borrowed $2,500 had been repaid and the little paper was on its way to becoming what Scripps called the greatest money-maker of any of the Scripps newspapers.[51]

Among the experiences that slowly crystallized Scripps' first principles of newspaper management while in Cleveland, the showdown with James E. and George H. taught him that men make money and that money does not make money. "It is the man that makes the newspaper, and not the man's capital. Everything else being equal, the more money that is spent on founding a paper, the less apt it is to be successful; and, even being successful, the less will be its success." [52]

Scripps drove himself hard during the first few months, taking the attitude that it was his job to see that the staff turned out a good paper rather than that he himself turned out a good paper. He worked from 5 A.M. until late at night, reading other papers, thinking, planning, driving his employees.

However, when the paper picked up a momentum of its own, Scripps reverted, as he put it, to his boyhood scheme of sitting on the fence and watching the other fellows work. He habitually came to the office late and left early. Thus he began with his first paper the principle of delegation of authority and labor. Sometimes he would take off for days at a time, secluding himself in a country hotel to read and dream and think. As a corollary, he sought to have other men impress their, rather than his, personalities on the paper. Shunning attention as always, he preferred that someone else represent his paper before the public, a practice he continued through later years.

Noticing that the paper sold best when it had the greatest number of individual items in it, he adopted and maintained the rule that every issue of every paper should contain a minimum of 400 or 450 stories.[53] Much of the variety of out-of-town shorts came from Ellen B. As exchange editor of the Detroit *Evening News*, she prepared a daily collection which became known around the *News* as "Miss Ellen's miscellany." A copy went daily to Scripps in Cleveland. The Cleveland success of her miscellany, under varying heads, also taught Scripps the necessity of having one or several

[51] *Ibid.*, pp. 230–48.
[52] *Ibid.*, p. 247.
[53] *Ibid.*, p. 284.

staff members comb other newspapers and magazines for bits of information that otherwise would not come to the notice of that paper's readers. He estimated that Ellen B.'s production lightened his load on the *Penny Press* by 30 per cent.[54]

Personally Scripps changed considerably between the fall of 1878 and the spring of 1880 while editing the *Penny Press*. In following his natural bent of withdrawal and contemplation, he learned that he did not have to be at his desk to think, that he could keep his business under control — whether riding, driving, rowing, or sailing. His health continued to be poor (he had chronic bronchitis), and he began drinking more and more. "I never got drunk. I never wanted to get drunk; but I could consume enough whiskey every day, and keep my wits about me, to make half a dozen other men drunk." [55]

A virile man with a strong attraction for women, he made himself even more attractive by improving the dress of his tall, well-built figure. Not yet ready for marriage, he formed several liaisons in Cleveland, maintaining at least one mistress. But he hated himself for succumbing to the demands of the flesh, and exhausted himself at physical exercise, especially rowing, to curb his sexual propensity.

Because his editing created situations that endangered his life, he started carrying a pistol. He practiced daily, drawing suddenly and shooting at a gate or telegraph pole. By letting others know he carried a pistol and could use it, he was convinced, he saved himself from the humiliation of being shot at or whipped.[56] The comfort of a pistol did not relieve him from the anxiety of what he called physical cowardice, but a discovery about himself did help. On one occasion, when his life had been threatened, he worriedly paced his room in the Weddell House. Suddenly he caught himself in the mirror and was startled by the face he saw there — pale, with a look about the eyes that made him appear a dangerous stranger. With practice, he learned to assume and cast off the pose at will, making it a protective coloration. "For the first time, then, was revealed to me why it not infrequently occurred that men — big, strong fellows — had backed away from me." [57]

Another characteristic, coming to the fore, drove Scripps to a new field. Always he was the creator, the inventor, the innovator, the starter. Once started, any project invariably bored him. By the spring of 1880, little more than one and one-half years after starting the *Penny Press*, he searched for a new conquest.

[54] *Ibid.*, p. 283.
[55] *Ibid.*, pp. 316–17.
[56] EWS to Nackey Scripps, Mar. 10, 1915.
[57] EWS, "Autobiography," pp. 259–60.

FOUNDING OF ST. LOUIS CHRONICLE

Walking tall from what he considered his Cleveland success, Scripps persuaded his brothers to enclose St. Louis next in the cordon of western papers that James E. envisioned. Not yet trusting his capacity or judgment, his brothers acceded partly because he needed a change of climate for his health. With their financial backing he left Cleveland in May, 1880, began publication of the St. Louis *Chronicle* on July 31, and returned to Cleveland the next spring with his tail between his legs.

During those same months, James E. added the Buffalo *Telegraph* and the Cincinnati *Penny Paper*, making the first tentative move toward what was to become the Scripps League as the first American newspaper chain. James E. conceived the idea of a group of papers, but he worked from Scripps' dream of forming a combine. James E., adapting to journalism the corporate and holding-company structure then coming ever more into use in American business and industry, formed the Scripps Publishing Company to hold the family's stock in the Cleveland, St. Louis, Cincinnati, and Buffalo papers; other persons held minority stock in each of the companies other than Detroit. The Detroit *Evening News* remained their financial base and outside the new corporation. Later, James E. limited the Scripps Publishing Company to the Cleveland *Penny Press* and each paper was incorporated as a separate corporation thereafter.

Simply told, Scripps reached beyond himself in St. Louis. As general manager of a newspaper, he yet lacked the acumen to assail an established and conservative city of St. Louis' 350,000 population with a newspaper of a type that flourished best in a smaller industrial city riding the crest of a growth wave. In St. Louis, too, he encountered Joseph Pulitzer, who had established the *Post-Dispatch* in the same year Scripps started the *Penny Press*, and on the same platform. Too green or too restrained or on too much of a shoestring to match Pulitzer's methods — which, Scripps charged, included bribing *Chronicle* carriers to transfer their routes and subscribers to the *Post-Dispatch* [58] — he failed to take into account that Pulitzer already was doing in St. Louis what the Scrippses had done in Detroit and Cleveland.

He also made the cardinal mistake that would doom a shoestring Scripps-type paper — starting big. James E., for instance, maintained that a newspaper would become successful only by starting small and economically.[59] Overriding James E.'s wiser counsels, Scripps insisted on starting the *Chronicle* on a grand scale. The *Chronicle* remained a chronic invalid until he sold it in 1908. All the while, in St. Louis, he sullenly blamed the failure

[58] Cleveland *Penny Press*, Aug. 9, 1881.
[59] JES to EWS, May 28, 1880.

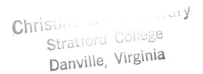

on everyone else, especially on James E. whom he always criticized for lack of vision and daring. Not until so many years had passed that no one cared any more did he concede that the chronic ill health of the *Chronicle* had been due to his excesses in trying to buy himself rich.[60] After the passage of a few years he saw more objectively than had been possible in 1880 that he failed in St. Louis because he lacked the means to carry out his ideas and because James E. lacked the man who could carry out James E.'s ideas.[61]

Scripps failed to form an effective organization in St. Louis. Blocked by frustration after frustration, he appears to have been a young man who sensed his own abilities but had not yet won the confidence of others. Hence, he could not exercise the personal leadership that would enable him to carry out his designs. Instead of following him, others resisted him. And the *Chronicle* was hobbled by a melange of uncoordinated plans and policies.

In adversity he showed himself to be mulish, egotistical, petulant, short-tempered, supersensitive, depressed, impatient, melancholy, disgusted — trying to run away when he couldn't have his way. He spent himself physically through hard work, and mental torture resulted from emotional stress, continued hard drinking, and sexual adventuring. His already poor health eroded into an illness which a physician was to say gave him but a few more months to live. Scripps suffered illnesses on other occasions when frustrated as in St. Louis.

He got along with no one. When he made a demand and his brothers acceded to it, he complained that they had forced him to accept their decision. For instance, he had prevented Sweeney from becoming business manager by convincing James E. that Sweeney was not to be trusted. Thus he got George H. as business manager, his own choice. When he and George H. disagreed, he convinced James E. that George H. was a failure. Bowing to Scripps' argument, James E. sent brother Will to St. Louis as a replacement for George H., only to be perplexed by Scripps' objection. Scripps lost faith in Stanley Waterloo, a St. Louis newspaperman who was his own choice for editor. Not once during Scripps' tenure did the paper show a monthly profit, and he blamed everyone but himself.

His favorite whipping boy was James E. Between the two men grew a constant attrition in which each exhausted the other's patience with incompatible and irreconcilable philosophies of newspaper management as well as irritating personal mannerisms. Each imperiously threatened to abandon the other unless his terms were met, thereby widening the natural breach between them almost to the breaking point.

[60] EWS to E. F. Chase, Feb. 17, 1906.
[61] EWS to JES, Feb. 2, 1889, in *Scripps* v. *Sweeney, Record*, 1:458 f.

From James E.'s point of view, Scripps was an arrogant young puppy trying to tell his successful older brothers how to run a newspaper. Still, James E. showed more patience, kindness, tolerance, and affection for the younger brother than could have been expected in view of the provocation. Strong-willed and supercilious toward Scripps, James E. reacted violently to many of Scripps' decisions and assumptions. For instance, Scripps ruffled him by arrogating to himself the Cleveland success. Scripps was so far out of line that Ellen B. curtly told him to mind his manners and keep his place.[62]

James E. in turn irritated Scripps. When Scripps exceeded his authority in arranging for a building and a press, and made grandiose plans that included scandalous $50-a-week salaries, James E. accused him of assumption, arrogance, visionary bombast, and drinking too much champagne. James E. further irritated Scripps by insisting upon the deference due his greater age and experience, but really angered him by saying Scripps' judgment was only "mediocre," [63] his ideas of journalism only "half crystallized," [64] that he wasn't worth much as a newspaper manager and was proving it.[65] Once, noting a looseness in style in the *Chronicle*, James E. said that issue was "a disgrace to anyone calling himself a journalist and not a bill-poster." [66]

Scripps poured out his woes in letters to Ellen B. She understood and loved her favorite, but firmly tried to make him act like a reasonable man instead of a child throwing temper tantrums. On one occasion when he announced his firm intention to secede from his brothers altogether (he made the threat several other times), she quickly reprimanded him. She said his "extreme sensitiveness" had led him to conclusions without foundation in fact, and reminded him that "your periods of depression and exaltation . . . are as sudden as they are variable." She argued that he must think of others, and pointed out that James E. could never be more than the nominal head of the concern. In time, she said, someone (implying Scripps) would be able to do more with the concern than James E. ever could.[67]

Within a few months, however, even she recognized the futility of the situation. Seeing that he could not unite the contending forces within the *Chronicle*, that he had reached an impasse with James E., and that he was nearing dangerous illness, she recommended that he leave St. Louis and the

[62] EBS to EWS, May 27, 1880.
[63] JES to EWS, May 25, 1880.
[64] JES to EWS, May 28, 1880.
[65] JES to EWS, July 14, 1880.
[66] JES to EWS, Jan. 22, 1881.
[67] EBS to EWS, Aug. 12, 1880.

concern.[68] A few weeks later Scripps returned to Cleveland. He left St. Louis against the protests of James E. and others, but ironically remembered the incident as his having been deposed by the directors, an action which left him feeling "wretched." [69]

Circumstances really gave him an excuse to leave St. Louis. James E. had left for Europe in the spring of 1881, and wanted each key post manned. Henry Little had assumed the editorship of the Cleveland *Penny Press* when Scripps had left, but now was needed in Buffalo. The Scrippses and Sweeney had earmarked a pudgy young reporter, Robert F. Paine, as the next Cleveland editor, but he had to be trained, and Little had to leave immediately. Preparing Paine to take the helm in Cleveland gave Scripps a good excuse to return to Cleveland, leaving the *Chronicle* in the hands of his brother Will and Waterloo. His expectation was that he would leave the concern after training Paine.

RETURN TO CLEVELAND

Shortly after his return to Cleveland, Scripps came face to face with a prison term. Hearing that the *Leader* and *News* were in financial trouble, the *Penny Press* sent reporter M. J. Haley to ask Scripps' old enemy, Edwin Cowles, about it. In the *Leader* report, Cowles kicked Haley down the stairs, yelling that the *Penny Press* was a blackmailing sheet. Angrily denying Cowles' story point by point, the *Penny Press* quoted him in a dialect indicating a speech impairment which it attributed to the loss of the roof of his mouth through a youthful indiscretion. Cowles immediately filed a criminal libel suit, saying the *Penny Press* implied venereal disease.[70]

Morosely conceding that there seemed no way out of the jam, Scripps moaned to Ellen B. that he would be sent to prison and thus disgraced. She replied sternly that there would be no disgrace in going to jail under those circumstances.[71] But he got no support from James E., who said Scripps "neither has my sympathy nor backing" and would have to fight alone.[72]

Scripps went to trial, defended by Judge R. F. Paine, father of the youngster Scripps was training for the editor's chair. When the court refused to admit as evidence the first *Leader* story which would have given Scripps evidence of provocation, Scripps refused to defend himself further, letting the case go to the jury then and there, and echoing Ellen B.'s advice when he orated that a jail cell would be no disgrace under the circumstances.[73]

[68] EBS to EWS, Feb. 17, 1881.
[69] EWS to JGS, Dec. 29, 1914.
[70] Cleveland *Penny Press*, Apr. 13, 16, 18, 19, 20, 1881.
[71] EBS to EWS, Apr. 25, 1881.
[72] JES to EBS, May 13 and June 18, 1881.
[73] Cleveland *Penny Press*, Oct. 18, 1881.

When the jury returned after twenty-nine hours of deliberation, the foreman announced: "Not guilty."

Meantime, Scripps had been spending as little time in the office as possible, mainly because of illness which Ellen B. said was hypochondria. In the doldrums, he complained that he felt like running away from Cleveland and from everything in his past and starting all over again. Her prescription was "vigorous application to manual labor, plain living, and high (not dreamy, fantastic) thinking. . . ." [74] Besides, she said, he found comfort only in hardship, never happiness in success.

Ellen B. replied with another's view of him:

You are altogether too exacting — wanting to be at the top of the tree without the trouble of climbing. If you would be content to grovel underneath, as I do, and pick up the acorns that fall, no one would interfere with you. But aiming higher you meet with obstacles and rivals and become disgruntled and misanthropic because the latter won't concede that an upward flying leap is as safe and sure as a steady climb.

However, looking on from a lower and more humble position it seems to me that your rebuffs and repulses have done you a "mighty sight" of good. I detect so much less of the waywardness, the impatience, the self-opinionativeness [sic] that used to stand in your way with others and spoil your best efforts. I recognize so much more caution, prudence, judgment with sundry other qualities that constitute the true manliness in your business transactions that I think you have profited by what you are pleased to term reverses and hairlines. Isn't such recognition a better offering than all the best wishes for happy returns for natal day? . . .[75]

Nevertheless, Scripps was a sick man, told by Dr. J. E. Jones of Cleveland that consumption gave him only a few more months to live. North Africa would be as good a place as any to die, the doctor said.

With that ultimatum, which he really did not take seriously, although he dramatized it on later occasions, Scripps left for Europe in the fall of 1881, taking Ellen B. with him. Scripps intended to study history, theology, philosophy, political science, literature, sculpture, painting, architecture, museums — all to fit himself for something higher and better than he had yet known.

"You know I have never sought to pursue the old customary road to the end success and I think in this new departure I may yet be able to cut across lots to a success which another man of my mean capacities might never hope to reach by pursuing the old slow tedious route." [76]

Scripps had come to a crossroads.

[74] EBS to EWS, Apr. 13, 1881.
[75] EBS to EWS, June 30, 1881.
[76] EWS to EBS, June 18, 1881.

SURCEASE IN EUROPE

Scripps was suffering frequent lung or bronchial hemorrhages and carrying only 120 pounds on his six-foot frame when he left in November, 1881, for twenty months abroad, but several months in Algeria restored his health. Both the coughing and hemorrhaging stopped, and his weight rose to 180 pounds. For the rest of his life he suffered no more such hemorrhages, and remembered Algeria with affection as the first place and first time he had ever been free from chronic colds.

Leaving Algeria, Scripps and Ellen B. toured the continent in 1882. Scripps lived in Paris several months while Ellen B. visited England. In December they began a tour of the Mediterranean and the Holy Land. Tired of wandering, they returned to America in June, 1883.

While abroad, Scripps was subjected to a drumfire from James E., who wanted him home. Knowing his younger brother well, James E. tried to dissuade him from chasing a literary will-of-the-wisp, because Scripps, having revived his earlier dream of being a writer, was toying with the idea of living out his life in Europe in literary pursuits, supported by a comfortable income from the *Press* and *News*. With an accuracy proven by Scripps' own methods in writing the disquisitions, James E. said Scripps was not cut out for literature, "your nervous irritability standing in the way of that patience in research and careful perfecting of work which are the highest necessaries." [77] Insisting that Scripps' best plan would be to choose one newspaper and settle down to it, James E. said he had always looked upon Scripps as his successor, that managing skill could not take the place of hard work, that his brothers had never asked Scripps to do other than assume independent management of some branch of the business, and that it would be absurd to expect Scripps to be accountable to James E. or anyone else. [78]

To all of this Scripps remained impervious for the moment, but James E. had swayed Scripps, who was a suggestible person, at least at that age. As Scripps worked hard in Europe — reading, observing, criticizing, comparing, analyzing, generalizing, synthesizing his old knowledge with his new — he formed conclusions that grew directly out of James E.'s arguments. His suggestibility is further illustrated by a comment made a few years later; he said he was so habituated to deferring to James E. that "I find it almost impossible not to be so influenced even against my own reasoning." [79]

Discarding the notion of a literary career with the argument that it was too late to begin one, Scripps decided he would own his own newspaper and never again lose his freedom. Convinced that women and whiskey had

[77] JES to EWS, May 4, 1882.
[78] JES to EWS, Mar. 1, May 4, July 19, Sept. 14, 1882; Apr. 23, 1883.
[79] EWS to JES, Mar. 27, 1888 in *Scripps* v. *Sweeney, Record*, 1:334–35.

botched his life, he further resolved that he would burn out the bad habits by throwing himself into work when he returned to America.

However unwillingly, he divested himself of the adolescent presumption that the genius of Ed Scripps automatically entitled him to preferment. Having left America a captious boy who refused to grow up, he returned with the resolution of a man and a whole new complex of objectives. He had stiffened his backbone while traveling with Ellen B.

CONTROL OF CINCINNATI POST

Returning from Europe in June, 1883, Scripps entered the second phase of his business career which put to the test the firmness of his new resolutions: to own a newspaper; to quit wenching and boozing; to work in the public interest; to make enough money in three years to allow him to retire to a secluded life; to get married.

Scripps eliminated the other family papers for one reason or another, and found in the Cincinnati *Penny Post* just what he wanted — a little paper on rock bottom but with potential. The paper had been founded as the *Penny Paper* by Walter and Albert Wellman in 1880. Early in 1881 James E. had bought 60 per cent of the stock, and later that year Scripps had bought out the Wellmans. During his absence the paper had been renamed the *Penny Post*. It has since been known as the Cincinnati *Post* and as the present Cincinnati *Post and Times-Star*.

By early July he carried out his first objective. Already holding a sizable block of stock, he concentrated a majority in his hands by buying the stock of business manager C. A. Worthington and cousin John Sweeney. That gave him 55 per cent of the stock, Ellen B., 5 per cent, James E. and George H., 20 per cent each. Buying additional stock in the St. Louis *Chronicle*, he worked out an arrangement with James E. whereby Scripps was to control the *Post* and be editorial director of the *Chronicle*; James E. was to run the business side in St. Louis.[80]

By voluntarily exposing a dramatic scene in which a former mistress tried to blackmail him, Scripps at least gave an earnest toward personal reform. A woman reportedly named Elizabeth Brown, who had been his mistress in Cleveland and St. Louis, appeared in his office on August 2, 1883, demanding that he take her back on pain of having their former relationship exposed. He called police, swore out a warrant for disorderly conduct, called in reporters from the other papers, and told them the full story, emphasizing that he had come to Cincinnati to lead a different life. Slumped in discouragement, he dashed off a note to Ellen B. that very afternoon, saying:

[80] EWS to EBS, July 6, 1883.

"It will hurt my personal character. It may ruin me in a business way but for that I do not care." [81]

The newspapers spread the story for all Cincinnati to read the next day, but to his surprise and disgust Scripps found that neither he nor the *Post* suffered. Neither condemned for his morals nor applauded for opposing blackmail, he snorted: "Am I not excusable under the circumstances for holding humanity in such contempt? Were I the worst of men and still successful, I would be the most applauded. Bah!" [82]

The woman left town and troubled him no more. For the next few months he left women alone.

But he could not cork the bottle. Basically an unhappy person, he could not make friends. When he had left Cleveland to start the St. Louis paper in 1880 he told no one goodbye, because he had made no friends. Lack of friendship drove him into solitude, which caused him to brood, which produced fits of despondency. The bottle helped. He explained his reasons for drinking:

I am just now going through one of my periodical depressions of spirit. That which you say cautioning me against drinking is all right . . . . Of course I can drink without becoming a drunkard. Of course I need never drink. But I probably will drink and that to a greater or less extent according as my life can be made more or less happy and natural.

So long as circumstances force me into my present uncongenial [*sic*] life the temptation will be very strong for me to drink. At times I feel very brave and strong, and hate to becloud myself with liquor. At other times I feel very keenly my isolation in this world of happier people than I. I see myself by force of my peculiar disposition regarded with distrust by my family as though I were a changeling introduced no one knows how into the bosom of a respectable household that desired only to get rid of me.

.   .   .   .

Perhaps one of the strongest inducements that I will have [for going away and spending restless energy in travel] will be the conviction that only in that way can I save myself from being what you fear, a boozy imbecil [*sic*].

.   .   .   .

My two great dangers are financial ruin and the whiskey bottle. I can only hope to escape them. [83]

In contrast to the environment that had proved benign for a Scripps-type paper, Cincinnati was an old town and slowing down. Cincinnati had built a population of 255,000 as a center of river traffic, but railroads were short-circuiting the city by the time Scripps arrived. The city's meat, whiskey,

[81] EWS to EBS, Aug. 2, 1883; second of two letters of same date.
[82] EWS to EBS, Aug. 16, 1883.
[83] EWS to EBS, July 7, 1883.

and soap manufacturing had been subordinated by the heavy industry of other cities.

However, a fortuitous blending of three factors was to tip the scales in favor of Scripps' success: his mental attitude; the competitive situation; and the happenstance of a talented staff. Taking over the *Penny Post*, which was to remain his principal base for the next eight years, Scripps had to overcome the stigma of a "blackmailing sheet" which he said the Wellmans had left upon the paper. He found the paper published in a disreputable hole-in-the-wall, and soon transferred it to more dignified quarters. With his money at stake more than anyone else's, Scripps relied on the basic principle of James E., rather than his own earlier theory of show and inflation: "I have insisted and still insist that success is not to be found by competing with the older papers in the fields where they have advantage over us but in creating a new field for ourselves. Lavish expenditure for telegraph, and $35-a-week writing is not appreciated by the common people whom we should seek for our constituency." [84]

A new field in Cincinnati journalism was Scripps' for the taking. Murat Halstead, one of the better-known nineteenth-century editors, made the morning *Commercial-Gazette* a respected voice of the Republican party. but emphasized opinion to the neglect of news. John R. McLean edited the morning *Enquirer* as a salacious gossip, a special pleader for the Democrats, and a flail for those whose names were written in the "son of a bitch" book he carried on his person. The afternoon *Times-Star* was Scripps' only direct competition, edited by Charles P. Taft (of the later political family) but financed by his father-in-law, David Sinton. It seemed to Scripps that the *Times-Star* was more dedicated to Sinton's business interests than to its equivocal republicanism.

Scripps plunged through the line with two attractions not to be found in the other papers — news and a willingness to fight political corruption. Scripps attacked under a barrage laid down by a competent staff, chief among whom was Milton A. McRae, the young advertising manager who was to rank as Scripps' chief lieutenant for the next quarter-century. Next was editor R. B. Ross, the tough-looking Scot who had helped Scripps break in as a reporter in Detroit. The reporters happened to be devoutly religious men: a young cub, John H. Ridenour, soon to become editor and later to become publisher of a Long Island newspaper; Lemuel T. Atwood, a lawyer on his uppers who also was to become a top man in the Scripps organization; and Delos R. Baker, who had been read out of the Methodist ministry for heresy and who considered that he would be doing the Lord's will by working for the *Post*. Harnessing the religious bent of his staff to the

[84] JES to EWS, Sept. 18, 1884.

idealism of his resolution of personal reform, Scripps emphasized religious news for a time. Despite the success of the innovation, Scripps soon reversed it, because he could not stand his own hypocrisy. Having no religion of his own, he had let his paper preach things he did not believe.

Within two months of his arrival, Scripps gave force to his resolution of public service in a head-on fight with the corrupt political ring headed by Thomas C. Campbell, a lawyer, and McLean.[85] The fight was brought on when Ross and a young *Post* reporter, F. B. Gessner, were charged with criminal libel because of a story saying that the city health officer, a Dr. Beck, sold to druggists the privilege of dispensing medicine to the poor. Campbell represented Beck, and the case went to trial.

Not content with legal action, the Campbell ring set a gang of hoodlums on Scripps and his men inside the courthouse itself. A dozen rowdies jumped McRae in the anteroom of the courtroom, and another group attacked Ross, beating his face bloody. As Scripps moved to McRae's aid, the gang turned on him. Contorting his face into the expression that made him look dangerous, he reached for his pocket. "He's going to shoot!" someone yelled. The hoodlums fled.[86]

Scripps issued a philippic against the gang in a two-column signed article on page 1. He called Beck a quack and scoundrel who had advertised his ability "to restore the seal of chastity of erring or unfortunate women." Both Ross and Gessner "needed a friend, and, by the Almighty, I propose they shall find one in me at whatever cost." Testifying that he saw Campbell strike McRae in the back, Scripps concluded with this declaration of war:

My attorneys caution me against making any indiscreet remarks about the case. I have told them that I will make no remarks on which I cannot trust my reputation as a gentleman and a journalist, but that I have no intention of showing the white feather. I shall do my duty in this matter as every citizen should. I small demand a fair trial and make a fair fight, and if, for penning this article, which I consider perfectly blameless, I am imprisoned in person, pounded to death by thugs, or ruined in my fortune, I will not be so much the sufferer as the tens of thousands of other citizens of Cincinnati.

If any friends of justice come to my assistance in this contest I shall advise them to leave me, on peril of their lives and their furtunes. But something ought to be done by the city at large, not perhaps to protect me and my friends, but to save themselves from public shame and disgrace.[87]

[85] Alvin F. Harlow, *Serene Cincinnatians* (New York, 1950), pp. 256 f., 414–15; Milton A. McRae, *Forty Years in Newspaperdom; The Autobiography of a Newspaper Man* (New York, 1924), pp. 41–45.
[86] EWS, "Autobiography," pp. 260–61; McRae, *Forty Years*, pp. 41–45.
[87] Cincinnati *Penny Post*, Sept. 1, 1883.

That particular case ended in a hung jury, but Scripps continued to fight political corruption in Cincinnati even long years after he had moved from the city. However, Cincinnati did not throw off boss rule until 1925.

He modified his objective but continued to work toward the establishment of an independent income in three years. Considering too much money vulgar, he had intended to establish the *Post* on a basis that would pay him no more than $5,000 or $6,000 a year, which he considered quite enough for any man; in his youth, he had idealistically held that no man should have more than a dollar a day. He also intended that the *Post* should never make a profit of more than $10,000 a year, everything above that being plowed back into the paper to develop "its power as a political and social organ." [88]

As a consequence of his collision with the Campbell ring, however, he abandoned all idea of making the *Post* "a safe little business," and started to build a personal fortune. "I have determined to launch out on a much heavier enterprise," he said. "I have been literally forced into an important position journalistically and nothing but pure cowardice could be given as a reason for my not taking advantage of the position. This situation brings increased responsibilities and risks, but there is no excuse for evading them." [89]

Scripps' early Cincinnati objective of a competence rather than a fortune obviously conflicts with his determination to become rich, which he had formed on the first trip to Europe. The two declarations illustrate his inconsistency.

To develop the *Post*, Scripps found a chief lieutenant ideal to his purposes in McRae, a large, assertive man a few years his junior. McRae had started on the Detroit *Evening News* and had been transferred to Cincinnati as advertising manager a few months before Scripps took charge. Scripps recognized McRae as a hustler who could help make the *Post* a success, and promoted him to business manager over Worthington. He and McRae were almost complete opposites in nature and temperament. Where Scripps detested trade, McRae was a businessman. Where Scripps wanted to be in the background, McRae loved being out front. Where Scripps did not care for association with famous or rich personages, McRae was in his element with them. Both markedly egotistic, they recalled their early relationship differently. Saying that Scripps took to him "with a vengeance," McRae recalled:

My association with Mr. Scripps from the start was of an unusual character and my position, instead of being irksome and distasteful, became a labor of

[88] EWS, "Autobiography," pp. 353–54.
[89] EWS to EBS, Sept. 11, 1883.

love. I believe it was due more to the nature of our teamwork and friendship for each other than to any other thing that the *Post* ultimately achieved its splendid position in Cincinnati. Mr. Scripps used to call me the "human dynamo"; if long hours and loyal service count for anything, I was fairly entitled to the appellation.[90]

While giving McRae his due as a hard worker, Scripps also held some reservations about him:

McRae attached himself to me. It was hard to get away from him when he was not at work on the streets fighting for dollars, dimes, and even cents in the way of advertising business. He monopolized to the fullest extent possible my time in the evenings and on Sunday. I was aware that he could not do this without neglecting his wife and children, and I resented it. I was frequently going and coming on the railroad between Cincinnati and Cleveland, Cincinnati and Detroit, and Cincinnati and St. Louis. Almost invariably McRae escorted me to the train, carrying my valise, and rarely did I arrive in Cincinnati without his meeting me at the train and carrying my valise and escorting me, either on foot, or in a cab, to my hotel. He talked of the *Post*, directly, or indirectly, all of the time; he talked of the advertisers he was meeting; he talked of his work; and he talked of himself. He never lost an opportunity to blow his own horn and to impress me with his great capacity. In fact, Mr. McRae was determined to take possession of me completely, and he very nearly did so.

It was also a fact that Mr. McRae regarded himself as my natural mentor and guardian. He seemed to regard me as a sort of impractical genius — one that, properly handled, could be made very profitable. Mr. McRae, I think, for over twenty years of the thirty that we have been together, considered himself far superior to me as a practical man of affairs.

. . . .

Mr. McRae was perhaps the most difficult to get along with of all my lieutenants. He was clever and shrewd; he could, and often did, force my hand and lead me into undertakings that I would not have gone into otherwise. The result on my own fortune of his energy and attention to my affairs, in season and out, is hard to calculate. I am willing to concede that I might have failed with the *Post* had I not had such a lieutenant as McRae in the business office. . . .[91]

Despite the disclaimer in his autobiography, Scripps' correspondence at the time shows a greater and more willing dependence on McRae than he cared to acknowledge later. During one trying period he wrote Ellen B.: "McRae came back last evening. I was never more delighted in my life at the sight of anyone. I felt ready to drop with fatigue and nervousness." [92]

Starting out with a $10,000 debt, Scripps and McRae put the *Post* on a

[90] McRae, *Forty Years*, pp. 40 f.
[91] EWS, "Autobiography," pp. 380–83. Scripps' appraisal of McRae was written in 1915, several years after Scripps, in anger, had virtually dismissed McRae.
[92] EWS to EBS, Aug. 12, 1884.

paying basis by February, 1884. Their first step had been to lop off almost half the paper's 13,000 subscribers, getting rid of out-of-town subscribers and making the *Post* strictly a local paper. By February they had pushed circulation to 20,000. All the while Scripps had had greater support from James E. than ever before, because he had knuckled down in one place and had made the paper pay its way.

By 1885 Scripps had achieved one of his dearest professional objectives: his paper had outstripped the Detroit *Evening News* in circulation. Through his position in Cincinnati and Cleveland he saw himself as the leading publisher in Ohio, with greater personal power than any other citizen of the state, and with more respect and goodwill of his patrons than any other American journalist.[93]

In the meantime, while spending most of 1884 in St. Louis in a vain effort to get the *Chronicle* on its feet, he again succumbed to temptation and came to a great disillusionment about women. As a young newspaper proprietor he had, for the first time, an entree to society whose belles taught him, at age thirty, that a young lady of breeding can be just as sportive as one from the other side of the tracks. Until that time he had cherished a chivalric distinction between nice girls, whose hems he did not dare touch, and those whose hems he raised.[94]

Once more worn out from overwork and disgusted with his human weaknesses, he escaped for four months in early 1885, touring the South to meet Democratic leaders who had risen to power with the election of President Cleveland. Visiting every southern capital, he acquired an abiding distrust of the Democratic party,[95] and yet he continued — with the exception of the 1896 campaign — to support the Democratic party.

During the years 1883–85 Scripps matured but also developed two neurotic manifestations that were to make life miserable — anxiety and hypochondria. Even though mounting success might tend to justify "my old conceit that I was born to fill a grander mission than most men,"[96] he was gripped by "a nightmare of morbid presentiment of evil to come. . . ."[97] For the first time he began to complain of shattered nerves. Discontent gnawed at him constantly. Convinced that he had heart trouble, he stopped smoking, but that did not last long, either. Always he wanted to run away. "I despise . . . all humanity."[98] Dragging a leaden weight of world weari-

93 EWS to EBS, Sept. 23, 1885.
94 EWS, "Autobiography," p. 397.
95 EWS, "Autobiography," pp. 397–98.
96 EWS to EBS, July 27, 1883.
97 EWS to EBS, Aug. 14, 1884.
98 EWS to EBS, Sept. 23, 1885.

ness, he ground himself between the millstones of unappeasable ambition and escapism.

MARRIAGE

Returning to Cincinnati in May, 1885, Scripps set out to lead a monastic life and wound up getting married.

He vowed complete and perpetual reform after backsliding in St. Louis, and fled to the country as the only means of avoiding the temptations of the city and the human companionship he abhorred. As a boarder he rented quarters in the country home of Col. Charles A. Gano, sixteen miles north of Cincinnati, where he intended to seclude himself while McRae ran the *Post*, read, exercise, and exorcise the devils of his flesh. In such isolation he carried out his vows, permanently, apparently, as regards women out of marriage and temporarily as regards liquor.

Shortly after moving to the country, he met an eighteen-year-old organist at a church social. She was Nackie Holtsinger, daughter of the Reverend Samuel K. Holtsinger, who was Presbyterian minister in West Chester. Soon he was calling at the parsonage almost every evening.

One evening, while he was returning home astride a Kentucky saddle horse which he had just purchased, a pelting rainstorm caught him just as he approached a tollgate on the road. Because of the rain and the hour he decided to jump the gate, but just as the horse neared the gate, lightning rent the heavens. Terrified, the horse stalled at the gate, throwing Scripps headlong onto rocks on the other side. Bruised, angered, and embarrassed, he walked to the farmhouse where the tollgate keeper lived. A woman opened the door and held out a lantern. To his tale of woe, she merely extended a hand to take his two-cent toll and closed the door in his face. The story is worth mentioning here only because the tollgate keeper was the grandfather of Roy W. Howard.

He and Miss Holtsinger were married in the parsonage on October 7, 1885, a secret marriage so far as his family was concerned. He had not even told his family of his engagement. Only the Holtsingers and Ganos attended the couple, Rev. Mr. Holtsinger performing the ceremony. Taking his bride on a wedding trip to the East, he informed his family from Old Point Comfort that he was married. James E. clucked: "Think of the few marriages in our family, and then to have one occur in this shabby fashion." [99] In December he gathered part of the clan — Ellen B., James E. and his wife, and one of their daughters — for an extended trip to Mexico with him and Mrs. Scripps, the third major trip he had taken in less than a year.

Frequent extensive travel was indicative of his growing affluence, but

[99] JES to EWS, Oct. 29, 1885.

Scripps also used the trips to provide McRae with a psychological stimulus. Before leaving on a trip, Scripps said, he would insist that McRae could not possibly accomplish a given objective, knowing that McRae would accept the challenge, carry out the scheme during Scripps' absence, and bear full responsibility for it.[100]

When he moved his bride into their country home in West Chester in the spring of 1886 he completed carrying out all the resolutions made in Europe in 1883. Well within his three-year limit he had established a fortune sufficient to support a secluded life, reckoning his worth at $250,000 and his annual income at $20,000.[101]

TURNING POINTS

The major turning point in Scripps' personal life and in his career came between 1885 and 1890. At the same time that marriage transformed his personal life, Scripps peaked as an executive in his mid-thirties. He had bullied and pouted his way to one-man control of the Scripps newspapers, inflated a premature design for making the Scripps League a big-time chain operation, split with his brothers after being deposed by James E. and ripped the League apart, and was forced to go it alone thereafter in building the newspaper institution that bears his name today.

The stories of Scripps in command and Scripps at West Chester must be told separately, keeping in mind that they were all part of a pattern involving:

1. The first appearance of the E. W. Scripps who wrote the disquisitions, in contrast to the miserable Eddie Scripps who had painfully inched up the jagged cliff of his ambition while eating his heart out because he could not realize nor yet make others recognize the latent ability he had sensed within himself.

2. His forging of the first effective newspaper chain.

3. His substitution of hard, practical, creative thinking for part — but only part — of the fanciful daydreams of earlier years. He continued to be a daydreamer, and often was so engaged when others thought he was deep in thought.

4. The emergence and implementation of his principle of one-man rule.

5. His self-avowal as an autocrat dedicated to absolutism at home and in business.

6. His perfection of the technique of iron-fisted executive leadership through remote control.

7. His enunciation of ideas, theologies, and principles of newspaper management which would be applied in building his own empire.

[100] EWS to EBS, Dec. 10, 1885.
[101] EWS to EBS, May 12, 1886.

8. His contempt for wealth as an end. He insisted that labor was the only worthwhile end — labor for the joy of doing and creating, employing the full faculties of man as an organism — and that wealth is only a by-product.

9. His adaptation of the Scripps newspapers to rapidly changing social and economic conditions that brought forth the modern newspaper.

10. His claim at the time of creating a "new journalism." The very term "new journalism" happens to be used by historians in describing the changes of the late 1880's, but is usually equated with Joseph Pulitzer.

COUNTRY SQUIRE

Marriage made a different man of Scripps between 1885 and 1890, settling him into the pattern of his mature years. He and his wife added to their family within the first year of marriage with the birth of James George on July 19, 1886, followed by John Paul in 1888. Scripps said it would be hard to find a family with less cause to be unhappy than they.[102] The first daughter, Dolla Blair, was born in 1890. Their Irish cook exclaimed, "Begorra an' this bates all the places I ever seed for breedin'," at a moment when Mrs. Scripps was pregnant; their cow had had a calf; the hired man's wife, a baby; and the cat, kittens.[103]

Scripps found fulfillment for the first time. His family, books, and farm gave to his life a meaning and direction it had never had before. His letters reflect a man proud of his pretty young wife and her versatility. Eager to make her happy, he seriously took into account the divergence in their interests owing to the twelve years difference in their ages. The city rounder metamorphosed into the country squire who comfortably reconciled a strong sense of morality and propriety with his hard core of individualism. Indeed, ever thereafter his personal code was that of middle-class Victorian morality, in spite of the freedom and license he advocated in theory in some disquisitions, to such an extent that in the early 1900's he sidelined one of his closest friends in the Concern because of a divorce. Although he continued to drink, he apparently stopped trying to run away from himself in a bottle.

Freed from daily business routine, he sealed himself in the world of books. He read extensively about government, dreaming of a political career — Congress by the time he was forty because he would need ten years to make the Senate.[104] Just as in Europe, his reading and thinking soon would explode in decisive new courses of action.

102 EWS to EBS, Sept. 9, 1888.
103 EWS to EBS, June 1, 1888.
104 EWS to EBS, May 12, 1886.

Having built a small fortune, he could indulge in the luxury of contempt for wealth as an objective. He decided that his children should never become aristocrats nor inherit great wealth from him.[105] A related attitude became characteristic — that wealth is an obligation, not a privilege, and should be used for humanity but not through charity. Putting this idea into practice, he beautified his West Chester grounds as a public park, built a road through it, and planned a bridge that would give his village neighbors direct access to the grounds.

Because an awareness of the contrary side of Scripps is essential to an understanding of the man, an otherwise disproportionate attention must be paid to the bile that trickled into his flow of milk and honey — the lame metaphor of trickle and flow being the just proportion. Never a man of equable temperament, he whipped himself into a ferment periodically, usually when irritable and impatient. The points at which he could not adjust to his role completely proved an augury.

Many times then and later he minimized himself by saying he was not cut out for the role of *pater familias*, a favorite term of his. Sometimes he chafed under the demands of a wife, such as having to allay her fears in a darkened room during thunderstorms, when he preferred to stand and drink in the display. Before they had been married three years, he was forced to study at night because his wife was jealous of his books, although one of his joys was having her read to him. Resentfully, he said his wife seemed to think he belonged solely to her, expecting him to "lollygag" at home all the time.[106]

Household responsibilities tried his patience, too. Servants would not do his bidding to his satisfaction, and he was convinced village tradesmen took advantage of him through servants doing his purchasing. "We are the royal family and the bounties and places at our disposal make us the unhappy centre of never-ending intrigue." [107] Blowing up at one point, he discharged most of the servants, employed others, and set out to show his young wife how to run a household. His autocracy gave way to subtle feminine assault, but he did not boast so much of that.

Despotism, growing from his belief that a strong man should rule all around him, brought him into constant conflict with his wife, children, mother-in-law, and servants. Particularly did he fly into paroxysms of rage when a child fell ill, especially with a cold. With his own dread of colds, he took every precaution known to prevent them, and gave strict orders that health precautions should be observed for the sake of the children.

[105] EWS to EBS, Mar. 26, 1890.
[106] EWS to EBS, Jan. 1, July 2, Nov. 21, 1888.
[107] EWS to JES, July 1, 1888, in *Scripps* v. *Sweeney, Record,* 1:375.

He also had difficulty getting to know his son Jim, who in a few years would want to be big enough to lick his Dad and would in time seize a part of his father's Concern in a rebellion. Scripps dealt heavily with the diapered toddler. Furious at his wife and mother-in-law for teaching the boy "every nasty disagreeable trick of a spoiled child," Scripps set out to make Jim understand he had to obey, even though this once involved him in a week-long bout with an eighteen-month-old child, which caused Mrs. Scripps to call her husband a brute.[108] Another time, when Jim at two and one-half years fought his mother at bedtime, Scripps spanked him "in a way that not one boy in ten thousand was ever spanked before." Jim did not whimper, but when his father laid him down, the baby "remained like a bended bow resting on his head and heels." [109] His wife predicted that his crossness with Jim would keep the boy from loving him or confiding in him. "I fear it myself," he confessed.[110]

Even among those who belonged most to him, Scripps did not feel wanted or appreciated, to such an extent that Christmas became an annual trial in which he felt he had no place.[111] His periodic discontent erupted when he asked his sister: "What was I born for? Not for business. I have demonstrated that by being capable and not liking it. Not for home serenity. I am not the serene kind. What then? . . . A monastery, with one monk and me the monk! Ah, that would be paradise! Perhaps?" [112]

In his country seclusion Scripps perfected his technique of remote-control management. Although he visited his papers frequently, he did not clutter his mind with details of daily operation. He set the policy and the goals, goading subordinates into achieving his personal desires.

Dashing the short distance to Cincinnati for periodic visits with McRae, he embarrassed his sophisticated manager by appearing in the "decidedly bizarre" costume of a countryman who gave no mind to his appearance. Scripps stuffed his pants into boots, slapped on an old slouch hat, and came in for lunch, without coat or tie, causing McRae to cringe in the knowledge that Scripps' dress would attract unwanted attention. Perhaps with a sigh, McRae charitably conceded, "After all, genius does rise above mere raiment." [113]

Scripps' principal objective was absolute journalistic independence, a principle that guided him from the time he first gained control of the *Post*. As

108 EWS to EBS, Feb. 22 and July 16, 1888.
109 EWS to JES, Feb. 2, 1889, in *Scripps* v. *Sweeney, Record*, 1:465.
110 EWS to EBS, Dec. 25, 1888.
111 *Ibid.*
112 EWS to EBS, June 1, 1888.
113 McRae, *Forty Years*, pp. 94–95.

a general but not invariable rule, he refused to borrow money from banks; when he needed money, and he built his whole organization on borrowed money, he borrowed from Ellen B., James E., and George H. Just as bankers might have pressured him, so might advertisers, and so he kept his dependence upon advertising to a minimum. In Cincinnati he held on to and maintained his independence, running what he called "a newspaper to serve the community." [114]

The personal changes in Scripps between 1885 and 1890 are best summarized by Ellen B. in her customary birthday letter, comparing his letters of 1880–81 with those of 1890:

I read you then [1880–81] a sensitive morbid man with health broken down, constitution impaired; harping always on a short life and an early death; a prey to doubts and fears, doubtful even of yourself at times; ready to throw up the sponge, cry out beaten, to hide your abject head in the dust, harassed by warfares within and without, mortified by want of appreciation from others, beset by petty enemies, counseled to your own hurt by well-meaning but short-sighted friends, hampered in your business ventures, miserable in your pleasures. . . . Well, I see you now — well fed and fat, serene of temper, aspirations satisfied, success won; the happy husband and father of a family to be proud of; their future to think and plan for, and leisure in which to do it. I don't envy you, but I am glad for you as having, I verily believe, done more or come nearer to the solution of the problem of life than any other of our family. Glad for you, your children, and for the world. For as we get near to the end of life we see more clearly (and wonder at our former obtuseness) how the individual is but a part of the great whole; and of moment only so far as it [he] helps to build up and form and perfect that whole.[115]

Confirming her interpretations, Scripps elaborated on the changes he had observed in himself:

You compare in your letter my twenty-sixth with my thirty-sixth year. As I can remember it all, I think the change for the better in my case has been even as much as you desire. But I believe the chief cause of it all has been the difference in the trend of my thoughts. At twenty-six I had more time for thinking than I have now and I then thought of myself so much that my head would ache and I would become utterly wearied of myself. Now that I have less time to think I have so many others to think of that I rarely become self-wearied. I believe, too, that my own deliberate determination to force ego out and altro [sic] into my thoughts, and not mere chance and circumstance, has been the cause of the change. I believe that the human animal can, by the exercise of will power alone, change the leopard spots and Ethiope skin of his whole mental

[114] EWS, "Autobiography," pp. 385–87.
[115] EBS to EWS, June 17, 1890.

and moral character — can in fact make a wise man out of the self-material of a
fool, a good man out of the self-material of a criminal. . . .[116]

FORMING OF SCRIPPS LEAGUE;
BREAK WITH JAMES E.

The turning point in Scripps' career came in 1887–90, during the period
of what the Scrippses called the Quadripartite. In 1887 serious illness forced
James E. to relinquish direct and indirect control of the four Scripps papers — in Detroit, Cleveland, Cincinnati, and St. Louis; the Buffalo paper
had been sold by then. To restore the equilibrium, James E., George H.,
Scripps, and Sweeney signed the Quadripartite agreement by which they
bound themselves not to sell any of their stock to outsiders and agreed that
upon the death of any signer one-half his stock would be purchased by surviving signers. Leaving for a two-year visit in Europe, James E. interpreted
the Quadripartite, and a related document known as the Basis of Adjustment, as meaning that all dissensions were allayed, all ambitions smothered,
all stock-grabbing ended, and the way cleared for the two junior partners to
succeed ultimately to senior status.[117]

James E. was hardly out of sight before a fight for power erupted between
Scripps and Sweeney, culminating in a showdown that meant one or the
other had to be discharged. Scripps had become president of all four companies, but actually had only his two southern papers under tight personal
control. The center of the contest was the Detroit *Evening News* and Cleveland *Press* where Sweeney was business manager and managing director,
respectively; Sweeney tried to entrench himself in virtual control through
placing his own men in strategic positions within the two companies. But
Scripps blocked him at every point.

To give but one example: Sweeney plotted with Dee, still editor of the
News, to fire John McVicar, whom Scripps personally had chosen as managing editor, and replace him with Sweeney's man from the Cleveland
Press, Fred Purdy. Learning of the plan through George H., who opposed
both Sweeney and Dee, Scripps armed McVicar with a secret letter. In case
Sweeney or Dee tried to fire him, McVicar was to produce the letter, which
was Scripps' authorization for him to assume complete editorial control
of the *News*. Sweeney and Dee did try to fire him, McVicar flashed the letter
and confounded both of them.

Intrigue, scheming, conspiracy, stolen correspondence all played a part
in the internal warfare of corporate journalism in which Scripps and Sweeney fought for mastery. With almost hydrophobic insistence, Scripps main-

[116] EWS to EBS, June 18, 1890.
[117] James E. Scripps to George H. Scripps, Mar. 9, 1888.

tained that Sweeney could not be trusted, that he was a rogue, scoundrel, liar, and financial villain straight out of Balzac, but he never did produce a bill of particulars. Sweeney and Dee maintained that Scripps had completely demoralized the Detroit *Evening News*. In his letters from Europe, James E. defended Sweeney. Arguing that Sweeney was a trustworthy associate and proven money-maker, James E. said any excess of which Sweeney might be guilty could be forgiven through attribution to a fear that Scripps was trying to get the better of him.

Actually, Scripps was jealous of Sweeney. Their rivalry may have dated from childhood, but Scripps' jealousy stemmed from the fact that Sweeney stood higher in James E.'s regard than Scripps did. As a matter of fact, James E. once said that if he had to choose between Scripps and Sweeney he would take Sweeney, whose business methods paralleled his own. In the light of the conflict, and Scripps' subsequent sense of having been wronged, it may be significant that the only time he ever told the story of the fourteen-dollar suit that shrank—the one he bought from Sweeney in 1872—was in his bitter account of what happened to him in 1887–89, his "History of the Scripps League."

The struggle for power ended when James E. returned for a brief visit in September, 1888, intending to restore harmony, but concluded that Scripps was right and that Sweeney would have to go. Scripps, James E., and George H. agreed to that decision in a board meeting. When the decision had been made, Scripps then maneuvered James E. into a surrender of James E.'s last vestige of executive power over the *News*, a nebulous but restraining post as general superintendent. James E. retained a determining reserve of power as the controlling stockholder, however. Scripps had won. He now was supreme in all four companies in name and in fact. Sweeney was beaten. His brothers had yielded under his maneuvering again.

At that point Scripps dropped a bombshell: he wanted to keep Sweeney. Incredulously, his brothers heard him explain that Sweeney was their most valuable man (indeed, many years later Scripps brought Sweeney into his own concern briefly), but should be in a subordinate capacity. He therefore proposed to hire him as advertising manager. Both James E. and George H. objected, but Scripps forced them to concede.

James E. cried out, "Ed, you have got the confoundedest mean way of rubbing in a thing on a man than anyone else I ever saw. It is bad enough to get into this boat without being taunted." [118]

As a counterpoise to Sweeney, Scripps persuaded James E.'s son-in-law, George Booth, to come into the Concern as business manager of the *News*, or claimed to have done so. George H. had first recognized young Booth's

[118] EWS, "History of the Scripps League," p. 112.

potential, and it was upon his suggestion that Scripps acted, with the approval of James E. In time Booth made his own mark in the newspaper business.

Having clawed his way to the undisputed top and consolidated his position by "my own devilish instinct to scheme," [119] Scripps knew his hour had come. "Now is my crucial test," he acknowledged.[120]

Then in his thirty-fifth year, Scripps was at the height of his vigor and intellectual power, having full control of his tremendous energy, drive, confidence, and ambition, all of which were vitiated at other times by emotional stress and lack of persistence. And his months of rest and reading at West Chester had fitted him all the better for the rigorous test he now faced. Reinvigorated by country life, he felt strong and compelling "among these poor nerve-worn mortals of the city" and could not "resist at all times the my [sic] natural and exaggerated spirit of a bully." [121] His final element of motivation was the certainty that it was now or never if he were to weld the four papers into the league or chain of which he had dreamed in earlier years.[122]

Aiming only at complete control, Scripps clutched the newspapers as a self-avowed "absolute dictator." [123] He worked from West Chester, traveling among the papers frequently and sometimes remaining long in Detroit, the real seat of government for the Scripps papers. He ruled with a heavy hand and arbitrarily by-passed the boards of the four papers, having played one member against another to such an extent that he could have gotten what he wanted by a simple wave of his hand, anyway. Brooking no opposition, he was prepared to act as judge, jury, and lord high executioner all in the instant of discovering disloyalty or obstructionism.

Spurning a salary, he threw himself into the work of building the business on his own basic principles of idealism and faith in the future. Contrary to the principles of his brothers, his intent was not to extract immediate profit but to make the business a bigger and better newspaper concern which would, inevitably, pay even larger profits in the future than could otherwise be expected. Steadfastly maintaining that he wanted neither glory nor wealth, he said his only interest in the business was to "see it grow into something worth admiring." From his point of view, all the Scrippses had more money than they needed and should now work single-mindedly for the "advancement of our great family of newspapers." For himself, he said, "I

[119] EWS to EBS, July 2, 1888.
[120] EWS to EBS, Sept. 23, 1888.
[121] EWS to EBS, Oct. 26, 1888.
[122] EWS to EBS, July 2, 1888.
[123] EWS to George Booth, Jan. 3, 1889.

don't mind the labor of making great newspapers and I feel sure that being done the profits are not only inevitable but more sure for not being regarded so much. . . ." [124]

He summed up his entire reason for being, in a defiant response to James E., who had attacked him because Scripps' policy had resulted in a sharp drop in *News* profits. James E. protested that he had thought Scripps had been "converted from the ranks of the d———d fools" who think business is conducted for any reason other than to make money. Scripps retorted:

No sir I am not "converted from the ranks of those d———d fools who believe that business is carried on for any other purpose than that of making money." I am still in those ranks. I believe that large businesses like all other large undertakings, from the building up of a great empire down to the breaking in of a wild young horse, are undertaken by men simply in obedience to a very simple law of nature which compels strong men to do great acts.

I consider moneymaking and great wealth as purely incidental to great feats of business. I believe beyond a doubt that our great family of journals may be made to grow into an estate as great as that of the Astors and Vanderbilts and from its character infinitely more honorable and powerful. [125]

Scripps put his theory of one-man rule into practice firmly, but seldom gently. James E. tried to restrain him, writing good-natured letters in which he urged compromise as an art of getting along with business associates, but Scripps haughtily scorned compromise except as a last resort. Moreover, Scripps proceeded on the thesis that the test of good government is not the method but the effectiveness of the governing. "That I am harsh and dictatorial and even cruel in my treatment of men, I have learned by finding so many men crying in my presence, but that I am not so at heart I know, because at such times I feel like crying myself." He insisted on absolutism, both as governor and as one of the governed. [126]

His experience with autocratic control led to the formation of another guiding principle of management. When he discovered that "the great secret of weakness in autocratic government . . . is an incapacity of almost any man to bear the strain of continual responsibility," he concluded that the secret of one-man rule thus lay in a succession of supreme commanders at about five-year intervals. [127] This he allied with an earlier conviction that he would retire at age forty, [128] which was the precursor of his later policy, not always adhered to, that every executive should retire at forty.

[124] EWS to EBS, July 8, 1889.
[125] EWS to JES, Jan. 20, 1889, in *Scripps* v. *Sweeney, Record,* 1:446 f.
[126] EWS to JES, Feb. 2, 1889, in *ibid.,* 1:458 f.
[127] EWS to JES, Apr. 8, 1889, in *ibid.,* 1:500-1.
[128] EWS to EBS, July 2, 1888.

In carrying forward his work, he recharted the course of his papers along a line that he anticipated would either make him stand out as unique among his fellows or as the "founder of a new journalism and perhaps something more." [129] His first step was a complete about-face on the Cincinnati *Post*. Whereas the *Post* previously had criticized Cincinnati for being slow, smoky, unenterprising, wicked, and corruptly governed, he ordered in late 1888 that the paper start printing boom stories — showing Cincinnati to be beautiful, healthful, and full of enterprising young men.[130] Actually, the idea for the changeover came from James E., who suggested that the St. Louis *Chronicle* finally could find a field for itself by booming real estate, railroad, wholesale, building, and other interests.[131]

Having tested the method in Cincinnati, Scripps applied it to Detroit and Cleveland. In Celeveland, where the old method had been to win by fear, the new was to win by favor. He got Paine to swing the *Press* around to "healing up old sores and making warm friends for it and its proprietors." [132]

In Cincinnati and Detroit he produced the innovation of making over the paper, filling it with state news for the first editions and local news for the city edition. The make-over was such a departure then that he had to urge James E. not to decry the plan until it had been tried.[133] It produced still more circulation.

Coming into power at a time when rapid industrialization was changing the American economy even more, Scripps saw that cheap newsprint and Linotypes would make the small paper a thing of the past. He took the present as an indicator of the future, and predicted — and planned accordingly — that the small Scripps papers would have to become metropolitan papers because their cities had become commercial capitals with which the papers must grow or give way to competitors.[134]

To hold the papers closer together and exchange ideas, he introduced what is now a regular part of the Scripps-Howard operation, annual conferences of editors. James E. said he had thought of bringing the editors together, but had encountered such opposition that he had dropped the idea, and commended Scripps' nerve and skill in carrying it off.[135]

But building up the papers cost money, and Scripps prodded his advertising managers into meeting guaranteed goals of minimum receipts. How-

[129] EWS to EBS, Jan. 8, 1888.
[130] EWS to George Booth, Feb. 20, 1889, in *Scripps* v. *Sweeney, Record*, 1:488–89.
[131] JES to EWS, Oct. 15, 1888.
[132] EWS to EBS, Feb. 14, 1888.
[133] EWS to JES, Feb. 28, 1889, in *Scripps* v. *Sweeney, Record*, 1:470.
[134] EWS to JES, Apr. 20, 1889, in *ibid.*, 1:517.
[135] JES to EWS, June 13, 1888.

ever, he did not produce immediate profits. With advertising and circulation bringing in more money than the papers had ever had before, he put the profits back into the papers, thus reducing the actual profits to be divided among the owners, and thereby agitating his brothers greatly.

Scripps' most imaginative and exciting work during the period of the Quadripartite was in making the Scripps League the first newspaper chain. He carried into execution an idea that had been in the air for a long time, possibly ever since the founding of the Detroit *News* in 1873. Although James E. had first given written notice of the idea of establishing a cordon of western papers, Scripps claimed authorship of the idea of making them an entity through a group organization. In 1889 Scripps said he was trying "to develop my boy's idea of the Scripps league — an idea now 15 years old." [136] With typical immodesty, he looked upon himself as the "maker of the league." [137] James E. seems to have conceded that the league idea did originate with Scripps, for in 1880 — while Scripps was founding the St. Louis *Chronicle* — he referred to the "grand design" of which Scripps had dreamed.[138]

Scripps charged full tilt toward realizing his dream the instant he triumphed over Sweeney in September, 1888. With James E.'s approval of a general-in-chief for all four papers, he took the first step toward forming the chain in October by formally adopting the name "Scripps League." Previously, the papers had been known informally in the profession as the Scripps league, Scripps papers, and the Scripps syndicate, the last having a particularly odious connotation at the time.[139]

Aside from the power of his personality, his chief instruments in making the four papers an entity were the New York Advertising Bureau and the New York News Bureau. The advertising bureau had been established a short time before to obtain national (then known as "foreign") advertising for all four papers; Scripps personally established the New York News Bureau in 1888. The Scripps papers are said to have had an advantage in getting advertising, in that they were among the few newspapers of the time that published honest circulation figures. Scripps looked upon the New York News Bureau as his "most daring experiment" and one that could lead to editorial control of the league as a single concern. He placed Ridenour, formerly of the *Post*, in charge of the New York office, and extended its control to Washington and foreign coverage.[140] Ridenour also was to develop

[136] EWS to George Booth, Jan. 3, 1889, in *Scripps* v. *Sweeney, Record,* 1:429 f.
[137] EWS to EBS, July 2, 1888.
[138] JES to EWS, July 1, 1880.
[139] EWS to EBS, Sept. 9, 1888; EWS to JES, Oct. 12, 1888, in *Scripps* v. *Sweeney, Record,* 1:400; EWS, "History of the Scripps League," p. 118; EWS to Milton A. McRae, Apr. 9, 1902.
[140] EWS to JES, July 1, 1888, in *Scripps* v. *Sweeney, Record,* 1:370.

a system whereby men in Europe would cull European papers for the best condensations and translations; Scripps preferred that method of covering Europe because he had learned through his travels that American reporters did an abysmally poor job of reporting European news, and vice versa.[141] Carrying the scheme further, he placed "agents" in Chicago, Washington, Detroit, Cleveland, Cincinnati, and St. Louis to report for all the papers.

He also centralized other functions. Holding that it was foolish for the four papers to buy supplies as so many small purchasers, he centralized purchasing and once bought newsprint at what he said was the lowest price they had ever obtained.[142] He applied the same rule to the editorial side, contending that it was absurd to pay four writers a total of $160 a week when a better writer than any of them could be hired for less than the total sum and write for all four papers.[143]

Although Scripps, estimating that the Scripps papers were read by 300,000 persons a day, concluded that the general idea of the league had been demonstrated correct in theory and comparatively easy to effectuate,[144] James E. returned from Europe in August, 1889, and aborted the League in its eleventh month. The rock on which Scripps and James E. split was Scripps' management of the Detroit *News*, always the pet and chief concern of James E.

Scripps' worst sin, in the eyes of James E., had been his expansionist plans for the *News*. Whereas James E. believed firmly in a small, four-page paper as a carefully nurtured business paying regular dividends, Scripps had rushed the *News* toward modernization, planning to print eight pages and maybe more. The thing that really threw James E. into a rage was Scripps' unauthorized decision to build a new pressroom and install a complete set of new presses.

Scripps had bulled through a virtual revolution of the *News*. He had instituted a whole new roster of executives, made the paper larger and longer, employed larger type, started the *Sunday News*, and striven to move the daily circulation up to 50,000, a level long since reached by his Cincinnati *Post*. With good advertising prospects, he and the others had determined to enlarge the *News'* press capacity because enlargement would produce additional advertising that in turn would produce an additional $25,000 – $50,000 a year in net profits.[145] The Scripps League also had sent a Workingman's Expedition to the Paris Exposition in 1889 — the era of newspaper stunts was gaining momentum at that time — at a cost of more than $50,000,

[141] EWS to JES, Feb. 18, 1889, in *ibid.*, 1:482–84.
[142] EWS to EBS, Dec. 9, 1888.
[143] EWS to JES, July 1, 1888, in *Scripps* v. *Sweeney, Record*, 1:370.
[144] EWS to JES, Apr. 8, 1889, in *ibid.*, 1:501.
[145] EWS, "History of the Scripps League," pp. 139–41.

which James E. found to his alarm was being footed almost entirely by the *News*.

And on the rock of the *News* the two brothers split for good, although the disagreement dragged out for over a year before the severance became final.

James E.'s position was this: He found upon his return that the old *News* organization had been destroyed; no adequate replacement had been instituted; the paper had been forced to pass a dividend for the first time; he had reached an age at which he had no interest in expansionist ambitions; and he wanted his newspaper interests confined to the *News*, which he felt he "must protect from all danger of being wrecked by wild or irresponsible management. . . ." [146] Actually, he had decided earlier in the year that Scripps was "a mere adventurer making a big dash on the chance of a success with an equal chance of failure." [147] Writing Scripps, James E. summed up his position by saying: "I don't dispute the sincerity of your belief that you have been a great benefactor to the concern, and I am sorry to say that I with equal sincerity regard your administration as positively disastrous." [148] Ultimately, James E. came to this bitter conclusion about Scripps:

First, Ed is unboundedly ambitious. He seeks to keep all our properties together to be at the head of them. He is not satisfied to stand on his own bottom but wants to build his fortunes on ours. He has for years persistently followed the policy of getting everything possible into his own hands and relinquishing nothing. I foresee that, if permitted to go on, in a few years more he will be the all-dominant power and the great capitalist of the concern.

I have no jealousy of him if he acquires power of his skill and genius and wealth by hard work and prudent saving but I am clear that his power will be secured not by his merits but by his intrigue and undermining and making tools of others and his wealth by equally wrongful means. He has got all Ellen's capital into his hands. His quadripartite scheme was intended to give him at a small cost a large share of ours. . . . I tell you he is a dangerous man for any who are not equally sharp and scheming to have anything to do with.[149]

Scripps' position was this: He had found the *News* in a declining position and had built it in two years into a paper that was able to spend more in one year than it had ever made in any year under James E. He also became convinced that James E. was badly scared by the size and nature of the *News*, fearing he could not run it himself and that Scripps would insist upon ruling it or ruining it. In addition, there was the ever-present, basic disagreement — Scripps looked to the future, his brother to immediate profit. Still, he conceded that he always admired the idealism of his brother as a

[146] JES to EBS, Aug. 26, 1889.
[147] JES to EBS, Feb. 17, 1889.
[148] JES to EWS, Dec. 21, 1889.
[149] JES to George H. Scripps, Aug. 29, 1892.

journalist but was always shocked by his brother's other side — that of the money-maker — and what he called James E.'s willingness to sacrifice the better for the baser passion.[150]

James E. immediately deposed Scripps as president of the Evening News Association, ultimately abrogated the Quadripartite upon which Scripps had been relying for a considerable though delayed reward, and shifted the scene of the fight to the Cleveland *Press*. Although angered by his deposition as president of the *News*, Scripps actually had been wanting to be relieved of that responsibility, but to be cut out of the *Press* was something else again. Always he had regarded himself as being the father of two families — what he called the children of his flesh and the children of his spirit, his newspapers. And he regarded the *Press* as his first-born child.

Being removed as president of the *Press*, deposed as a member of the board, and then having to fight off an effort to make him sell his stock was what really caused Scripps to explode in the 1889–90 fight with James E. He was angered, mortified, and filled with hatred because James E. had used "brute force" to wrong him.

Scripps was eliminated from the management of the two northern papers, although he owned stock in both, and was left with only the Cincinnati *Post* and St. Louis *Chronicle* under his control. In 1890 the two brothers separated forever, notwithstanding an overlap of stock ownership. In the split, George H. sided with James E., Ellen B. with Scripps.

Scripps was licked.

FORMING OF SCRIPPS-McRAE LEAGUE

Smarting from the twin stings of defeat and repudiation, Scripps characteristically tried to run away. He fled to the farthermost corner of the United States, buying a chunk of semi-arid mesa north of San Diego where he built "Miramar," a home that soon became his retreat from the world. By placing McRae under contract to run the *Post* and *Chronicle* at a profit, Scripps freed himself from all business obligations except those that he voluntarily chose to undertake, and kept the chain principle in force by naming his two papers the Scripps-McRae League to distinguish them from James E.'s two papers. For two years Scripps exhausted his energies in creating a home out of desolation, working out of his system the hatred and resentment he felt toward James E.

In 1892 George H. broke with James E., shifting his allegiance to Scripps and bringing the Cleveland *Press* into the Scripps-McRae League. At about the same time, Scripps became ready once more to turn his hand to building

150 EWS, "Autobiography," pp. 162–63, 444; EWS, "History of the Scripps League," pp. 147–48.

and extending a newspaper chain. In 1895 he and George H. signed a three-way contract with McRae, similar to the 1890 contract, and the new Scripps-McRae League started to rise.

Again, the stories of Scripps the empire builder and Scripps of "Miramar" must be told separately, each leading up to his retirement in 1908.

BUILDING OF "MIRAMAR"

Scripps' bull-headed determination to do the impossible, as well as his characteristic compulsion to create, produced "Miramar" as an oasis on the treeless, sage-covered mesa north of San Diego. A combination of circumstances caused him to pick that spot. First, there was the compelling desire to escape, to get away from the world. The mesa offered just that opportunity, a "lodge in a vast wilderness," as he saw it. Further, San Diego had only about 10,000 inhabitants and was sixteen miles away by a trail winding through sagebrush. Obviously, he would not be bothered by people. When he first saw the mesa in December, 1890, looking at it because his brother Fred wanted to establish what he called a lemon ranch and needed financial assistance, Scripps immediately likened terrain and climate to North Africa, the only place where he had ever been free from the colds that were the bane of his life. He and Ellen B. also wanted to help Fred establish a citrus orchard.

In addition, making a home on that desert seemed impossible. A few homesteaders had tried and failed for lack of water. Forcing his will upon a wild land happened to be just the antidote Scripps needed for the poison of hatred and revenge that then filled him.

He and Ellen B. bought about four hundred acres, thirty of which were his own, although he later came to own all the land. A whole Scripps colony soon moved into the general area — Ellen B. establishing a home in La Jolla, his brothers Will and Fred working at "Miramar," and others coming and going.

Beginning in February, 1891, Scripps spent eight years building "Miramar," drawing the plans for and supervising construction of the house himself. When he finished the first wing in the summer of 1891, he had intended only to build a cheap winter home, but as the challenge of the task grew greater, so grew his plans. Further, it developed that he alone (as he told it) was able to help the impoverished homesteaders whose dreams of irrigated fields had ended in despair. Some needed money to leave, and he bought their nearly worthless land, enlarging his tract to 2,100 acres. Others needed money to stay, and he hired them to clear the land and build the house.[151]

[151] "One of a Hundred Million," EWS Writings, 6:1.

Following the design of North African architecture as he remembered it, Scripps built three sides of a square around a paved courtyard. With the exception of one room known as the Tower Room, he built a one-story home of about forty rooms, determined that each child should have a sitting room and bedroom for maximum privacy, with room for all his poorer relatives. In the adobe east wing, completed in 1898, he gave himself a private suite of bedroom, study, and dining room, and let it be known that no one was to invade his rooms except Mrs. Scripps and she just enough to maintain her rights.[152] Studiously avoiding any ostentation, Scripps simply built a comfortable and pleasant home. In external appearance, the design of the alabaster house is simple almost to the point of austerity, although considerable changes have been made since Scripps' death.

Building the house was only part of the challenge. He wanted to make the land bloom. He planted a lemon orchard of one hundred acres, but gave it up because of drought, built dams to impound the sparse rainfall, and planted seven hundred acres of eucalyptus trees which he thought would be marketable as fuel.[153] He started every eucalyptus tree from a seed, nurturing the seedling in a greenhouse until it was about twelve inches high and then transplanting it to a nursery of about three acres. The thousands of trees raised in the greenhouse are to be seen on the "Miramar" grounds today, the orderly rows of planting still discernible when viewed from the proper angle. But his sole, overriding motive was to conquer and to create, his only real interest lying in the obstacles that had to be overcome.[154]

For the first few years he spent the winter at "Miramar" and the summer at West Chester, shuttling his family back and forth in a special railroad car. But by 1900 "Miramar" became his year-round abode, although West Chester remained his legal residence, and he seldom left it between then and 1917.

Happiness and tragedy marked Scripps' life during the 1890's. Three more children were born during the decade, one of whom, Edward Willis McLean, died at "Miramar" in 1899, just a few weeks short of his eighth birthday. Robert P. was born October 27, 1895, named for Bob Paine of Cleveland, and Nackey Elizabeth on May 16, 1898, both in San Diego. In the meantime, it had been discovered that Dolla (Dorothy), the first daughter, was mentally retarded. Because the sight of her agitated and depressed Scripps, Dolla lived most of her childhood in a special school in New Jersey. Her father later established Dolla in a home of her own at Escondido, north of "Miramar."

[152] EWS to EBS, Oct. 4, 1898.
[153] EWS to Gifford Pinchot, May 26, 1908; EWS to R. C. Allen, Apr. 19, 1910.
[154] EWS, "Autobiography," pp. 418–19; EWS to EBS, May 4, July 18, Oct. 7, 1895.

Scripps ran his family with a mixture of despotism and permissiveness. His despotism was shown most clearly in contests with his wife and in-laws in which he laid down the law that he would govern all around him by right of power, that he was dictator in his own family, and would exclude all from his circle who would not submit to his will.[155] Otherwise, he was indulgent toward his wife and, apparently, liberal toward his in-laws.

He deliberately tried to teach and train his children "to the 'king trade.'" Despising convention himself, he intended that his children "should not be servile to any sort of convention."[156] Although there was no mistaking who was boss in the family, and contrary to his one-man rule in business, Scripps sincerely gave his children rein to develop their independent powers to the full.

Hoping they would become original thinkers (he saw himself as one), he refused to place them in the stamping mill of a classroom. Except for brief interludes when Jim and John attended school and Nackey went away to a girls' school, Scripps employed tutors, but always for the single purpose of teaching certain facts, "never for the purpose of training or directing their minds along any channels, moral or other."[157] Always he encouraged his children to read extensively and intensively, sometimes laying out reading courses for them. He explained his purposes in a letter to Paine:

> In a general way, this is how I am trying to train my sons: I give them absolute liberty to enjoy life and the pursuit of happiness, so long as they do not interfere with the rights of others; so long as they do not, as minors, do anything to injure their own health. Naturally, like every other father I am teaching them morals and manners from my own point of view. I am trying to teach them how a master should behave, rather than how a servant deports himself. The chances are that they will be servants; but that is a trait I do not know and hence cannot impart to them.[158]

Indeed, Scripps himself was a teacher, in the broadest sense of the term, and his sons learned to think and argue in free-ranging conversations with him. Especially was this true as they grew older and took, or prepared to take, their places in his business. A 1907 dinner conversation was remembered thus:

> Topics discussed had a wide range; and E. W. Scripps' three-fold relationship towards his sons was quite obvious — parent, tutor and business associate and counselor. The bent of mind of each of the boys was even more obvious.
>
> Jim's was the practical mind — business organization, dollars, profits, rights of capital.

[155] EWS to EBS, May 23, Oct. 11, 1895; Sept. 30, 1898.
[156] EWS to EBS, Mar. 17, 1898.
[157] EWS, "Autobiography," p. 592.
[158] EWS to Robert F. Paine, Jan. 5, 1901.

John's favorite themes: minimum wage, living wage, editorial responsibilities and prerogatives.

Though "just a kid," Bob's thinking processes worked the faster, and he was invariably in the thick of any discussion, never hesitating to either disagree or agree with either of his brothers or his father. He generally upheld his brother John, but went much farther — minimum wage, rights of labor, free speech and the "Bill of Rights," assured independence of the editor, and, in general, "human welfare" subjects.[159]

Scripps helped fit his sons for the newspaper business by letting them publish a weekly, printed family newspaper, the *Sunbeam*. It was written mostly by the boys and their tutor, George H. Hazzard, but it sometimes carried a contribution known as "Observations of Mr. Spookle Wiseacre," which had a distinct Scrippsian cut.

Scripps used "Miramar" as a baronial retreat from the vexations of business.[160] Although he also dreaded the complications encountered at "Miramar," there at least "I can get on a horse or a buckboard and run away. . . ." [161] But escape to "Miramar" did not mean he was removed from involvement in business, for he spent long hours with reports and correspondence.

During the late 1890's his habit was to sleep until almost noon and then exercise out-of-doors; he ate breakfast about the time others ate their noon meal in the dining room where there were three tables — one for the family, one for business people, and one for employees; sometimes he worked all afternoon with his secretary (he had employed his first one in 1889), but ordinarily did not settle down to business until about 9 P.M. and the worked until about 2 A.M.[162]

Always fearful of catching cold, Scripps habitually wore a skullcap indoors to keep his head warm. He still dressed as carelessly as he had in West Chester — rough work clothes and soft, custom-made boots.

A "hat table" just outside his study was stacked with hats, and he grabbed one at will when he strode out of the house to take a walk, which he did several times a day. He tromped about the grounds with a five-foot bamboo staff fashioned by one of his workmen. Sometimes he walked extensively over the grounds; sometimes he circled the courtyard enough times to equal a mile, keeping track of the laps by transferring a gold coin from one pocket to the other.[163]

[159] Harry L. Smithton, "Notes."
[160] EWS to EBS, Sept. 17, 1894.
[161] EWS to EBS, Sept. 18, 1893.
[162] *Sunbeam*, Feb. 25, 1899.
[163] Mrs. Nackey Scripps Meanley, interview with editor, July 10, 1961.

Too direct to bother with bells, Scripps bawled out like a hog caller for whomever he wanted, family or servants. He usually had Japanese house servants, because he considered a servant's position beneath the dignity of an American. At various times he had rather large crews of men working on the ranch, housed in a bunkhouse and fed in a boardinghouse. Any tramp who wandered by "Miramar" was guaranteed two meals and a bunk for the night.

Although Scripps had been a good horseman in his younger years, he came more and more to traveling over the ranch in a buckboard drawn by a team of grays, Dick and Duke. As impatient there as anywhere else, he drove Mexican style — at a trot.[164] An apochryphal story has it that he once galloped a horse to death between "Miramar" and San Diego.

However, he seldom went to San Diego, except to get his teeth filled, order new boots, or play poker at the Cuyamaca Club where a doorman once tried to turn him away because Scripps' rough dress and shaggy beard made him look like a laborer.

To make a business trip, he rode by wagon to the Linda Vista flag stop a short distance west of the ranch and flagged a Santa Fe train. When he first began to use automobiles on the ranch in the early 1900's, he always had a wagon follow along in case the car broke down.

Where other wealthy men might patronize the arts, Scripps held art in repugnance and artists in contempt, but he always was willing to bet on a man, which led him to commission a youthful sculptor just to see what the young man could do. The sculptor was Arthur Putnam, a boy from the mesa who was as original and individualistic in his way as Scripps in his. To satisfy his curiosity about Putnam, Scripps commissioned him to shape four bronzes depicting the history of California. Putnam did the Indian, the Padre, and the Plowman — the first two on exhibit in San Diego, the third still at "Miramar" — but not the fourth.

Unremitting labor, tension, continually heavier drinking, and excessive smoking took their toll of Scripps, sometimes immobilizing him through nervousness and hypochondria. He imagined heart disease and temporarily gave up whiskey and tobacco; he suffered nervous attacks which he called "the horrors"; he feared insanity; he felt sorry for himself, victimized by others.[165]

All of this anxiety brought Scripps to another great moment of decision in 1899: Quit drinking or die. Whiskey, tobacco, and neurosis had almost destroyed his eyesight, and left his body weak and flabby.[166] But his condi-

[164] *Ibid.*, July 13, 1961.

[165] EWS to EBS, May 9, 1893; July 18, 1894; Sept. 15, Oct. 4, Oct. 11, 1895; July 21, 1896.

[166] EWS, "Autobiography," pp. 468–69.

tion did not bring him to the decision. Rather, he was shocked into it when George H. started dying from cancer, which meant that Scripps had to stay alive because Jim at fifteen was not old enough to succeed his father in the management of the newspapers. Scripps told a physician, an oculist, and a nerve specialist he would follow their instructions if they would keep him alive another six or seven years. Neither they nor anyone else ever believed Scripps' story that he had drunk a gallon of whiskey a day for many years.[167] The oculist attributed the blindness to nerves, but all of them told Scripps he might improve if he were to stop drinking and smoking.

As a result, Scripps followed this advice. He never did resume drinking to any extent, but soon returned to smoking, consuming sometimes twenty cigars a day, very mild Santa Fe's made for him in San Diego.

He cared for George H. until the latter's death at "Miramar" in 1900.

Scripps improved quickly, but soon recognized an inkling that his trouble might be psychosomatic. In June, 1901, he had a long session of eight days with a Cincinnati dentist and his eyesight almost failed him. Immediately afterward, he took his sons on a three-week trip to Yellowstone National Park, and so forgot himself and his troubles that his eyesight — with spectacles — became as good as it ever had been. Blindness and debilitating nervousness returned whenever he experienced emotional stress, either at home or in connection with business,[168] and this up-again, down-again course continued until ill health forced him to retire in 1908.

EXPANSION OF SCRIPPS-McRAE LEAGUE

By holding the Cincinnati *Post* and St. Louis *Chronicle* as the Scripps-McRae League, Scripps kept alive the germ cell of the first newspaper chain until he was ready to make that cell divide and reproduce itself into the largest number of daily newspapers that had ever been established by one man. He and his associates founded thirty-two newspapers and acquired fifteen others, some of which were short-lived, others still published today.

After withdrawing to lick his wounds in 1890, Scripps was ready by 1892 to start building the newspaper empire of his dreams. In 1892 he gained predominance in the Cleveland *Press* through George H.'s shift of allegiance and his and George H.'s purchase of Sweeney's stock, and acquired the San Diego *Sun*.

In 1895 the way was cleared for the explosive growth of the Scripps newspapers when he and George H. combined all their stock and signed a new contract with McRae. The three men pooled all dividends and salaries each

---

[167] *Ibid.*
[168] EWS to Dr. F. J. Langdon, Aug. 18 and Sept. 3, 1901; Dr. Langdon's letter quoted in EWS to Robert F. Paine, Sept. 3, 1901.

year; the total was then divided, with Scripps and George H. each getting two-fifths and McRae one-fifth. McRae ran the papers as general manager, but Scripps retained full control as editor-in-chief. He held stock for all three as trustee, and was the Number 1 man. Following his earlier-developed principle of one-man power (himself) and his theory of a succession of commanders, Scripps intended McRae to be general manager until 1900, president until 1905, and chairman of the board after that, each time giving way to a younger man. As controlling stockholder Scripps always would have final say, regardless of who the executives were.

The contract was the foundation of his independent career, what he called the third era of his life, into which he was forced by the break with James E. Carrying forward that career, he actually developed three groups or chains of newspapers. The Scripps-McRae League included the Cincinnati and St. Louis papers, and the name embraced another group of midwestern and southwestern papers in which Scripps' lawyer, J. C. Harper of Cincinnati, was his principal associate. On the West Coast, Scripps developed a completely separate chain.

Because a history of the Scripps newspaper concern is out of the question here, suffice it to say that his newspaper holdings included the following properties when he retired in 1908, thirteen years after signing the tripartite contract with McRae: Cleveland *Press*; Cincinnati *Post* and its sister, the *Kentucky Post*; St. Louis *Chronicle*; San Diego *Sun*; Los Angeles *Record*; Kansas City *World*; Seattle *Star*; Akron *Press*; Des Moines *News*; Spokane *Press*; San Francisco *News*; Toledo *News-Bee*; Tacoma *Times*; Columbus *Citizen*; Sacramento *Star*; Fresno *Tribune*; Denver *Express*; Evansville *Press*; Pueblo *Sun*; Terre Haute *Post*; Dallas *Dispatch*; Portland *News*; *Oklahoma News*; Memphis *Press*; and Berkeley *Independent*. In addition, he held a minority interest in the Detroit *News* and Detroit *Tribune*, at one time had controlled the ill-fated Nashville *Times* and had a minority interest in the Omaha *News*, and had taken a fling in Chicago, starting and killing the Chicago *Press* in 1900.

George H.'s death in 1900 precipitated a bitter family fight when James E. contested the will, which bequeathed George's newspaper stock to Scripps. Scripps and James E. finally settled their dispute in 1903, whereby George's 32 per cent of the stock in the Detroit *News* was exchanged for James E.'s interest in the other papers. But Scripps held on to his one share of Detroit *News* stock out of "pure, damn fool sentiment." [169]

Scripps contemplated a national newspaper made up of his separate papers, the common denominator being the Newspaper Enterprise Association which he founded in 1902. NEA provided news, features, and editorials

[169] EWS to Pat Baker, Jan. 9, 1920.

for the Scripps papers, but the autonomy of his editors, who looked upon NEA as syndicate filler, prevented the development of his national newspaper idea. Representing the idealism of Scripps' concept of journalism, the NEA will be discussed at more length in the section on Journalism.

In 1907 he performed what he reckoned to be his greatest service to freedom of the press by establishing the United Press. Countering what he considered to be a potential news monopoly through the franchise-ruled Associated Press, the UP report was available to any newspaper that wanted it, including Scripps' competitors.

The core of Scripps' journalism was his cry of earlier years, "God damn the rich and God help the poor." Giving his newspapers a spirit of protest, he branded them with independence and deliberately kept them small as a means of avoiding dependence on the "Interests" for sustenance through advertising. Although he himself became wealthy, Scripps studiously and deliberately avoided contact with other rich men. He avoided the common man just as much, even though he dedicated his papers to the common man's interest, and fought for reform and justice. He would die for the common man, he said, but be damned if he would live with him. Occasionally, one of his papers drifted from this line of Scripps' idealism and he jerked it back ruthlessly. Not even his closest friend in the Concern, Bob Paine in Cleveland, was immune from his purgative. In 1894 Scripps decided that Paine had made the *Press* much more influential politically than Scripps thought any newspaper should be. Believing that Paine was giving too much attention to present politics and "not enough to the newspaper as a newspaper, and not enough to things in the future of politics," Scripps ordered Paine to stop printing editorials and stories designed to influence readers politically.[170] His basic attitude was that newspapers should be honest and impartial witnesses. Similarly, he discovered in 1898 that the Cincinnati *Post*, under McRae, had reached some sort of *modus vivendi* with Cincinnati interests that made the paper complacent toward municipal corruption. He ripped things apart there, too, to get the *Post* back on the track, despite an immediate loss of profits.

Ironically, Scripps built his chain of four-page papers by following James E.'s principles, which he earlier had maligned so freely. He conceded on several occasions that he followed his elder brother's rules, summing it up by saying he had corrected his own abuses and fallen back upon the lessons learned from James E.[171]

Scripps built his empire on the principle of holding control through at least 51 per cent of the stock in each newspaper, letting the editor and

170 EWS, "Autobiography," p. 285.
171 EWS to EBS, Sept. 8, 1899.

business manager between them have all or part of the remaining 49 per cent. Sometimes other associates also held some of the stock. Usually in starting a paper he put up all the money. When the paper became profitable, the editor and business manager began repaying Scripps for the initial value of their stock. The incentive of profit-sharing undoubtedly had much to do with making a success of what might be regarded as shoestring newspapers. Furthermore, their initial capitalization appeared lower than it really was, because his editors and managers worked for a smaller salary, in anticipating an eventual share of ownership, than they would have otherwise; the difference between what they earned and what they would have earned represented a hidden capital cost.

To keep his newspapers true to course, he followed the invariable rule of making the editor supreme. The business manager's job simply was to handle the money. Although Scripps once again was following his boyhood discovery of how to get the other fellow to do the work, he worked hard himself even through the system of long-range management. Weekly and monthly financial statements came to his desk from every newspaper, and he knew exactly what was going on where. He also claimed that he could tell from those statements when the profit motive got the better of the service motive on any given paper. However, he intermittently went for long periods without reading his newspapers.

He kept in touch with his papers by making an annual tour of inspection. He also brought editors and managers to "Miramar" for periodic conferences about the council table, "with the 'old man' sitting at the head, the inevitable cigar between his teeth, talking, counseling, directing, often stirring his audience with his startling views of men and affairs." [172] Even in retirement he continued to meet editors in conference. After a few days with Scripps the executives would be worn out, but he seldom was tired. They were said not to be afraid of him, but were on their mettle in his presence.[173]

The only real unity in the chain was Scripps himself. Each paper was published by a separate company, but each bore the marks of his character, idealism, and personality. There was no central corporation, and Scripps was the only individual holding stock in all papers. Managerial centralization was effected through the central office in Cincinnati. A modicum of editorial centralization was effected through the NEA, which was an appendage of the Cleveland *Press* rather than a separate operation.

This unity in diversity obscures the true role of McRae who, despite his unquestioned contributions to building the League, was more an employee

[172] McRae, *Forty Years*, p. 96.
[173] E. F. Elfstrom, publisher of Fullerton (Calif.) *News-Tribune* who was Scripps' secretary from 1922 to 1924, interview with editor, July 15, 1961.

than an equal. However, he was the one who stood forth in the public eye, creating a national reputation as both a newspaperman and civic worker, while Scripps by preference remained in obscurity. There were occasions when the uninformed thought Scripps-McRae meant that Scripps was Mc-Rae's first name. "McRae has always been a nuisance," Scripps once said, "but I put up with him for many years because his most marked fault (notoriety seeking) has served to help me in my efforts to remain obscure." [174]

The 1895 contract had made Scripps and McRae partners to that extent, but Scripps drew a distinction between partner and partnership. "Our concern is not a partnership," he told McRae. "It consists of a number of corporations, each one subject to the control of the majority vote of its stockholders." [175] What it boiled down to was that Scripps had recognized McRae's ability and took full advantage of the ability but not of the man. McRae said Scripps had an ability to pick men, and upon finding one he could trust he rewarded him liberally; McRae testified that he had never found Scripps niggardly with him.[176]

Although Scripps and McRae complemented each other, an unbridgeable chasm separated them, because Scripps fundamentally was the editorial idealist and McRae the profit-producing advertising man. The chasm finally became a running sore in the organization because of the contradictory philosophies of what Scripps called Scrippsism and McRaeism.

Scripps in effect dismissed McRae in 1905 by making him chairman of the board.[177] Scripps complained that he had been put to the expense of creating the central office — with L. T. Atwood, the one-time *Post* reporter, in charge of financial affairs — because McRae had not performed all his duties. "McRae failed to deliver the goods he contracted to deliver," although Scripps agreed that McRae had delivered other goods, namely, a large volume of business and national prestige. "I contracted for a loaf. McRae did not give me the loaf. He only gave me half a loaf, and eked it out with a fish, which I did not contract for, and which I really did not want. . . . There has grown up — that is to say, there has existed — for many years a sort of antagonism between Scrippsism and McRaeism." [178] Scripps insisted that there "must be the most full and complete understanding throughout the concern that Mr. McRae and I have extremely different views on

[174] EWS to EBS, Mar. 22, 1924.
[175] EWS to Milton A. McRae, Mar. 31, 1905.
[176] McRae, *Forty Years*, pp. 92–93.
[177] EWS to EBS, Jan. 26, 1925.
[178] EWS to Robert F. Paine, Mar. 30, 1905.

certain newspaper matters, especially on the subject of editorial prece-
dence." [179]

Scripps "contracted the habit of overlooking Mr. McRae" [180] during 1906,
and then in November, 1907, McRae withdrew from management when
he and Scripps abrogated the 1895 contract. McRae's retirement did not
disturb their fairly cordial personal relationship at the time.

Only three months later, Scripps, too, retired because of failing health, but
it was only a partial retirement. He handed over control of business affairs
to his son Jim, then twenty-two, but retained editorial control until 1911. In
stepping aside (with one foot) in February, 1908, Scripps left his editors
and managers three injunctions for running his papers: (1) Make money;
(2) obey the Ten Commandments; (3) serve the workingman.

IN RETIREMENT

From this point on, the story of E. W. Scripps requires considerably less
detailing than even the little that has been possible heretofore, because so
much of his thought and life after 1908 is represented in the disquisitions
and commentaries that follow.

Retirement to Scripps merely meant letting someone else run the show
under his constant and searching eye, permitting him to release his creativity
in other directions. He recollected having told Jim in 1908, "Jim, so long as
I can wiggle either a finger or a toe I am going to be master not only of myself, but of what is mine." [181] His Letterbooks after 1908 show he was prepared at any time to make quick and strong decisions directly, rather than
through Jim. However, he drew a line between dollars and ideas prior to
1911, leaving dollars to Jim while he tried "to see to it that what our editors do and say will be in line with principles and policies consistent with
my views." [182] He relinquished editorial direction to his son John in 1911.
John, who had married McRae's daughter Edith, died in 1914, leaving a
son, John Paul.

In 1908 Scripps turned to writing the disquisitions. With a cigar clenched
in his teeth, he worked in his study, an end room which had no windows
in the end wall because he did not want to be distracted. His eyesight had
improved sufficiently for him to read. Never using an easy chair for reading,
he tilted back in an office chair while devouring books and periodicals, particularly the latter; he had an extensive subscription list of both American
and English journals. When ready to discourse, he called in a secretary,

[179] EWS to J. C. Harper, Apr. 20, 1905.
[180] EWS to L. T. Atwood, Apr. 14, 1906.
[181] EWS to EBS, Mar. 4, 1926.
[182] EWS to Judge Ben Lindsey, Sept. 7, 1911.

tilted back in his chair, shoved his spectacles up on his forehead, and started talking. Cigar ashes flaked his vest. He never, or seldom, used an ashtray. When he flicked an ash, it was onto the carpet.

Reaching out for greater intellectual pursuits, he tried to establish a correspondence society of men who read and thought, but found everyone else too busy. For stimulation, he kept up a voluminous correspondence with thought leaders across the country, several of whom visited him at "Miramar," some of whom he saw on a 1914 trip to the East. Soon after retirement, his list of correspondents, friends, and acquaintances was weighted in favor of reformers. Later, the list was weighted in favor of scientists. The early list included (the list being merely illustrative): Judge Ben Lindsey, James H. Causey of Denver, Francis J. Heney of San Francisco, Gifford Pinchot, Hiram Johnson, Clarence Darrow, Lincoln Steffens, W. A. U'Ren of Oregon, Fremont Older, William Allen White, Senator Robert M. LaFollette, Franklin K. Lane, William Gibbs McAdoo, William Jennings Bryan, and Max Eastman. Those who visited him found a man whose handshake was limp and with whom a conversation proved to be a monologue in a deep, gravelly voice. Only one man had the distinction of being able to talk Scripps down — Joseph Fels, the Philadelphia soap manufacturer, who visited "Miramar." [183]

Gradually his interest turned to science, sparked by the only person with whom he ever developed a genuine and close personal friendship, Professor W. E. Ritter, a University of California zoologist. Scripps' interest in science ultimately led to establishment of what is now the Scripps Institution of Oceanography at La Jolla, the Foundation for Population Research at Miami University in Ohio, and Science Service for the dissemination of science news through daily newspapers.

He continued to work hard in retirement, sometimes going until 2 A.M. Many evenings, however, he spent playing dominoes with his wife or listening to her read novels; neither she nor anyone else could ever read scientific works aloud to his satisfaction. He regularly spent Sunday afternoon in a four- or five-hour visit with Ellen B. in La Jolla.

The ranch occupied much of his attention as he continued his forestation program and revived citrus cultivation briefly. Another ranch a short distance away, Fanita Ranch, became a challenge to him, and he devoted so much attention to alfalfa that Mrs. Scripps jokingly called him Alfalfa Ed. He found a further outlet for his restless creativity by providing leadership in the construction of roads in San Diego County, some of which he built at his own expense.

More unhappiness seized him in 1916 when his daughter Nackey eloped

[183] Mrs. Nackey Scripps Meanley, interview with editor, July 10, 1961.

with Tom Meanley, who had been Scripps' secretary and whom Scripps disliked for reasons not specified in his documents; many times, it appears that Scripps disliked individuals instinctively and then justified himself by various means. Because he refused to have anything to do with his son-in-law, while providing for his daughter, the marriage marked a rupture in the family. He therefore made plans to move from "Miramar" to Washington, choosing the capital because of the crisis facing America through the war in Europe.

He did not move to Washington until America's entry into World War I gave him a plausible reason, however. There, for a few months in 1917, he supervised coverage and editorial treatment of the war.

Just as the Quadripartite marked the turning point in his career, World War I marked a turning point in his thought. Almost imperceptibly he changed into a conservative, remarking that he was becoming an aristocrat or oligarch. The reason for the change is not clearly delineated, but it appears to have resulted from his recognition of the incontrovertible and indispensable importance of capitalism in winning the war, and his further recognition that the America of his youth had passed into the role of a world power. Quite willing to accept the change, he realigned his premises accordingly; he stopped saying "God damn the rich."

Scripps' re-emergence brought on a violent conflict with Jim. They clashed on two points principally — Scripps' insistence on supporting the Wilson administration and his insistence that Robert P. now come into the Concern as editor-in-chief. Saying he could work for his father but not with him, Jim used his and his associates' stock positions to take out of the Concern five west coast papers — Los Angeles *Record*, Seattle *Star*, Spokane *Press*, Tacoma *Times*, Portland *News* — and the Dallas *Dispatch*.

The emotional stress, the unrelieved strain of hard work, and some resumption of drinking all preceded a stroke that sidelined Scripps in November, 1917. He later blamed the stroke on three "heart-breaking experiences" —John's death, Nackey's elopement, and Jim's defection.[184] On doctor's orders, Scripps left Washington and went to Florida where he discovered the pleasure of living on a yacht. Although he briefly established residence in Annapolis and spent occasional interludes at "Miramar," he lived mostly on a yacht thereafter, progressing through two smaller yachts to the large "Ohio," which became his floating home.

Looking upon Jim's papers as the "outlaw papers," which permanently remained beyond Scripps' control after Jim's death in 1921. Scripps came back from retirement in 1920, and in 1922 formed an entirely new newspaper combination — Scripps-Howard. In this case, the Scripps was Robert

[184] EWS to EBS, Sept. 11, 1925.

P., the one surviving son, teamed with Roy W. Howard who was transferred from presidency of the United Press to chairman of the board. Unlike the Scripps-McRae League, Scripps-Howard embraced all the E. W. Scripps papers.

Energetically directing the work of Robert P. and Howard, Scripps quickly replaced the gap left by the "outlaw papers," and his two successors further expanded the Concern. Between 1921 and 1925 Scripps-Howard added the Birmingham *Post,* Norfolk *Post*, Fort Worth *Press*, Washington *Daily News*, Knoxville *News*, Youngstown *Telegram*, Indianapolis *Times*, El Paso *Post*, Pittsburgh *Press*, Baltimore *Post*, United Features Syndicate, *New Mexico State Tribune*, United News Pictures, and Akron *Times*.

Having re-established his Concern, Scripps left its operation to Robert P. and Howard and lived out his life on the "Ohio," roaming the world and coming into port only reluctantly. Only at sea was he comfortable. The minute his feet touched land, for other than a visit in some far port, he suffered from extreme nervousness.

He lived aboard the "Ohio" in considerable comfort, always with several hundred books for diversion and enjoying the company of carefully chosen guests, either those invited aboard for dinner or those invited to take long cruises with him. His personal staff included a male secretary — at different times it was Jerry Clemans, E. F. Elfstrom, and J. R. Young. Another secretary, H. L. Smithton, ran his personal office in Cincinnati. Because of his precarious health, he had a nurse in constant attendance; she was Katherine Steelman, who had been Dolla's nurse at one time. Part of the time he had from one to three women readers, but none satisfactorily read the scientific works in which he was most interested, and his failing eyesight kept him from reading very much for himself.

Longingly, he would have preferred to have his wife aboard to read to him, but they had become virtually estranged. She had taken the side of Jim and Nackey, and always tried to change her husband's attitude, which only made him excited and angry. Because his doctors had expressly ordered him to avoid tension and excitement, he deliberately kept away from his wife, even to the extent of once refusing to read a letter from her until he could reach the presence of his physician in Washington. Another reason for the estrangement was that he refused to have any relatives around him who would not accept his headship of the family and obey his dictates.

Only Robert P., the youngest son, then in his late twenties, acknowledged that headship, and Scripps as a consequence centered his entire line of succession in him and his heirs. All the other grandsons were cut out of the succession to control, but not of inheritance; this included John's son John Paul, of whom McRae got custody when the child's mother died. To perpetuate his institution — and particularly to prevent its fragmentation through inheritance by female relatives, including his wife — he devised a "living trust" which has kept his organization intact.

As he had through all the years since 1872 he poured out his troubles to Ellen B., who outlived him by several years. Showing his respect for her, he sometimes brought the "Ohio" off the coast near her home upon his return from a long voyage, and fired a salute in her honor.

On the evening of March 12, 1926, Scripps had dinner guests aboard the "Ohio" while anchored off Monrovia, Liberia. During after-dinner conversation in the library he complained of feeling ill. Twenty minutes later he was dead of apoplexy, in his seventy-second year. Obeying Scripps' written instructions that he be buried at sea, his crew slid the body into the Atlantic Ocean which, one lavish admirer said, was the only tomb big enough for him.

SUMMARY

Sizing up E. W. Scripps is like trying to draw the contour of a mountain by placing one's palm on a boulder. Often the boulders are mountains in themselves, filling the landscape to the exclusion of other formations.

Understandably, then, only the obvious in Scripps generally has been glimpsed — his accomplishments in journalism. Sometimes, though, a distorted emphasis has been given to his candid, but possibly exaggerated, accounts of youthful sexual activity and his outlandish claim of a gallon of liquor a day. Some attention has been paid in the preceding pages to his accounts of his early sex life in recognition of the truth of his insistence that no one can tell the story of a man's life unless he includes that man's sex life in the story, but in awareness that Scripps made no similar record of his sex life after marriage.

In the field of journalism, he and his associates founded more newspapers than anyone before them. To serve his own papers and maintain freedom of the press against the emerging cooperative combine of the Associated Press, he founded one of the first of the modern press associations, now known as United Press International (UPI), which he hoped would be remembered as his greatest service to American journalism. With the intention of educating the public, he formed the Newspaper Enterprise Association, today one of the large syndicates and considerably changed from his original concept of a national newspaper distributed through the local papers comprising the Scripps chain.

To increase public knowledge and understanding of science, he endowed the foundation of Science Service for the distribution of accurate science news to newspapers. To broaden man's knowledge, he was the instrumental layman in establishing and determining the initial direction of the first basic private research laboratory west of the Mississippi, the Scripps Institution of Oceanography, which has become the core of the University of California's new Graduate School of Science and Engineering at San Diego. Later he endowed the Foundation for Population Research at Miami University (Ohio) to carry out studies in a field that had long commanded his earnest attention.

He predicated his work upon a faith in the Common People, known in his organization as the "C.P." and "the 95 per cent," and conceived of journalism in terms of service to man. In the process he built a fortune, but, more importantly, perpetuated an institution now in the hands of third-generation management. By contrast, most other moguls of the American press built institutions that died with them, or contracted greatly after their death, or expired in the second generation, or passed into the hands of others.

Because Scripps placed his greatest faith in small papers and did not festoon them with glamor, his papers often were, and some still are, known as the second papers in their cities; other Scripps papers are the front-runners in theirs. But the strength of what he built through a league system — a device whose mystery and potential few others have sought to master — can be seen in the fact that the Scripps organization has picked up the pieces after the passing of stalwarts in several cities where Scripps papers were published. Scripps papers did not carry the field in every city, of course, but a few examples will suffice to show their hardiness. It was a Scripps paper that absorbed the old New York *World* when it could not long survive the death of Joseph Pulitzer, and later incorporated the remains of Dana's newspaperman's newspaper, the *Sun*, to become the present New York *World-Telegram and Sun*. In Cleveland and Cincinnati, the two cities where Scripps did most of his on-the-spot work, his papers have survived as the afternoon papers. Similarly, Scripps' United Press absorbed Hearst's International News Service to form the present UPI. But other papers succumbed, in Houston and San Francisco, to name the most recent.

His successes rested not alone on his own efforts. Rather, the expansion and vitality of the Concern came from the labor of an army of young men (some critics looked on the Scripps papers as devouring the youth of a man). These men shared in the profits and were chosen by Scripps with an almost unerring judgment.

Even more, his successes rested not on a foundation of his making alone but on a family foundation. Scripps branched off from the foundation laid by James E. who, in the final analysis, was the man who taught Scripps the business. The constant conflict between the two, and especially James E.'s sneering and often contemptuous attitude toward Scripps, served only to goad Scripps to do his utmost. Counterbalancing James E. was Ellen B., who encouraged Scripps, helped him work out his problems, and bolstered the young man's flagging confidence. In their opposite ways, the half sister and half brother had more influence on his life than anyone else, but George H. often tipped the scales in Scripps' favor when the chips were down. It was the support of Ellen B. and George H. that cleared the board for Scripps in his final contest with James E., allowed him to checkmate the latter's king, and start a new game of newspaper chess in which he carved and controlled all the pieces.

An account of Scripps' material accomplishments merely scratches the surface, for he was an enormously complex man. Perhaps one episode toward the close of life comes closer to summarizing him than could any other single set of circumstances.

In August, 1922, he sailed his yacht into Huntington Bay, Long Island, to visit his son Robert P. while the ship was being repaired, and found that his associates had arranged for him to sit for a portrait by John Young-Hunter and a bust by Jo Davidson; Scripps considered this to be tomfoolery, for he had submitted even to very few photographs previously. The sittings irritated him, as so many other experiences did.

The portrait, now hanging in the living room at "Miramar," shows him in typical pose aboard the yacht. Wearing the skull cap he had worn habitually for years to keep his head warm because of his deathly fear of colds, he has pushed his thick-lensed spectacles up onto his forehead. Held in the absent-minded manner of one who is thinking far into the future or far into the past or far into the subject, the cigar is almost as much a part of him as his angry bellow at some negligent servant or as the usually untamed beard which had been trimmed to a neat goatee shortly before the sitting. Cigar ashes fleck his vest as always. In his hand, a newspaper. On his feet, the boots he wore to the last, sometimes to the discomfiture of associates more concerned with appearance than he was. Something of his massive bulk shows through, contrasted with the weak, almost-effeminate hands that caused men to remember his limp handshake. What doesn't show is the sensitivity greater than that of many women. Of the man himself, even in repose something of the power of his never-quiet energy is there. Thick eye folds suggest the shrewdness and knowing. The pensive, far-away look in the eyes betokens both the sadness that had fallen on his life and the many hours spent in thought.

The Davidson bust shows something quite different — sheer, bull-necked, ruthless power. Thick, strong head. Heavy, rounded shoulders hunched as for a lunge. Strong, implacable features. Explosive energy held by a thin leash.

Both show a man accustomed to getting his own way, ready to ride rough-shod over all opposition.

What went on during the sittings is also characteristic:

. . . Both my sculptor and painter kept talking about interpreting their sitter's character. I sneered at both of them and asked, "What the Devil do you fellows think you are, that you can come and study a man's face for two or three days or more, and then think that you can delve into his mind and into his heart and interpret his whole character, when you don't do anything more than extract from your own minds some ideal of a man or woman who in all probability never existed? [185]

Davidson began his work on the bust with this injunction from Lincoln Steffens, perhaps the most articulate of Scripps' admirers:

You must do a great thing with Scripps. He is a great man, and an individual. There is no other like him: energy, vision, courage, wisdom. He thinks his own thoughts absolutely. He sees straight. He goes crooked, but he sees the line he is on and his thinking sticks to that. I regard Scripps as one of the two or three great men of my day. He is onto himself and the world, plays the game and despises it. He is sincere, not cynical.

Really he should be done, not as a bust but as a full-length standing figure so as to show the power of the man, the strength he took care to keep from becoming refined; he avoided other rich men so as to escape being one; he knew the danger his riches carried for himself, for his papers and for his seeing. Rough, almost ruthless force, but restrained by clear, even shrewd insight; an executive, capable of fierce action restrained by the observation that a doer must not do too many things himself, but use his will to make others do them. And he did that, all right. Read some of his letters to editors, the young fellows he was driving so hard and yet leaving alone.[186]

Quite rightly, neither sculptor nor artist showed his man mellowed or softened by a sense of humor, for Scripps was a humorless man. Oh, he had a sense of humor, but so long subordinated to his deadly seriousness that it had atrophied. By his own testimony — accurate, as his self-evaluations often were — he laughed at people more than with them.[187]

Scripps disliked both portrait and bust. An intensely self-conscious and self-critical person, he winced as always under revelations of self. He wrote Ellen B. that all he could see in the bust was a man whom all women would like to see licked and whom all men would like to whip.

[185] EWS to EBS, Nov. 20, 1922.
[186] This quotation comes from a copy, in the "Miramar" files, extracted from the original letter, date not given, and is somewhat fuller than the version opposite page 692 in the *Autobiography of Lincoln Steffens*, which was credited to *Scripps-Howard News*.
[187] EWS to EBS, Jan. 18, 1925.

Perhaps after all, in this one respect, the artist did discover the character of his subject. At least it has been my experience in life that women always liked to laugh at my discomfiture, no matter what it was, while I have seen many a man back away from me when he thought I was dangerous [and] when I knew that I was only cowardly.[188]

His displeasure with the bust was made all the more acute when he saw in it what he called the "mean part" of President Harding whose face "somewhat resembles a typical satyr." [189] The portrait, he concluded, "certainly did make me look like a broken-hearted old man. . . ." [190] Truly he was a sad man during those last years, roaming the world in his yacht, brooding, awaiting and yet fearing death.

I run over in my mind my peculiar situation. I have a large family, but yet I feel myself alone, not only physically separated from my family, but spiritually isolated. I do not grieve over this or pity myself overmuch. I do not repine overmuch at my isolation. I was born to loneliness and to isolation. It was only by an act of self-compulsion that, years ago, after we returned from Europe, I threw myself into affairs and undertook to try to be "normal" by marrying and raising a family. As a family man, I was always required to exercise considerable restraint and control, since I was not naturally adapted for such a role.

I think it is more than probable that the "shipwreck" (if it can be called a shipwreck) of my domestic affairs was largely the result of my temperament. I do not reproach myself for this. I had nothing to do in the way of creation and development of my temperament. I struggled, more or less unsuccessfully, in the way of keeping up appearances. I am not a social animal, and it has been impossible for me to deceive anyone to any considerable extent.

Of course I regret, at times, the absence of the little children and the grown-up children who owe their existence to me. Not only habit, but something much deeper and much stronger, attaches me to my wife, and her absence would be much harder to bear than it is if I did not constantly endeavor to keep my mind employed.

.   .   .   .

I would not have you or anyone else waste any pity on me on account of my present sad and solitary life. Just as women say they enjoy a good cry, I can say I feel a certain sense of happiness in my sadness.

I suppose it's a strange thing for any man to be placed as I am in another way: I have no dear friends. There is no man or woman that I know of, outside of my own family circle, whose companionship I strongly crave. I even feel that the presence of any one of the few who are comparatively intimate with me would, by their presence, cause me more uncomfortable disturbance of mind than would be offset by the pleasure I would feel in their personal companionship.

[188] EWS to EBS, Nov. 20, 1922.
[189] EWS to EBS, Sept. 28, 1922.
[190] EWS to EBS, Aug. 21, 1922.

It is very easy for me to make acquaintances, and I know that wherever I may be the number of my acquaintances and casual friendships would only be limited by my own will.[191]

Claiming that he had seen himself in a mirror only occasionally and had never bothered to look at his profile in the mirror, he caught some back views of himself while Davidson was at work, and saw a perfect stranger. He said he no longer wondered why people cheered when he got beaten and why he had never sensed any real human sympathy toward himself.[192]

Both the portrait and bust were sent to Ellen B. in La Jolla, other castings of the bust being placed in all the newspaper offices. She was ecstatic about both. Saying that someone had spoken of the "fire and spirit" of the bust, she called it "a magnificent piece of work." She said everyone must get, as one of her visitors had put it, "the impression of intensity, imagination, spiritual awareness." [193] Those qualities likewise characterized E. W. Scripps, and the conflicting opinions also were typical.

She also considered the bust "marvelously successful" [194] as a character interpretation, the sculptor "producing a sense of virility and intellectual forcefulness which your ordinary companion sees nothing of." [195] She was all the more impressed by a photograph showing Scripps seated beside the bust. "There is no particular resemblance between the two. But the bust seems more like you than you look like yourself." [196]

Over and above everything else E. W. Scripps was the embodiment of a spirit and voice of protest. He protested directly in his disquisitions. In these his most intimate writings he emerges as a vigorous thinker who was in a position to leave an impress upon the thought patterns of his time; a humanist of some stature; a philosopher who generalized from experience and empathy; a social critic of penetrating view; an idealist who reared his head into the clouds but let not the fog obscure the reality; an experimenter, even with his nearest and dearest, to see what would happen to human beings under certain conditions; a shrewd analyst of his time and of the drift in time; and a minor prophet.

He also was a contrary old bastard.

[191] EWS to EBS, Dec. 21, 1918.
[192] EWS to EBS, Aug. 29, 1922.
[193] EBS to EWS, Dec. 1, 1922.
[194] EBS to EWS, Nov. 7, 1922.
[195] EBS to EWS, Sept. 13, 1922.
[196] EBS to EWS, Sept. 21, 1922.

SEARCH FOR SELF

Scripps constantly sought himself — who, what, and why he was. Consequently, more of the disquisitions deal with himself, his thoughts, his feelings, his reminiscences than with any other subject. Part of the heavy emphasis upon himself can, of course, be attributed to his strongly developed egocentrism, but only part. In his own way, sometimes bumbling but sometimes with sharp insight, he sought for the meaning of his own life, for the circumstances and conditions that had made him a successful and powerful man, as a key to the meaning of life in general. His quest for meaning also gave an introspective cast to many other disquisitions elsewhere in this collection.

Both autobiographical and introspective disquisitions are included in this first group, not to attempt any sort of connected autobiographical narrative but for self-revelations of character, attitudes, habits of mind, self-view, and world-view.

While recognizing the difficulty any man has in being absolutely and totally honest about himself and with himself, Scripps at least tried to be honest in his various accounts of his life. As a matter of fact, he was greatly concerned about the difficulty any man would encounter in writing a fully honest autobiography, a problem that seemed to take on greater importance to him because of his recognition that no one else could ever hope to write the complete story of any other man's life.

Despite his sometimes contradictory disclaimers to the contrary, Scripps had sensed as a young man with a feeling of personal destiny that someday the story of his life might be important. As the years advanced, his interest in such an account cropped up again and again, but each time with an increasing concern with the difficulty of complete honesty. His contempt for fame caused him to give short shrift to any consideration of a biography or an autobiography that would simply make him out to be a great man.

95

In addition to numerous disquisitions giving bits and pieces of his life story, Scripps wrote three frankly autobiographical accounts. The first, written in 1889, was the "History of the Scripps League," which told his story up to the break with James E., but with a disclaimer that he wrote it for any purpose other than as a personal *aide memoire*.

Next, he set about writing an "Autobiography" (sometimes called the "Autobiographical Notes") in 1915, which provides the skeleton of his life story but is devoid of development and broader relationships. His purpose, incidentally, was not to write a full autobiography, but to record some of the memories and events that were most clear in his mind. The autobiography provided the raw material from which came the various accounts that painted Scripps as a skirt-chaser, because he quite frankly recounted his youthful sexual experiences, saying that the biography or autobiography that does not include a fairly accurate synopsis of a man's sex experiences is not biographical at all. After finishing the autobiography, he negotiated briefly with R. M. Yost, a Los Angeles newspaper acquaintance, to get the manuscript in shape mechanically, with the design of giving his children typewritten copies, but he soon dropped the idea. In 1923 Scripps assigned Gilson Gardner to the task of editing the autobiography and disquisitions into a biography, and challenged him by saying: "You cannot help but be conventional."

You will probably select only that material which is creditable to me, and that which is conveniently respectable, or at most conventionally permissible in the way of admission of common frailties.

My friend Dr. [William E.] Ritter wrote a little book which was entitled *The Organism as a Whole*. He was considering the organism biologically, or rather, physiologically, and paid but slight attention to the psychological element.

My desire is to deal with an organism as a whole, primarily psychologically, secondarily what we call morally, and incidentally biologically.

To the physiologist the mouth is no more respectable than the anus. To the biographer the meanest and wickedest deed of his subject is no less characteristic than the loftiest and noblest of his deeds — and no more so.[1]

But Gardner failed to rise to the challenge, and when Gardner completed his work in 1925, Scripps described himself as "surprised and disgusted," saying, "the foolish fellow thought it was his duty to edit out of my [Autobiographical] Notes most everything of a personal character which he was idiot enough to think reflected upon my character, and then he transcribed parts of some of my disquisitions which he considered laudatory."[2] Scripps or-

[1] EWS to Gilson Gardner, Sept. 9, 1922.
[2] EWS to EBS, Oct. 5, 1925.

dered all his papers withdrawn from Gardner, but Gardner later wrote a biography on his own, *Lusty Scripps*.

In the meantime, Scripps had tried once more to write a completely honest autobiography. Ingeniously, in January, 1925, he decided he could write a full and truthful account by leaving out the names of persons and places. With the assistance of Miss Stella McGehee, who was part secretary and part literary assistant on the yacht, he put together an account entitled "The Short Story of a Soul." With considerable enthusiasm he set about the task, thinking that by leaving out names and localities a man might be able to tell the essentials of his life experiences "which would be a very frank statement of all those instances which had been character-forming, all of those instances and occasions when emotions of various kinds took hold of him and willy-nilly shaped his course."[3] However, he found that dictating the account was "most painful labor," and when he first saw the completed transcript, he was "disappointed" and "disgusted." He concluded that "the mere fact that I was conscious of writing the story of an individual made it impossible for me to the tell the truth, the whole truth, and nothing but the truth."[4]

Perhaps he unknowingly came closer to his objective in dictating individual disquisitions through the years, taking in only a limited field each time instead of trying to recall the whole story of a lifetime.

[3] EWS to EBS, Jan. 26, 1925.
[4] EWS to EBS, Feb. 2, 1925.

A Damned Old Crank

[*April 5, 1909*]

The other day a famous and notorious spiritualist or clairvoyant came to San Diego and for several days did a thriving business exchanging guesses for the dollars of the credulous.[5]

My oldest son, Jim, who is just breaking into business in a serious way, and who is pretty anxious just now to find out when a business boom is going to set in again and the revenues of our business increase, went to consult the faker. Jim didn't learn anything about business, I understand, but got the usual dose of information about himself personally, his family affairs, and the usual advice to a young man of business.

In order to convince Jim that he (the faker) had peculiar and occult opportunities for learning what the future is to be, the wizard told him some things about the past and the present that any man who knew that Jim's surname was Scripps could have told him. Of course, it didn't occur to Jim that on account of his own peculiarly large stature, strength of body, habits of dress, coupled with the fact that he was the son of a man who is locally conspicuous, would make it very easy for him to be "tipped off" to the faker long before he got from the anteroom to the sanctum. Nor did it occur, perhaps, to Jim that his own big, healthy body, open face, and rough and ready dress would invite from a shrewd observer a certain amount of pretended blunt candor.

Jim told me something about the interview, but very little, but he told me how the faker characterized me, his subject's father. Said the faker, "Your father is a crank; in fact, he is a damned old crank!"

"Why didn't you swat him one, Jim?" I asked. Quick came the reply, "Because, Dad, I had given up three dollars for what I could learn, and I wanted

[5] With changes, deletions, and additions from other Scripps material, this disquisition appears in McCabe, *Damned Old Crank*, p. 1 f.

to get my money's worth in the five minutes for which I had paid, and what he said about you was in the first part of his talk. If I had swatted him I wouldn't have got anything for my three dollars."

My son Jim is as canny about money as any proverbial Scotchman.

But really I see no reason why Jim should have swatted him for calling me "a damned old crank," or why I should feel hurt because Jim didn't swat him. There are some truths about a man that he does not like to hear, but there are also some truths about himself which are neither unpleasant nor uninstructive.

The word "crank" is used to define the character of a man who does not think and act in exactly the same way as the universality, almost, of his fellowmen. I am fully entitled, I feel, to the name of "crank" and I have no fault to find with being called an "old crank," and as I am almost universally judged to be peculiar, I am condemned as a crank. The word "damned" means the same as condemned. Hence I am a "damned crank," and "a damned old crank."

I am sorry that I am a crank and I am sorry that I am old, and I am sorry that I am condemned as a crank, because if most people or all people lived and acted as I do I believe the world would be a better world; and if all people thought and acted as I do then I would no longer be a crank, and hence people would not pass such judgment on me.

It is very unfortunate for the world that I am a damned crank; it is unfortunate to myself that I am an old crank, and that I am old at all. You see, I am sorry for everybody, including myself.

Wherein am I exposed to the public in the matter of my crankiness? There are some things about me that are visible to everybody [who] knows me. These are some of them:

I wear a full beard when nearly everybody else shaves clean; to that extent I am willing to appear like a man, and do not, like my fellows, make myself look like a girl.

I wear long boots, and I wear my pants in my boots, and because they are pants — not "trousers" — I give further evidence of being cranky, since most men who are as rich as I am call their lower garments "trousers." I have several good reasons for wearing boots, and wearing them in the way that I do; one of them is that it is easier to put them on and off; and by wearing my boots in this fashion I am entirely free from the pest of fleas; then I live in the country and tramp over rough ground and through brush and high grass and, by wearing my boots in this manner, I am saved the annoyance of getting my shoes full of loose dirt, pebbles, and sticky things in the grass and brush. But my main and great reason is that by protecting my ankles and the lower part of my legs from exposure to the cold air I frequently avoid taking cold, and because of this trick of mine I do not suffer half as much from colds as do the men who wear low shoes.

I am also cranky in the matter of the rest of my wearing apparel, as all my life I have been too busy with other things of importance to look after my dress much.

I have another cranky symptom: I am a busy man. I haven't much time to waste, and when I am walking I walk fast to save time; when I am driving horses I drive them on the run, and now in these days of automobiles I get the biggest, and strongest, and fastest and most durable, that is to say, the most expensive, machines, so that I can get over the ground fast and waste but very little time waiting for my chauffeur to patch up a weak, easily crippled machine.

I never go to the church or to the theater, or attend any social function, nor do I listen to public political speeches, not do I sit on the bleachers watching other men exercise themselves with baseball and football. I do not hunt or play golf. I am really not interested in any of these affairs and I have not time to be. But I play poker, just like common people do, so that in one respect, at least, I am not a crank. At poker I am an average loser, and therein I am like other people and no crank.

I give my money and my time to public works without desire or expectation of any profit. That is certainly evidence of crankiness.

No matter what my excuse is for doing these things, I am a crank!

I am one of those men who cannot rest or idle away my time. Perhaps the great and chiefest [*sic*] desire of most men is to have money enough to be idle and then be idle; as I must work and as I have no occasion to work for myself any longer, and in fact my health forbids me to do the only kind of work which is profitable to myself, I must do something, so I build roads and interest myself in other such things.[6]

Most rich men like to spend money acquiring reputations for being great lovers of humanity — that is to say, philanthropists. They seek fame and notoriety. I am a crank because I don't want the reputation for being good, or being wise, or any sort of reputation at all. I have so small a respect for humanity that I place little value on the respect or admiration or affection of any human being; in fact, I do not respect myself or make any effort to win or keep my own self-respect. But, of course, every wise man will admit that I am perfectly right in the low value I place upon fame, that is to say, the respect, the admiration, the love of anything so wretched as a human being; nevertheless, it is a fact that these few men who coincide with me in judgment on the matter are themselves cranks.

[6] When this was written in 1909, Scripps was a member of the San Diego County highway commission.

Even in my own profession and lifelong vocation I am a crank and always have been one; because it was easier to make money by being an honest journalist, I have been as honest as I could be. I have not sold out $10,000 worth of newspaper business goodwill for $1,000, or taken bribes from other rich men offered to me for services for which the would-be contributors expected to get a hundredfold return.

I have been cranky in other respects: I am one of the few newspapermen who happen to know that this country is populated by 95 per cent of plain people, and that the patronage of 95 per cent of even plain and poor people is worth more to a newspaper owner than the patronage of the wealthy 5 per cent. So I have always run my business along the line of least resistance and for the greatest profit, and because I have made money easier than any other newspaper publisher ever did make it, and made more than all but few other publishers, I am odd and cranky.

In another respect I am a crank: First, above all people, I love my wife, next I love myself, and take care of my own material and spiritual comfort; next in the order of my affections come my children; beyond these I love the whole line of my posterity that will extend generation after generation into the future. Now, I have provided for my wife every comfort and every happiness that I think she is capable of enjoying. Personally, I possess a home, in fact two homes, that are so nearly what I want that I would not exchange either of them for any other residence. I possess more wealth than I need; that is to say, my income is greater than my capacity for enjoying (spending) the same. Beyond this I own sufficient property to leave my children wealthy when I die, perhaps too wealthy for their own good. Now, I have provided for wife, self, and children; what other motive of affection will move me? The only part of my family that I have not provided for is my unborn posterity.

What can I do for posterity? I can do my best to make the world a better world for them to live in, and particularly to make my country a more enjoyable place for them. In fact, owing to my peculiarly fortunate or unfortunate situation in life, there is nothing left for me to do except to work for an unborn posterity, hence my occupation is an odd one, and because it is odd I am a crank — yes, a damned old crank. If I wasn't old I would have greater need of my services to make life enjoyable for myself, but being old and nearly done with life there is very little more for me to do for myself.

I have always been a crank. Think of this!

I am now lacking only a few weeks of being 55 years old; I was born the son of a farmer, on a farm; I lived there until I was 18 years old, or past. When I was 18 I went to the city to learn my trade of journalism. During the years 18 to 31 (13 years) — in fact, not quite so long, because I left the farm four months after I was 18 and went back to the farm two months before I was 31 — I was either a working newspaperman or traveling over the world. About eight years of my time were devoted to real office newspaper work in various cities; about five years were spent in foreign travel. When I was 31 I married and took up my home on a farm; from that time to this I have lived exclusively on my Ohio farm or on my California ranch. My farm life, then, is composed of periods of 18 years in Illinois, 24 years on the Ohio farm and the California ranch — a total of 42 years.

During the past 24 years I have perhaps not averaged more than 24 hours out of each month in cities, or in work in my city offices. As a matter of fact, although I have done much business work in my home, on my farm in Ohio and on my ranch, I believe that the time that I have actually expended on and devoted absolutely to my business has not averaged two hours per working day from the time I left the Illinois farm to the present moment; yet, I have been uniformly successful and my fortune has grown with such rapidity as to have been surpassed by percentage of increase by, perhaps, not more than 1,000 men amongst these 90 millions of people in the United States, the great majority of whom are rightfully accused of devoting almost their whole time to money-getting.

From the beginning of my first nest egg of capital — the eighty dollars I carried away from the farm sewed in my vest lining — my capital has doubled at least once every seven years, and during all of that period my expenditures have been relative to that of others of my class and standing, so great as to have been universally condemned as extravagant. In fact, I have never thought to save money at all. I have never denied myself anything that I wanted.

I have always lived in a way calling for expenditures many times larger than the average expenditures of men of my own wealth; so it may be observed that I am a crank in two respects; that is to say, that I have been an oddity in two respects. I have done large and successful business from the standpoint of an outsider and dweller on a farm, and I have amassed a fortune without resorting to the usual methods of saving and economy. Nor have I ever been a speculator; in fact, it has been a rigid rule of mine never to buy anything for the purpose of selling at a profit; in fact, in my whole lifetime, although I have bought much, I have never sold anything when I once became possessed of it.

Was there ever such a crank?

Another evidence of my crankiness: I have never in my life kept a set of books; I don't know anything about bookkeeping; in fact, I regard the usual bookkeeper and the usual set of books kept by businessmen as an intolerable and unbearable nuisance, and handicap to business.

I am a crank in another respect: I am a successful businessman and yet I know nothing about anybody else's business but my own. I am a businessman; I spend most of my time on my farm or my ranch, and yet the chief part of my life's energies has been devoted to the thoroughly unbusinesslike practice of library reading. For every hour I have devoted to my business I have devoted at least three hours to literature and on subjects entirely foreign to my own or any other kind of business. This peculiarity of mine, even if I had no other distinguishing marks, would well entitle me to be called a crank.

It is only too evident from all the above that I have one element in my character that is common and is universal — I have vanity! This whole essay is nothing but one long holler of boast, no matter what other virtues it may have in the matter of truthfulness and suggested philosophy.

Yes, I am entitled to be called a crank! Yes, an old crank! And further a damned old crank; and if Jim's faker only knew as much about future business conditions as he apparently knew about Jim's father he would have been able, if he had wanted to, to have given Jim three million dollars worth of information for three dollars.

Arithmetic and Humanity

[*March, 1914*]

Scripps wrote the following disquisition while waiting for his middle and favorite son, John Paul, to die of a lingering illness at the age of twenty-six. Scripps elsewhere attributed the death to endocarditis, which had its onset when John Paul had severe tonsillitis at the age of twelve.

Scripps' pride in this disquisition is indicated by the large group of influential men to whom he sent copies for their comments and reactions. The group included Roger Babson, Rudolph Spreckels, Francis J. Heney, Clarence Darrow, Ben Lindsey, Lincoln Steffens, Norman Hapgood, Gifford and Amos Pinchot, and W. E. Ritter. Steffens enthusiastically wired for permission to publish it, but Scripps as usual refused to allow publication.

To his longtime associate from the Cleveland Press, *Bob Paine, Scripps said he had shown the disquisition to a banker friend who looked worried when Scripps told him it was almost certain that three-fourths of the banker's ancestors had been bastards. "You see, Bob, I had this sort of an idea when I was formulating my disquisition. It seemed to me that it might be a petard with which one might blow into everlasting smithereens all the fool class and cast [sic] snobbery of at least this democratic country of ours."* [7]

They were sitting together, the old man and his wife — the old man not so very old and his wife not nearly so old. Although she had borne him seven children [8] and was already five times a grandmother, she was yet young enough in appearance to have passed for the old man's daughter.

Although two of her seven children had died, and there had been much real and more imaginary sorrows in her life, there had also been a great freedom

[7] EWS to Robert F. Paine, Apr. 8, 1914.

[8] James George, John Paul, Dolla Blair, E. W. (Ted), who died in childhood, Robert P., and Nackey Elizabeth. A seventh child had been stillborn in the early years of marriage.

104

on her part from many of the petty cares and daily worries. And the struggles born of feminine ambitions and vanities — temptation and even the opportunity of those social excesses which wear away so much of the bodily health and the nervous energy of most of her sisters of the class to which she belongs (the class of the protected women) — had not been hers. The woman had had no real labors to perform. Large as was her household, none of its cares had rested on her. Servants well selected and well-enough trained had always been able to do well enough the household work, and since there was no occasion to save expenses, the gap between well-ordered economy and all necessary accommodations had been filled up by her husband's ability to pay.

In the evening of the old man's life and the afternoon of that of his wife, they sat together one winter night, this couple who were, or who might at least have been, envied by nearly all who knew them. Successful had been the fortune-builder — successful in his fortune-building, and despite the toll of death, successful had been the family's rearing.

But on this evening the two sat face-to-face with an approaching sorrow. Death was about to exact a new toll. A son lay dying in the home of his father and mother. But even for this son life and been full; he had grown to man's estate; he had loved and married and had, before he was stricken, a grand baby boy.

The two, husband and wife, sat together. Even the greatness of their sorrow had been softened by its months' long approach, its certainty of coming. There was to be no shock.

The man had been fumbling over his papers — the correspondence of the day and previous days. The man was a rich man and was commonly reputed to be much richer than he was, and like other such rich men, his letters were often from the more unfortunate, and oftener still from those who had or thought they had a mission in this world — a mission to ameliorate the sufferings of others living, and still more to ameliorate the sufferings of coming generations.

The man was worrying; he was feeling uncomfortable; he was in fact doubtful as to whether he should say Yes or No to some appeal. He spoke to his wife about that which was on his mind.

Mildly protesting and mildly indignant she replied: "Why worry yourself now, Pa, about these things — the troubles of other people? Have we not enough at home of care and anxiety? There are yet three ungrown, unsettled children. We have five grandchildren now and maybe many more to come. Our son who is sick needs all our care. Have you not enough people at home to think about and care for without letting your mind wander out to seek other responsibilities and the care of others who are strangers?"

The evening drew on. The wife, as usual much earlier than her husband, retired to her own room, to her bed and to sleep. The man remained; he was restless; to be alone with his thoughts and the ever-approaching grief, possessed of the feeling of helplessness to stay the approach of death that was so soon to take away his child, was hard to endure. To read as was most times his custom was for this night impossible.

"After all," he thought, "is the wife right, or nearly right? What real difference is there between the sorrow for one death and that for another? How is it possible for grief to be selfish? Love, love between man and woman, may be selfish, but grief — no, there is no selfishness in grief.

"Who are these people, these thousands and hundreds of thousands and millions of our fellows, among whom there are only rare scores or, at the most, hundreds, whose lives have been anywhere near as fortunate as ours — to whom death, millions on millions of times, comes while young, younger or no older than is our son? Many of these do not need to die so early. If they could have but a portion of the care and the costly attention of physicians that are being lavished on this fortunate unfortunate boy of ours, many of these would live long lives.

"Fortune rarely smiles on individuals; more rarely does she smile on whole families for decades as it has smiled, and appears inclined to continue to smile for decades more, on this family of ours.

"Fortune's smiles will not last forever — perhaps for some of our children a full generation, perhaps for others for a shorter period, these smiles may continue. But eventually by the law of averages, all of this troop of our descendants which the vision of my reason exposes to me — this troop will go on marching generation after generation down centuries ever growing larger — will be in the main composed of unfortunates. Yet they will be our children. Generation after generation, our descendants will increase in number until they will walk the earth in companies of hundreds, later in regiments of thousands, in armies of hundreds of thousands, and sooner or later their numbers will first equal a quarter, and then a half, and then finally almost all of this our nation; and in the far distant future perhaps our blood will flow in the veins of most all of those, if not in all of those, who people the earth at that time."

The old man took paper and pencil and said to himself, "I will see how this thing works out arithmetically. For the present I will assume that all of our children and children's children, from generation to generation, shall prove on the average no less fruitful than we have been.

"Seven children have we had; two have died; one is dying. But I have five grandchildren now, and mayhap other of my children will live longer and win out to make up for the absence of him, the one about to die.

"I will then assume five adults to come from every marriage, and that all shall marry (and I must not entirely overlook the possibilities and even the probabilities of illegitimacy).

"Granting that we are to have 25 grandchildren, then successive generations will follow: 125 great-grandchildren, 625 descendants of the fourth generation; (then allowing for the living of the previous generations, counting on an average life of 45 years) during the period of the fifth generation there will be living of our descendants 3,875; (considering generations as governed by the child-bearing age of women, the length of a generation is assumed to be 33 1/3 years; as the period of the first generation has already been covered by our own lives I must reckon that the period closing the fifth generation will be 133 years hence) in the sixth generation there will be living 19,375 of our descendants; during the seventh generation, 96,875; eighth generation, 484,375; ninth generation, 2,421,875; tenth generation, 12,109,375; eleventh generation, 60,546,875; twelfth generation, 302,734,375; and finally at the end of six-tenths of the thirteenth generation our descendants will number something more than 800 million. (This figure has been assumed to limit the number of people that can live in the United States with any degree of comfort.)

"Reckoning a generation as 33 1/3 years and that the period of one of the 12 6/10 generations has already been covered by our own lives, the date at which our descendants will number all the population that should live in this country will be 11 6/10 times 33 1/3 years hence — that is, 387 years hence. I have but to live a few more years, and one-third of the whole period named will have been equaled by the difference between the date of my father's birth and that of my death."

Thus setting down figures, calculating, and thinking, time passed until the old man's time of retiring was reached, and without further thought as to the bigness or the littleness of the significance of his hour's employment, he went to his bed and easily fell asleep.

The next day came and with it the accustomed round of small duties, small employments, all to be gone through with, no matter how nearly hovered the shadowing wings of death.

In the evening the old man and his wife again sat together. After the usual evening hour of reading the two sat together, for a time neither speaking. Finally the man spoke to his wife:

"Ma, do you recall what you said to me last evening about my cares at home, and the wrongness of allowing my thoughts to wander out to strangers? After you left me last night, I sat here for another hour and I passed the time by thinking some and by doing a small sum in arithmetic. I figured that, providing all of our children were as fruitful as you and I have been, and providing all of their children were equally fruitful, and providing further that all of our descendants were on the average equally fruitful, we would have descendants living to the number of over 800 million, 387 years hence. The children of our children's children would be eight times as numerous as the present population of this country."

"Oh, Pa, you are crazy! That's not so; I know it's not so. I am sleepy and want to go to bed. You are always figuring, and you know figures make my head ache."

"But wait, Ma, there is still more to come. I have only given you the figures for 12½ generations or 11½ generations after this time. If two generations more were added there would be more than 25 billions of our descendants on earth if all continued to keep up the family record."

"Pa, you are certainly going crazy. Stop it!"

"But, Ma, making all due allowances for all the old maids and all the old bachelors and all of those who die young, still I cannot see how you can escape the responsibility of being the several times great-grandmother of at least half of the people living in North America 400 years hence."

"Pa, stop it; I tell you, stop it; I do not want to hear another word!"

"But, Ma, it's all true. Your children's children will by hundreds of thousands and millions (if we or they do not succeed in changing the present order of things so as to lift civilization up very much higher than it is now) be the poor, unhappy workingmen and women of the future, the miserably poor, the terribly sinful. They will constitute the mobs of future revolutionary times. They will kill thousands and thousands, and will be killed by thousands and tens of thousands — your children and mine fighting each other like wild beasts. Your descendants and mine will be in the prisons. Many of them will be worse off. They will populate the haunts of vice. They will be the harlots of their time. They will be the thieves, robbers, and murderers."

"Oh, Pa, you are horrible! What you say is not so. How can I sleep if you tell me such things?"

"But, Ma, I want you to hear. No matter what happens to many of our descendants, they will soon enough number at least half of all of the people in these United States, and they will be warring against each other. A few of them will be oppressing the many, and the many will be begging for, or fighting for, the bare necessities of life. The warfare of the classes in this country in the future will be between the few fortunates of our grandchildren's children and the great mass of the people, who, poor and ignorant and criminal, will yet be our children's children, who have descended from us."

"Oh, Pa, haven't you got through yet!"

"No, Ma, listen to me a little longer. You have loved your children — our children — so that you have always been ready to die for any of them. You love your grandchildren, it seems to me, even more than you have loved your own children. How about these others who are to be your children's grandchildren and your grandchildren's grandchildren? If you do not live to love them all, they will be loved by those you have loved, and they will only lack being loved by you because of your having ceased to live. Last night you reproached me for allowing my thoughts to wander from those under our own roof to strangers, as you called them. Do I show any lack of love of family, when all that I wish to do, and all that I am striving for with all of my might and main is to save my own children's children from the sufferings, physical and spiritual, that now have to be endured by those others who you say are not of my family? All these poor unfortunates that we see around us today are probably, and almost certainly, though we know not the line of their descent, descended from those who were your and my progenitors.

"After all, the human family is a family; it is one family. We are bound together by ties of blood to the stranger at our gate, perhaps as closely as are either of us to our own children. Anyway our brothers and sisters and all that great group of people who are our cousins and whom we call our near relations and to whom you are so willing to give love and aid, probably have no more of blood ties to us than these unknown others."

The old man took up his book, and his wife, who was not so old, and who was yet the mother of his children, sighed, retired to her bed and to sleep, having, as the old man thoroughly well knew, dismissed from her mind all thought of her husband's foolish arithmetic.

P.S. After the incident above narrated, the old man submitted two other problems to one of the mathematical experts of a state university:

Problem 1. Providing marriage was universal, providing that each family should produce three children that should come to mature age, and last, providing that all marriages should be exogamous, how many generations and how many years would pass before one married pair living now would become the progenitors of 800 millions of people — it being assumed always that descendants of other stock would supply the material necessary for continuous exogamous marriages?

Problem 2. Providing that marriage should be the invariable custom of one particular family springing from one couple now living, and providing each descendant of this couple should have two children, and no more, who should live to maturity, and providing exogamous marriages should be the invariable rule, how many generations and how many years would be required before the original couple would be the progenitors of all of the 800 millions who can live in comfort in the territory of the United States?

The answer to the first problem, the three-child problem, was that it would require 18⅓ generations or 611 years to produce the 800 millions — the descendants of the original couple.

The answer to the second problem was more startling. While it would be a fact that if the two-children family was universal there would be no increase in general population at all, still, if the exogamous rule is invariable, the descendants of the first original couple would double every generation. Therefore, providing that there was always material for exogamous marriages, it would require only a period of 29 generations or some 2,500 years to make it an accomplished fact that the original parents of the two-children family had become the progenitors of 800 million living beings.

On Friendship

[*December 30, 1915*]

The following letter to A. M. Hopkins was marked "not sent." Such a notation, however, is not considered as necessarily invalidating the content of a document as representing Scripps' attitude. Each such unsent letter must be measured against this general criterion: The "not sent" notation probably more often means that Scripps thought better of saying those things to that person at that time, rather than that he decided against saying them at all. The criterion does not, of course, hold up in all instances, because some unsent letters clearly reflect a deeper-than-usual pessimism, or betray some disturbance that invalidates them, or indicate that Scripps was not in form when he dictated.

Hopkins was a former editorial associate on the Cincinnati Post *who left the newspaper for the drug business in Cincinnati.*

"Miramar," Calif., December 30, 1915

Mr. A. M. Hopkins
c/o The Dow Stores
Cincinnati, Ohio

My dear Hopkins:

In a postscript at the bottom of your circular letter just received you tell me that you never expect to get another letter from me. Your expectations are so well justified that I am as much surprised at what I am about to do as you will be when you receive this.

Perhaps I do not know the real meaning of the word "friendship." Perhaps I have never been able to sense the thing. I have had many close and intimate acquaintanceships; I have felt a tremendous interest in many individuals. I have admired some of these, and have even respected a few; but I think my chief interest in my acquaintances has been that of observing and studying them — noting the underplay of the inheritance and environment

111

in the development of each individual. I have obtained considerable satisfaction in watching the effect of causes. How a certain man of my acquaintance will respond to a certain stimulant is a question I have been always asking myself. It is needless to say that I have not infrequently attempted to apply this stimulant in order to discover results.

I recall an article in the *Atlantic Monthly* a number of years ago. The article was a description, or an attempted description, of a wealthy man who had retired from the hurly-burly of the world to a home in the outskirts of a village in the New England mountains. The only occupation of this man was that of ministering to the welfare of the neighboring community, collectively and individually. His whole life seemed to be that of service. He sought to relieve the suffering of poverty without humiliating the object of his generosity, always taking care, when possible, to conceal the source of the benefaction received. Each young boy and young girl in the community with natural ability, who was lacking an opportunity from other sources, found his or her opportunity, knowing not from whence it came. Even men and women who were comparatively well-to-do, but who had no capacity to enjoy their lives properly, unaided, received what they wanted.

The writer of the article, who was a friend of the man described and who had an opportunity of knowing of all his friend's activities, once asked the question: "How is it your whole enjoyment in life seems to be in serving your neighbors while you live here in your big house alone and never come in personal contact with them?"

The man replied: "Oh, I love human beings well enough to die for them, but I do not love them well enough to live with them."

The name of the man was not given nor was it possible to identify him.

I often think of this man. I believe he was a real character. I believe that I thoroughly well understand his attitude. Do you think he lived an unhappy life? For myself, I do not think that he necessarily did live unhappily.

I cannot truthfully say that I have ever felt a warm glow of pleasure as the result of meeting any man or woman whom I had known in the past or who was, for the time being, on intimate terms with me. While I try (I really think through a sense of duty) to be cordial and kindly in my greeting and treatment of the few who visit me and the larger number whom I perforce must meet in moving around in the world, I am sure I am never thoroughly successful in completely deceiving anyone.

Sometimes I have asked myself whether or not things would be different with me and would have been different with me had I been less successful in exercising power and accumulating wealth. I am far from sure that you and others would be right in explaining the situation by saying that I have been too busy with my own affairs to have time for anything else. On the other hand, I am inclined to believe that my so-called successes in life have been largely the result of my incapacity to enjoy the things that you, and I suppose almost the universality of men, enjoy. It was perhaps because I had no other source of amusement that I have devoted myself almost exclusively during my lifetime to acquiring information by observation and reading, and, to a less extent, developing those plans that made me more than well-to-do.

Like the man on the New England mountainside, I am not lacking in goodwill and a certain sort of sympathy for a world full of people. I am also capable of suffering, and I do suffer on account of there being a world full of misery. In these days of the terrible war I am no less sad of heart than during those long months when I saw my son John suffering, slowly dying from a disease of the heart. I will even confess that, when alone, tears can flow; but it is only when I am alone.

I do not regret, as one of your friends did, the lack of friendship. I really feel that I have never needed a friend. I have never felt that my pain would be lessened in the least by the sympathies of another.

I am only capable of enjoying giving. I experience no pleasure in receiving anything that is given me.

I was never given to uproarious mirth; but rarely an hour passes, sick or well, in the midst of success or in the midst of failure, that I do not chuckle.

I do not think that you or even an ordinarily large number of men have more enjoyment in life than I have. I would like to feel that the great majority of men and women were happier in their minds than I am. Even if most people lived as happily as I live I think there would be no occasion for my being sad at all, and I think that I never would be sad.

In a previous letter I remember that I asked you to, someday, come to California and visit me. After what I have said, however, you can well understand that curiosity rather than friendship is the occasion of my invitation.

I have had opportunities to observe and study many life careers — the odd and unexpected (unexpected to me) developments of character.

How such a man as you were can be such a man as you are presents a very interesting problem.

I doubt if you see much in the development of my character to surprise you. From your point of view, at least, I have traveled the usual route from poverty to wealth, from unsophisticatedness to sophisticatedness, from illusion to disillusion. I do not believe that effect would follow causes in any such way in my case as is supposed to be usual in men of my type. I know that I am wealthy, but I do not *feel* rich; and if I do not feel rich how can my wealth alter my character?

As to being sophisticated: How can any increase in my possession of knowledge have affected my character when I am always conscious of being a fool, and when you and thousands of others know that I am a fool, and [when] in innumerable ways [you] seldom purposely reveal your opinions?

Never in my life has there existed for me a more perfect rainbow of illusions and aspirations than that which I find myself contemplating today, in the last half of my sixty-second year.

But you are the problem. What turned you from what you were to what you are? What is it that turns so many of the young men whom I used to know into something so different from what they once were? The best explanation, to me, of all this seems to be the part I have played with all of you in those early days.

A long time ago I discovered that I had certain hypnotic powers, that I had a capacity sometimes to turn a sow's ear into a silk purse and at other times to turn a silk purse into a sow's ear. It seems to me possible that I have not only had the capacity to see visions, or perhaps only illusions, but to compel others to see what I saw; often enough to see my visions even more clearly defined and apparently more solid and substantial than they were to me.

I have known brilliant minds to dim; forceful characters [to] have become weak and supine; optimism to turn into pessimism; and knowledge to turn into lethargy with no other, to me, apparent cause for the metamorphosis than the withdrawal of my personality, directly or indirectly applied. There must be a correlation [=corollary?] to this proposition; if I influence others, others must be influencing me.

The elements of character with which I was born included cynicism. I have always been at warfare with this element. The most effective weapon that I had in the combat was the youth, the vigor, and the love of the illusion of younger men, if not in years at least in spirit, with whom I associated. I have drawn perhaps more enthusiasm from others, more inspirations, in fact, than I have given. The companionship of age was always intolerable to me. Old institutions were distasteful to me. I have always noticed that, even up to the present time, my interest in my various newspapers has waned with their age.

When, twenty-five years ago (and then I was an old, old man of thirty-seven), I was called upon to take control of the two oldest Scripps papers, the Detroit *News* and the Cleveland *Press*, the managers of those two institutions were always complaining to me because I was so seldom in their offices, and because, when there, I was always impatient and critical of everything that was going on. It was very distasteful to me, the work I had to do in those two offices.

I once tried to explain my attitude by saying that I only liked young things and hard jobs, and that, while the Cincinnati *Post* and St. Louis *Chronicle* were not only comparatively young papers, but very difficult of management, the *Post* [*News*] and *Press* were well established and very profitable. "Why," I said, "all young things are pretty and all old things are ugly. Even a little pig is pretty; its actions are cute and friendly; while nothing can be uglier than a fat old sow. To me, the *News* and *Press* are two fat, greasy, dirty, old sows. As properties, they are magnificent; but as occupations, they are detestable."

A lot of the cute little pigs that I knew thirty or forty years ago (and you are one of them) have grown into commonplace pork — some lean and razorback, it is true, and some fat and stupid. The pity of it is, Hopkins, that we old fellows don't know ourselves how ugly we are.

Think of what a beautiful world this would be, what a jolly happy world it would be for the people who live in it, if no one was allowed to live beyond, say, thirty-five years of age. Of course society would not be so well or so poorly organized as it now is; of course civilization would not move on quite so fast in some directions; but then, the people of the world would not be conscious of their deprivations and of the "might-have-beens"; but what a jolly, exciting time everybody would be having.

When my son died last year and my sister endeavored to console me, I told her I needed no consolation, that I had loved my boy well enough to wish him all that was good in life and to wish that he should miss most of that which was bad. He had lived all through childhood, when to live was to enjoy; he had had his young man's dreams and ambitions; he had loved a woman and had not outlived his love for her; he had become the father of a boy to succeed him. Do you not believe with me that he had lived through that part of life which contributes 90 per cent of all the happiness of living and that he had only missed that part of life during which 90 per cent of all the misery that comes from living occurs?

While I live and dream and contemplate a whole rainbow of illusions, I know that I am only an encumbrance, and it is a pleasure to me now that duty and inclination and ability prompt me to live as a recluse, needing no friends and hidden from all enemies.

But, Hoppy! Hopkins! A. M. Hopkins! Mr. Hopkins! What has become of him? Certainly it was not old Hoppy nor even Hopkins that wrote the letter that caused me to bore my secretary with this long dissertation.

Yours sincerely,

E. W. Scripps

The Other Man Doesn't Know
and Can't Know

[*August 6, 1919*]

Recently I had a brief business interview with a man who has been my legal adviser for thirty-six years [J. C. Harper]. In an attempt to make him understand my own personal attitude with regard to certain business and editorial policies connected with my newspapers and now under consideration by me, I made this statement:

"My sister and I are both so advanced in years and so well-to-do personally that we cannot feel any selfish interest whatever in the prospects of larger or smaller profits of the institution, the major part of which we own."

To this the attorney replied about as follows: "This attitude of yours constitutes a real danger to every one of the minor stockholders in your various corporations." (The legal gentleman has nearly all of his own fortune invested in shares of these corporations.)

I wish to make these two statements the text of a disquisition on what I may call philosophical economics.

I have made a number of attempts in the way of analyses, both of my own individual character and the causes of the existence and development of the large institution that I have ruled over from its first inception. In every case I have been driven to the conclusion that, tested by all of the commonly accepted standards and measures, I was not an able businessman, and that all my activities had violated some or all of the rules supposed by the commonalty to govern successful businessmen.

I have compared myself with a large number of my contemporaries, my associates in the business world, and especially my own subordinates, with the result of finding that, even according to my own peculiar views, most of these men were my superiors. I mean by this that in any given case where

116

some important step had to be taken or some one thing had to be done, there was always some one of my associates who could do the thing better than I could myself.[9]

In the pure, abstract element of judgment had I any advantage over the others? I must admit that in few, if any, cases have I been sure that my own judgment was superior to that of others. I have felt that in almost any case where my judgment was adopted, and had to be adopted because it was my judgment, had it chanced that my judgment had been in the other fellow's possession and his judgment in my possession, and had I been as determined to have my own way, the results might have been better, or at least as good, in the matter of success or failure.

So finally I have been driven to the conclusion that it is at least quite possible that, to the extent I have been successful, my success could have been due to what might be called sheer force of character — a determination that could not be resisted or in the least deflected by an opposing will. My uniform or at least average success may have had the effect of producing in my own mind, and even in the minds of many others, an unjustifiably high estimate of my own intelligence.

Having thus arraigned myself and having made the farthest excursion possible for me in the direction of modesty, I will hereinafter attempt to be equally frank as an egotist.

If my attorney friend finds in my attitude with regard to the future financial prosperity of my institution a present danger to all of my partners, I can find nothing in that attitude that is new to me — any change in it that has been the result of increasing years. I can find something more — namely, that this attitude is the very germ from which has grown and developed the institution I have spoken of as it exists today. But for this attitude there could have been no such insitution.

From the first, in dealing with the infant plant, I have done with it what I wanted to do. I have done what I wanted to do, not because my reason told me that by doing so I would make the most money, the most friends, or the most pleasant conditions in which to live. If I have not been driven by blind instinct alone, I have nevertheless not turned aside from the course I chose to pursue because of encountering great, though not insurmountable, difficulties and dangers which might have been evaded.

I recall a meditation I indulged in late in my twenty-fifth year or early in my twenty-sixth year. At that time I was in the midst of great difficulties. I was in imminent danger of being imprisoned. I was being tried in court on

---

[9] Scripps stated this point of view in various ways at various times. Perhaps more frequently than any other way, he attributed to his own laziness his practice of letting someone else do a job when that person could do it as well as or better than he could.

a charge of criminal libel.[10] I had not committed the libel. I mean I had not written or even personally published the article which was alleged to be libelous. I was absent, not only from the office, but from the city in which my newspaper was published on the day the article was written and published. But many an innocent man has been convicted of crime and sentenced to punishment.

The subject of my meditation was the perils of free journalism. In those days editors were sometimes shot and killed, sometimes horsewhipped or submitted to other indignities. And then, there was always the danger of criminal proceedings and civil damage suits prosecuted by some person who resented disagreeable notoriety.

It was not long before the time of which I speak when a certain then supposedly wealthy man — a member of Congress, having influence with the Administration and owning a newspaper — had offered me, if I would give up my own little newspaper, the position of editor of his old and established journal and also a high-salaried government office in his congressional district.[11] The salary offered me was just ten times that which I was then drawing, and a year's salary equaled 60 per cent of all the capital invested in my paper.

This offer presented to me the opportunity of becoming immediately a prominent citizen and a respected member of that small coterie of wealthy, influential, and respectable citizens in my adopted community. According to my ability (in those days I had none of the doubts concerning myself that I have indicated in the opening paragraphs of this disquisition), I might rapidly rise, also in a financial way. I had rejected the offer.

Instead of being in daily attendance at the principal clubs of the city, I was daily attending court and facing a jury that would decide whether I was to go to jail or not.

I was then, as I was before and always have been, a coward, though a coward entirely successful in concealing his fear from others. I was really very much afraid, not only of being convicted of criminal libel, but, on that account, of having my first little venture in journalism ruined. My newspaper was still an infant and its income was considerably less than its outgo.

I faced and considered the situation. I wanted to find out for myself why I had done what I had done and why I was doing what I was doing. I decided that in some things, at least, I was not my own master; that, in fact, my conduct was governed by something entirely different from reason. I have

[10] Cowles suit, described in the previous section.
[11] In a letter to Ellen B. of Feb. 1, 1919, Scripps recalled the same incident, identifying the congressman as Richard C. Parsons, who was editor and part owner of the Cleveland *Daily Herald*.

put it to myself in this way: Now, supposing that I was in a certain situation and was inwardly prompted to take a certain course, and supposing it should appear to me that if I took that course I would only have one chance of succeeding and 999 chances of going to the penitentiary. What would I do? I concluded that I would take the one chance in a thousand.

I had recently had an adventure. I had, or thought I had, escaped being killed by prompt action on my part in an encounter. I had been threatened with bodily violence on several occasions. I put to myself this question: If I should some day have on my table an item of news that I considered legitimate, and some man of whose courage and determination I would have no doubt threatened to shoot me if I published it, what would I do? I did not make any determination or resolution as to what I would do. I felt sure that if I had one chance in a hundred of killing the other man before he killed me, I would publish the item. (I recall that for years after this I always carried a pistol and practiced shooting, because I believed I was just the kind of a man who might need the pistol.)

Therefore, I believe I am right in saying that my present attitude, in considering the subject which I discussed with my legal friend, is no whit different than it was some forty years ago.

It seems to me that the Scripps Institution, as it stands today, owes its existence rather to this attitude of mine than to any other quality of character that can be recognized as an attribute of myself. I have been inclined to think that it was only an accident or a chance that my mental attitude, or my temperament or whatever you may call it, happened to be something that fitted the times in which I lived — something that was a needed element, or at least a fit element, in such an organization as my institution was, has been, and is.

Something less than a year ago I had occasion to address a letter to a certain eminent person in which I disclaimed any other qualification as an adviser than that my temperament was such as to make me typical of and representative of a very large portion of his constituency.

For forty years I have conducted and controlled that institution of which I spoke to my attorney when I said that, relative to a certain other thing that I willed, its future financial prosperity was to me insignificant and, in fact, entirely negligible as a matter of consideration. It is not because I willed that my institution should grow to be a large and valuable property that it has so grown. It is only because I willed that it should express my attitude that it has grown to be a large and valuable property.

While I can now say that I am determined on a certain course of action — and so determined that I would take it even though I knew it would result in the destruction of my property, and hence that of my associates — I am perfectly certain that, by pursuing the course I have determined on, I will add to the immediate prosperity of the institution and to its future greater growth.

I have no means of knowing what the thoughts of other men are — the thoughts of men who have erected large business enterprises or who have in other ways obtained positions of great power and influence in the community. I think I have good reason to suspect that all such men follow internal promptings such as none of their fellows know of, and do that which they do because they want to do it. They are influenced very little, if at all, by what the mass of their fellows think of their actions, or by their own judgment of the profitableness or unprofitableness, in a financial way, of the course they elect to pursue.

That famous or infamous railroad and coal baron (his name was Baer) [George Baer, Philadelphia and Reading Railway] who, when he declared he acted by divine right in the ruling of the corporations over which he exercised control, might have been and probably was one of the most modest of men. Like myself, he may have thoroughly analyzed his character and judged of his individual abilities and discovered that there was nothing exceptional or great in them. He might have been and probably was a very religious man. Hence, recognizing in all humility his great imperfections, nothing could have been more natural than that he should consider himself as only a humble agent of divinity.

However, when I assert myself, owing to my agnosticism in all matters of religion, I cannot and therefore do not claim title to act as the agent of divinity.

Thinking versus Knowing

[*December 8, 1920*]

Within the past day or two I have read in an article written by a critic of our educational system a statement of a condition that I hadn't even heard of before. It was to the effect that of over three million recruits to our army in the late war the average of intelligence or mental development of all these men was only equal to that of a 13⅓-year-old boy of normal intelligence and tolerable mental training.

Some of our eminent psychologists have invented systems for testing the strength of or the development of individual intelligence.

It is tolerably common knowledge that either by reason of difference in inheritance or difference in education there is great difference in mental powers between individuals. Memory is only one of the elements of intellection. Quickness of reaction to stimuli is another measurable element. (For instance, one child being asked the sum of five and four would give a quicker response in the way of an answer than another.) The ability to distinguish colors and sounds can also be measured. There are a number of other elements of intellect that can be measured. I presume that either the Binet or the Yerkes system of test was adopted in order that the mentality of our soldiers should be measured.

When a child in our public schools is being examined in order that the teacher shall know to what grade or class he shall work in, the examination is for the purpose of finding what the child knows, what it has learned in the way of facts.

Of course it stands to reason that there is a considerable amount of correlation of the two mental elements of intellect, mental vigor and that of knowledge possessed — knowledge, that is to say, of things which are taught in school.

However, it is perfectly evident that the mind of a boy might be highly de-

121

veloped and that the boy should possess great powers of thinking effectually without his even knowing his letters or being able to read at all, and without his having any knowledge of mathematics, grammar, geography, or history whatever, or any other subject in an ordinary school curriculum.

I remember in my youth an old gentleman who had been and still was a successful merchant, who had polite manners, who was really an estimable and honest citizen, who had never learned to read or write, or even to make mathematical calculations by any of the ordinary rules which are adopted by our mathematicians.

I recall the youthful experience of my own. I had learned to read very, very young, probably before I was four or five years of age. I was very fond of being read to by my sisters and my mother. My literary tastes were, for a child, of a high order. I think that I had read or had read to me most of Shakespeare's works before I was ten years of age. Milton's, Walter Scott's, Longfellow's, and Tennyson's poems were familiar to me before it was necessary and perhaps before I would have been able to read them.

I suppose I was seven or eight years of age before I went to the country school. School attendance was very repugnant to me. I was not interested in schoolbooks or lessons. In school I spent almost all of my time in reading some book concealed behind my schoolbook or in listening to the recitations of children in other classes and listening to the teacher.

I never learned my lessons properly and in class recitations always failed. In the earlier days of my schooling we did not have school reports. Had there been such a thing I am pretty sure I never could have carried home anything but a row of goose eggs.

I could make some show of knowledge by remembering what other people in their recitations had said. It was literally impossible then, as it has ever since been, for me to learn anything by rote. Try as I did, I never could remember rules laid down in my grammar or rules given in my arithmetic.

I recall, however, that in time I was able quickly to grasp and retain in memory the principle of any rule in arithmetic and grammar, though I could not retain in my memory the exact words. And yet I not only have the reputation of possessing one of the most retentive memories, but it seems to me that it is almost impossible for me ever to so far forget anything that I have ever read as not to be able even forty years later on reading a book to recognize every word and sentence and even to remember where and under what conditions I had read the words.

It was in my fourteenth year, I believe, when one Friday afternoon (the last day of the school week when it was customary, I think, once a month for parents and other people to come into the school to hear recitations of the children) my class in arithmetic (I remember it was Ray's *Third Arithmetic* and I can see in my mind's eye now that very book, its length and breadth and thickness and the ornamentation of the outside cover) was called up to recite and the teacher called me to the blackboard. I was given a very simple sum in addition and failed. There was one girl in our class, her name was Alice Putnam, who was my particular bête noire. I know I thought she was a fool girl and I particularly detested her because she had a case of little-girl love for the boy me. To mortify me, I think, the teacher called on Alice Putnam to do on the blackboard the sum I had failed upon. She easily accomplished her task and won the praise of the teacher, who at the same time was looking at me with scorn in her eyes. I was properly humiliated. I felt awfully bad.

It had always been my habit to steal away from my brothers and sisters and from the attention of my parents, from work or play, and go and hide and read. I always kept a piece of candle hidden in my bedroom and seldom went to bed without lighting the candle and reading for a considerable time in bed. That night after my humiliation in the school I took my Ray's *Third Arithmetic* to bed with me. I had fully determined to show Alice Putnam and the teacher, too, that I was not a dunce. I recall that I began at the very first page of the book and I remember I read the preface and for several hours that night I read (reading an arithmetic!). I read carefully and determined that I should not pass a single line or paragraph or a single problem without understanding just what was meant, just what the problem consisted of, just how and why the figured results were as they were. I forget how many days in school and out of school, Saturdays and Sundays, I devoted to reading this book, Ray's *Third Arithmetic*. I do recall that I had a piece of broken slate in the book, and a slate pencil, and that frequently I would set out problems to be solved and figured out. I went clear through this book up to logarithms. At that point I stopped. I do not recall ever having opened that book again, but I do recall that after that time at class recitations I never made a failure.

Although I was two or three years or grades away from the time when in the natural school order I should take up geometry, I determined to get my mathematics out of the way, and as soon as possible, and so I got a book on geometry and I went through that. Later, I forget how long afterwards, I got into a geometry class and I recall that I didn't have to depend upon my book to keep along with my class.

And still later algebra came along and I remember I got sick and tired of mathematics, and I became a zero man in my class. I am trying to make the point in the above that, while I had no knowledge of even the simplest elements of arithmetic or other mathematics, I had a mental development far superior to any of my classmates who, until the Alice Putnam affair, had far more knowledge than I had.

I recall I had a craze for languages once; then I studied French and German and Latin and Greek.[12] I had a tremendous interest in this kind of classical study and, had there been opportunity or necessity for my becoming a linguist, I think I could easily have acquired eminence. But Greek was far more interesting to me than Latin, and French far more interesting than German.

To this day I have retained my knowledge of French (ability to read, but I could never speak it well), but I have almost entirely forgotten my German. Although I have forgotten my Greek letters, my memory is very retentive of Greek words, I think, even more than of Latin, although on account of my French I suppose I know more Latin words than Greek. My facility in languages and the fact that I have an English vocabulary which is far larger than that of the ordinary, highly educated college graduate indicates that I have a certain kind of memory. (I have formed this idea as to the extent of my vocabulary by testing myself with an unabridged dictionary and comparing results with figures that have been given of similar tests made amongst the large numbers of college men.) But, while I know a large number of words, it is almost impossible for me to quote literally offhand any passage or even line of a poem or essay the contents or the whole of which I am perfectly familiar with.

While I find many solid works in philosophy and science and history rather dull and stupid, I have never found a book in English which I could not read understandingly, or in French (if I devoted sufficient labor to the reading and understanding). Neither have I ever found a book of this sort so stupid and so difficult that I would not prefer to spend my time reading it than reading any of the ordinary books of fiction or to spending my time in idle desultory dreaming or thinking.

After reading the lines stating [that] the average mental age of the recruits in the American Army was only 13½ years, I sat for some time thinking.

A new idea presented itself to my mind.

I have always found it extremely difficult to talk to most men and to make any man understand just what meaning I was trying to put over. It occurred to me that the reason why I found so little satisfaction in associating with my fellows and being interested in conversation with them was that the other fellow doesn't understand me — he doesn't fully understand me. The words I use, if they have any meaning to him, mean something very differ-

12 In early manhood.

ent from their meaning to me. The other fellow knows perhaps all of the words I use but he has perhaps no knowledge whatever of the thought and intent that lie behind my words.

I have had great difficulty always in my dealings with my business associates, because probably 99 times out of 100 what I have said has been entirely misinterpreted. Many serious misunderstandings as to business have arisen between myself and others as a result of my incapacity to convey my meaning. One result of this has been that I have been driven to adopting a certain rule, namely, to disclaim all obligation on my part for any of my spoken words and to state to each person that I have dealings with that I shall not be bound by anything that I say until it has been put in writing and autographically signed by me, and, generally, and perhaps in every case, I write or dictate very carefully and very briefly what I say and then carefully revise it before attaching my signature.

I have had the misfortune all of my life never to be able to have any serious conversation with women without giving offense. With one exception I have never been successful in my serious dealings with the women of my own family. When it is only my desire to please, I succeed only in offending. These ladies don't know what I mean and I can't tell them what I mean. They invariably think I mean something entirely different from what I would like to convey to them in words.

Words are only a part of speech. Even as parts of speech, pure and simple, the meaning of words depends to a tremendous extent on context. What words mean depends so much upon emphasis and facial expression and tone of voice and gesture as to make them very poor implements for conveying meaning in written or printed form.

I remember Thackeray once attempted, or rather succeeded, in showing five distinct meanings to the two words "my dear." The word "my" italicized and "dear" in roman meant something entirely different from the words "my dear" with the "dear" italicized. I forget just how he carried his explanation through; I only know that the words "my dear" might express contempt, rebuke, pleading, mortification, and even a foul epithet on the printed page without the existence of tone, facial expression, or gesture.

But to get back to the caption of this essay, "Thinking versus Knowing."

What sort of a government could there be in a family household if, even all of the children being very intelligent, the children from the child of four to the son and daughter of, say, eighteen were by their majority vote to establish the rules of the family and direct the family's affairs?

What sort of a government can our states and nation have when the pick of all the young men between the ages of 21 and 31 only possessed the mental capacities on the average of a child of 13½ years of age, even if that child should have the best possible mind that could be possessed by one 13½ years old? And now, it being conceded that on account of natural law or on account of customary sex relations of male and female that women are, if not intellectually inferior, intellectually different from men, we have fully doubled our electorate in giving women votes!

For the past two years I have been cooperating with a party of eminent scientists in a scheme to launch a society for the dissemination of science.[13] My object in writing this disquisition is to suggest or to argue that thinking, or the power to think, really is more important than knowledge.

The "little man" in one of Dickens' stories kept declaring that knowledge is power. I forget just what was the argument of his adversary in the discussion.

I think there is no evidence that knowledge in itself is power. Knowledge is only an instrument which intellect can use. Knowledge can be compared with a kit of carpenter's tools. The carpenter's tools could not build a house. The carpenters can build the house with the tools. The possession of knowledge by a man or woman, the possession of a great many facts, scientific and otherwise, have no value whatever to anyone whose mentality cannot make good use of the knowledge — not necessarily what is called utilitarian use, but any sort of use.

I am wondering whether it would be to any advantage to the people of the United States, to the government of the United States, whether the people of the United States would be any happier if every man and woman in this country knew all that is known by every individual of our "Association for the Dissemination of Science."

Let us look at one spot in the economic field. Here are two farmers, we will say, both possessed of identically the same education, each in fact knowing all that the other knows concerning farming. Are we to suppose that both of these farmers will be equally successful?

Let us take any two young men, say, of twenty-five years of age, both of whom have had identically the same religious teaching, the same schooling, and have read identically the same books and have been subject to identically the same environment, both having the same knowledge of physical and moral and written law. Have we any reason to suppose that the moral nature or character of these two men will be identical? I think there is no doubt that the relative successfulness of the two farmers and the relative morality of the two young men will depend entirely upon the intellect and capacity to think rightly of the various individuals.

13 Now Science Service.

During a rather long period of time I have been mixing with thousands and tens of thousands of my fellows, some few of these fortunate and the great mass of them more or less unfortunate.

What has been the reason for this difference of fortune?

I have had very much to do with young men. I have sought generally to aid and serve all the young men I have come in contact with, as I suppose nearly every other man has as he passes through life. To some few of these young men I have been able to be of service, to some of them great service, to others smaller service. Some of them have acted as though they understood my advice and appreciated it and made use of it, but for the most part these young men, who have been deferential to me in words and polite, would give no evidence of my advice having had any effect on them.

It has not been those young men whom I personally liked the most and in whom I was personally interested who gained the most. In fact, it seemed that almost all the really lovable ones were the very ones I could do nothing for. There is an old saying that he who can take good advice doesn't need it.

It is possible or even probable that the young men who gained in association with me have been the young men whose mental development or inherited intellect was of such a character as to make them able not only to understand me but to make use of the facts and the knowledge I imparted to them.

I recall an experience I had in California a good many years ago. There were two schemes presented to the ranchers in my neighborhood for an irrigation system. I was personally interested as the owner of a ranch in the success of the irrigation project. I had given the subject personal consideration and had sought and obtained expert engineers' advice.

One of the schemes was a rotten, robbing promotion scheme; the other was a practical one. I undertook to canvass the voters of the district to get their vote for what I considered the better scheme. One of my neighbors, a man named Jordan, was also frequently employed by me on my ranch. I called on him to canvass for his vote. He and his wife listened to me attentively, but just before I was leaving there came to Jordan's house a little, petty politician whose character as a corrupt man was well known. It was also known that he was employed and was paid money to canvass the district.

I stopped to hear his talk to the voter, Jordan. The principal argument made by this canvasser was that I was a wealthy man and that Jordan was a poor man and that "we poor men" must be on the lookout to see that the capitalists didn't swindle "us."

After this chap got done talking, Jordan turned to me and said, "Well, I guess I won't vote. You tell me one thing and this man tells me another and how can I tell which one to believe is right?" And yet this man Jordan was really a good citizen, a responsible fellow, and not at all below the average in intelligence. He couldn't think straight. He had no capacity to weigh the arguments or to judge of the character and the ability of the two rival organizations who wanted to carry out the irrigation scheme.

I was not surprised to find that on election day my party was snowed under and at the time it was my conviction, I remember, that most of the voters voted against that plan which was advocated by the wealthy and more intelligent people of the district, simply because they were wealthy and intelligent.

I have taken part as a journalist in hundreds of political campaigns of cities and counties and states and the nation, in political elections and in referendums of legislation. I have perhaps been as often on the winning side as on the losing side, but I have not been able to recall a single campaign where a choice of the majority of the electors was based on intelligence and thinking.

I do not believe that 5 per cent of the people of the United States as a rule have their choice determined by thought. Some campaign slogan, some personal prejudice, some personal animosity, some purely imaginary or real personal advantage, single or collective, is the motive. Our political campaigns in small communities and nationally depend upon emotions for their interest. Instead of voters being influenced by their reason, they are influenced by their emotions.

Since the conclusion of the great war there has been a condition of great unrest amongst the working people of all the European nations and of the United States. The working people in all of these countries, who were anything but contented before the war, seem to be determined now to produce some sort of economic revolution. Even where political democracy of the highest and freest form exists, there is great discontent with the government and a disposition to (what is called) democratize industry.

The skilled mechanic who has spent four to seven years in learning his trade, and who recognizes that since his apprenticeship he has learned much of his trade, has little if any doubt but that he is fully possessed of all the knowledge and all of the capacity necessary to take a large and active influential part in the management and the financing of great and intricate business. They have not the power of thinking that will permit them to realize that whereas it only requires three, four, five, six, or seven years for them to learn their own trades, it generally requires from ten to twenty years for a man to learn the trade of business management to such an extent and to such perfection as will allow him to be considered even as a candidate for a managerial position.

It is this lack of power of thinking—perhaps I might say this entire neglect to think at all—that causes these workingmen to believe that a man who doesn't work with his hands doesn't really do any hard work at all or any work that requires any training.

A clerk even holding a petty position in the office of a great business institution may be in a position and often is in a position to learn the meaning of all the words used by his employer, the names of all the material, and even in a general way the mechanical processes of the factory; he may know prices of the things that are bought and what they are sold for.

In a few months a comparatively intelligent young man could learn the whole history of an old business and could learn even every detail of the conduct of the business.

Such a young man might be elected as the chief manager of a great institution and he might hold that position for a number of days, weeks, or even months, and it would be impossible for any member, stockholder, or customer of the concern to observe the slightest difference in the character of the business which had resulted from the change from an old and able and experienced man to this tyro. And yet it would be inevitable that utter and complete failure of the business would soon enough occur as a result of the young man's not having had his thinking developed to such an extent as to permit him to make use of all of the tools he had, namely, all of the knowledge he had acquired by, say, precept or instruction. No man of sufficient intelligence to have acquired the ownership of a great business would even think of turning over to his son—a young man, untrained, undeveloped by practice in the business and only verbally instructed—the control and management of his, the father's, business.

On the other hand no such man would nominate as his successor any old employee who had not had his powers of thinking correctly developed by having on occasions been trusted more and more with responsibility and authority.

A chief clerk in a business or even an assistant manager could never have the chance to be developed by the practice of responsibility and authority, and could not successfully succeed his employer. The mere fact that such a man had been long employed without ever having experienced responsibility and the necessity of thinking would be a detriment to such a man.

I have several thousand employees. Some scores of them have held high and responsible positions in my concern and yet I know no one of them, especially none of the older and most experienced of them, who is fitted to succeed to my responsibility.

Employees are always departmental employees. They have had the opportunity to think for their department, and that develops their thinking capacity in this particular form to such an extent that it seems there is no room in their mentality for them to think clearly or even to learn to think clearly for the institution as a whole.

Whenever I have had occasion to think of this matter at all when I have been in contact with men of the different departments of my business, I have always been struck with the evidence that, in my affairs at least, the men employed in my concern know little more about my business than any outsider, or they know so much of some one department of it as to cause them to become even less capable of development for general management than they were in their early connection with the business. The advice that I have often had urged on me by my own most loyal and intelligent employees with respect to the conduct of my business has shocked me often enough on account of its entire impracticability.

I have had to acknowledge frequently that no one could know so little about the newspaper business as a journalist and no one could know so little about journalism as a profession as one of the employees in the mechanical or business department.

The knowledge of some of these men, or most of these men, who are working for me and have been working for me for years, is not a power. It is really a weakness or would be a weakness to any one of them called upon to function as a manager of the whole concern or the manager of any other department than the one they are accustomed to work in.

I think it is quite possible that civilization, or material civilization such as exists in Europe and America today, is on the eve of a great setback.

We have discovered that democratization in politics is entirely possible. Democratic political government is possible because the few rule the many; the few who are capable of government are also capable by demagoguery (this term not used invidiously) to persuade the many to give their votes.

But we have for centuries developed political democracy out of original autocracy. Perhaps in centuries to come we may be able to develop a successful form of industrial democracy from present autocracy. But the transition from one form of industrial government to another must be long and tedious, and even if it is ever accomplished the few in this new order of events in industry will rule the many. The present owner and controller of great industry sometime may hold his position by reason of the votes of his workingmen instead of by reason of his stock certificates.

Perhaps all the evils that may flow from an eventual change from auto-cratic to democratic industrialism may be offset and compensated for by the necessity of workingmen learning how to think straight about business or more nearly straight than they can now think.

I can conclude by saying that it is my belief that humanity is really clut-tered up with so much more knowledge than it has thinking power to use that the first greatest duty or interest of nations is to teach or to compel its citizens to do more and better thinking.

A Great Bore

[*December 25, 1920*]

This is what Christmas Day has been to me ever since I got out of baby clothes into pants, or approximately a little later than that day. I remember standing at the sittingroom fireplace shouting up the chimney to Santa Claus on several Christmases. I remember my petition for suspenders and for copper-toed boots. I recall I sent the usual child's letter to Santa Claus on one occasion.

Then there was that memorable Christmas — that day of great mental anguish! One of my presents was a rather large piece of candy made in the form of a beefsteak. By coloration the candy represented streaks of lean and streaks of fat and part of the rib bone. But to me it was only candy, only sweet.

My mother, who was not only thrifty but careful of her children's diet, had objections to my eating too much of the candy and so broke me off a small lump which she permitted me to eat.

But, while she was not looking and there was no notice being taken of me, I got my hand on the candy and slipped out of the sittingroom up the stairs into what was called the boys' bedroom, where there were three beds that I and my brothers used to sleep on. Under one of these I crawled and began to gorge myself on the candy. However, I had not been long absent from the family circle until my absence was discovered and a search was made for me and finally I was pulled out from under the bed, all sticky and dirty with my beefsteak not half consumed. Of course I received the usual corporeal [*sic*] chastisement. But what I suffered from most was the mortification of being detected in such a selfish act.

Then there were the Christmases in the old farmhouse. But from the time of the beafsteak adventure there were no more joyous Christmases. Santa Claus, or the belief in him, had gone glimmering. The usual Christmas Day

132

opened as Christmas Days generally do open to the young. There were little presents, most of which were for one reason or another entirely unappreciated by me.

On one Christmas Day I received such an instrument of torture as to have made it especially memorable. It was a suit of red flannels, shirt and drawers, that my mother had made for me. The flannel that she used in this case must have been the most prickly sort ever manufactured. I was marched off to a bedroom by my mother immediately and made to put on those abominations. They prickled and scratched and hurt me even while putting them on. I was led back to the family circle squalling and protesting. The room was warm and the heat of my anger and the convulsions of my sobs made me sweat and increased ten volume the irritation of the flannel on my skin.

All day long I was watched and made to wear my flannels. I endeavored to slip away and throw them off on several occasions but I was always prevented. Even when night came I went to bed sobbing and dreading the day to come and the days thereafter, since my mother had told me that I must wear my flannels all winter.

There came other Christmases with simple toys and so-called useful presents — a new suit of clothes that didn't fit me (I have always hated new clothes whether I bought them ready-made at the village store or had them turned out by the most fashionable tailor), a new pair of woolen sox, maybe a quite unobjectionable cap, a tolerable knit woolen comforter to wear around my neck, or a pair of woolen mittens.

Then there was a Christmas dinner — a long table, all the family and some guests, plenty to eat, a large appetite. But I, the youngest, had to wait till the last to be served and then only a drumstick. I never got the wishbone; that was always given to one of my older brothers or sisters. The plum pudding was good enough. I would overeat and in the afternoon would be heavy and sometimes sick (I always had a delicate stomach even when I had a good appetite).

Other Christmases, I was getting to be a grown boy. I had become a good reader and liked good books, of which there were plenty in the house.

Then there was another awful calamity. My sister Ellen who happened to be absent, possibly at college or possibly at work in Detroit on a newspaper, who had had abundant opportunity to know my tastes and proficiency in literature, disappointed me, shocked me, and even disgusted me by sending me as a Christmas present a child's book written in words of one syllable. That my sister Ellen, of all persons, should so humiliate me was unbearable. I went to my bedroom and cried. I went out-of-doors and cried. It was hard work for me to keep back my tears at any time of the day even when other people were around.

I grew to be a young man. I had a little spending money. There were things that I wanted to buy with my money — powder and shot for my gun, skates, fishing tackle, perhaps more than all else, books. But it was a custom of our family each one to give the other a present and these presents took all of my hoard of savings.

And then the jollifications! Jollity, which was to me, if not wholly clownish, almost so in its simplicity.

Christmas set me always on edge. It irritated me. It spoiled my none-too-good disposition. While a youngster I imagine I never escaped a Christmas without one or more whippings by my mother; grown older, I was scolded or reproved or humiliated by being punished in some other way. I always dreaded Christmas at home and always felt a sense of relief when it was over.

As a young man I spent several Christmases in the city of Detroit where I was doing some kind of newspaper work. There were members of the family there. I tried to be decent and conform to the spirit of the day but it was a struggle.

After an experience of smoking a cigar when I was about fourteen years old, I resolved not to smoke until after I was twenty-one. I also resolved not to drink any alcoholics. However, my father always kept wine and bottled Scotch ale in our cellar. Occasionally I would steal a bottle of either wine or ale from his store and hide somewhere in the barn or elsewhere, taking occasional drinks.

But after I went to Detroit in my nineteenth year I drank nothing until my twenty-first birthday, when I took a small glass of claret wine.

But on the Christmas following my twenty-first birthday, after having spent most of the day pretending to be jolly and happy amongst my relatives, I managed to get away and foregather with some of my fellow reporters on the Detroit *News* and that evening I took enough wine and more than enough spirits — brandy or whiskey. I was sick all that night and miserable.

There were two or three other Christmases in Detroit. They were tedious days as there was no work to be done in the office as we did not publish on Christmas. Even in the theatres, or some of them at least, the plays were Christmas plays.

It was in my twenty-fifth year that I went to Cleveland and established the Cleveland *Press* the second of November.

I spent Christmas Day in Cleveland. We didn't publish the *Press* on Christmas. I spent most of the day with four or five of my printers and pressmen in a room in the old Johnson House Hotel in Cleveland, playing penny-ante poker. We all drank too much. Whenever I took the least too much alcohol it didn't make me drunk exactly but made me feel dizzy and slightly nauseated. So long as I kept upright I could endure the sensation. But as soon as I would lie down my head would seem to whirl around. It was almost impossible to get relief by vomiting.

This first Christmas Day in Cleveland, as I said, I took a little too much. I was able to eat a little supper but, on going to my room to sit down to read, my head went to whirling. All that night I walked the streets of Cleveland, trying to work off the effects but I couldn't get over my discomfort.

I went to my office the morning after Christmas without having slept at all. My head was aching and I was extremely irritable. I quarreled with and nagged my staff and printers. It was several years before I ever again permitted myself to cross the line of sobriety.

The Christmas of 1880 I spent in St. Louis, where I was publishing a new paper we had started, the *Chronicle*. There was only one of my family in St. Louis, my bachelor brother. But I spent the day alone in my room and that Christmas was memorable because it was, perhaps, the first not unpleasant Christmas of my memory.

Then there was a Christmas that I spent in Spain, at Seville, I think. On that day my sister, who was traveling with me, and I went to see a bullfight, which disgusted both of us.

Prior to this I had spent a Christmas in Algiers at a pension with my sister. All of the other guests at the pension were elderly people and English. I have no unpleasant recollections of this Christmas.

I spent one or more Christmases in Cincinnati which I don't remember anything about.

After I married and was on my honeymoon tour, which lasted some six months or more, I spent a Christmas Day either in Texas or Mexico — which, I don't recall. Naturally, all days were alike in being pleasant in those times.

There were several Christmases in my home at West Chester near Cincinnati. My wife's father was a minister. The Christmases there weren't so bad. I helped my wife and father-in-law and mother-in-law in their church celebrations.

There were two Christmases at Cincinnati when my two oldest children were just old enough to be supposedly interested in Christmas trees and toys.

Then came a long series of Christmases at "Miramar." The children had increased in number and Christmas celebrations were a matter of necessity. But all the ceremonial parts of our Christmases here were conducted by my wife or my brothers and sisters. They were generally noisy affairs and the most I could do was to wear a grin and pretend to be patient, while in fact I was in torture on account of anxiety. My wife's strenuous labors getting ready for Christmas generally lasted from two weeks to a month, almost invariably resulting in her being sick on Christmas or immediately thereafter. Some or all of the children were made sick by the Christmas excitement and overeating.

Time passed on and the children grew older, but Mrs. Scripps never failed to consider it her duty to celebrate Christmas by buying gifts, not only for all the members of her immediate family, but for all of her relatives and friends and all of the score or more of servants and other employees about the ranch or ranch house. I could always tell when Christmas was coming by the frequency of my wife's absences from home and their long duration — days and days and days together I did not see her in the daytime and only did see her at night when she was tired, half sick, and always indisposed. I think that at least two out of every three Christmases that have been celebrated at "Miramar" have resulted in Mrs. Scripps being ill for several days either on Christmas Day or immediately thereafter.

This Christmas Day, my sixty-seventh Christmas, finds me sitting alone in my house.

Death has robbed me of two of my sons. Another son, my oldest, is lying sick with an illness that he will never fully recover from, even if he gets over the acute attack. His mother is with him. My youngest son, Robert, called back by me on account of his brother's illness, is on the train.

My elder daughter is in her home, probably celebrating her Christmas and, I imagine, enjoying it, with her servants at Escondido thirty miles away. My younger daughter, whose husband I never wish to meet, is at her home on Fanita Ranch, which I bought a number of years ago. I am sure she is following in her mother's footsteps in the matter of Christmas celebration with her two boy babies.

My son Robert's wife and two children are at Robert's home in Cleveland, Ohio.

My dead son John's son and heir, John P. Scripps, who is orphaned of both of his parents, is at his grandfather McRae's home in the city of San Diego.

None of the children of my sick son are up at "Miramar" with me today, although for several days they have been with me on account of their father's illness. Doubtless, they are going through some form of Christmas celebration even in the house of sickness and imminent death.

I have a wife and four children living, who soon will be only three, and I have nine grandchildren. And I am spending this Christmas Day alone and, were it not for the one impending catastrophe, I should feel well content.

It is altogether probable that I will have to endure very few more Christmases.

If all the days of my life had been, on the average, as unhappy as all the Christmas Days of my life have been, I would certainly be able to write myself down as the least happy man on earth.

James George Osborn Scripps

[*January 7, 1921*]

This was dictated on the evening of the day Jim died.

| Born July 19, 1886 | Died January 7, 1921 |
| A born financier | Born a fighting man |

My son was born on my wife's twentieth birthday, being thirty-two years and one month and one day younger than his father.

His mother could not nurse him at breast. Only a few weeks after his birth, his mother was pregnant again. This second child died at birth; and a few weeks later the mother was again pregnant. Before Jim was five years old, a fourth child was born to live. A case of phlegma dolens occurred at this fourth birth and for more than a year the mother was an invalid.

Most of the care of Jim during his infancy fell to me and to his grandmother.[14] For the first year, I had the assistance of a physician who daily attended my house, and there were also nurse girls.

It was early in Jim's third year that I first punished him. He was born a fighter, and it was on account of this bellicose tendency which had brought him into contact with his mother that I punished him. That was the beginning, perhaps, of a conflict which, in one form or another, existed during most of Jim's lifetime.

I can remember that I only punished my son corporally not more than four or five times. This was because Jim was obedient to me, but the obedience was caused by his fear of his father. After my son was a grown man, he once told me that for years while he was a boy he cherished the hope of some day growing large enough to give me a licking.

Since I began reading Freud and considering the subject of psychoanalysis,

[14] Mrs. Samuel K. Holtsinger.

I have been able to realize the possibility of permanent impressions being made on a child's mind — impressions of hostility, of fear, and of affection toward certain individuals — that endure notwithstanding the obliteration of all childish memories.

Jim was a fighter. He was one of that kind of men to whom life would probably be dull even to the point of being unendurable were it not for antagonism. My son was a man whom William James would have called "tough-minded." He was not a sentimentalist. He dearly loved to view prizefights. His play was rough play. He enjoyed business because he enjoyed strife and struggle.

His disposition was not avaricious or miserly. Often in his talks with me, he has protested that he did not value money for the sake of money, and that all he found interesting in the business was "playing the game."

A good many years ago, my sister Ellen made me a little Christmas or birthday gift in the shape of a copper plaque which represents a middle-aged man sitting alone at a table, grasping a mug of beer with one hand and a long-stemmed clay pipe in the other. Beneath the man are these four lines:

> A little health, a little wealth,
> A little house and freedom;
> With some few friends for certain ends
> But little cause to need 'em.

On many occasions, my son spoke to me about this plaque, and he always told me that those lines represented his ideals.

For the most part, Jim's life was that of a solitaire.

He married young, and had four children. He was a good husband and a devoted father. He loved to play with his children — to play with his children and their toys.

From the time even before he got into his teens, his was a remarkable personality. At times, child as he was, he had all the gravity and maturity of a middle-aged man. At other times, he was boisterous in a child-like way. As he grew into manhood, these characteristics of his changed not at all. To the very last he was frequently as child-like as his youngest child, and he could have just as much sport with a child's toy, playing with his children, as his children had.

He was never happy when away from his home and his children; and whenever he was away from his family, he received daily telegraphic messages concerning his children. His anxiety on their account was continuous.

It was when Jim was seventeen years old, I think on his seventeenth birthday, that he called his tutor to him (I never sent my children to school but always employed a tutor for them [erroneous]) and told this tutor that he was done with books, done with study. Thereafter he kept his tutor for some time but used him as a valet sometimes and sometimes as a business employee.

There is no doubt but what, to some extent at least, Jim's deference and regard for his father was undermined because I was "a bookworm" — because I read and talked books.

I had two elder half brothers: James E. Scripps and George H. Scripps. Neither of these men were bookish men. My elder brother, who practiced the profession of journalism, once told me that, although on account of his profession he had had to read much, he had never considered book-reading as anything but the severest of all the tasks that he had been set to or had set himself to.

These two brothers of mine were, in many respects, of opposite character. The elder brother was ambitious for wealth and power but cared little or nothing for social distinction. The other brother played with business, and successfully played with it, solely as an occupation.

The men that my older brother associated with were men of great ability and some distinction. The other brother desired only the companionship of rather rough, uncultured men. My son, who never seemed to have inherited any particular qualities or characteristics of mine, seems to have acquired characteristics similar in the main to those possessed by these two half brothers of mine. Sometimes he would talk and behave as would one of them, and sometimes he would talk and behave as would the other.

Jim was a man of two distinct personalities. My older brother James, if he had few friends, had no enemies. He hated no one. It was impossible for him to harbor any enmities or resentments. The other brother never forgot nor forgave an injury. Jim was a good enough hater — too good a hater, I thought.

Jim was a born financier. He was always careful of his money, even as a child. He liked to "trade" — that is to say, he liked to measure his wits with other boys and men. He gloried in getting the best of the bargain.

Before he was ten years of age, I recognized some of Jim's characteristics. I felt pretty sure that as he grew older and developed mentally, he would take pleasure in the business of money-making. By the time he had thrown aside his books, I had become convinced of the uselessness of my attempting to teach him or train him to do anything or be anything but that which was in accordance with his natural bent.

He was only fifteen years of age when I gave him his liberty — that is to say, I discharged him from his obligations to me as a minor. At the same time I turned over to him the management and the control of my household and personal affairs and expenditures. He was fully competent to take over this work and he really enjoyed it. His overthrift sometimes caused him to make a few economic mistakes, but before he was sixteen years of age I was as willing to trust him in any minor business affairs as I would have been to trust a man ten years older.

When he was only a few weeks past twenty-one years of age, I put him in charge of my central business office, and only a few months later I gave him my full power of attorney; and for a number of years, for reasons of my own, I permitted him to exercise absolute control over all of my financial transactions, though I would never permit him to exercise control — full control or even partial control — over the editorial department of my newspaper properties.

I think it was in his eighteenth year that I furnished him money enough to found a small paper at Fresno, California, and before this I tried him out in subordinate capacities on two other properties.

Although I had given Jim my power of attorney, by which he was permitted to do any business which I could do, I still, on occasion, directed him. Occasionally there would be some matter in which we strongly differed, but always on such occasions Jim submitted to my absolute control.

Beginning early in his life, I began transferring property to Jim.

I think that by the time he was twenty-one years of age, he had personal property of his own amounting to upwards of $50,000. Rapidly from that time on, I made considerable additions to Jim's fortune — giving him, however, no more than I felt his services entitled him to. In fact, I treated him as a partner.

On one occasion, probably not later than his twenty-sixth or twenty-seventh year, Jim came to my office at "Miramar" and said, "Dad, I can afford now to tell you at any time to go to Hell!" He explained what he meant. He told me that he had obtained a fortune by that time, the income from which was larger than he felt he would ever have any occasion to need.

Beginning even in his years of childhood, I had endeavored to impress upon Jim that, as he was the eldest of my children, he was eventually to be the head of the family and the head of the business, and that he must consider himself responsible for the affairs of his mother and his brothers and sisters. Frankly and frequently, Jim told me that he did not desire this position — that he wanted to have only the responsibility for his own affairs and to have no other responsibilities than those pertaining to his own immediate family.

Jim was alway frank and outspoken. To the best of my recollection, Jim never told me a lie nor acted a lie. He gave me just as thoroughly to understand that he did not propose to be the keeper of his brothers and sisters as I gave him to understand that he *must* do so in duty to me.

Jim was truthful, and brutally truthful. Came the time when I and my son found ourselves openly and frankly in opposition and antagonistic. When this time came, Jim gave me no excuse for thinking or even hoping that he would be longer submissive to me.

Jim had become wealthy. He was a millionaire in his own right. Still, his wealth was perhaps not one-fifth as large as would eventually at my death be his share of the estate. He recognized this, as I did, and we talked together plainly on this subject. The time had come when it was no longer endurable for Jim to submit to the commands of any other man, even his own father.

There was a contest lasting for several years — lasting in its acute form for nearly a year. During all this time, I had a divided mind with regard to what I wanted my son to do. While the idea of an open rupture between us two was extremely repugnant to me, I felt that I would suffer even more keenly if my son should be utterly subservient to *anyone* else, even to his father. I felt that I would prefer to be defied by my son, and even antagonized and injured by my son, than that a son of mine should be soft and weak.

I am sure he enjoyed this strife.

I have described Jim in this writing as what William James would call a "tough-minded" man, as distinguished from a "tender-minded" man. I was a strong man and an able man myself, and Jim knew it. There was no occasion for his having pity, then, or sympathy for me.

Jim had a different code of ethics from my own. There were things that he would do and think right that I would not do because I would think they were wrong; and doubtless there were many things that I would do and think right that Jim would not do because he would not think them right.

I am absolutely certain that when Jim began to realize that he was perhaps sick unto death, he suffered no twinges of conscience. I do not think that he would have done at any time different from what he did do had he felt sure that death was just before him.

Jim is the fourth of my sons to die. One perished in infancy; another lived to be seven years of age; [15] and one died in his twenty-fourth year.[16] While apparently instinct had caused me to suffer greatly with each of these deaths, in no one of these cases have I felt that I had rational grounds for mourning.

My oldest son who has just died lived a full and strong life, has enjoyed life as men of his temperament can enjoy life, and has left behind a family of children that any man might be proud of. He has enjoyed a successful career, and he died almost suddenly, suffering but comparatively little bodily

[15] E. W., known as Ted.
[16] John Paul.

pain. He died at the best part of every man's life, namely at the close of the first half of the "three-scores-and-ten."

I have lived long enough to know that the chances are that a man who dies at thirty-five has had a greater portion of happiness and a smaller portion of misery than the average man experiences who lives to be seventy or even sixty or fifty years of age.

If this disagreement — call it quarrel, if one will — between father and son must result in any sort of unhappiness, it is going to be the father who will suffer and not the son. So why should my affection for my son cause me to grieve at his death?

I believe that if I had died and Jim lived, Jim would have suffered no remorse; nor would there have been any occasion for him to have suffered any remorse. Jim obeyed his nature, and I am not sorry today because Jim's nature was such as it was.

Perhaps I am as "tough-minded" as was my son "tough-minded."

A fighting man is fortunate if he can die fighting in the heat of battle.

There's one other instance that I can relate that might serve to illustrate Jim's character. I have said that Jim for the most part of his life eschewed books. Some two or three years ago, after a more or less heated controversy with Jim, some part of our discussion had called to my mind some of Shakespeare's words. I sent for my secretary to get a copy of Shakespeare out of the library, and I had him read to Jim and myself the "Seven Ages of Man," where Jaques says: [17]

> All the world's a stage,
> And all the men and women merely players;
> They have their exits and their entrances,
> And one man in his time plays many parts,
> His acts being seven ages. At first the infant,
> Mewling and puking in his nurse's arms;
> Then the whining school-boy, with his satchel
> And shining morning face, creeping like snail
> Unwillingly to school; and then the lover,
> Sighing like furnace, with a woeful ballad
> Made to his mistress' eyebrow; then a soldier,
> Full of strange oaths, and bearded like the pard,
> Jealous in honour, sudden and quick in quarrel,
> Seeking the bubble reputation
> Even in the cannon's mouth; and then the justice,
> In fair round belly with good capon lined,
> With eyes severe and beard of formal cut,
> Full of wise saws and modern instances;

[17] *As You Like It*, Act II, scene 7.

> And so he plays his part. The sixth age shifts
> Into the lean and slippered pantaloon,
> With spectacles on nose and pouch on side,
> His youthful hose well saved, a world too wide
> For his shrunk shank; and his big manly voice,
> Turning again toward childish treble, pipes
> And whistles in his sound. Last scene of all,
> That ends this strange eventful history,
> Is second childishness and mere oblivion,
> Sans teeth, sans eyes, sans taste, sans everything.

Jim listened to the reading and showed great interest in it.

The next day, or some days later, Jim spoke to me about this "Seven Ages of Man" and told me that he liked it and that he recognized himself as the fellow who was swearing "strange oaths." Of course, this was the very thing I had in my own mind at the time I called for the reading.

No, there is no occasion for mourning or for grieving on account of Jim's death. This, at least, is the conclusion of my own *reason*. But death is death; and a father is a father. Jim was once a baby in my arms, and for many years was the chief cause of all my solicitude.

I have not forgiven Jim, because I feel there is nothing to forgive; and I am perfectly certain that Jim has never felt that there was ever any occasion for him to forgive his own father.

We were just two men and we did what men do and what men should do.

A Blind Leader of the Blind

[*July 20, 1921*]

Such perhaps have I been!

I recall the story, heard or read by me in my youth, of a man who rather late in life became a famous surgeon. As I recall the story, this man was originally a blacksmith. Dealing with horses, he learned something of the ailments of horses. He became more or less successful in performing surgical operations on horses. Being occasionally called upon to perform minor operations on human beings, he made a series of successful operations. In some manner, and by some accident, he attracted the attention of some medical man or surgical operator and was induced to, and helped to, become educated. Naturally, he studied surgery and in time became a scientific and very successful surgeon.

Later in life he confessed to what his feelings were with regard to his early practices. He stated that he was always filled with horror at remembering some of the things he had done with his knife before he had learned anything of human or any other anatomy. When he had learned anatomy, he was able to comprehend how it was only by a mere chapter of accidents that he had not caused the death of his patients, who were as ignorant as he himself had been.

I began my career of a journalist as a boy in my twentieth year. I had no other qualifications for the profession than that of having indulged a great liking for literature — the reading of much poetry, especially plays. I had read some philosophical works; amongst other books, Tom Paine's *Age of Reason*, Locke's *Essay [Concerning] Human Understanding*, Bishop Colenso's once-famous work, later plagiarized by the great American orator, Robert Ingersoll, and a great many sermons (particularly Robertson's "My Father Was a Church of England Man" [?] and a number of theological works produced by English clergy). I had also read some novels by Dickens,

Thackeray, Marryat, Victor Hugo, Turgeniev, Goethe (*Werther* and *Wilhelm Meister*, [his work on] elective affinities, etc.). I had also read the village weekly paper and sometimes the Chicago *Tribune* and sometimes the Detroit *Tribune*. I also had acquired as much general and practical information as was consistent with my life as a farmer's son.

As a whole, I was both ignorant and emotional — peculiarly emotional.

Outside of a great many books of almost pure literature, I was as ignorant as was the vast majority of other young men and women, and old ones as a matter of fact, of the United States in the early seventies. Perhaps because of my general ignorance, my writing, when I began to write, was comprehensible by the readers of the papers that I wrote for and edited.

I had, naturally or by acquirement, literary capacity of a sort, but long before I had learned to think straight, and long before I had acquired a knowledge of facts, I set myself up as a leader and teacher of the populace. I was sympathetic and hence could feel. I was filled with personal enthusiasm and hence was able to communicate my enthusiasm to my readers. I was as well fitted to be a public teacher and political leader as was that blacksmith to be a surgeon.

But the practice of journalism compelled me to acquire some practical business ability. I had vast opportunities to observe. I had a tremendous hunger for books. Thinking was not only never hard work for me but a most enjoyable employment. I traveled much and far, and as I traveled I read and re-read the history of the various peoples whose countries I visited. I had the facility of introducing myself to all sorts of people and to engage them in conversations and particularly in discussions.

By degrees, I lost my facility to write matter for my own papers which would attract the attention and the interest of my public.

I became afflicted with a capacity to see not only both sides, but many sides, of the various questions in which the public were [*sic*] interested. I lost many of my convictions. It became difficult for me to be a partisan of any man or any principle. I never lost my emotional characteristics. My instincts of sympathy were constantly running counter to my reasoning. My instincts prompted me to take one course of action. My reason prompted me to take the reverse attitude. But I grew to doubt the correctness of my own reasoning. Logic was no guide to me because logic has to depend, not upon proved facts, but upon hypotheses, and hypotheses are only assumptions that are as likely to be wrong as right. Statistics may be used to prove anything. So can logic. But I was a journalist and was committed to my calling.

I determined to submit to pure instinct as my guide. I willingly submitted myself to a course guided by instinct.

But I became unable to write effectively for the public on subjects in which the people were interested and this because — well, because, perhaps, I knew too much of the fallibility of my instincts.

So I soon enough became dependent upon others to do the writing for my papers. The success of my journals depended upon the goodwill of my constituency. Therefore, I deliberately selected men to write for my papers and to edit them — men whose instincts, whose motives, were similar to, or rather identical with, those that were my own during my youth.

If I doubted my instincts, I doubted my capacity to reason correctly.

I grew to acquire a vast amount of what is called knowledge. I did not choose as my editors and writers men who had similar knowledge to or more knowledge than myself. In fact I recognized that not only a little knowledge is a dangerous thing but a great deal of knowledge is dangerous, at least for a journalist. A great deal of knowledge on the part of an editor is not a good thing for the newspaper business!

I admit that there was a period of several years during which my mind was greatly confused. During this period I at least thoroughly suspected myself of being a hypocrite. I felt that perhaps I was only playing the game, and that for a selfish purpose; but in time I began to realize that, after all, the duty of a journalist was not so much that of being a leader of the people but that of being a witness whose duty it was to tell the truth, the whole truth, and nothing but the truth, and leave the people to weigh the evidence and decide for themselves what was right and what was wrong.

Never did I purposely or willfully even consent to the publication of what I considered to be false or even to refrain from publishing matter that would be against my own personal interests. By this I mean that I did not publish, or cause to be published, something that I was sure was not true either as to facts or arguments or ideals.

I do not mean that I did not permit my editors and the writers on my papers to write things and publish things the truth of which I doubted. All I required was that these men should be sincere and that their motives should be comparatively pure and that their efforts should be in the direction that they thought was to the best public interest.

For instance, in some certain cases such as the question of woman's suffrage, while I myself had great doubt as to the wisdom of granting the vote to women, when it developed that almost the universality of my editorial staffs believed that a great public advantage would derive from women having the vote, I permitted my newspapers to heartily and enthusiastically endorse this, to me, more than doubtful reform movement.

I was once a Democrat, a believer in democracy. I believed that that would be the best government which depended upon the popular vote. In time I grew to doubt this. But as I never have been able to convince myself that

any form of government would be better than democracy, I have never re-
canted. Perhaps it is only as a salve to my conscience that I formulated the
theory that there really was no other government than democracy.

A king, a despot, a dictator, an autocrat are all just as much, according to
this theory of mine, dependent for their tenure of office upon their choice
by, or the consent of, the whole people as is the president of our American
democracy. This for the reason that no man can govern people against the
will of the people. The many are stronger than the one, and any ruler that
is not satisfactory to the many must suffer deposition.

In my youth I could not tolerate the idea of an aristocracy. Of course, I
only thought of aristocrats as those men in high position who acquired
their high position by birth. When I was a young man I hated the capitalists
as much as ever did a follower of Karl Marx. Later when I discovered myself to be a capitalist I confronted an embarrassing situation.

I had to justify myself. The way of my justification was this: I assumed
and proved to my own satisfaction that every capitalist had been elected to
his position just as much as any political ruler had been elected.

I argued that I and other capitalists had never had any power to compel
any man to work for us against his will. Nor had we ever had the power to
compel other capitalists, large or small, to place in our keeping, through
stocks and bonds, their capital. The money and the labor that the capitalist
gathers together to serve his interests are freely and voluntarily offered to
him.

Well, enough of this kind of logic and, forget it not, I am by profession at
least a despiser of logic.

My years accumulated. My knowledge accumulated. And my wealth accumulated.

And then came the great cataclysm, the World War.

And today the whole civilized world seems to be in a state of unsettled
equilibrium — if the present chaotic state of society can be called equilibrium.

The workingman, to whose service I always considered it was my duty to
devote myself, has, to a large extent by my advice and prompting, organized
into a great and powerful army that is using its power both to affect politics
and industry.

The workingman, because he has been a workingman, is necessarily ignorant in matters political and economic. Being ignorant, he is self-confident
and knows naught of his weakness or, perhaps I had better say, power to
vastly injure himself as well as all of his fellows in the nation.

Women have votes, and there are more women voters in the country, or
at least as many, as there are men. Some women are wiser in matters politi-

cal and economic than are some men, but no intelligent man or woman, who has had occasion to learn by observation and experience, can doubt that women are less capable as directors of business and less capable in matters political than are men.

By adding the women's vote, and sharing with the women the power to rule this country, this nation's capacity to rule itself wisely has been greatly decreased, and that too at this psychological and critical period when civilization itself may be considered as tottering.

In these United States, society is divided into two warring and apparently irreconcilable factions — Capital and Labor.

The arch of civilization rests upon two supporting columns — Capital and Labor. If either column breaks, the arch falls. Unfortunately the columns are not inert, unorganized matter but are composed of living beings and the living beings in each column are trying, if not to destroy the others, to greatly cripple them.

While I suppose there are really no capitalists who want to destroy Labor, there are many laborers who want to destroy Capital, while perhaps the majority of all laborers are too indifferent to their own welfare to have any thoughts as to the standing and future of Capital.

Too many capitalists really wish to, and are striving to, reduce Labor to the position of practically dependent slaves. And there are too many capitalists who are unable to comprehend that their own existence depends upon the support of willing Labor.

But to what extent have I contributed to this class warfare? Have not I, in conjunction with others, overdone things in the matter of inciting Labor to organize and unite so as to become strong? And to what extent have we inspired Labor to make unreasonable and impossible demands?

Have I not really been a demagogue? Not in the worst sense of the word. Not for selfish and personal reasons; but through ignorance and thoughtlessness.

A *fool* philanthropist may, and perhaps generally does, do more harm than the most unprincipled egoist.

To a large extent — too large an extent for my own peace of mind — have I been responsible for the adoption of a system of taxation of the rich.

Today I recognize that the heavy taxation of incomes and what is called excess profits is alike injurious to both Capital and Labor.

For many years I furiously attacked the railroad system of the country and helped to instigate that legislation which has resulted in something very near to a paralysis of the country's most needed of all enterprises, the transportation system. I have no inclination now to defend the old-time abuses of railroad management. I have only to confess a feeling that probably the cure of this old disease is worse than was the disease itself.

But "birds of a feather flock together." Once I was a poor man and hated the capitalists, and now I am a capitalist and I see the other side of the question.

But I am no more sure that my bias of today is to be depended upon than I am that my bias of a generation and a half ago was wrong.

I am still blind. I am unfitted to lead.

Can I even depend upon myself to be a fair witness on the stand, one capable of telling the truth, the whole truth, and nothing but the truth?

Mediocrity

[*November 28, 1921*]

My present secretary, F. G. Westberg, was telling me the other day of having met an ex-employee of mine — a man whose name I had forgotten, but who since being in my employ has, by speculation and good management, acquired a large fortune. This man told Westberg that his, Westberg's, present employer had the faculty of making more mediocre men successful than any other man he had ever known. When I came to think about it, it occurred to me that perhaps this man was right.

Of course, I have no means of knowing how many other mediocrities have been made successful by other men.

Also I don't know what this man's definition of mediocrity is. I presume, however, that my critic would define a mediocrity as being a man who had never acquired much fame while in my employ.

It is true I have never had any Arthur Brisbanes, Eugene Fields, Mel Stones, Amos Cummings, Whitelaw Reids, Joe McCulloughs [Joseph B. McCullagh, St. Louis *Globe-Democrat*], Henry Wattersons, etc. — men who, even as employees, became nationally more or less famous. But, if all my successful men have been mediocrities, so have I been a mediocrity — judged by an identical standard.

For instance, although I have had a long and successful career as a journalist, during which time my influence in the political field has often produced really spectacular results, my name has never appeared in the publication entitled *Who's Who in America*. [However, he soon did appear in *Who's Who*, his name appearing for the first time in the 1922–23 edition.]

Although my journalistic activities have been of such a character that perhaps half of the whole population of this country have been more or less influenced by me politically and otherwise, there are thousands of journalists whose names have become household words and tens of thousands of newspapermen during my lifetime whose personalities have been more conspicuous than my own.

I do not deny that there does exist in the public mind an idea of some shadowy force or personality behind the things that I have been doing, but this idea is not accompanied by anything mystical or mysterious or of much significance.

For a lifetime I have been recognizing the validity of Alexander Pope's declaration that "the proper study of man is mankind" [sic]. Always have I been studying man collectively and men individually and, as much practice tends at least to approach perfection, I can well suppose that I have an unusual power to judge of men.

I might be ashamed to acknowledge how often my own thoughts have turned to the subject of my own personality and how keenly I have observed and studied and reasoned on this subject of the why and the wherefore of my having been as successful as I have been and yet having remained so completely in obscurity. Here, at least, I am willing to admit that I have sometimes been chagrined and felt some degree of disappointment and resentment on this account. Still, I have never suffered greatly from a feeling of injustice.

As I have said, I have been sufficiently long a student of some subjects and have become sufficiently expert on the matter of judgment to know the full extent of my inferiority to the men whose characters I have highly esteemed. Then, too, point by point, feature by feature, I have compared myself with scores of other individuals with the result that I have been convinced that compared, whole man with whole man, I have been inferior.

Even in the matter of personal physical courage, although I have sometimes been exposed to great danger without flinching or showing or, perhaps at the instant, feeling any great pusilanimity, I have had to admit in all such instances the courage I had was only the courage of a rat at bay.

In all matters of morals, excepting in one special field, I know that my career has been, as near as humanly possible, free from reproach. But even here I have got to confess that I have been exceedingly fortunate in escaping from temptation. Perhaps almost universally I have done right because it wouldn't have paid to have done wrong — a sort of long-headedness.

The only reason I have been exposed to dangers physical is that I have been foolishly, temporarily at least, reckless. If I have encountered and overcome many difficulties in the way of business and other enterprises, it is because I have been equally foolhardy and reckless in entering into enterprises, thus being compelled to give up my natural slothfulness and exert myself mightily to save myself from disaster.

If I have been fortunate in any undertaking, it is because the then existing necessities compelled hard thinking, straight thinking, enduring toil and shrewd maneuvering — in fact, a whole series of accidents rather than anything else, accidents which in themselves presented such danger and difficulties that they brought into existence the full force of necessity.

I have not been a manly sort of a man, since from my infancy I have been pestered by two demons — slothfulness and diffidence. When I have rushed into a fray of any sort it has been the result not of design but of thoughtlessness.

Only in two particulars have I ever found myself a match for or superior to any sort of antagonist or opposition. I have a certain sort of bull-headedness and a perfect loathing for any sort of subservience to men or even conditions. Beyond this and perhaps because of this, I have acquired practice in the matter of submitting others to my control (something that euphonists [euphemists] would call executive ability).

Except for these two particulars, I have never found myself so placed relative to another man or other men who were not better able than myself to perform any sort of task, whether it was on the farm, running a printing press, writing an article or even [directing] all of the departments of that particular business with which I have been associated all of my life.

There are a few men of my acquaintance who know something about more things than I do. There are still fewer who do not know more about something or some things than I do.

As a boy I did write some rather startling articles, but I learned afterwards that my writing was very, very crude.

When I became an editor of a newspaper in name, I left it to others to edit my paper. From almost the first day of my installation as editor of a newspaper, almost the whole of the editorial staff recognized my actual position. I chose as a leader one of my nominal subordinates. Even in the community at large the public recognized . . . some one other than me as being the real personality, the real governing personality of my newspaper. These subordinates, each of them, would be more or less conspicuous characters in the eyes of the public, while only the unknowing ones came to me about their business with my newspaper.

As it was with my first newspaper venture, so has it been with one newspaper after another that has passed under my control, and so it is now with the comparatively great institution that I control by exercising little or no control over it.

These men, whom the critic I spoke of in the opening lines of this essay referred to, are not recognized individually as great men or as men much above mediocrity. The esteem that they enjoy, the privileges they receive, and the influence they exert are not the result of the recognition of their individual personal high qualities. They owe such public and private esteem as they enjoy to the fact that they are representatives of an institution that they consider to be great. But because of my own mediocrity and the mediocrity of my lieutenants, the greatness and the power of this institution which my men represent is not generally appreciated or estimated at perhaps more than 25 per cent of its reality.

In cogitating over these matters I have been almost persuaded, if not fully persuaded, to the belief that no small part of my personal success and no less the success of the institution as a whole has been due to the lack of appreciation for such qualities as I have and to lack of appreciation of the extent of the wealth and power of my institution.

"Uneasy lies the head that wears the [a] crown." [18]

The most sticks are found under the apple trees that are known to have the best fruit.

If the king was not known to be the king he would be in no danger and if all the boys in the neighborhood supposed that there were only sour apples on the tree there would be no clubs found under it.

There have been known cases where a neighborhood bully has started in to lick a stranger and found himself worsted because the stranger happened to be, though unknown to the bully, a prizefighter. Even a man possessing a mediocre mind might outwit one much shrewder than himself if his antagonist made the mistake of supposing him to be possessed of less than ordinary common sense.

Are all of the men in our concern mediocrities? Or are they only supposed to be mediocre because they do not "advertise"? A real cardsharp intent on fleecing the crowd in a game of cards must, in order to be successful, first convince his intended victim of his own stupidity.

Are not all supposedly great men, or most of them at least, mediocrities whom chance or some desperate emergency has forced into conspicuous positions?

Doesn't the job really make the man?

Is greatness inherited or is it the result of the various aggregate influence of environment?

If it is true, as my critic has averred, that I have been capable of making successful a lot of mediocrities, is it not possible that all mediocrities might be successful if there existed the necessities — a sufficient number of necessities — impelling a sufficient number of men whose success depended upon making other men successful?

In the above, I have demonstrated to the best of my ability my own mediocrity, that is to say, my original, inherent mediocrity. I acknowledge that I

[18] *King Henry IV*, Part 2, Act III, scene 1.

am no longer a mediocrity, that the conditions of my life have been such as to have resulted in my acquiring some elements of superiority — superiority, however, only in a few particulars.

Suppose a great general by some freak of fortune was reduced to the rank of private. Is it to be supposed that as a private soldier this transposed general would be one whit superior to the rank and file of those he served with? The probability is that as a common soldier he would be inferior to his fellows because his fellows would have learned their trade, the trade that the general had never learned, that of being a private soldier.

If for any reason at the start of my life it had been absolutely necessary for me, in order to succeed in what I wanted to do, to make myself conspicuous, and if my final success had required that I should become nationally famous, it is possible that because of the possession of one of my fundamental characteristics, viz. forcefulness, it is at least possible that I would have become famous, or (it amounts to the same thing) notorious.

Such have been some of the circumstances in emergencies of my life that I am now reasonably sure that I could, had I chosen to do so, [have] obtained some political office high enough to have been for at least a time recognized as a national character. That is to say, I might, had I chosen to do so, have stepped off of the ladder of comparative wealth and comparatively successful journalism onto a political ladder — not on the first rung, but a rung way up toward the top.

But all this doesn't argue against my mediocrity. Hundreds of thousands of other Americans might have, with the same or with similar series of accidents, traveled the same course that I have traveled and traveled maybe farther.

Now, are my men mediocrities? I will admit that originally they came into the world with no better stuff or no worse stuff than the average mediocre man. But conditions changed them. Their environment, of which I was a part, made them something different from mediocrities.

This institution of which I am the chief is anything but a mediocrity. It is an institution which is composed of an organization of human beings. It is an organization, and could not be an organization that had some large elements of greatness [unless it were] composed of men who in time [had] become men of much more than mediocre ability.

Have I made successful men out of mediocre men or have mediocre men made me a successful man?

I have had many newspaper children; that is to say, I have founded or bought a number of children. The career of each one of these newspapers has been as different as could have been the career of any of the sons of a given father. Some of these newspapers have grown and flourished; some of them have sickened and died. Some have flourished greatly and some less greatly.

I have been the father of all these newspapers. Each of them has shared and enjoyed equally my parenthood. Whatever advantage could be derived from my ownership or control, nominal or real, over them has been given freely.

Why, then, has the career of one newspaper been different from another?

When I have seen one of my newspapers [become] very successful, I have known that the reason for this success has been that one or two or more men who were serving that newspaper were possessed of unusual ability, whether acquired or inherent. The shrewdest investigation that I could make of such a paper would never reveal to me just what man or men on that paper were causing the results. Sometimes I have been convinced that the titular head or heads of such a paper were not the cause of the results.

But the fact that one of my newspapers succeeded wonderfully and another perished miserably has always been considered by me proof enough that on one of the papers there was ability and on the other paper no ability.

The fact that two of my newspapers have had such different careers is evidence sufficient for anyone, I should think, to prove at least my lack of great and dominating superiority.

The parents of every effect are thousands of causes. Amongst the causes of the effect of success or failure is perhaps something analogous to what biologists consider in thinking of the Mendelian law or principle.

If in one newspaper the individuals who are dominating are not success-builders, failure may result. If in another the dominating individuals have the success-building capacity, success may be the result.

I don't know that I ever met the man or woman yet who would admit that he or she had only mediocre qualities. This is because I have never been able to meet myself face to face.

Growing Old Sensibly

[*June 13, 1922*]

Of growing old gracefully we have heard enough and read enough of this silly prattle.[19]

Remarks of this kind are generally made by people who have had no experience in growing old at all — people who draw on their imaginations exclusively for depicting conditions or by people who have had some experience with age, being more or less advanced in years, but who are not past the period when they are free from foolish or even childish or, at least, adolescent vanity. Older people who speak of such methods are the kind of old people who make fools of themselves by dressing in raiment that is only really becoming to youth and by resorting to masseurs to smooth out their wrinkles and to manicurists to have their fingernails polished.

This kind of people can even be heard to say that one is no older than he feels, and they then proceed to mimic in their walk and in their talk, in their posing and in their employment, younger people in their environment. They are people who are never wise and who are never capable of becoming wise, people congenitally affected with the tendency to be continually arrested in development.

Perhaps there are some old people who do grow old gracefully, that is to say, who grow old naturally just as a child grows to the period of adolescence, to maturity, naturally.

But what is commonly understood by growing old gracefully is that one, while aging, should to a greater or less extent mimic as much as possible the activity of all sorts of exhibitions made by the young.

Grow old gracefully! One might as well talk of dying gracefully.

I saw my mother die and saw her die gracefully in her eightieth year. She fell asleep and ceased to breathe. There was nothing shocking, nothing ter-

[19] This disquisition appears in McCabe, *Damned Old Crank*, pp. 252–59.

156

rible in her activities and speech of the last few hours. She seemed to be unaware of the fact that she was dying, or at least not at all impressed by the
importance to her or to anyone else of her condition. But she was very old
and she succumbed to a disease that was painless.

I have seen others die, suffering terribly, and there was nothing graceful
presented to my sight. Pain, and terrible pain, distorted the features of the
faces, and that which the dying ones said actually ploughed deep and harrowed into the feelings of the onlookers.

One may grow old without suffering and one observing such a person might
say that he or she grew old gracefully.

But I saw one who was very near to me in blood growing old from her
middle age to extreme old age, suffering always, her hearing gradually diminishing to deafness and her sight gradually diminishing to blindness, and
yet she lived well into her ninth decade.

Could she grow old gracefully? I have seen the very old suffering from
poverty, and the very old possessed of great wealth, not one particle of
whose wealth could allay terrible physical and mental anguish.

Resignation! What is the difference between resignation and despair? In
either case the only hope is for death to cut short the pain of living.

Perhaps the nearest approach to that which is called growing old gracefully can be defined as growing old sensibly — enduring pain that cannot be
avoided, anguish that cannot be appeased.

My own idea of the best way of growing old is to grow old sensibly, recognizing the changing conditions physically and mentally — perhaps, I might
say, socially — conditions that change from day to day, month to month, and
from year to year, and making the best possible personal adjustment to all
of these conditions.

It is my opinion that the best period, at least of every man's life (I will not
speak of women), is the time when his children are being born to him and
when those little sprouts from himself are fresh and beautiful. Then the father can dream beautiful dreams of the future of these little ones. Then as a
rule, the father has himself had no experiences of old age and is still so strong
in body and spirit that he rather delights in than resents his own struggles for
his own existence and the welfare of those he most loves — mother and
children. He has no time to devote to foreboding, nor has he any inclination
thereto. How can he dread that which is going to happen to his offspring
when he has to suffer nothing himself — nothing worthwhile?

I, for myself, having experienced the joy of living in my own children,
have never forgotten this experience.

I believe that most fathers have had similar happy experiences or, at least,
have, during the period of the infancy of their children, had their sufferings

greatly mitigated. Then they suffered less than they have had to suffer later on; then they could hope more for their own future than they could have any reason to hope in those later years when their children had grown to manhood and to womanhood. All great accomplishments are really the accomplishments of youth, so that when youth, or at least comparative youth, is past, then there is nothing reasonable in hoping for a future better time for one's self.

Then comes the time when, if the father would grow old reasonably, he should live in the lives of his children; appreciate and sympathize with their hopes and aspirations and enjoy for himself those things that only his children can feel and enjoy. But time flies so swiftly. It is so long a distance to travel, that stretching from grandfather to children, that I more than doubt the commonly expressed view that grandparents more enjoy their grandchildren than they ever enjoyed their children. If there were no other grounds for this doubt, it could be found in the common expression that "we, the grandparents, have all the pleasure derivable from the little children and none of the pain and suffering and trouble." I have never lost by death a grandchild; three of my sons have died.

I know that when any one of my children was suffering even from a slight illness my mind was filled with anxiety to such an extent that I have spent many and many a sleepless night. When my grandchildren have been ill, it is true that I have been anxious about them, but my fears were not nearly so poignant. I wonder if there are any old men, or middle-aged men, or even comparatively young men who have forgotten the thrill and ecstasy of their early youthful love or loves. For all such I feel the greatest pity.

I know there are children who have spent no part of their lives outside of and away from cities, great or small, who have never run barefoot over green fields and through shady forests, and who have never seen more than a streak of blue or gray above them — the only sky they have ever known. For these, too, I have a feeling of pity.

An approaching thunderstorm; the sighing of a breeze through forest trees; the roar and groaning of the leaves and branches in a great woods when the storm was sweeping through it; the sight of fleecy clouds floating overhead seen by the boy lying prone upon his back in some comparatively deserted place; the rippling stream and the majestic sweep of some great river; the ever-recurring adventures of the boy with gun and rod, in boat or on horseback; each and all of these things are a rich store of memories of the country-reared child.

If I had the power I would procure these for every living child, that his or her youth should be spent in such a way as to have such a store of memories — the last and finishing touch of which would be the first boy and girl love affair, perhaps accompanied by a kiss or an embrace, or perhaps only the desire, such intense desire as to cause the whole frame to tremble, the knees to feel weak.

But I am not to write the beginning of life but the ending.

When a man's children are full grown then is the time when the process of growing old has fairly begun. Just imagine a man stopping at this period to think of growing old gracefully! He is a happier man if not a wiser one if he thinks not at all of growing old.

He has enjoyed so much living in his children that he knows, or should know, that there are any number of other young lives in which he can live, and in so living forget all about himself. There are young men who are only beginning their careers; there are young men who have started on their careers; and there are young men who are rearing their families and little ones and who are enjoying themselves thereby. The man who has passed through these periods can sympathize joyously or sadly with the triumphs and defeats of these younger ones.

If such a man with such experiences has chanced to be of the successful few, his opportunities are great — his opportunities to lend a helping hand to those who have both the strength in mind and body and strong ambitions.

While one's own children generally are few in number, so that all of them pass through adolescence in a comparatively short time, other fathers and mothers are also producing life, so that in any man's immediate environment there is a constant army of youth marching up from whom to select those to whom favors can be given and those who can profit by the aid of elders, so that no man need ever lack the inspiration, the wholesome urge, of youth around him.

I take it that no man can grow old more sensibly than by making full use of this opportunity of living with and in the lives of those who are young.

I have lived long enough to see babies grow into manhood, to see these men become fathers, and even a few of them grandfathers. If, perchance, I live many years longer, the distance between myself and even a new grandfather may be far enough to make me rather enjoy the companionship of these older young men than I have enjoyed the companionship of men whose children are yet young.

Growing old sensibly consists of doing many things, eliminating many things that were once pleasurable and taking on new occupations that are still pleasurable, though not so pleasurable.

More than half, I think, of all the pleasures and all the pains of human life are inextricably interwoven, or rather proceed from the second law of nature, but as a man approaches what is called middle life he usually loses the power to enjoy greatly purely physical occupations — such as sports of all kinds. Becoming a little older, the palate becomes less imperative in its demands or else wise physicians advise such things as changes of diet.

Then later comes the sad climacteric when a male of the human species can no longer find great joy in intimate contact with his chosen companion of the other sex.

There are some, I consider, very foolish men who are so nonsensical as to attempt in all possible ways to prolong certain pleasures. I do not consider that these men are growing old sensibly.

All too frequently — perhaps almost invariably — comes that period in the life of a man when, if he permits himself so to suffer, [he] does suffer from many disappointed hopes.

His family has ceased to be his family; his children have families of their own. His mate may have died, or, having herself passed the period of subordination of the sex motive, discovers that her interests in life have become different from his.

Somewhat synchronizing with this condition of affairs, the man whose life interest has been largely made up of business and professional pursuits, or purely intellectual achievements, finds that his power is so far diminished or his interests so desiccated that he is no longer able to practice successfully in his old occupation, or else his interests in the same have become so desiccated that he no longer covets achievement.

For these four great reasons a great majority of men find themselves, instead of growing old sensibly, compelled to live lonely lives, unoccupied or uninterested. Such soon perish.

I have known professional men in such periods who abandoned their profession entirely, and to abandon all interest in the same. I have known such older men to retire from business, thinking vainly that they will be contented to live on their income. I have even known scientific men to lose all interest in their science and become mentally inert. I take it that none of these men is growing old sensibly.

The man who finds himself aging, to grow old sensibly, should accept conditions as they are, pine not at all, and refuse to have or actually feel any sense of disappointment.

There are not only always the younger men with whom he can cooperate, but then the whole land is filled with children who are growing to be men and women, and then there are the future generations.

To grow old sensibly, one should always keep one's eyes turned from the past to the future, and continue to strive with all his might to serve those who are coming even more efficiently than he has served in the past, shoulder to shoulder. There should be no feelings of remorse, no feelings of regret, no feelings of mortification for past failures. If wrong has been done, reparation is impossible. If one feels that he has suffered ingratitude, he has not become sensible as he has become old. Such an attitude of mind is rather evidence of man's unworthiness, for he who has only served others that he might be served himself in return has really given nothing, and has only bargained for *quid pro quo*, and at best has only made a bad bargain.

If he has lived rightly and righteously and lived truly nobly, he has never considered even the word gratitude; hence, there can be no feeling of disappointment.

When one has grown old and life persists in him, and promises to persist so that he must continue to grow older and older still, he has yet his occupations, the occupations that he as an old man can excel all others in performing.

There is nothing that he can learn that he cannot turn to someone else's use, if not for the use of someone immediately near him or dear to him, still for some human being who may get profit by the knowledge gained by the labor of the most efficient of men, namely, the oldest of men whose minds have not suffered too greatly from senile decay.

The old man who has grown old sensibly is more sensible than any younger man can be — more sensible concerning not only his own needs and requirements but concerning the services he can render to others. Such a man cannot possibly govern his conduct by the opinions or wishes of others. In order that he should grow older and older, still sensibly, he must govern his own conduct.

Providing this old man has grown old sensibly, he has performed as well as he can perform all, or nearly all, of his duties to society — such society as was contemporary with him. He, of all men, may feel himself exempt from all commands addressed to him, all demands made upon him by others. To continue to grow old sensibly, he cannot fail to strive to increase the happiness of others or diminish the sorrow of others to the extent of his powers without ever imitating the folly of youth or overstraining his capacity. Sensibly as a man has lived, sensibly as a man has aged, there can be no guarantee against that man suffering greatly in spirit and in body before he is finally released.

If this old man is sensible, he will recognize the possible inevitable, and march boldly or totter along feebly to the end, being neither thankful nor of a complaining spirit.

Not Guilty

[April 13, 1923]

For a number of years I have been trying to avoid a certain class of literature. Perhaps the best description of this class might be covered by the word "socialistic." But there are many writers who are not socialists and who could not be described as socialistic who are writing books and magazine articles, the burden of all of which is a complaint of the inequitable distribution of wealth. Some of these writers deal gently with us rich men and try to convince us of the error of our ways in a language replete with sweet reasonableness. However, for the most part we are scolded and damned on account of our iniquity — the iniquity of our being individually wealthy — while fully 98 per cent of our fellow humans are suffering from poverty.

When I was a young man it was my habit, when visiting any comparatively large city, to visit the haunts of poverty and vice — the slums — and I have visited many of the large cities in the world. But for many years past I have avoided all such excursions.

If possible, I will never ride in any other automobile than a limousine. My excuse for this, the excuse I give to others, is that my doctors tell me that I must avoid exposing myself to drafts and any possible wettings in the event of my being caught out in a rainstorm. But my real reason for using a limousine is that whenever by chance I pass through the poorer quarters of a town, by drawing down the shades I can cut out from my sight scenes of misery. The sight of a wretched tenement house pains me more than a slap in the face.

My wife reads me many storybooks,[20] but whenever by ill luck she happens on one of those so-called realistic stories in which are given descriptions of low life and poverty, or when it turns out that the book is dealing with any

[20] Mrs. Scripps was not with him on the "Ohio" anchored in Yokohama Bay, when he dictated this disquisition.

162

of the vices of upper-class society so called — the vice of gambling, excessive drinking, and sex looseness — I always insist on the book being closed and laid aside.

Whatever any critic of mine say of me, he cannot rightly accuse me of being callous. I cannot determine whether I am entirely wanting in sympathy or whether by nature I am not too sympathetic. Meanness in others disgusts me whether or not such meanness is the result of pure misfortune or cultivated selfishness.

I detest poverty. I am one of those who believe that poverty is criminal and that for the most part all those persons who suffer poverty are to blame for their poverty. It seems to me so easy for anyone to escape being poor that he or she who does not escape it is to blame. Only fools commit real crimes and poverty is a crime. I could write bookfuls of arguments on this last thesis but the object of this disquisition is not to prosecute the poor but to defend the rich, to defend at least one rich man.

My parents were not poverty stricken; neither were they wealthy, or even what would now be called well-to-do. If I was not thrown into the world a poor boy, I at least went out into the world with no other possessions than something less than a hundred dollars, all of which money I had earned by my own labor.

I did not go out into the world with any ambition to become a rich man. Quite the contrary. I determined that I would not be a rich man even so late as in my nineteenth or twentieth year. I was resolved never to have an income, earned or unearned, to exceed three thousand dollars a year. I was still adhering to this resolution up to the latter part of my twenty-fourth year. Then something happened which caused me to change my resolution.

It was at that time that I became convinced that humanity was divided into two classes, slaves and masters — many, many slaves and few masters — and I determined, happen what might, that I would not be a slave.[21] That was nearly half a century ago. I did not determine or even think of becoming very rich. I recall that it was not long after my conversion that I put a limit on the amount of my wealth. I was in France or Italy at the time. There, from some personal experience and much more observation, it appeared to me that a man could not spend more than ten thousand dollars a year for all the comforts and luxuries even that such a man as I was could enjoy.

Then I began to work on "my own." With a very small amount of capital I founded a little daily newspaper.[22] I do not recall ever having asked any man to work for me. I do not believe I did ask anyone to work for me. All of my earlier employees came to me seeking positions. As I had very little

[21] London 1878.
[22] Cleveland *Penny Press.*

money I could afford to pay only the smallest wages or salaries. For several years, I think, the average pay of my employees (those that were not members of organized unions) was much less than other employers were paying for the same class of work. I only had one rule and that was to pay out less money every day, week, month, and year than I received. But for every applicant for a position with me whom I consented to employ there were literally dozens that were turned away by me.

Year by year my business increased in size, and year by year I paid higher and higher wages and salaries on the average. I do not recall more than a half a dozen instances where there was any negotiation or bargaining as to wages or salaries between myself and candidates for employment. Men and women sought employment in my concern and accepted such wages or salaries as were offered to them.

I do not remember a single instance where I increased the salary or wages of any man or woman for the purpose of inducing him or her to stay in my employ instead of going to some other employer who would pay them more. More than this I was extremely careful that no candidate for employment and that no one in my employ should be induced to enter my employ or remain in it by prospects of having wages or salaries later increased. As it is almost the universal custom to raise wages or salaries periodically, regularly or irregularly, by reason of long service, I always impressed upon everyone that no amount of service or no length of service should create an obligation on my part toward the one giving the service. To each and every one, whenever opportunity presented itself, I would say, "When you receive your pay envelope at the end of the week I have cleared the slate of all obligations toward you, and I consider that you are in no way obliged even to give me a day's notice of your quitting."

I would go on further to say, "In such establishments as this of mine there are very few large prizes in the way of promotion to honorable positions or to high wages and salaries, and when the time comes to appoint a man to an honorable position and one that to which will be attached high pay, I will give no consideration to any man on account of past services; I will select men for these superior positions who I think will be best fitted to do future work. The last thing in the world that I will ever consider will be seniority."

Notwithstanding all of this, the institution which grew up under my control and supervision never lacked men that I considered capable.

For the first seventeen years after I began work on "my own" I never but once gave any thought to my institution as a property. On that occasion I was called upon to appraise the value of the stock of one of my associates who was about to sell it to another stockholder. Of course, in appraising the value of this stock I must have recognized that my holdings represented a capital value.

It was seventeen years after I started my first business that I and one of my brothers decided to pool our interests.[23] In order to do this we had to appraise the value of our different stocks. Each of us made an appraisement. Our figures were very similar and I remember how greatly I was astonished at the size of them and how I turned to my brother and said, "Why, George, I'm a millionaire."

He replied: "Why, you damn fool, didn't you know that?"

After that there were a number of occasions when I had to appraise the capital value of my holdings. And on every such occasion that I can recall I was surprised at the mounting figures.

When the first annual income tax was inaugurated and I was informed of how much income tax I had to pay, I was not surprised and would not have been surprised had the figure been several times larger or even a half or a quarter of the figure named. I was not thinking much of such things.

But when the government issued a report showing how many persons had paid income taxes on certain amounts of income, I was surprised and chagrined to find that there were only 360 people in the United States who had confessed to as large an income as my agents had determined that I had enjoyed. The first impression made in my mind was that there were a lot of damn rascally millionaires in the United States who were evading their taxes.

I was in California at the time and I went to the president of my bank and presented to him this grotesque situation. "Why," I said, "there are more than 360 men in California alone who have larger incomes than my own." While I was discussing the matter with him, the president of the other large bank in town came in, and these two bank presidents assured me that they were convinced that there were not more than four other men in California who had larger incomes than my own.

Sometime later than this I ran across a statement appearing in one of my magazines, or in some book, to the effect that there were not more than 200 men in England who had as large or larger incomes than myself, only 90 in Germany, and only 16 in Japan. According to these figures, it would appear then that there are probably not over 2,000 people in the world, perhaps not even 1,500, who had as large an income as I had.

About seven years ago some documents emanating from the United States Treasury or Census Bureau gave the estimated figures of the total product of the United States. On comparing these figures with the previous annual report of my concern, it appeared that 1/10,000 of the net wealth of all of

23 George H., in 1895.

the citizens of the United States was represented by the net wealth of my own institution.

A few years later, taking such estimates of wealth and income as were made by various financial publications, I estimated that if these estimates made by other people were correct, my concern represented 1/6,000 of the total wealth of the country. I have no faith whatever in any of the published estimates of wealth and income made by the government or by financial experts or professional economists. But, making all possible allowances, it would appear that the best that can be said for me is that if the possession of large wealth is a crime, I am one of at least a thousand of the wickedest men in this country. Even a worse indictment can be made against me. By reason of the character of the business which is my personal property, as a capitalist I am ten times more responsible for the economic and political conditions in this country than any other ten men who have wealth equal to my own.

If poverty is not a crime and great property is a crime, then I am one of the worst of criminals. I maintain that by acts of neither omission nor commission have I ever ground the face of the poor, consciously or unconsciously.

Following, I will give a bit of personal experience. In the spring of the year 1908, when I was fifty-four years of age, I determined to retire from active business. In spite of all of my efforts in the way of resistance to tendency, I had become at that time aware that I was doing little more than chasing the dollar. Things had occurred which caused me to feel that increasing possessions only added to my personal discomforts. Then, too, I had grown very skeptical of my own capacity as a public leader.

In response to the question I asked myself, "Why should I continue my thankless task and profitless task of increasing my power for good or evil by a further extension of my journalistic enterprises?" I answered, "There is no reason why I should continue my labor."

I determined to follow a course of dissipating my fortune. I began wasting my money by spending large sums on two ranches which I possessed, fully convinced that personally I was unfitted to be a successful farmer. I also spent large sums of money in building and improving public highways, and devoted as much of my attention in spending a dollar — as much thinking and planning — as would have resulted in adding ten dollars to my fortune had I devoted an equal amount of time and thought to my business. I interested myself in local politics and affairs of public concern. Interested in various sciences as I had been for most of my life, I also applied considerable energy and a good many dollars to developing an institution for scientific research.[24] I had no desire to obtain public favor, and perhaps for this reason

[24] Scripps Institution of Oceanography.

my contempt of the public as such was reciprocated, if not by the contempt of the public, at least to some extent by the public ill will.

For about twelve years I continued my activities along these lines. Then an emergency occurred which caused me to resolve to return to active business. I took up my business affairs, rather yielding to an impulse or whim than to any great necessity. I had not found that the activities of the past dozen years had added anything to my personal satisfaction. The most I could say of them was that they had been used by me as pastimes.

In the past I had been a builder of business. Naturally, on my return to business, I returned to business-building. I had no desire to increase my fortune or to add anything to my reputation. The first task I set myself to was the founding of a number of new papers. As I say, I did not want to increase my fortune; I just wanted a job to do. [Expansion of Scripps-Howard.]

I had been told that the number of employees in my concern amounted to between three and four thousand, and that the concern's annual payroll amounted to $6 or $7 million. I figured that at least 10 per cent of this annual payroll ought to be saved by my employees and that taking the employees as a whole group the average savings should be 20 per cent. Thus, over and above my own resources, I calculated that between $500,000 and $1,000,000 a year ought to be accessible for my projected extensions.

Personally, I knew that the success of this new-planned extension or development would depend on its being generally known and recognized that my share of money to be invested was large, and that far more important than this would be the fact that all personally concerned should know that I, personally, held enough stock in every proposed new corporation to control it.

I thought out a scheme by which a series of intermediate investment companies, each of which would have half voting and half non-voting stock, and by having the stockholding in the new newspaper corporations made up on the same basis, I might control the new newspaper companies by holding a very small amount of capital stock in them [sic]. In this way I would afford opportunities to all employees to hold as much stock as they wanted to, from three-fourths to seven-eighths, while all the stockholders would feel that they had the advantage of my ability and prestige. I was willing to furnish all the money for any one newspaper or to furnish only so much as to pay for the stock that the others did not want.

Many years before this time I am speaking of, I had successfully put into execution a somewhat similar plan of doing business. I would first determine that two or three young men in my employ were worthwhile — worthy of being backed by me. I would next select some city for the location of some new newspaper enterprise. Then I would found the new institution entirely at my

own expense and I would offer to certain of my employees the right, if they
should prove successful in working with me in building up the property, to
buy from me 49 per cent of the stock at cost. These employees were not required to advance any money at any time, but they were required, in lieu [?]
of their prospects, to accept much smaller salaries than would ordinarily be
paid to men holding such positions as they held. They were given practically
unlimited time to pay for their stock, excepting that all the dividends that
should eventually be paid to them should be set aside to pay pro rata, according to their stockholdings, their share of the original capital invested plus
interest at the going rate.

Quite a number of young men whom I engaged in this work acquired in
this way considerable wealth. I do not consider my action in this matter as
generous on my part. I consider it just good business. My experience taught
me that 51 per cent of the stock of a newspaper, which was being locally
managed and worked for by the holders of 49 per cent, would be worth more
to me than 100 per cent of the ownership of a paper that was being conducted by salaried men.

About one-third of my enterprises failed and with them disappeared the
opportunity of becoming prosperous of all of those young men who had cooperated with me in the losing ventures. But so successful on the average
were the other two-thirds of the papers that my own share of the profits on
the total investment was enormous, while at the same time many of my associates acquired fortunes, considering what their opportunities would have
been had they been simply hired men.

Now, when I took up the reins of business, I chose three comparatively
young men to be my colleagues, to be in fact, under my direction, the managers not only of that part of my concern which had been established but that
part which I intended to create. Only one of three youngsters had any considerable experience in business and had proved that he had great business
ability [Roy W. Howard]. Another was my youngest son and heir. The third
was a young lawyer who had attracted my attention by some work he had
done for me. [Thomas L. Sidlo, general counsel and comptroller of Scripps-
Howard.]

I called these three men together and laid before them my plan of extension, offering to them half of all the increase of profits that they made in my
established properties on condition that they should invest all such money
as accrued to them in stock in the proposed new newspapers. I advised them
to canvass the employees of the concern, offering these latter stock in certain
investment companies to be paid for out of their savings, with the understanding that all of the capital accumulated by the investment companies
should be re-invested in stock in the new newspapers. I also notified them

that my intention was that two or more of the employees of each new newspaper should have allotted to them in the aggregate 20 or 25 per cent of the
stock of the paper on which they were working, and that these persons
should not be required to pay anything for their stock unless the individual
projects should be successful, while their dividends only should be retained
until they had each paid their proportion of the capital cost of the new
project.

Then I stated my plan was that there were to be two groups of stockholders,
the capitalist group composed of myself, each of the three men with me, and
the investment companies whose capital would be the savings of my employees; and the other class was to be the employees on the new paper. In
case of the failure of a given enterprise, all the money cost of that enterprise was to be lost by the capital investors, there being no personal obligation resting against the employed managers.

A further part of my plan was that not only would we refuse to let any individuals other than employees own any stock in a given newspaper but no
one but employees would be allowed to purchase stock in the intermediate
investment companies. Further, I stipulated that only men who had been
previously employed in the concern should be selected for the managers,
editorial or business, of any new project.

One of my three young men objected to my scheme of having the investment companies share in the risk of failure beyond the proportion of the
actual stock allotted to such investment companies. When I asked them
who should bear the loss on the 20 or 25 per cent of stock allotted to the
management, there was no other possible answer than that I should bear
this loss personally. That would mean that I should be discriminated against
and that my risk as a capitalist would be double that of any other adventuring
capitalist, large or small. I pointed out that, as the amount of money that I
could afford to invest would be limited, then further extension of the business would be limited by my inability to furnish money not only for my own
stock but by my risk of having eventually to pay for the loss of the non-con-
tributing stockholders. I pointed out further that this would be bad business
and that it would react more to the disadvantage of all the other stockholders
than to myself, since it would limit the number of projects that could be entered into, and thus the opportunities of all of our employees, and amongst
others each of the three.

Why, I said that my part in these new papers was really that of one of the
working managers of each new paper, since the whole prospect of success
of any newspaper would depend upon not only my capacity or skill in founding each new project but also upon my ability to direct each enterprise and
enforce those business principles that I alone had learned.

My young lawyer friend listened attentively not only to my plans but especially to the latter part of my argument. From the expression on his face I could see that he was analyzing all of my proposals and arguments. Finally his countenance began to crinkle with humor and at last he broke out into hearty laughter.

"Why," he said, "Mr. Scripps, what an absurdity your whole proposal is, or at least this idea of your being 'grubstaked' by your employees. Of course, I understand that you have no intention of getting your stock for nothing and throwing the capital risk on others, but what strikes me as absurd is that you should claim that justice and equity give you that right."

"Why," he repeated, "according to that plan, you propose not only that your employees should furnish all the capital but that they should furnish the management of the new papers. I know well your idea that most men are fools, but do you suppose your men are such fools as to willingly consent to any such scheme proposed to them? They would say to themselves, 'If we are going to furnish all the money and all the men, why should we let Scripps have any stock at all, why shouldn't we get together and start a paper ourselves and keep all the stock to ourselves?' "

The young lawyer, T. L. Sidlo, had proved that he was a pretty good lawyer, and for all I knew he might have proved some business ability. But still there are lots of things in human nature that he had not learned and he certainly did not know the newspaper game.

I started this disquisition by the assertion that I am "not guilty" of taking advantage of any of my fellow humans in building up my fortune at their expense. Why are there so few employers and so many employees? Why are not all men or most men working on "their own" entirely or collectively as fellow shareholders in some business?

After Sidlo had sufficiently amused himself at my expense, I said to my company, "If Sidlo isn't right he ought to be right, but then he isn't right." I went on to say that up to the time of my retirement, for a period of over twenty-five years, I had founded some new newspaper or other business on the average of once every year and out of my employees I selected as managers of these new projects men who would eventually become fellow shareholders with me. [Expansion occurred between 1892 and 1907, making the "average" misleading.]

"Now, for twelve years," I said, "I have been out of business, and during that time the concern has not only founded no new newspaper or other projects but it has actually abandoned a half a dozen businesses that I started before I retired. In the old days a great number of ambitious young men were eager to enter the employ of my concern, because they had observed that men in it had greater opportunities to rise and acquire wealth than had men employed in other institutions. But during these twelve years that I have been away those ambitious young men have ceased to knock at our door and many that have been with us have left us and have gone to work elsewhere. Also, during those years our employees accumulated many hundreds of thousands of dollars, perhaps even millions, in the way of savings which they had put into savings banks, bonds, life insurance, and often into very risky speculative enterprises. They have been doing this notwithstanding the object lesson that they have always had in plain view of them of the great many very successful and profitable newspapers that had been founded on very small capital.

"Now, Sidlo," I asked, "why haven't these young men got together and done for themselves what I had previously done for myself and other young men?"

I then put to Sidlo this question: "Supposing a group of such young men were to get together to start a newspaper, would you want to put any of your money in with them?" I forget the answer. But I know, of course, that he would not. I know myself that I would not invest any of my money in any business institution that was not controlled by one or more men of previously proven ability.

While there have been a number of cooperative institutions that have been more or less successful in the old countries, and even some in this country (U.S.), none of them have developed into great institutions, and those that have been successful have given to their shareholders returns in the way of profits very little if any more than ordinary interest rates. Only those business institutions that have been founded by one person and have been dominated by this one person for many years have ever developed into great properties.

I have often had occasion to remark that I would rather have, say, 1 per cent in an institution that was absolutely controlled by one man of mediocre ability than to own 10 or even 20 per cent of the stock in a corporation whose government depended upon the agreement of two or three or a dozen of the very ablest of businessmen. We have to put up with government by compromise and all sorts of political government, but no business institution that is run on the basis of compromise can successfully compete with a business that is thoroughly dominated by one man.

Personally I have no doubt but that a large majority of all men have latently or potentially great capacities, which opportunity alone would develop to such an extent that almost any individual might be molded into an oligarch.

This idea might explain the present situation in the economic world, a situation which gives to the few great wealth and power and leaves to the many only humble positions in society.

As wealth increases, it must of necessity organize, and organization itself means such division of labor as not only to require but to permit that only one in a hundred, or in a thousand, or in ten thousand, or one in a hundred thousand should be the actual employer.

Luck and chance are largely but not wholly responsible for the selection of the oligarch. No two men are identically alike. No two men have identical qualities for filling any one position. In ascending the pyramid that can be said to be at least analogous to all political, economic, and social organizations, at each step there are two or many candidates for positions on the next step upward. By one means or another, choice is made, because it has to be made, of one or a few out of the many to take the next step upward. And step by step the upward course is taken, and step by step the number of candidates for promotion is reduced.

These choices are made more or less unintelligently and are more or less haphazard, but choice or choices having been made, the man or the men who have been promoted have opportunities for self-development greater than their fellows left behind on the previous step (the job makes the man).

How many steps there are in the pyramid depends upon conditions that cannot be described or possibly even conceived by anyone. But on the higher steps there is only room for a few and on the suppositious top block of the pyramid there is only room for one.

The number of oligarchs then depends upon the number of pyramids. There can be an economic institution as small as a ten-acre farm or a cobbler's shop, and there are in existence economic pyramids as large as the Standard Oil Company, the United States Steel Corporation, etc. And between these lesser pyramids and these greater pyramids there are only a limited number of pyramids, and the number of oligarchs in the country or of the world at large are limited by the number of these pyramids.

Man is a gregarious animal. All gregarious animals organize themselves hierarchically. There is a great bull buffalo. There is a gander who is the point of every V-shaped flock of wild geese.

In human history we find despots, kings, prime ministers, and republican presidents. For every three or four or more men that gather together there is always one self-elected or group-selected leader.

I admit that there are no supermen and that therefore the most that can be said of any chief of a tribe of savages, despot, war lord, king, or president [is that he] must have all the defects of common humanity, and that therefore all history is only a record of human disasters.

On the other hand I maintain that each and every oligarch is not responsible for the fact that he holds his position as an oligarch. He has been selected by active commission or omission — the acts of his subordinates, or the subjects of a king, or employees in a factory.

A number of years ago I took off my little crown and threw it in the dust, and, later, conditions over which I had no control, such conditions as, say, my own personal temperament or the demands either articulate or inarticulate of my subjects, caused me to pick up the crown again and put it on my head.

Doubtful as I was of my ability on account of age and feeble health, I had to do what I did do, and while adding nothing to my own comfort and satisfying no craving for the exercise of power or the acquisition of further wealth, developments have convinced me that I have at least temporarily benefitted many hundreds of men while I have not benefitted myself in the least. Neither have I added to my comforts, nor in the least degree diminished my previously existing discomforts.

One thing that I know and that is that the more benefits I distribute, the less the sympathy of others I will enjoy and the more I will become the object of hatred of all who know me or know of me.

Several years ago I dictated a short disquisition entitled "My Ladder of Discontent." Briefly I outlined the story of my mounting disappointment and my increasing disgust with everything and everybody. I dictated one line that I intended should be the conclusion of my essay. This line was in effect: "What's the use of doing anything?" With this sentence I dismissed my secretary and fell to ruminating. After a few minutes I recalled him and added another line to the effect: "What's the use of doing nothing?"

I have more than grave doubts whether I have during my whole life performed a real valuable service for any individual or for any number of individuals. I am often assailed by even a more grievous doubt. I doubt if I have ever done anything from a good motive, that is to say, from a motive that was strictly altruistic.

The only excuse I can offer to myself is: I am an organism, a living organism, and hence I have been compelled to function. I am compelled to function and I am of necessity compelled to function so long as a breath of life remains in me.

The Wisdom of One to Whom Death
Appears Imminent

[*October 7, 1925*]

All or nearly all men and women who have arrived at the age of maturity of mind have had the experience of feeling that death is imminent, or has recently been imminent.

All men and women who have arrived at great age must, if they think at all, be aware that death is imminent, if for no other reason than that all know that life cannot endure beyond a certain period, toward which the aging individual is rapidly approaching.

It is not my intention to deal with this subject generally. I wish only to express the thought or feeling of one person who has had reason to envisage dissolution as being close at hand.

Some months ago I attempted in a disquisition, entitled "Much Good Pain Wasted," [25] to give a view of what occurred to my mind during the period of two or three hours when I appeared to be on the verge of death itself, and especially of the few moments when I realized that I was probably dying.

Since then I have suffered two similar attacks, neither one of which were as violent as the one I first described. The effect of these latter two occurrences has been to impress upon me the fact that the sword of Damocles was hanging over me, suspended by a very fragile thread and that, notwithstanding the fact that I generally enjoyed good health, considering my advanced age, I might at any moment be stricken again.

It was during the latter part of my seventieth year, when I was on my yacht sailing the Caribbean waters, something occurred to my mind which brought to my attention the possibility that I might live for ten or fifteen, or even more years.

[25] No disquisition of this title appears in Scripps' papers, although he did bemoan the "good pain wasted" in a letter to EBS.

174

On this particular occasion I was feeling, physically, very well. I was suffering from no depression; on the other hand, I had been feeling somewhat exuberant in spirit. But, this thought that I might probably have many more years to live not only startled me but produced a very uncomfortable or displeasing prospect.

To be entirely candid, I should say a thought that was uppermost in my mind was that I had not made due preparation for great prolongation of my life — due preparation of a material or financial kind. In very early youth, on account of frequent spells of illness, I had always assumed that I was not destined to have a very long life. This general attitude of mine had resulted in my never giving much care or thought to preparing for a life unduly prolonged.

Because I had expected not to live for a long time, I had been for many years making preparation for the various members of my family, so that they would not suffer overmuch as a result of their losing the care and support from me they had enjoyed during my life.

But I did not make due preparation for myself, preparation for my old age.

I have said the thought uppermost in my mind was my own personal danger of finding myself aged and no longer fit for fending for myself, without sufficient means to support myself in the manner that I was long accustomed to.

But this thought was only one that was uppermost in my mind. There were other things that I was thinking about. What would I do with myself when I could do nothing more for myself, or for anyone else?

At the time I speak of, I felt that I had even then outlived or exhausted all of my interests in life. Rich or poor, strong or weak, I had a conviction that if my life was to be long continued, life itself was going to be one long period of boredom.

Thoughts on this subject continued with me for several days and finally resulted in my making certain resolutions; in fact, since then I have prepared, as well as I could, for my own financial support for a period of time which I feel now will be the limit of my existence.

It was quite a difficult matter when it came to arriving at some plan or scheme that would provide interesting employment for myself for a full decade or more [of] continued existence.

Now, when a few weeks ago it was made apparent to me that I was probably unduly alarmed about living too long a time, I have been trying to readjust myself in such a way that if I were to live long, I would not be too uncomfortable. And I have even tried to bring about that adjustment which, despite all the individual instinctive impulse, causes me not only to be resigned to the prospect of early death, but to desire such an event. I have tried to do this, but in vain.

My reason tells me one thing. My instinct clamors a denial of all that my reason asserts.

I have always been a hypochondriac.

I remember once hearing an old gentleman say that the coward who feared death had to endure the suffering of a thousand deaths, while the man of courage died only once, suffered death only once. Well, I am that coward. Fear has caused me to suffer a thousand deaths, each one of which was more painful than all the little I suffered in the emergency I referred to in my disquisition "Much Good Pain Wasted."

And so I presume, that for a short time, or for a long time — for weeks, maybe for years — I must continue to live, desiring mightily, as far as my reason is concerned, the end, while at the same time I shall be shrinking and shuddering with terror every time that some real or imaginary symptom shall be interpreted by myself as a forerunner of death itself.

I know that always, without exception, those who know me know of my accomplishments and my opportunities for enjoyment and the existing ties of affection to which I am bound, would heap only scorn and ridicule on me, if they knew of my present attitude.

All of us human beings, I believe, are at certain times, and in certain ways, existing in a condition of absolute loneliness, and being what we are, gregarious animals, and especially and particularly gregarious in our most human quality, that of spirituality, we suffer because of our absolute separation from all the members of our kind.

There are times when I feel that I would exchange all that I have — all my possessions, material and spiritual — for one understanding and sympathetic friend.

When, painfully, I force myself to recall to memory all the bitterness I have felt toward others, all the hatred, all the antagonism, and how much of the mental activity of my life has been so employed, I feel something more than shame and humiliation, I feel a sense of sin — of great sin.

When I have tried to console myself by recalling to memory the many acts of charity and goodwill that I have bestowed on others, I feel not only that in doing this I am kidding myself, but the deepest mortification, because I am conscious of my own hypocrisy in the present as well as in the past.

Amongst other of my derelictions has been one — my persistence to determine to myself and to others that I am an atheist. If I were really an atheist, I would neither fear life nor death; nor could I reproach myself for any thoughts or actions of my own.

If I believe nothing, it is equally true that I disbelieve nothing.

William MacDougall made a statement in the early part of the book he wrote on *Immortality* [26] that for himself he preferred the idea of annihilation after death, and then he went on through several hundred pages giving evidence pro and con of the immortality of the soul and its reverse. Yet I am sure that even MacDougall, when he was writing that book, felt as I feel now, far from certain that his soul was not immortal.

I am lonely, and perhaps just because I know that no one can communicate in mind with me, by any words of significance, anything on the subject on which my mind is now dwelling. I can conceive of no other method of communication between two people, one of whom is suffering as I am having to suffer so much, than so simple an act as pressure of the hand, when the sufferer could be conscious of and certain of the affection and sympathy of the would-be comforter.

In conclusion, I will try to paraphrase a sentence that appears in the Anglican Prayer Book, "We are all miserable beings."

[26] William McDougall wrote approximately 40 books dealing with psychology and social organization, but none by this title appears in the Library of Congress Catalog.

An Attempt to Find the Cause of the Universal Fear of Death

[*October 27, 1925*]

Is not the cause of our fear of death the fact that we have been taught to fear death?

I remember reading a book by one Wilfred Lay entitled the *Child's Unconscious Mind*.[27] In this book the author indicated that the large part of what might be called the character of an adult human being is formed while the infant is practically unconscious, or at least when the mind was little developed, with not only reason absent but memory.

I recall hearing it said that the Jesuits say among themselves, "Let us have the control and the teaching of the child up to and including its eighth year, and we care not what influences based on religions other than our own, nor for how long a time the child, the adolescent, and the man may be submitted to these influences, the child will remain through life a convinced Roman Catholic."

I have frequently undertaken to analyze my own character and the various causes that have shaped it. For some reason or other — probably the influence of some other person before, or during the period of my dawning consciousness — I cannot recall the time when I was not what is commonly called an atheist. I do not believe in God, or any being equal to or similar to the Christian's God. I have thought I knew just what person it was who so influenced me.

Yet when I called upon myself to classify myself as to what school of philosophy or religion I belonged to, I have had no doubt but that I should be classified as a Christian.

My morals, or my moral convictions, are those common to members of the Christian religion.

[27] Wilfred Lay, *Child's Unconscious Mind*. Dodd, Mead, New York, 1919.

178

How is it then that actually disbelieving that there was such a personality as Christ as usually depicted and, further, actually disbelieving that there is any such an individual as a Creator and a Ruler of all the universe, including man, I do have moral convictions that can have no other basis than belief in God and Christianity?

Why do I fear death when I do not believe in immortality and creature punishment for disobedience of the commands of God and the teachings of Jesus Christ?

It has always been remarked by me that the Christian Sabbath, Sunday, has always been a day of embarrassment for me. Knowing or even mistakenly thinking that some day is Sunday, I cannot comfortably indulge in any mental or physical employment which Puritan Christians disapprove of. To play a game of cards on a Sunday, or a day I think is Sunday, always results in my feeling a sense of sin. There are many other acts or thoughts that on any day, at any time, I am restrained from, simply because religious Puritans disapprove of such actions and thoughts, and these, too, notwithstanding that the great majority of Christians other than Puritan Protestants do not disapprove of, and further, notwithstanding convictions based on my own reasoning, entirely approve such actions and thoughts.

I do not steal and I do not want to steal. I hate lying as the Devil is said to hate holy water. I believe that there has been no time in my life when any temptation to commit adultery could overcome my natural (?) inhibitions to such an act. Jesus said that the man who lusteth after a woman has committed adultery in his heart. I find that, in my mind, adultery is a word defining an act contrary not only to the teaching of St. Paul, but an act committed on some person, which the laws of my own country define as being adultery. In other words, it would not be possible for me to feel remorse for any thought or action on my part before I was married, where my partner was not herself married.

I believe that, paraphrasing something which Professor Sumner said in his book on folkways,[28] in 999 out of every 1,000 of my activities, physical and mental, I am prompted to action or thought, or restrained from action or thought, by what might be called Christian tradition, or what might be called, even, superstition.

Perhaps influences that bore on my child's "unconscious mind" or on the not yet fully matured consciousness — my youthful environment in fact — [have] given the impress to my ideas as to right and wrong. It appears plain to me that my convictions are often not only inconsistent but absolutely contradictory.

Now from the time of my very earliest recollection, I have been immersed

[28] William Graham Sumner, *Folkways*. Ginn, Boston, 1906.

in a sea of Christian environment. At bottom, Christianity is founded on two beliefs — one heaven, the other hell. Always I have heard by word of mouth and seen by printed page declarations that heaven is such a delightful place that life there would be infinitely preferable to life on earth. This being the case, why should a devout Christian fear death? Why do all men, of all religious beliefs, without regard as to whether their lives have been holy or not, fear death? Of course, there are many men who declare they do not fear death and many men have made this declaration in their writings. Yet I have never known personally anyone sane in mind and physically free from great suffering who has not feared death and shown by his actions and expressions fear of death when it had become imminent. There have been suicides, of course, but in the case of every suicide evidence has been found, or could be found, that the physical or mental pain of living has been unendurable.

All animals struggle to their utmost to avoid death.

Perhaps man's fear of death has been a carry-over from the time when man was not man, but an animal, into all religions.

It is easy enough for biologists to explain the expediency of this, of this so-called instinct of self-preservation, but such explanations they offer are only theories as to the expediency of such an instinct — the propagation or rather the maintenance of the existence of the species. The resistance of man and all animals to death may have a teleological basis. But there are teleological objections to a too-long-continued existence of an individual's life. There are a large number of living organisms that can only propagate themselves by death. Any individual man in his vigorous youth is prompted by reason or instinct to do something more than postpone the date of his death. Alcohol is a poison. All intelligent men know it is a poison and there are but few who do not know that its use at any time in life will shorten the period of life. I know, as do all smokers, that tobacco is a poison and that its use, moderately or excessively, but shortens the life. The patriotic man who volunteers to join an army, whose purpose is to carry on warfare, knows that he is not only courting instant death but that the military service inevitably results in the shortening of life by reason of hardships to be endured. And yet, men will drink, they will smoke, and many will cheerfully seek the battlefield.

In thousands of other ways, men, especially young men, with full consciousness of their actions, will do other things that they are sure are going to shorten their lives, and even which threaten them with imminent death — for instance, automobilists will run a race with a coming train to see which can reach the crossing first.

While death is always feared, it is only greatly feared when imminent.

It is the custom of man to avoid unpleasant thoughts. The contemplation of death is painful and so, being hedonists, all men exert themselves greatly to keep the thought of death out of mind —

(Excerpt from a letter written to my sister, Ellen B. Scripps, October 27, 1925, while off the coast of Martinique): ". . . I have been moved to write another disquisition on the subject of "Why Men Should Fear Death," and am answering this question, or trying to answer it by giving what personal evidence I can that men only fear death because from their very infancy they have been taught to fear death. It is natural that the parents of a child, from its earliest infancy, should begin to, and continue to teach the child to avoid all sorts of activities that may lead to death. Then, it is now, and has been through all the ages, the universal practice of humanity to make a great display of funereal rites, to weep and cry out and in every way possible create the impression that something dreadful had happened when someone had died.

"Most if not all of our beliefs have been the result of teaching, mostly the teaching of the very young by the older.

"It happens that I never read any Freudian literature, or any psychoanalyst's discussion on the subject of death, but I have not only read enough of such literature but have observed enough, to think that it is quite possible that while a man would instinctively avoid pain, which often accompanies death — pain or the semblance of pain — yet most men have at times suffered more excruciating physical pain than that which necessarily accompanies death.

"I have often enough said that while I have no desire to live I do greatly fear the pain that I would suffer in dying.

"Some of my recent experiences have caused me to doubt the truth of just such statements as these I have made. On several occasions I have fainted dead away. On several other occasions I have become unconscious on account of a blow or a fall. Had I not on any one of those occasions returned to consciousness, I would have been dead.

"The actual pain that I have suffered during the several recent attacks [29] has not been nearly so great as that pain that I have suffered on many other occasions. Then, it is not pain that I fear when contemplating death, but death itself.

"My contention is then that my fear of death, as well as that perhaps of everyone else, is something that has been instilled into my mind by some other human being.

"Several years ago I read a book by a psychoanalyst, Wilfred Lay, en-

[29] He had had heart attacks — or indigestion — the previous summer.

titled the *Child's Unconscious Mind*. In it he furnished great quantities of evidence to show that before the period of conscious reasoning, the child's mind is impressed with certain ideas and convictions which persist to the end of life.

"I recall that once some ten years ago when I was suffering a good many attacks of ileostasis, I sent for Dr. Pollock. I had sent for him on several other occasions, but the severe attack had passed before he came, but on this occasion I was so anxious that the doctor would have a chance of diagnosing me while I was suffering that I not only actually made the effort, but succeeded, in prolonging the actual pain until after the doctor should come. When Pollock came into the room and to the bedside, he placed his hand on the point underneath which the pain appeared to be located. Pollock looked at me with some surprise and said, 'Why, there's nothing here to hurt you. The bowel is not distended at all,' and he had hardly said these words before I was free from pain.

"You may remember the occasion when in the Iturbide Hotel in Mexico, I had suffered several weeks with an eye disease and when the doctors had been pumping me full of morphine, I found that after the disease of the eye had passed, and the eye itself looked perfectly normal, I felt the same excruciating pain as formerly, so soon as the effect of morphia had ceased. It was all imagination, that pain of mine. I know it must have been imagination. On other occasions I have suffered severely from pain that I was afterwards convinced was purely imagination, but at the same time I will have to assert that an imaginary pain hurt just as much as a real one.

"You have lived many years longer than I have and, judging from what I have seen of you and your attitude, I am pretty sure that you believe there is no rational excuse for fearing death. Perhaps you have lived long enough to not only have acquired the conviction that there is no reason for fear, but you have also acquired complete fearlessness of death.

"Even if this be the case I am sure that I do not envy you your condition of mind; if the sole or even the principal cause of this fearlessness has been so many more years of experience, I do not want to live and hence to experience suffering enough to desire or even to be resigned to death.

"But to get back to the subject of the why of the fear of death. I know that I do fear death. I know that I have a great deal better cause for fearing long life, but why do I fear death?

"The reason for this condition of my mind compels me to believe that this fear has been taught me and that it is not a matter of instinct but a matter of external influences."

JOURNALISM

Scripps impressed on his editors that journalism "is a gentleman's trade," and sided with the hoi polloi — a paradox that is merely superficial. Scripps' personal code made him a gentleman; instinctively he fought for the underdog.

Yet a deeper irony does thread through Scripps' journalism. Urging fearless advocacy of the inarticulate common people who, he insisted, did not have champions in most of the nation's newspapers, he preferred as editors youngsters from the street who could talk the language of and sympathize with the workingman. Whereupon he made capitalists of his editors by making them stockholders in the businesses they were expected to operate for a minimum profit of 15 per cent. Wryly, Scripps recognized that he had got rich in the cause of the poor.

Unlike William Rockhill Nelson, who regarded the reporter as the key man on a newspaper, Scripps looked upon the editor as "the one absolutely necessary element" in journalism. Unlike Joseph Pulitzer, who paid close attention to the details of news presentation, Scripps was more concerned with choosing editors as "captains" who would run their newspapers as entities. Unlike William Randolph Hearst, who published large papers in large cities, Scripps insisted on small papers in smaller industrial cities. Unlike many publishers who strove for large circulations, the better to enrich themselves through advertising, Scripps sought to make a profit on circulation, insisting that a newspaper could remain free, vocal, and fearless only if it scrupulously remained independent of what he considered to be the corrupting commercialism of advertising.

IDEALISM

Hoping that through his newspapers he was building an enduring social institution rather than so many business properties, he founded his newspapers on a blend of idealism and close business management.

185

His idealism made him a reformer, culminating in a governing philosophy of journalism that is set forth in "The Germ of a Scripps Paper," in which he said his newspapers rested upon a "moral principle" that he identified as the "spirit of protest." During the earlier years in Cleveland and Cincinnati, he had protested chiefly on behalf of organized labor. But about 1904 — when he added the voices of a growing number of newspapers from Cleveland to San Francisco — he broadened his views, joining the ranks of reformers who made the early years of the twentieth century a period of protest and reform. For instance, he established the Denver *Express* in 1906 at a cost of approximately $50,000 to aid Judge Ben Lindsey and other reformers. "There is only one reason for the existence of the Denver *Express*," he said, "and that is to fight the battles of righteousness against unrighteousness." [1]

Telling one of his editors that "if you have a real message for the people, the people will hear you," he maintained that an editor who had the "spark" could make a newspaper successful without elaborate equipment. But, he warned, elaborate equipment and brilliant writers could be a "positive injury" in the hands of a man who is not "a true journalist." [2]

He expressed his idealism in another way when he said a newspaper's editorials should be regarded as "the teaching department, the statesmanship department, the spiritual department" whose "sole aim and end should be to get two citizens to think straight and act politically and socially straight where before there had been only one citizen who thought straight and acted morally." [3] However, he seriously doubted the effect of an editorial, believing that a newspaper's impact comes through the news columns.

Contemptuously, he regarded newspapers that took the side of wealth as "organ-grinding for the great." But at one and the same time he could express honest admiration for the business management of the conservative Los Angeles *Times*, which fought organized labor, and bluntly tell the *Times* publisher: "I am as proud of not being your kind of journalist as you doubtless are of not being the same kind of journalist that I am. For many years it has been my greatest pleasure to perform that which I consider to be also my greatest duty — namely, opposing, more or less successfully, such doctrines as you and some other great editors have preached." [4]

Along with his idealism was a sense of responsibility and a frustrated awareness that neither he nor other American editors had the knowledge and wisdom demanded of them by their social responsibility. Convinced that the American people were led, if not absolutely ruled, by the men who ran the country's daily newspapers, he maintained that "all of the editors in

[1] EWS to Ben Lindsey, Jan. 25, 1910.
[2] EWS to W. H. Porterfield, June 20, 1905.
[3] EWS to EBS, Oct. 1, 1921.
[4] EWS to Gen. Harrison Gray Otis, Feb. 27, 1904.

the country are so profoundly ignorant of the fundamentals of all the subjects they deal with that many of their writings are marked by sloppy sentimentality and are hence unsound, uninstructive, and even unsafe." [5]

PRINCIPLES

Scripps translated his idealism into a set of working principles for the governance of his newspapers. To two cardinal principles he attributed much of his success: the "51 per cent rule" by which he retained control of every newspaper and thus averted shifts in the balance of power; and his invariable rule that each paper be sharply divided into editorial and business departments, with the editor having the final say. The working principles are best illustrated in "Scripps' Advice to a New Editor."

When he eliminated McRae from executive control in 1905, he formulated "the whole of my system and theory of the newspaper business" in five points which, at the moment, were intended to put McRae straight and keep him straight about who was boss and what the Scripps papers were to stand for. He said: (1) The papers are to be controlled by editors who are "so broad-minded and far-seeing" that they would be utterly beyond the influence of the average business manager; (2) business managers were to confine themselves to selling as many newspapers as possible and to sell as much advertising as would be consistent with reasonable profits, but only at such rates and of such character as the editors approved, and to keep expenditures within 85 per cent of total receipts; (3) the energy of the Concern was to be concentrated on those papers that could be conducted profitably and the others were to be eliminated; (4) that the firm was to abandon any idea of buying out rivals or consolidating newspapers or attempting any sort of monopoly; and (5) that there should be a continuing increase in expenditures for news-gathering.[6]

Many times he drummed home the dominant principle of editorial supremacy, especially in letters to editors, as when he said: "It is our duty as editors to keep watch and guard over our business representatives in order that their acts shall in no way and at no time be inconsistent with the moral tone and gentlemanly character of its [the Concern's] chief men, the editors." [7]

The gentlemanly character encompassed honorable dealings with competitors. Time after time he chastised editors for getting into name-calling fights with rivals. In the case of the Spokane *Press*, Scripps laid down an "irrevocable rule" that the *Press* should never attack the character of any

[5] EWS to Robert P. Scripps, Sept. 18, 1915.
[6] EWS to Milton A. McRae, Apr. 22, 1905.
[7] EWS to H. N. Rickey, who had recently been made editor-in-chief of the Ohio papers, Nov. 7, 1905.

competitor without the consent of the majority of the stockholders — which meant himself. On another occasion, Scripps personally overruled McRae peremptorily on what he considered to be a wrong course of conduct. He said that, when they were thinking about starting a paper in Salt Lake City, McRae sent out a prospective editor with instructions to get a job on a local paper and spy out the land. "I stopped this and wrote McRae to the effect that we did not want to trust newspapers in the hands of men who, even under our orders, would consent to do such things as he had proposed." [8] There was never a Scripps paper in Salt Lake City.

He expected Herculean effort of his editors in putting out a salable newspaper "with one lead pencil and a pair of shears." Scoffingly, he said, "The editor who thinks that he can make a good paper and a salable paper by hiring legs and lead pencils is, in fact, no editor at all. He is a mere simulacrum." [9]

The editor had to produce an interesting newspaper if he were to attract readers, for Scripps took this view: "Get your audience before you start preaching to them." [10] By that he meant that a newspaper had to be composed of 90 per cent of what the readers wanted and 10 per cent of what the editor wanted them to have. "In fact, my plan was to sugar-coat my pills — give one ounce of medicine to nine ounces of jam." [11] He sought variety through a large number of "items," as many as 400 in a four-page newspaper.

Concerned more with substance than with appearance, Scripps was interested in the honesty of his newspapers' content, not their makeup. As a result, most Scripps papers had a slapped-together look.[12]

EDITORIAL POLICY

Scripps was the spirit and inspiration of his newspapers, governed by an overriding purpose in journalism — "to bring about a more equitable division of the joint products of manual and mental labor and capital." [13] As a result:

. . . there was a thoroughly fixed idea of what the Scripps papers should stand for. They were founded in the belief that other papers served the classes, and it was their job to serve the masses. "C.P." was an abbreviation familiar to all the workers — the "Common People." Sometimes it was "the 95 per cent." There were those who profited by monopoly and exploited those who toiled. E. W. and his papers would have none of these. What was good for the masses?

8 EWS to Robert F. Paine, Apr. 6, 1905.
9 EWS to E. F. Chase, Feb. 17, 1906.
10 E. F. Elfstrom, interview with editor, July 15, 1961.
11 EWS to Nackey Elizabeth Scripps (Meanley), Feb. 21, 1915.
12 Roy W. Howard, interview with editor, May 14, 1962.
13 EWS to Robert P. Scripps, July 11, 1918.

What did the unions want? How make government more amenable to the people? How tame the grafting city government, the state legislature or the United States Congress? They were low-brow papers, spat upon by the nabobs and loved by the laboring man. They made no attempt at dignity, respectability or culture. The editor of a Scripps paper must be an Ishmaelite. He must be attacking something, a corrupt bunch of aldermen, a street car corporation; or it might be gas or water or electricity corporations. The editor or owner of the rival paper would have his safety deposit box stuffed with bonds and stocks in the utility company, and was proportionately disinclined to fight for lower rates, while Scripps, with a life-long rule to keep his money exclusively in his newspaper holdings, was free to lead the charge for the people's cause.[14]

Scripps' editorial policy generally went in the direction indicated by "The Principles of the Scripps Idea of Journalism." Starting out with his eye only on labor's grievances, he cut an ever-wider path to the left until he sometimes was called a radical and even a "Red." He shifted emphasis and attention as the political situation changed, but did not alter his basic point of view.

His editors did veer from that point of view sometimes, though. Sometimes, an editor might take a position antagonistic to organized labor. Or an editor might take a position more acceptable to advertisers, expecting to derive larger revenue as a result.

On such occasions Scripps either whipped them back into line angrily, or, as in one brief interlude, forbade editorial expression altogether. He had immersed himself in the building of "Miramar" during much of the 1890's, leaving operation of the papers in the hands of McRae. When he again turned attention to his newspapers, he found editorial writers discussing subjects they were not competent to handle and expressing opinions inimical "to the interests of the masses." At that point he issued "a sweeping order" that editorials should be abandoned altogether or made "absolutely non-effective." During this period he established the Seattle *Star* in 1899 with explicit orders to print only the news and not editorial opinion on any subject.[15]

NEWSPAPER ENTERPRISE ASSOCIATION

He rescinded the ban on editorials in 1901, and in 1902 formed the Newspaper Enterprise Association as the central editorial voice of his newspapers. Operating at first as an adjunct of the Cleveland *Press* rather than as a separate corporation, NEA was to use the combined resources of all the Scripps

[14] Gilson Gardner, *Lusty Scripps* (New York, 1932), p. 35.
[15] EWS to Paul H. Blades, July 21, 1902; minutes of Seattle *Star* stockholders' meeting, June 13, 1902.

papers in supplying editorials, news reports, features, and illustrations of a quality that the individual papers could not afford singly. It was headed by an executive holding the title of president and general manager.

Scripps had grand plans and a lofty mission for NEA, as outlined in "Principles That the N.E.A. Should Stand For," and excitedly looked on it as a prospective national newspaper; that is, the NEA material would be nationalized through the individual Scripps papers as local outlets. Something along this line had been done — but by no means an exact parallel — by the ready-print services that came into existence for country weeklies immediately after the Civil War, printing two of a paper's four pages, with the other two being set up locally, but producing regional rather than national editions. Nor did Scripps carry his plan so far as to encompass central printing of such a portion of all his papers.

As time went on, he more strongly interpreted NEA as being the "editorial head of each and every Scripps paper," even though the various Scripps editors did not know it. Indeed, he held the NEA to be superior even to the editor of the Cleveland *Press* of which, paradoxically, NEA was a subsidiary.[16]

To his exasperation and indignation, however, his editors were unwilling to accept the NEA as of such scope and power. From the very beginning, he had to cram NEA down the throats of some. One of the first to buck him was Paul H. Blades of the Los Angeles *Record*. Exploding at Blades for being antagonistic to the common people and organized labor, Scripps gave Blades a direct order to use NEA editorials and to start producing local editorials in the same spirit and same vein. Other editors resisted NEA so strongly that as late as 1910 Scripps accused them of "meanly" using NEA as so much syndicate filler. The intensity of, and perhaps the reason for, his reaction can be seen in his reference to NEA as the "most loved of my constructive works."[17]

Ultimately, in 1910 he laid down the unequivocal order that NEA was to voice the editorial opinion of the Scripps papers, and there was to be no local divergence from the policy so set. Seeking unity and consistency in the editorial stand of his newspapers, even though he was retired, he issued the order because his editors had split into two camps over — and his newspapers thus expressed two points of view about — Theodore Roosevelt's course in attempting to heal a breach between President Taft's conservatives and Senator Robert LaFollette's insurgents in the Republican party. Scripps decided the entire organization must act "harmoniously and consistently."

[16] EWS to E. F. Chase, Feb. 17, 1906; EWS to Robert F. Paine, Aug. 10, 1903 and May 8, 1905.

[17] EWS to Robert F. Paine and W. B. Colver, May 3, 1910; EWS to Paul H. Blades, July 21, 1902.

Therefore, he ordered: "Hereafter the president and general manager of the Newspaper Enterprise Association shall have authority in all matters of general editorial policies; to define and express the views of the concern, and copy bearing his 'must' must be published by all Scripps papers in good faith." However, he reassured his editors that NEA would express their opinions agreed upon in conference, since they chose the president and general manager.[18] In a separate letter to W. B. Colver, who was president and general manager of NEA, Scripps said he was not concerned with what the policy should be but with "the perfecting of an organization which will make it possible for the whole concern to have one policy." [19]

Somewhat more candidly, he told his Washington correspondent: "These newspapers can only stand for that which I in the main approve, and my approval depends upon judgments based on evidence." [20]

NEA became a commercial service selling its product to any newspaper in 1921, and what is now the Scripps-Howard Alliance, based in Washington, later took over responsibility for determining policy and producing editorials on national and international questions.

The 1910 episode was symptomatic of a drift away from the basic Scripps policies after Scripps retired. Watching the drift, Scripps tried without success to stop it. In 1910 he said: "The spirit of our institution is changing, or has changed. The spirit is less a public service, and more a personal private gain, today than it has ever been before." [21] A few years later he complained:

The business of a Scripps editor is to make it easier for the poor man to get all that he is entitled to and harder for the rich man to get more than he needs.

Having read few Scripps papers for several years, but having heard several conversations and having heard of many more conversations, I have come to the conclusion that the majority of the Scripps editors, either through zeal or selfish interest, are more anxious to keep up the profits and circulation of their papers than they are to give public service.

[18] "Unity of Editorial Policy," EWS circular letter to Robert F. Paine, Harry N. Rickey, W. B. Colver, J. C. Harper, John Paul Scripps, B. H. Canfield, W. H. Porterfield, Oct. 7, 1910.

[19] EWS to W. B. Colver, Oct. 8, 1910. Trained as an attorney, Colver entered the newspaper business as telegraph editor of the Cleveland *Plain Dealer* in 1894 and switched to the *Press* in 1896. After reportorial assignments in New York and Washington, he was editor of NEA from 1902 to 1904, and then participated in business and politics for two years. He returned to NEA as president and general manager in 1907, holding that post until 1912 at which time he became editor-in-chief of the Clover Leaf group (see below) for five years. He served on the Federal Trade Commission from 1917 to 1920, acting as chairman in 1918–19, and also worked with the War Industries Board. He became Scripps-Howard general editorial manager in 1924–25.

[20] EWS to Gilson Gardner, Nov. 15, 1910.

[21] "The Present Editorial Trend of the Scripps Newspapers," EWS circular letter to Harry N. Rickey, J. C. Harper, B. H. Canfield, W. H. Porterfield, W. B. Colver, Robert F. Paine, Apr. 9, 1910.

. . . .

I judge from what I hear, incidentally, that cowardice is a dominant characteristic of the latter day Scripps paper. . . . [22]

His bitterness about the change shows through in "Ingratitude?" which
has nothing to do with any personal resentment on his part. Aside from up-
braiding the editor of the Seattle *Star*, in that disquisition, for turning away
from the workingman in the 1919 general strike in Seattle, he had a violent
interview with the editor, whom he accused of caring more for advertising
than for public service.[23]

DELEGATING AUTHORITY

Not often did Scripps collide so violently with an editor, for much of his
success lay in his ability to pick good men, delegate authority, and leave
them alone. But they knew, and he knew, that the Scripps newspapers were
subject to one-man rule which, however, came to be reserved for crucial decisions only. During the 1880's, when he had first developed his one-man
rule principle, he had been dictatorial to the extent of personally approving
every expenditure and every hiring and firing. But he had to soften that approach as his league was expanded in the early 1900's. Because it took the
form it did — numerous papers scattered over more than two-thirds of the
United States — the league operated in many respects as a little democracy;
the men who ran the papers had to have considerable voice in management
policies in view of their financial interests in their own papers. Furthermore,
the extensiveness of the Scripps operation automatically created large areas
of decision-making, which had to be the province of the man on the spot.
But always in the background was the Old Man with the final word, as in a
dispute with an editor about the amount of advertising space in the San Fran-
ciso *News*: "You desired twelve columns. I desired ten. I rather think that
we will settle down to the ten column idea." [24]

Although Scripps sometimes denied he had been a good judge of men, the
record shows the contrary. He could not have succeeded with this particular
system of newspaper operation otherwise. Whereas many other newspaper
executives hired editors, Scripps took his editors as partners and put up all
the money, which meant, as he rightly said, that he bet his money on a man.

In choosing an editor, Scripps stuck to his basic philosophy of individuality and originality. For that reason, he preferred young men of much intelligence and little experience; he was convinced that a man who had had
experience elsewhere had been "trained," whereas Scripps believed in education through self-development, discussed in "An Old Hobby."

[22] EWS to J. C. Harper, May 25, 1914.
[23] EWS to EBS, Sept. 7, 1922.
[24] EWS to Hamilton Clark, Dec. 15, 1905.

Scripps formed his judgment of editors in careful interviews, usually at "Miramar." Sometimes these were private interviews with prospective editors; sometimes they were interviews arranged as soon as possible after an editor had been chosen by one of Scripps' senior associates; sometimes they were interviews hidden within a conference of editors.

What did Scripps look for in an editor? For one thing, he tested the man to see if he were a yes man, a type Scripps detested. If the man disagreed with what Scripps said, a faint sparkle of joy would appear in the older man's eye. In spite of the fact that Scripps in the final analysis ruled autocratically, he maintained: "It is only men who are capable of expressing themselves fearlessly, and I might say almost offensively, to those with whom they differ that I have cared to place in high positions." [25]

Scripps could rise to great enthusiasm when he spotted a new editor who was a cut above the average. For instance, in an editorial conference in January, 1907, he met Alfred O. Andersson, editor of the Dallas *Dispatch* which had been founded the previous September. Of him Scripps wrote:

Andersson is a bright, charming fellow who is earnest and sincere. In a way, he is intellectually and morally the peer of any editor in my concern. . . . He was very sensitive and I am quite sure that I more than once hurt his feelings by my plain speech and rough criticism.

I feel now that I have a greater interest in the future of the Dallas *Dispatch* than a mere business interest. I want Andersson to succeed; I want a man of his type and character to prove great ability for the purpose of getting considerable influence. I want more of the spirit of Andersson in our concern . . . Andersson just wants one thing, and that is to be a decent and honorable editor. . . . [26]

In delegating authority, Scripps became a great teacher of young newspaper executives, although few of them had much affection for him, nor did he seek affection. Delegation of authority allowed an editor to develop his own powers and ability, Scripps disclaiming that he had ever been able to develop a man except by giving the man an opportunity to develop himself.

I have all my life had my own plan of administration. It has several features. It proscribes from doing anything that another can do. It is to develop men rather by imposing on them responsibilities than by a too long and intricate course of instruction. Its aim is to limit the scope of action of the chief to a constantly decreasing set of subjects, each piece of detail being turned over to some other who has developed the capacity for it. Each year the chief should become less important to the *maintenance* of what has been established, with more liberty and greater capacity to enlarge and extend the business.[27]

[25] EWS to Amos Pinchot, Apr. 16, 1917.
[26] Memorandum of conference, Jan. 30, 1907, Letterbook E, opposite p. 17 f.
[27] EWS to EBS, Sept. 14, 1892.

Convinced that men, money, and method make a newspaper, he counted the man as most important. Experience taught him that the Scripps methods "aren't worth the powder to blow them to Hades unless there is one man on the paper who would have been able to succeed if there had never been any such thing as Scripps principles, plans, and methods." [28]

True to his credo that he would never do that which another could do, Scripps left his editors alone in carrying out the details of their jobs. He issued general instructions, offered advice when called upon, and kept a close watch on what they were doing. But he seldom intervened. He set down the ground rules, as of 1905, this way:

Sometimes I make suggestions, which I do not expect to be taken as orders or even advice. My suggestions are only points for your consideration. I never give advice until I am not only pretty willing, but pretty nearly determined, to have [it] followed. I hate to give orders. I think it is hardly worthwhile. I think it is more economical, in time and money, to give a discharge instead.[29]

Having concluded that "the great art of executive management consists in the least possible amount of management," [30] Scripps operated with as few rules as possible. At one point in his career, he had attempted to enforce a large, uniform body of rules, but as the league grew in size he discovered he had more rules than enforcement machinery. Consequently, he abandoned the network of rules early in the 1900's, and wiped them out entirely when he retired in 1908, because he did not "believe in the rule of the dead hand or the palsied hand." [31] However, the retired but not palsied hand could be laid on an editor's shoulder when necessary. For example, he noted that a west coast editor's policies were diametrically opposed to pre-retirement policies, and cautioned the editor not to dismiss the old rules lightly but to look upon them "as the outcome of a mind that has been very active and very rich in experience." [32]

Leaving the detail work to local managers happened to suit his predilections, for Scripps got his fun out of starting something. He was an idea man, not a detail man; routine bored him; few things commanded his sustained interest for long. McRae once observed that Scripps would start something and, regardless of whether it had been started aright, dump it on McRae or someone else, leaving them to take the blame or praise, depending on how it turned out. "I guess he was right," Scripps said.[33] Epitomizing this trait, he once wrote:

[28] EWS to Negley D. Cochran, Dec. 17, 1913.
[29] EWS to Hamilton Clark, Dec. 15, 1905.
[30] EWS to B. H. Canfield, Dec. 16, 1908.
[31] EWS to W. H. Porterfield, Nov. 15, 1909.
[32] *Ibid.*
[33] EWS to James G. Scripps, June 30, 1917.

Newspapers are a great deal like pigs; they are very pretty and attractive while they are young and innocent, but when they grow fat and greasy, they grow ugly and disagreeable. I give more voluntary attention, and feel a keener interest in seeing one of my baby newspapers make its first hundred or two hundred dollars a month, than I do to the big things and their thousands, more or less, of net profits.[34]

FOUNDING THE UNITED PRESS

An example of Scripps' way of starting something and leaving its development to others is to be found in the United Press. In "Driftwood" and "Founding of the United Press," he tells the story of how the UP came into being in 1907, but there is more to the story than that.

When Scripps formally organized the Scripps League in 1888, he established an embryonic wire service in his New York News Bureau, serving the four Scripps papers. After the split with James E., he converted the bureau into the Scripps-McRae Telegram Company, which provided the Adscititious Report under the editorship of Bob Paine in Cleveland until 1897.

On a small scale, his wire service paralleled a development that was in keeping with the general spirit of American corporate organization in the late nineteenth century — the formation of newspaper combines for the collection and distribution of news. Through monopolistic arrangements, larger combines were effected through the old United Press (not to be confused with Scripps' later UP) and the predecessors of the modern Associated Press.

The Associated Press first appeared in 1848 as a combination of six New York papers for the cooperative gathering of telegraph news, but the name Associated Press did not come into general use until the 1860's. By the 1880's the Associated Press of New York centralized national and international news, drawing upon its members' foreign and Washington reports as well as upon the reports of European news agencies, all of which were national monopolies involved in an international cartel, which it received through Reuters, a British agency. Through Western Union, the New York AP sold its reports to regional groups, all of which had AP in their titles. By the 1880's the strongest regional group was the Western Associated Press, composed of midwestern newspapers.

The old UP grew out of the first challenger AP faced. In an effort to break the monopoly of the California Associated Press, Henry George (who is better remembered as the author of *Progress and Poverty*) formed the American Press Association in 1871. The APA was reorganized in 1882 as the United Press. The old UP was formed by Walter P. Phillips, a former

[34] EWS to John Vandercook, Mar. 12, 1902.

AP man, as general manager; William M. Laffan, business manager of the New York *Sun*; and John R. Walsh and James W. Scott of the Chicago *Herald*. As a national agency, the old UP replaced the regional AP in the European cartel contract with Reuters.

On the surface, two competing press associations served American newspapers by 1890, but a secret trust agreement vitiated their competition. Members of the AP's ruling Joint Executive Committee, dominated by New York publishers and having representatives from only two inland papers, obtained UP stock through the trust agreement and profited from an exchange of AP news, which reduced the costs and increased the profits of the UP.

Discovering the secret arrangement which had greatly reduced the value of their memberships, members of the Western Associated Press started a ruckus in 1892. Rather than have western upstarts dictate to them, all New York papers bolted to the UP in 1893.

At that point a fight to the death erupted. The Western AP reorganized as the Associated Press of Illinois under the leadership of Victor Lawson, owner of the Chicago *Daily News*. His former partner and founder of the *Daily News*, Melville E. Stone, operated the AP from Chicago headquarters. Seeking members across the nation, the AP offered inducements as a cooperative with monopoly franchise rights which protected individual members against competitors getting the AP report; members also were forbidden to use any other news service. Because it was designed to be a national news agency, the new AP recaptured the Reuters contract, thus taking away from New York papers the foreign news which formerly had been available to them through the UP. For four years the AP fought the old UP at a cost of one million dollars over and above regular expenses.

By 1897 the AP had won the fight. All New York papers, except Charles A. Dana's *Sun* and Hearst's *Journal*, returned to the AP fold in 1897. The old UP died in the struggle, going into bankruptcy in April, 1897, and passing from the scene forever, discredited.

In 1900 an Illinois court ruled that the AP was a public utility, a decision which would have killed the monopoly franchise that was the heart of the AP's strength as a cooperative. As a result, the AP of Illinois was dissolved and a new AP incorporated under the laws of New York, from which the present AP dates.

Scripps had allied himself with the UP during the fight. Not only was it profitable for him to do so, for reasons that are brought out in the disquisitions, but two other reasons show through clearly in letters to his sister Ellen. Brother James E., with whom he was not on speaking terms during those years, was a prime mover in forming the new AP; Phillips and James

E. disliked each other. The second reason was that Phillips treated Scripps respectfully and courted him, even calling on him at West Chester, whereas Lawson and Stone did not. Besides, "the United Press people have not been modest in their claims that their Scripps was the best Scripps and had the biggest end of the Scripps concern." [35] By that time, Scripps had regained control of the Cleveland *Press*, giving him Cleveland, Cincinnati, and St. Louis, with James E. controlling only Detroit. Moreover, he equated all the AP publishers with James E. as "old fossils" and "graybeards."

When the old UP folded in April, 1897, Scripps faced a more agonizing choice than his disquisitions bring out. Even though the scheme to force McRae into accepting the idea of a separate wire service may have been in his mind, as discussed in "Driftwood" and "Founding of the United Press," it is clear that McRae almost pushed Scripps into the AP. Indeed, having once agreed to go into the AP if he could do so on his own terms, he had second thoughts which caused him to fear that the AP might accept his terms. For that reason, and also because he was "really ashamed" of himself for letting McRae talk him into negotiating with the AP at all, Scripps went to Chicago in May, 1897, for the showdown. He was certain that, if he were to go into a cooperative which was subject to monopoly rules, "I don't think I would be worth a cent . . . if I had my wings clipped and my spirit broken by anything like submission to anybody else's control." [36]

At any rate, he stayed out of the AP, and converted the Adscititious Report into the Scripps-McRae Press Association (SMPA), linking it with his own Scripps News Association on the West Coast and J. B. Shale's Publishers Press Association on the East Coast. In 1906 John Vandercook, editor of the Cincinnati *Post*, persuaded him to buy Publishers Press, and Scripps then found himself with three wire services covering the nation.

These he converted into one wire service in 1907, adopting the name United Press Association, the last word becoming "Associations" later. The intriguing question is why he reached back ten years and took the name of a bankrupt and discredited organization as the name of his brand-new service. No one in the organization today seems to know why he did it. None of his personal papers give a clue, except one statement in his autobiography to the effect that he intended his new SMPA in 1897 to be the successor of the defeated UP. The answer to the question possibly lies in the psychology of a complex man who thumbed his nose at the great and the mighty.

At any rate, he found himself in a new business. He and his men did not know much about running a wire service. "But I am in it, and we are in it, and this being the case, there is nothing else for us to do except to bend all of

[35] EWS to EBS, Aug. 23, 1894.
[36] EWS to EBS, May 24, 1897.

our energies to the upbuilding of a great news association, which shall be developed progressively from the old and routine lines of a news association into something better." [37]

From that point Scripps behaved characteristically. He had brought the new UP into being, he gave it initial direction, and then left it for someone else to develop and run. At first, he turned it over to Hamilton B. Clark, who had started out as Scripps' secretary and entered the newspaper business as one of the founding partners of the San Francisco *News*, and Vandercook, whose life was cut short by appendicitis in 1908. One or two others headed the UP for a few years, and then Roy Howard — "that young boy Howard," Scripps called him — took charge. With what he calls a "boys' brigade," Howard built the UP into a worldwide press association. The UP was Scripps' intellectual creation; it was Howard's operational creation. Scripps paid little attention to the detailed operation of the UP.

As with his newspapers, he set the large goals, however, and in this case he saw the UP as superseding NEA in one important particular — a national newspaper. He said: "I contemplate the upbuilding of an institution which shall itself be a sort of universal newspaper — that is to say, the main product of what might be called a universal newspaper." [38]

In other words, Scripps sensed at the time what now is clear in retrospect: The creation of national press associations in the early 1900's meant a nationalization of newspaper content in important degree. Both the UP and AP were national organizations, and Hearst added a third in 1909 with International News Service, which UP absorbed in 1958 to become the present United Press International. Previously, newspaper content had been of local and regional origin. But with national press associations, an identical account would appear in scores and even hundreds of cities in the same words on the same date. True, the press associations have long been recognized as a major influence toward standardization of American newspapers, news values, and news writing styles, but the nationalization of newspaper content which they effected is a factor fraught with implications in the development of a homogeneous American people in the twentieth century.

BUSINESS MANAGEMENT

Scripps the editor may have been noble of purpose and broad of vision, but Scripps the businessman was cold-blooded and hard-boiled. A dollar was a dollar, and fifteen cents out of every dollar taken in had to be clear profit. At the same time, he registered angry contempt when an editor or manager became a dollar-chaser instead of a steward in the public interest.

[37] Diary Notes, Aug. 28, 1906, Letterbook D, opposite p. 489 f.
[38] *Ibid.*

In spite of his many apparently sincere protestations that he detested business, Scripps on the business side was shrewd, tight-fisted, and scrupulously
honest. Some of his thinking about the business side of a newspaper will be
found in "The Newspaper Business in Relation to Other Forms of Business,"
and in other disquisitions in the American Business and Labor section.

Scripps was well aware that one certainly could question the sincerity of
his editorial motives in light of the fortune that he built. Yet his idealism
shows even in his business methods, for his thinking encompassed the newspaper as being a whole of delicately balanced parts. He once lamented that
he could not discuss the whole of his view with associates or friends, because
they talked dollars-and-cents, and "I have always preferred to consider my
newspapers from another point of view, but unfortunately I have never had a
companion with the right sort of vision of the peculiar interests which would
make my talk intelligible by them." [39]

To begin with, he took the position that anyone who attempted to run a
newspaper just to make money was bound to fail, that the only chance
for success lay in desiring to make a better and better newspaper. Categor-
ically, he once stated that he had "never founded a newspaper yet or bought
one as a purely business undertaking that met with any sort of success." [40]

Interwoven here was a certain amount of sentimentality about his newspapers that perhaps accounted for his refusal to sell a newspaper, a policy
that was breached only once during his lifetime, in the sale of the St. Louis
Chronicle in 1908. Over and over again he referred to his newspapers as the
children of his brain, knowing them as a parent might know a child, knowing
the spirit and soul of each, knowing why each existed, knowing why each
was weak or strong, knowing why people did or did not read one, knowing
why readers were influenced or not by each. Consequently, it seemed strange
to him that other newspapermen did not recognize what he called the real
entity of a going newspaper — the spirit or soul that was imparted to it by
the men who had helped direct it. "Long after you and I are dead — perhaps
for generations even," he clucked at Paine, "your life and my life are going
to be extended right along as the spirit and moving force of a number of
newspapers whose owners and editors of that future time will perhaps even
be ignorant of our ever having existed." [41] Possibly growing from that conviction was his iron-bound rule: He would discontinue a newspaper if he
could not obtain a competent management for it, but he would never sell
a newspaper, no matter how large the price. He would have been willing to
make an exception in the event he were convinced the new "owner would

[39] EWS to EBS, Feb. 1, 1919.
[40] EWS to Edgar Pennington Young, Apr. 19, 1911.
[41] EWS to Robert F. Paine, Aug. 2, 1915.

be better able and more inclined to serve humanity than I was." [42] Whether he was guided by that principle to the last letter in selling the St. Louis *Chronicle* to Nathan Frank in 1908 is not indicated fully in his personal papers, but he had strong reservations about selling the paper. A further illustration of the base line in his business principles was the order in which he ranked the departments of a newspaper: first and "absolutely important," editorial; second, circulation; third, advertising, the most profitable to the employee but the least valuable to the management, as he put it. [43]

Notwithstanding the strength of his views and guiding principles, Scripps demonstrated a flexibility without which his institution could not have endured, for his career spanned so many changes in journalism that the Cleveland *Press* of 1878 would have been an anachronism in the Scripps-Howard organization of the 1920's.

Scripps came into the field of journalism in the 1870's when the old political newspaper was yielding to the newspaper that emphasized news ahead of opinion. Indeed, the Scripps papers were among the first to establish themselves as independent of political party, a development that marked the 1870's as the beginning of what has been dubbed, with over-simplification, the independent press. As the *news*paper evolved from the party paper, the news-gathering apparatus was steadily extended, reaching its apogee in the creation of national press associations that extended their activities throughout the world. Contrasted with the limitations of hand-set type, steady technological improvements brought mass production techniques into the manufacture of newspapers. Going along with the capacity to produce a larger number of larger newspapers quickly was the opportunity to grasp larger circulations as urban population burgeoned. To accommodate themselves to the changing production role, publishers swung into line with a trend of the times — the development and growth of the corporation as the integral element of American economic growth. Mass production in industry generally was reflected in large-circulation newspapers — a trend which Scripps resisted, thus perhaps making his small newspapers something of a vestigial remnant. The United States had 574 daily newspapers in 1870, and 2,200 in 1909. Circulation had increased from 2,800,000 to 24,200,000.

When Scripps began his career, most advertising was local and static; that is, a local merchant would place an ad for a year and it would be set in type for a year. But an intensification of local business competition changed the nature of local advertising into a fast-paced element of commercial competition, with the newspaper serving as a major sales device of the department store whose rise and development was accompanied by an increasing enrich-

---

[42] EWS to Sam T. Clover, Los Angeles *Graphic*, Dec. 7, 1910.
[43] EWS to Harry Y. Saint, Spokane *Press*, Mar. 5, 1903.

ment of newspapers. At the same time, as the American economy gradually became nationalized after the Civil War, national advertising of national brand names became an increasingly important source of revenue for newspapers. National advertising also became one of the factors that resulted in a gradual decline in the number of newspapers, beginning shortly before World War I. A national advertiser tended to spend his money in only one paper in a two-paper town, say, and patronized the paper with the larger circulation, which thus became financially stronger and expanded its content to attract a still larger circulation, while the second paper went into oblivion.

Scripps recognized these changes during his time and adapted himself to them, although he unsuccessfully resisted the enlargement of his four-page papers after his retirement. Mention has already been made of his recognition of the trend toward metropolitan papers in the late 1880's. As of 1902 he assessed the situation this way: Current changes in the newspaper business were not much different from past trends, except that fewer new papers had been started; trusts, consolidations, and pools had not appeared in journalism as in other businesses because the newspaper was essentially a local institution; the only development along that line had been his own innovation, through the league system, that made a group of papers into one large, preferred buyer of the materials used in manufacturing a newspaper; an ultimate trust and combine would not appear in journalism until three or four great newspaper corporations published newspapers in all or most of the large cities simultaneously, a condition he had long predicted would evolve eventually; one reason for the small number of new newspaper starts was the development of the newspaper into a pure newspaper as contrasted with the old partisan journal; any city had enough people of differing points of view to justify an equal number of newspaper exponents, but when it came to news one paper was as good as a dozen; the public expected only truthfulness, enterprise, and industry in printing the news and did not care what the editor's views were; regretfully, he concluded that conditions made national advertising, a condition he had once deplored, now a business necessity.[44]

His recognition of and adaptability to change was exemplified in 1910 when he told his sons that the increasing supply of gold, which entered world-trade channels largely through mining in the British Empire, was the most startling of many changes that betokened a whole new era in world affairs. Because of the dawn of a new era, he told them:

Of one thing I am perfectly certain, and that is that so little adapted to practice and future conditions have been many of my general business principles,

[44] EWS to Milton A. McRae, Jan. 10, 1902.

that were you to undertake to practice the same principles that I have, you would almost certainly fail — I believe you would certainly fail.

However, you can depend upon it that the great majority, almost the universality of men in and out of business, will continue to practice the methods of their fathers, and will utterly be unable to comprehend how radically all conditions have changed. This should, if you are superior in your knowledge and wisdom to them, give you a great advantage.[45]

A careful and correct choice of fields was essential to the success of such newspapers as his. Scripps therefore confined himself to smaller industrial cities which he more precisely defined as "small metropolises." As of 1902 (when he had papers in Cleveland, St. Louis, Cincinnati, San Diego, Los Angeles, Kansas City, Seattle, Akron, and Des Moines) he identified as desirable cities for future Scripps papers Buffalo, Pittsburgh, Louisville, Indianapolis, Omaha, Denver, Salt Lake City, St. Paul–Minneapolis, Portland, San Francisco, Milwaukee, and Chicago.

Not by chance did Scripps limit that list mostly to western and midwestern cities, for he had an abiding distrust of the East. He called the East a "wilderness of conservatism, convention, and caste" with which he wanted nothing to do. Dividing the eastern "desert" into the three regions of New England, New York, and Pennsylvania, he considered Pennsylvania the most hopeless.

Because he did consider Pennsylvania the most difficult, he chose Philadelphia in 1912 when he was "persuaded by an ardent youth to lead a colony Eastward." The youth was Marlen E. Pew, who established the Philadelphia *News-Post* which continued until 1914. But Pew, working as a fighting Scripps editor, was constantly in trouble. Scripps said word went out from the Philadelphia "powers that be" that the *News-Post* must be silenced, that Pew was arrested twice and charged with criminal libel, and once "was taken from his bed at midnight and incarcerated." As a consequence, Scripps said, the experience "has shown me that if the East is not 'wild and woolly' it still is not a safe place for a man who has acquired the habit of being honest and candid in his journalistic experiences." [46]

Not until Scripps-Howard began expanding in the early 1920's did Scripps accept the East as a field for development. Scripps-Howard undertook this area at the same time it began planting newspapers in the South. As for the South, Scripps said in 1921:

I have had a strong inclination to plant one of our papers in every southern city that is large enough. I do not consider the opportunities for making money

[45] EWS to James G. and John Paul Scripps, Feb. 14, 1910.

[46] EWS to Robert J. Collier, *Collier's National Weekly*, Feb. 10, 1913, in response to a *Collier's* editorial expressing hope that Scripps would establish newspapers in the East.

in this section of the country as great as in other sections but I do believe that the southern states have suffered as much from a lack of the right kind of newspapers as from any other lack. Then, too, because of the scarcity of large cities and the comparatively great area of territory and a large number of states, it seems to me that here in the south it will be possible for us to exercise a greater amount of influence according to the money invested than elsewhere in the country.

. . . I know of no city in the north that has a better evening paper than our contemporary, the Birmingham *News*.[47]

Before the Scripps-Howard expansion, Scripps had or had had papers in Dallas, Oklahoma City, Memphis, Nashville, and Houston. Scripps-Howard added, before Scripps' death in 1926, Birmingham, Norfolk, Fort Worth, Washington, Knoxville, El Paso, and Baltimore. However, he grouped the Texas papers apart, with the result that Birmingham was the only Deep South city in which he founded a paper.

Scripps carried out his newspaper expansion through internal financing alone. He adhered to a rule on which he, James E., George H., and Ellen B. had agreed in the early days: Their business was to be a cash business; the corporations would be close corporations; they should borrow only from each other personally; their corporations should borrow only from one another.

Keeping his newspapers as close corporations led Scripps into a system of profit-sharing whereby his subordinates held a healthy share of stock in the newspapers they were running. He invariably held the 51 per cent, but divided the other 49 per cent among his associates. Each new paper was started with from two to four local stockholders. The editor and business manager each held 15 or 20 per cent of the stock, paying for it from dividends. Gradually, some of his associates amassed enough money to hold stock in several newspapers.

Here Scripps did not even pretend to altruism. He simply could make more money by holding 51 per cent and letting capable subordinates hold the other 49 per cent than he could by owning the entire paper.[48]

However, he made it a point not to talk anyone into joining him in a business venture. Taking in only those men who insisted upon an opportunity, he placed on them full responsibility for their participation, and thus protected himself against resentment if an enterprise failed.[49]

As the network of newspapers and minority stockholders became more complicated through numbers and changes through time, Scripps devised yet another system of profit-sharing. He set up individual investment companies in which employees, regardless of rank, could buy stock, the com-

[47] EWS to EBS, Nov. 29, 1921.
[48] EWS to Robert P. Scripps, July 11, 1918.
[49] Diary Entry, Mar. 12, 1907, Letterbook E, pp. 41–42.

panies in turn holding stock in the various newspapers. Again, he was not altruistic. Quite coldly, he reasoned that the papers paid out large sums in salaries, representing pure waste insofar as internal capital was concerned; an investment company could recapture part of the salaries and put that money to work for further expansion; at the same time the employee-investors would make more money. Ultimately, he had six investment companies, which were consolidated into the Scripps-Howard Investment Company.

The money for expansion came from profits that resulted from the strict economy—employees might have called it penuriousness—that was the key to Scripps' close business management. Again, he operated on an old family rule: Any well-conducted newspaper must operate at a cost not exceeding 85 per cent of receipts, which meant a 15 per cent profit.

Holding that the chief capital asset of any newspaper was its goodwill or reputation, Scripps held plant investment to a minimum. Seldom, at least prior to World War I, did the investment in a Scripps paper exceed fifty thousand dollars. Scripps also held the mechanical equipment to a minimum; his papers were not to exceed four pages, anyway. For many years he refused even to own the property that his newspapers occupied, but modified that policy as the years went by. Likewise, he refused to carry much insurance on his plants, having learned in two Detroit fires that flame and water do little damage to printing material. In choosing a site for a new plant, he sought one as near the center of population as possible, which placed it beyond the center of the business district. Thus, detractors sneered at Scripps papers as being in the neighborhood of blacksmith shops; defenders said that was because blacksmith shops were on the main routes of travel. Either reason would have accomplished Scripps' probable purpose — economical circulation.

Scripps placed great emphasis on circulation, because he intended that his newspapers should rely on circulation for much of their income. But in building circulation he would have nothing to do with gimmicks — prizes, contests, premiums. The only kind of circulation he wanted was that which came from the reader's desire to read the paper.

Scripps men and Scripps methods did not uniformly produce successful newspapers, however. In fact, he concluded, as of 1911, that about one of four papers would fail, and the other three would not be outstanding successes. He recognized four real failures — St. Louis *Chronicle*, Kansas City *World*, San Francisco *Report*, and Spokane *Press* — and said each one was due to "the folly of a local management in attempting to get rich quick, and attempting to buy itself rich, in fact, in making big papers and spending money." He ruefully conceded that, as the local manager, he had made the first mistake with the St. Louis *Chronicle*.[50] However, he did not found the Kansas City *World* directly, and he bought the San Francisco *Report* as an established property.

In determining the value of a newspaper property, Scripps used a sliding-scale formula which he called the "Rule of Three": If the circulation of the newspaper is equal to one in every five inhabitants of the city; if the paper has been making a 15 per cent profit for the last five years; if the circulation and its volume of business have been increasing as rapidly as the population of the city, then the newspaper is worth three times the total annual receipts of the paper, exclusive of real estate and capital reserve fund.[51] In arriving at a final valuation, he adjusted the figures up or down in each category as he calculated the worth of a paper, adding the value of real estate and reserve fund and deducting debts. Only some of his associates accepted the validity of the Rule of Three.

Another standard used in assessing a paper's value was the 6 per cent per annum rule — that is, that a newspaper's profit for a given year represented its ability to pay 6 per cent on the investment; hence, a paper with an annual profit of $3,600,000 would be worth 60 million dollars. Scripps said the Rule of Three resulted in a lower valuation for a long-established and profitable newspaper than did the 6 per cent rule, with the converse true for new or still-developing papers.

ADVERTISING

The final element on the business side was the one Scripps hated — advertising. He appreciated the importance of advertising in its place, but, still, it was a necessary evil. Indeed, advertising galled him so much that his dislike was almost obsessive.

His basic idea about advertising was that it should be local; he disliked national advertising for some reason, and eliminated it entirely from the Seattle *Star* when that paper was founded in 1899. Also, the advertising rates should be the same for all customers, with no preference shown large or regular advertisers. And the rates should be low enough to keep the advertising space full. His rules also excluded advertising by public officials, public utilities, or anyone known to have political ambitions.

His vigilance against advertising influence on his papers slackened during the 1890's when he was busy building "Miramar," but was revived. When he again picked up active management about 1900, he became furious at the conditions he found existing. Angrily, he ordered a sharp cutback in ad-

---

[50] EWS to E. F. Chase, Feb. 17, 1906.
[51] EWS to EBS, July 23, 1925.

vertising, banning what he called "dirty" advertising and reducing the volume of department-store advertising. His order against "nasty" advertising applied specifically to patent medicines advertised as cures for venereal disease. He explained his actions:

> Our business has got into such a condition that the advertising tail was wagging the journalistic dog. It was my imperative duty to cure this evil. It's been hard to make anyone believe that I was really desirous of reducing the volume of advertising receipts. There is a class of advertising that is good to print under ordinary conditions; yet even the best class of advertising becomes bad business when the proportion of gross receipts of a newspaper from advertising becomes abnormally large. If any body of men could have been trusted with such a condition, I think we could have been, yet we found ourselves stooping and demeaning ourselves to a contemptible extent. Dirty advertisements are bad for the newspaper as a journal. Overgrown, insolent, and impudent department-store managers threaten the very existence of a newspaper as a business. Hence my efforts to reduce the volume of advertising by attacking these two classes.[52]

His more important, and more enduring, action was in clubbing patent-medicine advertising. He issued the first order against dirty advertising in 1900, and in 1903 he appointed Paine, then still in Cleveland, as censor of all national advertising copy going into Scripps papers. The papers reputedly lost nearly $500,000 worth of revenue in one year as a result of the censorship.

With that action, Scripps became the first newspaper publisher deliberately to exclude patent-medicine advertising on principle, although a few national magazines had taken similar action previously. What he struck was the source, until about that time, of the largest volume of national advertising in the country. Patent-medicine makers of all types and stripes had developed national advertising to tap the lucrative market composed of gullible Americans who had little faith in physicians. Compounds were advertised to correct fallen wombs, cure gonorrhea, and open the bowels. The advertising copy contained words that were taboo in editorial columns because of the mores of the time. Some compounds were harmless enough, but others were vicious cure-alls, containing a high proportion of morphine, thus contributing to drug addiction, and others were alcohol flavored with herbs. He set forth his reasoning:

> Really I did not expect and do not expect much permanent profitable circulation on account of our elimination of dirty advertising.
> Whatever is gained on this account will be considered by me as surplus gain over and above what I expected.
> Our real gain, I have thought, would be the result of better papers, better news-

[52] EWS to Robert F. Paine, Jan. 19, 1900.

papers, which better newspapers would result from our editors being emancipated from the labor of catering to such disreputables as are these dirty advertisers.

.   .   .   .

While we will always humbly solicit and gratefully accept the patronage of men of our own or higher morality, we are pretty sure, so long at least as I am in evidence, to act in a way very offensive to that class of people from whom are recruited the largest numbers of advertisers.

. . . We despise braggarts and blowhards.

What else under the sun is an advertiser? How can we do more than tolerate the patronage of many of these vulgar fellows?

So long as I wasn't strictly in it I didn't much mind that very close association that was growing up between our papers and the advertising public but when I got into it all over and found that not only were the advertisers running our business but the meanest and dirtiest of the class were the most in evidence, I revolted. [This was the beginning of the final clash between "Scrippsism" and "McRaeism."]

The most that an advertiser can expect from us is the privilege of buying so much space in our columns and any action of ours as self-puffery or as cowardly subordination to this advertising class can only work future evil, since it is only a question of time when we will either get out of the business or become very disagreeable business associates with advertisers.[53]

ADLESS NEWSPAPERS

Because of his antipathy toward advertising, Scripps long nursed a dream of finding some way to publish a newspaper profitably without advertising. If he could eliminate advertising entirely, as he saw it, he could produce a genuinely free press and set a model which any other newspaperman could follow in establishing a newspaper with a relatively small investment.

He made his first effort toward an adless newspaper with the Chicago *Press* in April, 1900, personally directing its formation on the scene. As circulation grew, he became enthusiastic about the potential success of a paper that would free itself from the "counter-jumping crowd," as he called the advertisers. But his plan exploded, for Hearst, who had dazzled San Francisco with the well-heeled *Examiner* and New York with the extravagant *Journal*, blared into Chicago with the *American*. Then engaged in costly litigation with James E. over the estate of George H., Scripps — the advocate of tight-fisted little papers — was not about to extend himself to the point of vulnerability in the contest with James E. by jousting at the moment with "the brainiest and best financially equipped exponent of show, splurge, and bigness." [54] He quietly folded the Chicago *Press*.

[53] EWS to Robert F. Paine, Mar. 14, 1900.
[54] EWS to EBS, June 3, 1900.

Gingerly, he next tested the adless prospect with the San Francisco *News* in 1903. Unwilling as yet to subsidize a paper, he temporized by restricting the *News* to ten columns of unsolicited advertising, hoping to eliminate the advertising altogether in time. But the earthquake and fire of 1906 disrupted the entire newspaper situation. In readjusting to changed conditions, his local managers broke ranks and sought advertising profits; Scripps yielded.

In the meantime, his determination to go full tilt at an adless newspaper was triggered by, of all things, the Salvation Army. Commander Booth-Tucker visited "Miramar," and told Scripps the Salvation Army's *War Cry* made a profit of $60,000 a year without advertising. "Those fellows have succeeded in doing just what I have always had a hankering to do. They are running a great and successful business without being assisted or trammeled by advertisers. . . . Some day or another I am going to try this non-advertising newspaper business myself." [55]

Before trying it, however, he had to have just the right man as editor. He found him in Vandercook of the Cincinnati *Post*. Beginning in 1905 Scripps began laying plans for the adless paper which Vandercook was to edit in New York, warning him to keep the whole project confidential, "as an inventor's secret." After the purchase of Publishers Press Association in 1906, Scripps met Vandercook and others in conference at "Miramar" to discuss the future of their three wire services, at which time Vandercook's name was put forward as news manager for a proposed single news service. At that Scripps balked, saying, "I have no other candidate to be the editor of the proposed new adless newspaper." Losing Vandercook seems to have been the only reservation Scripps had about forming the UP, but he intended to release Vandercook only long enough to get the UP going. In another "Miramar" conference in April, 1907, at which the UP was formed, Scripps spent an entire day outlining plans for the new adless paper. Vandercook's death the next year sidetracked the project. Scripps had no other editor for the job.

Soon, however, he identified his man in Negley D. Cochran, who was retiring as editor of the Toledo *News-Bee*. Regarding Cochran as the most courageous of all Scripps Ohio editors since his own day and that of Bob Paine, Scripps began active planning of the adless paper with Cochran in 1910.

Their plans eventuated in the Chicago *Day Book*, which Cochran ran as an experiment in journalism from 1911 to 1917. Scripps financed it with income from a $500,000 inheritance from George H. Cochran was limited to a budget of $2,500 per month, plus the cost of newsprint. Using no more newsprint than a regular 4-page paper, the *Day Book* was folded into a daily magazine of 32 pages, each page being 7⅞ inches long by 6⅛ inches

55 EWS to Robert F. Paine, Mar. 26, 1904.

wide. It sold for a penny. Cochran as editor ran it with a managing editor, business manager, and reporter. Personnel varied; one reporter was Carl Sandburg.

Contrary to his usual practice, Scripps kept a close directing hand on the paper through voluminous correspondence with Cochran. The paper started slowly, but gradually increased in circulation. Final success would be determined by a circulation of 30,000, for at that point the paper would be entirely self-sustaining. Through the first few years circulation inched upward. Later, a steady growth to 20,000 by August, 1915, caused Scripps to conclude the *Day Book* had demonstrated its soundness as a business proposition, and to predict its final success.

And then Scripps killed the *Day Book* in 1917, clouding his reasons in tangled thought lines and emotional conflict. Ostensibly, he ceased publication because of the war, which had caused a prohibitive increase in newsprint prices, and because he needed Cochran in Washington. But to intimates he said he had decided he and Cochran were too old to carry the paper through to success. Perhaps most important of all probable influences on his decision, he had accumulated a heavy weight of personal problems through grief over John's death in 1914, resentment at Nackey's elopement, and growing discord with his wife. An undertone in his correspondence suggests that he simply had lost interest in the *Day Book* but would not admit it. His behavior pattern in earlier years would suggest that the weight of his emotional tensions had once again left him "disgusted" — a word he often used to describe his feelings in such situations, an emotional tone that he seems on occasion to have generalized.

He offered a confused assessment of the experiment. On the one hand, he contended that he had demonstrated to his satisfaction that an adless newspaper could be made into a profit-paying property, *provided* one had the right man as editor. But, he conceded on the other hand, the man who could make an adless newspaper successful probably would be more valuable running a traditional newspaper. And then he contradicted himself: "The *Day Book* failed just because I and Cochran were not able to put it over." [56]

Whatever the reasons, and notwithstanding any and all rationalizations offered by Scripps and others, the *Day Book* must be reckoned a failure as an experiment in adless journalism.

In the meantime, he had in 1913 considered turning Pew's embattled Philadelphia *News-Post* into an adless paper, but killed it instead in 1914.

Scripps' associates revived the idea of an adless newspaper with the founding of the Washington *Daily News* by Scripps-Howard in 1921. The genesis of the Washington *Daily News* is to be found in Scripps' thinking as early as

[56] EWS to James G. Scripps, June 30, 1917.

1914, although the idea itself — an adless paper in Washington — seems to have come from Charles R. Crane, a businessman who was interested in the same sort of project and whose Chicago *Press* (not to be confused with Scripps' earlier paper of the same name) had been absorbed by the *Day Book* in 1914. The Washington *Daily News* came out originally as a twelve-page, penny tabloid, but eventually accepted advertising.

"THE CONCERN"

Scripps grouped his multitudinous newspaper operations into an amorphous entity called "The Concern" — an empire that hid the emperor from public view. It is not surprising that he was so successful in hiding his identity in this extended and intricate series of local partnerships, for only the Cleveland *Press* and Fresno *Tribune* bore his name in the publishing corporation's title. Other papers were published by corporations carrying the newspaper's name — Post Publishing Company in Cincinnati, Express Publishing Company in Denver, and so forth. He even erased his name from all letterheads about 1900. As a result, only newspapermen and knowledgeable laymen could know of E. W. Scripps as a newspaper magnate.

He denied that he was the Concern, but conceded that he was the spirit of the Concern. Whatever the amorphous concern might have been, Scripps looked upon his newspapers as an institution that had never purposely been directed toward financial success. At one point, he told Paine: "Our concern, Bob, does not belong to you and me and the others who, with us, have made it. It belongs to the people; it belongs to the future; it belongs to younger and stronger men than we are." [57] His conviction that his newspapers were a social institution was so strong that once, during the rift with Jim, the son asked whether the father thought more of his newspaper children than of his flesh-and-blood children. "I had to, in candor, frankly acknowledge that my newspapers were at least better worth thinking about, as their existence was far more significant in this world than my children, save as and excepting my children, or some of them, should be a worthy part of my newspapers." [58]

The Concern consisted of several groups of newspapers. The core had been the Scripps-McRae League, a name rather vaguely attached to the Scripps papers. But after Scripps in effect fired McRae in 1905, he never once referred to his operation as Scripps-McRae. Rather, he referred to it as the Concern, the Scripps institution, the Scripps system of newspapers, and the like.

The Scripps-McRae group included the Cleveland *Press*, Cincinnati *Post*

[57] EWS to Robert F. Paine, Sept. 29, 1908.
[58] EWS to EBS, Feb. 1, 1919.

and its adjunct the *Kentucky Post*, Columbus *Citizen*, Toledo *News-Bee*, Akron *Press*, and St. Louis *Chronicle*.

His lawyer, J. C. Harper, became interested in newspaper investment, and beginning in 1906 the Harper group came into existence: Denver *Express*, Pueblo *Sun*, Evansville *Press*, Terre Haute *Post*, Nashville *Times*, Memphis *Press, Oklahoma News*, and Dallas *Dispatch*.

The west-coast group, in which his principal major associates were W. H. Porterfield and B. H. Canfield, included the Seattle *Star*, Tacoma *Times*, Spokane *Press*, Portland *News*, Los Angeles *Record*, San Francisco *News*, Sacramento *Star*, San Diego *Sun*, Fresno *Tribune*, Berkeley *Independent*, and Oakland *Mail*.

In addition he was affiliated with yet another group of midwestern papers known as the Clover Leaf, although he had a controlling interest only in their Des Moines *News*, Kansas City *World*, both of which in some ways were tied in with Scripps-McRae, and the Omaha *News*. At one time, however, he anticipated that he could use NEA as a means of controlling the other Clover Leaf papers: St. Paul *Daily News*, Minneapolis *Daily News*, Duluth *Star*, St. Joseph *Star*, and the *Rural Weekly*. The dominant figures in the Clover Leaf were Will Kellogg, who had married brother Will's daughter, L. V. Ashbaugh, and B. D. Butler.

Naturally, the reach of such an organization varied from year to year. In 1915, for example, Scripps said he had a circulation of one million, and reached about three million through NEA and from one-fourth to one-third of all the people in the United States through the UP.[59]

Scripps worked without any sort of superstructure holding his varied enterprises together. He headed the whole organization, exercising control through subordinates and by making decisions based on the regular weekly and monthly reports that came to his desk.

When he fired McRae by making him chairman of the board in 1905, Scripps did effect some degree of consolidation, however. For instance, all his papers had not been served by one purchasing unit. Further, the Ohio papers operated as a unit in obtaining national advertising, but Porterfield, representing the west-coast papers, had to make annual trips east to get "foreign" advertising for those papers. Telling McRae that in the future they would use more of the league system of operations, Scripps formed a Foreign Advertising Bureau, which later became the National Advertising Department and is now the General Advertising Department, to serve all papers. He also formed the Newspaper Supply Company in 1907 to centralize purchasing, and it eventually became the present Scripps-Howard Supply Company.

[59] EWS to Secretary of the Interior Franklin K. Lane, Nov. 4, 1915.

Also upon McRae's retirement, Scripps formed what he called his "cabinet" — not to advise him on what to do but on how to do it. "I have decided what to do." [60] As of 1907, the cabinet was composed of Paine, Harper, L. T. Atwood, Jim, and John. Cochran's biography of Scripps says the first cabinet was composed of Ellen B., McRae, and Harper,[61] but Scripps' personal correspondence does not show the word "cabinet" until 1905. During the earlier years, however, he did leave considerable authority in the hands of, and place much reliance on, both McRae and Harper. Throughout his life, of course, his closest adviser was Ellen B.

In 1907 Scripps appointed Paine as his editorial secretary. The position seems to have been roughly analogous to that of a general editor-in-chief without portfolio. Scripps issued a general order "to whom it may concern," saying that Paine's requests for information should be read as emanating directly from Scripps himself. On a limited scale, Scripps also began using a system of editor-in-chief for regional or group papers.

Atwood, who ran the day-by-day business affairs of the Concern from the central office in Cincinnati, operated with the power of attorney, which Scripps had withdrawn from McRae in a huff. Atwood was secretary of several of the individual corporations, and extended that role to the extent required by central-office operations. He also was the connecting link between Scripps and the Clover Leaf, a post that Scripps regarded as more diplomatic than administrative.

Although Scripps personally supplied the only element of unity in the whole Concern, several other elements worked toward cohesion: annual conferences of editors; the central office; NEA; UP; Newspaper Supply Company; and the National Advertising Department.

Intending that his sons should be his successors, Scripps groomed them carefully for the job, but when personality clashes erupted, he became greatly concerned about the succession. Indeed, throughout his correspondence dealing with problems associated with the succession runs a thread strongly suggestive of a feudal prince arranging the succession so as to head off future revolts. Reportedly he said in 1915: "I have forged Excalibur. Who is strong enough to wield it when I am gone? Would it not be better to hurl it back into the waves?" [62]

He finally arranged for the future with the E. W. Scripps Trust which he had drawn by Newton D. Baker, who had been Secretary of War during World War I. Telling Baker that he regarded the Concern as a public trust and not as a property, he asked that Baker handle the matter just as he would have handled a public question while serving in President Wilson's

[60] EWS to Robert F. Paine, Mar. 29, 1905.
[61] Negley D. Cochran, *E. W. Scripps* (New York, 1933), p. 61 f.
[62] Gardner, *Lusty Scripps*, p. 59.

cabinet — without reference to Scripps' foibles, biases, friendships, or enmities, but with reference only to the good of the country. Working with Scripps as with Wilson, Baker should, he said, do the best thing possible for the present generation and generations yet unborn.[63] The trust set up under Scripps' will later was contested in court twice, but stood up each time.

Because of the rupture with Jim and disagreement with Jim's widow, Scripps lost the Seattle *Star*, Spokane *Press*, Tacoma *Times*, Portland *News*, Los Angeles *Record*, and Dallas *Dispatch*. In the meantime, the St. Louis *Chronicle* had been sold, and the Kansas City *World*, Fresno *Tribune*, Nashville *Times*, Berkeley *Independent*, and Oakland *Mail* killed.

Thus, the Scripps-Howard combination started out in 1922 with the Cleveland *Press*, Cincinnati *Post*, San Diego *Sun*, Akron *Press*, Des Moines *News*, San Francisco *News*, Toledo *News-Bee*, Columbus *Citizen*, Denver *Express*, Evansville *Press*, Terre Haute *Post, Oklahoma News*, Memphis *Press*, Houston *Press*, UP, NEA, and the various central-office operations.

Beginning in the early 1920's, under Scripps' goad, Scripps-Howard expanded by adding the newspapers already listed in the biographical introduction, but the depression of the 1930's and local conditions since World War II caused the suspension of some papers, consolidation of others, and other readjustments until as of mid-1965 Scripps-Howard included the Albuquerque *Tribune*, Birmingham *Post-Herald*, Cincinnati *Post and Times-Star* and its Kentucky edition, Cleveland *Press*, Columbus *Citizen-Journal, Rocky Mountain News*, El Paso *Herald-Post*, Evansville *Press*, Fort Worth *Press*, Indianapolis *Times*, Knoxville *News-Sentinel*, Memphis *Press-Scimitar*, Memphis *Commercial Appeal*, New York *World-Telegram and The Sun*, Pittsburgh *Press*, and Washington *Daily News*. It also embraces UPI, NEA, United Features Syndicate, three radio and two television stations.

SCRIPPS AND HEARST

Scripps' only competitor in developing a national newspaper chain (an offensive word to chain people, whether in foodstores or newspapers, who prefer "group") was William Randolph Hearst. The only point of similarity between them, aside from multiple ownership and their establishing of wire services, was that Hearst first made his basic appeal on the side of the underdog. But before many years passed, Hearst's sincerity became distrusted because of the sensationalism that marked his papers and what some considered to be the shallowness of his editorial pages. Where the Scripps organization has demonstrated a staying power, the Hearst organization has been cutting back steadily in recent years.

Scripps and Hearst were diametrical opposites. With cymbals clashing,

[63] EWS to EBS, Oct. 1, 1921.

Hearst took a town by frontal assault; Scripps infiltrated. To illustrate: Hearst's entry into New York journalism in 1895, a plunge that resulted in the competitive orgy known as yellow journalism, was described as having "all the discreet secrecy of a wooden-legged burglar having a fit on a tin roof." [64] Scripps preferred what he called a "still hunt," as in Los Angeles where he advised the *Record*'s managers to let the rivals huff and puff while the *Record* unobtrusively built up circulation, even if it meant denying to advertisers that circulation had increased; he desired that the opposition should "have no idea of the possibilities of penny journalism until I have got the field pretty well filled. . . ." [65]

In 1911 executives of the respective groups showed the contrast of methods: A Hearst executive said, "We want every man, woman, and child to know that Hearst is here." A Scripps executive said, "We want each of our subscribers to think he is the only subscriber." [66]

Will Irwin, in a muckraking series in *Collier's* in 1911, further contrasted the two publishers this way: He said Arthur Brisbane, Hearst's pre-eminent editorial writer, gave the Hearst papers a tone of "insincere sincerities," whereas Scripps — having learned that nothing is more profitable for a newspaper than truth — had "commercialized sincerity." [67]

A final evaluation of Scripps in journalism certainly is not to be found in comparing or contrasting the gravel-voiced titan of "Miramar" with the squeaky-voiced mogul of "San Simeon." But where is such a final evaluation to be found in one so full of contradictions, so facile of thought, so fertile of imagination, so prolific of ideas, so bold in experimentation, one whose associates invariably called him a genius?

Roy Howard simplified the problem when he said, "There is no journalistic slide rule to measure him by. He was unique." [68]

[64] Will Irwin, "The American Newspaper . . . The Fourth Current," *Collier's National Weekly*, Feb. 18, 1911, p. 17.

[65] EWS to Milton A. McRae, July 25, 1902.

[66] Will Irwin, "The American Newspaper . . . The New Era," *Collier's National Weekly*, July 8, 1911, p. 16.

[67] Will Irwin, "The American Newspaper . . . The Fourth Current," *Collier's National Weekly*, Feb. 18, 1911, p. 24; "The American Newspaper . . . The New Era," *Collier's National Weekly*, July 8, 1911, p. 16.

[68] Interview with editor, May 14, 1962.

The Germ of a Scripps Paper

[1915]

This selection was taken from Scripps' "Autobiography."

What is the fundamental principle and spirit of one of my newspapers?

It is everything that is human; it is nothing that is remarkable.

This principle, this spark of life and vitality and vigor, is a moral principle. As a whole body, my newspaper is as full of corruption, of weakness and immorality as is any human being. But despite the existence of these elements, there also exists the moral principle that I speak of. That moral principle is a spirit of protest. It is and always has been in evidence by reason of iconoclastic activity. If there is anything in it that is constructive, it is hardly discernible, even to me. So much of my newspaper work has been that of protest against what is, and of effort to destroy existing conditions, that there has been little time or energy to direct toward constructive work.

Against what has this spirit and activity of protest been directed?

It has been directed against all that is in social organization. As against the old thesis that "Whatever is, is right," I have set up the antithesis that "Whatever is, is wrong," and must be changed. Otherwise there can be no human progress; otherwise there can be only stagnation, inertia, and perhaps retrogression.

I have protested against the governmental system that had to be wrong because it was old, and [that] originated under old conditions of society, of material development or lack of development, and of ignorance of the science of today. I have protested against undemocratic government carried on under falsely named democracy.

I have protested against great usurpation of power on the part of the rich and the intellectual that is used to oppress the less fortunate.

I have protested against the inequality of opportunity.

215

I have protested against outworn theology and superstition, against old creeds that were almost universally repeated and proclaimed hypocritically by non-believers.

I have protested against all sorts of authority, save that exercised by a man for the sole purpose of benefiting mankind; against all authority that was not based upon the voluntary and present desire of those who submitted to it.

I have protested against all sorts of legislatures whose members obtained position by corrupt practices, by chicanery, by false pretenses.

I have protested most especially against the rule of the lawyer and the usurpation and oppressive use of the power of the courts, and against the claims of the courts to the sacredness of their office.

Thirty-five years ago, as a journalist I was as unformed, undeveloped, and plastic as a newborn babe. The spirit that moved me as a journalist, however, was the spirit of protest. It moved and exercised itself unconsciously, that is to say, unconscious of any purpose well-defined or even possible of definition. I had no end in view. I can almost say that I was absolutely deficient of any conscious or unconscious, general or particular, moral principles such as I recognize myself possessed of today.

I just grew by fighting, fighting because it is my nature to fight; and fighting that which, whatever it was, antagonized me. It was natural that I fought that which most antagonized me, although I did not for a long time stop to think what particular class of people and conditions were antagonistic to me. I resented authority, and as authority found itself in the hands of usurpers, I fought the usurpers, selfishly and egotistically, never recognizing, for a long time at least, that there was a real principle at stake, that there was anything else at stake excepting a personal victory. I hunted and fought instinctively, as the wolf and the lion and as the fish in the sea hunt and fight, because it was my nature as it is theirs to hunt and fight and devour prey.

Therefore it would be a mistake to suppose that a Scripps newspaper rests on any broad foundation of a large and well-ordered body of ethical principles.

Because I was a poor man and a workingman, and because I felt that in common with these other poor men and workingmen I had natural rights that were being trampled upon by richer, more intellectual men, I fought in the blind fury of resentment; I fought so furiously that I passed out of the ranks of the poor and oppressed and advanced well into those of my opponents, still cutting and still slashing, but still holding my own, preferring rather to remain alone in my own little circle than to join forces with the new men I had around me, as against my old associates, and refusing also to give up the spoils of my bow and spear to return to those I had left behind me, groveling in their slavery and their misery, grumbling much but daring not enough.

Just as I, a man, had found myself isolated, surrounded by a host of enemies that I chose to be enemies, courted by those whom I would not have as
friends, so has my newspaper organization advanced well into the ranks of
great and powerful corporations and combinations.

THE FUTURE OF THE ORGANIZATION

What has the future in store for me and my newspapers?

I cannot stand still and they cannot. Standing still means stagnation, tor-
pidity, disease, and death.

We might permit ourselves to be absorbed and to become a part of the
militant aristocracy, that little band of the few and mighty who stand holding almost all the world at bay while enjoying wrongly acquired possessions.

Not for long will we be allowed to occupy our position of splendid isolation. Not for long can we keep our hearts in sympathy with the slaves of
whom we are the champions, if we live in splendid palaces and feed around
princely tables. Already we have grown suspect of our followers and supporters. Already have our followers and our equals grown restive of our position among them and isolated from them. It is only a question of time, perhaps, when our position will be the hardest of all men's. We shall become
the common enemies of both contending forces. Capitalism will desire to destroy us, the disturbers of their peace; serfdom will recognize us as not of
their kind.

We must either fight on farther, or retreat and be destroyed as cowards,
and should be destroyed.

The whole press of the United States outside of the Scripps newspapers,
with very few exceptions — journals of comparatively little influence among
the governing classes — is now subject to and dominated by capitalism.

This press has, for the most part, been founded by men who, temperamentally unlike myself and my associates, were fit members of the army to
which they now belong. It has been possible for these papers to be absorbed
by capitalism without being destroyed as properties.

It is my conviction that it is impossible for us, even if we were willing, to
join the army of plutocracy, since the mere fact of our attempting to join
with these people would, by the destruction of our properties, eliminate
us from the capitalistic class. Our position might be likened to that of Cortez
in his invasion of Mexico; like that of Caesar who, landing in the island of
Britain, burned his ships behind him; that of Napoleon, who kindled the
flame of war in Europe and could only exist, being a soldier, so long as warfare continued.

We can only hold together, having supporting us the army of our followers, so long as we fight hard and win battles for them; so long as we fight
against privilege and successfully and by degrees transfer continually some

of the privileges of the few to the many. There is only battle ahead, and certain destruction behind. But it is my opinion that continual victory is as certain a result of fighting, as destruction is of retreat.

The political world of the United States is ripe for and prepared for change, revolutionary change, and it is only waiting for leadership that can organize, leadership that has the weapons and ingenuity, the capacity for stratagem and tactics of the dominant class, as well as the confidence of the great mass of the dispossessed. This is a time for great men, for brave men, and for men who know how. This is an opportunity for the Scripps papers and the Scripps army of men to do great deeds.

This institution, in the hands of a man or of men strong and powerful, and devoted to that principle which forms the germ of its original existence, can become a mighty instrument for progress and for the improvement of mankind.

Scripps' Advice to a New Editor

[*1911*]

This is a composite of two documents, an account written by Paul C. Edwards [69]
in which the full text of Scripps' letter has been interpolated, taken from his
Letterbooks.

Edwards, born at Knightstown, Indiana, in 1882, was educated at Stanford
and began his newspaper career on the San Francisco News *in 1908. He became*
managing editor of the Dallas Dispatch *in 1910, edited the Houston* Press *from*
1911 to 1916, and then edited the Dispatch *again until 1919. He served as*
editor-in-chief of the Scripps-Howard southwestern group from 1919 to 1922
and in a similar post on the West Coast from 1922 to 1931, during part of which
time he was editor of the San Diego Sun. *He ended his career with Scripps-*
Howard as associate editor of the San Francisco News.

The first time I saw E. W. Scripps was in 1908 when I was city editor of the
San Francisco *News.* That was just two years after the great earthquake and
fire of 1906. The city still was in ruins and the streets littered with ashes,
powdered mortar, and horse dung from the four-horse teams of the drays
that did all the trucking in those days. Winds swept clouds of this mixture
up and down the streets. The *News* had built a new, one-story building on
Ninth Street near Folsom to replace the building that had been destroyed by
the fire. The door of the editorial room opened right onto the street and when
it was opened a gust of dust-laden air almost invariably swept in. One mid-
day this door was flung open and a strange apparition came in with the cloud
of dust.

He was a man of better than medium height, wearing a linen duster showing grease spots and a cap that was equally in need of the laundry. His dark
trousers were stuffed into knee-high boots that were dusty and well worn.

He strode to the middle of the room and shouted, "Where's Bill Pierce?"

[69] Letter to editor, Feb. 21, 1962.

I was sitting at my desk and motioned to the door of the composing room. Pierce was composing-room foreman.

The apparition, with no further word, flung open the composing-room door and repeated his query, "Where's Bill Pierce?"

Pierce came running, greeted the visitor gladsomely, and for fifteen minutes the two leaned over an imposing stone, chatting with animation and evident enjoyment. Then, as suddenly as he had appeared, he left, without so much as a goodbye.

As he went out, I had a less startled look at him. His face was adorned with a scraggly, brownish beard, he held a half-smoked cigar in his mouth, the suit under the linen duster was obviously tailor-made and of excellent quality. One eye was cocked in a manner that gave his expression a kind of leer, but his glance was penetrating.

When the street door slammed behind him, I dashed into the composing room and asked Bill Pierce, "Who in hell was that guy?"

"Why," said Bill, "didn't you know? That was E. W. Scripps, the owner of this joint!"

Not until three years later did I see E. W. again. That was in May, 1911, when I went to "Miramar" to see him as the prospective editor of a new Scripps paper at Houston, Texas. Here I must digress to tell how I happened to be chosen for that assignment. I had gone to work on the *News* after four years at Stanford University. I had switched from the *News* staff to take a job in the United Press bureau in San Francisco at the behest of Roy Howard, who had begun his newspaper career in Indianapolis, Indiana, at precisely the same time as I when we were selected to be high school correspondents for the Indianapolis *News*.

Robert F. Paine, former editor of the Cleveland *Press*, had retired and was living in San Francisco. He couldn't stay away from printers ink and came to the *News* office every day. A task he assigned himself was to condense the entire UP report into a column of three- and four-line paragraphs. One day he came to me and showed me a telegram. It was from one of his "boys," as he called a number of young fellows who had worked for him in later years. The sender was Alfred O. Andersson. He asked Paine to recommend someone for a job on the staff of the Dallas *Dispatch*.

"Want the job?" Bob asked.

I thought it over a little and then said "yes," not revealing that one of the most moving considerations in my decision was that I had a college sweetheart in Fort Smith, Arkansas, just an overnight train ride from Dallas. So I went to Dallas and formed an association with Andersson that eventuated into his recommending me as the founding editor of a new paper in Houston. By that time I was managing editor of the Dallas *Dispatch* at $35.00 a week. The editorship of the proposed new paper was to pay $25.00 per week. I had wed my Fort Smith sweetheart in the meantime, and a competence of $25.00 a week presented problems to a newly married couple, even in those days.

Andersson thought I should go out to see E. W. before starting in Houston. At first, E. W. was reluctant to agree, because, for several years, because of his health, he had refused to consider any specific problems of the concern. Matters had to be laid before him in purely hypothetical terms shorn of personalities and details. But he finally consented, and my wife and I took the train for San Diego. In view of my first encounter with him it is not hard to imagine my nervousness when we arrived at "Miramar" and I was about to "beard the lion in his den."

We were received cordially and hospitably by Mrs. Scripps. It seemed they had the impression at the ranch that we were a newly married couple combining our honeymoon with the trip. We were assigned a large bedroom with bath and a Japanese boy to look after our every want.

My first meeting with Mr. Scripps was at dinner that evening. He spoke to me in a kindly fashion and shook hands. I noted that his handshake was very limp. He sat at the head of a long table, his wife at the right. We did not know all the others at the table and were not introduced. After we finished eating, all the others withdrew, and E. W. asked me to remain. Before leaving Houston, I had steeped myself in facts about the city — its history, its government, its economics, etc., so I was ready for the quiz that followed. He shot questions at me in rapid fire order. I thought I fielded them pretty well. Presently, he dismissed me.

"Be at my office at nine o'clock in the morning," he said.

He was at his desk when I entered the office at 9 A.M. "Take this chair," he commanded, indicating a comfortable seat at one end of the desk. He picked up a paper and glanced at it. I didn't know until later that it was a brief biographical sketch of me which Andersson had sent him.

"I see," he said, "that you spent the best four years of your life up at the so-called university, Stanford, run by that old charlatan, David Starr Jordan." I made no reply. "I see also that you claim to be a self-made young man. I want to tell you that your background has been aristocratic, your experience with the so-called upper classes. You have not had to earn your living with your hands. And until you divest yourself of the ideas the sort of life you have led has instilled in your mind, you cannot hope to be a successful Scripps editor."

Well, this was a pretty brutal start. I wondered if I were going to be dissected in this manner all morning. I decided it was not for me to start an argument with the great man, so I held my peace. Later I learned this was a disappointment. He was trying my mettle and found it wanting. He must, however, have read something in my expression, possibly shock, because a little smile came into his face, he lighted a cigar, and leaned back in his chair.

Then he began talking, only occasionally directly to me, and for the ensuing two and a half hours I sat rapt by what he was saying. He began by reviewing his early days with his half brother in Detroit, how he began formulating his newspaper philosophy, how ultimately he decided to have a newspaper of his own and how he went about gratifying that ambition. Then he told about starting the Cleveland *Penny Press* and the great success he had in building circulation. I could see he was still proud of that record, and I was to wonder later if he derived some satisfaction out of learning that the Houston *Press*, in its first year, came nearest equaling that record than any other paper that had been started. [Scripps did, indeed. He said only the Cleveland and Houston papers had been the exception to the rule that it took three years to establish a paper by the Scripps method.]

From telling about Cleveland he launched into a general discussion of the growth of the whole concern — how he formed an association in Cincinnati with Milton A. McRae. He talked very frankly about McRae, as he did about all the other men who had become prominent in the Concern. And he spoke just as frankly about himself, his weaknesses as well as strengths, his mistakes and disappointments. Through it all ran the thread of his philosophy and his newspaper principles. When noon came he dismissed me rather brusquely. I suppose I had not spoken as many as a hundred words all morning.

"Be back here at nine o'clock in the morning," he said and walked out.

At luncheon Mrs. Scripps was not in her accustomed seat. "Where's Ma?" he asked, and was informed she had been out with the new ostler. [She was a horsewoman.]

Presently, she came in. "How was the new man?" he demanded.

"I thought he did very well," Mrs. Scripps replied.

"Does he know how many paces to ride behind?" her husband inquired peremptorily, and was assured he did.

After lunch he asked if I would like to look over the ranch. Of course I was glad to. In a car with a chauffeur we drove for an hour or so. He showed me with some pride the roads and dams he had built on the place, and particularly the orange orchard.

"They told me," he said, "that I could never raise oranges on this place. So I blasted out holes with dynamite, filled them with good soil hauled in from elsewhere and planted my trees. You see, I raised oranges."

I was told later that after the first crop he lost interest. He had refuted the advice given him. During our trip around the ranch he was kindly and understanding, apparently appreciative of my interest. After dinner that evening we chatted pleasantly for a few minutes.

Then he went out into the colonnade around the patio, yelling, "Ma, oh,

Ma, where are you? Come on." Mrs. Scripps read to him every evening on account of his poor eyesight.

Next morning at nine o'clock he began where he had left off the day before, and talked without pause until noon. He analyzed the respective abilities of his sons James and John and paid his uncomplimentary respects to the professors who were running what is now the Scripps Institution of Oceanography, which he and his sister Ellen had largely financed.

"My son Bob (who was then of high school age) could do a better job of operating that place than they do," he said.

His commentaries on the Concern brought things pretty well down to date, and I began to think he was through. But at noon he ordered me to be back in the office at nine the next morning.

In the intervals while I was talking with him, Mrs. Scripps was very nice and friendly to Mrs. Edwards. The ranch was run pretty much like a business or hotel. People were going and coming all the time, the servants were busy with many duties.

On the third morning I took my usual place beside his desk, but instead of beginning again to talk to me he called his secretary. I thought I was about to hear him dictate his morning correspondence.

However, he began, "Take this letter."

[*Scripps then dictated the following letter in Edwards' presence, a fairly common practice with him.*]

"Miramar," Calif., May 20, 1911

Mr. Paul C. Edwards
"Miramar," Calif.

My dear Mr. Edwards:

There is about to be born a new Scripps newspaper, and it is proposed that you are to be its editor.

You have come to me to learn something of my general policies and fundamental principles of journalism as well as to seek particular advice on the subject of this enterprise.

From what you tell me there is to be a comparatively large number of stockholders. I think that this division of ownership and the large number of stockholders, each one having his own peculiar aims and opinions, is a handicap.

No one person has so large an interest in the new paper as to offer exceeding great reward for success or to make final failure unendurably painful.

Such of the stockholders as are named are of two classes: One class — those who have money — can afford to lose their 'prorata' in case of failure, and those of the other class have nothing to lose except their time. I presume you are the only one in this latter class.

Of course, while you have little or nothing to lose by failure, you have a tremendous amount to gain by success. By succeeding, and making your 10 per cent of the stock worth anything, you must make it worth from $10,000 to $20,000. The great advantage to you of this would be that it would be a first and very substantial step on the road to financial independence, and to a certain extent will make you a capitalist. It will remove you from the ranks of the great majority of newspapermen who have no other status than that of wage-earners.

However, the greatest advantage you could gain will be — in case of the success of the newspaper — that you have demonstrated that you are one of the very, very few men who have real ability as an editor. Of all the vast army of journalists in this country perhaps only a small fraction of 1 per cent of them have ever proved (perhaps by reason of lack of opportunity) that they are really fit for any other position than that of hired men.

You are twenty-nine years old now. In one year — if you are a man of the first order — you might have a successful paper, but if in two years, or even in three years, you succeed in establishing your paper as a profit-paying concern, and gaining the confidence and respect of the community and establishing yourself as a worthy member of the newspaper association to which you belong, you may well enough expect to go far in the way of becoming an important influence in the country and a man of considerable personal wealth.

My advice to you is that you shall consider all of your fellow stockholders, and especially those who are strong enough to actually dominate the control of the newspaper, both in its editorial and business policy. It will not be safe or wise for you to follow my individual advice unless the same is fully sanctioned by the controlling element in your association. I warn you that you must consider the real character of these men. While you might in the beginning obtain their consent to any line of policy, and while you might be allowed for a considerable length of time to pursue such line of policy, you must always hold in mind that the condition of the minds of these men and their attitude will be radically changed at some future point of time — at the time when your non-success, or apparent non-success, will show up strongly or at the time when your success will be such that the stockholders of this paper will regard it as being a valuable property. Your associates may be very willing to let you go on finding your own way, playing your own game with this paper so long as it is purely experimental, and so long as it has not determined any real intrinsic value. But when the property becomes a property and is valued as such by its stockholders, every man among you will make it his business to protect his own interest by maintaining the value or increasing the same. Young journalists and young journalistic institutions are naturally honest and fearless. It is only when they are far advanced and have a more or less considerable capital stake that mind-corrupting influences begin their work.

My advice to you is to start right and to keep going on right, and that your own greatest effort should be to avoid temptation. In other words, so conduct your paper that never at any one time will you be tempted to color in the least possible particular your editorial policy for the purpose of maintaining the patronage of advertisers. I have found it infinitely more easy to resist the temptation to do cowardly and crooked work for the purpose of getting a new patron than it is to resist the temptation of doing the same thing for the purpose of maintaining patronage that I have already got.

Therefore, I would advise you to consider the majority of the advertisers that you have a prospect of getting as being your enemies. Right from the start deal with the advertiser as an individual and with the whole class of advertisers in such a way that you will never get any of their patronage as a result of his or their individual or collective goodwill. The only kind of advertising that your paper can afford to receive or that any young paper can afford to receive is that which results from the commercial instinct and the selfish promptings of the customer. You want no man's advertising who can, as a purely business proposition, refrain from patronage.

I warn you against allowing your advertising business to grow too rapidly.

I have told you that while many of the new papers that have been added to our concern, by foundation or purchase, since the early days of my career, have, in respect to volume of business — that is to say, cash receipts — grown more rapidly than did those papers that were founded in the early days and were more or less directly under my personal and daily supervision and oversight; not one of these papers have in their early days grown in circulation and in influence in their communities even half as rapidly as did the Detroit *News*, Cleveland *Press*, and Cincinnati *Post*.

I believe the reason for this has been that the young men who have been engaged in the founding and building up of these new papers have regarded them as purely business institutions — as commercial ventures.

For myself, both in those early days and even up to the present time, I have never regarded a newspaper in any such light. It is true that eagerly enough I sought for increasing revenue and that I have also been determined always to make my papers profitable; that is to say, independent and self-sustaining. But my purpose in doing this has been solely that of seeking means for making my papers largely read and hence influential.

One thing, and only one thing, in a business way have I ever considered as of very great importance and that was the growth of my newspapers in circulation, the development of their character as influential organs of public opinion being proved by this growth.

Naturally, as I concentrated all my efforts on the one object of obtaining circulation and dissipated no part of my energy in acquiring revenue from advertisers, I had to be, and was, successful in rapidly building up circulation.

While there have been other reasons for my always desiring a small newspaper, my chief reason has been that there is a large profit in the small or little newspapers while there was small profit or no profit, or actual loss, in the sale of large sheets, and therefore both as editor and as owner I had the inducement to sell as many papers as possible and my business managers, because they must of necessity be commercially minded, have themselves been anxious to increase the circulation because there was a profit in such increase.

Given a large paper, whether there was little or no profit or actual loss in the sale of the paper, the business office and even the editor himself is compelled to look to the development of the advertising business to secure funds not only to pay a profit from but meet running expenses. In fact the smaller the circulation—providing the advertising public could be kept in ignorance —the larger the profit would be. Therefore, on large papers the whole effort of the counting room has been to obtain advertising, and even when they have made an effort to obtain circulation it has been only for the purpose of extending its billboard space or the price to be charged for the same. Necessarily, the editors have been compelled to take a similar view and act accordingly.

As I said, you want to avoid temptation. I consider a small paper as one of the very best guards and guarantees against temptation to any evil practices of commission or omission.

I would advise that you use your influence to get your associates to, in the beginning at least, abstain from all expenditure on account of advertising. I would even advise against putting in any advertising type to start with at least, and I would not have an advertising solicitor or permit any man to solicit advertising in the beginning.

The most that I would do would be to make an announcement in your paper (perhaps keeping it standing) that whenever you had a circulation that would warrant your demanding an advertising rate of, say, thirty cents per inch you would open your columns to advertisers and solicit business, but that before that time you would prefer to receive no advertising patronage whatever.

I would advise you to use your influence to have the paper started as though there was no desire or expectation of ever taking advertising at all. Have your office organized to begin with strictly for the purpose of making a newspaper that the people want to read and getting it well circulated.

The economies that would result from this course would, I believe, during the first year of your existence fully equal all the possible income from advertising during the same period of time, so that the first cost of founding your paper would be no greater as the result of your spending nothing and getting nothing on account of advertising.

Then before the time shall have come for you to solicit advertising you would have created a personality for your paper and established all of its principles so that every advertiser whose patronage you should thereafter obtain would come to you with his business well knowing that you were independent and resourceful and that he would have no possible reason for hoping or expecting to influence your editorial course by his patronage.

You must remember that that particular class of men that make up the advertisers are men of extremely sordid minds. Their lives are given up to dollar-getting. They presume that every man is equally sordid. They presume —and they have a perfect right in this country to presume—that newspaper publishers are venal and that they have but one object in view and that is to obtain advertising patronage and make a profit. Every new newspaper is regarded with suspicion by the business public. No really intelligent advertiser would waste much money in patronizing a newspaper venture that may — and probably will — eventually fail. The vast majority of newspapers founded do fail and go out of business.

The principal cause for patronage of a new newspaper, I have found by past experience, is that while the advertisers regard any new newspaper as a venture that will probably fail, they also recognize the possibility of such a new paper being a success, and some of them, more crafty than the others, are prone to cast an anchor to leeward by patronizing (using the word in the most contemptible sense) a new newspaper in order that in case of its future success such early patronage may put them in a position to demand special favors and consideration on account of their presumed friendly acts during the trying days of the beginning of the new paper.

I really do not know what your own personal views are on many subjects. You tell me that as a whole you like and admire the policies of the Scripps papers. As the principal owner of these papers I am going to tell you that there is much in the management and conduct of our papers that is contemptible in the extreme. While they are to a certain extent independent, it is noticeable that their independent dealing with public questions is in direct proportion to the amount of business interests involved. They are often very independent in dealing with questions when advertisers will not resent their actions in so doing. Where the advertisers are either indifferent or divided in their opinions they can be, and are, very radical.

I would advise you to begin your course as editor of this paper with one object and only one object in view and that is to serve that class of people and only that class of people from whom you cannot even hope to derive any other income than the one cent a day they pay you for your paper. Be honest and fearless with them, always without regard to the goodwill or the ill will of the so-called business community.

As a man of experience in these affairs, and one having perhaps many times more experience than any other man has ever had, I will tell you that it is absolutely certain in the end that you will get far more patronage and far better patronage from the advertisers by taking this course than you can possibly hope to get by any exhibition of flunkyism. It is the weak man who really admires the great athlete. It is the rascal who has the highest opinion of the gentleman. It is the sordid, money-making businessman that courts and fawns on the man with a newspaper that appears to be or that actually is influenced by higher motives.

In time, if you succeed in getting a circulation, advertising patronage will come to your paper. When it does, remember that in all Scripps papers the editor, and the editor alone, is responsible for every line of matter in the paper — advertising as well as news and editorial matter. He, and he alone, therefore can shape the business policy of the paper. The advertising patronage of any Scripps newspaper is that, and only that, which the editor of our papers chooses it to be.

When you come to dealing with the advertisers, as a matter of business policy, I advise you never to accept from any one advertiser so large an amount of custom that, if he should withdraw his patronage, it would materially affect your receipts or even your profits. The advertiser is the enemy. The big advertiser is the mortal foe of honest journalism. I would rather go through a dark alley with a thug than to couple up, in a business way, as a young newspaperman, with a big advertising patron.

It is customary and imbecile with the general newspaper business manager to seek to get the patronage of large advertisers; that is to say, of advertisers who use a large amount of space, and it is no less imbecile, of course, that lower rates per inch are given for a large amount of space than for small amounts. Ten dollars a month received from ten advertisers is a far better asset to a newspaper than the patronage of one man that gives you twenty dollars a month. Hence, the smaller the advertiser the more desirable his business and the lower his rate should be.

Remember another thing — that the big men of the future are the small businessmen of today, and that the big businessmen of today are generally approaching the end of their careers. As a young man and as a young newspaper you and your paper should keep your eyes continually on the future. The men whose patronage is going to be of great worth to your paper in the future are the so-called little fellows in business today, and the men who have but small amounts of money to spend for advertising.

But as editor of the paper it would perhaps be better almost that you should ignore even the existence of an advertiser except as a necessary and disagreeable intruder into your columns.

I would advise you, especially during the period of time when you will be engaged in building up the circulation of your paper, that you should not even think of the future when the advertising patronage of your paper will be an element in your business.

Speak your mind — or rather write it — freely on every and any subject. Don't be afraid of damning a bad Jew because he is a Jew. Treat men connected with any other religious sect in the same way. What is good, praise. What is evil, condemn.

I do not here advise you to set yourself up as a universal judge and arbiter of affairs in your city. That would be foolish. This is a democracy: We are bound to, both of us, accept the rule of the majority. As an editor you must keep your ear to the ground.

You must know what the majority of your people think is right and if you disagree with the majority it is not your province to take a club to them but it is your business rather to persuade them to your way of thinking if you can, but always evincing a willingness and even a desire to voice public opinion. This is pure demagoguery, but I want to tell you that pure demagoguery is pure democracy, and that you need suffer no shame on account of [it] either.

While you are a poor man and have been a poor and struggling boy, you must not forget that all your training and association has been by and with the aristocrats, intellectual or financial.

As the editor of this paper you must, in order to succeed, strip yourself of all the vanities of your class and be not only able but glad to be one in the ranks of the vulgar masses.

You cannot deliver a message to the masses from an elevated pulpit or dais; it is only by standing on the same level with these men that you can appreciate their sufferings and aid them in their efforts.

You may be, and probably are — most men are cowards — something of a coward; at least very timid, but whether you are frightened or not you must act the part of a courageous man. It takes courage to found a paper. It takes more courage than most men have got. Sometimes I think that courage is even more necessary than is either intelligence or honesty in conducting a newspaper.

A drunken bully with a pistol in his hand may terrorize a whole community of which the main portion may have more real courage than the bully himself. But the man with the gun who gives evidence that he is ready to kill any man that opposes him is the man that the community fears.

A fearless editor has in his paper a more powerful weapon than any pistol. If he has courage as well as a good conscience he can safely defy any man or any combination of men in any community.

Be diplomatic, but don't be too damned diplomatic. Most men fear to speak the truth, the bald, whole truth, to any man or community because they fear that such men in the community are not prepared to endure such frankness. I think this is a mistake. It is rare indeed when the circumstances are such that a conscientious man can lose anything by fearless, frank speech and writing.

Sincerely yours,
E. W. Scripps

For an hour and a half I sat listening to him dictate the letter which was subsequently filed among his disquisitions. [It was filed in the Letterbooks, not with the disquisitions.] It was a summary of all that he had told me the two previous days about his ideas of journalism and the operation of his newspapers.

When he finished, he said, "See that Mr. Edwards is furnished the top copy of that letter before he leaves 'Miramar.' "

Then he turned to me. "Edwards," he said, "you are welcome to stay around here as long as you want, but I am through with you and I don't want to see anything more of you. I haven't worked so hard in years as I have with you these past three days and I am exhausted. It will take me weeks to recover. Now goodbye."

The letter was duly delivered to me that day, and literally clutching it to my breast as a prize, I left "Miramar" with Mrs. Edwards immediately. As we journeyed back to Dallas I could not help reflecting upon my unique experience and making some estimate of the remarkable character with whom I had spent three most important days of my life. I was a little disturbed by the remoteness of this man from the people to whom he had dedicated his life and his resources. There he was on his ranch like a potentate, master of all he surveyed, seeing only those he wanted to see. He had no close friends; when he traveled he was obliged on account of the sensitivity of his nerves to isolate himself from all except his retinue, yet there he was in his retreat, the ruler of an empire whose purpose he had dedicated to bettering the lot of the workingman.

There seemed to be an anachronism here and it troubled me for awhile, but the more I thought upon it the more convinced I became that he was sound and sincere in his principles, that he believed in the rightness of his purpose and that he was, indeed, a friend of the people, a democrat in the true sense of the word.

So I went to Houston some months later to start the *Press* [September 25, 1911] firm in my intention to carry out his ideas to the fullest possible extent. And I did. It is to that fact and not to any ability I might have had that I ascribe the success of the paper in its early years.

Principles That the N.E.A.
Should Stand For

[*September 24, 1907*]

"Miramar," Calif., September 24, 1907

To the Directorate
of the Newspaper Enterprise Association

Gentlemen:

I favor the appointment of W. B. Colver as a new general manager of the Newspaper Enterprise Association — Marlen Pew should remain as managing editor of the same until Colver shall have tested his own ability and that of Pew.[70]

I wish to have a personal interview with Colver soon after his taking office.

I desire him to personally visit and become acquainted with the young papers of our organization, especially those of the West and extreme South.

I feel that he will not eventually succeed unless he is thoroughly permeated with the spirit of the new generation of newspapers and unless he succeeds in conducting the N.E.A. from the standpoint of those newspapers and those sections of the country in which they exist.

In my interview with Colver I propose to impress upon his mind the necessity of his adhering to certain general principles and certain details.

The primary aim and object of the N.E.A., like that of our newspapers, is to serve the great majority of the nation, namely, that class that are not possessed of wealth. The manager of the N.E.A. is never to consider economic questions from the standpoint of the stockholders of the different newspapers. That is to say, he is not to conduct the N.E.A. for the purpose of profit — for the purpose of getting copy for our newspapers at a cheaper price than

[70] With considerable editing, part of this disquisition appears in McCabe, *Damned Old Crank*, p. 142 f.

that ordinarily paid by newspapers for copy. In fact, the profit value of the product of the N.E.A. being purely an incidental item, it is not to be considered by the manager of the N.E.A. at all.

The object of the N.E.A. is not to get copy cheap; it is, in fact, to get copy so costly as to be out of the reach of any individual newspaper member of the N.E.A.

We have created the N.E.A. for the purpose of spending large sums of money in the direction of benefiting the common people of the country.

While the N.E.A. must of necessity have become a great news-gathering association, it is not our object to displace by its product the product of the telegraph news association, or the local reportorial staff, or the state or section special telegraphic correspondence.

In its news-gathering capacity, it is to collect those articles of information which lie outside of the field and beyond the scope of the ordinary "get-copy-quick" agencies. The field of news-gathering for the N.E.A. will be largely the North American continent, and still more largely the territory of the United States.

Its mission in a news-gathering way is to present to the people of all of the communities in which we have membership all of the news of all the country, so that the readers of our newspapers will, to a certain extent, become less provincial and more national, and to some extent more cosmopolitan.

Besides being a news-gathering institution, the N.E.A. will be something else, something that I desire it to be, something even more and greater, namely, a great leader and criticizer, if not molder, of public thought. To state this more simply, I would say its editorial department is to be more important than its news department.

But if the Newspaper Enterprise Association is to mold public thought, in what form, it may be asked, shall it mold it?

I desire it to mold public opinion, or criticize the same, in some of the following ways.

1. Thrift is not the greatest of virtues.

Great wealth is not a blessing either to a nation or to an individual. Capital is a danger; large capital is never acquired by individuals as a result of perfectly fair play.

Capitalists must exist, but the danger of their existence can be minimized by constant attacks and public ill will. Keep the capitalist busy defending what he has got, and the very activity enforced upon him makes him a better citizen and more considerate a neighbor and employer. Capitalists resting secure behind the fortifications of ancient and obsolete, or modern, corruptly obtained laws, become vicious, arrogant, and harmful alike to themselves and the community.

2. The nation and the people of the United States as individuals are too rich to be healthy and strong, either as a nation or as individuals. The wealth of the nation creates envy and invites attack from foreign foes, while it enervates the people and makes them less capable of resisting such attacks.

3. Whether the people of the nation desire it or not, the United States must be a warlike nation; it must fight and conquer or be conquered. The Pacific Ocean alone divides Western and Eastern civilization, the old and the new races. For centuries to come the great wars of the world will be fought on the shores of the Pacific Ocean, and the United States' western boundary is the frontier presented by Western civilization to an enviable and mighty foe. The battles of the future are to be fought with the Pacific Coast ports as the bases of operation of all the great future wars. Our people should not be taught to hope for, much less to expect, international peace, since, if they entertain such thoughts, they are destined to not only a rude and shocking awakening, but a very early experience of this sort. The United States must be the most warlike of nations, or cease to exist as a nation and a republic. It should be our duty, through the N.E.A., to arouse in the minds of all the people in the nation a full comprehension of this inevitable war in order that the people may prepare for it.

4. The battles of the Pacific and the wars of the future will be naval. Unless the United States can dominate the Pacific, it must be conquered by Asiatic peoples. Naval warfare is less horrible and less expensive, both directly and indirectly, than land warfare.

The United States must have the most powerful navies of all the seas, powerful in equipment, and more powerful in the selection and training of efficient men.

Naval officials and the rank and file of the fighting men on board the ships must be selected from the best material the country affords, and this can only be accomplished by their enjoying the very greatest rewards for service, financially and socially. The people of the United States should be so well instructed as to conditions as to understand this so that the time may soon come when, instead of its being difficult for the nation to obtain recruits for service in the Navy and to keep the same after enlistment, appointments in the Navy should be so coveted that all but the most efficient and most patriotic of our citizens could be eliminated.

5. New brooms sweep cleanest. No great harm to the nation, and hence the vast majority of its citizens, would be suffered by the elimination by lawful process of the wealth and privileges of the present plutocratic governing classes. France lost nothing and gained much by the elimination of the old regime and the bloody terror of France was a health-giving surgical opera-

tion. The people of the United States should proceed by lawful ways, and the people of the United States should be taught that there are perfectly lawful and proper and moral ways of ridding themselves of their present masters. Old laws that protect wealth and property improperly acquired or uselessly employed can be substituted in this democracy by laws that will work no such evils.

The people of the United States should be taught that there should be a revolution in the country, a lawful revolution, a revolution by laws, and they should be taught how best to obtain this revolution.

6. Organized labor is an effort in this direction. Organized labor is not socialistic, though it cunningly but unconsciously trades on socialism. There is more room for individualism in labor unionism than in any form of democracy yet invented. But the individualism of labor unionism is a different kind of individualism. It is a healthier individualism. Individualism is understood by the purely commercial or capitalistic class as only one form, and a low form, of individualism. Its one expression is the right of every man to get richer than his neighbor. The individualism of labor unionism is the individualism of real democracy. In labor union organizations, men obtain position of power and influence not as they do in our present commercial republic, by mere possession of wealth, but by force of character and intellect and by the greater force and the nobler one of justice and goodwill toward their fellows.

7. The possession of wealth, no matter how much, whether it be greater than a competency or only a competency, whether it consists of land and goods, of money in bank, or paid up or partially paid up insurance policy, weakens every man that has such possessions, makes him a more selfish man, a more timid man, a man less apt to be a soldier, a man enslaved by the greater capitalism and the greater capitalists of his fellows. Life insurance is not only the greatest of modern vices, but it is the most costly. The husband and father who insures his life eventually imagines that he is securing the future of his widow and children, and is therefore less alert and less bound by necessity to protect his wife and children by the most obvious and most necessary of all means, the teaching and the training of the children to be self-supporting. The system is costly because there is no form of thrift wherein the money paid into the investment brings so small a return.

Life insurance is the scheme and the design of the most crafty capitalistic class to get the largest possible share of the laborer's wage at the least possible cost.

I would have the N.E.A. thoroughly exploit and develop those ideas.

8. The American people have the modern vice of all people, to a greater extent than any other people: They think more of the present, of their own

immediate lifetime existence, than any other people have ever done. Hence, they are more improvident as a race. They consume a small part and waste a larger part of the inheritance of their children and their children's children.

The spirit of race is naturally strong, but not strong enough to overcome modern chaotic social conditions. Self-preservation is the first law of nature, and the propagation of species is the second.

Our children and our children's children will have to encounter perhaps the greatest struggle for existence that has ever been encountered by any people. All of our legislation and all of our stewardship of natural resources should be undertaken with this idea in view. [Theodore] Roosevelt has sounded a note of warning and the people's respectful attention and appreciation of his acts prove that the people will only need to be reminded of their duty in order to perform it. Our N.E.A. should never lose sight of this cause.

9. That great and useful institution, the public school, including all of its forms, from the kindergarten to the university, has become a national abuse.

What are we teaching our children, and by whom are we having them taught, and for what purpose? The children of a nation of some 80 million people are all being taught the same thing, when no two of them will have the chance to make use of the same information or even the kind of information, beyond that of the most rudimentary character.

What are we doing for our school children physically? Their long hours in school, their unnatural employment in youth, and their whole hygienic treatment are destroying the greater part of what would be otherwise a physical excellence. Our boys are hardier, but through our girls we are destroying the larger half of a possible population and crippling to a very great extent the remainder.

Our American women are less fitted for motherhood and less fertile than any other women the world has known save that of a few small classes of ancient Greece and Rome.

Through the N.E.A. we should at least inform the readers of our newspapers, the fathers and mothers of this and the next generation, just what the effect of school life is and the physical condition of the boys and girls.

The original American stock is already in a process of decay and degeneration, both in numbers and in quality.

There is every reason to believe that a similar condition will be revealed in the descendants of the present American stock unless it be we reform a much-lauded institution, the public school.

10. City life is so bad a condition, physically speaking, that he who founds a family in one city might as well castrate his children, so far as the future of his progeny [is] concerned. Our newspapers, our city institutions, thrive in

proportion as the city in which one of them is located grows in numbers. To this extent they are carrion birds, living on corpses. It is to the immediate selfish interest of the proprietors of every newspaper that the city in which their certain newspaper is located should grow in numbers, and it is selfishness and greed and not civic pride and patriotism that [cause] our publishers to do all in their power to bring within the city gates men and women and children to be consumed and destroyed.

What can any one or fifty newspapers do in a warfare against this most marked form of race suicide? They can do little or nothing in a year or a generation, perhaps, but it is possible that they can do much in the way of disseminating that information which will, sooner than we now dream of, cause a checking of this evil and an alteration in the line of future progress of our people.

For thirty years and more I have watched and studied the great and the popular newspaper, the immediate and the future effect of its teaching. I believe that few people aside from myself have any idea of the tremendous, the almost invincible, power and force of the daily press. I am one of those who believe that at least in America the press rules the country; it rules its politics, its religion, its social practice. I believe that if all of the newspapers' editors of the United States were of one mind on any one matter of what the public ought to do, and if they had the courage of their convictions, it would only be a question of a short time before the nation as a whole would think as these editors think and do that which these editors think that they ought to do.

The members of the N.E.A. are only a small fraction of the press of the United States, but they are a very conspicuous fraction, and a very influential one. It is my conviction that the modern press of the United States, including its vices and virtues, is more than half the product and development of that organization which constitutes the main portion of the membership of the N.E.A.

The power for good or evil, then, of the Newspaper Enterprise Association in the future is not at all in proportion to the relative circulation and business standing of our clientage [sic] in the N.E.A., but it is in exact proportion to the courage and ability which we display. It is not in proportion to our moral sentiment nor in proportion to our great wisdom that we will be effective. Our influence will be in exact proportion to our force and ability, whether it be rightly or wrongly exercised.

11. The N.E.A. is itself a type and a model; it is not to be subject in the least degree to any outside journalistic influence; it must imitate no other thing in journalism; it must not seek to be different from any other institution. It must simply be what it is itself, because of its own spirit. It must be original not because it seeks conspicuousness, fame or prosperity; it must

be original only because it expresses itself not with bravado or what might be called courage, but simply because its expression is a necessary, and *the* necessary, function of its existence.

Yours sincerely,

E. W. Scripps

Is Honest Journalism Possible?

[*December 29, 1908*]

A writer in a recent number of the *Atlantic Monthly* magazine — presumably a New York editor — started a discussion on this subject.[71] This writer seemed to infer that reasonably honest journalism was possible. Mr. [William Marion] Reedy, now the editor of the [weekly] St. Louis *Mirror*, discussed this same subject before the Missouri Press Association and concluded that American daily journalism at least could not be honest.

Lord Northcliffe — the brilliant, comparatively young, and successful publisher of a number of English daily papers — told the New York *Times* that "American newspapers are getting worse every year."

Even Frank Munsey, the erratic publisher of various magazines and daily papers, has taken his seat upon the judicial bench. The editor of perhaps the most untrustworthy of all American great national weeklies — the *Leslie's Weekly* — states that the newspapers are not as accurate as they were fifty years ago.

President [Arthur T.] Hadley of Yale has also indicted our American press. What Hadley says is really funny. Hadley complains of a journalistic propensity to indulge in rhetoric rather than in logic, and yet Hadley's remarks are all rhetorical, and seemed to me to be logical absurdities.

As would be expected, Reedy, the humblest and most democratic of all of the journalistic critics, because he is a journalist himself, and, hence, a man who has had to think so rapidly and continuously as to make it impossible for him to become acquainted with all the fundamental premises, expressed the most commonly held opinion concerning the press.

Reedy dwells particularly upon the fact that newspapers are owned by men who do not edit them — that is to say, who do not write them. For the newspaper writer's shortcomings, he has the excuse to offer that he writes for

[71] An edited version of this disquisition appears in McCabe, *Damned Old Crank*, p. 222 f.

a living, writes under orders, and writes what his employer wants him to write and not what he, the writer, thinks.

Reedy also has a very commonly held opinion that newspaper owners are part and parcel of the plutocratic clique, and that by choice they suppress some news and distort other news happenings, and generally try to create a public opinion that is favorable to plutocracy.

Reedy also is a victim of a very common delusion — a delusion so common as to be practically universal. This delusion is that a newspaper can only be founded at great expense of capital, and, hence, that it is impossible for one of the non-plutocratic class in these days to found or purchase a newspaper property.

There are tricks in all trades, especially in our trade. I am a newspaper owner. Newspaper owners do not like competition. They want as few newspapers in existence as possible. It is but natural — even if to be natural is to be dishonest — for newspaper owners to desire to create the impression that it requires tremendous sums of money to found a newspaper, and that even when founded a newspaper is not a very profitable property.

Yet, as a matter of fact, although I do not know the full history of all of the great newspapers in the United States, and only know in a general way the history of a large majority of them, I can say that I am not personally acquainted with the history of a single great and successful and influential American newspaper, the first cost of the founding of which has been equal to the cost of founding any third- or fourth-grade business in the locality where the newspaper was founded, at the time of the founding of that paper.

As a matter of fact, no great newspaper has been founded by the aid of large capital. As a matter of fact, no more substantial obstacle to success can be presented to the founder of any newspaper, than the possession of abundant capital.

It has been said that there has been more money lost in journalism in America than has ever been made out of it. I think that it is at least possible that this statement is a true one. But the losses have all been made as a result of an attempt to found newspapers by means of capital, or the attempt to own and conduct newspapers by the sheer force of capital.

In journalism, money does not make money. In journalism, money makes for failure.

I know that I am frequently accused of being paradoxical when I utter opinions about those subjects of which I am most accurately informed. If I were governed by the principle of Machiavelli — that is to say, if I desired always to dissimulate — I would know no better means to obtain my ends than by always speaking truthfully concerning my own business and my own profession. No one, especially of the laity, ever believes a word I say concerning journalism.

Now here is a proposition that I have made frequently, and in making it, I have been both sincere and truthful:

Given one man, or two men, or a collective staff of men of a certain ability, and it being proposed that this man or these men should found a newspaper, and the question being further proposed whether they should be endowed with no more capital than enough to purchase an old, almost worn-out, second-hand office equipment, together with a cash capital sufficient to barely feed and clothe and house the man or men for a period of two or three years on a standard of living expenses not superior to that of ordinary day-laborers — what would my judgment be as to the chances of success as between the two methods, that is, large capital and limited capital?

I would say that the newspaper founded on large capital would not have one chance of success, where a paper founded on the smallest possible capital would have a hundred or perhaps a thousand chances. In fact, my conviction is that there would be no chance at all for the success of a newspaper founded by men who had relatively large capital, and who intended to use relatively large capital in the foundation of their newspaper.

I have been interested in a proprietary way in between thirty and forty daily newspapers. Some of my newspapers have been remarkably successful, some of them have been absolute and complete failures, some of them have succeeded moderately, and some of them have been founded and conducted at so little expense as to be considered as small failures.

On the average, however, whether coincidences played a great part or not, my newspaper successes have been in inverse proportion to the amount of original capital accessible or employed.

The most pronounced failures that I have had experience with have been those in which either large capital was available or in which there were managers who supposed that large capital would be put eventually at their disposal.

Therefore, I would say that journalistic honesty does not necessarily suffer because of the original natural dishonesty of men who eventually become capitalists. Young newspapers, that is to say, papers that have not yet become so profitable as to corrupt the morals of their owners, are, for the most part, the most honest newspapers. The young and struggling newspaper has to establish itself, and the first thing that an intelligent young owner of a newspaper, or owner of a young newspaper, learns is that it pays to be honest. His older, more successful, and more profitable rivals in the journalistic field, having not only become corrupted by wealth but no longer depending entirely for existence — for their daily bread — on continued and growing public confidence, may be dishonest, and hence cannot compete with a poor, young publication for the public favor on the grounds of absolute honesty.

If, then, it requires but a small capital to found a newspaper, and if honesty is a good business policy, my critic will ask, "Why is it that the daily press of the United States is almost exclusively owned by capitalists, and why are its practices almost invariably plutocratic or dishonest?"

I can answer this first question very easily: There is no more valuable and substantial property in the world than a successful newspaper. In every community the property value of the most successful newspaper in that community is greater perhaps than the property value of any other single business institution in such a locality. If it is not greater, it is at least greater than any other but a very, very few local business institutions.

It is impossible to have a very successful newspaper in a town of 50,000 population whose capital value is not equal to $200,000. It is impossible to have a successful daily newspaper in a town of 100,000 population which is not worth $500,000. It is impossible to have a very successful newspaper in a town of 500,000 people that is not worth more than $1,000,000.

One can see, then, why the great and successful newspapers in the United States are owned by millionaires. One cannot own a newspaper that is worth several millions without owning many millions of dollars worth of property. A newspaper cannot be a very great and successful newspaper without being worth several millions of dollars.

I have said before that the founding of a successful newspaper not only does not depend upon the publisher owning a large capital, but rather depends upon the publisher originally owning a very small capital. The publisher's capital — his greatest capital, that is to say, the overwhelmingly largest proportion of his capital — consists originally and perhaps indefinitely and continuously in his ability, that is to say, what newspapermen call "brains."

The successful publisher, the publisher who has succeeded, then, is necessarily a capitalist, because he is possessed of the unearned increment and intelligence, of brains, of, if not a finer sort, at least of a sort that enables him to produce a very valuable commodity with a comparatively small outlay of effort.

Now, then, as to the second question: Why should great and successful newspapers, that is to say, newspaper owners, be dishonest? Are they? I will not presume here to answer this question.

I will only presume that Mr. Reedy, in common with the vast mass of humanity, consciously or unconsciously, holds the belief so tersely expressed by some French philosophers in the last part of the eighteenth century, *la propriété est le vol*, literally translated "property is theft." A thief, of course, is dishonest. If property is the result of theft or dishonesty, then the man who owns property is dishonest. A man who owns a little property may be considered a little dishonest, while the man who owns a great property must be considered very dishonest. A man cannot own a great and successful newspaper who does not own a great property, and, hence, the owner of such a great and successful newspaper must be very dishonest.

I do not think that Reedy or his associates would confess to the charge that they believed "property is theft."

However, it is a fact that the mere possession of wealth by one man and the lack of such possession by another man results in the two men having distinct and often diametrically opposite points of view on very many subjects called "moral." The rich man and the poor man on the average are never in agreement on any subject of property rights — markedly is this the case when they are considering the subject of dividing and appropriating the respective shares of the profits of the joint efforts of labor and capital.

The writers — the employees of newspaper owners — have necessarily points of view that differ from those of their employers. The owner of the newspaper, the employer, requires his employees to write those things which the employer either believes or wants his readers to believe, and, as he is human, he will not allow his newspaper to be used to controvert his own opinions. Nor will he pay to the writer money in the way of wages to produce matter which he does not want to appear in his paper.

As an editor originally and a newspaper owner latterly, I have often, in fact, I have always, been in a quandary on a certain subject.

Whatever the opinion of others may be of myself, I have thought I was honest. I have felt it my duty to express my own honest convictions through my newspaper. But a newspaper is a large institution. The amount of space in it devoted to reading matter is many times larger than that which I, or any one man, can fill. I, the owner or the editor of a newspaper, must employ many assistants.

I not only want to be honest, but I want my editors and my writers to be honest. By a careful selection in my staff of men, I have been able always to have around me a set of men who agreed with me on many, many important matters connected with our calling. But it is impossible for any two men to agree on every subject. It is impossible, or almost impossible, to find a newspaper staff of men numbering from twenty to a hundred or more who will agree on any one subject. But a newspaper is a single entity — an individual. It as a rule is compelled to have only one opinion on any one subject. Now what has occurred when, as an editor, I have been directing the policy of my newspaper, and when there daily occurred, and had to occur, differences of opinion between myself and some one or more of the writers who were subordinate to me? If I waived my opinion in favor of that of my subordinate, I, who was responsible for the utterances made in my paper, would have been insincere and permitted my paper to express opinions contrary to my own. I would have been dishonest, would I not? Of course, I have never done this. I have required my subordinates, the writers of a given article, to express my opinion, which, in many a given case, was contrary to his own. In doing this, have I compelled the writer to be dishonest?

However, in order to continue my arguments, I will concede that Mr. Reedy's criticism of the press is a just one, that the press is plutocratic, and that it is unfair in its dealings with the public, that it shows partiality in its dealings with the wealthy, and a far too great amount of indifference to the rights and welfare of the masses.

The possessor of great wealth may be, and frequently is, corrupted. No matter how good and moral a man may be, the possession of great wealth must have a certain amount of corrupting influence upon him. The possession of wealth isolates a man to a great extent from his fellows. This isolation results in a constantly diminishing sympathy for human kind. The duties connected with the administration of a large property are so absorbing and so strenuous as to permit a man, who is the possessor of wealth, no time to think of even his own misfortunes, and much less of the misfortunes of others. Perhaps only the very rich men are those who fully appreciate the fact that the most unhappy men are those who are farthest from the center of the general average. The very rich and the very poor are, if not equally unhappily situated, at least far more unhappily situated than the great mass of men who occupy the intermediate space between wealth and poverty.

There are other reasons than that of mere personal absorption of [in] business affairs, which tend to make wealthy men unsympathetic with the masses. "Birds of a feather flock together" not merely because they want to but because they have to. Excepting in rare incidences, there can be no close, congenial intimacy, mutual affection, and confidence existing between a very rich and a very poor man, or even between a tolerably rich and a tolerably poor man. The mere possession of wealth so modifies a man's personal character as to make it possible for him to only find congenial fellowship with men whose characters have been modified in a similar way.

There is not only a community of interest but a community of social feeling between the capitalists of any locality, section, or country. The successful journalist, that is to say, when he owns his newspaper, is a wealthy man, a capitalist by necessity. His associates are necessarily other capitalists. The greater this association of capitalists is, the more completely does it minister to and give satisfaction to the natural, normal, human social instincts. A social capitalistic class quickly crystallizes and solidifies into a social caste, and the journalist who has become a capitalist is inevitably estranged from the larger community.

Mr. Reedy and hundreds of thousands of American citizens are condemning the American press because it is unfair to the poorer class, and is a false witness in every case being tried at the bar of public opinion between capital and labor.

This criticism may be as just as the condition is necessary.

What would one think of a poor man who had a case in court against a rich man, who allowed his rich antagonist to employ the lawyers on both sides — who would allow his rich antagonist to employ and pay his, the poor man's, lawyer fees?

Yet, this is just what the poorer people of the United States do in every case that is tried between labor and capital before the bar of public opinion. A modern, up-to-date great newspaper is published in the form of a great and bulky document. The white paper used by the publisher in many cases costs at the paper mills more money than the reader pays for it. This being the case, all the other expenses, the employment of great staffs of writing journalists, of printers, of other mechanics, the cost of rent, machinery, and the wear and tear on the same, the telegraph tolls, and all the profit of the business of making a great newspaper, is borne, not by the readers of a newspaper, but by the advertisers, men in business, men who are capitalists.

When a man attempts to get something for nothing, or anything at less than cost, he is certainly fooled, and as certainly, I think, deservedly fooled.

The public, that is to say, the readers of newspapers, can only procure reliable advocates and, to them, friendly newspapers by employing and paying their own journalistic servants, and not accepting gratuities from the capitalistic, the advertising class.

I have said before that President Hadley's comment on the press was funny. Professor Hadley says that the "average editor will work for the average reader."

I will say that the average editor will work just hard enough for the average reader to get that reader to continue to read his paper and, hence, the advertisements of the newspaper's more liberal customers, the merchants.

But it would take a whole essay, perhaps a whole book, to include in it all the things that President Hadley does not know about the newspaper business.

But the really, to me at least, funny thing about President Hadley's position is his inference that the public can get, by demanding it, an honest newspaper, or a "logical" one, as he puts it.

How can the public demand something, the existence of which it does not know?

What does the great mass of the people in the United States know that they do not learn from the newspapers? In this day and age, the public gets 99 per cent, at least, of all its information concerning public affairs from the daily newspaper press. If the whole press is bearing false witness on a large number of important facts, the possession of which is the right of the public, how can the public know that it is the victim of false testimony? Has not one got to prove first to the public mind that the press, as it stands today, is false and dishonest, before that public can demand an honest and truthful press? What other means can exist in these times for conveying to the public this proof, than the press?

Is there any considerable degree of greater honesty on the part of the weekly and the monthly publications than that of the daily press? I, for one, do not believe there is. So far as I have been able to observe, the weekly and monthly press of the United States is infinitely more cursed by plutocratic principles and methods than is the daily press.

President Hadley's advice or suggestions suggest to me the question of "how to bell the cat."

An Old Hobby

[*March 4, 1909*]

The subject is "education."

My friend and old partner, M. A. McRae, has been visiting with me. It has always seemed to me that McRae had a hankering for the footlights. At one time he had a well-defined amateurish ambition for the stage.

Now that he has retired from his employment as a newspaper business manager, he is gratified to find himself welcome on the lecture platform. One of his favorite subjects is "education and application." McRae is a man of far more than average intelligence. But it requires only a few minutes conversation with him to convince any of his hearers that McRae holds to that definition of what education is, which is so commonly held as to be almost universal.

By education he means training. He would educate a man into being a lawyer, a doctor, or a businessman, or into any other sort of specialist. In fact, he would mold his subject while he or she is yet youthful or plastic, into one or another form.

In common with almost the universality of his fellow countrymen and women, he believes that education — that is to say, this sort of training — in schools by means of books and professional teachers is unqualifiedly a good thing.

However, he has a little more sense than the commonalty, and therefore he does not believe that education is of any benefit to an individual who does not make a useful and profitable employment of his mind and energies after they have been trained. Therefore, he advises young hearers that they must make application of their education.

There is one thing very certain that Mr. McRae regards as education that formal and conventional production of the ordinary schools and colleges [*sic*]. It is evident that he believes that every boy and girl will be better fitted for any and all possible employment by reason of having his or her whole youth devoted mainly to what might be called "school life."

246

Mr. McRae has not, I believe, the remotest idea that his matter-of-course acceptance of all his theories on the subject of schooling or so-called education are purely the result of a mental bias impressed upon him in his own childhood and youth.

Mr. McRae is certainly a practical-minded man. He is fully able to comprehend that there should be a definite sort of education or training for each vocation — one sort for the doctor, one for the lawyer, and one for the mechanic; but he holds, I believe, the common idea that it is well enough to get this special sort of training and education after each and all of the parties interested have passed through a period of identically the same sort of schooling.

Incidentally, I must say that McRae as a father is giving practically the same sort of schooling to both his son and daughters.

Conventionality and habit make us all more or less inconsiderate. Although McRae has known me for twenty-five years and known of my practice and methods in my own family and business, it seems to have hardly ever occurred to him that all my actions in the main have been consistent with my oft-expressed theory that education is the reverse of training and that schooling and training are injurious in all cases where they are not directed toward an end, or rather toward the pursuit to be [sic] of the subject.

I have not only failed to send my children to schools of any sort,[72] but have prevented them in one way or another from attending such schools. I have had tutors in my house for my children, for the purpose of teaching them certain facts, but never for the purpose of training them or directing their minds along any channels, moral or other.

Mr. McRae, however, has seen the tutors in my house and presumed that this scheme of mine was practically in the nature of a private school system, maintained by my own purse but in every way producing and being intended to produce the same results as those produced by ordinary public and private schools.

Although I have been under his personal observation for so many years, he evidently has never taken notice of one peculiar feature of my system.

After a discussion the other day, he turned on me and said practically, "Why, Ed, your own course of action contradicts all your contentions. In all your business affairs you have appointed to positions men who have been previously trained for the same." He meant by this, men who had been trained by others, perhaps.

Then I called his attention to little facts in the history of the business in which he has spent over one-quarter of a century. He himself was the first important appointee of mine to a position of responsibility. I reminded him

[72] On the contrary, he did send Jim and John to school for short periods. Most of the time, though, he did use private tutors at "Miramar."

that when he was appointed business manager of the Cincinnati *Post* he was not only a very young man but, to my knowledge, had never even temporarily held a position as an executive with authority over any institution, with subordinates subject to his orders and direction. It is true that he had had some experience as a personal solicitor for advertisements to appear in directories and newspapers, and, hence, he knew something of the newspaper business. However, instead of this being considered an advantage by me, I considered it a disadvantage, and today I consider that Mr. McRae's greatest handicap through life has been that he had a sort of training direct and indirect in publication offices, based on very false and very common theories. Had I placed any value on McRae's training, I would have kept him in the advertising department, in a position where he would personally solicit business. But I did the reverse of this. I gave him a position as far as possible removed from that where he would have had the opportunity to put in practice his training. In fact, I told McRae that instead of going out to seek for a business manager of the Cincinnati *Post*, a man who had had training in office work and business management, I took him in preference, not because of his knowledge or training in the business, but because of his lack of it. In fact, I chose McRae because he knew nothing of business management, and because [he] therefore [had] no preconceived notions and no training by anyone else, I felt I could depend upon him better than I could upon anyone else to carry out my ideas and to literally obey my instructions during the interval in which he was being educated, that is to say, in which he would be developing his own mind originally, to such an extent as would enable him to manage the paper instead of having it managed by myself through him. Should he ever stop to think seriously on this subject, he would find that I never endeavored to educate him or to train him. It is true that I presented to him my theories, but I never compelled him to practice them. It is true that I limited his authority, but never to an extent further than that of forbidding him to incur debts which I could not pay.

I also called McRae's attention to the history of every other important appointment that I made or caused to be made. Neither [Robert F.] Paine nor [L. T.] Atwood came to us with the least previous training. While he himself, when in authority, had trained up men to various positions to which he afterwards appointed them, I never took for, and appointed to, any position a man who had had any previous training where it was possible to get someone who had not such training. The fact that W. W. Thornton succeeded McRae as president of the company [in 1905] after many years in a position subordinate to McRae is in no way to be considered evidence of inconsistency on my part. In fact, Mr. Thornton was the only man of whom I knew and whom I considered strong enough personally to be president. Could I have found a man with even inferior personal qualification to Thornton and who had had no opportunity of being trained by McRae or anyone else, I would have taken that man. Perhaps in my eyes Mr. Thornton's chief merit was that, notwithstanding the fact that he had so long occupied a position in which, had he been plastic he would have been molded by McRae, he gave every evidence of being a man of education and not at all of training — a man whose development was a matter of original growth and not at all a matter of training. He seemed to me to be so strong a man that even Mr. McRae's powerful and forceful individuality had made no impression upon him. I think that subsequent events have proven that while Mr. Thornton was going to school with Mr. McRae, he was learning nothing from his preceptor more than he would learn and did learn from every other specimen of humanity which came under his observation. In other words, Mr. Thornton neither preached nor practiced, as I understand them, any of the McRae doctrines. More than this, I can say that he neither preached nor practiced any of my doctrines. Thornton is Thornton, and not a reflection of a Scripps or a McRae or any man that I personally know. It is possible, however, that, unknown to me, he has gone to school to some other man or men and that he is a disciple or a pupil of such person or persons, although I do not think so.

I called McRae's attention also to a large number of other capable and forceful young men in the concern and especially to the fact that of all of these that I have appointed not one had had any previous training for their positions by me or intentionally by any other man in my concern. As a matter of fact, I never took a man from either the Cleveland *Press* or Cincinnati *Post*, or Detroit *News*, to put in charge of a new business. Whenever I did take a man from one established newspaper to place him in charge of a business, I always chose the man from the newspaper where the opportunities for training and bias had been least. I believe my only appointment resulting in a direct transfer of a man from one established office to a new one was that of [Boyd F.] Gurley of Denver [Denver *Express*]. However, I chose Gurley not because of his long service or because of any training in a desk position, a position of responsibility. In all my offices there were subordinate editors who had been trained in editorial duties, but I chose none of them. I took Gurley, a reporter on the [Los Angeles] *Record*, because he seemed to me to be the right sort.

I told McRae that when considering a new appointee for a job, my practice was to ask, among others, several questions. (1) Have you had much schooling? (2) Have you had any experience in another office in this kind of work? (3) Are you married? A negative answer to all of these questions I considered to be decidedly in favor of the candidate.

I cannot now say that in my various actions of appointments and promotions, I have been consciously influenced by any rule. I mean by this that I would not reject a candidate who had graduated from college just because he had graduated, or that I would reject a candidate who had been employed in another office, or that I would reject a married man as a candidate for a position of responsibility in so serious and difficult a task as that of founding a new newspaper.

Perhaps all that has occurred has been that my attention has been attracted to men who would never have attracted my attention had they been handicapped by training in a higher educational institution, or a training as a subordinate but important staff member in some other newspaper office.

In fact, those meritorious points which I desire in a man to fill a responsible position are points not possessed by men who have had their personality rubbed out by the disciplining hand of some powerful superior.

Captain Mahan in his biography of Lord Nelson [73] dwells at length on the peculiar features of Lord Nelson's career. A chapter of accidents resulted in Nelson's never having, during his whole career, been subordinated to a chief officer "on the spot." As midshipman even, his luck began. By some chance he happened to be senior in command of every undertaking. Not standing high with the Admiralty Board, he was left in the lurch, in the outskirts as it were of the British Navy, commanding very small vessels in distant parts of the seas where there was no occasion of there being great ships and, hence, high naval officers. This chapter of accidents continued during his whole life, so that at no period, I believe, did he ever enter a naval engagement of any kind where he did not either have absolute control or practically absolute control of his own actions and those of his subordinates. The story is told that in one important naval engagement there was a superior officer on another ship whose signals Nelson could not see, since he placed his glass to his blind eye.

Mahan also discoursed on the careers of other great military captains, pointing out that in each case similar fortunate chapters of accidents had occurred to these men. In fact, Captain Mahan concludes with the statement that history proves that discipline and training unfit a man for leadership.

What McRae calls education, I have before said, is really training, and Mahan says, as I say, that no man can escape being spoiled and more or less unfitted for really important work by being educated, that is, trained.

So far from being opposed to education, I am one of only a very few who believe in education, that is to say, in the drawing out [of] the natural development of a human being — solely the development of the being as it exists, when at birth it begins an individual life.

The so-called educationists, on the contrary, believe in pouring into the

[73] Alfred Thayer Mahan, *Life of Nelson*. Boston: Little, Brown and Co., 1897.

mind of the subject pupil the thoughts and the individual characteristics of the teacher. These same educationists believe in training. They believe in suppressing some of the natural tendencies of the individual, in developing other natural tendencies, and adding to these latter some purely extraneous thoughts, ideas, and tendencies.

McRae, looking at my children as he sees them growing and judging of them, and looking over the concern of which I have been so important a member, frankly says that it appears to him that I have proved to a certain extent the truth of some of my theories.

However, I am sure that he considers that the most part of the results of my accomplishments has been accidental and that perhaps the reason why I have been so fortunate is that, despite my expressed theories and scheme, I have not lived up to them entirely, and that even if I had endeavored to do so, circumstances have made it impossible for me to prevent that which he called education, and also training, of the subjects that have come under my control and influence. Beyond this, he doubtlessly considers also that my own peculiarly fortunate situation in the world has allowed me such opportunities in the conduct of my family and business affairs as perhaps no one else of his acquaintance has ever had.

Perhaps it will never occur to him that my peculiar opportunities have been the effect and not the cause of my system.

The other day he said to me, "Ed, does it ever occur to you that your own position is unique and that perhaps nowhere else in the whole country is there a man who lives as you do, remote from actual contact with your business, directing its affairs very little personally, while the whole institution moves on so successfully? Why, this is the very matter Hearst spoke to me about. He expressed a wonder that you could live as you do out here in California and have your business scattered all over the country and doing as well as it does do."

Mr. McRae expressed wonder at the fact himself. But I do not believe it has occurred to him that in all probability the real cause of this situation is that consciously and unconsciously I have been governed by some of my fundamental and extraordinarily uncommon views.

I have let my children from childhood lead natural lives; that is to say, I have left them alone to grow and develop as nature would have them develop, untrammeled, unbent, undwarfed by any other agency than a purely natural one.

I have selected here and there partners, chiefs of departments, selected them and left them alone to grow and develop along their own natural lines. (It is true, that I have selected, so far as I was able, men who I hoped would have, and who in many cases have had, a natural bent of mind which, developing, developed along lines that were consistent with my own business practices — not entirely consistent, but merely enough consistent to make the whole system harmonious.)

As it happened, my children had such natural characteristics as enabled them to develop in a way that McRae considers at least good enough. It is possible that they might have had such natural characteristics as would have caused them to develop in a way that would make me very unhappy.

For the most part, my partners and other associates in the business have happened to have those natural qualities inherent and inherited, capacities, and tendencies which have enabled them to develop naturally to their own advantage and to the advantage of the concern as a whole. It must not be forgotten, however, that there have been instances where very capable men in my concern have developed along lines of natural tendencies, which has made it impossible for them to harmonize with me and the concern and which led to their elimination from the concern and their subsequent successful development elsewhere.

It will be observed that I recognize the value of education. It will perhaps be also recognized that I believe that the only assistance any man can give to a child or another man in the way of the latter's education is that of presenting opportunities and removing natural and artificial obstructions.

I consider one of these artificial obstructions to real education of youth to be the ordinary and almost universal school, college, and university systems prevailing among civilized peoples. I educated my sons, then, not by training or precept of my own, but by forbidding others to meddle with, to distort, or trammel their natural growth.

Having had no control over the youth of my partners and associates, I have been unable to assist at their primary education, and so I have been driven to another course, namely, that of selecting my company from among men who had not been trained in my business and my profession to too great an extent by anyone else. I consider that my whole duty has been done to my child when, having caused his being, I have watched over and guarded him against the dangers of the natural, physical world and the impertinent, intermeddling busybodies amongst my fellows who would, if they were permitted by me, gladly undertake the task of molding my children to a pattern entirely inconsistent with that intended by nature.

I consider that I have best served my young business associates in my concern and myself when, having selected some new member of my business family, I give him every opportunity to grow in his own way and at the same time exert myself to shield him from the influences of all his human environments, especially of other newspapermen who, by force and personal contact, would seek to divert such a man from the course he would naturally pursue if left alone. In order to do this, I have never failed to impress upon the minds of my young friends that they must stand upon their own bottom, that they must not depend upon me or anyone else for instruction or guidance, or for any more financial assistance than just enough to carry them over that infantile period of a newspaper history when paternal support is necessary.

Just as the newborn babe must derive its nourishment from its mother's breast, so must a new newspaper for a brief period of time depend for its capital on its founder or founders.

That newspaper business which for too long a time depends upon its founder's capital and upon his fatherly direction and control can never successfully develop. Just as oversolicitude of parents may ruin the physical and mental stamina of a child, so will overmuch governmental control and too great a supply of capital destroy the chances of what might otherwise have been a successful and magnificent newspaper enterprise.

As with my mind's eye I glance over my family of newspapers and newspapermen, I am impressed with the idea that therein can be found proof for some of my ideas. Those are the most successful newspapers and those are the most successful men who, for one reason or another, have had the least occasion, or rather the least opportunity, to depend upon me for money and for personal advice and instruction in times of emergency in the ordinary course of their affairs.

Selling N.E.A. Service

[*March 13, 1909*]

Mr. John P. Scripps
"Miramar," Calif.

Dear John:

Several days ago you told me that a question and dispute had occurred on the subject of the sale of N.E.A. product to clients. You asked me to read the correspondence and give a decision.

I declined to even hear from you an account of the affair and, of course, refused to read the correspondence.

To you as to others I have made it plain that I feel that I owe to the concern and to the young men in it that I should cease to exercise control or even a large influence in the direction of our newspapers. Unless I shall so cease to act, my successors will, being free from final personal responsibility, fail to develop to the full their own large natural capacities to govern themselves and safely direct an institution which is sorely in need not only of strong men but of many strong men.

A few days later you came to me with the same subject and desired me to put in written form — into the form of one of my disquisitions — my general views on a subject of this character. I consented to do this under the condition that you and others should understand that I was only submitting some of my own personal views. I stated that it might be well for you to gain my views along with those of other men of practical experience, not for the purpose of guiding yourself according to advice but for the purpose of enriching your own mind with the largest number of facts possible to be obtained on which to base your judgment, or rather from which to deduce your own personal conclusions.

It is not worthwhile here considering the original cause of the institution called the N.E.A., nor any of its purposes.

It is sufficient that the N.E.A. is in existence. It is an implement in the hands and entirely under the control of men on whom has been imposed the duty of conducting the newspapers which I have founded. It is the duty of these men to continue or abolish this institution, according to their own best judgment. If they continue this institution, it is their duty to conduct it without regard to the policy of the past controller and in the way they think best.

I warn you and I warn every other man in this concern against shirking responsibility and the necessity of hard and laborious thought on no other and better ground than that an old and much overestimated man had, at one time in the past, held an expressed opinion on any subject.

I cannot too often remind you that I, the very person whom you are prone to depend upon for advice and assistance and on whose wisdom and experience you place so much reliance, am myself convinced that there are now in the concern a number of men that I know who have proven that they have greater natural capacities than I possessed when I was at the same point of age and experience where they now stand. The independently reasoned out conclusions of these men — conclusions unbiased by my own precepts and instructions — cannot fail to be of far more value than the judgment of a man who bases all his conclusions upon his memory.

But even if all the above were not the case and if there were not a man in the concern who was not my inferior, still the fact remains that you youngsters have got to run the business and conduct the newspapers for the good or evil of the people, and the sooner you are compelled to think and act for yourselves, the sooner you will find your places and the better you will perform your duties.

Now as to N.E.A.

The first great and important duty of all of our newspapers and the Newspaper Enterprise Association and the United Press is to serve the interest of the nation at large and those very communities in which our newspapers are situated.

It is true that you have got to conduct all of your newspapers and other institutions in such a way, that is to say, so profitably, as to be able to furnish the living expenses of all persons attached to the concern and also to make the concern sufficiently wealthy and powerful in the business community to maintain its entire and absolute independence. You must make your newspapers pay in order that you may make good newspapers, but you will never respect yourselves nor will the public respect you if you conduct your newspapers solely for the purpose of making money.

The Newspaper Enterprise Association is a part and element of and in every one of our newspapers. It is not, at least at the present time, an individual institution existing for the purpose of being a profitable business or an organization of public influence.

The primary and only cause for the existence of the N.E.A. is that of its being a part of our newspapers. There is danger that the mere fact that the Newspaper Enterprise Association is a corporate entity and has an individual organization will have a tendency to cause it to attempt to set up housekeeping on its own accord.

The sole aim and object of the Newspaper Enterprise Association is to serve the Scripps newspapers and the allied institution of the Clover Leaf. Even in the case of the Clover Leaf the alliance is based exclusively on the idea that the Clover Leaf papers have identically the same journalistic policy as that of the Scripps papers.

Then when it comes to a question of selling the N.E.A. service to any other paper, this question is to be decided not by the organization, that is to say, the management of the N.E.A., but by those newspaper corporations of which the N.E.A. is a part of their editorial staff.

Every newspaper that has a part of its whole in the N.E.A. should exercise a complete and absolute control over the N.E.A. in its particular community. Beyond this there are groups of papers. The Ohio group, for instance, should not only control the territory of Ohio but neighboring territories in other states. The California group should have absolute control over the state of California. The northwestern group should have absolute control over the northwest section of the country.

The N.E.A. report should therefore only be sold to other newspapers by the N.E.A. organization in such territories where there are at present no Scripps or Clover Leaf newspapers, or in such occupied territories where the local representative or member of the association gives consent.

For example: The president and the full board of trustees and manager of the N.E.A. all together have no moral right and should have no legal right to sell its report to any Indiana newspaper against the protest of either Evansville or the little Terre Haute cripple.

There are two reasons and only two reasons for our selling our report to any other newspapers than to charter members. The first of these is to obtain a larger revenue for the purpose of improving the report, and the second (which I consider far more important) is to secure to other communities, to other American citizens, the advantages of learning the truth about many important matters which they would not learn if they had to depend upon the good faith and enterprise of their local newspapers. The owners and editors of our newspapers should welcome every opportunity to give the public at large the advantage of our work for the public interest without regard to the financial rewards of such service. We can make enough money out of our own newspapers to enable us to serve gratuitously, if need be, sections of the public outside of our own peculiar fields of influence.

I have, from the beginning of the N.E.A., been averse to selling our report to any other newspaper for one reason only. This is the reason:

The pursuit of this plan might cause the development of what would
be practically a newspaper syndicate. The manager of this newspaper syndicate would then by degrees grow into considering that the N.E.A. was
an individual profit-making or loss-saving institution. Once possessed of
this idea, the manager of the N.E.A. would inevitably cater to the general
demands in furnishing both newspaper and editorial utterances. The N.E.A.
would then be conducted for the purpose of obtaining the largest number
of customers and the greatest possible revenue, instead of being conducted
solely for the purpose of being a valuable aid to the editorial staffs of our
own newspapers.

Such is the peculiarity of human nature that no man or set of men can
be depended upon to consent to occupy a restricted field when there is a
larger field in sight. Even if the manager of the N.E.A. could fully possess
the proper idea, his staff of writers, being conscious that their writings
were going into a large number of other newspapers than Scripps papers,
would inevitably to a greater or lesser extent compose their articles so as to
make them acceptable to the greatest number of newspapers and not solely
to make them acceptable to the Scripps newspapers. In other words, both
greed and vanity would work to the injury of the character of the N.E.A.

So large is the interest of all our newspapers in the United Press Association that every newspaper possessed of intelligence will see the expediency and almost the necessity of giving the United Press support in nearly
every possible legitimate way.

Therefore, it is probable that the whole band of newspapers composing
the N.E.A. will voluntarily surrender their rights of individual protest in
communities and sections when it comes to a matter of giving N.E.A.
material to the United Press, since the advantage of such a course to the
whole concern will far outweigh the disadvantages of any member of our
whole community of newspapers.

I recognize that there are some young men in the concern whose experiences have so far been limited and whose employment so narrows
their point of vision that they cannot be depended upon to take broad
views in every case. However, our system of having group editors-in-chief
with supreme authority should be sufficient to guarantee broad-minded
actions rather than narrow-minded. [H. N.] Rickey, [B. H.] Canfield, [J. C.]
Harper, and Crawford, I believe, have authority to speak for the editorial
departments of every individual newspaper vitally concerned.

I know enough of Mr. Rickey and of his peculiar opportunities to take
broad views to convince me that he is so far open to reason that he cannot
fail to see the justice and wisdom of any editor's contention when it is

well grounded. I believe that the chances are that Canfield, Crawford, and Harper would, after an individual discussion with Rickey on any subject, be more apt to be convinced by Rickey as to the reasonableness of any action than by anyone else except perhaps myself.

My advice to you, John, is that you go to school to these men younger than myself and older than yourself in fitting yourself for your future work, rather than to me. I hope that you will develop qualities which will fit you so to stand in relation with our editors as will make your cooperation with them valued by them and valuable to the concern. As soon as you have reached your majority so that you have the legal right to act as a trustee, I believe that no harm will result from your becoming one of the trustees of the N.E.A. With four other men on the board, that board might, and I believe will be, the gainer by including even so young a man as yourself. In all cases I want the youngest possible men in the concern to be introduced into positions of such responsibility as will give full play to their youthful vigor and energies and novelties of ideas and methods.

However, you must know that you must not depend upon me or my position of control for your position, but entirely upon your own capacities. You must prove your own fitness rather to others than to me.

Yours affectionately,

E. W. Scripps

Driftwood

McRae told me the other day that Victor Lawson, owner of the Chicago *News*, was making over a million dollars a year out of his paper, and that Lawson was just building himself a million-dollar home.

Lawson is fifty-nine years old — four years older than I am. We began journalistic work almost if not exactly at the same time; perhaps a year or two before I started the Cleveland *Press*, Lawson started the Chicago *News*.[74]

It appears, then, that he was my predecessor in one-cent journalism. However, the Detroit *News* was the progenitor of all the cheap western papers; it was founded as a two-cent publication on August 23, 1873.

There are and have been some points of similarity in the beginnings and careers of Lawson and myself.

We are both native-born Americans of foreign stock; Lawson's parents were Scandinavian, while my father was English.

Lawson got into journalism by accident; he had to take a newspaper in payment of a tenant's rent debt. He was a businessman naturally and only had editorial work thrust upon him by disagreement with and separation from his partner, [Melville E.] Stone. I went into journalism naturally enough, but have not and never had any natural qualifications as a businessman, and only the accident or series of accidents that compelled me to give attention to business affairs gave me a business career.

Lawson started in the very rapidly growing city of Chicago, while my

[74] Melville E. Stone founded the Chicago *Daily News* in 1876, using the New York *Daily News* (not to be confused with the modern New York *Daily News*, dating from 1919) as a model, although he followed also the pattern set by the Scripps' Detroit *News*. Lawson came into the concern as business manager with two-thirds of the stock during the first year of operation. Stone sold out to Lawson in 1888.

first resting place was Cleveland. Chicago has grown to be a city five times as big as Cleveland, and his Chicago property is five times as large a property as my Cleveland property.

Circumstances forced Lawson into the press association business at exactly the same time that I was forced into the same business. In fact, it was because of the spirit of the Associated Press, which found expression in such a businessman as Lawson (who was its president), that prevented me from voluntarily becoming a member of that association. It was to combat the spirit of commercialism and monopoly that I founded the association known as the United Press. But Lawson has a membership in a mutual association that is not run for profit, while I am the majority stockholder in a corporation that is intended to make a profit.

It is odd how things shape themselves! Considering the aim and object of these two associations, they should occupy exactly opposite positions in the matter of organization, but it is the spirit of the man that rules and not the form of government that is significant.

I have sought to secure the freedom of the press and especially to arm myself in warfare against monopoly, and by the very instrument of monopoly — the use of one-man power.

Lawson may be, and probably is, four or five times as rich as myself. Lawson is a confirmed hypochondriac; I have been hypochondriacal most of my life. We have both been devoting a large part of our energies to keeping alive.

There are two more famous and more wealthy newspapermen in the country than Lawson and myself; they are Pulitzer and Hearst.

I have felt, and probably now feel, a certain amount of jealousy toward my three distinguished contemporaries. All three of these men are many times more famous than I am, and even many times more famous in proportion to their successes than I am.

Hearst's one great ambition seems to be for notoriety; Pulitzer loves it. But, so far as I know, Lawson covets seclusion even more greedily than I do.

There has been a marked difference in many points between Lawson's and my own career. Lawson does not like partnership, and he only had one partner and eliminated him; the whole groundwork of my own institution has been an extended series of partnerships.

I have been a rolling stone, Lawson has been a fixed block. Lawson has devoted himself exclusively to his papers in Chicago, while I have wandered all over the United States. Lawson has stuck to one task, while I have scattered my energies. Lawson runs his own business and probably will till the day of his death; I have never done anything about my business that I could get someone else, partner or employee, to attend to, and although I am four years younger than Lawson, I have so far removed myself from the center of business activity that I am practically retired.

Lawson's career is true to the classical business ideal; my own is the reverse of this.

Today McRae tells me that Lawson is building a million-dollar home in the great city of Chicago, in a city where the climate is extremely inclement, and where human misery is gathered in millions of units. My own home, in the matter of cost, is perhaps as consistent with my fortune as is Lawson's consistent with his; its probable cost would be about one-fifth that of Lawson's. My home is in the middle of a wilderness, and is situated where the climate is the most delightful known in the American Republic.

THE SIMPLE LIFE

McRae, who has always been my partner, my admirer, and my flatterer, tells me that since he retired from active business he has been devoting his attention exclusively to the study of the relation of wealth and contentment. He declares that I am the only rich man that he knows or knows of who leads the "simple life." My home is built in that fashion and in that place that best suits my taste, and that too without regard to any of the customs of my class. As a matter of fact, while I spend money freely and lavishly, as compared to the custom of other rich men, the expenditure is all for the purpose of comfort and not at all for luxury or display. McRae also notes that both the situation of my home and the manner of its conduct have not the least relation to business advantage, either of convenience or credit-making display.

About a year ago Dr. McClellan,[75] the president of an eastern college and a member of the commission which has in charge the distribution of the Rockefeller educational fund, was visiting me, and while sitting on the roof terrace of my house, looking over the court and grounds, told me that he was personally acquainted with Mr. Rockefeller and with his several homes, and he said that the richest man in America had no home that was equal, in point of all advantages that a rich man might enjoy, to my place. And he further said that he had seen no home-place in this country which, from appearance, indicated that it could be more desirable than was mine; and yet, he said, he could easily see how, by a little effort of will in a man's freeing himself from the conventionalities, there might be many thousands and even millions of pleasant homes where at present there was the re-

[75] Perhaps Thomas McClelland, president of Knox College, Galesburg, Ill. The General Education Board, which John D. Rockefeller established in 1902, made a grant of $50,000 to Knox College in 1908. However, President McClelland had no connection with the General Education Board. The Rockefeller Foundation, which was not established until 1913, has no record of a Dr. McClellan as having been with either the board or the foundation.

verse. He said that it only required that a man should adapt himself to natural surroundings rather than make an effort to conform himself to an unending series of houses and habits which originated in other lands and in other days where nature wore a different garb and when customs were adapted to conditions no longer existing.

HOME-BUILDING

While a home is the first requisite of every man, whether he be alone or the head of a family, it deserves and should have attention only to its main essentials, and it deserves far less, even infinitely less, of attention than is almost universally given to it.

Convenience, that is, straight comfort, compared with the financial ability of its owner, can be obtained easily and without much cost, and it may be maintained by a trifling small portion of any man's attention.

That which occasions nearly all the labor of home-building and home management, and which detracts from the home the greater part of its possible comfort, is the effort to make needless display and to conform to the trivial and ought-to-be obsolete conventions of society. The servant problem is easily reduced to the simple matter of good manners; there is hardly any distinguishable difference between the master of and the servant in the house, as human beings. Friendship and mutual kindness are as necessary to pleasant living when it applies to the mutual relations between employer and employee as it is to any other social relation. Servants engage themselves to work for wages, but servants only do good work for employers whom they love. [Often enough, on other occasions, Scripps complained of his servants. He usually bellowed at them, for that matter.]

During my life I have had financial relations with many thousands of men: I have been employee and employer. I have been the partner of many men; I have contested many actions of law; and my whole business career has been one of contest and competition, in one form or another, with other men.

Just as the formal wage-paying and wage-receiving transaction takes place between master and servant, so does money-getting and money-giving-up mark and form a conspicuous element in most of the transactions between human beings. Yet, I have learned that the mainspring of all the greatest endeavors in any and every man's actions has been something other than the desire to retain and the objection to giving up money. A loyal servant and ally will render more than double as much service for me than he would for money of mine.

My competitor, whether in peaceful business or in the warfare of litigation, will put forth a hundred times more effort for the hate he bears, or for the love he has for my enemy, than he will for the money that he hopes or expects to obtain.

Many a time in my life have I made valuable use of the hatred of other men against some enemy of my own. I have learned, too, to have a wholesome fear of the friends of my enemy.

We sometimes speak of cold-blooded business and businessmen. I have known of none such business or men. Love, hatred, pride, vanity, and ambition are the things to count on always and everywhere — in the counting room, the courts, legislatures, and the boudoir.

Money-getting is not the ruling passion of men; the ruling passion may, however, be measured or signified by money as is the value of the commonest material commodity.

The Newspaper Business in Relation to Other Forms of Business

[*February 19, 1910*]

In the *Quarterly Journal of Economics* for February, 1909, appeared an article entitled "A Year After the Panic of 1907," by A. D. Noyes, a writer on finance of recognized ability. This copy of the *Journal* missed my eye until it was a year old, but even at the time of reading it I was so much impressed by the article that I failed to discern it was not fresh.

What particularly struck me was the author's statistics concerning the volumes of various businesses during the period of most severe depression after the October, 1907, panic broke out.

There appeared a time when the volume of business being done by the large concerns was not more than 28 per cent of what it had been in the previous year. In many kinds of business during the whole year of 1908 the volume of business was not over 50 per cent of what it had been previously. Many staples, such as iron, copper, and tin, were quoted as having market prices of half or less than half that of previously existing prices. The selling price of stocks in many of the most substantial business corporations had fallen to half or less than half of the previously existing prices. Even in December, 1908, the average volume of business in the country was not over 75 per cent of what it had been fifteen months before.

For many years I have caused to be kept data of my own business. I have a controlling interest in 25 newspaper corporations. A number of these were quite new concerns when the panic broke out. However, for purposes of comparison I took the 13 oldest of my corporations, those that had been existing long enough to have been established, or at least to have proved their power to stand alone. These 13 ranged in annual volume of business from a maximum of some $900,000 down to as low as $20,000. The oldest of these 13 newspapers in 1908 was thirty years old; the youngest, four years old.

264

During 1908 the total volume of business done by these 13 papers was just 1.03 per cent less than the volume of business done by the same papers in the year 1907. In December, 1909, the volume of business done by these 13 papers was several per cent greater than that of any other previous month before or since the 1907 panic.

The year's business of 1909 of all my 25 newspaper corporations and one other, the United Press, showed an increase of 16.5 per cent over the aggregate of the business done by the same papers during the year of 1908.

Taking the two years together, then, the average increase of business was approximately 7½ per cent. During these two years only one new business was founded and that such a small affair as to not affect the percentage showings by probably more than one-quarter of 1 per cent. During the whole time that I have been engaged in the newspaper business, some thirty-five years, taking into consideration the new investments that I have made, the volume of my business has doubled sometimes once in five years and sometimes once in seven years. At an average rate of 10 per cent per annum increase, it would take practically seven years to double a given amount. It will be seen that taking the two years of 1908 and 1907 the average increase of my business was only something like 25 per cent less than what would have been required to double the volume every seven years.

Considering the fact that there were no new papers founded, this item alone might account for almost the whole of the falling off of growth of volume of business. In fact I am inclined to believe that, everything considered, the panic of 1907 had but a very slight, if any, effect in the matter of retardation of the growth of my business.

At the present time I have only got the statistics for one month of the year 1910, but this shows a growth in the volume of business of over 24 per cent over the same month of last year. It seems probable that the increase in volume of business, this year over last year, will not be less than 16 per cent, and it may even be as high as 20 per cent. Therefore, taking the three years together, the growth of volume of business will be from 32 to 36 per cent.

Even allowing for the compounding calculation, the growth of volume of business during the three years, including the period of depression, has been practically up to normal.

What does all this mean? Other business institutions, as a whole, all suffered in loss of business, by reason of the panic, from 15 to 80 per cent; that is to say, from 15 to 80 times more than we suffered. During the year 1908 so little recovery was made by other businesses that in the last month of 1908 the average business was 25 per cent lower than the previous high tide. In the case of our business, such recovery had been made that in December our volume of business was greater by several per cent than it had ever been before.

I have no definite information of general business conditions over the country for the beginning of this year, 1910. However, from such general information as I get from the journals, I judge that, with rare exceptions, business volume has not yet got back to what it was in 1907.

In the case of my own business, it appears that the volume of business has increased to such an extent that it is 40 per cent greater or more than 40 per cent greater than it was in the high tide of the prepanic boom. What are the deductions that I should make from all of this?

1. Is the newspaper business itself such a peculiar one as not to be subject to the ordinary loss occasioned by business depression?

2. Is my business peculiarly remarkable in the fact that it is officered by men who, by reason of their youth, energy, and peculiar capacities, are far above the average of men similarly employed in other lines of business?

3. Are the rules and methods established by me and practiced by my successors at all responsible for this most remarkable condition of affairs?

I will undertake some analysis of the last of the three propositions, by putting questions and answering them.

What is the most remarkable characteristic of the Scripps newspaper business?

I would answer it by saying that beyond all question, the characteristic most to be noted is that it is not a debtor concern; that is to say, it is not doing business on borrowed money, on money procured by the sale of bonds. The amount of outstanding indebtedness of the concern, as an aggregate to other than owners of the concern, is not perhaps 1 per cent of the aggregate value of the concern. For the most part corporate as well as private business is done on a capital half or three-quarters of which is furnished by outsiders lending money in one form or another, but generally in the form of bonds.

The next most noticeable feature of our business is that, so far from our having any water in our stock, the face capital of our corporations does not aggregate 10 per cent, perhaps not even 5 per cent, of the real value of the concern, as indicated by its immediate ability to pay dividends and its perfectly evident prospects of great increase in profits.

A third characteristic of our business is the custom of rapid rotation in office; that is to say, a rotation which is equivalent to elimination. The result is an almost universal employment of new brooms and of young men during only that period of their lives when they are most vigorous, self-confident, and determined.

Personally, I am responsible for the two conditions; namely, the small capitalization and the rapid elimination of old men and employment of only young men. For the third condition, namely, the absence of debt, I cannot claim that I am responsible — at least by intention. By temperament or instinct I am opposed to debt. By practice and by the use of my reason I have always sought to be a debtor; that is to say, I have been anxious to borrow all the money I could get at the going rates of interest to invest in a business which I knew so well how to handle on a profit of several times greater than the ordinary interest rate.

As to the first proposition, namely, "Is the newspaper business in itself a peculiar one?" I have also something to say. I consider that the newspaper business as a business is a peculiar one. The most remarkable feature in its peculiarity is the fact that its capital value is composed at least 90 per cent of goodwill; that is to say, public prestige. In this respect it has the peculiarity of a profession. It is the prestige, the public confidence, which gives the large remuneration to lawyers, doctors, engineers, and all other professional men. In nearly all manufacturing and mercantile business from 90 to 95 per cent of their basis of value consists of actual stock, or material, patent rights, or other franchises. But in no other business excepting the newspaper business, that I can think of, is the percentage of value represented by goodwill or public prestige to the extent of 90 per cent.

But there are five thousand other newspapers in the United States. Some of them are very valuable and have made their owners very rich, but on the average I doubt if there is not more money lost in the newspaper business in this country than there is made. I mean by this that the aggregate capital invested in newspapers does not yield an average profit equal to the going interest rates. It is possible, even, that there is no profit at all made on the whole, but even a loss. It has been said about the gold-mining business that more money or capital is put into the various forms of mining enterprise every year than is taken out in actual gold. The same has been said of the newspaper business, and perhaps truthfully.

On the other hand, it is said of all gas companies that it is almost impossible for investors in gas production not to make a profit, and that, taking the aggregate of all the capital invested in gas production, a higher annual profit is made than in any other business. It would seem, then, that there is nothing peculiar about the newspaper business which accounts for our prosperity and our growth. We have not discovered, then, a secret which we are keeping under cover, and from which we are profiting.

I am inclined to believe, however, that we are profiting by various conditions and by various practices which are almost universally recognized as valuable, but which are almost universally not taken advantage of. I am rather inclined to ascribe the prosperous condition of our business to three things which I will set down in the order they merit.

1. That the stockholders are determined to do business at present and immediate profits.

2. That we employ only very young men, men who have not elsewhere, under other employment, earned a right to prestige — young men who have practically been working for us at apprentice wages while they are doing their best work; and further we do not load ourselves up with older men who are employed simply on account of their prestige long after the period of their greatest usefulness.

3. That we not only keep water out of our stock but capitalize our corporations at the smallest possible amount, and because of our small capitalization we force ourselves to abstain from all extravagances, all expenditures, the purpose of which is display and show of prosperity. In this way we are also forced to depend almost entirely for advance in public esteem on work actually done — first, in producing a popular newspaper, and second, in selling the newspaper and getting advertising. In fact, this very idea of small capitalization artificially induces us to make skillful use of the only valuable element in any business, namely, human effort. The man who depends upon his own right arm and his own capacity to think right has an infinitely better chance than he who depends upon capital inherited or obtained otherwise, or on repute falsely based upon inheritance or some accident resulting from conspicuousness in a community, large or small.

We have an instance of this latter kind of repute being made profitable in the case of William Jennings Bryan, in his newspaper the *Commoner*. The *Commoner* does not depend upon its own prestige, or goodwill, but upon the fame or notoriety of its editor. If Bryan should die or if some other person should purchase the *Commoner*, the whole goodwill value of that institution would cease.

Not only are my newspaper properties many times more valuable than Bryan's, just as Bryan is many times more notorious than I am, but so far as my death or elimination from my concern ruining the property or even injuring it, recent experiments are convincing me that the concern will gain as much by the elimination of the "old man," myself, as it has gained in the aggregate by the elimination of all the scores of other old men who were once connected with it.

The Principles of the Scripps Idea of Journalism

[March 2, 1910]

"Miramar," Calif., March 2, 1910

Mr. H. N. Rickey
Mr. W. B. Colver
410 American Trust Building
Cleveland, Ohio

Gentlemen:

You have asked me to reduce to writing, or have reduced to writing, the principles of the Scripps idea of journalism.[76]

They are so few and so simple that they can all be known and easily understood by anyone who has had a quarter of an hour's conversation with me. If they are not generally known and fully comprehended by all such persons, it is simply because my words have not been taken at their face value, or, to put it in another way, I have not been credited with meaning what I have said.

Before undertaking to enunciate the principles that govern me as a journalist, I should take cognizance of and make remarks concerning a business principle which is a necessary underlying foundation of such a newspaper institution as I have attempted to create. This principle is that a newspaper's income should not only be great enough to pay its going expenses, including the wages and other compensations necessary to secure and retain the employment of men of considerable ability, but they should be great enough to guarantee a profit, in ordinary times, of such dimensions as will rapidly make a reserve fund.

A newspaper fairly and honestly conducted in the interest of the great masses of the public must at all times antagonize the selfish interests of

[76] Part of this letter appears in McCabe, *Damned Old Crank*, p. 145 f.

269

that very class which furnishes the larger part of a newspaper's income, and occasionally so antagonize this class as to cause it not only to cease patronage, to a greater or lesser extent, but to make actually offensive warfare against the newspaper.

In order to maintain a newspaper's entire independence, it is necessary that the newspaper should be so conducted that its revenue from the advertising class will be the smallest possible that that class can afford to get on with. The advertising patronage that such a newspaper should have should only be a result of the necessity of the newspaper's patrons to get publicity for personal and selfish reasons.

The man who carries a gun, and is known to carry a gun, seldom needs it. The newspaper whose reserve of capital is large, and is known to be large, is almost wholly free from the danger of boycott by advertisers who would certainly resort to pressure in order to subdue a newspaper whose treasury was small and whose existence depended from day to day upon its advertising patronage.

As to editorial principles:

The first of my principles is that I have constituted myself the advocate of that large majority of the people who are not so rich in worldly goods and native intelligence as to make them equal, man for man, in the struggle with individuals of the wealthier and more intellectual class.

The press of this country is now, and always has been, so thoroughly dominated by the wealthy few of the country that it cannot be depended upon to give the great mass of the people that correct information concerning political, economical, and social subjects which it is necessary that the mass of the people shall have in order that they shall vote and in all ways act in the best way to protect themselves from the brutal force and chicanery of the ruling and employing class. I have sought to give these people all that information which will strengthen them in their unequal contest with their masters.

In furtherance of this latter policy I have sought to teach the common people the value — even the necessity — of combination. Although I fully recognize the many evils inherent in trade unionism, I have advocated its extension, the perfecting of its discipline, and its comprehending political activity.

Whenever there is a contest between the ruling classes, including not only employers but government officials on one side and the wage earners, the poor men, and even the moderately well-to-do men on the other side, I have chosen to be the associate, friend, and fellow-striver of the second party. I have assumed, for purposes of guiding my own conduct, that the first party is mainly wrong and the second party is mainly always right. Even when the leading men and measures in my party are of more than questionable worth and morality, I have assumed that there are enough other newspapers and enough other forces arrayed against us to insure that no general and far-reaching injustice will result even from the temporary successes of men and measures in my party that are intrinsically bad. I do not "stand for men" — all men — as Henry George is said to have done. I have been an uncompromising partisan of that great majority of our people who are strong only in numbers.

It is not one of my journalistic principles to reform all the political and other social movements of our people. Even when I cause to be published arguments and matters of fact, the purpose of which are to persuade the masses of men to be temperate or totally abstemious in the use of liquor, it has not been for the purpose of saving souls; it has only been for the purpose of making my partisans more efficient in their struggle with their antagonists.

In a municipal contest between the great majority of the citizens — the working class — and the capitalistic element, I would aid my partisans even did I know that their success would give the city poor government and that the success of their opponents would give the city a good government.

In fact, I have not a whole series of journalistic principles. I have only one principle, and that is represented by an effort to make it harder for the rich to grow richer and easier for the poor to keep from growing poorer.

It can be said, and it can even be proved to the satisfaction of most men, that there is no difference in my business principle and the business principle that governs the majority of newspaper owners, and it also can be said and proved to the satisfaction of the same people that the ethics of my journalism are no better than those of the most venal and selfish of my profession.

It can be said that the net results of making money in order to make an independent newspaper are the same as if I were to make my newspaper serve only to make me money. It can be said and be believed by very honest, serious-minded men that it is no less wicked to be radical partisans of one party than it is to be radical partisans of the other.

However, you do not ask me to furnish arguments in defense of my principles and my motives. You only ask for their enunciation.

Our experience has taught us that there is nothing in our business principles that would conflict with our interests no matter how selfish we were. Our experience as journalists has also taught us that our joy of battle has been the greater because we have chosen to struggle with the unconquerable.

So long as our business and journalistic principles have secured and are securing for us the two main essentials of a happy life, it seems to me that there are no good reasons why we should seek to change our location in the business and ethical field.

On the other side of the line, which divides us from our enemy, are crowded hundreds of newspapers competing one with another for the favors of the rich and the great, while on our side of the line there are few to compete with us for either honor or profit.

I believe that in the foregoing I have fully and completely outlined the principles of the man who presided over and led the forces that created the Scripps newspapers. I believe, also, that unintentionally while I have been dictating I have indicated sufficiently good arguments to support my theories.

I accept Rickey's suggestion that Mr. Paine should elaborate more or less in detail special rules that would naturally be deduced from the general principles that have so largely influenced the institution in which he has spent his whole adult life.

Yours sincerely,

E. W. Scripps

[Perhaps in pursuance of the suggestion mentioned in the last paragraph, Paine reduced the principles and policies of the Scripps papers to more concrete terms in a letter to Colver, dated December 9, 1910, and filed in Scripps' personal Letterbooks. Paine wrote:]

GENERAL POLICIES

Loyalty to the Masses. — Loyalty to what is right and best for the common people, especially including legitimate labor organizations.

Contents of the Paper. — The editor does and should make the paper and is responsible for all its contents.

Number of Items. — Variety and character of news items should be sought and, other things being equal, the paper containing the largest number of items will win the best reception from the public.

Quality of Items. — Those items are the most valuable which will interest the largest number of readers. Conciseness, intelligibility, and originality will count rather than high literary excellence.

Quarrels. — Quarrels with competitors are to be avoided. In fact, continued quarreling or nagging with anybody is not desirable.

Size of Paper. — Success of a newspaper depends very little on quantity of contents compared to quality of contents.

Finances. — The paper will succeed best when the editor is wisely, and hence profitably, spending in his department 35 per cent of the income from circulation and advertisements.

Main Aim. — To attract and hold fireside readers, avoiding things offensive to such, should be the main aim.

SPECIAL POLICIES

The Tariff. — Treat it as an economic question. Revise schedule by schedule on expert information. We should give [President] Taft credit for his stand for the Beveridge plan for a permanent commission. [Senator Albert J. Beveridge of Indiana, ranked as a Republican progressive of the era, fought Old Guard efforts to raise tariff rates. The Old Guard put through the Payne-Aldrich tariff bill of 1909, but the bill also created the Tariff Commission.]

Conservation. — Should be a matter for federal management. [Gifford] Pinchot's ideas on the subject seem to be of great worth.

Railroads. — Demand full information, physical valuation and stronger, more definite authority for the Interstate Commerce Commission. Final solution, government ownership.

National Incorporations. — Favor it, with provisions against stock watering. Demand fullest publicity. State regulation of interstate business is an impossibility. We might pay some attention to Rudolph Spreckels' scheme to require big corporations to publish names of all stockholders at regular intervals.

Ship Subsidy. — Support a plan for building a national commercial fleet, to be leased to private companies or communities in numerous seaports. See Senator [Francis G.] Newlands' measure.

Central Bank. — It might be a good thing, if the government were to own and administer it. Sixty per cent of the directors should be government appointees, the President, Secretary of the Treasury, and Speaker of the House among them. Stock should be sold to the people, especially postal-savings bank depositors. No stockholder should be permitted to own or hold over 5 per cent, and never more than 10 per cent should be owned or held by the people of one state.

Defense of the Panama Canal. — The U.S. government should fortify and defend the canal. It would be fair and creditable to back up Taft's position in this matter as set forth in his recent message.

Income Tax. — Favor it.

Non-Partisan Judiciary. — Work for it.

Initiative, Referendum, and Recall. — Favor them.

Employers Liability Act. — Favor it.

Direct Primaries. — Favor them.

Currency Reform. — Don't damn it simply because [Senator Nelson W.] Aldrich [Republican, Rhode Island] may favor it.

Alaska. — Government should conserve its resources and try out the policy of government building and operating railroads, terminals, docks, etc.

Enlargement of Navy. — Favor it, with an effort to secure a better class of men for the Navy, through establishing better conditions and more opportunities for advancement.

Government Inspection and Control of Mines. — Favor them.

Female Suffrage. — Favor it.

Parcels Post. — Favor it.

Government Plans to Locate Immigrants. — Favor them, and include reforms in immigration legislation.

Government Control of Interstate Telegraph and Telephone Companies. — Favor it.

Congressional Franking Privileges. — Should be reduction and reform in them. The matter of distributing free seeds ought to be left to the Agricultural Department, for instance.

Court Injunctions. — Work for radical reform.

Contempt of Court Cases. — Demand that such shall not hold save when the act occurs in a courtroom during prosecution of court business.

Labor Unions Not Criminal Trusts. — Stand by organized labor in its demand that anti-trust laws shall not apply to labor unions.

Politics. — Fight for a clean-cut division between conservative and radical progressive ideas, even though it be necessary to encourage a new party.

Some Ideas and Plans

[*April 10, 1910*]

I have sometimes defined myself as being the parent of two sets of children — the children of my brain, or intellectual effort, and the children of my flesh. The first-mentioned family began to appear before the second, and has continued to have numerical additions made up to the present time. I have a family of newspapers, and a family of boys and girls.

Owing somewhat to my peculiar temperament, and perhaps more to the fact that the birth, continued existence, and development of my newspapers have been caused by voluntary effort and self-sacrifice, my feelings and affection for and interest in my newspapers as individuals has been little, if any, less than my affection for and interest in these children of my flesh, whose very existence has taxed neither my willpower nor my capacity for self-sacrifice.

Now amongst certain rather primitive or barbaric peoples there has existed a custom that has sometimes been described as patriarchal and sometimes as primogenital, by means of which only one of a man's children could become his heir. All the other children, the wives of the decedent, and even the mother of the fortunate one designated as heir became the slaves and chattels of the heir. This was a beastly custom.

The patriarchal system might have been and perhaps was necessary to a certain stage of the development of human society.

Primogeniture has in many countries and for long periods of time been an element in the social order that has worked not all too badly.

However, I have no patience with either the patriarchal or the primogenital systems. I would not have any young man submitted to the absolute control of his elder, even though that elder be his father. I would not even have a young man trained to consider with deference the opinions and desires of his elder, just because that elder chances to be a parent.

The whole object and intention of a title to property, and power by indi-

275

viduals in society, is to best serve the interests not only of the title-holders, but of all society. Therefore, it is desirable that only the most fit should by inheritance become possessed of wealth or political power and influence.

Physiologists have learned that the firstborn, so far from having any superior advantages in body or mind over others of his father's children, has if anything a poorer chance, first of life itself and second of a robust, healthy body and mind.

Few parents live long enough to be able to fully determine the exact relative qualities of their children, and hence the selection of the favorite heir can at best be but a gamble.

My idea is that at the parent's death all of his children should inherit equally that parent's estate.

Now I have two sets of children: my newspapers, and my boys and girls. I would not in life by orders or argument, or any sort of influence, subordinate the children of my flesh to make them the servants of my newspapers. That is to say, I would not compel my children to learn how to become newspapermen, or even ask them to work with and for my newspapers.

On the other hand, I would not turn over as chattels to the possession of my children solely for their use, enjoyment, and amusement, my newspapers, if there was any possible way of avoiding such a course. However, society through its laws must recognize my newspapers as simply property, and a part of my estate, and hence as subject matter for inheritance by my children. These newspapers are property, and they must be owned by individuals. These individuals must be my children, or the children of some other man.

I could exchange these newspaper properties for other forms of property during my lifetime, so that these other forms of property, rather than these newspapers themselves, would become the inheritance of my children. But in order to do this, I must during my lifetime disassociate myself from these children of my brain, and suffer greatly in mind by reason of the alienation.

I have all along been prepared to make this great sacrifice of personal comfort in the interest of my newspapers, providing it should appear to me that my children of the flesh were either unworthy of being trusted with the control of the newspapers, or undesirous of assuming their ownership and control as a pleasant duty.

If none of my sons were capable of conducting my newspapers in an honorable and efficient way for the service of the public, I would certainly during my lifetime choose other men to become owners of these newspapers — in part giving and in part selling to these new owners, so that while the children of my flesh would lose nothing of the value of their inheritance, my newspapers would have the advantage of being owned and conducted by competent and worthy men.

However, the time has already come when I am become convinced that, of all businessmen I could select worthy of the trusteeship of these newspapers, among my sons the choice would lie. It is also now apparent to me that one or more of my children would prefer to have their estate consist of newspaper property rather than any other property.

Owing to the conditions under which my family has grown up and to the peculiar opportunities my children have had to learn the newspaper business, it is evident that they are and will be better trained and better instructed in the newspaper business than in any other line.

Now that I have decided, for various reasons, the equality that must exist between all of my children (except my eldest daughter) [77] in the matter of inheritance at the date of my death, and that I have further decided that the best interests of my children and my newspapers will be served by my children becoming the owners of the newspapers, some other problems are presenting themselves to my mind.

One of the parables of Jesus relates to the action of a certain vineyard owner who on a certain day employed a large number of men to work in his vineyard. Some of these men began work at the first hour of the day and labored all through the day. Their number was added to at various hours of the day, some even coming so late as to work only during the last hour of the day. When the day's labor was performed, the owner of the vineyard called in all of the men he had hired during the day, and to each he paid exactly the same sum. On this there arose complaint on the part of the men who had worked all the day that their wages had only been the same as the wages received by men who had worked for a much less amount of time. According to the parable, these complainants were rebuked by their employer.

This parable is for the purpose of teaching a lesson in morals, the wisdom of which lesson I am not convinced of.[78]

However, I had recognized that to a very large extent law and custom of modern civilized people are very similar to the ruling of this vineyard-owner parable.

Especially in this country, there is an almost overwhelming popular opinion in favor of a perfectly equitable division of an estate among all the children of the decedent, without regard to the fitness of the individual members of a man's family to administer property and without regard to the amount of service and the length of time of such service given by the children of the decedent during the latter's life, performed in the interest and for the benefit of the common estate.

Necessarily, everything else being equal, the eldest child of a family must contribute a year or two more of work toward the family's fortune than the

[77] Dolla, who was mentally retarded.
[78] Matthew, 20:1.

next-born. Each succeeding child will have an equally long period of time wherein he serves more than his brother or sister who follows.

So far, beginning very early in life, each of my children has been called upon by me and has willingly and voluntarily contributed services, helping me in my labors. It is possible and probable that this condition will continue until the time of my death, or until the time of my absolute and complete abdication. Now I do not think it will be just for me, nor just to my newspapers, or to my children, that I should continue up to my death in full possession and ownership of all of that property, the building of which I began alone, but which to a greater or less degree for a greater or less length of time, has been the joint work of myself and my children.

On the other hand, I feel that for various reasons I should begin the distribution of my estate amongst my children at the earliest possible time. For the same reasons, I think it is wise that I should from time to time, as rapidly as practicable, give to each of my children the actual title to that part of my property which might be continued in undivided estate — that part which is clearly and unmistakably to be recognized as the result of each individual child's personal effort.

In fact, I hold it would not be right for me to permit my oldest son, who is nearly ten years older than my youngest son, to labor for ten years longer than my youngest son and at a certain given time in the ages of both divide my estate so that each would have an exactly equal share. In the same way, I feel that it would be just and equitable that each child should receive, during my lifetime and during the period of his service, compensation not only in proportion to time served but in proportion to ability, that is to say, value of work done.

I believe that no worse injury could be done to any young man than that he should habitually accustom himself to the idea of reaping where he has not sown, or reaping anything else than what he has sown. For this reason I feel that the sons of all rich men who have constantly in mind and knowledge that they are to be heirs and possessors of property that they have not created are at a disadvantage. However, there is nothing that I can do, that I ought to do, which will remove this disadvantage that my children must suffer. The most that I can do is to cause that condition of affairs which will give relatively, amongst my children, rewards greater or less according to the time of their service and the value of their service in and to the institution which I govern.

But because of the difference in ages, the extreme youth and hence incapacity of some of my children, and the more advanced age of others, I cannot adopt the plan of giving to each of my children in exact proportion to his services. I must establish a certain minimum as an amount to be distributed to each of my children, without regard to their services. I propose that this minimum income shall be well within the income that they would be reasonably certain of deriving from their share of my estate if I were to die at any moment. Therefore, I think that each of my children should receive from me directly or from my estate what would be called an allowance, and that this income should be equitably apportioned according to their ages, necessities, and their state of mental development.

In a certain practical way I have done this. Beginning at a very early age, with each of my children, I made them a personal allowance. In each case this has been increased, both with their added years and their own capacity to make use of the money given them and my ability to allot them money.

Naturally enough my younger children, at a given age, received more than my older children did, because my estate and my capacity for giving has been increased since the time that my older children first received their allotments.

The maximum allowance that I should make each of these children should be limited by other considerations than my ability to make the allowance. The principal idea governing me in this matter should be what I consider to be to the interest of the child himself or herself. It might be possible for me to make an allowance, the maximum of which would be so large as to utterly and completely discourage the child from making any personal effort on his part or her part.

I do not believe it would be possible or that it would be even fair to have a fixed minimum or maximum. I think that each individual case should be considered. I must always remember that the acquirement of property, so far from being the chief end of man's effort, is really not more than of second-rate, or even third-rate, importance. Therefore, equity and justice to my children compel me to consider a great many more things than the mere apportionment of daily allowances of money.

The amount of money that I could and should allow monthly to each of my children under present conditions is between $50.00 and $1,000 per month. I doubt the wisdom of any of my children, at the present time, making use of more than $500 per month for living expenses. If, for any reason, I should make a larger allowance, I think that it would be fair for me to require that all above $500, just at this time anyway, should be preserved by a child of mine in the way of capital.

I think that each of my children should always hold in view the possibility that for some reason or another the whole of their father's estate might be annihilated. I think that each of them should make an unceasing effort to build up so much of an individual estate as to not only secure them a competence in case of the destruction of my own estate, but to enable them to render a fair amount of assistance to their mother and other less fortunate members of the family. It should be each one's business: (1) to secure his own independent fortune; (2) to secure an independent competence for each of his brothers and sisters; and (3) to care for the common fortune — the parental estate.

No man who ever waited for "a dead man's shoes" was worthy of receiving anything from the dead man, or really capable of taking care of what he did receive. I have a contempt for, and the world has a contempt for, any man who makes the first object of his consideration an inheritance, no matter how large it may be.

Now remains the question of considering ways and means of the segregation of the family estate. I have rejected the simplest and the commonest custom of leaving all of this to the last will and testament.

I have already decided, and have made a beginning in the way of making a personal division, by means of absolute and direct gifts of property, and by affording other means to my sons of entering into partnership in business ventures of my own. I have made a beginning, but little more.

The time has come now when I and the two of my sons who are of mature age [Jim and John] are being forced to consider a plan for the further development of this scheme for the segregation and partition. I have thought of, and broached to my sons, the idea of forming the whole estate into a corporation and making absolute gifts of certain shares of stock to members of my family. This scheme has not been entirely acceptable. The worst of it is that it contemplates the gift from a father to a son rather than the payment of just compensation for services rendered, or a fair share of the profits in proportion to each man's services. I myself believe that in the long run the happiness, the contentment, and the success of my children, each of them, will be served by the practice of independence in character and fortune-building. It will be better for my children, each of them, to refuse to accept something for nothing, even from their own father, especially during his lifetime. It would be better for them, also, to accustom themselves to the idea that a property inheritance from their father is accompanied by such an inheritance of duty and an obligation of trusteeship as would in their minds greatly detract from what would otherwise be purely selfish gain from such inheritance.

I predict that he or she, among my children, who first actually and really succeeds in regarding an inheritance as being entirely a neutral thing so far as desirability or undesirability is concerned will be the one who will stand above all the others in the possession of fortune and the exercise of power, and in the general enjoyment of life.

I do not want to give, and I feel that my sons ought to be unwilling to accept, anything for nothing.

Owing to their opportunities, their natural ability, and the training they have had, both of my older sons now are fully capable of paying their way;

that is to say, they are capable of performing such valuable services that, being justly compensated for the same, they need feel no dependence upon their father, and no sense of obligation for financial assistance.

I do not presume to say that both my oldest sons are equally competent to render services of equal value. In my own mind, I am convinced that they are not.

But I have said before that few parents can live long enough to fully appraise the character and competence of their sons. No two men have identically the same idea, either, of the relative value of any other two men. Often during my life's experience I have seen men whom I had at one time supposed inferior prove themselves to be very superior. More often, still, I have found men that I rejected entirely because of their lack of value demonstrate elsewhere very superior capacities.

I recall that the consensus of opinion in my own family was that of my father, namely, that of all his children, I was considered the least efficient, and the one who would develop the least capacity for doing great work. My appraisement of the value of my sons to the concern should not be considered by them, or others, as very significant. These sons of mine, each in his own way and in his own time, will demonstrate his capacities, and it is reasonable for me to expect that my higher opinion of one might be to the detriment of that one, while my lower opinion of the other might be his greatest advantage.

Now, while I find it not only difficult but impossible to correctly appraise the relative merits of my children, and their consequent relative share in the profits of our joint enterprise, I have no doubts in my own mind on several subjects:

1. I believe that my sons together, or some of them, are so competent that, in the future, the newspapers which I own will be more prosperous and successful if I abstain from too much of their management, and delegate almost the whole of the authority to my sons.

2. While I am insistent in my ideas that my sons should not permit themselves to accept something for nothing from me, I am, on the other hand, determined not to accept anything for nothing from them. In other words, I am determined to treat them as my partners and to share with them fairly the profits of our joint efforts, and the profits of the joint products of my previously acquired capital, and their present and future labor.

It is perfectly evident to any man of affairs that no human mind is capable of accurately appraising and hence dividing the products of several men's labor into capital.

For a great many years I have adopted as a rule of business practice a plan whereby I have furnished the capital and such assistance as I chose to give voluntarily, and then divided equally with one man, or one set of men (or nearly equally, in case of corporations 49 per cent to 51 per cent) the profits of any enterprise that I went into, or undertook, or continued with a partner or partners.

At this late period, my plan having worked so well as it has in the past, I feel that it is unnecessary to change it.

Now I propose to have a sort of equal partnership; myself being the party of the first part, entitled to half the profits, and my sons being the parties of the second part to divide amongst themselves, perhaps according to my decision, the other half. I propose that at some given date, say January 1, 1910 [*sic*], to have the value of my newspaper estate fixed and appraised. From that date on I propose that half of all the increase of the estate shall be considered the property of my partners.

It shall be understood that I am giving my partners, my sons, nothing. I am parting with nothing, myself, to transfer to them. For instance, at no time can my aggregate wealth be found to be less than it was at the date mentioned.

Further, at no time shall the aggregate of the wealth my sons hold (inclusive of all the money they have received from that date) be greater than the amount of my wealth at that time, in excess of my wealth at the date, say of January 1, 1908 [*sic*]. Beyond this, to protect myself from any inconvenience, and to prevent my sons from any unwise speculation, I must stipulate that the final proof of property growth shall be net cash divisible profits, or else real estate, not including buildings.

I am thoroughly determined that a fair proportion of all profits must be "fluid," that is to say, cash income usable by me in my lifetime. My sons have longer to live, and therefore will, after a reasonable time of waiting, be in a position to fully enjoy a cash income.

For the purpose of having some sort of a standard, I propose that the capital be considered on a 6 per cent income basis.

For my purposes, I propose that all of the property that I am assessed as being worth January 1, 1908, shall be reckoned as allowing me an income of 6 per cent. If, for instance, I am assessed as being worth 3 million dollars, there shall be due to me an annual income from that date of $180,000, at least. Then, not until I have been paid in cash an income equal to $180,000 per annum from January 1, 1908, shall there be considered to be any cash income to be provided for my partners. Beyond this, whatever is the aggregate cash income received by my partner sons in any period of time, it shall not be greater than the aggregate of my cash income over and above $180,000 per year.

It is my idea now that there should be no considerable division of stock interest of any kind until after a cash divisible income has been obtained. In other words, for the purpose of dividing as between partners, there must be no increase in the value of property considered until the actual increase in value has been proven by the property's capacity to yield income, say at a rate of 6 per cent.

While it will be manifestly evident that there may have been a great appreciation in the value of the property, my partner sons should wait until this appreciation has been proved by cash profits before demanding or even consenting to the acceptance of their share. It may be unwise at this time to attempt to further work out the details of this whole proposition. There may come a time when, considering the underlying principles that have dictated my determination in the foregoing, and in justice to my sons, I should make some sort of a written contract, and perhaps add a clause or codicil to my will.

The most that I think I can do and should do at this time is to let my sons understand that the principle of my dealings with them is to be that, in some form or another and in some practical manner at the earliest times possible, they are to receive in *unequal* amounts, in proportion to their ability and service, a fair share of the products of their joint labor with me and their joint labor with the capital I have created, and that I will appraise this share in accordance with an old and well-tried rule and plan of mine, that of giving half a dollar out of every dollar that is made as a result of the joining of my capital and labor with the labor of my partners.

I do not propose, at least at this early date, a scheme of such entire equality with my young and untried partners as will give them an equal voice with me in determining any question as to the fairness and propriety of the time and manner of the division. Until such times as my sons are capable of, whether they are willing to resort to such a course or not, but until they are capable of, man for man with me, compelling me to do justice whether I will or not, I will not, and should not, in the interests of all parties, consider their position [as] of entire equality with me.

It is my conviction that the time when they should be in this position should not be far distant in the future. According to nature, the time must come when they will arrive at a full equality of power, and hence of rights with me, and further the time will come when their power, and hence their rights in and control of the institution which is the major part of my estate, will be greater than mine, and when I must be dominated even as I now dominate in this family of men and institutions.

It seems to me now quite possible that my adoption of this scheme and plan must inevitably result in a tolerably fair and equitable division of the results of my lifework amongst my children in proportion to the merits, the capacities, and the services of each.

It is only proper for me to say here that I consider that a rather remarkable condition of affairs exists in this family. While one of my daughters is conceded to be absolutely inefficient and necessarily subject to guardianship, I have no reason to believe that my younger daughter and youngest son may not be fully the equal of either or both of my two eldest sons in capacity to own and control property. But for her sex, I would consider that young Nackey might well outstrip all of her brothers in proved business capacity. I have no doubt but that she will be able to take care of herself and not only to successfully control an inheritance but to increase it. Therefore, I doubt whether it will be necessary or even advisable to exclude her from the ownership of newspaper stock and reduce her inheritance to an entirely different kind of property.

If, by chance, my life is so prolonged as has been that of other members of my family — prolonged beyond the period when I can be of very great use to the newspapers — I believe it will be better that I should part altogether with the individual ownership of any newspaper stock, and I believe that it will be decided that my estate should consist wholly of other property than stocks.

I abhor the idea of the "dead hand," and I consider that the control by the "palsied hand" is even more dangerous. I should count as the best evidence of my own success of life the fact that, before it was ended, my sons should, with or without my voluntary wish or even consent, take from me all of my newspaper possessions.

On Managing Men and Newspapers

[*August 21, 1911*]

"Miramar," Calif., August 21, 1911

Jas. G. Scripps
Jno. P. Scripps
San Diego, Calif.

My dear Sons:

I wish you to consider the two following propositions: [79]

1. That this concern of ours should develop from its cubs its great men, though it may be wise to make a few exceptions to this rule.

2. That great men as a rule result from their having exceptional opportunities very early in their careers, and that their successes depend upon this condition more than upon the possible fact that they have exceptional natural gifts.

ARGUMENTS

The Jesuit brotherhood of the great Catholic Church has been from its beginning and for centuries the most powerful and effective organ of the church. Its almost invariable custom has been to recruit its membership from very young children, almost infants. (There is a saying amongst the Jesuits that, "Give us a child, its teaching and training, for the first seven years of its life, and we have small fear that it will ever cease to be a good Catholic.")

The Jesuit takes the young child, teaches and trains him, and molds his mind while it is plasticity itself. The boy continues in the Jesuit school; taught and trained nothing else but the ways of Catholicism and Jesuitry; and when the boy has grown to young manhood, while he is eminently fitted to practice the priestly profession, he is almost incapable of pursuing any other vocation successfully or even with sufficient energy to make existence possible.

For centuries the great Mohammedan power, which was the greatest mili-

[79] Title of this disquisition supplied by editor.

285

tary power in Europe and Asia for a long period of time, had as its most effective military arm a body of soldiers called janissaries. The troops of the janissaries were practically exclusively composed of men whose parents were of other races and other religions than that of the Mohammedans.

In their great wars of conquest the Mohammedans sought always to annihilate their enemies, to kill all of their soldiers, and to take as slaves their younger women and all of the children. These children, or such of them as were very young, were reserved for special treatment by the state. To them was given a peculiar education and training. On them more than upon the children of Mohammedan subjects were impressed the teachings of the Koran and faith in Mohammed. As a result, these children grown to manhood were the most zealous and the most faithful of Mohammedans, and the most courageous and willing to sacrifice life on the battlefields.

The great advantage of the system of recruiting the very young in our particular class of journalism is that these boys or young men come to us with opinions unformed and with no practice in other journalistic methods. It is during their term of plasticity of mind that they are young and vigorous and are inclined to throw into the work the whole of their energy — unthoughtful, unbiased, willing, and glad to follow and learn from a leader. As these young men grow up together they become mutually familiar with the ways of thought and the practices of each other, and hence "team" well together and have comparatively small reason to waste their time in contentions as to objects to be obtained and as to methods to be practiced.

They have learned such things as are of great value to themselves and to the concern, and such learning and habits as they have acquired rather unfits them than fits them for successful careers in that other class of journalism which is most antagonistic to ours.

While we must fully recognize the existence of genius and the fact that in the ranks of the many there are a few brilliant and exceptionable men, we must also recognize that these exceptionable men are so few that perhaps out of every thousand men who come to us not more than one such exceptionable man may be present.

But while there are only a few geniuses, a far larger proportion in the ranks of the so-called common men are men who only need great opportunities, great necessities, and great inducements in order that they shall develop to such an extent that it is almost impossible to distinguish between such as they are become and the genius born.

Young as you are yourselves you have still lived long enough to have been able to learn by observation that the best and most effective work by any man is done during that period when he is acquiring reputation. Reputation once won has a high market value so that he who employs men of great repute must pay such an excessively large price for their services that great financial and business skill is required on the part of the employer to derive any financial profit from such employment.

The great profit to the employer comes from the labor of those men who are acquiring reputations by such valuable work as, [at] the time of its being done, is unrecognized by the workman himself, his immediate associates, or his employer. While there is a possibility, therefore, of great gain from unrecognized capacity or genius, there is little profit to be derived from the work of the workman, the value of whose work is known by all.

There should never be employed in any department of a modern newspaper (save in the mechanical department, subject to the rules of organized labor, and hence the individuals of which are in no way accessible to the conductors of the journals) any man who cannot be considered by his employer as his possible successor in the control and even perhaps the ownership of the institution, in part or as a whole. This rule itself would disqualify for recruitment almost every man who has lived long enough to acquire outside of the concern a great reputation. For such men coming to our concern late in life, without fortune and without practice in controlling such forces as we have, must serve long before they can rank very high even in the councils of the concern, so that the period of their vigorous manhood will have passed and by age alone they become unfit to take commanding positions.

The man who brings to you a reputation and who offers for sale his services is the man whose reputation is so general and so well known that the market in which he can sell his wares is large. You not only have to compete in this market but at any time after your employment of him has been going on, another employer may bid higher and take him away.

Military history from the days of old Greece and Rome up to quite modern times is full of the records of the so-called mercenary soldiers, rank and file and officers of the same. The military history of the Middle Ages, and more particularly that of Italy, abounds in such instances. Some petty king or ruler, either by legitimate inheritance or by usurpation, would customarily employ some band of soldiers of fortune under some renowned adventurous captain, and would with these hirelings rule for a time his people, and even make wars of conquest upon his neighbors.

It was the custom of these men to sell their services to the highest bidder, so that — they having served one political ruler for a time — if the opponent of this ruler, the ruler of some other and adverse state, would offer a higher price for the services of the mercenaries they would go to him and give to their new employer not only the results of their original prowess but all that they had learned from their late employer.

As civilization progressed and the science of statesmanship and war both advanced, the time came when all people learned that only native soldiers and captains, only men whose greatest interest in their rulers and in their nations was patriotism, were recognized as fit military bulwarks for any nation. Now in all civilized countries the employment of mercenary soldiers has ceased. Such mercenaries as are still employed by such great nations as England and France are for the conquest of and the rule of alien peoples of barbarous customs.

It has been my own observation that the men who have most effectively cooperated with me and served this institution are those who have worked harder for the glory and success of the concern than for wage, and who have had even far more interest in the causes which I have fought for than they have had in their own selfish and immediate advantage represented by wage and glory.

I believe today that most of the effective work that is done in the Scripps papers and the strongest support of this institution is rendered by an army of men whose labors and whose personalities even you are unacquainted with.

Of one thing you can rest assured, that whenever you have a successful and vigorous newspaper, you have not only on it one or two able chiefs but a large proportion of subordinate chiefs and men serving in the ranks who have unusual capacity, many of whom are fully capable of occupying positions of highest trust, great responsibility, and authority. Do not make the mistake of relying too much upon your chiefs. Give them great credit and treat them generously, but do not fail to recognize that the chief strength of the chief is shown by his ability and his practice of gathering around him very able men.

So far for the first proposition. Now for the second.

From the Scriptures I quote: "Many are called but few are chosen." [80]

From the beginning of this institution many men have been called to positions of trust and responsibility and authority compared with those that have long retained such positions. However, this does not prove that many of those [who] were called to positions of trust and lost them had not greater ability than those [who] maintained their positions and subsequent promotion. It has been because there have been but few high positions to be filled that the ranks of candidates have been decimated.

In the competition for place where there was only one place for a dozen men, only one could be chosen, and I am far from believing that even in a majority of cases the man who was, luckily for himself, chosen was the most competent candidate.

The fact of the matter is that opportunity and practice of responsible positions are so advantageous to the individual that any one of a dozen really capable men will, as a result of the advantages of his position, rapidly outgrow the strength of all of his whilom competitors who had no such opportunity.

[80] Matthew, 22:14.

While I have called many to positions of trust who have failed ultimately purely on account of their natural inborn lack of capacity, the number of such failures is small as compared with the number of those men who have not succeeded with me because I failed to give them opportunity.

I know that I have been credited far more than I deserve to be with a capacity to judge of men and make selections. This has been because so many have been more or less successful in the positions to which they have been appointed by me. For the sake of my own prestige and the value of that prestige to myself, I have not willingly and at all times or even very often made the confession that I am quite willing to make to you men.

I do not believe that I have any abnormally great capacity to judge of men and make selections. To anyone else but you I would be ashamed to own what frivolous and utterly inadequate grounds many of my appointments have rested upon. Even at the times I have made these appointments I have been fully aware that I was making the wildest and most absurd of guesses. I have wagered large stakes on the chances of my putting my hand into a "grab bag" and pulling out a good man in the first human object my hand touched.

Nothing at all but one long-continued series of failures would have been my portion were it not for the fact that, however much I might lack in judgment in selection of men, I had the advantage of two things: first, my own capacity to adapt myself to almost any sort of man; and second, the fact that if all men are not born equal, the great majority of men have such equality of capacities that in order that one should outdistance the other in the race he needs but the opportunity of a start.

I believe that the greatest and most valuable thing that I have learned as a manager of men is this which is a secret to most men; viz., the opportunity to grow has more to do with a man's development than all of his inherited and acquired characteristics.

The agriculturist and the horticulturist, especially he who has studied tree growth, knows that while there are no two seeds of a single species of plant that are identical in the quality and vigor of the seed itself, the main consideration for the development of the future plant is not the quality of the seed but the opportunity for the plant, that comes from the seed, to grow. It is the good deep soil as compared with the poor thin soil; the fertilizing and cultivation and irrigation of the soil, rather than the vigor of the plant; it is the freedom that the plant has from being crowded by weeds or other plants of its own variety; the abundance of air and sunshine that counts.

It is the opportunity that you boys have had to early acquire knowledge of conditions, and of the use and the necessary use of your own minds and wills and the control of others, that has given you opportunities that are far more valuable for your future development than all that you have inherited physically and mentally and materially from your parents.

In Captain Mahan's life of Lord Nelson [81] — the great English admiral — he dwelt particularly on the fact that young Nelson's early misfortunes were the chief causes of his later great successes. . . .

[*The material here deleted repeats what Scripps said in "An Old Hobby" about Nelson's career.*]

Mahan actually expressed the belief that no great man had ever been the result of any other great man's training and teaching, and that the habit of subordination, obedience, and discipline was fatal to the development of any sort of greatness.

Long before I had read Captain Mahan or even ever considered my historical reading on this subject, I had acquired as a result of my own experience and observation the conviction that youth, vigor, freedom, and independence altogether formed a more wholesome asset for any man in a commanding position than could all of the training and teaching and consideration of authority and precedent, wisdom of thought, and experience that any man could supply.

I have often heard the story of the old Indian warrior's test of his children. He would throw his baby boys into a rushing stream, and those that would sink and drown he felt he was well rid of, as only those who were fit to live would survive the ordeal and swim ashore.

I have always considered the system of promotion by seniority and even by slow testing out as fatal to any organization of men.

You know my theory of planting an acorn and letting it grow or die. It is the theory of the Indian father.

My idea has been to plant a newspaper with some man or men in charge and let it die if die it must or, growing, grow as the result of the growth of the men who made it and not as the result of my managing the men who managed the paper.

You know it has always been my system — everything else being equal — to choose a man for any certain employment who had no past training and experience in the employment. I have called this "the making of men." It should be called the "system of letting men make themselves" with an opportunity furnished by me.

Looking over our concern today, we will find that a great majority of our men have made themselves and their reputations in the concern. Still there are successful men in it who came to us from the outside, and men who had acquired positions on top after long training in subordinate positions.

[81] Mahan, *Life of Nelson.*

We might say that exceptions prove the rule.

I am more inclined, however, to believe that there are other reasons for accounting for the success of these men. Among these is a condition which I have sometimes called "momentum." The organization of a newspaper while it is young consists of little else than a few tools and one man, in which the man is everything. But as the organization of the newspaper grows it becomes complex, so that the body of the organization entirely outgrows the head. This organization can grow to such an extent that a biological paradox occurs — it can grow to such an extent that it can exist without a head, or with something that is practically the same, a nominal head, or a figurehead. The organization that furnishes the life of a well-developed and matured newspaper becomes so powerful that it requires really a great genius to occupy the position of headship and control the organization instead of being controlled by it.

I have seen from time to time various of my newspapers grow until the organization had almost sloughed me off. Finally, I lived to see the organization and institution as a whole grow to such an extent that my headship became so insignificant that when it was eliminated there was not even no shock but not even a perceptible nervous tremor throughout the whole body.

Therefore, to attach, as a head, to such an organization as a newspaper that has been matured and that has acquired not only a personality remote from any individual but a "momentum" that can hardly be affected by any individual, some man that you call a head — an editor, a business manager, or even a superior officer like the chairman of a board — can produce nothing but an imperceptible effect.

Thus a [C. A.] McGrew can come to the [San Diego] *Sun*, a Harry Brown to the Cincinnati *Post*, a Harry Rickey to the Ohio league, and win great personal glory and renown, and yet possibly be properly credited with no virtue whatever.

While great individual industry and capacity and many years of labor may be required to build up from nothing a great newspaper, I hold that it requires even far superior ability on the part of a man maliciously and disloyally inclined to seriously affect the vitality of such a newspaper and destroy it even with long years given to such employment. It is true that a willful iconoclast might so attack the organism of a newspaper that present profits should disappear and actual losses take their place. But in such a case it only requires to use the knife and cut off the diseased head and replace it with a head of ordinary or even lower than ordinary ability in order that a newspaper should regain its vitality, force, and its capacity for profits.

I call your attention to these latter remarks in order that you should not vex yourselves and worry yourselves too much with the mistaken idea that it is always absolutely necessary to instantly and immediately secure for any one of your papers or your concern as a whole a chief of approved ability.

You must always hold in mind and consider the vital force and importance of an organization and especially its momentum.

Any "nincompoop" could be put in as a nominal head of one of our long-established newspapers and the bad effects of such an action would be long in showing itself.

Here is another consideration that may in an emergency, if well thought out and considered, be of great value to you: In some great and serious emergency, some period of time when comparatively very large sums of money are required to come quickly, you can take any well-established newspaper and reduce its whole expense, whatever it has been, 25 per cent or even one-half, and thereby enormously increase the cash profits, and you can do this for a period of time of three months, six months, or even a year or more, and after even the most severe course of blood-letting, it will only require a short period of healthful and proper management in order that such a paper should entirely regain all of its past strength and prestige.

Learn to value at their true worth these two qualities of "organism" and "momentum" and you will be able to face fearlessly and overcome with safety the most serious emergency that can in all probability occur to you.

Affectionately,

E. W. Scripps

Founding of the United Press

[*September 27, 1912*]

"Miramar," Calif., September 27, 1912

Mr. Roy W. Howard
World Building
New York, N.Y.

My dear Howard:

In your letter of September 14 you asked me to give you an account of the founding of the United Press, and the reasons for the same.[82]

My serious and personal experience with press associations began with the founding of the Cleveland *Press* in '78.

The old Western Associated Press was similar to the present Associated Press in being a monopolistic and close corporation. Neither the Detroit *News* nor the Cleveland *Press* could at first obtain its service.

There were several efforts to establish a respectable press association service for the few new and poor — financially speaking — newspapers of that day. I remember that one time we had to depend upon what was called, I believe, the American Press Association. It was managed by a man whose name has now slipped my memory, but who was the editor of the New York *Daily Graphic,* an unsuccessful illustrated daily paper.[83]

Between 1873, the date of the foundation of the Detroit *News*, and 1883, when, on returning from Europe I took charge of the Cincinnati *Post*, I can remember that we had a great deal of trouble to get a very poor news report. On my return from a two years' trip abroad, coming to Cincinnati, I found that there had been organized a very substantial institution then called the

[82] Title of this disquisition supplied by editor.

[83] The APA was founded by Henry George in cooperation with John Hasson. The New York *Daily Graphic*, of which Scripps speaks, was published from 1873 to 1889 and is not to be confused with Bernarr Macfadden's sensational tabloid, the New York *Graphic*, 1924–32.

293

United Press. I believe it was already managed by Walter P. Phillips, but was completely dominated and controlled by the Chicago banker John R. Walsh who, a short time ago, died in the penitentiary. He had become interested with Mr. [James W.] Scott, the founder of the Chicago *Herald*. Scott and Phillips were Walsh's puppets. While it was presumed that the United Press was a mutual association conducted by all of its members, it was in fact a one-man concern. Walsh was an unscrupulous fellow, and Phillips was an easily managed tool of his. Scott was indebted to Walsh head over heels, and was equally with Phillips amenable to Walsh.

I believe Walsh was in real control of the United Press, owing to its debts, real or fictitious, to Walsh's bank.

After the Walsh regime — I think by reason that the New York syndicate had taken up Walsh's bank debts — the New York syndicate came into the control of the United Press. The syndicate was composed of Pulitzer of the *World*; Whitelaw Reid of the *Tribune*; [Charles A.] Dana of the *Sun*; and, I think, the *Herald*'s representative. These new controllers of the United Press were, if anything, worse than Walsh had been. They proceeded to milk the U.P. in good form.

As I remember it, the U.P. was for a time run mainly for the purpose of saving these four New York papers some part of their cable and special telegraph expense.

During the Walsh regime, Phillips made my acquaintance and began to cultivate me. He was looking for an antidote to Walsh. He gave me every favor he could. I had had great difficulty in getting any good report from the East. I made an arrangement with Phillips by which he gave me the use of all of the United Press wires at a rate that was not, I think, equal to the cost of telegraph operators. From New York and Washington, I remember, for one-quarter cent a word for filing, he delivered my special reports to all of the four then-existing Scripps papers.[84] A New York dispatch would then cost one of our papers only one-sixteenth of a cent a word.

Later, when the New York crowd got hold, he told me the inside of their manipulations, and showed me how I could get my share of the swag. They had adopted the system of exclusive franchise. For my papers he gave me a field of 100 or 150 miles around the city of its publication. I was allowed "protest" with the understanding that I wouldn't exercise it,[85] not to prevent service, but only for the purpose of reducing my rate. We made such use of this opportunity as to bring our actual net cost for receiving the report down to about $20.00 a week per paper. The right that I had to use the wires for my own then-called Scripps League Service to the Scripps papers at one-quarter-

[84] Detroit *News*, Cleveland *Press*, Cincinnati *Post*, St. Louis *Chronicle*.
[85] Presumably this meant a publisher's right to prevent by protest the distribution of the UP report to a competitor within his publication zone.

cent filing rate was made use of to such an extent that in reality the Scripps papers received a subsidy, or what was equal to a subsidy, of $40.00 to $50.00 a week each to take the U.P. report.

Of course, I soon enough recognized that we were all grafting the United Press out of existence. By various means, especially that of cutting rates, the United Press had pretty well done up the old Western Associated Press.

A number of disgruntled United Press clients, together with a large number of the old Western Associated Press men, began to organize a revolt. The Scripps papers were the backbone of the United Press in the evening field in the Middle West. The United Press was on the rocks, and the western press association was in a moribund condition. Senility marked the old institution, and corruption the new one; and competition had reduced the whole press-association business to an absurdity.

Finally, a time came when it appeared to both sides that the Scripps papers held the balance of power.

Phillips froze to me and brought me all sorts of messages and promises from Dana *et al.* I think Dana was really Laffan.

I remember that the Laffan service [86] was then going, and Laffan's share of the graft consisted in the United Press paying cable and other telegraph tolls for what Laffan received pay for from Laffan clients.

About this time the insurgents sent me word that they were going to form a new press association and that, if I would join them, I would become the actual owner of one-quarter of the stock of this new association. But as the new association was composed of such men as Victor Lawson, Lawson's men [Frank B.] Noyes [Washington *Star*] and Charles Knapp [St. Louis *Republic*], my brother James, and a whole raft of what I then considered old fossils, I did not accept the proposition.

Soon after that, the insurgents really got together and formed a powerful organization, ten of them putting up ten thousand dollars apiece as a war fund, while others promised more.

The new Associated Press of Illinois was soon enough formed, and rapidly attracted to itself nearly all the stronger papers in the country outside of the New York big four [*World, Herald, Sun,* and *Tribune*], and in the big four itself, I knew from Phillips, there was warfare which mainly consisted in warfare of the three others against the Dana-Laffan element.

Finally, the crash came to the United Press, and Pulitzer, Reid, and Bennett [James Gordon, Jr.] — I believe it was Bennett — went over to the Associated Press.

In an instant I found myself a very insignificant factor. Mr. McRae felt that I had maneuvered wrongly and made a desperate effort to climb in the

[86] After the dissolution of the old UP, William M. Laffan, business manager of the New York *Sun*, operated the Laffan News Bureau until 1916.

band wagon and carry me with him. My brother James was very anxious to have my papers in. He had already taken the Detroit *News* in. McRae, who was very intimate with Knapp, Lawson, Noyes, and [Melville E.] Stone, was treated very kindly by them, he said. Late as the day was, they offered to let us come in on the ground floor. To convince him that it would be wise for me to submit, they outlined to him their policy, which was to establish such a monopoly as would make it impossible for any new paper to be started in any of the cities where there were Associated Press members. I recognized the value of all this, but I was just at that time feeling very cocky. I considered myself a sort of man-of-destiny. I had ambitious plans of planting a score or more of new papers. I pointed out to McRae and my brother George that, while under the proposed conditions no one else could start new newspapers in our towns, we would never be able to start another new newspaper.

I was informed that, as I had refused the offer made, I would never again have as good an opportunity.

However, later all of the old United Press members and clients were notified that such of them as would join the Associated Press prior to a certain date, I think, in '97 — or it might have been some time sooner or later — would be admitted as sort of second-class members.

The United Press had been whipped to death and I knew it. McRae was panic-stricken. My brother George . . . although he had a good deal of faith in my ability, because he was much beset by McRae and my brother James, was a little shaky. I was determined not to join the Associated Press, but I felt that it was necessary to have my brother George's full support. I saw the Associated Press was strongly organized and I knew the character of its men. I knew that most of them thoroughly disliked me, and that all of them were arrogant. I feared that, if they knew too much of my plans, however, my brother James would warn them of the danger of leaving me out, and would induce them to make terms with me.

Therefore, I chose McRae as our representative to deal with Lawson, Knapp, Stone, and Noyes. I didn't tell McRae of all my plans. I made him promise to keep away from James E. Whenever McRae is scared, he always shows that he is scared. I wanted those fellows to feel that I was scared. I wanted them to be arrogant and sassy. I wanted them to say such things and act in such a way that it would anger my brother George and arouse the spirit of bulldog which he possessed. McRae was just the man for that job.

McRae went on his mission. He came back to us overjoyed. He had had the promise that if we would be good and humble and submit our request at the next meeting of the directors of the Associated Press, we might be voted in, and probably would be.

The meeting was held in the Auditorium Hotel in Chicago. McRae, George, Paine, and myself went to Chicago. McRae was jubilant; Paine was downhearted and disgusted; both for the same reason. They both thought I would submit. In the meantime, George was fully informed of my plans, and it was a peculiar characteristic of his that he always thought best of the plan that was about to be abandoned. On our way to Chicago he began to talk to me about our ability to go it alone.

Arrived at the Auditorium Hotel, I determined that there should be no doubt of my having surrendered. Without McRae's knowledge I sent my card by my secretary to each — Knapp, Lawson, Noyes, and Stone — to request an interview. Some of them sent word that they couldn't see me till after the meeting. Others ignored the message. George knew of my messages and how they were treated, and he got his mad up.

We waited in our rooms until the time when Mr. Stone was to notify McRae that he would be received as our ambassador. At the last moment before Mac was to appear, George and I gave him our ultimatum, which was that all of our papers were to be received in the association, and in each case we were to have a class A-1 position, or we wouldn't come in. McRae was astounded at our presumption, but he had nothing else to do but go with our message. He went and did his best, but came back with the report that no other place was open for us but that of humble clients.

I had prepared my scheme, and even the form of the telegraph announcement to be sent out to all the U.P. clients. We were going into the associated press business, and solicited patronage. Immediately after the rejection of our offer we put on the wires this announcement.

In the meantime, we had a news association organization built up under the old arrangement with Phillips. It was called the Adscititious Report and was managed by Paine. We had the nucleus of an organization: We named this the Scripps-McRae Press Association.

On the Pacific Coast the United Press had never done any business, and as I had several papers there, I had organized a little service for my own Pacific Coast papers and had some clients. It was called the Scripps-Blades Service.

Prior to this Chicago meeting there had been formed a sort of organization of a few small eastern papers [that] knew nothing of my plan, and [that] knew . . . they would not be permitted to join the Associated Press. At about the same time I launched my Scripps-McRae service the Publishers Press Association went into business.

I went soon to New York to meet the Publishers Press Association at a conference at the Astor House.

Laffan had determined to keep up his old report. I tried to get the Publishers Press to disband and become clients of mine. They declined.

I saw Laffan and tried to make a combination with him, but he had a contempt for a western man and a western institution.

Finally, I contrived alliances with both the Publishers Press and Laffan. The Publishers Press and the Scripps-McRae and the Scripps-Blades associations agreed to cooperate. The Publishers Press was to have the Atlantic states for territory; the Scripps-McRae Association to have all the territory between the west line of the Atlantic states and the east line of the Pacific states; the Scripps-Blades Association was to carry the Pacific states. A combination was made with Laffan by which we would pay him $200 a week for the use of his cables.

My expectations of clients were greatly disappointed. I confined myself in my two associations to the evening field. The Publishers Press had both the morning and the evening report, but there were very few clients to be got. Immediately there was a tremendous increase in the press-association expenses of the Scripps papers. Such papers as the Cleveland *Press* and the Cincinnati *Post*, that had previously been paying not over $20.00 a week for their reports, jumped up to over $1,000 a month.

Mr. Paine was appointed manager of the Scripps-McRae Association. Walter Phillips was employed for a time by Paine so that we could have the benefit of his practical experience and of his services in soliciting clients. The Phillips arrangement was soon concluded.

From almost the start the Scripps Association (formerly Scripps-Blades) of the West — Blades having dropped out and [Hamilton] Clark having taken his place — was a fairly good business. Paine always claimed that the Scripps Western Association milked the Scripps-McRae. For my own part I have no doubt that the principal reason for the success of our western association was that Clark was an infinitely better businessman than Paine, and that I was able to control the western association far more thoroughly than I was the Middle West.

From the beginning, however, we had trouble with the Publishers Press. Its management was guilty of all the vices of the old United Press. It bought dollars for $1.10 and $1.20 apiece. It slushed around and tried to cover too much territory. It sold exclusive franchises. It got into debt to people who made an improper use of their influence over it. Finally we found that it was not only unreliable, but that it was being corruptly used. Then John Vandercook appeared on the scene, and he was authorized to act as my agent to negotiate for the purchase or the control of this Publishers Press. At first a large price was demanded, $300,000 or $400,000. John was anxious to get it at any price as he felt sure there was a fortune in the business. The result of these negotiations showed us that the Publishers Press was really on the rocks itself, that it was being conducted at a loss, and that it was in debt.

It was very evident to me that, if I ceased to cooperate with them or if I put onto them the whole expense of paying for the cables and gathering news from all over the country, the institution as it then existed would break up. I was afraid it would be seized by someone else. I forgot whether Hearst was then looming up or not. Finally I sent them an ultimatum by Vandercook that I would give them $150,000, with which the Publishers Press could pay off its debts and, I suppose, some of its managers get a little rake-off; or I would cease to cooperate with them and commence to compete with them.

The offer was accepted. Ham Clark, who had been very successful with the Scripps News Association of the West, was allotted a share of the Publishers Press, he paying his share of the actual cost. The next step was to consolidate all of the three associations [SMPA, Scripps News Association, Publishers Press] into one.

This was done by appraising the value of the three associations. The new United Press Association was organized, and issued preferred stock guaranteed to the amount of the appraised value of the three original associations. This preferred stock was divided amongst the original owners of the three different associations, and the new concern issued common stock. If any, I think very little actual money was paid into the new corporation.

This is my memory of the financial and business history of the present United Press.

I am not sure about my dates — for instance, the exact date of the origin of the so-called Adscititious Scripps League Report, the date of founding the Scripps-Blades, afterwards the Scripps Western Report, the date fixing the limit when my papers could enter into the new Associated Press, the exact date of the meeting at the Auditorium Hotel at Chicago, the exact date of the organization of the Publishers Press, and the date of the purchase of the Publishers Press.

Now as to my motives for founding the United Press.

For nearly a quarter of a century I had had personal experience with various press associations, and from my brother James I had learned the story of the old western press association in which he was a charter member back in war times when he was the chief owner of the Detroit *Tribune*.

I had been convinced of the correctness of the proverb that what is everybody's business is nobody's business when applied to a purely mutual press association, considering the membership as a whole. Clique rule is an inevitable outcome of all mutual institutions, I believe. The inner circle gets in its work in the way of graft as well as in the way of improper influences, control, and use.

My experience with the [old] United Press also had taught me that there was little to choose between an ordinary stock company of this kind and a mutual association so far as proper and honest conduct was concerned. But there was an additional danger in a stock-company association, in that contending parties must form, to be followed by strife for stock control. I had known many newspapers to fail because of quarrels amongst stockholders and the constant shifting of balance of power. The [old] United Press suffered more from internal strife amongst the stockholders than from any other cause.

I believe in one-man control — in other words, the 51 per cent rule — just as firmly as I believe in the distribution or the sharing of profits amongst all of the important and capable administrators of a business.

Providing the one man is fairly intelligent and is possessed both of reputation and character that makes him dependable, it is better that he should have final authority not by agreement but by his own individual power and title.

I proposed to avoid the dangers of a mutual concern as well as the dangers of shifting balances of power of the company of stockholding ownership.

The [new] United Press as it now exists would never have existed had identically the same stockholders held all the stock and had not one man had the power to decide any important question. It is almost impossible to find two men [who] will always agree, and it is absolutely impossible to find four or five. It is possible to find one man who can control weaker men who are his fellow stockholders, or enough of them to keep control. But in such an organization as ours it is desirable to have all the men strong and capable. It would be impossible for you, myself, Clark, and [C. D.] Lee [president of UP, 1910–13] to pursue one consistent line of policy if each of us held an exactly equal share of stock in the concern, especially when one or more of us could not be in daily attendance on the business.

But I had not only a selfish but also an altruistic motive in founding the new association. I do not believe in monopolies. I believe that monopolists suffer more than their victims in the long run. I did not believe it would be good for journalism in this country that there should be one big news trust such as the founders of the Associated Press fully expected to build up.

I not only wanted to start a new paper if I chose, but I wanted to make it possible for any other man to found a newspaper in any city in the Union. The men who hold controlling interest in the present Associated Press and Mr. Hearst would inevitably combine into a trust were it not for us.

Perhaps my greatest reason, however, for my objecting to becoming an integral part of the press association in the crisis was that I knew that at least 90 per cent of my fellows in American journalism were capitalistic and conservative. I knew at that time, at least, that unless I came into the field with a new service it would be impossible for the people of the United States to get correct news through the medium of the Associated Press. I determined to be as free in the matter of gathering telegraph news and printing what I wanted to print as I was in gathering local news and printing what I wanted to print. In those my youthful days of pride, I swelled up with vanity at the thought that I was to be the savior of the free press in America. Of course, I have learned now that it requires more than one man to guarantee such freedom. However, I confess that even now I feel no small sense of satisfaction on account of the results of my effort.

I believe, too, that I have done more good indirectly with the United Press than I have done with it directly, since I have made it impossible for the men who control the Associated Press to suppress the truth or successfully disseminate falsehood. The mere fact that the United Press can be depended upon to disseminate news that is of value to the public and that is against the interests of the plutocrat band makes it not only not worthwhile but positively dangerous for the Associated Press to withhold any information from the public. If a United Press paper in Cleveland gets a piece of news that the Associated Press client there doesn't get, there is a kick from the Associated Press paper to the management. If the Associated Press should attempt to give only real news to its client papers in towns where there were United Press papers, then other Associated Press papers in other towns would kick because they didn't get as full service as did those Associated Press papers in United Press towns.

I am convinced that no such political situation as exists in this country today would have existed had it not been for the direct and indirect results of the United Press work.

I really thought, Howard, in those callow days of the nineties, that a very large number of the publishers of American newspapers wanted to be and would be, if they could, really the friends of the people.

Yours sincerely,

E. W. Scripps

How to Find New Editors
for Old Papers

[*September 23, 1914*]

This disquisition appears to have been edited in Scripps' hand.

When I told my son [Jim] that I proposed the formation of a disquisition, based upon the experience of the Philadelphia *News-Post*, he replied substantially: that he knew my general theory of the supreme importance of the editor — that, in fact, the editor was, if not the whole of the newspaper, the one absolutely necessary element. Further, he admitted that he now knew that there was no use of trying to found a newspaper until he had found its editor. But he added, "What I would like you to do would be to write a disquisition on the subject of how to get another editor to take the place of one who has died, or has been otherwise eliminated from an established and growing newspaper."

I recognize that I am many more times expert in the creation of a new newspaper than I am in administering an established newspaper and causing it to continue in growth.

I like new things. I like inventions. There is something very interesting and attractive to me in the excitement of bringing into existence something where there has previously been nothing.

During the last half of my life most of the pleasurable sensations that I have enjoyed in the construction of a newspaper have been overshadowed by my being able to forecast and appreciate the irksomeness of my future duties, in having to administer, guard, and care for the infant property after it has become full grown.

I have never had any hankering to purchase a previously existing newspaper — one weak and ailing, which needed reforming and reconstructing,

302

or one already well-established and perhaps only needing careful administration.

I have been something like an old hen who, having hatched a brood of chickens, would be wonderfully enthusiastic in scratching for the chicks, and brooding over them, and watching that the hawks did not get them, but who, as soon as the down of the young began to disappear and be replaced by feathers, not only lost all interest in them, but was more inclined to greatly compete with them for the food that was thrown into the chicken yard. In fact, as soon as one of my new newspapers began to make profits, I have only been too glad to hand it over to some hired man to manage, and squeeze more and more profits out of it.

Still, as each of these newspapers was my property and I had an interest in its profits, I have been compelled to exercise oversight of it, and from time to time select successors of editors and business managers.

The sum total of my experiences has caused me, rightly or wrongly, to conclude that the man, who as editor, was successful in founding a newspaper, was almost invariably unfitted to continue successfully as editor of the established newspaper.

Another conclusion of mine has been that, everything else being equal, a man who had been the chief editor of an established and successful newspaper for any length of time, was not only unfit to take part in the founding of any newspaper, but unfit to take over the editorial management of a similar newspaper property that had just emerged from the chicken's down to the pin-feather stage.

Everything else being equal, I have also found that a subeditor, formerly trained in an established property, was even less fit to take over a new property.

It has been my experience that I have been most successful when I have substituted the founding editor of the new newspaper by one of his subordinates.

Also fairly good results have been obtained by taking a subeditor from some other new and small property to replace the founding editor of the newspaper just launched.

Nearly all of my personal experiences have been to provide the founding editor, his immediate successor, and the third in line. Only in two cases have I been called upon to appoint the fourth and fifth editors in old, established, and very profitable newspapers.

My most notable successes were the appointing of Pat Baker from foreman of the [composing] room of the Detroit *Evening News* [87] to the chief edi-

[87] He appointed Baker editor of the *News* in 1888, always claiming it was his own wisdom that led to the choice, although family correspondence suggests strongly that the idea came from James E. He made Rickey editor-in-chief of the Ohio papers in 1905.

torship, and the appointing of Harry Rickey to the editorship of several Ohio papers. In both of these cases I recognized that the spirit of editorship in the Detroit *News* and in the Cleveland *Press* and Cincinnati *Post* had become detached from any individual, and had become absorbed by the whole editorial staff of the various properties. The papers were dominated by what the French call *esprit de corps* rather than by the spirit of any one man. In such cases, one does not require so much editorial genius as a fairly good executive head, to direct the forces, or preside over the work of the staff.

As I know that Jim had in his mind the cases of such papers as the Los Angeles *Record* and the San Francisco *News*, I cannot see that any of the previous cases that I have referred to can be identical to those of these two papers. These two papers, and the others in the concern, have been, in a sense, established, each of them enjoying a fairly large circulation and public prestige. But these, and others of our papers, have not yet arrived at the point where considerable financial prosperity has been achieved.

In such cases as these, something more is required than a mere executive administrator of a growing concern. The editor of such a paper as one of these should have something of the spirit and capacity of a founding editor, coupled with the qualifications of a plodding executive.

Such papers as these represent large potentiality in the way of prosperity, but the prosperity has not yet been dug out.

In such properties as were once the St. Louis *Chronicle* and the Kansas City *World*, I now have a very clear idea as to what course should be pursued. It is not an editor that would be wanted; it would be an axe.

Having had small experiences — in fact, never having made a successful demonstration of my capacity to meet the situation that Jim has in view — I must acknowledge that my counsel to him should be considered by him as of little worth.

Still I must recognize that the purely administrative qualities are extremely necessary in these two cases.

Notwithstanding the extraordinary large field of my operations, or observations as a newspaper publisher, I am compelled to recognize that, as an administrator of established properties, the sum total of my son's experience has been even greater than my own. Therefore, I am bound to believe, and I do believe, that Jim is better able to make selections of editors in the cases of the *Record* and *News* than I am myself.

It is easy to find in the staff of a successful newspaper one to promote to the editorship of the paper; just because of the newspaper's being successful, there must, of necessity, be a number of men on the staff who are themselves capable of producing great success. The reason why it is difficult to discover, on the staff of a paper that is competely unsuccessful, a man capable of being a successful editor, is that the paper's unsuccessfulness demonstrates that there are few or no really capable men on the staff.

However, in dealing with such papers as the San Francisco *News*, and the Los Angeles *Record*, the general manager has one great advantage that he would not have in such cases as the Detroit *News* and the Cleveland *Press*. In the case of the latter two papers, the momentum of the business is so great, the force of the *esprit de corps* so strong, that these papers are going to continue to be successful, no matter who holds the editorship, and, therefore, it is impossible, except after a long period of time, to discover whether a new editor is making good or not. On the other hand, in the cases of the Los Angeles *Record* and the San Francisco *News*, where the two papers hang suspended just about halfway between ultimate success and ultimate failure, an editor can always instantly demonstrate his ability or lack of ability.

"Necessity is the mother of invention." Opportunity is a tremendous developer of latent qualities.

A man who appears to be and probably is very mediocre, put into the position of editor of the *Record*, under the stress of necessity might and probably would develop capacities unsuspected by himself or anyone else; in fact, a considerable experience of my own has led me to believe that "the job makes the man."

Many or most of the successful men in my concern could and would have lived out lives of mediocrity had not my need for captains been great and my supply of ready-made material small, so that I was compelled to promote men, often, who had given no evidence of their fitness for holding important positions.

I consider that one of the best demonstrations proving the truth of my contention that the job makes the man is that furnished in the case of the man who is now at the head of the Scripps newspapers [Jim]. Nothing but the absolute necessity of my choosing my successor, while Jim was a very young man, would ever have resulted in his becoming a newspaper publisher at all. I think that it is quite probable that, but for my own necessities and his, he would never have developed any unusual business qualifications. The development of both Thornton and Rickey was owing to similar conditions of affairs.

Jim's necessities, in such cases as the *Record*, San Francisco *News*, Tacoma [*Times*], and Spokane [*Press*], will, almost beyond the peradventure of a doubt, throw up one or more strong characters whose exercise of authority and responsibility will develop them into still greater men.

Although we are engaged now in an effort to relieve my personal estate and all of its component parts of the embarrassment of debts and other obligations, I have a feeling that a success in this direction will relieve Jim of the sharp spur of necessity, and thus curtail his fullest development. I am almost persuaded to regard as elements of good fortune the several hard newspaper business nuts that Jim has to crack, or that have to be cracked by someone. It is from the most difficult fields of operation that will be developed, from young men, the strong and able captains of the future.

I might advise Jim to confide, to a certain extent, in these young men who are taking new responsibilities the views I hold on this subject, so that each of them will be able to understand that, as difficult as his position is, his opportunities are in exact proportion to his difficulties.

In Gibbon's history of Rome are to be found many fine examples of the theory I am trying to develop.

After the Roman Empire had been founded, life in the central quarter, or Rome itself, became so easy and luxurious that those young men who grew up there, notwithstanding the fact of their being close to the throne, and having such "pulls" as even actual heirships to empires, became so flabby in character that they were unable, sometimes, to seize, and, more frequently, to hold an imperial scepter. On the other hand, the generals and governors in outlying Roman provinces, where warfare or struggle was constant, grew strong in executive ability and in the habits of mastery. Thus, for a long period of time the imperial scepter passed from hand to hand among these generals who, when opportunity presented itself, returned from their distant provinces with their armies to overthrow the weaklings on the imperial throne and set themselves there.

The Case of Roy Howard

[*January 15, 1917*]

Whenever, which is often enough, I find myself in retrospective mood and indulge in reviewing my past, my thoughts generally center about some man or group of men—youngsters whose lives I have more or less molded, molded in part for my own business purposes and perhaps, even in a larger part, experimentally.[88]

A very large part of the enjoyment that I have experienced in my life's activities has been derived from the curious and inquiring attention that I have given to the development of my young helpers.

I am inclined to dispute the truth of that vulgar saying that "you can't make a silk purse out of a sow's ear." I put but very little reliance on that equally vulgar and, too often, sneering comment that "blood will tell."

I am inclined to think that the so-called science of eugenics is no science at all. At least, I am pretty well convinced that it is impossible for one to learn enough about any man's progenitors to make it possible to predict anything concerning the mental characteristics of the offspring of any pair of men and women.

It was about thirty-two years ago that I went to live in the country house of an ex-colonel of the United States Army, which house was situated quite out in the country, some sixteen miles from Cincinnati, on the old turnpike leading from Cincinnati to Dayton, Ohio.

On this turnpike, not a hundred yards from my host's home, was a tiny little cottage occupied by the keeper of a tollgate. The tollgate keeper had a family of several children, sons and daughters.

Now, it is easy enough for anyone to form an opinion of the general characteristics of a tollgate keeper and his family. Certainly, tollgate-keeping is

---

[88] This selection appears in both McCabe, *Damned Old Crank*, p. 217 f., and Cochran, *E. W. Scripps*, p. 222 f.

anything but the occupation of an industrious, ambitious, and enterprising man.

Being fond of taking my exercise on a horse's back at that time, I kept a saddle horse. It was provoking to me to always have to stop my ride and to call the tollgate keeper, wait for the tollgate to be raised until I had paid my little fee; and I will admit that I seldom submitted to this indignity. Sometimes I would make my horse jump the tollgate, and sometimes the hedge fence at the side of the road, into the adjoining field, passing around the tollgate, and jumping the horse back again into the pike.

I never made the acquaintance of the tollgate keeper, or any member of his family. Being a newcomer in the neighborhood, I knew nothing of the past of the family.

It was not until many years afterward that I learned that there was a man in the employ of one of my newspapers who was a son of one of the daughters of this family.

The great occasion I had to encounter this tollgate was that it extended straight across the road that led from my lodging-place to the door of the young lady who afterward became my wife.

The occasion of my learning the origin of Roy Howard, and my subsequent interest in him, was my wife's mother writing my wife, informing her that a son of my wife's old schoolmate, the daughter of the tollgate keeper, had become a reporter on one of my papers [Cincinnati *Post*].

It was something about the association of young Howard with a very important incident in my life that caused me to be especially interested in him. I am inclined to believe that Roy Howard's whole career has been greatly influenced by this interest I felt in him.

What could be expected of a tollgate-keeper's grandson?

Had I not known so much about his origin, I would have had no more curiosity about, or interest in, him than I would have had in any of the other hundreds of my employees. Although I did not see young Howard until perhaps several years after I heard of him, my interest in him certainly had its effect in the way of opening opportunities for him.

I do not recall having seen Howard until he had made considerable headway in the way of promotion. When I finally met him for the first time, I think it was at "Miramar" [1908].

He was a striking individual, very small of stature, a large head and speaking countenance, and eyes that appeared to be windows for a rather unusual intellect. His manner was forceful, and the reverse from modest. Gall was written all over his face. It was in every tone and every word he voiced. There was ambition, self-respect, and forcefulness oozing out of every pore of his body.

Since those days Howard has learned to affect some degree of deference in his speech and manner in my presence, but in my first interview with him he did not reveal, and I do not believe he experienced, the least feeling of awe. However, on the other hand, so completely and exuberantly frank was he that it was impossible for me to feel any resentment on account of his cheek. He passed from his reportership on the paper to a subordinate position in the United Press Association, an institution that I had newly organized and launched.

Prior to my organizing the United Press Association, I had for several years maintained two small sectional news associations, one for gathering and disseminating the news of the Middle West, and one for doing the same in the Pacific Coast states; and later I had bought a similar association for gathering and disseminating the news of the eastern states. These three associations I combined into the United Press Association.

In organizing the United Press Association, I organized it by buying up the other three associations, paying for the same in preferred stock of the new institution, so that some ten or twelve years ago the United Press Association started on its career with what was practically a mortgage debt of $300,000 and practically not a dollar in its treasury. I distributed the common stock of the new organization, 51 per cent to myself, and 49 per cent to several young men that I had selected from among my employees, who were to conduct the new concern.

At the time Howard took employment in the United Press, he might have been twenty-one or twenty-two years of age. Of course, he was only an employee. I do not suppose he or anyone else ever thought that he would be anything else but an employee.

Fortunately, Howard had demonstrated his ability to be a good assistant to the general manager while the institution was still in almost an embryo state; its first manager, John Vandercook, died as the result of a surgical operation. Learning of this, I immediately gave attention to the appointment of his successor. I had no idea of appointing Howard. If my remembrance is correct, I had not seen Howard even then. [He saw Howard in February, 1908, and Vandercook died in April.]

I suggested to my associates several names, any one of whom I would have been willing to appoint as Vandercook's successor, had the other men who had worked on the association agreed. I was surprised at being urged to let Howard be tried out for a time, at least, on the job.

Certainly, at this critical point in Howard's career, he owed everything to the fact that he was the tollgate-keeper's grandson.[89] My fancy was tickled

[89] This appears to be a slight exaggeration after the fact. The short, dapper Howard had gone to work for the Cincinnati *Post* and talked himself into a job as special correspondent in New York, where he was when Scripps bought Publishers Press in 1906. He became news manager of Publishers Press in New York and then New York man-

with the idea. My propensity to try experiments demonstrated itself again. I recall that I was much amused, and that I told my wife about what I had done. However, Howard made good.

Pretty soon he appeared as a candidate as a purchaser of some of Vandercook's stock. Then there were other changes, and Howard got more stock. Of course, Howard had no money to start with, and in this case as in many other similar cases I assigned stock to a man for the purpose of inspiring him to greater effort. Howard continued to make good, and as he made good the United Press made good, and began to grow into [a] property that had an actual value.

There were other changes, and Howard continued to buy stock until now he has 30 per cent of the institution, [which] is making a clear net profit of over $100,000 a year.

Howard gets a salary of $7,500 a year, and beyond this he received last year a bonus of $7,500, based upon an arrangement by which the manager's bonus be proportioned to the volume of profits. During the year 1916, Howard's share of the profits as a stockholder was $32,000; his salary and bonus amounted to $15,000. Hence, his clear net earnings for the year were $47,000.

But this is not all. Perhaps largely owing to Howard's efficiency as a manager, the United Press is rapidly growing in volume of business and profits.

It was only a few weeks ago there was a sale of some common stock. The price paid was on a company valuation of $1,000,000. Just about a year

---

ager when the UP was formed in 1907. The next year, Hamilton B. Clark, UP president, had Howard exchange jobs for a short time with Max Balthasar, San Francisco manager, to permit each to find out what went on on the other side of the continent. In taking over in San Francisco, Howard paid his first visit to Scripps at "Miramar." "My God, another little one," Scripps said when Howard was introduced. "That was like being hit by a custard pie," Howard recalled. Both Vandercook and Clark had given Scripps the impression that Howard was a man of such drive and talents that he likely would succeed one or both of them. Thus, when Vandercook died, Scripps was motivated by those recommendations in letting Howard be appointed general news manager of the United Press. However, he had some reservations — but not many — about Howard because of his youth. He had more serious reservations, because he thought Howard appeared to have a frail constitution, and because Howard had not yet won the full confidence of the key executives in the Scripps concern. But the thing that really turned the tide in Howard's favor was a letter he wrote to Paine in 1911, assessing Woodrow Wilson and the upcoming 1912 presidential campaign. When Scripps saw the letter, he fastened upon the conviction that Howard was a man who could take an executive position anywhere in the Concern, even as editor-in-chief of the all-important Ohio papers. Scripps said the letter showed Howard to be a man of "clear, cold, calculating, and masterful" intellect. Howard became president of UP in 1913. Although he may have owed his initial appointment as news manager to his being the grandson of the tollgate keeper, he owed his promotion to president to the effect his 1911 letter produced on Scripps. Although Howard has been quoted as saying he thought Scripps never had any real affection for him, Howard was one of the very few lieutenants (Paine was another) whom Scripps addressed by first name in the salutation of his letters.

before this time, another sale had taken place — Howard himself having bought this stock on a valuation of $750,000. I now feel that at the respective times, the valuations were not excessive, but rather modest. So it would appear Howard's 30 per cent of stock increased during the year 33⅓ per cent. It was in the beginning of the year 1916, Howard had 30 per cent of the $750,000 worth of property, or $225,000. Now he has 30 per cent of a $1,000,000 property, or $300,000. By stock appreciation, he made $75,000. So it appears during the year 1916, Howard has made a salary of $7,500; bonus, $7,500; cash profits, $32,000; by appreciation, $75,000; or a total of $122,000.

See how this tollgate-keeper's grandson has flourished.

But there is another item to be added to all this.

Owing to the extension of the business of the United Press, and owing to the fact that the greatest important news in these times is connected with the European war, it has been necessary for the manager of the United Press to go to Europe frequently.

The statesmen of Europe deem it extremely important that the American people should be kept well informed in all the controversies going on between the belligerent nations. They are, therefore, bound to give much attention to the American press, or, rather, the representatives of the American press. The United Press is, next to the Associated Press, the largest medium for the dissemination of news in the United States. Consequently, Mr. Howard has not only had no difficulty to coming in contact with both the political and military leaders of the countries which he has visited, but has been warmly welcomed by them.

Owing a great deal to his peculiar personality, Howard seems to have gained some personal favors amongst these men. He has had interviews with premiers, foreign secretaries, generals, and civilians of the higher grade.

Lord Northcliffe, the giant journalist of England, has been particularly intimate with Howard, and, owing to Northcliffe's relations to the powers-that-be in England, Howard of the United Press is favored above all other American journalists and journalistic institutions.

So far, Howard has not come into contact with royalty itself, though I have very little doubt but that he is yet to stand before kings.

The other day, Howard called on me at "Miramar," and spent an hour or two talking with me.

While he occupied the seat at the end of my table, where I usually place my most favored guests, I could not restrain myself from looking him over, up and down, and laughing uproariously, as I kept comparing in my mind that little old tollgate house with this friend and intimate of a belted earl, the great statesmen, and famous generals. It is characteristic of Howard that when I told him the cause of my mirth, he indicated neither confusion nor resentment. He seemed to have his own fancy tickled by it.

I do not believe that in this respect Howard will ever change. Of course, he is an upstart, and a very innocent upstart. He wasn't to blame for his origin, and, in fact, there was nothing blameworthy in his origin. I do not think he would ever be ashamed of his origin. I do not think either that his success in life or his position in life will add anything to his vanity or his self-respect.

As I indicated in some part of the foregoing, right from the start Howard's self-respect and self-confidence were so great as to make it impossible for it to increase.

Doubtless to himself, his present situation in life, his successes and his prosperity all seem to be perfectly natural — and to be no more nor no less than he expected, if he ever wasted his time in forecasting, of which I have very much doubt.

Ingratitude?

[*February 17, 1919*]

The following letter has been shown me:

Seattle, Wash., February 2, 1919

Dear Mr. [J. C.] Harper:

That part of your letter of January 21 to R.P.S. [Robert P. Scripps] that referred to the labor situation interested me greatly.

I refer particularly to this part:

"Bolshevism cannot prosper where people are employed at good wages and under conditions that mean as large a measure of contentment as is consistent with progress. On the other hand, Bolshevism thrives just as the I.W.W. thrives, on unemployment, poverty, damnable working conditions, and the vulgar flaunting of wealth and extravagance."

I believe we have all been thinking along that line. It is wrong.

Before saying what I wish to say in contradiction of part of your statements, I wish to refer to my own activities in the labor movement in order to forestall any idea that I have suddenly gone over to the "capitalistic class" because the Bolsheviki endanger my profits.

When I was 20 or 21 years old I joined the Knights of Labor, then nearly dead, but having a brief revival on account of the big street car strike in Cleveland. I went in with a fellow who printed a weekly labor paper and we turned it into a daily to fight for the strikers. We got 60,000 circulation and succeeded in boycotting all the papers except the Press. The paper busted after the troops came and took charge of the situation. However, I worked for many weeks trying to keep it alive and only quit when it was no longer possible to eat. After I became editor of the Los Angeles Record I made many fights for labor in a community that was by no means sympathetic. I did the same in the northwest. In fact, the Seattle Star and other northwest papers really established union labor in the northwest. I was accused many times of being an I.W.W. This charge was often printed by the Seattle Times in 1910, 11 and 12. I was arrested on local charges

313

of contempt and on federal charges of conspiracy growing out of these fights for the workers.

All right; I think that's all admitted. My only purpose in referring to it is to establish my claim that I am not prejudiced against labor.

A general strike has been called in Seattle. It is a sympathy strike for the purpose of aiding striking shipyard workers. Thirty thousand shipyard workers went out when their demands for more money were refused, the employers and the government both claiming that it was impossible to grant these demands. The leaders of labor have managed to engineer the general strike to support the men already out. There has been no attempt on the part of employers to cut wages. The strike started because wages were not raised beyond the mark set during the war.

Today the real center of attack by the strikers and the Bolsheviki, in particular, is the Seattle Star. In the event that they really decide to "take over the industries," as they claim they will do, the first newspaper office they will attempt to seize will be the Seattle Star, which they consider a traitor because it has not advocated everything they are preaching.

These same conditions apply to Tacoma. A series of strikes, which will cause a general strike there, also, began last week with a walkout of newsboys. The only paper they are permitting to be sold in Tacoma is the Union Record, of Seattle, the organ of the labor leaders. Probably this will be the only paper sold in Seattle soon. With all heat, light and power off we could not print anyway. In addition to this, even the printers have voted to strike. The stereotypers, after demanding $8.00 a day, suddenly announced that they were going to strike anyway. The Union Record probably will be permitted to run, as the leaders have a plan up their sleeve to announce that newspapers may be printed "but not for profit." Under the claim that all other papers are "capitalistic" the Record will be the only one "not for profit."

Bolshevism may thrive, as you say, on unemployment, poverty, bad working conditions, etc., but doing away with these things will not prevent Bolshevism.

Seattle labor has been and is today remarkably prosperous. It has had so much money that it didn't know what to do with it. It has been so prosperous that never in the history of Seattle has there been such trade in luxuries. For six blocks around the Labor Temple the streets are crowded with the autos of workingmen attending their meetings. There are no slums, no hovels, no unemployment, no poverty, no damnable working conditions in Seattle. And, believe me, there is no "vulgar flaunting of wealth and extravagance." "Wealth and extravagance" are in hiding or have gone to California. There never have been oppressive working conditions in Seattle, comparable to other cities. Labor has been and is wonderfully prosperous. And today Seattle is designated by the Department of Justice as the chief danger spot of Bolshevism. The Department of Justice is right.

In a few days in Seattle, unless something in the way of a miracle happens, this city will be without heat, lights, transportation, telephones, newspapers. Worse than that, it will be without food. Many persons in poor health will die in a day or two. The unions have consented to keep the hospitals going, but that's about all. Even worse than that is the fact that both sides are armed and seem to want to fight. Yesterday I attended a Bolshevik meeting where they talked about "taking control" and then I went to the police station where they had 800 police and soldiers armed with carbines, six-shooters and clubs. Street fighting is almost sure to start.

Everyone talks about the "revolution." The strikers don't seem to know what it is all about, but they are excited, elated and enthusiastic. They call Mayor Hanson a tool of the capitalists and open threats are made to "get" him; and I know that Hanson has fought all his life for the workingman.

Many circulars are being distributed headed "Russia did it" and "Overthrow the rotten system," etc. I enclose one of the latest.

Numbers of discharged soldiers are making Bolshevik speeches. I myself have seen soldiers, still in the service, refuse to salute officers and have seen the officers stop soldiers and threaten them for this refusal. Camp Lewis is flooded with Bolshevik literature. The Bolsheviks admit that soldiers at Camp Lewis will be called out in the event of disorder, but they believe that their agents among the soldiers and general conditions have caused such disaffection among these troops that they won't fight. Personally I believe they will fight, if ordered. However, it remains to be seen.

Soldiers already under arms here and kept at the police stations are old regulars from Fort Lawton.

Today preparations are being made to close all schools, courts and business of every kind. People are cleaning out the grocery stores and markets.

There is no question at all that the leaders intend to ruin Seattle if they cannot rule it.[90]

Therefore, I say that we have been going on the wrong theory in figuring that prevention of the evils you point out will stop Bolshevism. Here we have 30,000 workers who have quit and about 40,000 more who are going to quit, not because their wages have been lowered; not because they are hungry or unemployed; but because a higher scale wasn't granted, above war-time wages. And this in face of the fact that thousands of soldiers are out of work and are being kept out of work by this action.

In my opinion we have been counting on some things that may sound all right but are not in existence when it gets down to the practical business of publishing our kind of newspapers.

I also want to say that all we have to do is to hold onto certain ones of these theories and in some places on the map, at least, the time is coming when we will not even be permitted to print papers.

As an illustration of this latter statement, I doubt if we will soon be permitted to publish in Seattle and Tacoma, provided, of course, that the strike goes on. And what is happening in the northwest is going to happen in other places, later on.

Yours truly,

B. H. Canfield

[90] The 1919 general strike in Seattle was broken, and Mayor Ole Hanson claimed he had defeated Communist efforts to overthrow government and organized society.

Canfield is one of the Scripps editors, and at present chief of an important news and propaganda association that I founded many years ago [NEA].

Something over forty-five years ago I entered journalism. No matter what my purposes were for that step, almost at the beginning of my career I adopted a line of policy which I have since persisted in. I believed that the common interests of men, rich and poor alike, would be served by increasing the individual shares of the working people in their proportion to the total product. I knew that under our form of democracy the poor people, who formed a vast majority of the electorate, had it in their power to improve their condition if they only knew how. I found that the press — daily, weekly, and monthly — of the country was devoted exclusively to the interests of the well-to-do. The well-to-do were instructed by their press in all matters political and economical, while the poor were left in dense ignorance. As a rule, the working classes had been schooled and could read the newspapers. But they did not read the newspapers. The two principal reasons for their not doing so were: first, that the price of subscriptions to all journals was so high that few of the workingmen could afford to purchase and read the papers; and second, the writers of the then-existing press had such a superior education that, while they were able to write in a way to be understood and appreciated by the really educated and wealthier class, there was neither profit to them nor inclination on their part to write down to the common herd. The publishers of the journals of that time, for one reason or another, sought only the patronage of the well-to-do and intellectual classes.

From my observation and because I had myself enjoyed somewhat of knowledge and culture, I concluded the vast majority of the wealthy class were not so superior after all, in intellect and wisdom. In fact, in my youthful conceit I felt a vast contempt for those who called themselves of the better and higher classes.

I was no philanthropist or humanitarian in those days. My contempt and antagonism toward the upper classes was, I must admit, far greater than was my sympathy for the dumb, stupid, and inarticulate masses.

In those days my knowledge of the world outside America was so limited that I was unable to make comparisons and to realize how infinitely better was the lot of the American workingman and poor man than was that of his fellows in other countries.

The line of conduct I adopted as a journalist and which I have since persisted in has been that of instructing and educating the common people of my country and arousing in them a great discontent with their lot and antagonism toward the employing and governing class.

It needed none of my reading of history and philosophy, which, subsequently to those days, I indulged in, to convince me that those people who were in the upper classes and who were themselves rulers, were satisfied with conditions as they were and had no great inspiration or incentive to bring about any changes in the social order.

I had the conviction that necessity alone would be the cause of the amendment of the manners and customs of the employer and the wealthy, ruling class, and I proposed to force upon this upper class the necessity of amendment.

Not only the prosperity but the bare existence of the upper classes depended upon the labor of their inferiors — the contented and productive labor of these people.

I proposed to do all I could to promote the greatest possible discontent on the part of the working classes: to encourage strikes; to encourage the working people to vote against candidates for public office who were careless of their interests, and for candidates who made the greatest concessions to them.

Trade unionism in this country was, in those days, quite weak. I never failed to recognize, even from my earliest days, the faults of trade unionism. But it was an organization through which I felt that I could exercise comparatively a great influence. I therefore heartily espoused the cause of trade unionism. I did all in my power to bring workingmen's strikes to a successful conclusion, or at least to produce such results as would cause the employers to become more and more reluctant to provoke such strikes and to make greater and greater efforts in the way of concessions to forestall them.

I began publication of a series of small newspapers very cheaply conducted, so that they could be sold to the public at the smallest price consistent with the country's coinage — namely, one cent.

Without any exceptions the daily papers of my youth were all selling for five cents. A dollar a day was the common wage of my time. A five-cent paper cost 5 per cent of the workingman's daily wage, whereas a one-cent paper cost only 1 per cent of his wage.

At first, I must acknowledge, the principal appeal of my papers to the public was their cheapness. I never in the early days, or even in my later days, have experienced the gratification of feeling that any great proportion of the working class loved me or respected me because of the service I was trying to do them.

But I made a great discovery, which was that a newspaper that had the patronage of the working class had a better business opportunity than a newspaper that had to depend upon the upper class alone for its patronage. There were at least ninety-five possible readers for a one-cent paper to every five possible readers for a five-cent paper.

However, it was not long before many other shrewd men took advantage of my discovery, and soon enough there were one-cent papers published in every reasonably large community in the United States. Also soon enough the publishers of these papers learned that their prosperity depended upon their catering not only to the interests of, but the prejudices of, the vulgar crowd.

The result of this new kind of press has been a great revolution in the economic and political fields of this country.

I never nursed the illusion that by taking the course I determined to take I would become a great public leader of the people. In fact, I never thought of such a thing because I never desired such a thing.

I never loved publicity. At heart I was an aristocrat or perhaps even worse, a snob. I did not like the crowd. It was always a painful thing to me to be an object of public attention. I did not love my workingman for whom I loved to work. I never chose the companionship of the common people — the plain people. I was so much unsocial that the old saying, "Birds of a feather flock together," has never been applied to me. If I had to be with men and women I preferred the companionship of strong men and women — men and women of affairs and intellect and culture. But there has never been a time when social intercourse with my fellows has been necessary or even pleasant. Of course, there have been numerous occasions when I have been vastly self-weary and when even the companionship of books has palled on me and when, for a change, I have been glad to welcome the companionship of one or two, or even three or four, people at the same time. But there has never been a time when I would not prefer absolute solitude to mingling in a crowd, even no larger than half a score.

[*Scripps here repeated, as he did many times, the story of the New England philanthropist who loved the common people enough to die for them but not enough to live with them.*]

I never coveted or expected gratitude from those whom I served. I never expected to receive either fame or any great amount of friendship from them. I have neither been despondent nor surprised by my experiences.

However, I cannot claim that I have always been free from resentment. There are times without number when I have been injured in my feelings by discovering that I not only lacked the love of my proteges, but that it was only necessary for the latter to have an opportunity in order that they should reveal their ill will and even antagonism to me.

In time I grew wealthy and in time I became a very important element of the ruling class, a large employer and a man of considerable political influence.

Human nature being such as it is, there should be nothing remarkable about the fact that I should be the object of envy and suspicion now that I am in my present position. However, in the earlier days of my career, when I was still a very poor man, when all the powers that then were in the political, social, and economic worlds were arrayed against me, the only people that I feared and had occasion to fear (for I never felt that I was not superior to any enemy or combination of enemies of the ruling class) was the rabble. On two occasions of my young manhood I had to meet and defy (successfully) mobs bent upon my destruction, or at least the destruction of my newspaper properties.

Now, Canfield, the man who wrote the letter above transcribed — whose age is somewhere between forty and forty-five, I believe — has apparently just discovered that which I knew as a young man and which all of my subsequent experience has impressed upon me; namely, that the mob is not only ungrateful, but vindictive; that the objects of my solicitude and the solicitude of my papers for the last forty-five years are not only ready but anxious to turn upon us and rend us.

I made this discovery that Canfield has just made before Canfield was born. It appears that Canfield has concluded that my whole life is a mistake, and that there must be a right-about-face in the policy adopted by my newspapers in order that society itself should not be destroyed.

Doubtless Canfield has read some books; it is possible even that he has read some books of history.

Perhaps he has read the Bible. Jesus has not been the only man who has prayed his Father in Heaven to forgive his enemies because they knew not what they did. But Jesus' teachings did not destroy society.

History's pages are filled with the stories of martyrs and near-martyrs, and are also filled with the stories of great men who performed great services for their peoples and who lived to see the fruition of their work and rejoice in them, notwithstanding the invariable experience of all of them; namely, that the people whom they have served so well had no knowledge or appreciation of the services that had been rendered.

Canfield's case is an example of many of my own personal experiences — not more remarkable than other cases, but one which I choose to comment on.

Some seventeen or eighteen years ago Canfield came into the Scripps concern, a young, callow youth. It was by accident that he attracted my attention. He was anything but a remarkable young man. I remember my first seeing him and the very unflattering impression his personality made upon me. He appeared to be about as little fit for a responsible position as could have been any man. He had been pitchforked into the position as editor of the Los Angeles *Record* at a time when that property was in bad condition and after there had been many changes in the editorship. At the time, I was very tired on account of several months' tiring work in the East. Fully intending to displace Canfield by a better man as soon as I got around to it, I left Canfield on his job. However, I very soon noticed that the Los Angeles *Record* was being conducted more nearly according to my views than it had ever been before. Canfield is perfectly justified in the claim he makes in his letter of being a loyal friend and servant of the workingman. It was because, and just because, of his attitude in this respect that I permitted him to continue in the editorship of the *Record*. It was because of this characteristic that I was patient with him and overlooked many faults that I would not have endured from any editor less loyal to the clientele that I considered to be my own.

Time went on and Canfield developed ability, both as an editor and as a capable servant of the people. I left him in charge of the *Record*, and he was holding this position at the time of my retirement from active work in the spring of 1908.

For a time — I do not know how long, maybe several years — he continued in his post, until suddenly one day I was surprised to learn that my son James, my successor in the control of my properties, had promoted him to a very important position in charge of the editorial management of three or four of our northern Pacific Coast papers. I must admit that I was somewhat shocked as well as surprised at this step having been taken. I did not consider Canfield anything like fit for so important a post.

However, I had had trouble in my own time with the editorship of my northern papers, Mr. [E. H.] Wells, Canfield's predecessor, having developed considerable reactionary spirit as he had become comparatively rich and prosperous.

Therefore, I let it go by without remonstrance on my part — this new deal of my son's.

Soon enough I learned that Canfield was running true to form — my form — and I was very much gratified in my mind to learn that my son, notwithstanding my fears as to his probably soon-developing reactionary or conservative ideas, had chosen for so important a position such a thoroughgoing radical as Canfield appeared to be.

Later, Canfield was promoted to his present (at the time of writing) position as general manager of the Newspaper Enterprise Association, succeeding W. B. Colver. Colver, I learned, was considerably — almost too much — devoted to propagandism and was developing something of the spirit of the "highbrow."

It has only been lately that I have learned that by the favor of my son and by reason, I must concede, of his natural abilities, Canfield has made use of his opportunities and become comparatively wealthy. For something over a year I have been hearing various rumors and have been growing doubtful as to Canfield's ability to keep the faith while developing his wealth.

Now comes this letter. Canfield frankly exposes the ingratitude of the workingman toward him and his paper, the Seattle *Star*. Considering that Canfield is a very shrewd and able man, I am perfectly certain that long before this experience of his in Seattle he had come to the conclusions that he sets forth in his letter on this subject.

I am sure that he has been restless and uncomfortable because of his having for so long a time to continue that policy which was the root cause of his ever having become an element in the Scripps institution.

I have known men who, being under some debt or obligation to their fellows, have sought and even succeeded in making a payment of this debt by picking a quarrel with their creditors. In fact, this practice is, I believe, a very common trait with all men. I have had managers and partners in my business who could never discharge an old employee without first having a quarrel with him.

Mr. Canfield perhaps has seized upon this opportunity of the general strike in Seattle as a psychological moment to openly confess what he considers to be the errors in my ways.

Let me present a few points of history.

Had I, when I first realized that ignorance and weakness, ingratitude, and all sorts of vices were necessarily companions, adopted the views that Mr. Canfield now holds, I would not have founded the Cleveland *Press* — the parent stem of the whole Scripps concern of today.

Later, when my office on Frankfort Street in Cleveland was assailed by a mob which filled up the whole of Frankfort Street and three contiguous blocks of streets for the purpose and intention of destroying the Cleveland *Press* plant and perhaps doing me bodily harm, had I at that time abandoned the people to their folly, there would have been no Cincinnati *Post*, and no other of the nineteen Scripps papers, which still exist and which were founded after the mob incident in Cleveland, would have been allowed to come into existence.

Still later, after I had founded the Cincinnati *Post* and the St. Louis *Chronicle*, when in Cincinnati and in Cleveland I was battling against corrupt political rings and my life was not only threatened but a price put upon my head, and when the mass of the people refused to give me any confidence and support, had my spirit grown weary, there would have been no Los Angeles *Record* founded or any other of the west-coast papers.

I have suffered many defeats in journalism, even having to abandon newspapers that I had founded. There would have been none of these defeats had the working people, for whose interests I had been fighting, been even intelligently selfish, let alone loyal and friendly.

But for my determination to spread the gospel of my propaganda of the rights and wrongs of the common people to a much larger field than that covered by my own newspapers, there would have been no Newspaper Enterprise Association, which is the last (so far) rung in the ladder that Canfield has climbed.

From the altitude of Canfield's present position, a very high place in the institution that I have founded and through which he has developed, Canfield now proclaims not only the uselessness of my life work — the folly of it all — but its so great sinfulness that repentance and reform and change must be made in the whole institution.

Let us suppose that that Seattle mob of strikers and revolutionists completely wrecked the Seattle *Star* plant and destroyed it as a property. When a clergyman has performed the last sad rites over some dead human being, he seeks to console the bereaved ones by saying, "The Lord giveth and the Lord taketh away."

What is that property, the Seattle *Star*, but the capitalized goodwill, friendship, and support of the workingmen of Seattle, who composed the mob that threatened the existence of the property? Even had the Seattle *Star* plant been destroyed and the property thoroughly annihilated, still the patronage and goodwill of the workingmen of Seattle has been such that, over and above the value of the plant and the personal property, in the way of salaries and dividends, I, Canfield, and other stockholders in the Seattle *Star* have received during the existence of the paper, several hundred thousands of dollars which we have taken to ourselves and incorporated into private property located at points far distant from Seattle itself [*sic*].

Even had the mob in its folly and anger destroyed the Seattle *Star* as a property, it would only have done, in a moment of error and ill temper, mischief the dollar value of which would equal only a small portion of the benefits that had previously been heaped upon officers and employees of the Seattle *Star* company.

Now that I am in my sixty-fifth year, weakened by age and disease, I find myself a large stockholder in a great institution — practically the controlling owner of an institution which has an aggregate value of not less than 20 million dollars. Personally, I believe it has a value 50 per cent or more greater than the sum named.

Practically the whole of this institution has been developed from and grown out of some ten thousand dollars which I took to the city of Cleveland a little over forty years ago and with which I founded the Cleveland *Press*.

Besides this property of great value, I and other stockholders, in the way of salaries and dividends, during the past forty years, received many millions of dollars.

The whole of this great value — the whole of the property and the income — has been the capitalization of and coinage of the goodwill, the friendship, the patronage, and the confidence of millions of workingmen and their families.

It is true that I feel that I have rendered to the workingmen of the country even a greater service than they have rendered to me. But it is nonetheless a fact that the capital wealth of the Scripps institution consists of the confidence and goodwill of men and women who, still largely ignorant, still largely undeveloped mentally and morally, may, in periods of excitement and under the influence of foolish and vicious leaders, at any time turn and destroy individual elements of the property and perhaps in a great upheaval destroy the whole of it.

Notwithstanding this fact, the Scripps institution and the working people of the country are at the best, considering our side of the controversy, equal partners in the concern. The populace gives us money in the way of support for and in consideration of the services that we are under obligation to render these same working people.

Personally, I feel that neither I nor my heirs would have any right to any money derived from the sale of our property except for services well and loyally performed — services to the workingman and woman not only of the various communities in which we publish our papers but of the whole country.

Concerning the Founding
of New Newspapers

[*April 23, 1922*]

ONE

First and foremost, the fact must be recognized that a new newspaper can be successfully founded in any city, large or small, old or young, providing only that the editorial direction of the new paper shall be vastly superior to that of any newspaper formerly existing in the community.

I am here considering a newspaper as a property.

The Hearst and Pulitzer and the Ochs newspapers in New York are, in the sense I am considering, new newspapers as compared with nearly all of their contemporaries. Joseph Pulitzer made such changes in the old *World* as to practically make it a new newspaper. There is no connection between the Hearst *Journal* and the old *Journal* which Albert Pulitzer founded many years ago. The *Times* established by Adolph Ochs was not at all a continuation of the *Times* founded by the Jones brothers. [Henry Raymond and only George Jones founded the New York *Times*.]

The Hearst paper in Chicago has not only outlived but has absorbed all the Chicago morning papers except the *Tribune*.

The Chicago *News* is a young paper compared with the Chicago *Journal*.

There are many successful newspapers in the United States that have changed hands or ownership a number of times without their value being seriously affected — prosperous papers that continue to be prosperous.

TWO

The best community in which to found a new paper is one that is comparatively young and whose population has in very recent times greatly increased.

The reason for this is that there is such a thing as "the newspaper habit." Once a man has been accustomed to reading a certain newspaper for a number of years, he forms such a habit with regard to this paper that he will not discontinue his old newspaper in order to take another newspaper, even if the latter is in every way — even considering the personal bias of the reader — doubly as meritorious.

In every old city there are old, well-established newspapers. The people in such a city have all acquired the habit of reading one or the other of the old papers, and it is difficult for a new newspaper to attract their patronage. Especially in the case of an old city whose population is growing slowly (and mainly by natural increase), it requires a very long time to establish a newspaper. The son and daughter of a man who has been reading a certain newspaper, after [they] have grown up and established their own homes, have acquired the habit of reading the paper that their parents have read before. While it is easier to get such young people to take on the new paper, it is much more difficult to obtain such people as customers than it is to obtain the custom of a fresh immigrant into the town.

When a new paper is founded in a comparatively young city, we find that there are very few permanent residents of that city who have become very firmly attached to or habituated to any paper previously published. To a newcomer in a growing town, all the papers published in that town are to him equally old, established papers, and hence he makes his selection of the papers entirely on the merits of the different papers.

There were only 40,000 inhabitants in the city of Seattle when the Seattle *Star* was founded twenty-four years ago. It is probable that there are not over two or three thousand people in Seattle today who were reading the newspapers of that city when the Seattle *Star* was started.

The population of Los Angeles was perhaps not much over 80,000 when the *Record* was started. If the *Record*'s circulation as compared to the size of . . . Los Angeles today is not relatively equal to the Seattle *Star*'s circulation as compared with the present population of Seattle, it is because the editorial conduct of the *Record*, so far as the general public is concerned, was far inferior to that of the Seattle *Star*.

The San Francisco *News* was established long after the city of San Francisco had become a large and well-established city. In the matter of circulation, the San Francisco *News* has depended for its success or failure upon the merits of its editorial conduct.

There is the case of the Birmingham *Post*. The growth of our Birmingham paper, such as it has been, has been due to the editorial conduct of that paper. I think the Birmingham *Post*'s contemporary has been somewhat at a disadvantage since the latter (the Birmingham *News*) is such a good paper — that is to say, it has catered to a class far above the average intelligence of that community. (Personally, I found the Birmingham *News* a very satisfactory paper. As a matter of choice, there is no doubt that I or a man like me, settling in Birmingham, would take the *Evening News* and would refuse to read the Birmingham *Post*.)

THREE

Our concern has had practical experience only in industrial towns, and hence, everything else being equal, the value of our experience would be greater in industrial towns than in any other.

We are experimenting with newspapers in two cities, Washington and Norfolk, which are not industrial towns in the sense that Cleveland, Detroit, Birmingham, and Memphis are industrial towns.

FOUR

In any city where there is established an evening newspaper whose circulation in the city is equal to one in five of the population, it would be extremely difficult to successfully found a newspaper. It would be better business to buy an established newspaper.

FIVE

Everything else being equal, the opportunities for the growth of a new newspaper [are] affected by the character of the population of the city in which it is published. One native white American is a better prospect than two or three Negroes or comparatively recent immigrants from a foreign country.

SIX

In appraising the value of a city for a prospective new newspaper, too much emphasis should not be placed upon the size of the population outside the city of publication but within access by rail or otherwise to the office of publication.

It must be remembered that in almost any community, the value of the newspaper for advertising purposes by the merchants of a town is, to begin with, almost exclusively dependent upon its local circulation. At best, the advertiser does not get as much even as one-half of the returns from his advertising in the newspaper read outside of the city limits as he does from the same paper read within the city limits.

(Some exceptions to this rule exist. For instance, the city of San Diego is so related to the county of San Diego that the country circulation of a San Diego paper is almost as valuable to the advertising merchant as city circulation. But there are very few such communities.)

A large suburban population is, however, a valuable asset to a newspaper with regard to its long future growth and establishment.

It must always be remembered also that, as a rule, the cost of circulating a large city newspaper in any district much outside of the city is so great that there can be but little if any profit derived from such circulation.

When the Norfolk *Post* has been long established on a profitable basis, it is doubtful if it will ever pay to get any circulation in any of the cities or towns divided from Norfolk by water.

There is a local sentiment in every community that impels the people of such communities to prefer their local, inferior papers to a superior metropolitan paper, and also to prefer to patronize the merchants of their own towns, although they have inferior stocks of goods, than to patronize the stores in a larger city.

SEVEN

Costs and editorial ability. — It has long been my conviction that, everything else being equal, the more money spent in the establishment of a new newspaper and in its conduct, the less the prospects for its success.

By the expenditures of large sums of money, an inferior editor can secure a certain showing in the way of circulation as will both deceive him and the employing company. There are only a very, very few men who have such executive ability as to permit them to profitably expend any money at all. Few as there are of men of real editorial ability, there are fewer still of men who have, coupled with any sort of editorial ability, financial or executive ability.

It is the writers of newspapers that cause the people to desire to read these newspapers. While the universal curiosity of humanity is such that all men desire news items, still it is a fact that newspapers that are merely purveyors of news have no chance at all in competition with other publications which give less news but occasionally publish articles of news value (or of no news value) which have a strong appeal to the emotions and common instincts of humanity.

I recall my youthful experiences on the Detroit *News,* Cleveland *Press,* and Cincinnati *Post* — all newspapers which quickly achieved great popularity. I know that in the case of our first newspaper, the Detroit *News,* one man, a writer of great ability, supported by two reporters of somewhat less ability — all three of these men being peculiar geniuses, much given to idleness and only occasionally contributing rather startling articles — were the real authors of the success of this paper. I doubt if there was an average of more than one or two a week of these popular articles published.

The man who carried the Cleveland *Press* through was a $15-a-week, morphine-eating, whiskey-drunk reporter. My own personal contribution (in the way of writing) was far less valuable than this other man's. Later, this first genius was followed by another, and for years it was this other man who made the Cleveland *Press* famous.

It was a wild-eyed, eccentric, ex-Methodist minister, who had been ex-communicated, who did more to make the Cincinnati *Post* a success than all the rest of us put together, although there were two or three other embryo geniuses — just boys who, because they had original ideas and no journalistic training, could not help but be amusing.

I think the really great editor is the man who can secure and keep on his staff one, two, or three writers whom he permits to express themselves with the least possible restraint.

My own experiences have taught me that it is only rarely that a successful writer will be an efficient editor. Charles A. Dana was a great writer and he made the New York *Sun* a great success, but every writer on the old *Sun* had to write according to the Dana model or style.

I have had plenty of experiences with men who could not only write well but who could tolerate or develop or allow the development of other writers.

EIGHT

Every newspaper should be built up about an editorial personality. The first thing to do is to become aware of the existence of an unemployed genius. The next thing to do is to establish a newspaper for that genius in a city in which there are peculiar opportunities for exploiting his peculiar kind of genius. After these two things have been accomplished, it is only necessary to furnish the cheapest possible newspaper plant, all things considered, and to secure as a business manager for the property a man who is peculiarly fitted to sell the kind of a newspaper his editor can make, and to sell advertising space to those merchants who can profit by selling goods to that class of people who buy the kind of a paper the editor publishes.

There is more in this last statement than the ordinary man may be inclined to think. But consider this: Suppose your editor is peculiarly fitted to deal with sporting matters. It stands to reason that his paper will interest men interested in sporting news, and it also stands to reason that the sporting men have need for a different kind of goods than would, say, a Sunday school teacher. Or again, supposing your editor gains the patronage, to a large extent, of the poor and laboring classes. This class of people doesn't habitually buy pianos and high-powered automobiles.

I have known many managers of advertising and advertising solicitors who have wasted a tremendous amount of energy and thought in trying to gain the patronage of so-called high-class advertisers — usually called "leaders" — who can gain little or nothing by advertising in a paper that has almost a purely workmen's circulation.

By the same token, I have known many an editor who eventually failed by "trying to carry water on both shoulders" — making an effort to keep a large, general circulation and at the same time being popular with the "highbrows."

The Organism as a Whole —A Disquisition

[*June 8, 1922*]

On board yacht "Kemah"
At Huntington Bay, Long Island
June 8, 1922

Dear Bob [Robert P. Scripps]:

I have invited you, temporarily to a large extent at least, to lay aside some of your personal activities as editor-in-chief of our institution for the purpose of your having more time to study the past history of our institution from its birth, its growth as an organism of capital, and especially to measure and weigh quantitativably and qualitativably [*sic*] its present resources in the way of liquid capital such as money and bank deposits, its fixed capital in the way of real or tangible property such as land, buildings, machinery, *et cetera*, and its credit so-called.

Beyond this, I shall invite you to give further attention to the subject of what some of us call the spirit of the concern — what you yesterday in your talk with me defined as its conscience — but what has for a long time been called the "Scripps' Principles."

I have told you on more than one occasion that I have been confused and perplexed whenever this question of the Scripps' Principles has been mentioned and particularly when I have been asked to define them. On many occasions have I been actually startled and caused to have a feeling of resentment when someone has spoken in my presence in favor of this or that course of action as being necessary in order to be consistent with the Scripps' Principles. I have been equally surprised and caused to feel resentment when someone has stated that this, that, or the other course was inconsistent with the Scripps' Principles.

I have just finished reading the third chapter of Aurel Kolnai's *Psychoanalysis and Sociology*.[91] Kolnai is a German and his work is translated by

[91] Aurel Kolnai, *Psychoanalysis and Sociology*, trans. by Eden and Cedar Paul. Harcourt, Brace, New York, 1922.

Eden and Cedar Paul. The author is just about as devoid of lucidity as it is possible for a German to be. It is just as disgusting as all Freudian literature. But oddly enough in such a volume as this it seems to me that I have discovered not only the key to my perplexity concerning the subject of the Scripps' Principles, but a far better definition or rather exposé of that idea that I have been trying to impress upon you — namely, what I mean by our institution being an organism — than any I have been able to so far formulate myself.

All myths, as you know, are commonly supposed to have had their origin in some actual personality and the activity of some person. But Kolnai suggests the manner of the growth, the necessity of the growth, and the cause of the growth of the myth.

I think you are sufficiently familiar with the Washington myth, the Jefferson myth, and even the Lincoln myth; to all of those personalities have been given attributes which were not personal to them but which were demanded to satisfy the minds and the wishes and the yearnings of the populace. Each of these characters, in fact, as recognized by us of today, is a composite of the wishes of many thousands and in some cases of many millions of the common people — the masses.

I imagine that if Washington or Jefferson or even Lincoln should come back into the world today and learn from contact with living persons, each one of them, what sort of man the general public had grown to suppose him to be, he would be even more startled and even feel more a sense of resentment — much more startled and much more resentful than I have ever been when I have found myself burdened with sentiments, ideas, motives, and actions, many of which I know that I have never had, and many today incapable of possessing.

Even during my short life, tradition has taken charge of my personality and modified it and molded it into a form that never existed and perhaps never could exist — in fact, translated it into a tradition.

It is a fact that our organism can never see nor feel nor hear me as I am. In fact, they have molded me into a sort of a composite, not only of their own wishes, but the wishes of hundreds of men — maybe thousands — who have preceded them as elements and even organs (such as glands) in the organism as a whole.

At the last conference, you may recall that I made the statement that for many years, even before my retirement, I had become only an element in the organism, controlled by the organism — that is to say, controlled by just such men as I then had before me.

Both you and Howard and, in times past, such men as McRae and Paine and others have urged me to make my personality recognizable by the public.

I have given you what I thought my many good reasons for not permitting this to be done. Just today I have been thinking that possibly by my taking this course I might be retarding the natural and consistent growth of the organism such as I might recognize — retarding a growth that I greatly desire.

I have approved of and desired the title of "Scripps-McRae" to be affixed to our concern rather than the title of "E. W. Scripps" just because my personality would be so largely concealed thereby.

However, in spite of my desires, intentions, and negative processes, the organism has proved itself stronger than myself. It demands, if not an expressed personality, at least a personification of its ideals.

Is a living personality preferable to a dead one? If so, as you are destined to remain living for a longer time, it would be better for the concern to be personified by yourself than by my own personality.

If there is power, however, in tradition, and if the more ancient the tradition is the more power the organism will enjoy, then it might be better for it to be personified by myself.

Your business and your duty in the concern is not to gratify or to seek personal credit by assuming a purely filial attitude. Your duty is to the concern and not to me.

Amongst other things you should consider this subject and after duly weighing all considerations, you should act.

It is my business and my duty to give you a free hand to do what you wish to do. You will recall how often I sought to impress upon you your duty to treat with kindness and respect and, at least to a reasonable extent, generosity all of those men who have actually built their own lives into our institution. I imagine that you may be able to observe that I have been prompted in my advice to you by my feelings with regard to the solidarity of the concern and of my being only one of its elements — a person selected and elected by the other elements in the concern to a position of power, of control, and to the duty of directing.

I do not mean by any means that all of the people connected with our concern have at all times felt that I was fit. The most that can be said on this matter would be that the very fact that they remained as a part of the organism, and desired to remain a part of the organism, was their vote that they preferred to serve under me than under anyone else. Now, wisely or otherwise, it is the tendency of most men, even of all men, to regard a man's son as an extension in life of the man himself.

Perhaps it could be said that your position at present at least is vicarious. According to the growth and development of the organism will be your own status in it. But very slightly, even by your own immediate entourage and much less by the public at large, will your own personal merit, great or small, affect your position in the public thought, the small public or the large public.

If the concern grows strong and acquires great influence . . . you, personifying it, will be believed to have grown strong and great.

Washington became a great figure in history because the little nation that he led in war has grown into a great nation. Jefferson's name is one to be conjured with because the party of which Jefferson was the spokesman became a great political party. And yet I and many men as wise and learned as I am, and more wise and more learned, believe that Jefferson's contemporary, Alexander Hamilton, was the greater of the two men.

[*As further illustrations of his point, here deleted, Scripps goes on to cite examples provided by William I of Germany, Admiral Dewey, and James Gordon Bennett, Jr.*]

Like Washington, I was in at the beginning and perhaps only touched the spark that fired the cannon that in time made considerable noise.

Perhaps by chance or by reason of a temporary phase of my own mind, I gave the first direction to the institution.

After that I did the much less important work of putting behind the little organism my force, consenting to rather than compelling a cooperation with a continually increasing and continually changing company of other men whose inclinations caused them to pursue, journalistically, courses similar to my own.

After that first initiative, a large part of my attention was actually necessarily diverted from a course preferred by it, namely, purely editorial work, to business considerations.

Why, Bob, before I had reached my thirtieth year I had impressed upon me a reputation — even I can say several reputations — which always appeared to me as almost laughable in their eccentricities . . . there were two main reputations: one, a liberal in politics; and, two, a wizard in money-making. The net result of these reputations was a constantly increasing stream of recruits to the band of which I was captain.

As there were too many recruits of a certain caliber to be accommodated in the first and then the second and then the third of my enterprises, I was driven almost by necessity — a necessity perhaps derived [as much] from my acquisitiveness as from that which was altruistic in my character — to founding more and more newspapers and auxiliary institutions.

(There is just one thing that causes me, since dictating the foregoing, to hesitate and think again as to the correctness of the statements made there. That thing is that I recall that even in those days when the first of my newspapers was in actual process of being born, I was planning not only such an institution as we have, but one far greater — one that you, yourself, may not live long enough to see fully developed.)

I have often tried to explain to myself what I was, what I was doing, and why I was doing what I was doing. On such occasions I have compared myself to a savage driving down a great flood stream, sitting on a floating log, holding only a dead branch of a tree with which I could do a little steering of my log, just enough to keep it off the rocks, and just enough paddling to force it into some quiet haven for a breathing spell for myself.

But why didn't I ever stop in one of those quiet havens, I would ask further, and answer it by saying, just because I was possessed of what one would call the devil who would not only permit me to but compelled me to push out again and again into the deep, rushing water.

Here it appears I have been presenting a whole bunch of metaphors and allegories or other figures of speech.

But still, Bob, the devil which was in me, or perhaps was not in me but around me in that spirit organism of which I was a part, was the cause of all that was caused.

To such an extent that I know not of, you have been finding yourself and are finding yourself, and I hope that you will be able not only to recognize facts, but face them squarely.

Neg Cochran told me once of a quatrain of advice sent to you by Clarence Darrow. I will not attempt to paraphrase in rhyme this advice, but will try to do so in plain prose as follows:

So long as there are so many good men in the world who want to work and want to work for somebody and so long as there is so much good work to be done, there is really no excuse for your not being at least the titular boss of the biggest work in journalism that has ever been accomplished.

Affectionately,

E. W. Scripps

The Wisdom of an Old Penman

[*June 1, 1925*]

Well, boys, I'm here. My old friend who holds the chair of journalism in this university tells me that you want to hear me talk about newspaper work. First and foremost I want to tell you that a college is about the last place in the world where a man should go to learn journalism.[92]

A good many years ago, long before any of you were born, I was in Paris traveling with a friend who was also a newspaperman.

One evening my friend came to my room in my hotel to tell me of an adventure. He happened to see in the lobby of the hotel a man who was a great American newspaperman, the owner of one of the leading papers in this country. He had never met him before but he recognized him from the numerous portraits of him he had seen in American newspapers and magazines. This man was well along in years. My friend, who had a trait pretty well in common with all young newspapermen, namely, cheek, went up and introduced himself to the great man and told him that he himself was in the newspaper game.

The old fellow turned his fishy eyes on him and stared for several moments and then, "Working in a newspaper office, eh!!! ————house, eh!!! I'm a prostitute, you're a prostitute, we newspapermen are all prostitutes." As to what else he said it doesn't matter.

Whatever else you think about newspapers I can frankly tell you that this old publisher and editor is a good deal nearer right than you want to think or than you do think. Looking over your faces here I believe that a great many of you would immediately turn your backs on journalism if you knew how great a risk you're going to run by being properly designated as "no gentleman" if you further pursue the calling that you've elected.

Are there no clean honest gentlemen engaged in the profession? I'll say, Yes, but not many.

[92] This disquisition appears in McCabe, *Damned Old Crank*, p. 237 f.

There are very few opportunities for a man to be both a gentleman and a journalist. There is only one position in the newspaper business that a man can hold that is not only profitable in the long run but which a man can hold and have the choice of whether he is to be a gentleman or not. That position is ownership.

When you go out to seek a position as a reporter and you find one, how are you going to know whether the owner of the paper you are going to work for is a gentleman? How can you know whether the city editor under whom you are to work directly is a gentleman? All you can know is that you are to obey orders, to do as you are told, and if required lie and not to question why. If the owner of your paper is a gentleman and your immediate chief is a gentleman, it is probable that you will be working on a newspaper that is to have a short life.

I will not repeat the words of this old gentleman my friend met in the lobby of the hotel in Paris, I will not say that I have been a prostitute, knowingly, willingly, all the time.

As you know, I have been successful. I have done many things that I wouldn't want my son to do.

I have climbed the ladder from cub reporter to editor and owner, and the only consolation I have now is that I have been less of a rascal than most of my colleagues.

However, let me tell you this one thing. I do not think that as a class we newspapermen are worse than the average run of other men in business. I honestly believe that owing to our peculiar position we are constantly being impressed with the idea of our responsibility, and hence we are constantly straining to be less bad than we would be if we did not have this feeling of responsibility.

Stop and think of it. A paragraph of a half dozen lines thoughtlessly dashed off without the least bad intention may make a whole family unhappy and drive a wife away from her home, a husband to drink.

The power of the press is mighty. But, if it is great for good, it is great for evil.

Praise given to a man who does not deserve it, blame bestowed on a man who does not deserve it, may result in an honest candidate for the judgeship being defeated and a rascal placed on the bench.

A paragraph that you contribute to your paper may set afloat an impression that will grow and grow for years until a whole community at some critical time condemns the good man and supports the bad man.

As a reporter you must obey orders or get the sack. As a reporter you are instructed by your chief or by your fellows as to the policy of the newspaper on which you work so that without any direct orders you will comply with that policy, whether you think it right or wrong. You will probably not think about the rightness or the wrongness of the item or the article that you write; you will almost certainly think only of its effect upon your pay envelope.

Walter Bagehot, journalist, philosopher, and historian, in one of his books makes a statement something like this: "I worked on a number of journals in London. These journals all had different policies, some antagonistic to others. When I changed my position from one newspaper to another I'd have no idea of changing my views on politics or any other subject, but I always found that very shortly after I began my work on the journal the environment so affected me that I had thought and wrote as my fellows on the journal thought and wrote. I had no influence on the journal, it was the journal [that] molded me."

Personally, I have had a similar experience. I have owned several newspapers. Did these newspapers reflect me and my judgment? I can answer, Rarely. The community molds its newspapers. I go from one of my newspapers to another fully determined to carry out a certain policy, but although I owned the newspaper I couldn't control the newspaper, but the newspaper controlled me.

Oh, I admit that in certain particulars I could and did control the policy of my newspapers, but community feeling, the staff *esprit de corps*, and more than all else the traditions of the newspaper had a greater effect on me than did I have on the newspaper itself.

I have been well acquainted, not personally but through their newspapers, with two great journalists.

At one time one of these was the owner of a newspaper that made him considerable wealth. This paper was a blackmailing sheet in the large sense and in the meanest sense, too. One day, a very wealthy, a very respectable merchant of the city came into this man's newspaper office and told him that if he didn't sell his paper and leave the city in a week he would shoot him. The paper was sold and its publisher and editor moved to a different city. He conceived the idea that now he was rich enough to be respectable, so he founded or bought another newspaper, and although its founder and first editor has now long been dead, the paper has been respectable and powerful.

The other man had made a great success in a small western city. He had accumulated enough wealth to buy another paper in a much larger city. This latter paper was, as we say, on the rocks when he bought it. But he was a very skillful man and soon enough its publisher made a success and became very famous. He continued to own both papers, but even years later anyone reading first one of his papers and then the other would never dream that one man owned both of these papers.

Gentlemen, the trouble with journalism is its hermaphroditic character.

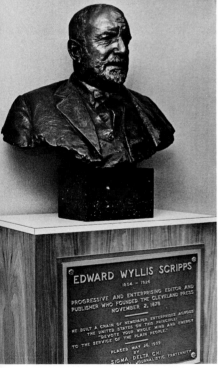

Scripps about 1885

Scripps about 1912

Upper left: *E. W. Scripps*
Upper right: *James E. Scripps*
Lower left: *L. T. Atwood*

Opposite page
Upper left: *Robert F. Paine*
Upper right: *Milton A. McRae*
Lower left: *George H. Scripps*
Lower right: *John S. Sweeney*

Scripps on his yacht

It isn't all a profession, it isn't all a business. Perhaps originally, or to speak more correctly, a few decades ago, journalism was a profession much more than it is now. Men practiced the profession for the love of it or for the love of the little or large influence or power that the calling brought with it.

Why, I can remember the time when in this country, taking the press as a whole, it cost more money to run all the newspapers in the United States than there was money received in profits by all the newspaper owners.

But now times have changed. Everywhere, all over this country in the various communities, the owners of newspapers in these communities are amongst the wealthiest members of their community.

The newspaper business has actually become what is called "big business." Newspapers have become or at least are becoming recognized by the public as properties rather than as organs of public opinion. We run our newspapers for the most part practically with the same end and object in view as do bankers and manufacturers, owners of coal mines, big department stores, for profit.

There was a time in this country when newspapers were run for the purpose of molding public opinion and their owners were esteemed lucky if they gained an incidental profit. Now newspapers are run for profit and only incidentally are molders of public opinion, leaders of the people in politics, and teachers.

Out of every dollar expended by newspaper publishers, on the average 90 cents is spent for the purpose of getting advertising revenue, and only 10 cents is spent in payment for news, instruction, and opinion-creating.

The poorest paid employees of a newspaper are the men who write. The largest compensation in the way of salaries or commissions are paid to the men who sell advertising space.

We publishers of newspapers pay to the various members of our staff the largest salaries to those men in the editorial department whose writings get us the most readers. That editor is esteemed to be the greatest who procures the largest number of readers for his paper and the greatest amount of goodwill on the part of the advertising customers. I know it to be a fact that most of our great newspapers sell their newspapers at a price less than the cost of the white paper used. The modern American newspaper is little more than a billboard carrying advertising. The more people who take our papers the more we are able to charge for the advertising space in the same.

Why, gentlemen, journalism is business pure and simple.

It is my recognition of some of the facts that I have stated, and others, that makes me feel very humble.

Dollar-chasing is anything but an ennobling pursuit.

Well, but what of it? The business is as it is, and it is our business to make the best of the situation that exists. If our publishers, your future employers, seek for and obtain an enormously large number of readers for the purpose of commanding a profitable advertising patronage, that at least incidentally gives to our newspaper writers an enormously large audience to whom we professional journalists can deliver whatever message we have to deliver. These businessmen engaged in newspaper work are giving us our opportunities to do good or ill service to the public. We can so teach the ignorant until they become less ignorant. We can to a very large extent mold public opinion according to our own views.

In reality journalism is statesmanship. The government of such a democracy as ours is practically a government by newspapers. There are comparatively few readers of books. There are more readers of magazines, but practically everybody reads the newspaper. What the public knows, it learns through the newspaper. Whatever the bias of the public mind may be, it is very largely the result of newspaper writers.

The teachers in our public schools and colleges, the ministers who preach sermons in our churches, the orators who address public meetings all exercise more or less influence in molding the minds of the people, but all of these influences are slight compared to the mighty force of the daily press and its auxiliary, the weekly and the monthly publications.

What do men know of men and events in the world — what can they know except what they learn from our newspapers?

Let us call ourselves, if we will, mere parasites sucking subsistence from a big commercial enterprise, yet we can easily enough recognize that our situation can give us opportunities to render services good or ill to the public. If journalism has fallen from its highest state of being solely employed in directing the public mind for the benefit of the public and become a mere dependent on capitalism, it may even be safely asserted that it has gained as much or more than it has lost, because without journalists there could be no newspapers and without newspapers there would not be so many millionaires.

I have often enough been reproached as a newspaperman for not being more patriotic and more loyal to the people, by men and women with perfectly good intentions but very small economic intelligence — men and women whom I can best describe by calling them economic imbeciles.

Such people as these insist that I ought to, and such men as you are ought to, teach and preach, preach and teach, and they tell me that we are very wrong in furnishing reading matter that will degrade and corrupt the minds and characters of our readers. If you have not already learned the fact, you will eventually learn that men and women do not like being preached at and taught, and that the moment that the average reader finds under his eyes some article intended to instruct and guide his or her opinion, he or she will skip that article to read something else.

If we do not amuse and entertain our readers we will have few readers or none at all. We will have no audience listening to us.

The public mind is such as it is at any given time. As patriots and altruists it is our business to improve that public mind in the only way possible. In order to instruct the people we must conceal as far as we can our intention to do so. We must slyly insinuate into the baser sorts of minds lessons that will be valuable to them and facts upon which they will be compelled to base their judgments when they are called upon by their votes, or by that sort of clamor which is called public opinion, to indicate their wishes and their demands to their servants in their official positions, executives, legislators, and the judiciary. We must keep our audience interested, whatever else we do, and then craftily work upon their minds.

The general public may be considered as a class in a kindergarten who are furnished with playthings and games which are unsuspected by the pupils of teaching them those things which their teacher desires them to learn.

A most salacious account of the proceedings in the divorce court may have and generally has concealed in it such valuable information and moral lessons that will do the reader more than enough good to make up for any possible harm.

Saying the worst we can say of the ignorant [sic] and base-mindedness of journalists, it must be apparent to any intelligent person that the men who are employed to write for newspapers are wiser and better instructed and more moral than is the great mass of the readers of the newspapers.

The daily press is intended for the great mass of our citizens and not for the highbrows, as we call them.

You and I all think that we are superior people and that, in fact, we belong to the highbrow class, and therefore I think we are right in concluding that the more people who read what we write the better it will be for the people as a whole. I started out by saying that there is only one extremely profitable job in so-called journalism, and that is the job of owner. I have also intimated that a man can only be both a gentleman and a journalist by being an owner of his newspaper. If independence is one of the chief elements of a gentleman, then in journalism the only man who can be independent is the owner of a newspaper. All employees must be subordinate to the will and wishes of their employers.

Now, I am only a has-been in the field of journalism, but I have been a journalist. I have also had peculiar opportunities for observing the quality of work done by many journalists. When I began to write for the newspapers I conformed in all things to the practice of other journalists. I was then as good a man and no better man than any of my fellow journalists. By degrees I began breaking the bonds of convention. I began expressing myself in my writing, not according to form but rather according to my personal inclination. I began writing the things that other people didn't write, writing the things that other people didn't write about, and finally I found that I had thrown to the winds all customs and conventions, and plainly expressed what I thought (but not about everything). However, I ceased to imitate, to at least a very large extent, any other newspaper writer.

I wrote as I thought and expressed myself in my writing as I would in my talk amongst intimate friends. Of course, I do not know what you are being taught in this school by your teachers. I only presume that you are being taught to write and express yourselves in the same or similar form as do other journalistic writers. I presume that in your studies and in your classes you are placed in possession of models in writing (the writings of other men and advised to imitate this writer and to avoid the style of another writer).

For the moment I have been allowed to be one of your teachers, and while I am acting in this capacity I am going to advise you to imitate nobody in writing, I am going to advise you, at least so far as your city editor, managing editor, or owner will permit you, to express yourself fully and completely and in your own style, and never in the style of another writer.

I know how difficult a task it will be to do this because I know how long and hard, and sometimes vainly, I strove to do the same thing.

I have had great advantages in being able to observe the beginnings, the development, and final accomplishment of many writing journalists. By experience and observation I have learned that those writing journalists who let themselves go, as it were, and wrote as nearly as possible, considering the limitations of the English language, what they thought, using the language and style chosen by themselves and not at all using the language and style of any other writer, rose quickest and highest in their profession.

You've all read books; you've all your favorite books and authors. If you have thought about the matter at all you must become aware that there is but little similarity either in the style or thoughts expressed by any two of the authors that have pleased you most. Think of Kipling and Meredith, of Milton and Browning, of Irvin Cobb and Wodehouse. I think the greatest blemish on the American press today is the likeness of the newspapers, taken as a whole each to another, and of all the writings in any single publication. Take one of the most commonly used phrases, "spread like wild fire" — I doubt if there is any newspaper writer today who has not used that phrase many times.

Fifty years ago and more, one might read an editorial by Dana or by

Halstead, or Henry Watterson or Joe McCullogh [Joseph B. McCullagh, St. Louis *Globe-Democrat*], and without looking at the title page of the paper he would know whether he was reading the New York *Sun*, the Cincinnati *Commercial*, the Louisville *Courier-Journal*, or the St. Louis *Globe-Democrat*.

Why, forty years ago, in reading any article, I would know whether it had appeared in one of my own papers or some other paper, and I would also know, which would be more easy to understand, in which one of my own papers the article had appeared. Today, with very few exceptions, you could read an article in any public paper published in any city from New York to San Francisco, and you would not be able to make a guess as to what paper it appeared in or even in what section of the country the paper in which it appeared was published.

Ben Franklin, who was himself a newspaperman, in *Poor Richard's Almanac*, said that "honesty was the best policy." That honesty in journalism is the best policy you might all reasonably doubt. However, I think none of us have reason to doubt that honesty is a good enough policy, though at times, because we are all frail human beings, the best that most of us can do is to be as honest as we can afford to be.

Forecasting

[*June 10, 1925*]

This is to be from a purely business point of view, but will deal with possibilities more perhaps than probabilities.

In 187[7] the total amount of money that the whole Scripps family could gather together was $30,000. [At the time the Detroit *News* was incorporated.] Fifty-one years later, in 1924, the net profits, excluding war taxes, from the investment and growth of this capital, the net cash profits of the Scripps Newspapers, exceeded 7 million dollars.

In the fall of 1878 the Cleveland *Press* was founded with a capital of $10,000 plus $2,500 obtained by loan. It was on this Cleveland foundation the Scripps-Howard concern was built and that, too, without any borrowed capital, and without any capital obtained by selling stock to people who had other income than salaries and dividends obtained from this concern.

In 1924, the net profit of this concern as given to me by H. L. Smithton [by then his private secretary, operating from the central office in Cincinnati] was $3,200,000. I am not certain but I think that this was over and above war taxes paid.

Since the date of the foundation of the Cleveland *Press*, only once did a period of five years pass without the volume and the profits of the business doubling.

From 1908 to 1917, a period of nine years elapsed before the volume and profits of the business were doubled, although it did not take so long a time for the profits to double.

One out of three of all the Scripps papers that were founded or bought failed absolutely or practically.

Beginning with November 2, 1878, I have had records kept of all the statement history showing month by month the circulation of each of our papers, the volume of money received for circulation and the volume of money received for advertisement, the gross volume, and showing the expense of each important department of the papers and the monthly gross expense and the net profit or loss of each paper and of the concern as a whole.

Some thirty years ago, using the data furnished by the statement history and having access to similar statements from the Detroit *Evening News*, I made an estimate of the value of the concern as a whole, and I found that including all the different properties the minimum value of the concern as a whole was not less than three times the volume of receipts of any year.

Comparing this statement with individual papers, I found that the value of any going concern — an individual property that had been making profits for five years — whose circulation of papers was making an annual increase, was worth much more than three times its gross receipts for one year.

In the year 1921 I took for each year the gross volume of receipts for each year dating from 1890 or 1895, multiplied this volume of business by three, and presuming that I had sold at the conclusion of any one of those years, I set this figure aside, presuming that I had sold the property at this price, and that I put the money out at 6 per cent compound interest, and then compared the gross sum of the principal and interest with the year 1921 the value I would have put on the concern at that time [*sic*].

In estimating the value of the concern in the year 1921 on the basis of 6 per cent, the profits of 1921 I found that if I had sold at any one year and invested the money at 6 per cent compound interest, my loss would have been enormous as compared with the gain I had made by keeping the property [*sic*].

I next made a series of calculations for various five-year periods, and in each case I found that even if in any year I had sold the whole group of properties on a basis of five times the annual business, I would have still been the loser by so doing.

At this time I estimated that any going newspaper that had been making a profit for the last five years, with a circulation growing proportionately with the growth of the population in the city in which it was published, was worth at a conservative figure not less than five times its volume of business for one year.

I have not during the past fifteen years figured on the proportions of increment value compared with the cash profits, but prior to that time it was common for me to make such figures, the result being that for every dollar I received in cash in the way of dividends, there was three dollars of value by increment.

It was during these earlier years that taking all of my newspapers, those that were profitable, those that were losing, and those that were merely staggering along, . . . there was an average increase in the value of all the newspapers of not less than 10 per cent a year; hence, I came to the conclusion that any one of my newspapers was not actually losing money that was making 6 per cent on the capital value in cash divisible, was actually making more than 16 per cent in cash and increment.

It has been owing to the indivisible profits of our business far more than to accumulations of capital from earnings that the wealth of the concern has so vastly increased.

Now it is an almost universal tendency among men to desire quick results in the way of profit, so that it has been an almost universal tendency on the part of all my minority stockholders to desire to sell their stock at any price regardless of [its] actual value whenever they could sell this stock at a profit of 100 to 200 per cent on assumed costs. I say "assumed costs," because in case of my own personal experience, none of my minority stockholders ever paid anything for their stock out of hand or out of money accumulated by their personal savings. In every case they were allowed to purchase their stock from their dividend earnings.

There must be a good and sufficient reason for the almost universal tendency of the owners of newspapers or newspaper stocks to vastly underestimate the actual value of the newspaper stocks which they own.

One of my lieutenants, Earle Martin, some four or five years ago was anxious to buy the Washington *Times*. He came to me one day and asked me what value I would put on a newspaper that had a certain circulation, a certain value of business, but had never made any money. I told him it was worth less than nothing to me.

There are few men, whether they are newspapermen or only ordinary businessmen, who do not believe that they could buy a losing newspaper and by better management make it a profitable one. A number of men have accomplished this feat. No man in the Scripps family or who has been connected with the Scripps concern has ever succeeded to my knowledge in performing this feat. The doing of such a thing is a possibility, but there are perhaps ten times as many chances of doubling the value of a profitable paper to one chance of making a going losing concern pay anything at all.

It is a trait of human nature that every man considers himself a wiser, abler, or more capable man than any other. The founder of a newspaper who has built it up into a large business finds it impossible to conceive that any other living man can so ably conduct a newspaper as he himself.

I have never known or known of a newspaper owner who did not attribute to his own personality, his own peculiar capacity, the success or profitableness of his newspaper. Such a man is incapable of segregating the two entities, the first, of course, himself, the second, his newspaper. Such a man cannot properly, reasonably, and fairly value his newspaper as a business or as a property.

When for any reason, especially when by reason of old age, the owner of a newspaper wishes to relieve himself of the work and worry of conducting a newspaper and begins to contemplate relief from servitude at the best possible price, there is another element that is almost certain to influence such a man's final determination. A newspaper is a creation, a part of himself, and even in contemplation of separating himself from it, he desires that his newspaper shall continue as a monument of his own past work.

He greatly desires that his successor in ownership shall be as nearly capable as himself. A similar trait in character is shown by all wealthy men in making their last will and testament. These men do not choose, as a rule, as heirs their needy friends or relatives to be the depositors of their wealth, but they prefer to make as their heirs men who have proved, by their capacity to accumulate wealth, their fitness or ability to be successful in administering the wealth of the testator.

An owner of a newspaper who contemplates the sale will consider the matter from several points of view, first: (1) He wants to sell for the largest possible price; (2) he wants to sell his newspaper to men capable of successfully conducting it; (3) he wants his successor in ownership to be a man to be relied upon to have the same principles of journalism that he himself has had.

More peculiarly in the case of newspaper property than that of any other property does the creator of the same regard the property in a way somewhat similar to that in which a man regards a child of his flesh.

I think it is impossible for any man [who practices] journalism to regard his property in the shape of a newspaper in the same way as he regards his property in the shape of real estate, stocks, and bonds.

But while there is a common market value for almost all kinds of property, there is no such thing as a market value for a newspaper. Every man who is selling a newspaper is compelled to value it without the assistance of the market, so called.

The buyer of a newspaper must be one of two sorts of men: first, the sort of man who knows nothing about journalism as a newspaper or business; second, a man of experience in the newspaper business who knows so much about his own previously owned newspapers as to know that it is always possible that a large part of the prestige, goodwill, and income is owing to the owner who is selling, to his personal and business relations in the community, to the various sorts of prestige he has won.

Of the latter class of men there are only a very, very few, and among this class there are still a fewer number who have acquired wealth enough to purchase from the would-be seller at a really fair valuation of the property to be sold, and those who are so placed financially are generally men of such age as to be themselves thinking of selling rather than of buying.

There will be soon placed on the market a certain well-established and very valuable newspaper. According to my estimates there are only three possible buyers, all of whom have passed sixty years. There are only three men who are considered capable of conducting this business successfully, and who could furnish the purchase price. I am convinced that when this property is sold it will not be sold for as much as one-half of its actual value to anyone.

A SCRIPPS-HOWARD POSSIBILITY

My present valuation of the Scripps-Howard concern is not less than 60 millions, and is probably more than 100 millions.

I am, through the E. W. Scripps Company, the voting control of all the Scripps-Howard Newspapers and other corporations, but I do not own more than 30 or 40 per cent of the whole institution.

It has been my purpose and desire for a number of years past to not increase my holdings any more than is actually necessary to secure the control of the whole institution to my estate. Means have been adopted by me to attain this end without having to greatly increase my personal holdings or those of the estate.

My desire is and has been to extend the growth of the concern indefinitely and to distribute the shareholding not only of new properties but of my old properties amongst such of my employees as are willing to make the sacrifice in the way of savings, but more especially in much larger blocks to men of great ability who are to have the largest possible opportunity to develop themselves and demonstrate their capacity.

I want there to be a king in the concern, a Cabinet, a House of Lords, and a House of Commons, and the largest possible commonalty.

The present annual turnover has been estimated for me by Smithton to be $25,500,000. I have roughly estimated that, of this, more than half accrues to the employees and stockholders.

No man or woman who has intelligence enough to be an efficient employee or stockholder should save less than 20 per cent of his or her annual income. Therefore, there should not be less than $2,500,000 usable for the purchase and founding of new newspapers.

I would not think it risky business for the concern to invest as high as 25 million dollars at the present time in going and profitable newspapers. To finance such an investment would, I think, be quite feasible. With such credit as we have, I think it would be easy to issue and sell from 10 to 15 millions of bonds of the E. W. Scripps Company. If this 25 million was invested in the purchase of newspapers on an eight-year purchase rate there should be little or no risk to this company.

There are a number of individuals in the company who together might, without calling upon the concern's funds, raise 5 millions of dollars. These persons should and would probably prefer to take stock direct in the purchased companies.

There would still be left 5 millions if the investment amounted to 25 millions. This, if offered to our employees, would furnish them a very great inducement to increase their savings to be put into investment companies which would in turn be put into the investment properties.

But my idea, however, is not to take one step and stop. If the new investments would turn out as profitably, say, as the investments in Youngstown and Pittsburgh, there would be no occasion to seek for an early return of bonds issued.

I think one provision should be made in case we embark on the course I have suggested and that is that every investor direct in the stock, that every investor in the investment companies, should agree for an indefinite period of time to devote one-half of all dividends from either the newspapers or investment companies in further similar investments.

I think it is hardly possible that if this scheme is adopted . . . before the next ten years is past, the turnover of the institution will amount to less than from 25.5 millions to 100 millions, and that the capital value of the institution as a whole will have increased to between 3 million and 5 million dollars, and that then the billion dollar goal will be in sight.

ADDENDA

No. 1.   I think that the greater the success of the concern will be, the worse it will be for the people of the United States.

No. 2.   I think it is bad for journalism that dollar-chasing shall be its main pursuit.

No. 3.   But we are men and women, and we all have the acquisitive instinct that rules us more than does reason, and so I will conclude by saying that if we want to get rich, we might as well pursue a safe and sure path to that end as any more difficult path.

SECOND ADDENDA

Don't worry about our ability to get the men to serve as privates, sub-officers, and generals. The concern will develop them more rapidly than you can use them, and the more rapid will be the tempo of the man-developing machinery.

New York—1876–1925—And Me

[*September 4, 1925*]

Signed by Scripps.

Of all the cities in the world the one I most detest is London. Next in order of my detestation comes New York.

I first saw New York in the late summer and early fall of 1876. I was twenty-two years old. I had two dollars in my pocket and my home town was Detroit, Michigan. I got back to Detroit somehow.

In those days I counted myself a journalist. After I got older I called myself a newspaperman.

The most wonderful paper in my opinion in America in those days was the New York *Herald*. It had a circulation of 80,000 — double that of any other newspaper in America. Now I own several newspapers which have much larger circulations than did the *Herald* have in those days.

Of course, the greatest living editor of that time — forty-nine years ago — was Charles A. Dana (Greeley had been removed from this vale of tears). We used to talk in those days of the great quadrilateral in journalism, namely, Charles A. Dana, Murat Halstead, Joseph McCullough [McCullagh], and Henry Watterson.[93] Personally I never met Dana, though of the other three I have recollections of intimacy.

Forty-nine years ago Whitelaw Reid was editor of the New York *Tribune*, but that paper had already begun to slide down.

The Jones brothers, owners of the New York *Times*, having led the fight to the finish against Boss Tweed, had a most respectable position and mark in journalism.

[93] Charles A. Dana, New York *Sun*; Murat Halstead, Cincinnati *Commercial-Gazette*; Joseph McCullagh, St. Louis *Globe-Democrat*; Henry Watterson, Louisville *Courier-Journal*.

A twenty-two-year-old boy, I walked the streets sufficiently to stand and look at every one of the office buildings of the different New York papers.

Already I had begun dreaming dreams.

After Greeley, Bennett, and Dana — some fifteen years after my first visit to New York — there appeared in this city one Joseph Pulitzer, a Viennese Jew or half Jew. I didn't like Pulitzer. Only a few years before Pulitzer's coming to New York I tried conclusions with him in the city of St. Louis to find out whether J.P. was a greater journalist than myself. I found out and I didn't like J.P. any better for what I learned.

Pulitzer, with a very little money, a great deal of gall, and some credit bought the New York *World*. He made a most amazing, rapid success of the *World*. By the 1890's the *World* had become recognized as the greatest American newspaper. It was compared with Old Thunderer, the London, England, *Times,* by its many admirers.

A new star of journalism had arisen in the West by the time I reached California, where I had chosen a winter residence. This star was William Randolph Hearst. In time Hearst drifted on to New York. He bought the old *Journal*, a paper founded, I believe, by Albert Pulitzer, brother of Joseph Pulitzer.

At this date William Randolph Hearst is recognized as the greatest of American newspapermen. I own more newspapers than Hearst, but Hearst owns bigger newspapers than mine. I really do not know what Hearst is worth in the way of money, and to be perfectly frank, I do not know what I am worth. I only feel pretty sure that Hearst controls newspaper property valued at two or three times the value I put on my newspaper holdings.

But Hearst's star actually arose after I had retired from business, or thought I had retired, some thirty-five years ago.

All the old great journalists of New York have disappeared, followed by Pulitzer.

The greatest figures in New York journalism today are, I suppose, William Randolph Hearst of the *Journal* and *American*, Adolph Ochs of the New York *Times*, and Frank Munsey who, besides several newspapers, owns, I believe, a string of grocery stores. I think that the Jew, Ochs, has more ready money than any other newspaperman in the United States. I think his net profits are perhaps larger than mine and Hearst put together.

I consider myself a glittering example of what may happen to a man if he succeeds in living long enough. Victor Lawson was another equally good example.

Neither Lawson nor myself were ever very articulative. Victor Lawson died the other day about the age of seventy-four. I am now seventy-one years old. It is only because Lawson and I lasted so long that the tide of fortune carried us so far.

Forty-nine years ago I was having a great time in New York with two dollars in my pocket, and a large amount of cheek. By the aid of the latter I got into the hotels and left them without being arrested. I can recall a hot coffee and doughnut stand down underneath the old New York *Sun* office building. I remember I had several ten-cent breakfasts there.

Now I have a suite of rooms on the fifteenth floor of the Ambassador, and a suite of attendants.

I have come in and gone out of New York perhaps not more than a dozen times in my life. I hope this will be my last incoming.

I wonder if I very much differ from the hundreds of other successful men who come into New York. I suppose that most people who know us or know of us at all think that we sit around here gloating over and enjoying our achievements. Well, I suppose all the other fellows have their troubles, too, and so there is no use of my complaining because I and others are misunderstood.

I mustn't let one event in my life pass unnoticed.

By just keeping alive I have attained the great distinction of being the oldest editor-publisher of eminence in this country. Now if I can keep alive another ten or fifteen years, and maybe not even so long, I may attain the greater distinction of being the oldest editor-publisher in the world.

Really I do not see why I should not have as good reason of being proud of this distinction as of any other distinction that I had, or have, or may acquire.

I suppose if a man requires some feeling of pride for his happiness, he might as well be proud of one thing as of another.

REFORM

Scripps took his place for a time among the Progressives who engineered major political, economic, and social reforms between, roughly, 1904 and 1917. Among them he acted as adviser, tart critic, friend, theoretician, disseminator of ideas, and morale-builder in their moments of despair.

The offhand mention he has received in histories of the period shows that he did not loom large among reformers. He deserved his obscurity, although it could be attributed in part to his preferred anonymity; as he once said, if he wanted to change something he would prefer to disseminate his ideas among men who would take action, and let them have the credit. As a voice from the wings, then, he may have had some importance in the reform movement; in direct action, he was of no consequence, aside from any effect his newspapers might have had.

The Reform movement of the early 1900's [1] was a widespread protest against conditions that had come into existence as America had been transformed into an industrialized, and hence urban, nation. Industry had produced huge aggregations of wealth, a class of *nouveau riche* had appeared thereby, Big Business had consolidated giant corporations, concentrated wealth came to be depicted by some as the nation's invisible government through political corruption, bosses dominated political conventions, city bosses ran cities as political principalities. As wealth had been accumulated by stronger individuals who believed in survival of the fittest as a natural law governing mankind, they produced an imbalance of wealth which was accompanied by human suffering. Women worked long hours in sweat shops, children toiled in mines, workingmen's families could not afford to live

[1] Discussions of the reform movement are to be found in Merle Curti, *Growth of American Thought* (New York, 1951), p. 605 f.; Richard Hofstadter, *Age of Reform* (New York, 1960); Eric Goldman, *Rendezvous with Destiny* (New York, 1956); Harold U. Faulkner, *Quest for Social Justice* (New York, 1931); and Louis Filler, *Crusaders for American Liberalism* (Yellow Springs, Ohio, 1950).

elsewhere than in crowded and unsanitary tenements. The growth of cities presented or accentuated social problems. The demands for reform interacted with an upheaval in American thought in which new ideas challenged the old assumptions of laissez faire and Darwinism. The protest was expressed in politics as progressivism, and was reflected in such terms as realism in literature, social justice, sociological jurisprudence, social gospel, and in more insistent demands by trade unionists, suffragettes, and prohibitionists. Radicals, in addition, preached revolutionary doctrine.

From the various demands came child labor laws, shorter working hours, improved working conditions, the secret ballot, laws regulating campaign expenditures, direct primaries, direct election of United States senators, civil service, the initiative, referendum, and recall, minimum wage and maximum hour laws, workmen's compensation and employer liability laws, woman suffrage, federal regulation of railroad rates, federal standards for food and drugs.

Among the many voices from many quarters demanding change, the Progressives have been the most noticed. Members of both major political parties, but many of them Republican, they were conservative men, many having inherited wealth. Generally speaking, the Progressives attacked political corruption, sought to ameliorate some conditions through social legislation, and resisted the misuse of power which had been acquired by others through wealth.

The Progressives came to Scripps for advice and/or money. They got advice.

To be sure, he contributed some money to some of their causes, but he did not believe in giving anybody anything; he maintained strenuously that a gift harmed rather than helped the recipient. Deciding that it was all right for a person to give money to a good cause if he had nothing else to give, Scripps preferred to contribute the support of his newspapers rather than money to reform.

In approaching reform, Scripps abided by what he had earlier said was his overriding purpose in journalism — to bring about a more equitable division of the products of labor of all kinds. Adjusting the inequities perplexed Scripps greatly, causing him — along with most of the Progressives — to be of two minds about a great many things. While he could seriously condemn the inequities, he at the same time fervently believed in survival of the fittest, the very argument used by the opposition; hence, he could defend aggregations of wealth on the ground that nature placed strong men in control, as in "Is There an Unearned Increment?" Where he parted company with the "plutocracy" was in the use that was made of the wealth and power so obtained. One of his guiding tenets was that one should use the talents bestowed upon him to the best of his ability for the good of those with lesser talents. In other words, he had a sort of *noblesse oblige* attitude with regard to his wealth, his intellectual endowment, and his newspapers.

Thus, he could say of himself and other reformers: "We do not love the poor devils who are suffering from the present system so much as we detest the ignorance, the meanness, and the cruelty of the oligarchy that rules in the capitalist army." [2]

Because he saw the "oligarchy" as the enemy, he was more exercised on behalf of reforms directed toward the judiciary than toward any other, for reasons brought out in "Contempt of Court," "Government by the Judiciary,"and "Reform of the Courts."

In a way, of course, he was a strange bedfellow for the polished gentlemen of the Progressives. "I am conscious of the fact that most people regard me as a sort of barbarian — respectable as such, but nevertheless troublesomely uncouth and abnormal." [3] Nonetheless, he took his place in their ranks, a place that can be suggested by mentioning some of those with whom he was in contact. Joseph Fels, the Philadelphia soap manufacturer who financed the cause of advancing the single-tax theory, traveled across the continent to meet Scripps at "Miramar." Through personal visit, frequent correspondence and the San Francisco *News*, Scripps supported Francis J. Heney, who was prosecuting municipal graft cases. Gifford Pinchot, Theodore Roosevelt's lieutenant in the conservation program, visited "Miramar," and he and his brother Amos were in intermittent correspondence with Scripps. Hiram Johnson, who succeeded Heney in the "boodling" prosecution, also visited "Miramar." Scripps carried on a correspondence with and entertained at "Miramar" William S. U'Ren, known as the father of the "Oregon system" of political reform; Scripps found U'Ren to be a man of sweetly serene and irresistible optimism who made everything seem more worthwhile than it had been before. Louis Brandeis called at Scripps' Washington hotel. Fremont Older, William Allen White, and Senator Robert M. LaFollette conversed with Scripps at "Miramar." Charles R. Crane, treasurer of LaFollette's National Progressive League, united with Scripps in the dream of an adless newspaper. In Chicago, Scripps visited Jane Addams and felt she was trying to do the same thing through settlement-house work that he was trying to do with his newspapers. He admired and supported Tom Johnson, the reform mayor of Cleveland.

Of all the reformers, Judge Ben Lindsey of Denver had the greatest command on Scripps' affection. The two exchanged relatively frequent, long, chatty letters. "Lindsey's very character is a medicine to a sick soul," Scripps said. [4]

[2] EWS to Max Eastman, Dec. 8, 1914.
[3] EWS to EBS, June 14, 1914.
[4] EWS to Lincoln Steffens, Apr. 22, 1908.

Scripps' principal contact with the reformers was through Lincoln Steffens, who gained a national reputation as one of the "muckraking" magazine writers of the day. A close bond of admiration and appreciation united the two men, but Scripps pleaded for Steffens to write his letters on a typewriter, saying he would rather saw wood all day than read a letter in Steffens' hand.

About 1909 Scripps' interest slackened. He said:

My greatest embarrassment and the cause of my being constantly confused as to my own course in modern reform politics arises from the fact that nearly all of the self-constituted saviors in this country are anything but democrats; they are Y.M.C.A. men or some sort of church men; they are capitalists, many of them grown so rich as to afford to be decent if they only knew how. They are aristocrats. They are men who feel that they have a duty to save and serve, and to guide the majority of their kind. As a matter of fact I am just as guilty . . . in many respects. I doubt if it is any of my business, or any of the business of these men, to save the people. If there is anything in democracy at all, such men as I have described, if not undesirable citizens, are at least members of the class who need serious rebuking and putting down.

I don't know that there is any better reason for considering [them] as hypocrites and designing, selfish men than there is for suspecting you or me being members of the same class. In fact I think we are all tarred with the same stick.

Sometimes I feel that I have either got to abandon my democracy or withdraw from the ranks of the reformers.[5]

Trade unionism advanced during this period, but Scripps' support of organized labor has been sufficiently emphasized, although he seems to have had almost no contact with labor leaders during the years in which he wrote the disquisitions.

Scripps was not afraid to tinker with the ideas of the far left, either. Syndicalism and anarchosyndicalism he placed beyond the pale. Bolshevism he dismissed as preposterous, but not until after he had played devil's advocate in an 84-page disquisition. But socialism he found intriguing.

Scripps was not a Socialist, but he did give careful attention to socialism in a period when it registered strong gains as a political party. Trying to make up his mind, he wrote disquisitions that developed the Socialist ideology and then disquisitions that countered that ideology. His final personal conclusions were that he was too much an individualist to be a Socialist, because Socialists were collectivists; that he would like to be a Socialist, but he realized socialism and natural law were in conflict; that he had never been able to find any excuse for socialism whatsoever; and that socialism was inevitable.

Flirting with but not seduced by socialism, he was one of nine men who

[5] EWS to W. H. Porterfield, Mar. 31, 1909.

financed the publication of Max Eastman's Socialist magazine, *The Masses*. Eastman remembered Scripps as follows:

. . . We never took a walk; we never took a drink; we never went driving. We sat in his study smoking an endless chain of mild, made-to-order Key West cigars and talking from three to ten hours at a stretch.

I can still see the kindly-outrageous old tyrant sitting there slanting back from his desk, squinting quizzically through the smoke, laying down the law as though he knew everything on all subjects, and yet as strongly intimating — whether with the intellectual mirth in his eyes, the deprecating gestures, the occasional wistful question — that, like the rest of us, he probably knew nothing at all. Every once in a while, he would get up and walk over into an alcove and come back with a manuscript. It would be a "Disquisition" by himself on the subject we were discussing. He would read it to me with an expression of delighted surprise at the wisdom he found in it — a surprise which I fully shared. Scripps had a mind like Montaigne's — fertile, discursive, full of extremely rational doubts and speculations about everything under the sun. And though he lacked the sublime gift of language, his Disquisitions had the same qualities of personal candor, intellectual daring, and ultimate unanswerable doubt that Montaigne's Essays have. But instead of publishing them, he locked them up in an old black steel box to lie there until his grandchildren were grown up.

Montaigne may seem far afield, but there is certainly no American, least of all among those who attained wealth and power, with whom to compare him.

.   .   .   .

Those talks would last from ten to one usually and be subject to renewal afternoon and evening. Upon dismissal, as I staggered from the room groggy with nicotine and sheer exhaustion of the brain cells, he would say "thank you for the conversation," as though I had some choice in the matter.

.   .   .   .

. . . He cared more about the thoughts he locked up in that iron box than those he expressed in his newspapers. His purest passion was for scientific truth.

.   .   .   .

It was instinctive with him to champion every measure directed against what he called the "wealthy and intellectual classes." He always linked those two adjectives in describing the chief enemy; and both adjectives, by no mere coincidence, exactly fitted him. A war like that against himself would defeat, if not destroy, most men. In most times and places it would defeat any man. But in American newspaperdom from 187[8] to 1917 — and in E. W. Scripps — it produced an enormous personal fortune and one of the most powerful weapons ever wielded in behalf of the underdog.

There was a developing class struggle in America in those years, and the Scripps papers, without getting tangled in the doctrinal formulation of it, took the side of the rising class of wage labor. E. W. stoutly and constantly championed the cause of the trade unions in his papers. But he had the good sense to leave socialism alone or dismiss it with the remark: "Class warfare must be perpetual." Indeed, he saw through socialism more clearly than any other critic I met in those days. He surprised me by saying: "Your propaganda will probably in the long run succeed." And then he added: "The thing you'll get will be as different from what you are talking about as modern organized Christianity is from the visions of Jesus. . . ." [6]

After *The Masses* failed financially — Scripps and Eastman had had a good laugh about trying to establish a Socialist magazine on a capitalist basis — Eastman published the *Liberator*. To bring Eastman's ideas before industrialists, businessmen, and educators who were not in sympathy with such ideas, Scripps donated one thousand dollars for subscriptions for such men. He hoped thus to expose them to ideas they would not encounter elsewhere, even though he personally did not like the ideas in the *Liberator*; they made him uncomfortable and he wished there were no such point of view as Eastman presented.

From similar motivation, he had contributed to the Fels Fund for advancing the single-tax theory, not because he favored it but because it would make the common man think.

As for woman suffrage, he thought it monstrous. Woman was inferior and was happiest when kept inferior. Notwithstanding, he placed his California papers at the disposal of Ellen B. in fighting for woman suffrage in California, and his papers generally supported the movement.

The really important point about Scripps with regard to reform is that his thinking ranged far beyond the here and now, the adjustments that were being made in the existing system. Unable to find any existing system — in actuality or theory — that suited him, he was not above constructing his own theory of a re-organized society. To the world's numberless Utopian schemes, he added his own, given here in "An Unutopian Utopia."

World War I changed much of his thinking about reform. Having always been convinced that capitalism was a good system, he ceased theorizing about competing systems when he saw what capitalism accomplished for the country during the war. Also, by the start of the 1920's, organized labor was on a sound footing, and he decided it no longer needed "wet-nursing" by Scripps newspapers.

As he lived out his last years on his yacht, he once told a confidant, "I'm just a conservative old millionaire."

[6] Max Eastman, "My Friend E. W.," *Freeman*, Jan. 11, 1954, p. 274 f. Reprinted by permission.

Rich Men Beware!

[1891]

The Gay Nineties were also the unhappy nineties, with strong undertones of unrest and fear of revolution. The outstanding political protest movement was that of the Populists, who formed the Peoples party in Cincinnati in 1891, adopting a platform that contained many radical proposals, including inflation, government ownership of railroads, graduated income tax, Australian ballot, shorter hours for labor, initiative and referendum, direct election of senators, single term for president and vice-president. It was against that background that Scripps wrote the following.

In the United States of America every man over twenty-one years of age is a voter and a soldier. Under the Constitution the majority can by their votes change and make almost any law. The majority of the people in three-fourths of the states can alter the Constitution itself.

Thirty thousand men own one-half of all the property of the United States. And nine-tenths of the other half at least is owned by one million people.

Yet there are 66 millions of people in the United States.[7]

The total value of all the property in the United States is not less than 66 billion. That sum would be $1,000 for every man, woman, and child in the country.

The average productive value of all the property in the United States is 4 per cent. Four per cent on $1,000 is $40.00.

The average family among all classes has a membership of five. The average family of the majority of the people who are workmen's families is nearer seven. Seven times $40.00 would be $280, the annual income over and above wages of every workingman's family, if the property were evenly divided. That amount is fully equal to if not more than usual average wages of the unskilled workingmen and agriculturalists.

[7] The 1890 census showed a population of 62,900,000.

There are 66 millions of people in the United States, including women and children who have nothing, while not more than one million own virtually all. The vast majority of so-called property owners own in one way or another as much as the forced sale value of all their property.

Anyway, there are 11 million voters and as many fighting men who own virtually nothing, while one million people at the most hold all the property.

Peaceably and by votes these 11 million can take all the property and spare the capitalists a few million mercenary allies. By force of arms the majority can enforce their laws and changes of Constitution. For a whole generation past, capitalists have been reducing their number by elimination. The larger preying on and absorbing the capital of the smaller holders [sic].

During the same time capital has waged a bitter and successful warfare against labor at every point on the farm, in the factory, in the mine and in trade; in the legislatures, in Congress, and in court.

When labor makes a legislator or a judge, capital buys the legislator and judge and makes him a tool.

This generation of Americans [has] been educated in our schools, by the press, and by experience. Unlike former generations, this world has the mighty power of knowledge and power to reason back of its physical brute strength.

The whole laboring population of this country is discontented and in mental revolt. The only safety of capital today lies in lack of organization, sympathy, and unanimity of this great army of discontented.

The growth of workingmen's societies from small and scattered local unions to larger and better-organized federation alliances, etc., should be sufficient indication to the wise to show how speedily this large body is crystalizing into larger and yet larger bodies of common interest and common purpose. In time crystalization will be perfect and there will be one large body that will include under one head and one management the majority of voters and fighting men.

Napoleon conquered Europe disintegrated and taught his opponents the necessity of that alliance which of necessity had to conquer Napoleon. Capital has conquered labor piecemeal and has taught labor the necessity of alliance.

If rich men will quit beating poor men in their strikes, in their attempts to get just laws, and in their effort to get justice in courts, and in place of trying to add to their already useless surplus hoards, turn around and be as generous in the future as they have in the past been niggardly, and as just as they have been unjust, the great alliance, the great warfare, and the utter defeat of all capital and all consequent beneficent social organization may be averted.

As a former workingman, as a recent employer of many workingmen, as the intimate acquaintance of thousands of workingmen, I know the class well. Today I would trust them to give me justice, fair treatment and kindly consideration man for man sooner than I would trust that other class — that class to which I now belong.

The time will come — is coming perhaps quicker than we dream of — when capital will have so heaped up its measure of iniquities and bitter wrongs against labor that it will only get justice of a sterner sort when each capitalist will be convicted and punished for the crimes of capitalists as a whole.

It is better for the capitalists to settle with the workingman now than later on. It will be better for the country as a whole and hence far better for the workingmen to have this change come about slowly and peacefully and without those sudden revolutions in our laws and customs which cannot fail to work great injury.

I have but small expectations of great immediate results from the new party born in Cincinnati, but I hope sincerely that its success will be great indeed and immediate, because the sooner our coming rulers get control of us the less embittered will they be, the more apt they will be to proceed with calm consideration and the less apt will they be to rush thoughtlessly and angrily into innovations of an injurious character.

The workingmen as a political party have to succeed sooner or later for the reasons: (1) The workingmen have a terrible grievance that can only be cured by political supremacy; (2) because the workingmen are the vast majority of our voters and because they are educated and intelligent; (3) and because capitalists individually and collectively are oppressing laborers more and more every day and more and more every day arrogantly, unblushingly, and openly.

Rich men beware!

One of the Rich Men

Contempt of Court

[*October 16, 1908*]

I believe that this attitude is almost universal amongst the laity. A short time ago I had occasion to discuss this matter with three young but eminent lawyers. One of them has acquired a national reputation as a political leader and representative of radical reforms, and is now the controlling factor of one of the two great political parties in one of the great states. Another is a young man who has acquired eminence as a member of a state legislature because of his having drafted and secured the passage of a bill, the object of which is to prevent combinations in restraint of trade in his state in cases and under conditions not governed by the general law of the nation. The third holds an enviable position in the local bar of a city and is recognized not only as a lawyer of great ability but of the very highest moral qualities.

It is needless to say that all three of them belong to the Democratic party. They are all sincere and vigorous fighters against the system of special privileges — what they consider the worst of all national evils.

The object of all these gentlemen was to arouse in me a greater interest in the affairs of the party — local, state, and national — and to secure from me more effective cooperation in the affairs of the party with which I have been more or less identified all my life.

I have frankly told them that I had very little faith either in their ability or their desire to accomplish anything like serious reform and betterment of political conditions, and that I had very little faith in the party which they so ably represented and of which I have been so long a member, for the very reason that they and men of their caste, the lawyer caste, assumed a position of leadership of the party and were acknowledged generally by the party to be fit.

With the best intentions in the world, and with intelligences so great and so discerning that they were abundantly able to recognize the existence of present evils, they were unfortunately so biased temperamentally and by training as to be unable to recognize that the chief and really the only sustaining prop of all existent evils was composed of the law that they practiced and the judges who hold their positions solely by their being members of the legal caste.

In every state legislature, and in all the national congresses, the lawyers frequently compose the majority, and universally compose the dominating and controlling voice of legislation. Even when good laws have by chance been passed by these legislative bodies, the chief award to the practice of law consisted in fees obtained by lawyers from clients who sought to evade the laws.

From the lawyer caste come the judges, and the judges universally practice and are guided by two systems of law: one, law by enactment of legislature; and the other, law judge-made.

At the hands of judges, any good law — good for the people as a whole — has only a chance of being treated in one of two ways by the judges: first, the law is either decided to be unconstitutional because it is contrary to some precedent existing in some former judge's decision, or perhaps only because the judge recognizes that it is not in harmony with his own individual views, views that have been formed by reason of his lawyer training; or second, the judge so interprets the law, so twists it about, as to cause it to operate in a way or in a direction extremely divergent from, if not directly opposite to, the intent of the legislators.

All of these men were perfectly willing in a general way to recognize my contention as to the evil of judge-made law, and one of them, the most eminent perhaps, frankly admitted that the whole system of judge-made law was the most serious blemish of the American legal practice.

But none of them will concede my contention that of all citizens most unfitted to serve in a judicial capacity, it is the man trained to law by education and practice of the same.

It would be a wonderful thing indeed to find any lawyer or any doctor or any shoemaker or any man practicing any vocation who would believe that his training would unfit him for any position of public trust or emolument.

It has been a long time since I read [Alexis] De Tocqueville's *Democracy in America* — twenty-five years at least — but I recall in a general way that one of the declarations he made in that book was that the custom of the American people to glorify the lawyer caste, to make of members of this caste its principal officers and legislators and interpreters of the law itself, would inevitably in time work out into a most serious condition in this Republic.

I remember reading somewhere the declaration made by a very intelligent and remarkably sincere member of the legal profession, who was so peculiarly gifted as to be able to see faintly at least what none of my three young lawyer friends were able to see: the principal and fundamental weakness of our present legal situation. Honestly, he could not apparently sustain the thesis that justice and legal judgment were identical. He made the declaration that law courts were not intended to secure justice, but only to settle disputes.

The reading of this statement by me had the effect of giving me the very first good and sufficient reason for continuing my old practice of upholding the law of the courts.

The settlement of any dispute I recognize as being far more important to any race or community of men than the mere meting out of justice on the basis of any philosophy invested by any man or set of men.

Individuals must suffer for the common good. It is a bad thing for a community to be torn asunder by unending disputes, and hence doubts as to the property and other rights of every individual composing it. Almost any settlement of such a dispute is better than no settlement.

The judge who has received his training in the legal profession will base his decisions on premises entirely different from those upon which a judgment would be based by a judge selected from any other class or caste.

It is not so important to select a premise upon which to base a judgment, as it is to have a judgment rendered. So long as the whole people or community are willing to accept as good enough premises for judgment the lawyer's code and practice, just so long may we tolerate, with what equanimity we can, the kind of judgments we get.

But the time has come when a very large number of the American people are showing not only by their utterances but by their actions that they are unwilling to have their disputes settled by judgments based upon the premises of lawyer-judges employed. Not only are the courts being held as objects of contempt, but the laws themselves are not even generally respected. Perhaps the law made by legislatures could and would willingly enough be assented to, providing the lawyer-judges would judge according to legislative law or statute law. That part of the law that is in most universal contempt and for which contempt is the most reasonable is the judge-made law, the law of precedents.

During my lifetime, I have been almost constantly a litigant. I have always had the lawyers with me; I devoted a large amount of my time and attention, in cooperation with the lawyers, in preparing cases and prosecuting them.

The most remarkable part of all my experience has been that the very briefest amount of time and attention was given to the statute or statutes bearing on any of my cases. In the law office and in the courtroom, the great and all-consuming matter of importance was judicial decisions, decisions made by other courts in cases similar in some way to mine. Decisions of judges in many states of the Union were hunted up and quoted.

Decisions of judges dead and gone long years ago, decisions that were made before even a fractional part of our present statute law had been formed were given the gravest consideration. Decisions of old English judges, decisions made by old English judges before even Parliament's right to legislate had been conceded, decisions of ancient Roman courts were always read with respect and maturely considered.

It always seemed to me that, everything else being equal, and there existing such an infinite mass of judicial decisions collected during the ages, victory was to be expected to perch on the banners of that litigant who could assemble the largest number of precedents. Of course, some discrimination is made in the matter of precedents, as to the particular court or particular state in which the court had sat, or the particular time.

But in this matter of selecting and discriminating, a very peculiar condition seemed to exist: everything else being equal, the older the decision was, the better. That is to say, decisions made when society had not evolved into its present form are esteemed better than later decisions. Then, too, except in cases where the Supreme Court of the state in which my trial was taking place had given a decision (because, of course, in case of appealing this case, it would go to this Supreme Court, which could not be expected to reverse itself), I have found that precedent decisions were considered more valuable if they had been made in more remote states and states where conditions were as dissimilar as possible from the conditions in which my case was being tried.

It is all precedent, precedent, precedent, from the attorney's opening argument to the judge's final instruction to the jury.

It would really seem to one situated as I have been that the courts did not recognize the right of a state legislature to enact a new law, or, anyway, a law that would be in the least in conflict with some dead and gone judge's decision, some precedent that this judge had established.

The most [that] courts and the lawyers seem to do is to admit this legislation as a sort of a necessary evil, something that intrudes itself on their attention, but something that is relatively of very little importance.

The statute law must have a place in the court, but must be suppressed as far as possible, or molded or twisted into some sort of shape that will be consistent with precedent. If the statute law is too obstreperous and too rigid in its form and attitude to be easily impressed, it is incontinently thrown out of court by being declared unconstitutional and an end made of it then and there.

The laws in America are not bad; they are pretty nearly up to date; the civil law and the criminal law, for the most part, mean what they say and are tolerably easy of comprehension even to a plain man of ordinary education. Most any jury, guided by the statute law, even without the assistance of a trained exponent of the legal profession, would come to an absolutely correct decision in probably 999 cases out of 1,000.

This would indicate that the lawyers are not such bad lawmakers. However, there may be and certainly is a great deal of sophistication in the minds of lawyer-legislators. They recognize well enough that the laws they are drafting and enacting into statutes are of comparatively little importance in the real working out of their professional practice. Beyond all doubt, there are plenty of these lawyer-legislators who so influence the drafting and form of a law as to make it good bait with which to fish for future clients. There are plenty of lawyers who, in their capacity as lawmakers in legislation, are still, nevertheless, lawyers serving their clients, and who are molding the laws for the benefit of present and prospective clients either by injecting into them clauses or expressions the direction of which they know better than do the laymen in the legislative hall. A successful lawyer-legislator may even, recognizing that in the face of overwhelming public opinion it will be impossible to prevent the enactment of a certain law that will be detrimental to their clients, craftily inject into the statute some word or some principle which will secure its eventual annulment by the courts later on a decision of unconstitutionality.

This existence of a caste in legal profession, a caste that divides its field of operations into three parts — one of making the law, one of practicing the law, and one of deciding the law — makes of this caste a class of men tremendously powerful in the nation. They have a power so great as to make them finally, wholly, and entirely responsible for almost every evil existing in the land. Their power is so great that it is only matched by, or perhaps surpassed by, the power of wealth — the power of the clients, the supporters of these same lawyers. Generally speaking, the lawyer's training and environment is such that he is unfitted to be a businessman — that is to say, a wealthy man, a man of affairs; that is to say, to be a master amongst men. For that reason he is necessarily a servant, a servile tool of the master class, the men we call plutocrats — that most dangerous element that has existed in all times and exists now everywhere and in every community of mankind.

Capitalists without their servant lawyers could not exist in dangerous form. The lawyer is and always has been an effective instrument of oppression and of wrongdoing in the hands of monarchy, of nobles, and of captains of industry.

If there is any such thing as absolute democracy and of real freedom of the people, if there is such a goal to be obtained, the road to that goal lies over and through the ruin and annihilation of the legal caste.

Contempt of law and contempt of court under present conditions, so far from being a vice on the part of the people at the present time, is a virtue.

Now, we all know lawyers, we all reckon amongst our nearest and most respected friends members of this profession; as a rule and as a class, their intellectual development is far superior to the average. Wisdom and goodness are, if not invariably, almost invariably companions, and are seldom found far apart in any man.

This being the case, why should one express such sentiments as above, as against them as a class and as individuals?

The most virtuous of men have each vices. A great virtue in any man generally has a companion vice. No man can be good all around; no man can be altogether virtuous. A man cannot have the virtue of great bodily and mental strength and at the same time the virtue of meekness, of humility; of complete, that is to say, comprehending sympathy with the weak and unfortunate.

A blind man cannot — that is, one who has been blind from birth — comprehend the sense of seeing.

A robust man whose digestion is perfect cannot sympathize with a dyspeptic, since, never having felt the pains of internal anarchy, he cannot know what his brother, a dyspeptic, suffers.

The so-called fortunate man, the man of large intellect and physical strength, a man who by reason of his strength, bodily and mental, can never have suffered the pains of long-continued poverty, cannot, try as he will to be kind and considerate to the unfortunate, ever be able to extend to them true sympathy because he knows not of their condition.

The lawyer, trained to live by the law, trained to highly esteem his vocation, trained to practice it according to the code of the profession, cannot possibly comprehend how, if he has been and is doing only those things that he has been taught to believe [are] right, doing only those things which other and greater men than he in the profession have esteemed to be right, while they have at the same time succeeded in securing the esteem and the confidence of their fellowmen — such a lawyer, such a man, cannot himself be his own critic or the critic of his class or profession.

Modern law and the beginning of modern practice of law had an ecclesiastical origin; they both came out of the church of Christ.

To whatever depths of immorality the ancient church descended, its principles and teachings were moral. In the beginning of the law practice, in England anyway, the law courts were really ecclesiastical courts. The priest or the bishop or the archbishop sat in judgment and decided differences and contentions and disputes between members of their flock. The bishops and elders were ex-officio courts of last resort. When litigants came before these courts, as they were for the most part ignorant, unlettered clowns, they were unable to fully explain their cases to the court — that is to say, they were unable to do it in the brief time which such a court could give to any case. For the purpose of saving time, the court, who was the bishop, would appoint some of his subordinate priests, perhaps one on each side of a case of dispute between two men, to inform themselves fully as to the merits of the dispute, so that they could present more thoroughly and more quickly for the bishop's decision, the points at issue.

In time, it grew to be the custom of these litigants to make gifts to priests who took charge of their cases. In time, these gifts became regular and invariable, and their amount was in proportion either to the importance of the case, or the wealth of the litigant.

Theoretically, however, these priest-lawyers had no other interest in the cases that they handled than to enable the bishop to arrive at a correct and just decision.

Justice was the only object sought for by the church in its courts.

When the clericals passed their business over to the secular courts, along with it they passed a code of ethics one part of which was that the lawyer-successor of the priest was to be paid stipulated fees without regard to the result of the trial, without regard to the judgment finally rendered; and another part was that the lawyer was morally bound not to take any step that could possibly result in an injustice. He was not bound to withhold any evidence that would be detrimental to his client, or prevent any evidence being produced by the other party.

For a long time this sort of practice was ostensibly continued in the English court. It has only been in very recent times in England that a lawyer could maintain his position as a reputable member of the bar and be known to have won or attempted to have won a case for his client when such a judgment was unjust.

Even today there are many lawyers who will refuse to defend or prosecute an unrighteous case.

One might imagine, . . . as all lawyers are really members of the court, and as the sole reason for the existence of the court is to obtain justice, that it would be the duty of every lawyer not only to refuse to support a bad case, but to insist personally in an effort to have a bad case beaten.

However this may be, the practice in America, the code here, not only justifies but applauds and rewards the attorney who will resort to any legitimate device (and few lawyers recognize any device to be illegitimate) to to secure a judgment for [his] client.

The lawyer who has the least bit of squeamishness on such an account as this will have no practice. Even those clients who have no doubts in their minds as to the justice of their cases are never willing to rest all their chance of success upon the righteousness of their cause. They not only desire all the natural advantages of their position, but they desire every artificial support.

Thus, we will find the most notoriously unscrupulous lawyers employed in prosecuting most righteous cases.

Trickery, chicanery, and all sorts of corruption are so common and so universal in the practice of law that, protest as they will, all lawyers know that successful practice of law requires constant resort to trickery, to corruption, and to all sorts of unfair practices.

There is no man who has had much experience with the law who does not know, of his own knowledge, that his attorneys constantly do, and must constantly do, things which are revolting to the conscience of any upright man, and often even to himself as a client.

We make our judges out of great lawyers — that is to say, out of lawyers who are at least above the average in the practice of the law. We generally make our judges of men who have been employed by wealthy individuals and corporations.

These men, as lawyers, have not only the ordinary frailties of human nature, but they are men who have been developed and trained in practices that are immoral. They are men who have practiced law so long, and practiced the vices of the law so long, that their morals have been vitiated. For the most part, they will not condemn as wrongdoing what 99 per cent of the ordinary jurymen would condemn.

These men have grown accustomed to serving clients — the selfish interests of clients. No ordinary man is so immoral at any time as he is while he is a litigant. Lawyers learn to know men who are litigants. As a rule, they see most of men in their worst attitude. Lawyers, like other men, are subject to the influence of environment. The environment — that is to say, the client environment — of a lawyer is the worst environment possible.

Contempt of lawyers, and especially contempt of lawyers' veracity, is so universal that even women and children and the most ignorant of men recognize as synonymous the terms "lawyer" and "liar." The joke is such an old one and such a common one and such a matter-of-course one as to be incapable of arousing mirth in the minds of any except the most ignorant; it is a platitude.

Lawyers know they are liars; they know they are known to be liars; they feel it no disgrace to be known to constantly practice falsehood and false pretense.

From among these men we select our judges.

These judges settle our disputes, and in so doing, do well; they are serviceable members of the community. So are undertakers, so are garbage-men, so are hangmen, all of them useful to society. But perhaps the most contemptible of all, the profession most worthy of contempt of all of them, is that of the lawyer.

Government by the Judiciary

[*November 11, 1908*]

Scripps wrote this disquisition shortly after the presidential election of 1908 in which his newspapers had unsuccessfully opposed William Howard Taft. An issue at the time was the use of labor injunctions by means of which the courts sided with management in labor disputes.

Four months after writing this, he read J. Allen Smith's Spirit of American Government *(Macmillan, 1909), and said that, had he read the book first, this disquisition would have been "rank plagiarism."* [8]

I presume the object of any government is to make social life tolerable. Amongst other things: First, the government must take care of military matters and advance and maintain the interests of the people, both by offensive and defensive warfare. Second, it must make the rules, the laws so called, of a nation — the agreements as between man and man and different units of a community, large or small, as to the relations one to another. Third and lastly, it must interpret these rules and finally settle and dispose of all disputes between any two or more members of society or groups of members of society.

There have been a number of kinds of government tried. The sole object of society acting as a whole is to discover that system which will put into possession of office the best men — that is to say, the men who are able and willing to so conduct government as to procure the greatest amount of well-being amongst all the people.

It has often been said that the best government is a pure autocracy, providing there was any way of securing the best possible man to be the autocrat. One-man power is a principle of government that has been tried

[8] EWS to Gilson Gardner, Mar. 21, 1909.

in every possible field of human association, with the results that there have been many successes and many failures.

The first unit combination of society or national life is the family. All government is but an extension of that of the family unit. The family may be likened to the cell as it is understood by the biologist. The nation may be considered a fully developed animal organism.

Notwithstanding the protests and objections to the one-man-power principle in the family that [are] being made in these latter days, and that [have] probably always been made, no other satisfactory form of family government has ever been tried on a large scale successfully.

In the family, the male parent fights offensively and defensively for the good of his dependent. He lays down the rules (that is to say, the laws) of the family, and he interprets these rules of his own and decides all disputes.

The male parent of the family is warrior, legislator, and judge.

All manner and conditions of men have in times past been selected as the governing head of the community as a nation. The conquering warrior chief has ruled principally. The priest, God-vicar, has often been a successful head of a large and successful community.

Even in olden days, the legislator, the lawgiver, and law interpreter and decider in disputes, the judge, has often been a nation's chief.

In recent times, under the guise of, under the system of government called, democracy, the legislator, the judge — men learned and skilled in the matter of making laws and interpreting them — has more often than any other been the real chief of government, although, oftener than not, his office has only been real and not ostensible.

Most of the governments of Europe, monarchial or other, are really governments by legislators who are, in fact, judges.

In this government of the United States, this government that is or is supposed to be more nearly democratic than any other in the world, the judge is the government, and to a very large extent indeed is recognized as the government.

The fathers of this country who framed a constitution, and in doing so attempted to divide the government into three parts — a trinity of equals — attempted something that is inconsistent with humanity. They arbitrarily defined or attempted to define a distinction between a legislator and a judge. They proposed that one body of men should make the laws and another one interpret them, and that still another should enforce them.

That one body of men should make and interpret the laws is a natural and human system. It is not entirely inconsistent with humanity that the lawmakers and interpreters should be so incapable, so unendowed with physical force, as to enforce them. Therefore, it may be possible to have such a distinction as between the executive on one side, and the legislative and judiciary on the other, as could not exist as between the legislative and the judiciary.

However, as neither the lawmaker nor the interpreter, the legislator nor the judge, can exercise any control save by depending upon the greater power, that of the warrior chief, while the warrior can rule more or less successfully without the aid of either legislator or judge, there can be no such thing as equality between himself and the other party.

Mankind, in common with all other living things, maintains itself in opposition to all existing forces by one or both of two methods: physical force or mental cunning.

Being a comparatively weak animal, man himself during his whole life has had to depend more upon craft than force. Hence, he has developed more skill and more offensive and defensive power along the line of craft than he has along the line of physical force.

The men who rule mankind rule by reason of possession of one or the other or both of these qualities: physical force and mental cunning.

The cause for the existence of the government system called democracy has been that the majority of men have preferred government by craft rather than by force.

It is apparent to all men that as between one man of great physical power and small intellect, and a man of great intellectual gifts with inferior physical powers, there is no question but that sheer brute force is at a disadvantage.

In our American democracy we have almost eliminated the warrior. At most he is used as but a policeman. His part in the government, his influence over the government, is almost nil.

On the other hand, the lawyer, becoming statesman, chief executive, legislator, or judge, rules.

I have elsewhere expressed my contempt of and my discontent with the courts — that is to say, the men who become legislators and judges.

Most of the people of the United States, I am persuaded, share my views to a large extent. There may be one very good reason for this. Every man wants to be at the head of things, and there are only a few lawyers, a small minority of the people as a whole, who can be our rulers. We have Hobson's choice, but we are nevertheless discontented because the most of us are not qualified to be Hobson's choice.

Under our system of government, notwithstanding the great effort of its framers, there are no adequate checks and balances as between the alleged three branches of the government.

According to our system, our government is a government of law, so called, and is supposed not be a government of men at all. But there can be no law not framed by men. Men must interpret the law. A government by law, then, is a government by men who make and interpret the law: it is a government of the lawmaker and the judge.

It has been contended that the Constitution does not confer upon our courts the right to determine the legality (i.e., the constitutionality) of law. But, as a matter of fact, our courts do determine these questions and the people almost unanimously approve, tacitly or otherwise, of this so-called encroachment.

Under our system, no law passed by any legislative body is a law without the sanction of court. No man or body of men except judges can interpret the law — that is to say, to declare what it means relative to any given case. Our courts can and have frequently enjoined our executives from action in their executive capacity. They have, by mandamus proceedings, compelled legislators to adopt laws which they, the courts, desired adopted and which the legislators only adopt under compulsion.

In all or most monarchies there is the royal law, the monarch's law of *lèse majesté*. This is a law by which the monarch enforces punishment of any fellow citizen who, by word of action, is disrespectful, or supposed by the monarch to be disrespectful, to him.

In our democracy, no president of the nation and no governor of a state can so punish a man without the sanction of the courts. In theory, a legislature may punish a man or a body of men who act disrespectfully to their body, but this is a course seldom resorted to by a legislature, and even when it is resorted to, the legislature is powerless to act against the decision of the court.

Finally, then, the courts have a power far in excess of the two other coordinate branches of the government. They cannot only punish a citizen for being disrespectful, but the courts and the courts alone can determine whether their acts are lawful or not. Although a subordinate court's decision in such a matter may be overruled by a superior court, still, as all the courts form one branch of the government, the judiciary, the higher court, the court of last resort, is a court, and is really that court denominated as the judicial department of the government.

As a matter of fact, the Supreme Court of the United States is the supreme ruler of this government, as the supreme court of each individual state is the supreme ruler of that state.

The fact that these courts do not at the present time exercise all the functions of government does not in the least derogate from this principle.

Year by year and decade by decade, this democracy of the United States is developing, although not fully observed and realized by all of our people or the majority of them, into a system of oligarchy, of a government by the majority vote of a small number of judges.

Some of the more intelligent individuals of this democracy are beginning to faintly recognize this condition, as has been proven in the last campaign.

There were not many real issues at stake between the partisans of Democracy, so called, and of Republicanism, so called. The real issue recognized by the people was the choice of men, the choice as between Bryan and Taft, and all through the campaign there ran this note: "During the next four years, four of the present members of the Supreme Court of the United States are to be retired on account of age, and as the other members of the court are old men, it is possible that a full majority of the Supreme Court will be appointed by the next President. Now, who is the most fit man, Bryan or Taft, to appoint these judges?" In fact, perhaps the greatest issue in the last campaign was the issue of what manner of men are to be Supreme Judges — that is to say, supreme rulers of the land.

The decision of the last campaign was undoubtedly a decision in favor of the present system of government by judges and in favor of the system of the encroachment of the judiciary on the powers of the other two departments of the government.

It seems to me probable that the people of the United States will continue to develop more and more in the direction of preferring judge rule, and that it is only a question of time when the principal business of national and state and local politics will be that of choosing judges — choosing the real rulers of the country as a whole and all of its sections.

It seems to me that there is only one escape from this government system, if it is desired to escape from it, and that is to revert to militarism and monarchy.

What this nation desires, and all that it desires, or all that any other nation desires, is to have the best possible class of rulers. They must be ruled because they are men. The only question to be decided is whether the rulers shall be men of intellect — that is to say, craft and cunning — or men possessed of physical power.

Under present conditions of civilization and under those conditions which will probably endure for a century or more, it seems to me that there can be no question but that the choice will be in favor of the gown as against the sword, of the brain as against the muscle.

If all I have said in the foregoing is true, it seems to me, then, that the most important political question put up to each and all of us hereafter is to be the kind of men that we shall select as judges.

For a long time now the most intelligent part of our citizenship — that is to say, the men personally most skillful in business affairs — have recognized that the chief object of their solicitude is the personnel of the courts.

The great political machine dominated by capital which controls the state of California, I have been told, considers the personnel of the judiciary as the one thing of paramount importance. In its partnership cooperation with all other state institutions and all manner and sorts of politicians and place-hunters, it is ever ready to trade all other public offices for just two sets of officers: the lawmaker, the legislator, and the law-interpreting officer, the judge.

It seems to me that we have, in the case of the Electoral College, an example of political evolution, an evolution which is tending toward the results that I have pointed to.

It was originally intended that the members of the Electoral College were to be selected for the purpose of themselves, the members of the Electoral College, naming the president. In a very short time the Electoral College has by custom lost all power, all authority, and all responsibility. It has become a mere messenger, carrying the vote of the people to the national government. In time, it may be that the office of President of the United States may, by the growth of custom, degenerate into nothing more than the agent of the people in appointing Supreme Judges who shall be, in fact, nominated by something like a national convention or some sort of conclave of a very few citizens of the country who, by reason of their wealth or other qualifications for having influence, will name the judges that are to be appointed. Thereafter, although we may keep up our present theoretical system of choosing electors to elect a president and of further going through the form of electing the president, still both presidential electors and elected president will be nothing more than an old, worn-out form used to arrive at the desired end — namely, the choice of the nation's rulers as an oligarchy in the form of the Supreme Court.

Is There an Unearned Increment?

[*November 18, 1908*]

Good-intentioned reformers — that is to say, men who feel themselves be-longing to the only class that can be called reformers — are, as a rule, in a constant state of actively striving for some end they desire, political or so-cial, or floundering in a slough of despondency, disgust, and utter weariness with their kind because a great mass of the latter refuse to adopt the views of the former. The term "reactionary" is an opprobrious epithet, and yet he who would alter, make over, or form again political and social conditions on old or past models is himself attempting re-form, and hence he is a reformer.

But the reformer — that is to say, the man who wants to reform society into a condition that does not at present exist or never has existed, to form con-ditions better (different) than ever yet existed — is the only man who is gen-erally and publicly considered to be entitled to the name of "reformer."

There are a great many different kinds of reformers; there are a great num-ber of them. There are a great many objectives of reform. Even are there abundant cases of conflict between one kind of reform and another. There are all kinds of men having all kinds of religious and other ethical standards, who are strongly moved by their desire to get a change for the better.

Yet, notwithstanding all this, there are several traits or characteristics that are common to all individuals and all movements of reform. First, the proposed movements are what might be called altruistic in their objective, and all reformers not only pretend to be altruists but really are altruists. In this country and in Europe, at least, there are other common characteristics of reforms and reformers. They are all or nearly all based upon Christian religious beliefs.

A man or even a nation of men does not have to be Christian in his or its belief to be thoroughly Christian in thought and action. The Christian's point

376

of view is about the only point of view of the great mass of humanity outside of the pagan world, so called.

For many centuries have European peoples been trying to evolve governments and social conditions exactly in conformity with principles deduced from the Bible by ecclesiastics.

It is noteworthy that the most radical, the most determined, reformers are not only outside of the pale of the Christian church, so called, but consider themselves to be atheists. These men may long have lost all faith in the church, or may from their birth have been lacking in churchly training or conviction, but nevertheless, having been born into a world which had no other ethical point of view than the Christian, they have been so formed by their environment as to have no other than a Christian point of view.

It is well known that there is a warfare between Christians and scientists, and no even ordinarily equipped scientist can fail to recognize that much of Christian theory and practice is absolutely in opposition to natural law.

The fundamental theory of our own American government, that all men are born equal, is based directly on Christ's teachings. Yet nothing is more palpably evident than the converse of this proposition. While most persistently reiterating in speech this political and Christian dogma, no man, even the most devout of Christians, fails to prove by his acts that the proposition is a fiction, pure and simple.

No two men are alike; no two men are equally possessed of the same faculties.

The reformer is trying to construct a political government founded upon the first principles of Christianity. He is trying to produce a social condition based upon the same principle. He is always striving and always failing.

Since all men, or, rather, since the great majority of men profess with their mouths certain fundamental political and Christian doctrines, our reformers take it for granted that the convictions of the masses of the people are in accordance with their professions. Having taken this for granted, and having recognized a fact that is scientifically proven to exist, namely, that the human mind is logical, the reformer can see no reason why he should not easily succeed in getting the people as a whole to adopt political and other social arrangements in conformity with the professed dogma.

The real reason and the only sufficient reason for this ever-continuing failure lies in the fact that mankind has adopted a profession of ethics at variance with its convictions. In fact, men do not believe what they say they believe, and this is proven every day by every living man, and on election day, when the democracy selects its rulers, it invariably votes against principles that it professes.

There is no "peace on earth and goodwill toward men." Such a condition is in direct conflict with every known and suspected natural law. There must be constant warfare on earth and constant, adverse strivings (hence ill will) between all men and toward all men in order that mankind shall be, as it is and must be, an integral and a consistent part of the universe.

Life — that is to say, all that is — is movement, is energy, is action and re-action; in other words, is conflict, is warfare, a state of complete, absolute unrest.

Rest, quiescence, even comparative rest or quiescence, is death, non-ex-istence.

It is not such a far cry from all the above to the caption under which the whole of this follows.

Is there an unearned increment? By "unearned" is meant that no labor has been performed. What we mean by saying that a man is possessed of an un-earned increment is that he is in possession of something which was not pro-duced by his labor, physical or mental. The common man would perhaps call an increment unearned by its possessor when that man has not performed some sort of physical labor to obtain it.

The very phrase "unearned increment" is intended to convey the idea that some man or men are in possession of property to which they have no good title. But the phrase also carries with it the meaning that this man or these men have a title at least acknowledged by law and custom.

The use of the phrase suggests in reality and argues the principle that the holders of this title should be dispossessed and their property of this charac-ter turned over to and placed in the possession of others, perhaps the whole people.

A common law, rule, existing amongst all mankind, civilized and pagan, Christian and unchristian, is that "plaintiff in ejectment must first prove title." That is to say, it is not sufficient for one man or one set of men simply to prove that the possessor of a certain piece of property has not a good title to it, but the person or persons who desire to get possession of the same property must prove that his or their title is good.

I will not attempt here to answer the question which leads this article. I doubt if I would have the ability to give a satisfactory answer to it. However, I wish to formulate a few statements which possibly, by inference, may serve as a partial answer.

The statements and arguments that I will make will be based upon my own experience and observation. They will proceed from my own individual point of view. Neither I nor any other man can hold a conviction or express an opinion that does not proceed from an individual point of view attained by that individual's personal experience and observation.

Generally speaking, I will make the declaration that so far as my observa-tion and experience are concerned, no man can profit in the least by being placed in the possession of any property he has not earned — that is to say, which he has not acquired as a result of his own knowledge. This is a broad and sweeping statement which I know would be contested vehemently by many, by most men, in fact, and the vigorousness of the contesting would be in exact inverse proportion to the contestant's own material possessions. The few, the very few, who would instantly recognize the perfect reasonableness of my statement would be those whose possessions are large and whose world experience has been wide and frequent.

In my own particular and peculiar business, I have learned that success is directly in proportion to the nicety with which a division or the sharing of the profits or proceeds of the business shall be proportionate to the effectiveness of — that is to say, to the work or labor performed by — individuals laboring at the common task.

I have learned to make some rough sort of distinction between the various classes and qualities and quantities of labor performed.

Nothing is more apparent to me than that a successful newspaper, for instance, would be an impossibility were it so planned and conducted as to divide equally, share and share alike, the common products of the business between each and every person employed in producing the same.

I have learned also that as one would increase the number of individuals who by their vote would control the conduct and management of a newspaper, the chances of success would be decreased, and in case of success, the amount of profit produced would be decreased. While it is possible to assemble together in one joint partnership two or three or four individuals who would be so nicely complementary one with the others as to make it possible to produce a business success by an equal partnership amongst these people, the chances are all against success in the matter of selecting and assembling such a co-partnership. Given three men of an extremely high quality of ability and put them in charge of a newspaper, their chances of success would not be nearly so great as would be the chance of success on the part of a partnership composed of only two men of even less ability. The chances of success of this equal partnership of two men would be far less than would be the chances of success in the case of one man of still greatly inferior ability who would be able to control absolutely the property.

Two heads are not better than one. I can imagine the possibility of an equal co-partnership of, say, six of the most successful newspapermen in the United States, in the foundation and conduct of a given newspaper. But just because of the superlative capacities of each, I cannot imagine, even as a possibility, a successful outcome of their joint efforts.

My experience and observation have taught me, in my own business, however, that no one man can make a successful newspaper. He requires, in or-

der to make his newspaper succeed, not only the assistance but the cooperation of a number of men who are his equals or superiors in many qualities —
in any and all qualities excepting the one quality of ability to govern.

In the case of a newspaper owned by one man, or controlled by one man,
but whose product is the result of his own as well as that of the labor of a
number of other men, the proprietor's position not only appears to be but
is insignificant. He only performs one part of the many parts of a common
task. Being one man as against many, the sum of his intelligence and capacity
must be really small as compared with the sum of the whole capacity of the
working force. His functions are as necessary, however, to the existence of
the newspaper body as is the head of a man necessary to the existence of
a whole man. But because of his insignificant position and because his labors
are of a peculiarly unobservable sort, it appears perfectly apparent to almost all onlookers, even those onlookers most intimately connected with
him, that his share in the product of the common labor is monstrously disproportionate. To a greater or less extent, his possessions are considered in-
crements unearned by himself.

The only proof of the moral soundness of his title to these possessions is
founded upon the deduction that but for his existence and such labor as he
did perform, the newspaper would not have existed. There have been abundant proofs and evidences of this condition of affairs given by dissatisfied,
minority stockholders and greatly famous employees of a succeeding or
successful newspaper seceding from the original institution and attempting
to form a new organization and a new newspaper. These enterprises have almost invariably proven failures, because they have left out of their organization the absolutely essential element: the man who could govern and would
govern, and hence lay hands upon the major portion of the common product. Of course, if the seceding organization carried with it a ruler, another
candidate to receive yet-to-be "unearned increment," the success of this organization would only prove the original contention.

There is the unearned increment, so called, of our nation, of our state, of
a city, or of a community, which is always in the possession of some one or
more individual citizens. The question presents itself to my mind whether
or not it is possible that this so-called unearned increment is ever in the possession of a man who has not earned it in some way not perfectly and plainly
apparent to the common and uninformed. I am inclined to hold the view
that the mere possession of this property called unearned increment is proof
that some labor, valuable on account of either its quality, quantity, or character to the community as a whole, has been performed by the man who possesses it, and that his title to it is just as moral and good as is the title of the
newspaper proprietor that I have described.

The foundation doctrine of democracy is the foundation of Christianity, and as I have said before, both doctrines rest upon not only an unscientific basis, but upon a basis that is false to natural law.

Neither democracy nor Christianity recognizes the inequality of men, their unequal rights to power and possession. They are far, very far indeed, from recognizing that not only the common good but the mere existence of society depend upon not only the rule of a few individuals, but upon the so-called oppression and selfish aggrandizement by and of those few.

The growth and development of a municipality — always accompanied by a large growth of so-called unearned increment — is a slow process comparatively. The whole institution of a municipality is so complex and so large that it is impossible for any individual citizen of any municipality to know all the workings of a community and the part played by each individual in it, just as it is impossible for a common, private soldier on the battlefield to know of all the movements of his army, the thoughts and acts of those few men on whose thoughts and acts depend the issue of victory or defeat.

Then, too, comes in the question of time. The young man of today who looks upon some aged citizen in a community enjoying enormously large possessions in the shape, say, of very valuable lands, is pretty apt to feel certain that the wealth of this man is mainly constituted of unearned increment. He is in no position to know what part in the past development of the city this man has played, or as to whether or not the city as he knows it would have existed except for some sort of labor performed by this ancient and a few of his contemporaries.

As an example of this mental attitude of the young citizen, I have opportunities to experience and observe similar cases directly relating to myself. As an old man who has retired to an almost secluded, private life, I am receiving the major portion of all the products of a newspaper which I founded thirty years ago [Cleveland *Press*]. For almost twenty years I have been personally unknown to the hundreds of men who are daily laboring to continue the life and prosperity and profits of this newspaper. For a number of years I have performed no other function in the conduct of this property than that of holding absolute control of its stock.

To the young men, and even the older men, working on this paper in this year of 1908, it must appear to many of them that my services are absolutely nil. To most all of them it must appear that my share of the profits are enormously disproportionate to the services I perform. With this latter idea I am inclined myself to coincide.

What can I do to right this wrong, if wrong there is? If the scheme is wrong, unnatural, unscientific, a solution of the problem ought to be easy. I know that it is not easy.

The institution, this paper that I speak of, while it is of more value to me perhaps than anyone else, in the way of its returning to me a larger income than it returns to anyone else, is really of more value to each and every one of those who are daily employed upon it than it is to me, since every day they derive from it almost the whole income, and in most cases all of the incomes.

If I should attempt to divide my stockholding with other men, say, men who are employed on the paper, I would — being the actual owner of record today of only a bare controlling majority of the stock — part with control. The newspaper would lose its head. It would lose its government. It would be impossible for the stockholders to establish a new, governing head, since the new head would not control except by the consent of many. So far from there being one man in control of the property, there would be one man under the control of many men, and human nature is such that it would be impossible for any man in control to submit voluntarily to the rule of men whom he controlled, and it would further be impossible for these many stockholders to have a mind and an object so common as to make government — that is to say, they would have to make anarchy.

There is another course. I might part with the whole of my controlling interest to another man more vigorous, more active, and who so managed the property as to make it not only more valuable to himself but to all of his collaborators.

But how am I to select this man? It is impossible for me to select him. The man must select himself and prove his capacity to hold and govern the property by proving that he is strong enough to win it away from me either by craft or force.

To return to the municipality and the old man in possession of so-called unearned increment, what is his position in his society? Can he, any more than can I, dispose of his holdings, by his own voluntary act, to a more fit successor? If he gives what he has to the whole people he is committing a sin against Nature and against the community, since whatever virtues a democracy may have, it is possessed of the vice of impracticability in business affairs — at least, comparative impracticability. Its best ability is impracticability as compared with the ability of the able individual who has had the power to grasp possessions.

The only man who can become the heir to this old man's property without himself becoming a vicious and injurious element to the community is he who would relieve the old man of his possessions by force or craft. Even his legal heir-successor, as history-long experience has shown, on the average is an injury to society.

The so-called unearned increment in any municipality, state, or nation is in reality an earned increment, or it wouldn't exist, according to my own convictions.

I know well enough the stock argument of the increased value of real estate as a result of an incoming population. It would be impossible to frame an opposing argument which could be comprehended by a whole people, even a majority of any human community.

Yet, while the expressed belief in an unearned increment is almost universal, its reality is to be doubted since, if it were real, humanity would not tolerate the existence of such an increment. The mere fact that civilized society feels itself unable to make any proper, any beneficial, disposition of this so-called unearned increment is at least partial proof that society really recognizes that the increment was earned, and that its possessor had a moral as well as a legal title.

The fact is, men know that their professed moral attitude is a false one. They know that individual proprietorship of property is essential to race existence and the advantages of civilization, and they know also, by convictions which they cannot formulate in words, that no man possesses any property that he has not earned, and that not an infinitesimal fraction of such property has been earned and acquired by the owners without the community as a whole being benefited thereby.

It is comparatively easy for any common man to recognize that the founder and owner and the builder-up of any manufacturing institution which can be called property has benefited the community, as well as himself, and that thereby he has won a fair title to his property. It is less easy to the common man to learn in what ways and by what right a man has title to some other forms of property which are only the resultant of an exchange, by the owner of a factory, say, of his factory for other forms of valuable property, say, real estate.

Almost everybody knows, even the Socialists admit this frankly, that there are various classes of labor, and that a variability in the amount of rewards is permissible and moral, because it is advantageous to the community.

Even a majority of mankind recognizes that there are two general classes of labor in any and every industrial institution: one class, intellect or managing; and the other class, pure manual or other physical labor. Men recognize the community value of strong, intellectual men, leaders and rulers in the community — so-called captains of industry.

It is also commonly recognized that the ruling class, by necessity, is very small numerically.

What they do not recognize, especially in municipal life, is that this small ruling class in any community has performed far greater service to the community as a whole than have all the other individuals outside of this class. These head men, who have made and are making great and prosperous cities possible, are just men of such character that I have described as the owner-manager of a newspaper. Their work has been an absolutely essential element in the creation of a successful municipality. The work of the others has also been absolutely essential, but, by the very nature of conditions, the common good of all requires that this small class of men shall not only exercise control over the whole mass but that they should be armed with the power that makes their control inevitable, namely, the power of material possession of wealth greatly out of proportion to their numbers.

During the very recent past, I have been called upon and compelled by circumstances to give my attention to one small and growing city. Unconsciously — that is to say, with no conscious object in view, such as the holding and formulation of the views and opinions that I am herein expressing — I have been studying the conditions of this municipality. For a period of eighteen years I have known the community. For the greater part of this time, fully two-thirds of it, I knew of this community as a stagnant, retrograding, inefficient community. Its population was decreasing, rather than increasing. Possessed of great advantages — perhaps, everything considered, greater natural advantages than any other city that I know of — it was making no profitable use of the same. It was standing still.

A few years ago there began a change in the whole spirit and movement of the town. What was the cause of this change? There had been no improvement in natural resources. There had been slight, if any, improvement in artificial resources — that is to say, in the way of transportation facilities. But a change came over the community. Inactivity, even lethargy, had prevailed, and activity and a spirit of progress began to show itself.

What was the cause of this?

Did the whole town, each individual in it, wake up of a sudden by the initiative of each individual? No, the community of men and women remained almost the same. Some children grew up to manhood, and some old men and women died.

So far as my observation has gone, I have seen no such change in the spirit of the community — that is to say, in the spirit of each individual of the community.

I have seen a few, very few, new men appear on the scene. These have been active men, naturally. They began to move themselves and in moving they agitated those immediately around them. As these few exercised themselves, they grew stronger, and the movement that had been set up amongst their neighbors continued. It was easier for these few to keep adding more and more to the energy of this movement until the movement spread throughout the whole community.

A new San Diego has been born, and a new ruling class, very limited in number, has evolved. A dead little city has developed into a rapidly growing larger city, and just because the forceful few who started this movement are growing in force and are adding to their number from original, native stock and outsiders — that is to say, immigrants — this growth bids fair to continue for a long time, until a great city will grow up in the place of a small town.

Yet a few years more and there will be a ruling class of very wealthy men in the city of San Diego: men whose wealth will at that later time be considered to be composed almost entirely of unearned increment.

I, who have time and leisure and disposition to study and to put my imagination at work, if I am living at that future time, will be able to understand and appreciate the real title that these new rich men will have to their property. I will be able to understand that of the hundreds of millions of dollars worth of property that will have been created, only a small share, no more than a rightful share, will be found in the possession of the men whose energies were necessary in order that these hundreds of millions of dollars worth of property should have come into existence.

So far as I can see the work being done in the beginning, I will be able to understand the value of the work when it is done, whereas the few of the present citizens of San Diego and the many citizens of the future San Diego will have had no knowledge of the manner of work done, or that such work was done, and hence no possible appreciation of the necessity of the labor being performed by the men who did perform it at the time they did perform it.

Today the state of California is, or is supposed to be, governed by a great railroad corporation, unjustly and unfairly, it is claimed and believed by many good men and intelligent men amongst whom I would like to be numbered.

The Southern Pacific Railway Company is now a tremendously great property, and the possessors of this property wield a proportionately great power, political and social, in this state.

We of this generation of Californians, a few of us natives of this state, fewer still of us have had any opportunity to learn of the great sacrifices made, the great labors performed, by the originators and builders of the original transcontinental and California railways [sic]. We simply behold the great possessions and the great power of the present institution, and we cannot believe, even if we are attempting to do so we refuse to believe, that the labors performed by these pioneer transportation men were anything like in proportion to the reward they and their successors have received for their labors.

We all perfectly well know that perhaps nine-tenths, perhaps 99 per cent, of the property value of all that exists in California would not now be in existence were it not for the labors of the men who built our railways, whose aggregate possessions in this state cannot be valued at more than a very small percentage of the total value of the wealth resulting — that is to say, produced — by the building of these railroads which now compose the institution called the Southern Pacific Railway Company.

One thing is noticeable, and that is that notwithstanding the common outcry, notwithstanding the almost universally expressed condemnation of the Southern Pacific Railway political machine, a very large majority of the people refuse to express that condemnation at the polls where they have the opportunity every year, in one form or another, to express their condemnation and to take the necessary steps in a direction which would eventuate in the transfer of the property or the value of the property from its present holders to other hands.

The public's attitude, expressed by votes on election day, toward this great railway corporation is that of acknowledgment not only of the right of this corporation to rule, but of the opinion that, individually and collectively, the citizens of this state will be advantaged by that rule.

Neither the Christian ethics nor the democratic principles confessed and acknowledged by almost a totality of California society [are] strong enough to overcome the effects of a natural law.

Advancing Democracy

[*March 27, 1909*]

Much contempt and ridicule is heaped upon "parlor Socialists," "armchair strategists," "impractical reformers."

I suppose that every contemptuous expression might be applied to any remarks that I would make on subjects above named, or similar ones.

In every department of society, social, political, military, economic, scientific, etc., etc., are a number of men whose names are more or less conspicuous, who assume to be and are frequently assumed by others to be experts.

Let any man with not-long-clamored-for and obtained public reputation for expertness on any subject attempt to express an opinion and to gain a public hearing, and he will immediately be set upon and abused as a fool and an interloper by self-professed experts.

Nothing is more natural than the opinion of most men that no one man is capable of thoroughly mastering and comprehending more than one department of knowledge — one classification of it.

As a matter of fact, any man of that great mental capacity which makes him a master in any department of knowledge and life activity must be so constituted, first, as to be able to grasp, understand, and intelligently expound views on almost any other important department or classification of knowledge and action; and second, that such a man is necessarily so developed and trained in mind that he cannot and will not attempt to express an opinion for the purpose of leading others on any subject, in any department of knowledge, until he has mastered it sufficiently to satisfy himself that he is able to speak intelligently. This being the case, his thoughts, and hence his advice, have great public value.

Now, as I have never held a public office and have not gone through all the experiences of a candidate, successful and unsuccessful, it is taken for granted that I am no expert on political matters. As I am not a college professor or a well-known writer on political or economic subjects, it would

387

naturally be presumed that I have no valuable thoughts to express or advice to give on such subjects.

I am not a lawyer by profession, hence, it is presumed that I am not able to form a good judgment on constitutional law.

My name is not conspicuous as a statesman or a public leader. That being the case, it would be presumed that my views of great government affairs are crude and perhaps false.

When a man is universally considered by his neighbors as being incompetent for any particular class of work, the effect on him of this public opinion is to cause him to coincide with the public views even himself. Human nature in him compels him to be modest to this extent.

The most important affairs of my life are bound up in what might be considered social and political problems. This being the case, such subjects are of the greatest interest to me. I have perhaps devoted more of all my thought during all my life to these subjects than all the others that have been brought to my attention.

Because I simply have not spoken or written much or presumed to be a leader of men and an adviser of the people, why am I less able to form correct judgments than are those other men who fill the whole country full with their noise of declamation?

If democracy means what the great mass of people in this country and other countries believe it means, I am not a democrat. I do not believe that all men are born equal. I do not believe that all men ever should or can have each and every influence and equal control over the affairs of any nation. I know that the average judgment of any body of men, large or small, on any subject, is far lower in the scale of correctness than the judgment of one or a few more men in the crowd. In fact, it seems to me that the general idea of democracy is a sort of socialism — not a material socialism, but an intellectual socialism and equality of all. If the common idea of democracy, the right of the majority to rule, that is to say, the right of the many to have the same influence on the whole body politic as the exceptionally few and able, is correct, then in the end there would be no difference between socialism and democracy. Because, if the majority, which are mediocre in mental and physical capacities, and hence productiveness, have both the power and right to govern, then they will certainly, by mere force of numbers, subordinate to their control and use the abilities of the minority, and at the same time appropriate from these latter, not only all of their property, but all of the gratification to be derived from their superior abilities.

Both democracy and socialism are scientifically absurd.

But if democracy means only equality of opportunities, freedom from suppression of personal privileges other than that derived by the very nature of the individual, then I am a democrat.

Even such democracy as mine is, in these days of democracy, an ideal that is not only not obtained but not obtainable. It is only something to be striven for and approached very slowly and by infinite pains and struggling. It is because democracy is only an ideal, something that must always be struggled for and never obtained, that it is in perfect accord with natural law. Life itself is only an expression of energy and of effort — the heat caused by friction of opposing forces. An ideal once arrived at and perfectly accomplished is only a symbol of death, since, being accomplished, there is no more struggle for it, no more friction in overcoming obstacles, hence, no more heat and no more life.

The aim of democracy, then, is not the goal of individual equality amongst men — the common level of socialism. The aim of democracy in government, large or small, of many or few, in each and every department of life work, where community acts rather than the individual, is to select the man best qualified to govern the community in that department of its affairs where a man of his qualifications is required.

It stands to reason, in the light of all that has been taught us by the biological science, that hereditary monarchy or any other hereditary public office is bad politics. No matter how well qualified any man may be to hold the office of king or any subordinate office in government, there is not one chance in a million of any one of his sons, much less his first born, having the same qualifications. Then, too, even if the son had identically the same qualifications, the change of times and institutions might, and almost certainly would, require a different sort of talent to exercise governmental power during the lifetime of the son than that which was required during the lifetime of the father.

The aim of democracy is not only to obtain for the community the best sort of ruler but to obtain for every member of the community the opportunity to serve his own best interests whether he considered his interests a part of that of the whole community or his own individual interests, without at least infringing upon the domain of another man.

The end and aim, then, of democracy is to put every man in exactly the right place — the ablest man in the nation at the head of the nation, and the humblest and the weakest individual in such a place as will make his own life full and satisfactory without affecting injuriously the lives of any of his fellows.

A true democracy, then, is a body of men, always in flux, in which each individual is constantly moving from place to place, upward or downward, in the social scale and from one point to another point where he is most fitted to serve the community and where his capacities can be exercised to the greatest benefit of himself and the whole community.

Reform of the Courts

[*April 28, 1911*]

"Miramar," Calif., April 28, 1911

Judge Frank M. Gorman
Hamilton Co., Common Pleas Court
Cincinnati, Ohio

My dear Judge:

Do you recall the day something over a quarter of a century ago when we two were, comparatively speaking, "cubs" and were enjoying the honor of being patronized and "worked" by a little bunch of "little-great" men who were attempting to resist the power of the already infamous [John R.] McLean? I believe we called ourselves the "Committee of Fifteen." [9]

I remember one instance in that campaign from which I learned a lesson that has ever since been impressed upon my mind. I was young and enthusiastic as well as "green." The old fellows who were steering us were so hearty and apparently sincere in their loquacity that I took it for granted that they were patriots, and I knew that they had a great deal of money. (I have since learned to believe that it is almost as difficult for a rich man to be a patriot as it is for a big animal to go through a small opening.) I proposed that each of us who could should contribute a substantial sum for our campaign expenses and offered my donation of one thousand dollars. My proposal was met with a stony stare. I do not think that our Committee of Fifteen as a whole ever handled as much as a thousand dollars.

Soon after these times I lost sight personally of nearly all my colleagues on that committee. Business engagements for a considerable period of time and lately a more or less broken constitution have prevented my having any considerable personal acquaintance in Cincinnati. It has only been in the last few months that I have rediscovered you in the person of a very honorable member of the smallest group of men in these United States, that is to say, that little band of judges who are both square and intelligent. In no other

---

[9] This has reference to his early days in Cincinnati.

class of citizens in this country, I believe, so numerous as the legal profession, is it possible to find so few such men — square men and intelligent men — as in your profession.

There are in the profession plenty of square men according to their convictions, such as William Howard Taft, Supreme Judge Lurton [Associate Justice Horace H. Lurton of the U.S. Supreme Court], Elihu Root, etc., and the number of intelligent lawyers is legion.

The sad thing is that there are so few square lawyers having intelligence enough to recognize the necessity of twentieth-century conditions. For the most part, few of them have arrived at an attitude of mind and heart that would make them fit nicely into any condition of civilization less remote than several centuries back.

I was proud and glad to learn that I once knew the young man who, since becoming a judge, has had the courage that you have evinced, but I have been surprised beyond measure to find a Cincinnati judge who had progressed so far in common sense and human sympathy as to be able to recognize the anachronism of the idea that a judge should not be subject to public opinion. I am bound to infer that you have advanced to this position, since I have recently received from Mr. J. C. Harper an account of your public address on the subject of the recall of the judges.

I do not consider that the adoption of the recall plan — even the recall of judges — is going to prove a panacea. At most, the system may mitigate one of the greatest evils of this time — the almost universal public contempt for the legal profession and hatred of the courts.

I am one of those who believe that wolves should not be used as sheep dogs; that tariffs should not be made or revised by its friends, i.e., its beneficiaries; that capitalists or rich men should not have control of the law and system of tax assessment and collection; and that lawyers, the greatest part of whose education consists in acquiring medieval lore, and whose chief modern employment consists in earning wages by practices — nearly the whole object of which is to defeat justice — should not be entrusted with the judicial office.

You see, if you are remarkable in being radical as a judge, I am entitled to some notice as a radical in my class.

Lately I have been both in close and rather intimate relations with two California lawyers whose learning and ability and standing at the bar is now well recognized. They are Francis J. Heney and Hiram W. Johnson. I find that Heney is no whit less a radical on this subject than I am, and is outspoken in his opinions. Johnson does not go as far, or at least has not in his speech with me. He has not been so general in his condemnation of the whole judicial system. But he knows California, and he knows conditions here and he has been frank and open in his statements that at least the highest judiciary of this state is mentally and morally unqualified to exercise the tremendous power imposed on them by their offices. Of all public officials, Johnson believes that the judiciary is more in need of subjugation to popular will than any others.

I consider that the recall of the judiciary may serve (I am not sure it will serve) as a sufficient spillway to the great reservoir of public discontent which is rising so rapidly that there is great danger of the dam bursting, causing a revolution, and a more or less extended period of anarchy.

The people can by peaceful means and with comparative rapidity change unpopular executives, legislatures, and minor administrative officers, but at present the people have no way of suppressing that exercise of legislation which the courts have usurped. They can put out of office one judge and fill his place with another man belonging to the same caste who — except in such exceptional cases as yourself — can be counted on to continue to practice the abuses of his predecessor.

I believe that it ought to be admitted that I hold a position in this country that well fits me to be a far better than the average judge of the real temper of the great majority of our people. I do not pretend to be a great popular leader, or even a popular leader at all. A lifetime of experience has disabused my mind of all idea that I have great power just because I have a great audience. I have learned that it is only by voicing public opinion that I can content the public. When, misled by my own judgment or desires, I have attempted to get great masses of people to adopt my own private views, I have failed, but when I have succeeded in discerning the real attitude of public opinion and voiced it, I have become instantly aware of public approval.

If I was not the first, I believe I am among the very first, of journalists, who have freely criticized the judiciary, collectively and individually, and the "System," and you are probably aware how far I have gone in this direction.

I have ways of learning quickly enough when I am outrunning the people and when I am going in a direction that they disapprove of, and I assure you that no public effort that I have ever made has met with such hearty public approval as that which I have made in the direction not only of trying to reform the judiciary but of attempting to drive the judges out of the legislative field that they have usurped.

The common people of this country no longer trust the courts. It is not that they doubt that justice is to be obtained there; it is that they know that practically unjust treatment at the hands of the courts is inevitable.

I don't feel myself at liberty to name a name, but I know that in a certain great city in this country at the present time there is warfare between the people and the courts, and that the great majority of the people are convinced that the courts are their enemies, and that they (the courts) are fully determined to use all their great power not only to prevent common justice but to perpetrate mortal injury. Their feelings against these courts are identical to those of a conquered and oppressed citizenry toward a wicked, bloody, crowned tyrant. So deep are their convictions in this matter that it is more than possible that there are many violent and desperate persons who are restrained by no moral sentiment from feeling that assassination even would be justifiable.

Where in any country there is a feeling remotely approaching such a condition of mind as this is, it is not worthwhile to stop and consider points of law. There is real danger existing when a majority of the people are bitterly opposed to their government and the methods and practices of those who govern them.

To a greater or lesser extent a similar feeling of discontent pervades the great mass of the people of the whole country, and only willful blindness on the part of the great men — the statesmen and the jurists of the nation, of the various states, and of our smaller communities — is to blame for permitting this dangerous condition to continue to grow more and more dangerous.

You are in a position to know that the long bondage of the city of Cincinnati to corruption, vice, and thievery has only been made possible by the attitude of the bench and bar of that city and a part of the bench of the state.

Suppose we succeed in removing ["Boss" George] Cox and his gang. Did we not at a previous epoch remove John R. McLean and Tom Campbell? How much did we gain by exchanging these tyrants for your present oppressor?

Will it ever be possible under the present system to obtain from the men who have been trained for the bar judges who will be just, even if the people do have a chance to exchange one sycophant for another on the bench?

I do not know how far a reform of the judiciary and the judicial system would go toward curing public evils. I am not sure, but I think the evils of capitalism — that is to say, the evils of our present economic system — are the great evil.

You know how it is and always has been in despotic monarchies. The people have been willing to believe that the king was good but that his ministers and judges were bad, and it has always been the practice of the public to attack the king's ministers and judges rather than the king himself.

Perhaps in these days capitalism and the economic system [are] not charged by the public with all the things that they are guilty of, and perhaps the less guilty tools of the real rulers (the courts) are too much condemned.

However this may be, the almost universal feeling of contempt for, and hatred of, the courts is so great that some reform of the latter may serve to check the rising tide of popular discontent and be a precursor of other more vital and necessary reforms.

In all past times criminals have been at warfare with the law and society, but today the law is making criminals of so many that we have got to admit that society itself is at warfare with the law; that there are only two parties in existence — the custodians of the law and the criminals — society having been almost wholly absorbed into criminality.

Sincerely yours,

E. W. Scripps

Belligerent Rights in Class Warfare

[*May 1, 1911*]

Scripps said this disquisition did not represent his convictions. Nonetheless, he prized it as an exercise in formulating "a possible mental attitude."

The occasion of his writing it was the murder trial of James I. and John B. McNamara of the Structural Iron Workers Union in connection with the dynamiting of the Los Angeles Times *building on October 1, 1910, in which a number of non-union employees of the anti-union* Times *were killed.*

During a weekend recess of the trial, Clarence Darrow, the defense counsel, visited "Miramar" with Steffens. In the course of discussion, Scripps proudly pulled a copy of the disquisition from his drawer and read it to them.

He also sent copies to editors-in-chief of the various Scripps groups, asking for their private reactions which he would hold confidential if they wished. "Everybody damned me for it except [B. H.] Canfield [editor-in-chief of the Pacific Northwest group] and [W. H.] Porterfield [editor-in-chief of the California papers]. Canfield said 'amen'; Porterfield was afraid to say anything." [10]

In transmitting a copy to Paine, who then was writing an occasional NEA piece from San Diego, he wrote:

> *I have just perpetrated a bit of radicalism in the form of a disquisition which I am sending you.*
>
> *I am wondering just how far it would be expedient for us to go with the ideas that I have suggested.*
>
> .   .   .   .
>
> *If you are moved to produce any editorial matter on this subject I do not wish you to send it out until after we have conferred together. . . .* [11]

But he was more cautious in writing other associates about it. He told W. B. Colver, head of NEA, that he had sent it around just to draw out Colver and the others on the subject. He was very careful to tell J. C. Harper, his Cincinnati counsel, that the disquisition was not his own conviction.

[10] EWS to Robert F. Paine, Apr. 8, 1914.
[11] EWS to Robert F. Paine, May 1, 1911.

Scripps was so proud of his production that he sent a copy to Judge Lindsey in Denver, giving him permission to let Theodore Roosevelt read it, hoping to learn Roosevelt's private opinion of such a subject. However, a search of Scripps' files failed to turn up a letter from Lindsey indicating that Roosevelt had read it.

Most of us who have even the most general knowledge of ordinary events, such as is gained by reading current journals of the day, have a pretty well-defined idea of what the rights of a belligerent are, though it may be as difficult for others as it is for myself to define the meaning of this term.

A belligerent is a man who is carrying on any sort of warfare against any other man or a number of men, whether he is acting alone, the member of a small band, or is a unit of a great national army. I believe that I have read somewhere some writing on the subject of the right of revolution. The people of all nations are recognized by international lawyers to have the right to revolutionize their government, that is to say, that successful revolution is right and lawful because it is successful.

However, those who are engaged in an attempt by force of arms to revolutionize a government and who fail in their attempt are acknowledged no right in law or morals. The successful revolutionist leader is bound to become a national hero and to receive honors and rewards for performing those deeds for which he would have had to submit to condign punishment and even forfeiture of life if he had failed. In this case success is legal and failure is criminal, not only according to the scientific law of biology but according to all human law under all systems of civilization.

From the above it has been further deduced that the criminality of an unsuccessful revolutionist is in inverse proportion to the extent of his effort or to the nearness of his coming to success.

For instance, in the neighboring country of Mexico a few months ago when a revolution was begun by a few scattering bands of patriots, or self-seekers, the men leading and composing these bands were recognized — and properly recognized — not only by the Mexican government but by the individual citizens of other civilized countries as being criminals of the worst class — murderers, robbers, arsonists, and such.

Arrested by the police or by the soldiery of the government, they were entitled to no consideration on account of their moral or patriotic motives; they were bound to have been, and ought to have been, punished only as individual criminals violating the law against life and property. But when these first few small bands of disturbers were joined by other individuals and when numerous other bands bearing arms against the government sprang up and when by direct agreement or tacit assent all of these bands formed themselves under the direction of a central organization and chief, and proclaimed some man as chief magistrate (president) of Mexico, and after there had been many skirmishes and small battles and much property destroyed, it appearing that the revolutionary force was large in numbers, it began to appear to the governments of other civilized nations that there was a prospect of the revolution finally being successful.

At about this time certain men prominent among the disturbers of the public peace began to demand of their opponents, and of outside neutral nations, the rights of belligerency.

Up to this time no nation has formally recognized this movement as a real revolution and hence no nation has bound itself to consider any individual revolutionist as a real belligerent, or in fact anything other than an individual criminal.

Under this condition of affairs by reason of the comity that has existed between all civilized nations, the government of Mexico would have a right to pursue into a foreign country any individual revolutionist and demand — that is to say, requisition — the return of such refugee to Mexico for trial and punishment for any violation of the statute law of Mexico.

It is extremely improbable, however, that any country would now grant extradition to such a fugitive, since although such country has not yet recognized the revolution and the rights of belligerency formally, still public and official opinion does actually recognize a real condition of legal warfare.

There have been cases where our own government — the United States — has recognized revolution and the belligerent rights of revolutionists long before such persons had established anything like the claim to recognition that the insurgent Mexicans have. One notable case occurred in Panama.

A few years ago practical recognition was given to the Nicaraguan insurgents under conditions no more favorable to Nicaraguan insurrectos than such as exists in Mexico today.

I think — though I am not sure — that the granting of belligerent rights to insurgents has other advantages than the one I have above spoken of in regard to extradition. I presume that if belligerent rights were recognized, the government of the United States would allow its citizens to sell such munitions of war and other commodities to the insurgents as they now have the right to furnish to the Mexican government.

I have given all the foregoing for the purpose of hinting at my own idea of what belligerent rights are, and on what foundation of broad general human law they are based.

I suppose that the broad moral base on which is founded this idea of legality of revolution and the rights of belligerency of revolutionists can be clearly understood by anyone of ordinary intelligence and information.

The difference between the act of a man bearing arms taking life and destroying property for selfish personal reasons, self-aggrandizement, or in the spirit of personal spite, and that of another man taking up arms and killing men and destroying property for the purpose of serving others or saving the whole nation or a great section of the nation, is extremely great.

In one case the man is an enemy of society and seeks the good of no other person than himself. In the other case the man undertakes great labor and risk for no selfish gain and offers himself as a possible and even probable martyr for the benefit of his kind or his country, or his section or class.

According to the law of any civilized nation, however, no such discrimination is made or can be made as between the acts of these two individuals. They are equally guilty one with the other and are treated equally by the government.

John Brown was hanged at Harper's Ferry for attempting to do, and failing to do, just what over a million of his fellow citizens a short time later succeeded in accomplishing. Although John Brown suffered physically the penalty due a bloody-handed murderer, posterity has not only acquitted him of any crime, but has insisted upon regarding him as both a hero and a martyr.

Can society afford to deal with its John Browns at any time in any other way than it did the John Brown of Harper's Ferry?

Would we not be offering a premium for wrongdoing to every harebrained visionary if we allowed in our treatment of criminals a distinction to be made between the man of good motives and the man of bad motives?

Of all the great number of assassins of kings, presidents, and public officials in times past and of all those men who pronounce themselves anarchists and who are recognized as anarchists by the rest of society, few if any have ever committed their deeds of violence for personal gain or as the result of personal vindictiveness. For the most part they have evinced possession of a heroic character and of a spirit of being willing martyrs, sacrificing themselves for what they — right or wrong — believed to be the good of their fellows.

Christ has said: "Greater love hath no man than this, that he lay down his life for his friends."

Have not all of these bloody assassins, as we call them, then given the greatest evidence of their love of humanity?

Today in nearly all civilized countries there is going on to a greater or lesser extent a revolutionary warfare between the classes.

In the United States this warfare has already proceeded to such an extent that the insurgent revolutionists are known to have destroyed the lives of many individuals and to have destroyed many millions of dollars worth of property.

However, this revolution, far progressed as it is, has not yet taken the form of what could be called a political revolution.

There is actual war going on for the purpose of destroying one government and setting up another, but this existing government, however powerful it is in the existing political state, is not the political government of any state or any municipality in fact. The government that is being attacked is the government of plutocracy which at present governs the government and hence is in fact the government.

The warfare is between the employees of capitalistic institutions and capitalists and their institutions.

While the insurgents thoroughly well recognize that their enemies form the real government of the country today, they also recognize that it is not as political officers and governors that they face on the field of battle the insurgents.

Perhaps never before, and certainly never before to the same extent, has there been the same kind or class of insurrection as that which is going on in this country today. There is no international law, there is no common moral law well and generally recognized which can be applied to this present condition of warfare. Speaking in the narrow political sense, this warfare is neither legal nor illegal; it is extra-legal.

While in the prosecution of the war there are acts performed by both parties of belligerents that contravene statute law, the great majority of the movements of both parties are outside of or not considered by statute law.

The courts have, as many of us believe, illegally attempted to embrace within their jurisdiction the control of these movements. The Constitution of the nation and the constitutions of the various states have been strained, and many statute laws have been twisted and distorted by judges for the purpose of seeking some valid excuse for intervention.

To any unbiased onlooker who is tolerably well informed concerning the motives and movements of the leaders and the rank and file of the two opposing forces now engaged in warfare, there can be no manner of doubt but that both sides have adopted not only tactics of warfare, but the moral — that is, customary — rules of warfare.

A perfectly humane man as a private soldier or as an officer may shoot to death a man in the opposing ranks, or order the same to be shot to death, and feel no moral compunction. The same man, private soldier or officer, aside from his military station, would not, acting in his individual capacity, dare or wish to render even small bodily injury to any other person. At the same time that he is granted or assumes belligerent rights he adopts an unordinary, a purely military, code of morals.

In this warfare that is now going on between the employers and the employed in this country there is no doubt but that the soldier, the militant, the belligerent, moral code has been adopted by not only the officers but the rank and file of the opposing forces.

Members of each party are willing by act of commission or omission to destroy the lives, and many of the lives, of their adversaries.

Large employers who lock out their employees perform an act which has its identical counterpart in warfare by name of siege. The military commander who surrounds a city or fortification and cuts off supplies of food — and if possible, water — and thus causes the death of a part or all of the besieged acts with identically the same object in view — that of killing — as he has in prosecuting a pitched battle.

There is no man of such intelligence as to be a great capitalist or a great employer of labor who does not know that the one certain effect of a long-continued lockout or strike will be the death of many innocent non-combatants — children suffering from lack of nourishment or other necessities of life — while large numbers of adult men and women are compelled to bear such hardships as to eventually shorten their lives. And yet few, if any, employers of labor have any moral scruples whatever on the subject of strikes and lockouts. They are moved solely by selfish interests as a rule and really depend upon the havoc of starvation, which includes the death of babies, as a means to coerce into submission their employees.

There are many other acts, some of which even trench upon and violate statute law, which employers, as individuals, or in combination, have caused to be performed in order to subdue their servants.

Capitalists in the shape of railway stockholders are notoriously reckless of human life, as shown by their neglect in adopting life-saving mechanism and such rules of conduct of their business as would greatly reduce the amount of death and injury caused. It is known that the number of deaths and cripplings that are being caused in this country annually that could be prevented by no more severe sacrifice than a small reduction of dividends amount on the whole to figures such as have rarely been equaled in any of the great battles of history.

On the other hand in the army of labor, and especially of union labor, the leaders and privates are only restrained from visiting retribution upon their enemies by their fear of law. Protest, as all great union leaders do, against the idea that they countenance violence or desire violence, it must be apparent to anyone that their scruples in this regard are so slight that as a body, and individually, union men are quite willing always to condone the offense of a violent member and are even anxious to save him from suffering penalties for such violence.

Let us take the case of McNamara, secretary of the Structural Iron Workers Union who is now under arrest under the charge of having caused the Los Angeles *Times* explosion.

For the purpose of this disquisition let us admit that he is guilty — that he did plan the explosion and directed it, and paid for it. This explosion caused the death of twenty or more innocent men. These men that were killed should be considered what they really were — soldiers enlisted under a capitalist employer whose main purpose in life was warfare against the unions.

If belligerent rights were accorded to the two parties in this war, then McNamara was guilty of no greater offense than would be the officer of any band, large or small, of soldiers who ordered his men to fire upon an enemy and killed a great number of the same.

If McNamara did plan and execute this deed he did it not as an individual seeking to vent personal spite; he did what he did do with just the same motive and in the same spirit as that which prompted the leader of the first band of Mexican insurrectos who first fired upon the Mexican government's soldiers.

McNamara had nothing to gain personally by this act, but he did run great risk, as has been proven, by undertaking the action.

Is he a martyr, or a patriot, then?

It cannot certainly be said that he was simply a malicious criminal committing murder.

Suppose society should adopt by convention, custom, or statute law a rule recognizing the rights of belligerency in this warfare that is going on. What would be the effect of such a step?

However, instead of our government recognizing any such mutual belligerent rights, it will for a long time at least persevere in recognizing the common law rights of only one of the parties in this war. It has formed an alliance, and will continue the alliance, with capital. I think the inevitable result of this course will cause the working classes of this country, who form the vast majority of its people, to recognize as its chief enemy the government itself — through its agents, the courts and various executive and administrative offices, the government taking the side of the capitalist employers as against the great majority of the whole people.

If there was any way by which the government in this case could be neutral and in which the officers and privates of the capitalist army had to meet on equal ground the workingmen, it is possible that economic peace might be established at the cost of some, but not much, bloodshed and destruction of property without political revolution ensuing.

Such are conditions, however, that it is hopeless to expect the government to alter its course in any particular.

But how about the people at large? Already to some extent the public does recognize the belligerent rights of the workingmen. As a whole the public does not visit the same condemnation on the warlike act of a labor organization as it does upon an individual action.

Whether McNamara may be proven guilty or innocent, in popular esteem he will never descend to rank with the common thug and murderer whose deeds are prompted by desire for robbery or vengeance.

It is customary even for the most liberal of newspapers, the most liberal of the clergy, the most sympathetic (toward unions) of private citizens to publicly deprecate all sorts of violence in labor troubles. Good citizens patriotically are demanding or are supposed to be demanding that we shall uphold the law at least to the extent of not countenancing any open violence.

If the leading citizenry should adopt another course and should by their actions and their words and in all other ways express themselves to the effect that they consider that in the main employers and capitalists fully merit all that they suffer as a result of their acts of oppression and of warfare against labor, it is highly probable that the government would soon take notice of such public opinion, and that long before the government took action in accordance with such public opinion, capitalists and employers generally would seek for, and find, ways of peaceful cooperation with the men who are or should be their partners — the workingmen under their direction.

The public as a whole has its rights. This is often enough proclaimed by the demagogues of the wealthy and the intellectuals in their protest against the violation of law and order committed by striking workingmen. But who is there to voice the public protest against the actions of great corporations and great employers who solely and alone cause those conditions which result in strikes and riots and bloodshed and in secret conspiracies and the use of bombs?

Are not the real disturbers of the peace of the country the very selfish and very few who oppressively and unfairly take to themselves the greater share and far too great a share of the joint product of labor and capital and management?

To show what an excessively large proportion the capitalists get of the common product we need only cite reports of our government officials at Washington.

The value of the annual product of the United States amounts to practically 30 billion dollars a year.

The average income of the wage-earners, salesmen, and professionals ten years ago did not exceed $600 per individual per annum. We may assume that this scale has been raised to $700 today.

If the 30 billion dollars of annual income of the country were divided equally between every living human being in this country, the share of each would be something like $300 per year. The annual income, then, of a family of five would be $1,500. Allowing for a family to consist of one breadwinner and wife and three children, the annual income of that family would not be over $700. This leaves, then, some $800 per annum for each family of wage-earners to go to swell the income or fortune of the comparatively few capitalists and employers there are in this country.

Perhaps not more than 85 per cent of the whole people of this country have an income of $700 per year. Hence, it would follow that 15 per cent of the whole population takes as its share of the product of the whole country not less than between 60 per cent and 70 per cent of the whole annual product of the country.

Recent reports made by certain state and municipal officers of New York City indicate that the minimum living wage of a family of five in New York should not be less than $900 per annum. In fact, a less wage than this requires such a family to lack nourishment and even tolerably sanitary homes, and yet in that city the annual average wage per person is not over $600.

Here is a condition of inequality that exists in a democracy where the majority rule or can rule, where there is no hereditary monarch, no great standing army and long-continued habit on the part of the people to submit to oppression.

The conditions as to the two parties are so unequal as to property and so unequal numerically that it is absurd for any of us to imagine that peace and harmony can possibly exist and that warfare of some sort and revolution of some sort is not only inevitable and necessary but right.

The weakest army of the two numerically is so weak that it stands as only one to nineteen against its opposition. All it has on its side for allies are obsolete laws, medieval courts, and ancient customs and conventions.

Imbecile arrogance on the part of these weaklings is constantly inflaming the passions of their antagonists.

It seems to me that this country will be fortunate indeed if it escapes a revolution no worse than that which is threatening it from the propagandists of the Socialist doctrine.

ADDENDA

[May 18, 1911]

Since writing the above it has occurred to my mind that some considerable portion of the public, even among the insurgents, might condemn the author (whoever he is) of the Los Angeles *Times* building explosion for having aimed his blow in such a way as to destroy the lives of innocent workingmen at the same time that it destroyed only the property of the enemy of union labor.

Such critics might complain at the clumsiness or the carelessness or the heartlessness of the deed that left the person of the enemy unscathed while it worked such execution among his innocent servants.

One might well raise the question (having adopted the ethics of warfare, on which are founded belligerent rights) as to which party — the owner of the Los Angeles *Times* or his servants who suffered death — was most guilty in its conduct toward the party of revolution.

[Harrison Gray] Otis, the owner of the *Times*, at least based his whole conduct upon a principle, the morals of which principle may be considered by one party as good and by another bad. Still he was contending for a principle and all his actions were direct expressions of his conviction of principles. It is quite probable that Otis has been as willing to risk his life, liberty, and happiness in his fight for principle as his antagonists have been.

On the other hand, the victims of the explosion were themselves members of the working class and had voluntarily enlisted to serve Otis for pay in his warfare against all their fellow workingmen. For practical purposes the presumption must be that these servants of Otis were traitors to their kind and received pay for their treachery.

In warfare it has always been recognized that the renegade in case of capture was entitled to harsher punishment than that due the ordinary antagonist.

But warfare has to be practical. The leaders of the army of the insurrection must, in order to be successful, strike the most effective blows and must have an eye single to win the cause and must exclude from all consideration feelings of personal vindictiveness.

In the present warfare of classes the enemies of labor are so few in number that they would be perfectly incapable of alone prosecuting warfare, offensive or defensive. Their only chance of success lies in suborning, corrupting, and making selfish use of individuals from the opposing camp. In order to discourage desertions from the labor army to become the hired soldiers of the capitalist army the generals of the labor army must resort to every possible means. Once let it be known that it was the intention of the labor army to spare the lives and persons of the capitalists in every case, and on the other hand to visit condign punishment on all workingmen found serving the capitalist army, the capitalists would soon find it impossible to recruit soldiers.

Then, if McNamara did the deed and if his object was to win the battle for labor he perhaps could not have delivered a more effective blow than that which destroyed the lives of nineteen of Otis' servants, while sparing the life of Otis himself.

Monstrous Mother Nature

The time is out of joint: O cursed spite,
That ever I was born to set it right! [12]

Hamlet was a fool and I am a fool for thinking, each of us, that we had been
set such a task. But Hamlet was no more a fool than is every man and woman
now living and every man and woman who has lived for lo! these many milleniums.

Each and every one of us is constantly being made cognizant of conditions existing that are affecting adversely and disagreeably his own life and
the lives of everybody else around him. Then, too, we all think we see or
know of a way of remedying every one of these evil conditions.

Here is a poor man and his family, suffering from poverty and disease. We
feel sure that if somebody and everybody has done his or their duty, the
man would not be poor, there would be no disease in his family, and they
would not suffer.

All around us young children are dying like flies from preventable disease
and accident.

Not less than 10 per cent, probably 20 per cent and possibly 30 per cent,
of the energy and productivity of the working people in this country and
every other country is lost utterly on account of petty physical ills that might
be prevented if the sufferers knew what can easily be learned in the matter
of protecting their health — acting each one singly to guard himself from
disease or collectively, as society, in protecting the whole mass of the population from epidemics.

For instance, I have always been peculiarly susceptible to "taking cold."
I am no less susceptible now. For years I suffered the loss of from a quarter
to a half of my time every year and a vast amount of discomfort by reason of
acute colds, followed by long periods of bronchitis.

[12] *Hamlet*, Act I, Scene 5.

Something like twenty years ago I began to act on the knowledge I had gained from experience and instruction. I took care to protect myself by proper clothing and bathing and avoiding, as far as possible, contact with others who, having colds, might infect me. Notwithstanding all the care I took and although I greatly reduced the number and duration of the attacks of colds, I too frequently suffered from colds contracted by associating or mixing in crowds with others who did not know that colds were infectious and who, even if they had known such a thing, were careless of the welfare of myself and others.

Colds affect different people very differently. A large number of people, perhaps the great majority, are so constituted that an attack of cold is of very little inconvenience to them. Such people, for one, two, three, or four days, will have what is called a slight cold, which interferes very little with them and which seldom, if ever, causes them to be seriously ill. Suffering so little themselves, they cannot conceive that others should suffer more. Nothing is more common than for a man to laugh at and treat scornfully anyone of his fellows who attempts to protect himself. He is entirely unaware of the fact that a disease germ, which may come from a person who is slightly affected, can enter another host who is so constituted as to suffer extremely from its presence — perhaps even suffer death.

It is now nearly two and a half years since I have had a cold. During these two and a half years I have been able to protect myself from exposure to a large degree. Because of what I have learned, I have also been able, by the use of antiseptics, to kill the infecting germs soon after coming into contact with me and before they had entered fully into the mucous membranes.

During a period of seven years I have not had more than four or five colds. Nor have any of these colds been severe or even long enduring. This has been because, as soon as I discovered my condition, I have gone to bed — sometimes taking medicine — and remained there three or four days, and for at least one or two days after all symptoms of the cold had left me.

It is possible that during the past six or seven years I have thus devoted as much as two weeks' time to curing colds contracted. I doubt if there are more than four or five men in a thousand who have not lost more time as a result of cold-sickness during these six or seven years than I have, although I am far more susceptible to the disease than the average man. Had I not taken the precautions I have taken, both to avoid colds and to cure them, I would certainly have lost, while I was in a condition of severe illness, more than twenty times as much as I have lost. Should everyone take the same precautions I have been taking, not only to avoid taking colds but to avoid giving them to others, the sum total of all the time and energy lost as a result of colds in the community at large would certainly not be 10 per cent of what is lost at present. I think it is altogether possible that the disease might be thoroughly stamped out in the whole nation.

There is no doubt that consumption is an infectious disease and that it can be entirely stamped out.

Smallpox is a rare disease in any civilized community today.

Scarlet fever and diphtheria and many other diseases have been dealt with in such a way that the mortality on account of these diseases is small indeed compared with what it would be were it not for the preventive measures generally adopted.

Syphilis and gonorrhea are working havoc in even the most civilized nations and yet it is a peculiarity of these two diseases that it is not only possible but easy to guard against them. Activity on the part of the government and a very little knowledge and care on the part of individuals might very quickly eliminate these diseases from and keep them out of every civilized country.

Ignorance on the part of any adult individual in a civilized nation is inexcusable. A thoroughgoing administration of the machinery and funds devoted to education in the United States would result in completely obliterating what is called illiteracy in this country, at least in the case of all males and females who are not congenitally mentally or physically so defective as to warrant their being charges of the state and confined in institutions.

But ignorance and illiteracy are not synonymous terms by any means. The vast majority of the people of this or any other nation are lamentably ignorant, notwithstanding that comparatively few of our people are illiterate. They are not only ignorant but misinformed concerning most of the things which would be of value to themselves and society.

For instance, how few of the individuals of the great majority of our people who are workingmen and women have learned that their wages are, after all, only a share in the sum total of all production and that, therefore, the share that can be allotted to them, even by the most just of employers, the most capable managers amongst their employers, and the most just and equitable laws, must be limited by the amount produced by the workingman and woman themselves.

While it is true that the relation between the capitalist, so called, on one hand and the wage- or salary-workers on the other is at present monstrously inequitable, it is also a fact that 80 cents out of every dollars worth of production goes to the wage- and salary-workers and 20 cents to the capitalist. This being the case, even if all of the income of the capitalists was diverted to the workers, the latter *en masse* could only have their incomes increased by 25 per cent. Some — a small percentage of the employing class — get more than 20 per cent of the total product; some 30 per cent; some 50 per cent;

some 80 per cent perhaps. But by far the larger proportion of the whole employing class get less than 20 per cent of the total product. Many more than half of the employers in the United States receive as net incomes from their businesses not more than they could obtain as wage- or salary-workers.

Neither in our schools nor in our press — the two great educators of the public — are children and men and women taught this most important lesson, namely, that the wage fund is one that must be produced by work.

In England, where, prior to six years ago, the average wages of mechanics, miners, railway men, all sorts of factory-workers, farm-laborers, sailors, and fishermen were not more than six dollars a week, such was the condition of business that twenty-five cents a day could not have been added to the average wage or salary scale without wiping out the whole of the profits of capital and management.

In those days the average income of the workingman of England was less than one-half the average wages of the workingman in the United States. But the per capita product of an American workman, on the average, was at least two and one-half times as much as the per capita product of an English workman. There have been various reasons given for the greater productivity of the American workman. Chief among these is the greater use of labor-saving machinery in the United States than in England. The engine horsepower per capita in America was three times greater than that employed in England.

How few of the workingmen in America have any idea of how much they owe to mechanical contrivances, which permit employers to get along with from one-half to one-third the number of hands that the English employer has to use. Even in this country, as I know by my own experience in introducing labor-saving machinery, many intelligent workingmen regard with disfavor labor-saving machinery.

Another reason that is given is that our American workmen, getting better wages, are better fed and housed, and, on that account, are more fit physically and mentally to do good work.

A third reason given is that the American on the average is better educated than the Englishman, and hence, on account of his greater intelligence, is more productive.

All of these things and many more should be taught, or better taught, by our educators in the schools and in the public press.

The vast majority of our people are ignorant and are kept in ignorance on another subject that I myself consider the most important of all subjects. This subject might be called independence or self-reliance. The great mass of children are taught, in the family, in the schools, and in the press, directly or by inference, that wage-earning or salary-earning is, in the main, not only to be the common lot of the people as a whole, but a most desirable lot.

They are taught servitude and obedience. They are taught to submit to discipline. They are taught to be dependent and not independent. Why, they are even taught that their dependence is independence. They are taught the dignity of labor — not the dignity of labor for oneself, but the dignity of labor for a master. They are taught that a capacity to earn wages or a salary will enable them to be independent. Independent of what? Of whom? They are taught that a man who obtains a wage, for which he is dependent on some employer, is independent, because he can pay his house rent and pay for food and clothing and fuel and some other things.

A great majority — an overwhelming majority — of our people have been taught as children, and are being taught as men and women, that some other man can manage them and direct their work better than they can manage themselves and direct their own work.

They are kept in ignorance of the fact that, everything else being equal — intelligence included — a man working for himself can enjoy the whole of the fruits of his labor and not have to part with a large fraction of it to his master or employer. They are kept in ignorance of the fact that their own natural disposition would prompt them to produce 50 per cent or 100 per cent or 300 per cent more if they were working for themselves and enjoying all the fruits of their own labor, because their experience in the way of loss and gain, according to how they performed their labor, would teach them greater and greater capacity for production.

They are taught the most outrageous fallacy that "money makes money," and they are kept in entire ignorance of the fact that men, and only men, make money or anything else that is desired.

They are taught that the mere possession of capital is an advantage, without regard to the fact that money can only be advantageously used by the man who makes the money.

They are taught that capital — original capital in hand — is a necessity for the beginning of any independent enterprise. They are never taught the truth, namely, that nearly every great fortune, as well as nearly every small fortune, started with nothing but the labor and the brain and muscle of the maker of the fortune.

They are kept in ignorance of the fact that ninety-nine young men out of every hundred who start life with a fortune grow poorer and poorer more or less rapidly as they continue to live, and that only a very small proportion of the men who have grown rich and are growing richer had anything else to start with than their physical strength and the intelligence they acquired in their extreme youth.

Is it possible for all men to become wealthy? No.

Is it necessary for any man to be poor who started life with a healthy body and a sane mind and who has encountered no accident to his health or otherwise? No again.

Would it be possible for any man in this country to become very rich if all men worked for themselves, either in some infinitely small personal enterprise or collectively on a large enterprise? No again.

Considering human nature to be what it is supposed to be, would it be possible for there to exist any great enterprise, such as a railroad system, a great ship, a large and hence economically managed factory or mine, which would be owned by the workingman, from laborer to chief executive, in proportion to the ability and productivity of each worker? I think not.

Are such great enterprises absolutely necessary? I think not.

Would the sum total or the average of happiness in the country be greater in the proportion that each man was his own employer? I think so.

Could the population of a given territory be as great under this latter condition as under the existing system? I think not. But, on the other hand, I think the population of the United States might be and would be, in the course of a few generations, several times greater than it is at present, and that the average happiness of all the people living in this country would be greater and the sum total of misery and discomfort of all the unfortunate far less.

What is the use of large aggregates of population? In the case of warfare, the larger the population, the more soldiers there will be to fight.

Under present conditions, the larger the population of a country, the larger will be the number of possible employees of any employer and the greater will be the number of consumers — the people who will buy at a profit the goods produced for a great employer by a great number of employees.

The larger the population of a given city, the larger the rents that can be exacted by the men who own land favorably situated in the city.

But are the workingmen and salaried men in large cities really getting larger incomes than the workingmen and salaried men in small cities, towns, villages, and hamlets?

Is the average enjoyment of the citizens of a big city greater than the average enjoyment of the citizens of a small city? Is the percentage of sufferers in big city less than that in a small city?

The average incomes of the people in a large city are smaller than those of the people in a small city.

The average incomes, all things considered, of the people who do not live in either cities or towns, but in the country in farming sections, are greater than those of the people who live in any kind of cities or towns.

Do the schools and press of our cities teach the children and people these truths? No. All of the children and people of a city are taught that it is a good thing for them and for their city that its population should increase.

Europe is crowded. Europe is so full of people that the lands are not sufficient to produce the food needed by the inhabitants of Europe. The average incomes of the people of the United States, Canada, Australia, and South Africa — the people of European descent — are 100 per cent greater than the average incomes in England, 120 per cent greater than the average income in Germany before the war, perhaps 130 per cent greater than the average incomes of the people of France before the war, and more than 150 per cent greater than the average incomes of the people of Italy. Similar conditions as to the relations between America on one side and other highly civilized parts of Europe on the other in the matter of the average incomes of the people exist. Europe is overcrowded. Other large sections of the earth's surface are comparatively extremely underpopulated.

On the average, the immigrant from Europe is enormously benefited, economically, by his emigration. Yet the nations of Europe — or the governments of those nations — keep their people in such ignorance, or rather so thoroughly misinform them, that they are unaware of their misfortunes.

War is horrible and unnecessary, apparently. Plagues can be prevented. The ravages of disease are from four to ten times greater than are necessary, that is to say, ordinary preventive measures could by this much reduce sickness and mortality.

The social evil — controllable or preventable sexual disease — destroys many lives and prevents the coming into existence of many more human beings.

Peace is possible; famine unnecessary; disease reducible; individual wealth and comfort can be increased enormously — my friend Professor [W. E.] Ritter would say infinitely.

But then what? No wars, no plagues, little disease, no famine, no poverty; every healthy man and woman marrying and bearing children —

Let us have all these blessings and let us enjoy them — but for how long? Perhaps at the end of a single generation, certainly at the end of two generations, the world would be so full of people that it would not be large enough to furnish them food.

With no birth control and no great mortality on account of war, famine, and disease, and with all healthy men and women paired off in marriage, the population of the world would double, at least, every ten years.

Then, ten years hence there would be on the earth 3,200 billion people. Twenty years hence there would be 6,400 billion. Thirty years hence, at the end of one generation, there would be 12,800 billion.

Oh, in truth the world is out of joint.

But what is the use of being a reformer?

An Unutopian Utopia

[*April, 1919*]

Scripps continued to toy with some of the ideas expressed here until the last year of his life, but he said he would not want his wife, sister, or daughter to read this disquisition.

I have recently tried my hand as an apologist for bolshevism [in a disquisition not included among these selections]. I have also made an attempt to indict Mother Nature. Anyone reading these essays would be driven to conclude that I am very much discontented with things in general and everything in particular connected with conditions surrounding and governing men and society.

It is easy to criticize, but there are people foolish enough to think that a critic who blames the work of others ought to be able to do better work himself, if he only had the opportunity.

Now, I intend hereinafter to set down suggestions that might be made in the way of improvement, if one had the power to make changes in the existing order of things. I will not attempt to classify or group my suggestions, or arrange them even in the order of their significance — presumably their importance.

PROPAGATION OF THE SPECIES

The first thing that presents itself to my mind is that Nature is too prolific in the way of producing human beings. She causes so many of these to be produced that she is unable to make more than a very small proportion of the whole number even tolerably comfortable.

It is recognized that it is entirely impossible to depend upon individuals to correct the work of Nature and restrain her exuberance in the matter of producing too many human children.

Every orchardist knows that Nature cannot be left alone in the matter of producing tree fruits. Take, for instance, an orange tree. She consumes too much of the food that she furnishes the tree in making trunks and branches and twigs, the usefulness of which for man consists only in bearing fruit.

She is so wasteful in this respect that far too large a proportion of her effort is given to making wood and leaves, so there is left very little stuff to put into the fruit itself. The amount of orange material that can be produced from an orange tree developed by Nature with a free hand, and uninterfered with by man, is comparatively very small.

In the second place, when Nature has produced her tree, she tries to produce too many individual oranges — more individual fruits, in fact, than the sap of the tree will feed. The result of this is that probably 90 per cent of all the oranges that start to grow perish for lack of nurture at various times, beginning with the very infancy of the fruit, all the way along up to the time of its maturity. Further, she is so persistent in her efforts to produce fruit that she clings, right up to the last, to too many of them, so that none of them have sufficient nurture to develop more than half or perhaps not more than one-quarter of their potential size.

From almost the instant the young orange tree starts its growth, the orchardist has to begin to contend with and against Nature. He must prune and cut away many suckers and branches of the young tree. He must persist in this course during the whole growth of the tree to its fruit-bearing maturity, and thereafter, during the whole of the tree's life, always he must be cutting and pruning away many limbs and twigs. Then, too, as soon as the tree begins bearing fruit, he must be careful to resort to infanticide in plucking off or killing a larger number of the young oranges, leaving only such a number on the tree as he knows the tree will be able, through its sap, to properly nourish, so that the fruit that is left can grow to its full size, or at least to a useful size.

Now, suppose that we deal with mankind as a whole as the orchardist deals with the orange tree. Instead of letting every human infant born grow to a stunted maturity, crowding the earth's surface to an undesirable extent, suppose we begin right at the start and destroy in infancy the life of every babe that, for any reason at all, we suspect is incapable of developing into a perfectly sound and useful individual.

If all the fit males and females of the species — those that we could be almost certain, even in the period of infancy, were potentially capable of the best development — were allowed to grow to maturity and therefore to breed, the whole world would be overcrowded in the course of a generation or two. Therefore, we should destroy not only all of the certainly unfit and all of the possibly unfit, but by far the greater proportion even of those who are perfectly fit.

There are two ways of preventing redundancy in the production of children. One is infanticide; the other is that process called birth control (the use of contraceptional [*sic*] methods). The latter method, of course, is not only more humane but less wasteful. An enormous amount of time and expense, physical discomfort, and, finally, excruciating pain, accompany every childbirth. It would be absurd, then, to permit children to be born only to destroy them at their birth.

Then, too, the parental instinct (the instinct of the propagation of the species) is only a little less compelling than the instinct of procreation. No mother would fail to suffer terribly by reason of her child's death, even on the day of its birth. Few fathers could submit to this ordeal with equanimity. On the other hand, it is known that neither man nor woman suffer any mental anguish at all on account of the destruction of sperm or ovum while still in the cell state.

Therefore, it should be society's rule that no adult persons who, for any reason, are suspected of being unable to be parents of sound and healthy offspring should be allowed to be parents. There are methods of sterilizing both men and women so they cannot become parents, and of doing this in such a way as not to deny them any of the instincts or pleasures of sex intercourse.

Society should first make a selection of all men and women who are presumably perfectly fit for parenthood and, further, make a classification of these candidates for parenthood according to their qualities and characteristics, so that only a sufficient number of men and women of each group of qualifications should be produced to fill the needs, or the approximate needs, of a given society.

If in any one class or group of these individuals there were too many adults, the number of children allowed to be born to these parents should, according to needs, be limited. If in another group the number of adult candidates for parenthood was comparatively too small, then such parents should be induced to increase the number of their offspring.

Now, it is a generally accepted fact among physiologists that the firstborn, and possibly the secondborn, child of every mother is, as compared with later-born children, inferior, physically and mentally. (Dr. [Charles S.] Minot stated, in an extensive work on this subject, that it appeared, even in the matter of birth, that practice makes perfect, and that the physical woman in some way seemed to learn, by practice in having children, how to have the best ones.) So, as it appears that, under present circumstances, there must be a redundancy of children born, the first, and possibly even the second, child born of a woman should be destroyed at birth.

When there are so many to be selected from and so few needed, there would really be no risk taken by society if all the first- and secondborn children of mothers were eliminated. There would be still far more than enough human beings left after the most excessive culling.

But after birth, in infancy and even in very young childhood, there is room for innumerable accidents which may so cripple a child, physically or mentally, as to make him of doubtful usefulness in the future. Perhaps up to the age of ten or maybe twelve years, children are so incapable of thinking or so little inclined to think, and hence be[ing] possessed of fear and dread, that any child could have its life ended without suffering itself. So there would be no cruelty to the child itself in having its life snuffed out. The parents, however, would suffer excruciatingly, and human suffering is the main thing to be guarded against. Therefore, only such children as were badly crippled should be eliminated — those whose sufferings even parents of ordinary intelligence would recognize would be greater if they lived than they (the parents) would suffer from the child's death. We all know of the thousands and hundreds of thousands of lives spent miserably by individuals whose sufferings might have been avoided had it not been for existing laws and customs and unintelligent parental affection.

SEX PROBLEM

Chastity is a sin against the laws of Nature and, in the case at least of all males, there are heavy penalties to be paid by sinners. Now, right here becomes apparent one of monstrous Mother Nature's most malignant activities.

The male amongst men, when the individual is most sane, most healthy, and not at all corrupted, begins to feel the promptings of instinct many years before he is capable of being the parent of sound offspring. In the new order of society, where all sex matters would be controlled for the benefit of society as a whole, and where it should be necessary to prevent, rather than encourage, the production of too many children, the age of parenthood, both for women and men, might be set at a later date than is now considered moral, legal, or expedient. Perhaps it would be decided that no man should be a father or take the first steps toward fatherhood until after he is twenty-four years of age. Here, then, is a period of ten years between the age of puberty — the time of the prompting of instinct — and the age when this instinct should be permitted to result in parenthood.

During this period of time, the young male is prompted and, I imagine in the vast majority of cases, is compelled, to resort to practices that have the effect of causing him to suffer continually from self-mortification and shame, or to resort to intercourse with females, the vast majority of whom are diseased in such a way as to infect and frequently permanently injure their male companions.

Society would then be bound, for humanitarian reasons, to take some course to protect not only the physical bodies of its young males, but their moral and spiritual characters. Some form of hetaer[ism] should be adopted for the benefit of these young men.

There now exist in some primitive societies in the Southern Hemisphere and probably in the East certain sexual practices. The young men are not allowed to marry until they arrive at a certain age. All the young girls and widows, I believe, are permitted to have free intercourse with these young men for a certain period of time (perhaps children born to them suffer infanticide), until the young men are old enough to choose wives. Amongst these people monogamy is the custom, too. When the young men arrive at marriageable age, they select their wives, of course, from among these girls, and thereafter their wives lead, presumably, perfectly chaste lives, bearing children for their husbands.

Chastity is not a natural virtue. It may be considered a natural sin. The growth of the ideas of monogamy, marriage, and individual families has been much treated of by sociologists. It is generally supposed that in the earliest form of society there was promiscuity and complete incontinency. Later still was supposed to have come the system of community wives — a condition when all the women of any tribe or community were common to all the men of that same community. It was only later that the first form of exogamy seems to have appeared, when the women of one community became the wives of the men of another community. It is said that it was only after the idea of personal property developed in man's mind that polygamy, and next monogamy, came into vogue. At this time man began to consider woman as property and he resented other men making use of his property. Later still, under the stimulus perhaps of religion, came the idea of female purity as being a virtue and a valuable attribute of a woman in the eyes of the man who desired her as property.

From such crude beginnings, it is argued, have arisen the traditions and customs not only of monogamy and polygamy but of chastity, first of unmarried and later of married women.

Now, our proposed new and greatly more humane society would, of course, be bound to secure as much happiness — that is to say, pleasure — to all of its constituents as possible. Boys and girls and young women and young men, before the age of parenthood had set in, might be permitted entire freedom in every respect, excepting that precautions in the way of contraceptional [sic] practices should secure society against the birth of children from too-young parents.

Another, and perhaps, for reasons of our peculiar customs and traditions, better method might be adopted. A certain and sufficient number of young women might be set aside, on account of physical or intellectual blemishes or on account of there not being so many mothers needed, as hetaera[e]. They could be sterilized so as not to be capable of bearing children, and could be permitted the liberties of polyandry if they so chose. It might be that women of any age might elect to lead a certain kind of life. Widows in particular would be candidates for this body.

It might well be that custom would become such that these women would not suffer at all from the stigma of social inferiority. Their position in life and society should be in every way as respectable as that of the child-bearing women.

Women of this group could not only save from suffering every young man, but permit widowers who did not elect to marry again and men who had wives incapacitated for any reason to perform all the marital functions to live normal lives, comfortably and respectably.

There could be developments and refinements to the above-mentioned various methods and practices, such as would eliminate entirely from society by far the major portion of all the immorality, so called, of existing society.

At present the laws and customs and religions are united in a vain effort to enforce, as a moral law, a course of action that is not only diametrically opposed to Nature's law but is actually impossible, considering not individuals but society as a whole.

Before leaving this subject I wish to have it regarded from a purely scientific, biological view.

A rule of Nature is, Use or lose. A child or a man or a woman who does not thoroughly exercise his or her body inevitably must lose muscular strength — must lose, in fact, a large amount of muscle (or perhaps never develop it).

The organs of the body that are not used must of necessity atrophy, either wholly or partly.

Only that boy grows into perfect physical manhood who thoroughly (but not excessively) exercises his body.

It is well known by physiologists that the procreative organs of men and women may be, and frequently are, greatly atrophied by non-use. This is perhaps the main reason why there are many childless men and women. Statistics that have been gathered show that college graduates, male and female, in this country, have so few children that they fall far short of even reproducing themselves numerically. The number of children born to college-graduate women is, as a rule, considerably less than the number born to the average woman.

I have been told that in the schools where young boys are being educated for the Roman Catholic priesthood, it is a custom to take such a course with the boys — to deal with them in such a way — that every part of their bodies and minds is developed to the greatest degree possible at the expense of their genital organs. Boys are kept with boys; the greatest precaution is taken against what is called the solitary vice. Their diet, their physical exercise, and their mental employment are all, so far as possible, so regulated as not only to prevent bad practices but to prevent all sorts of suggestion — everything, in fact, which might permit sexual development. I have been told that it is entirely possible, by these means alone, to eunuchize a boy.

On the other hand, physiologists tell us that young girls, kept entirely segregated, not only from boys but from adult men, in school and out of school, as much as possible, are generally from two to three years late in the development of their secondary sexual parts, particularly the breasts, and that with them the period of menstruation begins a year or two years later than it does on the average with girls living an ordinary life.

The idea of the new society would certainly be to compose itself of the soundest and the healthiest and the mentally most sane and balanced members. Motherhood, then, would be, above any other thing, sure to receive very great attention. Girls would not only be mentally but physically trained and developed, above everything else, for this function.

I cannot say (and scientific men who have devoted themselves to the study of sex pathology acknowledge that they are not sufficiently informed to say) whether or not the control of sex instinct in women has the same effect as it does in men. There is a perfectly good reason for this. Society as it is has developed certain institutions of taboo and command. Society insists upon not only physical chastity in unmarried women, but so-called purity of mind on the part of all females, especially while they are children and unmarried girls. This being the case, every girl and woman is bound to protect her good name by declaring, by acts and words, her innocence and even her ignorance concerning the sex feeling. Even if any girl had as strong animal propensities as those of a boy, and if continence caused her as great suffering as it would cause a boy, she is bound by taboo to conceal these facts from everyone, even her mother, sisters, or her most intimate friend. On the other hand, there is no such strict taboo in the case of males. Social taboo imposes no such penalty on the unchastity of men as upon that of women.

Men are more outspoken with each other on sex subjects than are women, and far less restrained in their attitude on this subject in dealing with boys than are women in dealing with girls. As men set the example, boys follow it. Boys are more frank with each other, probably, than are girls, Most fathers and older male relatives or friends of boys advise them frequently and explicitly. Mothers and older female relatives and friends are so governed by social habit as to be more reticent in dealing with younger females. Perhaps there are few men who do not, sooner or later, tell their wives more or less of their youthful experiences, knowing full well that their wives will not be surprised at all or shocked very much. Imagine, if you can, a young wife being equally frank with her husband concerning such matters, even in a case where she had had much experience.

In fact, it is taken for granted, almost, by all men and women that young men have been unchaste, while the presumption that every young wife comes to her husband not only physically but mentally pure is equally taken as a matter of course. Every old physician of much practice, many schoolteachers, governesses, and especially those who have had much experience in so-called "social work" know that a very large percentage of young girls acquire much sexual experience before marriage. A very eminent and distinguished man who for a number of years held the position of judge in a juvenile court once told me that, by reason of his having to deal with boy delinquents in a certain large midwestern city, he had learned from these boys that far more than half of the girls in the high schools of his city were codelinquents with the boys. He stated that personal inquiries he had made of officials and others in large cities indicated that the condition of affairs in his own city was not at all unusual. One man whom this judge considered well qualified to speak on account of his information had told him he was convinced that fully 90 per cent of the young women who were or had been patrons of the public and private schools of his city had ceased to be virgins before the marriageable age.

Some years ago I read in a respectable publication — a magazine — a statement of a very eminent physician to the effect that when there was a case of seduction among boys and girls, the seducer was generally the girl and not the boy. He accounted for this, giving a physiological reason. Girls generally become sexually mature at an age two or three years younger than do boys; the girl's instinctive craving comes sooner than that of her boy companions, who are naturally approximately her own age, and hence, as between the boy and the girl, she would be the teacher of the boy.

Mere protests of horror on the part of people generally are no disproof of conditions as stated by the above witnesses.

I know myself that many men have told me that their first experiences of a certain sort were the result of the teaching of some young person of the other sex.

Most men who have had experience have learned that adult women are at least as passionate as adult men and perhaps more so. Everyone who knows anything about such matters knows that prostitutes can accommodate and give satisfaction to many more men than can any man have dealings with women.

I think it is fair, then, to presume that the sex instinct of girls and women is no less strong than that of men and that, therefore, restraint on the part of females costs as much suffering as does restraint on the part of men.

I think we have every reason to believe, too, that mentally, morally, spiritually, and physically, girls and women are as much demoralized as are men by all of the sex taboos.

Boys and girls, young men and young women, widows and widowers, and particularly adult unmarried women, must all suffer, either physically in some form or other or spiritually, on account of the social necessity of concealment without hypocrisy and of each individual's feeling that he or she is unworthy because the law of Nature cannot always, or perhaps even generally, be defied.

But the suffering of the young on this account must be far greater than that of older persons, who have reconciled their consciences or more fully developed reasoning capacities.

I remember reading, within the past year or two, a book called, I think, *Defense of Aristocracy*.[13] It was written by an Englishman, although he had an Italian name — Ludovici. He contended in favor of the domination of the aristocratic class. It is not worthwhile here to give all of his arguments. But this author particularly dwelt upon the great difference, mental, moral and physical, between the flourishing, well-nurtured classes in England and the common herd. He particularly dwelt upon the almost universal ugliness of face and feature, the unshapeliness of body, and the uncouth mentality of the crowds to be seen on the streets of London or any other great city.

Doubtless all of us in the flourishing, well-nurtured class have made similar observations. I imagine that, to a large extent at least, the mass of the common people — the crowd — have been as much affected disadvantageously by the lack of regular and natural sexual functioning as by the lack of food and mental culture.

Among other advantages enjoyed by people of something more than sufficient means of livelihood are the opportunities of sex functioning, at least somewhere near the extent that Nature requires.

It is known that we have the double code of morals. Society does not require the same morals of men as of women.

I recall that a few years ago I was on a much-frequented avenue in an eastern city. I had an idle afternoon. I was past my sixtieth year and hence cannot be too much suspected of a certain motive. I began to notice the crowd of pedestrians and occupants of automobiles. As for a number of years I had been almost a recluse, seldom going to public places, never attending a theatre or church, lecture or concert, I had not kept pace with the development and extravagances of fashion. My attention was first called to the female apparel; the fashion of the clothes of the women was startling

[13] Anthony Mario Ludovici, *Defence of Aristocracy*. Constable, London, 1915.

to me. I could almost fancy that I was beholding a carnival where all the women were dressed as for a fancy dress show. To me it appeared that the dresses were very ugly. Then I began to take note of the faces and figures of the women — so much of the figure as the clothes would permit me to see or imagine. The costumes of the women were such as to almost universally either conceal or distort their figures. However, the faces were in sight, the hands were in sight, and the gait of the walkers furnished some indication of their physical strength and, hence, symmetry. I determined to make a count of the really pretty women I should meet — women who appeared pretty notwithstanding their outrageous garments — and compare the number of these pretty women with that of the whole mass. I soon discovered that there were practically no pretty women walking on the street. Fleeting views of passing automobiles did reveal the faces of some women whom I thought might be beautiful. But in a period of perhaps half an hour I did not see one really beautiful woman.

I next determined to take a count of those women who were not, to my peculiar taste, positively ugly. I can say that it appeared to me that there was not one woman in a hundred that passed me amongst the pedestrians who did not appear somewhat repulsive to me.

Finally I determined to take a count of men. I set up a model in my mind for comparison's sake. I required a certain degree of tallness, not much below six feet; a full form, not fat and not too slender; regularity of facial features; a walking gait indicating physical development; intelligent-looking eyes.

With this standard in my mind I took note of the men. Amongst the thousands of men who passed me I saw some scores of men up to the standard — men whose female complements should have been women of beauty of feature, of figure, and of spiritual expression. While there were scores of handsome men on the street, there were no beautiful women.

Lowering my scale, I took a count of men who, being not handsome, were passably of good appearance in stature, figure, face and facial expression, and gait — men whose female complements would be women who were not bad to look at. Perhaps one-third of the men that I observed came up to the new standard. There were at least ten men of this class to one female complement.

How much of all of this difference was due to the comparative immorality of the men?

There is a phrase used frequently by the French — *beauté d' diable* [sic]. This term is applied in description of young girls of perhaps from fifteen to eighteen years of age. We all know that if ever in her life a woman is granted the compliment of beauty, it is generally at some point in her career between her fifteenth and twentieth years.

Why are the great majority of women better looking or less ugly at this age? Is it not possible (I think it is probable) that at this age the destructive effects of sex restraint or sex excess are not so apparent?

Rabelais, in one part of the history of his hero, recounts a conference held by him and several friends, among them a physician. The young man is considering the question of marriage. There is much discussion, pro and con, as to the advisability of marriage. On the whole, the young man is inclined to avoid the risks and dangers of conjugal life. However, he complains of the persistence and the uncontrollableness of his passions. He seems to think that he would be well off if he could be entirely free from them. He appeals to the physician for advice as to some method of freeing himself from his natural tendencies. The physician tells him that he only knows of three ways of getting relief: First, he suggests castration, but the youngster will not consider this for a moment. Next, the physician tells him that if he can keep himself constantly drunk with wine, he will be impotent. There is something attractive in this idea, but it is not wholly satisfactory. Lastly, the physician advises him that he can get the better of his tendencies by frequent submissions to them. If fact, if he should go to a woman every time he had a disposition that way, he would at least have a temporary respite, and would not suffer the pains of incontinence. This plan is enthusiastically accepted by the youth, being entirely agreeable to him.

In fact, Hobson's choice was made. There is only one way to escape from suffering. Suppressed passion is, of all things, the most painful of all pains endured, and the cause, perhaps, of more human suffering than any other one thing.

Healthy and vigorous men and women, thoroughly effective and fit to enjoy life, and enjoying life most completely — the men and women, in fact, of the society that I would have in existence — are those men and women, and only those, who function sexually freely, but never excessively.

There is a sanity and equilibrium, mental and physical, in such men and women which enable them to enter into and accomplish all their life's works with utmost satisfaction, so that, being living beings, mere living is a joy in itself. It is probable, as I have intimated before, that most of the wretchedness and misery and suffering of society, individually and collectively, is the result of Nature's law: a demand greater than the supply permitted by society and, in fact, permitted by Nature herself, since if the supply is fully sufficient to meet the demand, then overpopulation and other forms of suffering and death itself are inevitable. This new society would and should avoid the pain and suffering of overpopulation by the various means set forth above.

If these pages ever fall under the eye of readers, only those of either sex will criticize the writer for dwelling at such length upon a subject that all men and women pretend to believe (and really do not believe) to be the dominating element in the lives of all healthy normal men and women, who are not themselves healthy and normal men and women.

EDUCATION

The next most important problem that will have been solved with this new society will probably be that of the education of the minds and bodies of the youth. Then education will be education, and will become something entirely different from training. Education will be the drawing out of, and the development to the largest possible extent of, both the minds and bodies of infants, children, and youths.

Training will be considered as a thing apart from, though certainly concurrent with, education. The young will be trained — that is to say, each child will have impressed upon him habits suitable to his probable future activities in life. Then will have ceased the present absurd and wasteful practice of trying to stop round holes with square plugs; of trying to make all plugs on one pattern, while the shapes of the holes to be stopped are of a great variety and number.

From the earliest infancy of the children, psychologists and physiologists will inspect and test, at frequent intervals, the peculiar mentality and physiology of each individual, in order to discover the peculiar excellencies and deficiencies, mental and physical, of each subject with regard to any and all life vocations. In this way it will be discovered in what vocation each child would be most effective on becoming an adult, and both the education and training, mental and physical, of each and every child will be planned and regulated so as to make him or her the most perfect possible workingman or woman in his or her to-be station in life.

ECONOMIC SYSTEMS

What should be the economic system in the new society? It certainly should not be struggling competition of a life and death character between individuals. On the other hand, there should be no suppression of the spirit of emulation and ambition.

There might and probably would be a fairly equitable distribution of the necessary things and the good things and the things of luxury amongst all the people.

Whereas at present those who perform the hardest toil and do the most disagreeable work are those whose wages are the least — whose per capita share of the total product of society is the smallest — in the new society there would be a reverse order. The wages, or the proportion of the whole product of society, received by each member would be greater and greater in proportion to the hardness and the disagreeableness of the task performed.

In the new society every man's and every woman's individuality would be respected — their rights as well as their duties. The independence and freedom of action, bodily and mentally, of any individual would be no greater than those of another.

There would be no such thing, and could be no such thing, as what is called socialism. Instead of giving to each, according to his needs, and taking from all according to their ability to give, each person should only have that share of all that is produced which his labor, mental and physical, entitled him to have.

There would be no abandonment of the principle and practice of individual ownership of property. But there would be a complete abandonment, both in law and practice, of the principle of inheritance and of the right to give what has not been earned or to take what has not been earned. There would be no necessity of statutory law governing these matters. Custom would make it as shameful to accept a gift as law and custom make it shameful for one to steal. Both parents and friends would be moved by their very affection not to impose benefits on their children or on their friends, since, by so doing, they would be doing acts harmful, and not beneficial, to those whom they loved most.

No, this idea is not an absurd one. We do not have to wait milleniums for a new reform society to find men and women who not only hold this idea, but who, to the greatest extent possible, practice it. Particularly let us notice the common practice of nearly all parents in requiring of their children, to a greater or less extent, some sort of *quid pro quo*. Children are rewarded for their goodness with some kind of munificence. Children are punished for their badness by having withheld from them something that would otherwise be given them — perhaps a loving smile, perhaps a dainty in the way of food, some toy, some treat in the way of a holiday.

Later, when the children, especially the boys, have grown older, they are encouraged or compelled to earn some money or some small object of property which they are allowed to keep as their own. Well-to-do or wealthy fathers of grown sons invariably attempt, more or less successfully, to induce their sons to be self-supporting — to enter into some business or profession through which, by their own unaided efforts, they shall accumulate property of their own. Rarely indeed do fathers give to their children any considerable amount of property, except by devise or bequest. Then, and then only, do they give away what they (the fathers) can no longer use. While I have known many fathers — most fathers, in fact — who desired to secure their widows and daughters a comfortable subsistence after they (the fathers and husbands) had died, I have known of but few wealthy men who did not regret the fact that their children were to inherit such large means as not only to make it unnecessary for them to be actually industrious, but to submit them to the great temptation and exposure of corrupting influences of all kinds. I can hardly believe that any wealthy and so-called successful father would not prefer that the laws and customs of inheritance should be different and that a son, or the husband of a daughter, should be compelled to succeed in winning for himself and his family a fortune incomparably smaller than what his inheritance was to be rather than that his children should owe their wealth to the receipt of an inheritance.

Personally, I will say that I have been, to some extent, successful and fortunate in this respect with regard to some of my children.

ECONOMIC PRODUCTION

In the new society there would be no advantage of any sort to anyone in the possession of unearned wealth, because customs and practices would be such that all could acquire, by their own individual labor, everything that would be needful to them.

I do not mean by this that under the present system — social, economic, and political — inequalities in the matter of wealth could be destroyed, or that the present distribution of capital, considering the system in existence, is altogether bad.

In the new society the idea would prevail that in the economic field as many as possible, perhaps a large majority, of the people would be independent workers. Farmers would own their own farms and work them; men skilled in mechanics and trades would have their own shops and produce and sell their own wares; doctors and engineers and all sorts of professional men would each be paid proportionately, according to his ability, and labor in his chosen calling.

There would be many industries, however, that could not be owned and operated by individuals or by partnerships. Among others would be transportation systems, such as our present railroads. These would require the labor, physical and mental, of many men and women and many kinds of men and women.

How could such an institution be successfully conducted by vast numbers of men working as parts of one organization, without there being vast differences in the value of services rendered, either as a result of the different positions held by different men, or the difference in the capacities of men, and without justice requiring that there should be corresponding differences in the compensation of the men carrying on the enterprise? It would be impossible and very undesirable.

And yet, a great railroad system, engaging the labors of tens of thousands of men, could and would be conducted in such a way as to give the best kind of public service and in such a way that every man working on the system would receive a fair and equitable share of the proceeds. This hypothetical railroad would be owned jointly by all the men working on or for it. The proceeds — the product of the railroad in the way of money or its equivalent — would be divided amongst all the employees, each one's share to be assessed, first, as nearly as possible according to the ability and industry shown by the workingman, and second, according to the laboriousness or disagreeableness or danger of the position held. Naturally, the most capable of all the men would be the chief executive. Naturally, his services would be many times the value of those of the average man working on the railway system. Naturally, also, the least capable men would be employed on tasks requiring the least capacity, mental or physical. Everything else, however, being equal, some deduction should be made from the share of the most capable men who held the most honorable positions, because the honorableness of the position is at least a part of the reward received. Everything else being equal, naturally something should be added to the compensation of those men whose work was the most toilsome and disagreeable or hazardous — something added so as to make the compensation for such work somewhat larger than would be their share of the total value of the work done by all the men on the railroad system.

By these means the whole company of men employed on the railroad would produce an aggregate income greater or smaller, according to the physical and mental effort made collectively, and hence the shares of all the persons so engaged would be greater or less according to the amount of the whole work done and according to the exercise of thrift and intelligence and polite behavior toward the public of all the railroad men. Under these conditions, each man employed on the railroad would feel and would know that the amount of his compensation would be fairly proportionate to the amount of physical and intellectual effort put forth by him and, in some cases also, according to his agreeable and polite behavior toward the customers and possible customers of his railroad.

This whole idea can easily enough be denounced as Utopian and impossible. It certainly can be denounced as thoroughly and absolutely impractical in any society that exists today — society made up of units many of whom are ignorant, many more of whom are congenitally lacking in intelligence, each of whom has been trained from infancy to regard the other as a contestant and competitor, even as an enemy. The bolshevists of Russia are trying to introduce an economic scheme among a people who, of all Europeans in the Old World or the New World, are the least prepared to understand and put into action a scheme of complete cooperation. I am only speaking of a scheme to be applied to a society from which has been culled all of the congenitally inferior; all of the victims of accident and disease; all of the mistaught, misinstructed, and otherwise unsocially inclined individuals. The society, if it should successfully carry out such a scheme, and had eliminated from it all mental and physical defectives, would be composed of men and women who had been born of healthy parents and who, all of them, from their infancy, had been really and thoroughly educated and, at the same time, trained to habits of mind and body fitting them, at least in a large general way, to best perform as adults the work they had to do.

ECONOMIC WASTE

In the new society there would be waste as there is in the present society. No matter how highly developed in every way this new society may be at any one time, there will always be room for improvement. Successive ages, even into infinity, can never see society completely developed. Therefore, waste there will be always — waste of human energy, physical and mental, waste of all material things. But comparatively early in its existence this new society will have eliminated perhaps not less than nine-tenths of the present waste. Conditions will be such that any number of men and women can and will be supplied with all the good things that men know of now at one-tenth the cost of labor now required to supply the same number.

Everyone knows that waste — tremendous waste — is going on all the time and that the waste in some countries is far greater than in others. For example, in Germany, up to the time of the late war, the average income of the workingman's family was not more than one-quarter of what it was in the United States, and yet, apparently the health and vigor and the comforts of the poorer-remunerated half of the German people were at least equal (and some believed better) to those enjoyed by the half of the people of the United States whose family incomes were the lowest. This, then, indicates that for one reason or another wastefulness has been, and probably is, four times as great in the United States as in Germany.

The per capita cost, measured by money, of the sustenance, housing, and clothing of the average working classes of Japan and China was, up to only a few years ago, not one-twentieth, perhaps not more than one-fortieth, of the per capita cost for sustenance, clothing, and housing of the average workingman in the United States.

It is said that what one man has done, another can do.

It certainly would not be claimed by any American that, man for man, Chinese or Japanese were better in any way than Americans.

Here in America, with regard only to the actual necessities in the way of food, clothing, housing, and intellectual enjoyment, our people are wasting many times more than the lowest cost of all the things necessary for health, comfort, and pleasure. In the matter of clothing even the poorest of our families are wasteful on account of the pursuit of fashion. Rarely indeed does any man, woman, or child actually wear out his or her clothes. Father's pants are sometimes cut up by a mother in order to make some child's article of wearing apparel. The father, even when he is a hard-working man, seldom continues to wear his clothing as long as it will furnish a decent covering to his body and keep him warm. So soon as the edges of an outer garment become frayed and ragged or a hole is worn in any part of his clothing most exposed to wear (maybe a patch or two is made once in a while or a frayed edge clipped with the scissors), even the poorest workingman discards his old clothes and buys a new suit. "A stitch in time saves nine." And perhaps, ninety-nine times out of a hundred, the raggedness of a child's or a man's apparel is premature or altogether unnecessary, because of the lack of a stitch in time.

Costly meats (all meats are comparatively costly and perhaps unnecessary, considering the experiences of a good many people, including the Japanese) are consumed when much cheaper meats, just as nourishing, are unused, and when much cheaper and equally nutritious food could be obtained in vegetable form, at least to a large extent.

It is probable, too, that not more than half, perhaps not a quarter, of all the foodstuffs purveyed by butchers, bakers, grocers, and venders of vegetables in this country ever find their way into the human alimentary canal. The garbage can or its equivalent is infinitely better fed than the average human being and consumes the major portion of the food purchased by all classes and conditions of men.

Not only is there great waste by reason of food purchased and not consumed, but there is also great waste by reason of far more food being put into human bellies than is good for the systems of their owners. (But of course the greatest waste is on account of the consumption of foods that cost the greatest amount of labor to produce instead of foods that can be produced by the smallest amount of labor.)

Is is impossible to observe the outside of almost any house in America — the millionaire's mansion or the poor man's cottage — without seeing that a great part of the cost of the home, in many cases the greater part, has been occasioned by its owner's demand to make some public display of affluence, whether he possesses affluence or not. Such waste is not only condoned by the public, but generally praised. The occasion of the waste is frequently esthetic taste. The owner or occupant of a house not only desires to make a display of his ability to be wasteful, but he desires beauty in itself, for his own enjoyment and for the pleasure of his neighbors.

It is impossible to go into any house — mansion or cottage — without observing that the most expensive furniture is that which is least used and least needed.

I recall going to a furniture store in San Diego many years ago for the purpose of buying a bed for a temporary habitation I was just about to occupy. The bed was for my wife. I bought a $40.00 mattress, some pillows stuffed with the finest of feathers, some sheets of fine material and, to support these, I bought a $5.00 bedstead. I also bought very cheap blankets and comforts.

The proprietor of the store was amazed at my purchase. Then he began to talk about his trade. I remember his telling me about the usual custom of his patrons in the then little city. He stated that he had supplied furniture for many of the houses and cottages and that he knew it to be a fact that, in the majority of the homes, the furniture in the parlor and dining room cost twice as much as all the furniture for all the other parts of the house.

In the room where I am working I have a table of hand-carved oak, for which I paid $100. I have another smaller table at which my secretary writes, on which my wife and I play dominoes and cards, on which we take our breakfasts, and which, in fact, is used ten times as much as the hand-carved contraption. This table cost $2.00.

My two tables have cost $102. Had the cost of both been $4.00, or at most $6.00, they would have been just as useful. So it appears I have actually wasted $96.00 on tables.

It would probably be difficult to find a house in this or any other community in the United States in which the cost of the furniture has not been from five to ten times greater than was necessary, even considering necessity from the esthetic point of view.

Although the furniture in my bedroom, on account of polished mahogany, mirrors, and other things that I never either use or need, cost me between $1,500 and $2,000, I could have furnished the room at one-half the expense and in all probability made it more appealing to the esthetic eye than it is at present.

It is not necessary to pursue further this subject of waste. Some waste is observed and known by everybody. More and more waste is observable, according to the keenness of the observer's mind.

GROWTH OF THE NEW SOCIETY

In the new society, two of the three positive checks to overpopulousness have been eliminated and their places taken by carefully selected and therefore more sane methods. But there remains, after famine and plague have been eliminated, war.

However far distant in the future is to appear the new society, it certainly will not appear as a world phenomenon. Like all other things great, it must have a small beginning; that is to say, conforming to the growth of all organisms, material or social, it would begin as a small thing. Probably it would originate in a single family household. From generation to generation this family's cult would continue and its followers would be the descendants of the first household plus some proselytes largely acquired by

marriage and to some degree by friendly intimacy, and minus some rene-
gades — some individuals of atavistic tendencies, members of the family
too weak in moral character and intelligence to resist the influence of the
surrounding mass of the old society.

The new laws and customs being in opposition to those of the old society
— being considered crimes, in fact — they would only be practiced secretly or by means of evasion. Infanticide would have to be made to appear as accident or, at first, it might not be resorted to at all. Instead of
disposing of the unfit children and adults by causing their deaths, the children could be put away by desertion — for instance, by surreptitiously
imposing them on orphanages. Older and unfit persons could be ostracized,
first by the family and later the community.

The family, as it grew from generation to generation in numbers, could
adhere first in a single community — a thing easily to be accomplished
through the existing laws and customs of land tenure. More and more land
could be acquired as the family community grew. Only members of the
family community would be permitted to live on this land, in its houses, in
its village, and on its farms. Visitors and travelers would be unwise to oppose the community by any sort of force. There would be means, perfectly
legitimate and entirely unoffensive, of discouraging their presence.

By reason of the energy, thrift, and intelligence in the new and growing
community, the power and possessions of its individuals would rapidly increase. By reason of its moral principles and its intelligence, its populous-
ness — notwithstanding the great numbers eliminated — would increase
two-, three-, four-, five-, or perhaps even tenfold more rapidly than
that of the surrounding old-society communities. It would be probable that
each individual pair would multiply in each generation threefold. It would
be possible for each such pair to multiply in each generation four- or five-
fold. In the youth of this new society the aim would be to cause the most
rapid possible growth of the fit. The age of marriage would be the lowest at
which it is possible to produce children — perhaps females eighteen and
males twenty years of age [sic].

Because of the great attention given to physical and mental training and to
health, and especially because of the great care that would be given to matters of maternity, mothers might well bear ten or twelve children without
suffering in health or being worn out nearly to the extent that are mothers
of a half or a third that number of children under conditions existing in the
society of today.

As it is right to presume that, in the early days of this community, it would
be impossible to protect it fully from disease and mental and moral corruption coming from the outside, and that probably many cases of atavism

would occur, it would be safer to calculate on not more than a threefold increase per generation.

Starting with the original family which is to initiate the new society as being composed of six adult children, and assuming strict adherence to exogamy and that all the wives and husbands of members of this family shall be proselytes to the cult, the result would be that in each generation there would be a sixfold increase of the family or community. Although each pair only multiplies itself threefold, only one of the pair would be of the original family and hence the family itself would increase sixfold. Thus, there would be 6 children of the first generation, 36 of the second, 216 of the third, 1,296 of the fourth, 7,776 of the fifth, 46,656 of the sixth, 279,936 of the seventh, 1,679,616 of the eighth, and 10,077,696 of the ninth.

The new society, being intelligent, would be not only wary, but so naturally friendly of disposition that, instead of giving offense to the members of the old society in which they were growing up, they would win and hold the respect and the affection and the confidence of all the outsiders who came in contact with them. For the most part all of the laws of the old society, with but one or two exceptions, though not all of the customs, could be implicitly obeyed. Even for a very long time infanticide could be avoided. For instance, the parent community could avoid shocking existing society entirely by having, at some distance from the parent community, a daughter community in the shape of institutions for the particular care of ailing children, institutions of learning for the young, sanitariums for defective adults, and homes for the aged, all of which could be so admirably conducted as to secure not only the goodwill but the laudation of the general public. In this daughter community, or perhaps communities, all of these children or other persons could be so educated and so treated as to fit them to be acceptable members of the general run of the old society. The cult of the new and parent society would neither be taught nor practiced.

The plan of the growing new society would be to adhere and spread over a contiguous territory, always striving unostentatiously and unnoticed to acquire by purchase more and more land.

Members of the old society who occupied lands and homes scattered over and in the midst of the territory of the new society would, to a certain extent, be proselyted by marriage and by the peculiar influences of environment which are so strong as to hardly ever be resisted. Thoroughly objectionable members of the old society could, by gentle means or appeals to selfish interest, be induced to migrate, willingly and voluntarily.

Whole territories as large as any of the existing states of the American Union could and would become completely appropriated by the new society and this, too, all unnoticed, or at least not objected to, because trade and all other forms of amenities between the new and the old society would not only be kept up, but so developed as to make the people of the nation as a whole either entirely ignorant of the peculiarities of the new society, or respectful and friendly toward it.

But the time having come when the new society would be composed of millions of individuals, the time will also have come when there would be a condition of crowding.

Since the practice of exogamy will have been kept up during all this time, there could never have been, nor could there ever arise, a condition of antagonism between the old society and the new. Always half of the members of the new society would come into it after they were adult, out from amongst the old society. In fact, at least half of all the adults in the new society would be the brothers and sisters and sons, uncles and aunts and near cousins, of the great majority, if not almost the universality, of the old society.

Instead of there being a feeling of animosity on the part of the old society toward the new, there would have grown up a feeling entirely the reverse.

While it is probable that the whole population of the United States, by the time the new society had 10 million, would be as much as 400 million, all of these 400 million would have grown so permeated with respect, admiration, and even affection for the new society that they would have by degrees adapted themselves more and more to its customs and practices and even its cult, and would have gone a long ways toward having been assimilated and even absorbed by the new society. At least all of the health and educational practices of the new society, having been so thoroughly demonstrated to be good, would have been universally adopted.

Already, by statutory law, a number of states of the American Union have adopted the system of sterilizing the criminal class. Already it is almost universally recognized in America that defective men and women should be discouraged and, as much as possible, prevented from becoming parents. Custom frowns upon the marriage of persons tainted with insanity. Long before the time it would take to cause the new society to increase to the number of 10 millions, even were there no new society in existence to set the example, the laws and customs of civilized people not only in America but in Europe, would be such as to secure the people completely from epidemics and, to a large extent, from death on account of preventable diseases.

It is more than probable that with such a new society in existence for two hundred years or more in which to make a practical demonstration of its cult, this cult would have been universally adopted not only in America but amongst all other highly civilized peoples.

The reform and revolution that I have indicated as being the result of, and initiated by, the formation and building up of a new community and society are probably inevitable, even without the setting up of such an example. Either there must be such a reform or revolution or else the world of men will quickly progress toward complete destruction of all forms of civilization to a time when warfare, plague, famine, and barbarism, with consequent depopulation, will everywhere prevail.

WARFARE

The world is peopled at present mainly by three great families or races: the white or European race; the Mongolian, including Mongoloids; and the African or Negro. There are smaller families or races, such as the aborigines of North and South America.

It seems practical for all of these families or races, except the white or European race, to intermingle their blood — to miscegenate. For the present, at least, there is an absolute conviction on the part of most white people — those of the highest intelligence and greatest wisdom as well as the masses — that the white and colored races cannot miscegenate advantageously to either or to the world's society as a whole. Yet the time must come when one of three things must happen: The white and the colored races must be mingled and become completely absorbed in a common mongrel stock, or the colored races must be completely eliminated, or the white race completely eliminated.

Peace! There can be no lasting peace on earth so long as there are different races of men on earth, because men must multiply, and with such rapidity as to forever cause crowding and conflict between races.

The League of Nations — the supernation that is now struggling to be born — is in reality not a league of all the nations at all or of all the peoples. It is in fact nothing more than a league of nations of white men, into which may be admitted, but as entirely unwelcome and unnecessary members, some nations whose nationals are of the colored race.

It has been for a long time the fashion of some very respectable men among the learned class and of a very large number of pseudo-moralists to "pooh-pooh" what is called the Malthusian doctrine. An Englishman named Malthus wrote a book containing a statement which any thoughtful person cannot disbelieve. Malthus defined or named the three main causes that have so far prevented an inordinate growth in the population of men — the three positive checks to such growth. These he denominated war, famine, and pestilence.

Universally, mankind wants to eliminate war.

The greatest effort is being made in all civilization to stamp out pestilence and a large number of other diseases that would not be denominated as pestilence, and to minimize the number of deaths caused by accident.

Every possible effort is being made by peoples all over the world to prevent famine.

If the growth of population is no longer checked by the prevalence of wars and disease, then there can remain only two other checks — famine and birth prevention (perhaps infanticide also). But birth control can be, is, and will be only practiced by the most intelligent and most fit to survive of people of all races. It will naturally be practiced many more fold by the most intelligent of all races — the white race — than by any other races. The inferior races, then, will multiply the fastest. The inferior part of the white race will also continue to multiply.

In the end, after the white people have been annihilated, war, plague, and famine will all remain.

If it is admitted that it is desirable that the happiness of human beings on earth should be increased, that the greatest possible number of human beings should be healthy in body and mind, then we have only to consider means to accomplish that end.

Is it not possible that the world wants its wars, and more wars — wars between nations composed of inferior peoples? And it is just amongst these inferior peoples that warfare can be depended upon to exist if the people of superior nations do not intervene.

We want famines and more famines, providing that the people who starve to death and are eliminated are the people of inferior qualities in all races, and especially the people of all inferior races.

Plagues themselves might be considered beneficial, since they rage most extensively and destructively among inferior peoples, were it not for the fact that plagues, unlike famine and warfare, cannot be kept within bounds. Plagues originate and develop among inferior peoples, but spread to other lands and other nations and are there very destructive. If all of the inferior peoples were wiped off the earth's surface by warfare and famine, plagues would destroy eventually and soon enough [sic].

I am writing of a new society — not necessarily an un-Christian society or an irreligious society. There is nothing in the teachings of Jesus the Christ that need be ignored by the new society in order that it should thrive and redeem the world. However, on the other hand, for the most part all of the dogma of the dogmatists of the Christian Church would have to be eliminated. All that Christ taught is good. Most, perhaps all, of the interpretations of Christ's teachings by the theologians, have been untrue, unscientific, un-Christian, unnatural, wicked. Christ's Christianity was good; the Christianity of theologians and dogmatists is wholly bad.

In the new society, every man and every woman would be developed into the most expert soldier. From infancy upward, militarism should be developed and taught to every individual. Each should be taught how to make weapons of war and how to use them most effectively. At first the object should be solely to prepare for a defensive war, but in time offensive warfare would have to be fully prepared for. So thorough and complete should be the education and training of the men and women of the new society that anyone among them would be more than a match for any two or five or ten or twenty of their possible — aye, of their certain-to-be — antagonists.

What is needed most by a good soldier? First, a sound body and second, a well-developed mind. These qualities are no less desirable possessions of the individual for peaceful occupations than for warlike pursuits.

What is next most desirable? Intellect so well developed as to make possible a rapid increase in the number and quality of inventions — mechanical, chemical, and what might be called psychological. (Psychology, perhaps, plays a larger part in warfare than do muscles and machines.) But this intellectual development — capacity to invent improved machines and new chemicals and better and more effective reasoning (psychology) — is even more advantageous in times of peace than in war. In fact, all the physical and mental education, training, and exercise which is good with which to make a soldier is even better with which to make a citizen, a father, and a mother.

In the new society, which will be possessed of infinitely effective machines and methods, it will be so easy to provide all the necessaries and comforts and even luxuries of life that but a comparatively small amount of time and labor will have to be devoted to obtaining these objects. The result will be a great increase in the amount of time and labor that can be devoted to purely cultural ends, and among these cultural ends should be knowledge and understanding and efficiency in warfare.

When our new society has grown so large and so strong and effective as to have assimilated and become an integral and in no way, perhaps, superior part of society as a whole, and when many other nations have become thoroughly assimilated also (and I fear me long before that time), the white race will stand face to face, in a life and death struggle, with all the other races. Not all the other races combined. These other races will be so backward as to not only make effective combinations between them impossible, but as to cause them to be continually at warfare amongst themselves.

The white populations will have grown so numerous that in order that they shall increase in number at all more and more territory will be required. This demand for more territory will not come all at once. It will be a growing demand. The territory will have to be taken. It is a natural right that the superior should prevail over the inferior and that any people with institutions and customs, such as to permit two of their number to exist on a territory that is only sufficient to supply sustenance and room for one of an

inferior race, should take from the inferior people such part of their territory as is needed by the superior. For instance, what justice would there
be in killing or preventing the birth of two members of this new society
I am speaking of in order that one savage, one semi-barbarian, or even one
less fit member of an inferior race, should continue in existence?

Sooner or later the crucial moment will arrive in this world when either
two white men must die or be forbid an existence, or one Negro must die
or be forbid an existence. Sooner or later the time will arrive when either
two Europeans must die or be forbid an existence or one Asiatic must die
or be forbid an existence.

Can anyone doubt what the answer will be to such a question, if it is
raised?

The new society will be militarily so perfect that warfare between its superior people and the inferior people of other societies will in hardly any
way at all resemble the wars of past history. Rather it will resemble the
later phases of the war between the white Americans and the red aborigines of this country.

As it will be impossible for the inferior races to successfully stand against
the people of the new society, there will be little or no opposition to the
armies, so called, of the new society. The inferior peoples will withdraw and
make room for the superior peoples, but rarely striking a blow in despera-
tion as our American Indians did. They will gradually die out by so-called
natural deaths, thus receding before the invaders of their territory. But few
redskin Indians perished on account of the bullets that were fired into their
bodies. The weapons used by the white men which were most destructive
in removing the old occupants of the territories they acquired were not such
as soldiers use on the battlefield.

POLITICS

Scripps linked his interest in reform with an active and moderately effective part in national politics. Before about 1904, he had confined his participation to local and state politics for the most part.

During his early years in Cincinnati, he had envisioned a possible political career, dreaming himself into the United States Senate, forming a small political party in 1883 which he said Senator George Pendleton of Ohio took away from him, and imagining that he might be the Populist candidate for governor of Ohio in 1891. Other than the momentary flirtation in 1891, Scripps as a Democrat would have nothing to do with populism. In a way, this is anomalous because the Populist war cry, as uttered by Ignatius Donnelly — "From the same prolific womb of governmental injustice we breed two great classes — paupers and millionaires" — was at the core of Scripps' beliefs. Otherwise, it is not anomalous, because the Populists called for government ownership of railroads, and Scripps strongly opposed government ownership of any industry.

Nor did he compromise his beliefs when the Democrats appropriated most of the Populist creed, especially in the 1896 presidential campaign when William Jennings Bryan urged free and unlimited coinage of silver. Besides distrusting Bryan, Scripps personally was a Gold Democrat.

Clues that will help to dispel beforehand any confusion arising from the apparent conflict of Scripps' professions and his political interests are to be found in a few of his incidental remarks. For instance, he wrote in one disquisition that he had been using "crowbar and pickaxe" for thirty years in trying to break the "dam" of classic political party alignments to let democracy gush through, knowing the flood would catch him among the first; "I have always known that personal ruin would follow personal success." [1] Varying an earlier remark, he said, "I didn't count myself so much a

[1] "What of Tomorrow?" EWS Writings, 3:230.

friend of the poor as I counted myself the antagonist of the foolish members of my own economic class." [2] Although he had contributed to the single-tax movement in an effort to stimulate the thought of workingmen, he personally regarded the single tax as "an impractical fad that had been turned into a public nuisance by a lot of very impractical men and women." [3]

His best summation was this: "The longer I live and the more experience I get, the more it seems that my business interests, my friendships, and my morals get mixed up in a tangle of antagonism." [4]

In municipal politics, he ordered in 1904 that the Cincinnati *Post* and the other Ohio papers take a stronger position in combating Boss George Cox of Cincinnati, involving details that are discussed in "What of Taft Today?" And in 1908, while there was considerable agitation against bossism in American cities generally, he went out of his way to become acquainted with E. H. Hardy whom he identified as the political boss of San Diego, only to conclude that Hardy was not the bad sort he had anticipated.

In President Theodore Roosevelt, Scripps found a man who was both willing and in a position to adjust the economic and political inequities against which Scripps railed. He held Roosevelt in high regard, although the tone of "Triumphant Mediocrity" might cause one erroneously to conclude differently. Roosevelt began a liberalizing program that used government regulation to curb economic excesses and to bring irreplaceable natural resources under conservation controls, along with the more sensational trust-busting that marked his administration.

Scripps' marked interest in national politics began with the 1908 campaign. Roosevelt, announcing that he would not be a candidate for a third term, designated his former Secretary of War, William Howard Taft, as the crown prince, certain that Taft would continue the Roosevelt program. The Democrats nominated Bryan for his third try, and Hearst formed an Independence League with candidates of his own choosing.

Taft's nomination by the Republicans perturbed Scripps considerably. He personally disliked Taft, but part of this may have been from animosity toward Taft's brother, Charles P., who owned the competing Cincinnati *Times-Star*. On the other hand, McRae was a strong Taft man, and claimed that the Cincinnati *Post* gave Taft his first nomination for president. In the campaign, the Scripps papers supported Bryan, but Scripps did so grudgingly.

Against the remonstrances of his Progressive Republican friends and those of some of his business associates, Scripps voiced serious reservations

[2] "The Future in America," *ibid.*, 10:303.
[3] "Another Venture in Politics," *ibid.*, 8:185.
[4] EWS to John S. Sweeney, Aug. 24, 1906.

about Taft. Early in 1908, he predicted that Taft would not continue in the Roosevelt tradition but would land in the camp of the ultra-conservatives of the Republican party. Both Heney and Harper urged Scripps to support Taft, to which he replied: ". . . that Taft was only a very respectable member of a very bad political organization: an organization stronger than Taft and stronger than Roosevelt, an organization that would control a man and not be controlled by him; and that Taft's very virtues made him the most dangerous of all the possible candidates for the presidency." [5] Although he regarded Taft as standing for some things that were essential to the public welfare, Scripps was positive that Taft was instinctively reactionary and would be more serviceable to the anti-Roosevelt interests than to any other.

Bryan, as Scripps saw it, still was the idol of the people who befriended the Scripps papers; the common people needed a champion, but the nation also needed a defender against the other nations of the world. Were there no danger from foreign countries, he would have supported Bryan heartily. Of Hearst, who Scripps thought in early 1908 would be the candidate of the Independence League, Scripps said he might be Machiavellian and Napoleonic but had a better platform than Bryan's and was of such a nature that the nation need not fear foreign aggression with Hearst in the White House. [6]

When Taft received the Republican nomination, Scripps again predicted:

It has seemed to me that the passing of power from the hands of Roosevelt the courageous to those of Taft the simply efficient is to be a distinct gain for the reactionaries and a great loss to the Progressives. It has appeared to me that our party [the reformers] was showing signs of weariness and coming apathy, and that all the inspiration of enthusiasm and confidence was passing to the opposite side. [7]

General goodwill attended the inauguration of Taft in 1909, which Scripps reflected in the mellow tone of "The Election and Its Relation to My Business." Scripps' equanimity in the face of a Republican election leads only to the conclusion that he was willing to use his newspapers as battleships in class warfare, but it was so much more comforting to do so in an atmosphere of business stability, especially when the country was recovering from the depression of 1907.

With Taft in office, Roosevelt lost himself for a year on a big-game hunt in the wilds of Africa, and Taft's course almost immediately proved that Scripps had accurately gauged his man, for the new President's policies

[5] EWS to Lincoln Steffens, Apr. 22, 1908.
[6] EWS to Lincoln Steffens, Feb. 3, 1908.
[7] EWS to Rudolph Spreckels, July 4, 1908.

promptly resulted in a party split. Taft swung into the camp of the Republican Old Guard, who rammed through Congress the Payne-Aldrich tariff bill. The bill precipitated a rebellion in both houses among midwestern Republicans, who came to be known as insurgents.

Taft's divergence from the Roosevelt policies was shown more dramatically in a momentary sensation known as the Ballinger-Pinchot controversy, of which Scripps may have been a remote activator. Fragmentary evidence in Scripps' papers suggests, without corroboration from other sources, that he may have helped fuse a time bomb that exploded the Ballinger-Pinchot controversy as a political issue that would force Taft to show his hand. Broadly speaking, the controversy really extended over a period of about three years, but the politically significant part of it came during a Congressional investigation between January and May, 1910. Today it is simply a dreary, antiquarian piece of business, of interest here only because of Scripps' involvement and its effect upon his course. Historians differ as to the importance of the episode. Some hold that it was of no consequence in the eventual rift between Roosevelt and Taft; others, that it contributed to the rupture that resulted in Roosevelt's running against Taft on a third-party platform in 1912, which cleared the way for Woodrow Wilson's election.

Scripps' involvement began in September, 1909, when he had a long and earnest conference at "Miramar" with Gifford Pinchot, chief of the United States Forest Service. Not only was Pinchot a close personal friend of Roosevelt but he was an architect of Roosevelt's conservation program, the main purpose of which was to protect the country's natural resources in the name of the people against exploitation by corporations.

At that period, because of his conviction that Taft would ultimately align himself with the "oligarchy," Scripps expressed a deeper interest in politics than he ever had before, saying, "I am doing my level best in blowing hard to keep the spark of revolt alive." [8]

During the conference with Pinchot — which ostensibly was to deal with Scripps' success in forestation on the semi-arid "Miramar" mesa — Scripps and the chief forester did little else but discuss national affairs, especially Taft and Roosevelt. Communicating his predictions of Taft's course to Pinchot, Scripps found that Pinchot "was not yet prepared — *not yet*, mind you — to hold the opinion that I do of Taft." Pinchot reportedly told Scripps he would wait several months before making up his mind, but was sure Taft would be forced to declare himself and his attitude. Whereupon:

. . . I told Pinchot that I wanted him to take an active part when the right time came, to join us in an effort to convince Roosevelt that, as he had been re-

[8] EWS to W. H. Porterfield, Dec. 28, 1909.

sponsible for the present administration, he (Roosevelt) owes it to the public to frankly state whether he considered that Taft had or had not been faithful to his pledges formally or tacitly made.[9]

In the meantime, Pinchot's suspicions that Taft would depart from Roosevelt's conservation program had been growing stronger by the month, and Pinchot found himself constantly at odds with an old antagonist, Secretary of the Interior Richard A. Ballinger. As head of the General Land Office during the Roosevelt administration, Ballinger had, to Pinchot's way of thinking, shown animosity toward conservation. Shortly after Ballinger accepted the Interior portfolio, he had thrown open to public sale hydroelectric sites on western rivers — sites that the outgoing administration had frantically withdrawn from sale in the closing months of Roosevelt's term as a conservation measure. By pressing the issue on Taft, Pinchot had obtained a reversal of Ballinger's action.

At the same time, Ballinger — a Washington man who reflected the western desire to use resources now — had pursued a course which, if successful, would have opened valuable coal lands in Alaska to development by Morgan-Guggenheim interests, but was blocked by a young Land Office field investigator, Louis R. Glavis. In the ebb and flow of administrative actions, Glavis was blocked in his investigation of the land patents involved. He then appealed directly to the Forest Service, a bureau of the Department of Agriculture, because most of the coal claims lay within the Chugach National Forest. Through Pinchot's intervention, Glavis laid his case directly before Taft on August 18, 1909, trying to convince the Chief Executive that the claims were fraudulent. Taft forwarded the Glavis report to Ballinger with whom he conferred on September 6, at which time Ballinger — in company with Oscar Lawler, an assistant attorney general assigned to the Interior Department — presented a bulky report. After going through the Ballinger report in a few hours, Taft met with the Secretary again on September 7, informed him there was nothing in the record to speak against him, directed Lawler to prepare for the President's signature a letter exonerating Ballinger, and ordered the dismissal of Glavis for unjustly impeaching the integrity of a superior.

An appeal to the people then became necessary, in the opinion of Glavis who consulted with two of Pinchot's subordinates in the Forest Service, with the result that he laid bare the whole story in *Collier's* of November 13, 1909.

From that moment a Congressional investigation became inescapable, and was provided for in a joint resolution forming a joint committee. The

[9] EWS to W. H. Porterfield, Sept. 7, 1909.

President was requested to transmit to Congress all documents upon which he based his conclusions in the Glavis-Ballinger matter.

Scripps offered to pay Heney's expenses if he would go east to defend Glavis before the committee, but Heney could not take the case. Brandeis represented Glavis and *Collier's* in the hearing.

In the meantime, Pinchot's two subordinates — Overton W. Price and Alexander C. Shaw — had continued to make information available to *Collier's* as well as to other magazines and newspapers about the Alaska coal claims and Ballinger's actions. Ballinger sued *Collier's* for libel.

Early in January, 1910, Pinchot precipitated another crisis, which made him personally an issue, by writing a letter to Senator Jonathan P. Dolliver, a Republican insurgent from Iowa. Pinchot wrote that he had reprimanded his subordinates for a breach of propriety, but defended them strongly on moral grounds. Pinchot said the information that had been made public should have been made public, unless the people were not entitled to know about the source, nature, and progress of claims for portions of the public lands. "It is abundantly evident," he said, "that the action of Price and Shaw was taken with the single object of protecting the property of the people of the United States."

Dolliver read the letter in the Senate on January 6, the same day Taft forwarded to Congress a report of 717 printed pages that contained the documents on which he rested his exoneration of Ballinger and dismissal of Glavis. Pinchot knew how to time a play for publicity in appealing to the court of public opinion.

Taft fired Pinchot immediately for violating an administrative rule against communicating directly with a member of Congress without permission, and thereby provoked a political scandal: Taft had dared to fire Teddy's close friend. The result was a prediction of a tempest within the Republican party. Which may well have been exactly what Pinchot was trying to provoke — a showdown between Taftism and Rooseveltism — for his mother greeted the news of his firing with, "Hurrah!"

And it apparently was what Scripps had had in mind. For, a few months later, after a second conference with Pinchot, Scripps quoted Pinchot as saying he had written the Dolliver letter with Scripps' advice in mind; the reference will be found in the second letter to Colver grouped with other documents under the heading "Scripps Tries to Energize a Reform Party." However, neither Pinchot's autobiography nor biography even mentions Scripps in connection with this matter.[10] Assuming that Scripps' quotation is accurate, it is possible, of course, that Pinchot merely flattered him. Thus, Scripps' role in the controversy might be dismissed out of hand were

[10] Gifford Pinchot, *Breaking New Ground* (New York, 1947), pp. 391–458; M. Nelson McGeary, *Gifford Pinchot, Forester-Politician* (Princeton, 1960), pp. 113–89.

it not for one troublesomely salient point — that was the way Scripps operated, to plant an idea with another man, and let the other man follow through, assimilating the idea as his own.

Speculation aside, Pinchot clearly worked closely with Scripps' men, especially Gardner and Colver of NEA, during the hearing that began on January 26, 1910. Their involvement became clear in connection with the dramatic appearance of a secret document.

As the hearing progressed, Brandeis sniffed falsification in the Taft documents, and finally put his finger on it. Taft's letter exonerating Ballinger and ordering the dismissal of Glavis had been dated September 13, 1909; Congress wanted all the documents upon which Taft had based his decision; Taft's 717-page volume carried an 87-page summary prepared by the Attorney General and dated September 11; Brandeis knew Ballinger had not submitted his first documents to the President until September 6, which would have made it impossible for anybody to write a detailed report on such a mass of evidence between September 6 and September 11. Brandeis finally spotted evidence within the report that showed it had been prepared *after* September 11; in other words, the administration had predated its report, and thus placed damaging evidence in the hands of Brandeis.

What Brandeis still did not know was that there was yet missing from the President's papers the letter prepared by Lawler, but, sure that other papers were missing, he kept calling for them day by day. Finally, the story of the Lawler letter came to light. It so happened that a young stenographer in Ballinger's office, Frederick M. Kerby, had worked for James R. Garfield who had been Roosevelt's Secretary of the Interior. Kerby told Garfield, Pinchot, and Brandeis about the Lawler letter, and that the rough drafts had been burned.

Gardner and Colver were informed of Kerby's information, and they kept the secret. Neither they nor Brandeis put pressure on Kerby to come forward and tell what he knew. All waited patiently.

After an agonizing week, knowing he would lose his job, Kerby told the story of the Lawler memorandum through NEA stories to the Scripps papers, which appeared on May 14, 1910. Kerby later was given a job as a reporter in the Scripps organization. A flustered administration "found" the overlooked letter and sent it to the committee.

When the hearing ended late in May, the three reports that were filed — one by seven Republicans, one by four Democrats, and one by a single member — had the cumulative effect of clearing the name of each principal involved, holding the coal lands from entry, and giving the Taft administration a black eye.[11]

11 *Ibid.*

In the meantime, as the Ballinger-Pinchot controversy broke into the open through the hearing, Scripps had considered the situation a political emergency and saw it as the time to get a definite commitment from Roosevelt, then still in Africa. To accomplish that, he called Gardner from Washington for a conference at "Miramar"; it was decided that Gardner should leave at once for Africa, meet Roosevelt when he emerged from the interior, inform Roosevelt of what had been going on, and find out what Roosevelt intended to do. They arranged a private code, to permit Gardner to inform Scripps immediately of Roosevelt's attitude if the latter preferred not to speak for publication.

Gardner went to Khartoum, carrying a private report from Pinchot, and chartered a steamer to take him up the Nile to meet Roosevelt's steamer. Gardner met Roosevelt — they were friends, by the way — and dined with him on a river steamer amid the skins and bones of animals brought back from the safari.

Getting the information he wanted, Gardner filed two messages from a beehive hut cable station in a small native settlement. For immediate relay to Scripps he sent to Colver the one-word message, "hen." This told Scripps that Roosevelt was angry and would take action when he returned to America, but would not comment for publication immediately. At a dollar a word, payable in gold and in advance, Gardner also cabled a 100-word news story.[12]

Gardner's story appeared in the San Diego *Sun* on the same day that Hiram Johnson visited "Miramar" while campaigning for governor of California in sympathy with the Republican insurgents. When Johnson asked what Scripps thought Roosevelt's course would be, Scripps told him he interpreted the dispatch to mean that Roosevelt would come home "a thoroughgoing 'insurgent.' " Johnson said such a course would insure his own election as governor, for it would convince California Republicans they need not give up their republicanism to vote for him. A day or two after Johnson left "Miramar," Scripps received the "hen" message, whereupon he advised Johnson that confidential information from Egypt substantiated his interpretation of Gardner's story.[13]

Thereafter, Scripps became more active and more interested in trying to fuse a coalition party of Progressives from both major parties. His thoughts had first turned in this direction after the "Miramar" conference with Pinchot in 1909 and a conversation with Congressman Irvine Lenroot of Wisconsin in San Diego a few days before he saw Pinchot. Lenroot had told him the thirty insurgents in Congress had organized and were working as a unit, but would wait for the 1910 Congressional session to show where

[12] Gardner, *Lusty Scripps*, pp. 186–89.
[13] EWS to W. B. Colver, Mar. 18, 1910; EWS to Hiram Johnson, Mar. 26, 1910.

Taft really stood. Eagerly grasping the idea, Scripps had argued that the popular men of the Republican party were out of power, and that it was time for the Progressives to organize, saying a new party would sweep up the "liberal and patriotic" elements of both parties except for the "moss-backs and millionaires." However, Scripps had blundered in his first effort to bring about such coalition; working through Steffens, and possibly at Steffens' suggestion, Scripps had sought to bring together at "Miramar" a group of men interested in political reform, even offering to pay traveling expenses and make up in money for the time that some of them might lose from their jobs; suddenly he had decided that "Miramar" was out of the way for the men who must attend, such as LaFollette, and suggested an eastern meeting place; this had offended some of the others, and Scripps had had difficulty explaining that he was not backing out.[14] The high point of Scripps' efforts came in 1910, represented in "Scripps Tries to Energize a Reform Party."

The lead was taken away from him, naturally, and a new party, the National Progressive Republican League, was formed in LaFollette's home in Washington in January, 1911. Scripps declined to join the League, writing LaFollette that he would be of more help as a friend and supporter.

Trying to form a national political party from his adobe hacienda was Quixotic. He did not know what he was doing, he did not have sufficient personal standing to carry it through, and he made his effort from a remote corner of the country. As a gentleman dilettante bumbling into a game where professionals played for keeps, he was as incongruous as a child riding a Shetland pony onto the field during an international polo match.

He was less Quixotic than defiant, however, when he insisted that "Wobblies" and Socialists have soapbox rights in San Diego in 1912. During the first half of that year, San Diego seethed with unrest as public officials, backed by businessmen formed as vigilantes, tried to suppress speeches by radicals; vigilantes reportedly treated the radicals brutally. Just how Scripps became involved is not clear; one version is that he opened a vacant lot, which he owned in town, for the radicals to use as a hustings; another possible explanation is that hoboes, then feared as Wobblies automatically, customarily received two meals and a bed when passing "Miramar." Whatever the reason, Jim, who maintained an office in town, learned that armed vigilantes planned to march on "Miramar," and he placed an armed guard (one man) at the ranch. One night the vigilantes invaded the grounds — to attack Scripps, the story goes — but the guard turned them back with the threat to kill any man who advanced a step farther.

The political significance of the episode is that Scripps withdrew his per-

[14] EWS to Benjamin Ide Wheeler, Sept. 8, 1909; EWS to Joseph Fels, Feb. 3, 1910; EWS Letterbook No. 27, *passim*.

sonal friendship, but not his political support, from Governor Hiram Johnson when the Governor took no action against the vigilantes, whom Scripps
called a "crowd of cowardly scamps," and at the same time took no action
to prevent two attorneys, who had represented free-speech advocates, from
being sent to jail and fined for what Scripps called technical violations of
the law.[15]

In national politics, Scripps became disillusioned as the 1912 presidential
contest took shape. Right down the line he had stood for LaFollette first
and foremost, as the candidate of the Progressive party, without diminishing at all his respect for Roosevelt. But early in 1912 LaFollette was shunted
aside — one pretext was that he had shown signs of nervous exhaustion in
speaking to a publishers' group in Philadelphia — and some of his former
strong supporters had switched over to Roosevelt. Roosevelt then made it
clear he would seek the Republican nomination. In disgust, Scripps called
the whole maneuver a betrayal of LaFollette, and Scripps' respect for Roosevelt plummeted.

Looking over the remaining field — Roosevelt, Taft, Wilson, Bryan,
Governor Judson Harmon of Ohio — Scripps became thoroughly disgusted. Should the Republicans nominate Taft and the Democrats Harmon,
he should certainly personally prefer to back a Socialist candidate.[16]

In a momentarily pessimistic mood he advised his son John, who had editorial direction of the papers, that the Democratic party was not democracy
but was simply one of two political organizations representing the 5 per
cent of the people who ruled the 95 per cent for the benefit of the 5 per cent.
He then elaborated:

We know that only folly causes any of the 95 per cent to place reliance on
members of the 5 per cent.
We are of the 5 per cent ourselves.
We can only help the 95 per cent by hurting ourselves.
We are unfit to be the leaders of the 95 per cent.
But we know that the only hope of the 95 per cent having their conditions
ameliorated is by their forming a party among themselves.
The only party or a fraction of a party in this country that is entitled to the
goodwill of, and the confidence of, the common people, is the Socialist party.

.   .   .   .

Socialism, not Marxianism [sic], is inevitable and, I believe, will be the dominating force in this country before the youngest of my children is as old as I am

15 EWS to Hiram Johnson, May 27, 1912, Jan. 17, 1914; EWS Letterbooks Nos. 29
and 30, passim; "Life and Death of Edward W. Scripps," Editor and Publisher, Mar.
20, 1926, p. 6; Theodore Schroeder, Free Speech for Radicals (New York, 1916), pp.
116–90.
16 EWS to Gilson Gardner, Jan. 24, 1912.

now. [Eugene V. Debs, the Socialist candidate received almost 900,000 votes in 1912, more than double the Socialist vote of 1908.]

.   .   .   .

From what I know of our editors, I believe many of them are near Socialists, some of them real Socialists (whether they know it or not) and most of them possessed of such temperaments as will cause them to become Socialists when they know what socialism is and when it is no longer disgustingly unrespectable to be known as a Socialist.

I suppose the Scripps papers could define their position in this way:

They are not Socialists.

They hold that socialism is not so awful[ly] bad.

They believe that socialism can be made better.

As between socialism and plutocracy they prefer socialism.

And lastly they regard socialism as inevitable anyway.

[Scripps withheld the letter for a week, during which the Democrats nominated Wilson, and he then added the following as a postscript to the letter.]

However, I send you this just to let you know what is down in the bottom of my personal and private mind. If I were in your place of responsibility, I would be thinking only and not saying anything much.[17]

Reluctantly, Scripps personally went along with the editors in supporting Woodrow Wilson, keeping his hands off editorial policy. As he told Paine: "We [he and Paine] are biased, and all twisted up, and ossified in that shape and are not the best persons to plan and execute the policy of our newspapers in this emergency." [18]

At the same time, he insisted that Gardner, writing from Washington for NEA, should be allowed to advocate the election of Gardner's friend Roosevelt, who bolted the Republican party to form the Bull Moose party, even though the papers editorially supported Wilson.

Once Wilson was elected, however, his New Freedom program won Scripps' support, for it more nearly accorded with Scripps' beliefs than that of any previous administration. In protecting individual freedom against political and economic domination by extra-governmental forces, Wilson's views paralleled much of what Scripps had been preaching. The closest union of the two views came in the Clayton Act, which labor called its Magna Charta and which protected labor unions from anti-trust prosecution, limited the use of court injunctions in labor disputes, and legalized strikes, picketing, and boycotts.

[17] EWS to John Paul Scripps, June 29, 1912.
[18] EWS to Robert F. Paine, Aug. 9, 1912.

Unlike many other publishers, Scripps did not court the prestige that mantles one who has a private audience with the Chief Executive. Rather, he preferred, and expected, to see only about three persons during a visit to Washington in 1914. But Gardner arranged a constant stream of visitors to Scripps' hotel room. Brandeis called on him three times. About a dozen congressmen came in to talk with him. For the first time he met Bryan, who was Secretary of State, and had several chats with him. After the last visit, Bryan said he wanted to talk with him again; Scripps replied that Bryan would have to hunt him up, because Bryan was too busy a man to meet Scripps on such occasions as Scripps could spare for interviews.

Having rejected several suggestions that he talk with President Wilson, Scripps thought he was about through with Washington notables when his telephone rang shortly before breakfast one morning, and presidential secretary Joseph Tumulty invited him to have lunch with Wilson that day.

"I replied that I wouldn't take lunch with anybody. As I hadn't had my breakfast, I was, of course, in no amiable mood." [19]

After eating breakfast, Scripps began to have uncomfortable second thoughts about his brusqueness in dealing with a President of the United States. At that point, Tumulty telephoned again, asking Scripps to see the President later in the morning. Scripps accepted; Gardner piloted him into the White House, and he entered the President's presence.

"For the first time in my life, I believe, I was stumped and embarrassed, and sat like a ninny for a moment or two until the President started to talk. . . ." [20]

During the conference, Scripps proposed that Wilson create a new cabinet position, to be called Secretary of the People, as a means of communicating the administration's views and policies to the public. A similar idea has been broached many times since, and in recent years as a cabinet post for public relations. Indeed, that very suggestion had caused the President to invite Scripps to his office, for in the preceding few days Scripps had advanced the same idea to Bryan, Secretary of the Interior Franklin K. Lane, and Oliver Newman, who had covered the Wilson campaign for NEA and had been appointed one of the three commissioners governing the District of Columbia, all of whom urged Scripps to make an appointment with the President. Interwoven with the proposal was Scripps' idea that Wilson should use the Scripps concern as his medium for reaching the people. The suggestion of the cabinet post met a favorable reception with Wilson, who had already demonstrated an adeptness in using the press as a means of marshaling public opinion, both as governor of New Jersey and as President. Wilson followed it up to the extent of sending Lane to "Miramar" the next year for a more

[19] EWS to EBS, July 1, 1914.
[20] *Ibid.*

exhaustive discussion of the idea. In the end, Wilson dropped the suggestion, but during the war he did create George Creel's Committee on Public Information.

Leaving the White House, Scripps still worried whether he had been guilty of a serious breach of etiquette in refusing to have lunch with the President. At his hotel that evening, he put the question to Gardner.

Thoughtfully and hesitantly, Gardner said, "No, but I think you made a record." [21]

For the next three years Scripps was more closely involved with national politicians than at any other time in his life. While continuing to support Wilson, he also urged Gardner to devote himself to re-energizing the Progressive party around Roosevelt, a pleasant enough task for Gardner who at times functioned within a group of Roosevelt advisers. [22]

However, Scripps' contrary individuality kept him from meeting Roosevelt. In July, 1915, Roosevelt declined an invitation to visit "Miramar," but asked Scripps to meet him at the Grand Hotel in San Diego. Scripps refused to make an appointment to see the former President, because he did not like to make appointments to see anyone. [23]

Secretary of State Bryan did accept an invitation to "Miramar," however. When Bryan arrived about midafternoon — some hours late — Scripps told him he appeared "too disgustingly done up" to be of any amusement to Scripps or of value to himself; Scripps told him to go take a bath and rest; Bryan did so, and reappeared two or three hours later, fresh enough and "decent enough" to be good company. Suggesting a short drive, Scripps was disconcerted to find Mrs. Bryan going along, too; Scripps had definite ideas about a woman's place. After dinner, Mrs. Bryan, disregarding Scripps' suggestion that she was tired and should go to bed, joined the two men in Scripps' study for a three-hour chat. Let Scripps tell the story:

I discovered that Bryan was the locomotive and that Mrs. Bryan was the engineer, and that she kept her hand on the throttle and her mind on her business every minute.

It was she who suggested subjects, and it was she who kept Bryan to the subject, and it was she who stopped him when she thought he had said enough. She indicated the times when I should speak, and to what question I should give reply, or what suggestion I should make. Her gentle purr, "Now, Will, this; now, Will, that; and Mr. Scripps, this; and Mr. Scripps, that" ran through the whole course of the three sections [drive, dinner, chat] of our conference.

The next morning at the breakfast table, and even after they had gotten into the auto by which I was sending them to town, not going myself, Mrs. Bryan

[21] *Ibid.*
[22] *See* McGeary, *Gifford Pinchot*, p. 219 f.
[23] EWS to Gilson Gardner, July 28, 1915.

reminded her husband of not less than half a dozen things which she wanted him to say to me, and what Mr. Bryan wanted to hear me speak about.

· · · · · · · · · · · · · ·

It occurred to me that possibly the United States has had, for a period of some two years or more, a lady for Secretary of State.[24]

During the conference with the Bryans, Scripps detected what he thought were codes in Mrs. Bryan's expressions and gestures, and cues in her words, for the guidance of her husband. Throughout the conversation she had called her husband "Will," until Scripps finally brought the talk around to what he really wanted to discuss. Having determined from Bryan's previous remarks that he was not pro-ally, Scripps pointedly said that Bryan should know Scripps disagreed with him to the extent that Scripps favored a large navy and perhaps even enlargement of the army at that early moment. Bryan started to loose a flow of comment, but was stopped short when Mrs. Bryan's gentle "Will" cracked out as an imperative, "William!" [25]

The Scripps papers supported Wilson so strongly in 1916 that Scripps claimed they had determined the outcome of the election, a claim which finds some substantiation in the view of two practical politicians of the time. Postmaster General Albert Sidney Burleson reportedly wrote Gardner: "I want you to know that I know that it was the Scripps papers that determined the election." [26] How could this group of smaller newspapers have such an effect? Amos Pinchot, who had some influence in progressivism, tells the story this way: Roosevelt's Bull Moose party, the party of the Progressives, broke up in 1916 when Roosevelt refused the nomination and threw his support to Charles Evans Hughes, the Republican nominee. With the Progressives disheartened and disillusioned, Pinchot wrote: ". . . Scripps . . . again effected a telling political intervention by sending Gardner into Progressive-Republican states where governors, senators, and congressmen were up for election, with the message that the Scripps papers would support them in the exact proportion that they withheld support from Hughes' campaign. It was in these states, especially Oregon [Hughes carried Oregon], Washington, and the Dakotas, where Gardner had sowed the seed of Republican revolt in ground already harrowed by rage at Roosevelt's attempt to turn the liberals over to Lodge and then to Hughes, that Wilson won the doubtful electoral votes that swung the victory from Hughes." Pinchot called Gardner the Colonel House of the Scripps organization, likening him to Colonel Edward House who was President Wilson's

[24] *Ibid.*
[25] *Ibid.*
[26] Gardner, *Lusty Scripps*, p. 193.

personal agent.[27] Scripps' personal assessment of the campaign is to be found in "Scripps Views Wilson."

While in Washington during the war, Scripps became more firmly convinced than ever that America faced a real danger of social and economic revolution, possibly a bloody one, that could be headed off only by reforms rather than repression. Hoping to see Wilson on the merit of his idea alone — Scripps perhaps could have seen him at any time merely by presenting his card — he called first on Secretary Lane, trying to impress upon him the imminence of social revolution. Lane minimized the idea. One might suspect that national political leaders privately looked on Scripps as a crank on the subject of revolution. He did have a brief audience with the President later, but did not record the conversation.

Some grounds for Scripps' fears could be found in that there was some unrest in the country, signalized by the extremists — Socialists and the Industrial Workers of the World (I.W.W.). Added to that unrest were the activities of pacifists and conscientious objectors. All of these factors led to hysteria that produced espionage and sedition acts under which more than two thousand persons were arrested and many sent to prison for long terms, including the Socialist leaders Eugene V. Debs and Victor Berger, the latter a congressman from Milwaukee. Even LaFollette brought criticism upon himself by being one of the six senators who voted against the declaration of war.

Scripps' stroke in the fall of 1917 took him out of action for the rest of the war, but when he recovered he became furious after realizing what had happened to civil liberties during the war. In November, 1918, he urged President Wilson to grant general amnesty to all who had been imprisoned. Among other things he said he was proud to include LaFollette, Debs, and Eastman among his friends.[28]

With that letter to Wilson, Scripps had created a generally embarrassing situation. As the story got back to him it was this: There was a desire to keep the matter quiet, but somehow word of Scripps' letter to the President leaked out. Rather than have the President face the political dilemma of amnesty or no, there was a desire to bring cases before the Supreme Court

---

[27] Amos Pinchot, *History of the Progressive Party* (New York, 1958), pp. 121, 222–23.

[28] A copy of Scripps' letter to Wilson is not included in the Letterbooks, perhaps because Scripps regarded the letter as confidential. In a letter to EBS of Feb. 25, 1919, he said that he had sent the letter to Justice Brandeis, who might have been embarrassed by references to him in the letter, and that Brandeis later reported that the letter had reached and had been read by the President. A letter from Wilson to Scripps, a copy of which is attached to the letter to EBS, confirms the existence of the Scripps letter. Scripps described the contents of his letter to Wilson in a letter to Frederic C. Howe, Apr. 1, 1919.

where the sedition and espionage acts could be held unconstitutional, the prisoners thereby released, and the President saved the necessity of action. However, the situation developed in such a way that the President felt obliged to answer.

In February, 1919, Wilson wrote Scripps from Paris, saying he had "felt very much embarrassed to answer" Scripps' letter at the time of its receipt. Not having "formed a satisfactory judgment" about general amnesty at the time he had received Scripps' letter, the President said, he had merely acknowledged receipt, "trusting to your insight to understand." But, the President promised, "I shall take up the question of amnesty when I get home." [29]

Scripps was not satisfied. On May 16, 1919, he cabled the President:

MR PRESIDENT, FILLED WITH SYMPATHY FOR YOU DURING THESE WEEKS AND MONTHS OF YOUR STRENUOUS ENDEAVOR AND HAVING UNLIMITED CONFIDENCE IN YOUR CAPACITY AND MOTIVES, STILL I AM MORE ANXIOUS TODAY THAN WHEN I WROTE YOU LAST NOVEMBER THAT YOU SHOULD TAKE STEPS EVEN BEFORE LEAVING EUROPE TO GRANT AMNESTY AND PARDON TO THOUSANDS OF AMERICAN CITIZENS WHO HAVE BEEN CRUELLY PUNISHED FOR HOLDING AND EXPRESSING VIEWS DIFFERENT FROM YOURS AND MINE. THERE IS REAL DANGER THREATENING BECAUSE OF THE EXISTENCE OF DISCONTENT, NOT ONLY ON THE PART OF ACTUAL SUFFERERS AND THEIR FRIENDS, BUT ON THE PART OF A VAST NUMBER OF YOUR FELLOW CITIZENS WHO RESPECT AND LOVE YOU.

But Scripps was a voice in the wilderness. In 1919 the Supreme Court upheld the constitutionality of both the espionage and sedition acts in the Schenk and Abrams cases, respectively. Dissenters may have been pardoned individually, as Debs was by President Harding, but there was no general amnesty. On the contrary, the country experienced a wave of hysteria — mostly because of Communists — immediately after the war.

Scripps tried his hand at politics again in 1920, having his papers start, long before the two major party conventions, an editorial campaign that was designed to arouse the rank and file of both parties to such an extent that they would wrest control of the conventions from the Old Guard. Convinced, too, that the country needed a type of engineering — in social, financial, and industrial matters — rather than politics in meeting postwar conditions, Scripps took a look at both Herbert Hoover, who had made a reputation for his handling of food during the war, and Henry Ford. Not caring which party might back either man, he sent an emissary to each, sounding them out. When the reports were in, he assessed them, and decided to back Hoover. Hoover had reported that he did not know whether

[29] Woodrow Wilson to EWS, Feb. 5, 1919, copy attached to letter from EWS to EBS, Feb. 25, 1919.

he was Republican or Democrat. Scripps then developed a strategy of building up Hoover to such an extent that the Republicans would nominate him for fear the Democrats would, inasmuch as the Republican convention was first on the schedule. Before the conventions, however, Hoover destroyed the whole plan by announcing that he was a Republican, which allowed the Republicans to nominate Warren G. Harding without the slightest fear that the Democrats would nominate Hoover. With the original plan smashed, Scripps backed Governor James M. Cox of Ohio, the unsuccessful Democratic nominee.

That about ended Scripps' active interest in politics. In 1921 he called on President Harding and former President Wilson, comparing the two men in "Two Presidents." It was his third visit with Wilson — 1914, 1917, 1921.

He did, however, stir himself to a modicum of interest in 1924 when La-Follette came forth as the Progressive candidate for president. Because Robert P., by then running the Scripps-Howard papers, was backing LaFollette, Scripps agreed to see the Wisconsin senator. But he did so on the quiet. Not wanting anyone either in or out of the Concern to know that he was personally interesting himself in politics — and he really was not — Scripps had LaFollette brought to his yacht, the first time he had seen him since LaFollette's visit to "Miramar" in 1912.

During a conference of about an hour and a half, at which he did most of the talking, Scripps showed how much of a conservative he had become as a result of the changes that World War I produced in his thinking.

He literally jumped at LaFollette, saying he was disappointed in him, and demanding: "Are you, if by any chance you should become President, going to carry into the White House the same spirit that you showed in the Senate?"

LaFollette asked what he meant.

"You're always on hair trigger," Scripps explained. "You're always jumping in as the advocate of the workingman and the poor man. You're always jumping on us millionaires. You're not only partisan in details but you're partisan in generalities."

LaFollette said he would go on being LaFollette.

Scripps remonstrated, accusing him of having his mind only on the present.

"You're standing back with a club just watching and waiting for some head to hit," Scripps rejoined. "It appears to me that you're never thinking about anything except today, tomorrow, or the day after."

Scripps closed the interview by telling LaFollette he could expect more support from the young men then running Scripps-Howard than "I would be either able or willing to give . . . even if I felt strong enough to run my own machine." [30]

The full extent of Scripps' swing toward conservatism showed when he expressed content with the election of Coolidge. And yet there was a note of mellowness in his appraisal of the political situation, and his feeling that the world pendulum was swinging toward conservatism:

It is perhaps because I am now an old man and because of the development of my own business that I am not only able to be content with the apparent subsidence of radicalism [all over the world, as he saw it] but to be even content with Coolidge and all that Coolidge means. I have often enough in late years acknowledged that I had ceased to be a Democrat and that I had even become to a very large extent a reactionary.

Of course I am biased, but I have at least sense enough to know that I am biased by my own personal situation.

I think, however, that I am too wise and too well informed to believe that ever again in any part of the Western world will we ever get back to that old conservative spirit which ruled before the days of the Great War.

When I sit by myself thinking about general conditions, political and economical, I have to acknowledge that perhaps the world might have been the better if the tide of revolution which started in Russia had slipped over the whole world. [In a later letter he said it would take a century before the world would know whether communism had been right or wrong for Russia.] I certainly am not regretting anything that has happened so far. I wouldn't turn back the hands of Time for a day. Still, Ellen, I have been awfully afraid for a number of years past that progress toward democracy might be too rapid.

My own experiences of at least a half a lifetime have tended to develop in me a feeling of antagonism toward all forms of rebellion against authority and against overviolent attacks on old convention.

Perhaps it is just these experiences of my own that have been biasing me and I can fully realize that for this very reason my opinion has been adversely affected.[31]

By gradually slipping into acknowledged conservatism in old age, Scripps, of course, followed a law of nature, which in this case has the added blessing of making him understandably consistent for once.

But in earlier years, Scripps bumped into himself coming and going in politics more than in any other area. A radical who sidestepped populism, a Democrat who distrusted Bryan and wished he could be a Socialist, who said he was not a Socialist but advocated that his editors support socialism, who held that socialism was not so bad, who held that socialism was an absurdity, a Democrat who worked up his greatest political enthusiasm — prior to Wilson — over Progressive Republicans, who held that socialism

[30] EWS to EBS, July 12, 1924.
[31] EWS to EBS, Nov. 8, 1924.

was inevitable, who contemptuously predicted Taft would be just another puppet for reactionaries, who felt better as a businessman at Taft's election — that was Scripps' ball of contradictions in politics.

As one who once saw himself as "the most particular kind of an individualist," Scripps seems never to have found a political party, political thinker, or combination that satisfied the diverse elements within his thinking. Taking an independent course in each separate direction would harmonize with his general nature; being a disciple of any "ism" or a member of any doctrinaire in-group would not. The consequence would appear to be that in politics he had to take Hobson's choice, to use one of his pet phrases.

The Election and Its Relation to My Business

[*November 6, 1908*]

While acknowledging a really extraordinary amount of chagrin, not perhaps as a result of the election of Taft, but as the result of the overwhelming preference shown by the public to that system of government which the Republican party stands for, I must acknowledge that, as a businessman and as a capitalist, I feel a great sense of relief — a great increase of self-confidence and confidence in our business concern.

Had Taft been elected by a small plurality, and had this small plurality been on account of Bryan's vote being cut down by the great Socialist and independent party [Independence party] vote, I would have felt in every way satisfied, because I would rather trust Taft, or a man of his sort, to take care of the business interests of the country than I would Bryan, while I would at the same time have felt certain that a large and growing tendency toward socialism or other methods of protesting on the part of the people would have been a warning to the party in power so clear and so definite as to make it or its leaders more careful and more considerate of the public at large.

But the present situation is such that the party in power, and the clique in control of the party, and especially the great captains of industry and financial magnates, will feel themselves so thoroughly well entrenched as to become arrogant and impudent.

I believe that it is quite possible that Taft's majority is stronger and greater than would have been that of Roosevelt if Roosevelt had gone before the people unstultified by any previous pledge such as he made of not again being a candidate. In fact, I believe that Taft was popular largely because the public had been educated to believe that he was a more conservative man than Roosevelt, and because they have been convinced that, while

458

being guided in the main by Roosevelt's moral principles, he would so modify the application of them as to hamper not at all the great business leaders of the country, and only to cause the worst element of capitalists to be a little more discreet and careful rather than honest — careful of appearances [rather] than of acts.

I am rather inclined to believe that no other candidate of the Democratic party could have polled as many votes as Bryan did. Had a "safer" man, say, like Governor [John A.] Johnson [Minnesota], been the candidate, that fact alone would have caused such an alarm of the possibilities of Democratic success as to have driven many Democratic voters out of the party and have caused the business elements to have been even more active in their efforts to defeat him. Bryan carried a vast amount of votes, too, on account of sentimentalism that neither Johnson nor any other man could have carried.

In fact, I am willing to concede that the great majority of the people, Democrats as well as Republicans, are very well satisfied with the present condition of things political.

A Democrat of habit, of sentiment, and a sentimentalist like myself could afford to support and vote for Bryan just because we felt that his election was next to impossible, and that, while it would be a good thing from our point of view for the country to have the Republican candidate win, it would be a better thing to have him win by a small majority instead of a large one.

Not a few of my business and personal friends chaffed me on the question of my Democracy for some time before election day, declaring that they were certain that if I had it in my power to individually cast the deciding vote as between Taft and Bryan, I would cast that vote in favor of Taft. I can say that I believe that these people were mistaken, but that I am mighty glad that this alternative never came within less than a million miles of me.

Taft will suit his party. If the people of the United States will elect Taft in these comparatively dark days of after-panic depression, what will they do four years hence when, barring some extraordinary accident, business and general prosperity will be greatly advanced, and would have been advanced no matter who had been elected president? Taft is not the kind of man to make many mistakes. It has grown the custom in this country of giving a good president a second term. Taft will be his own successor, if he lives and if there does not exist or grow up in his mind some obligation to make way for Roosevelt in 1912. In 1912 Taft will, if he lives, be re-elected, or else Roosevelt will be. He will probably serve until 1916, when Roosevelt may come back.

There will be at least eight years more of Rooseveltism tempered with Taftism. The new system may be called Taft-Rooseveltism. These two men together as a team, or one or the other, certainly do stand for the things that an overwhelming majority of the people of the United States stand for and desire.

In 1896 we settled the money question forever, or almost forever. In 1908 the people of the United States have put their final stamp of disapproval on socialism and everything socialistic, sentimentalism, Bryanism, and all sorts of innovation reforms.

For eight years, at least, there will be a steady progress along present lines. It is probable that it will be twelve years before there can be any possible chance of a political revolution of any kind, no matter how moderate, in this country.

The businessmen and capitalism and plutocracy — in fact, the government of the United States — have received an overwhelming vote of confidence.

There is one advantage of this situation, at least, which presents itself to all men: capitalist, poor man, employer, and employee. There is no occasion for any doubt as to what is going to occur in the business world for some time. We know where we are at, and we know where we are going to stay for some time. The businessman and the capitalist, the poor man and the wage-earner, can now make safe calculations not only for the immediate future, but for a considerable period of time into the future. There is no need now of holding off from any proposed business or other project to find out what is going to turn up in the political world. Nothing new is going to turn up. Absolute certainty has taken the place of not only doubts but possible doubts.

A citizen of the United States does not have to be a sound political economist, trained in the lore of this complex, brain-wearying science in order to prognosticate the future. He simply has to deal with twenty years of past history of business, and to reckon to a certainty that with some modifications, some exaggerations, of good and evil, the future will be a repetition of the past.

As in '73 and '93 the country recovered, somewhat slowly, from the effects of the panic, we will get through the depression caused by the panic of 1907 more rapidly because we will be more confident. Progress and the extension of business will not only go on and increase until in the course of three, two, and perhaps one year more, our business affairs will be up to the standard of 1906 and the early part of 1907, but after that, prosperity will continue increasing until the condition of affairs in this country will be the marvel of all commercial and industrial history.

The capitalist real, or the capitalist of credit, needs only to be possessed of ordinary, good business judgment in order to make his prosperity safe and certain, the result of almost any good investment. That is to say, the average capitalist will make huge average gain. Of course, there will be exceptions.

Of course, accidents will happen, and, of course, even the shrewdest businessman may make wrong guesses occasionally.

This is a time when I would say that it would be wise for a man to embark all his capital and all the capital he can acquire by credit — a reasonable credit — in any of the standard enterprises or in enterprise in which such an investor has become proficient and expert.

Now, as to my own trade as a journalist. I must humbly admit that I have been proven a very false prophet indeed. My judgment has been biased by my personal sentiment.

Where I thought to find a huge majority of the people of the United States suffering from some form of discontent and a very large minority indeed in a condition of mind almost verging on revolt, I have found that identically opposite conditions prevail.

As an editor, I have been preaching to an imaginary audience which I supposed was willing to listen to me, glad to hear me, sympathizing with my views, and eager for the leadership of such men as myself. I find that there has been no such audience. The people who have been reading my papers in large numbers have not been attracted to them by my prophecies of woe and my clamor of grief. I can imagine, even, the blush of mortification, but the people for the most part who have read such utterances in my paper have only been entertained because they were amused. They have read my paper, perhaps, though mainly, because of the more sane and wholesome parts of the news that were devoted to the real news of the day and the comments on real and not imaginary conditions and facts.

Where I have been willing and thought it was my duty to weep with those that wept, I have perhaps been only a lugubrious nuisance in the midst of a cheerful and far from heartbroken company.

The people do not want my sympathy, and they do not want my leadership and my help, apparently. The most they want of me is to give them all the news of the day and the most cheerful and entertaining literature.

I feel that I have been overwhelmingly voted a bore.

The people do not want me for a Moses. They want me to be a cheerful, prosperous, intelligently selfish businessman, cooperating with (and not antagonizing) the other members of my class.

Elsewhere I have truly said that a new era had begun in my concern with the new, young men. We, a bunch of "Old Men of the Sea," have been riding the shoulders of these youngsters, much to their discomfort, perhaps.

It seems particularly fortunate that the young captains of my concern, who are causing the concern itself to take a new departure, happen to find themselves in charge of the government just at a time when the world of business and world of politics has been swept clean of all old nuisances, of doubts, misconceptions, and sentimentalities.

I have been too long developing in myself that spirit which has become so evident of late years for me to change my disposition and my trend of thought. I can't change it. The times require of this concern of mine, for which I am responsible, not only a change of men but a change of motives, of methods, of practices.

Optimism instead of pessimism — youth and energy and hope instead of age, of caution, of timidity — [is] required.

Perhaps the best advice that I can give to my successors is that, so long as they cannot bury me bodily, they had better bury out of sight and out of thought all that there was or is of me other than the purely physical.[32]

Even my advice might be listened to or read as one who would read some droll but ancient bit of history — the philosophy of men who were wise in their times, but whose even greatest wisdom was infantile, was puerile, as viewed from the present day's greatly increased knowledge.

[32] Strictly a passing thought, considering his watchful eye on the course of his papers.

Triumphant Mediocrity

[*April 5, 1909*]

This disquisition appears to have been edited in Scripps' hand.

What is there about Mr. Theodore Roosevelt that is remarkable?

He is a scion of an old Dutch family of New York. What are the most remarkable characteristics of these old Dutch families of New York? It seems that they are: first, Dutch, not English, French, Irish or Scotch, or African, or Chinese, or Japanese; and second, that their founders went to Manhattan Island a long time ago, but few people know of anything else that any of them did to make themselves remarkable. The mere incident that they obtained land on Manhattan Island, or somewhere else, and that later generations built up a great city on that island, causing these lands to enhance greatly in value, may have redounded greatly to their profit and notoriety, but it gave no evidence of any other superior qualities, physical or intellectual.

The citizens of old New Amsterdam did not even seriously attempt to defend themselves against the invading English. In the days of the American Revolution they certainly had opportunity to discover to the world any great qualities they possessed, but the old Dutch families distinguished themselves most by going through that little affair without attracting any particular attention.

Whatever else could be said about Theodore Roosevelt, it cannot be said that he is a typical Dutchman; on the contrary, Roosevelt is the antithesis of everything that is Dutch and old, so that even if the old Dutch families are entitled to any credit at all, Roosevelt is undeserving of any credit on that account.

Roosevelt, as a boy and young man, was a typical child of the city, that is to say, he was not robust of body. The indications even are that he was a

463

neurotic. He has always been a restless, excitable, perhaps even hysterical character.

Apparently Roosevelt has spent the greater part of his life, first, in trying to recover, and second, in trying to maintain his health by all sorts of physical exercise and out-of-door sports. Yet he never attained a high degree of physical development — he does not have a commanding figure, a sonorous voice, or a faculty of expressing himself in words or writing in such a way as to indicate that he has a powerful and discerning mind. As a rancher he was active, but apparently futile.

He started out to be scientific; he went a little way into biology, far enough at least to have some of his papers on this subject accepted and printed — mark this well — after he had become notorious as a politician. As to biology, he not only did not take a leading place, but rather lagged somewhat behind the textbooks.

Roosevelt got a place on the national Civil Service Commission. In this position he made himself somewhat conspicuous, but it is well known that he was not even one of the authors of this great reform or change in the government's system of employing its servants.

He was a police commissioner in New York, and talked a great deal about enforcing the law, such as it was, without regard to what the laws were, but no great or even any small reform of importance in the police department or morals of New York dated from Roosevelt's epoch.

He was in no way qualified by expert knowledge on the subject to fill his later position as assistant to the Secretary of the Navy; he held down this job for only a short time and, for this reason, didn't have the opportunity to attract much attention.

Was he the author of the Rough Rider regiment, organized at the time of the Spanish war, or was the scheme someone else's, only offering Roosevelt an opportunity to play the spectacular part? The "Rough Riders" was a name fortunately chosen for the purpose of getting advertising. The whole Spanish war was an affair such as to add nothing to the military glory of the country, but even in this little adventure the American Army, from its base, the commissary, to its chief, the fat [General William R.] Shafter, disgraced itself and the country. In this whole little war there was only one spectacular event — the charging of San Juan Hill — and this attack had nothing to do with the eventual and inevitable victory of the Americans; the Rough Riders were at San Juan, but they were led by Doctor or Colonel [Leonard] Wood and not by Roosevelt. The Rough Riders didn't capture San Juan Hill, but Roosevelt captured a great deal of glory, such as it was.

Later, as governor of New York, Roosevelt did not distinguish himself as one of the few great governors of the state, but he talked much and made himself some (for him) fortunate enemies, and thereby acquired a position in the office of Vice-President. The accident of the Czolgosz incident [assassination of President McKinley] made Roosevelt President and gave him an opportunity of making a great noise in a place where he could be heard all around the world.

Much has been said about the Roosevelt policies! What were they? Were there any Roosevelt policies? Were not the Roosevelt policies made by someone else and appropriated by Roosevelt? Upton Sinclair in his book *The Jungle* suggested an idea to Roosevelt which he exploited in a tremendously noisy campaign against the beef-packers. Perhaps someone knows who the author of the anthracite coal mining strike intervention was. [Attorney General Philander C.] Knox and McKinley, or McKinley and Knox, began the trust-busting business in the case of the Northern Securities merger, which continued through two administrations and finally became known as the "Roosevelt policy" of curbing and regulating great capitalistic combinations.

The movement for the conservation of America's natural resources was not organized by Roosevelt.

There is good ground for the suspicion that [William] Nelson Cromwell, a great lawyer-promoter, was the real author of the Panama canal construction by our government.[33]

Whether Germany, or England, or France should have sent the plenipotentiaries of Japan and Russia to Portsmouth to arrange their peace — whoever it was, it was Roosevelt's opportunity.[34]

Roosevelt has been a voluminous writer, but he has never written a book nor an article whose character was above the most stupid mediocrity, nor a book nor article that would have sold except for the reason that its author was the most thoroughly well-advertised man in the United States. Since Roosevelt's retirement from the presidency, as editor of the *Outlook*, he has written one article on socialism — the article in question is trite and shows on the face of it that Roosevelt has no more knowledge on this subject than such as has been picked up by casual reading of other newspaper and magazine articles, written themselves by men whose mental bias was even greater than their ignorance on the subject. His denunciation of socialism is based upon the assumed (by him) truth of vulgar slanders. He appeals to the mob, as a demagogue would. He has said nothing that would cause an avowed Socialist to reconsider his convictions. He has said nothing that will prevent any reader of his from embracing the theory of socialism; on the contrary he has increased the number of potential Socialists, since some of his readers

[33] Cromwell was attorney for Philippe Bunau-Varilla of the New Panama Canal Company, a French concern that the United States bought before beginning construction of the canal.

[34] The peace treaty ending the brief Russo-Japanese War was signed in Portsmouth, N.H., in 1905.

will yet find out the falsity of Roosevelt's charges and, presuming that Roosevelt is capable of knowing and saying everything possible against socialism, they will presume that it is unnecessary to search for further evidence on the part of the prosecution.

All of the above may be considered a rather complete indictment of Roosevelt on the charge of mediocrity.

If, then, Roosevelt is a mediocre man, why is he famous?

Perhaps several answers might be given to this question, but two are enough:

1. While Roosevelt is of the mediocrity, he is the very prince of the mediocre, he stands out pre-eminently as the representative of the great majority of his fellow citizens — those who can't think deeply and those who can think incorrectly.

2. The other answer can best be given by using Roosevelt's favorite adjective, "strenuous."

Roosevelt could put more nervous energy into and make a greater personal display and create a hundred times more noise refereeing a dog fight than men like General Grant could in the direction of a hundred great battles.

That Roosevelt thought rightly and that he acted rightly, for the most part, during all of his career, has been perfectly natural and was to have been expected of him, because he thought and acted in a way considered right and proper by the vast majority of his constituents — that is to say, the men and women of mediocre capacity. He was not ahead of his times; he was not above the majority of his people in intellectual grasp or moral principles; in fact his greatest eulogist could find nothing better to say of him than that he was "delightfully human," by this meaning that he was so startlingly commonplace that all the people could understand him. He stood so near[ly] on the level with the great majority of the people that he gave no offense to them by reason of his possession of greater advantages than the common man. He could not be vague in his utterances because his convictions were so elemental and commonplace as to make their expression easily understood by everyone.

There are men in this country who have reputations for being great engineers, great doctors, great lawyers, great chemists, great astronomers, great mathematicians, great this, that and the other thing. Most of these great men are entitled to their reputations, perhaps, but how can any man know whether any other man is great in any particular department unless he (the critic and judge) is himself a great man and expert in the same department? How can the ordinary layman, who knows nothing of biology, for instance, be able to determine what another man knows about it? The party of the first part cannot intelligently examine the party of the second part by a series of questions and examinations when the party of the first part knows nothing whatever about the subject and cannot determine whether the party of the second part is giving correct or incorrect answers.

Who, but a great statesman, could judge the character and ability of another great statesman? One good businessman can judge of another good businessman's ability. The endorsement by one successful doctor of a brother medico is of great value, since the man expressing judgment has himself knowledge of the science of medicine.

The universal praise and laudation of Roosevelt by the mediocrity might be considered evidence that Roosevelt himself is of the mediocrity.

But why is it that Roosevelt is either hated and admired or loved and respected by so large a number of the really great men and women of this country? Why is it that he is almost universally considered a great man by people of our own country and people of other lands? Perhaps it is just simply because he is the most strenuous and most energetic man in public life today except one, perhaps — the emperor of the German nation. Exhibitions of force and of energy and of courage, no matter what form the exhibition takes, are pretty sure to attract the wondering admiration of all observers.

What of Taft Today?

[*February 12, 1910*]

This disquisition appears to have been edited in Scripps' hand. Scripps circulated this disquisition among his editors-in-chief and Gardner, his Washington correspondent, with a letter saying:

> *A few days ago I found in myself a somewhat changed attitude toward President Taft. I attempted to sum up in a disquisition the causes of this change.*
>
> *The essay is halting and crude, perhaps just because of my own unpreparedness and surprise at myself.*
>
> *I am not even sure of my historical data.*
>
> *Still, I feel inclined to send to you and some of my other associates my essay. I want to see how it strikes men who have so much more opportunity than I have to see and feel things, and who have neither time nor inclination to theorize.*[35]

It seems to me that either there is a very distinct change of policy developing in the administration, or else that a lot of us have been more or less mistaken in our judgment of Taft, being carried away, as it were, by our zeal and overhaste to continue the prosecution of the Roosevelt policies, or, perhaps, [being] biased by our prejudices. I have not believed that a man of Taft's breeding and training could serve the masses.

During the past twelve months I have been reading Gideon Welles' *Diary* concerning Lincoln's term as President.[36] This reading called back to my memory things that I used to hear talked about when I was a boy.

While Lincoln was the choice and hope of the radical abolitionists of the North and while he undoubtedly owed his nomination to the balance of

[35] EWS to Gilson Gardner, Feb. 14, 1910.

[36] Gideon Welles, *Diary of Gideon Welles, Secretary of the Navy Under Lincoln and Johnson*, 3 vols. Houghton Mifflin, Boston, 1911.

power which these people held and threw to him, he was not, if I remember rightly, nominated on a conspicuously abolition platform, and it is more than doubtful whether he would have been nominated at all had there been an attempt to have nominated him upon such a platform.

However, from the time that Lincoln was elected until the day of his assassination, he aroused more indignation and resentment on the part of many of the most radical and most influential members of his party, because of his slow and conservative course, than the indignation and resentment which has been felt toward Taft by the radical Roosevelt supporters. But in the end Lincoln turned out all right.

I am going to try the part of an apologist for Taft. I am going to presume that Roosevelt was fundamentally right in his judgment of him. I am going to try to explain, myself, how Taft might at heart be the kind of man that Roosevelt thought him to be and still fully capable of pursuing the course that he did during the first eight or nine months of his administration.

It was said, and it is possibly true, that Taft had no ambition or desire to be a candidate for the presidency or to be elected president. Against his personal wishes, let us assume, he was forced to become a presidential candidate. Under these circumstances he might well feel that he was freed from a considerable amount of responsibility — especially responsibility to that element in his party which has most severely criticized him.

It must not be forgotten that for many years Taft had been a very conspicuous public figure. During all of that time he had been the object of the most fulsome and flattering comment on the part of the public press and public speakers.

All of this being followed by "the office (of president) seeking him instead of his seeking the office," it would only be natural for Taft to feel that his overwhelming victory at the polls indicated that he, as much or more than any other president, was a representative of the people and trusted by them. That he should have had what is called the "big head" could not be surprising.

Perhaps Taft is a slothful man naturally, and hence has trusted so much to others that he has been imposed upon, and will be imposed upon.

All of us have had large personal experience with forceful, demonstrative, and pugnacious men who have taken infinite pains to overcome by force of will conditions which could more easily have been overcome by gentle words, or which might never have existed had gentle means only been employed. Perhaps the most pugnacious man who has ever been in public life was Roosevelt. It might have well appeared to Taft that most of the opposition Roosevelt encountered was unnecessary and only caused by Roosevelt's mannerisms. It might easily be imagined that Taft proposed to avoid these mistakes of his predecessor's and to adopt an entirely different course with the full expectation and intention of arriving at the same ends as his predecessor was aiming at.

Taft was a lawyer and a judge. As such, he was better able to understand and judge of the qualities of lawyers than any other class of men. Everything else being equal, he could tell a good man who was a lawyer quicker than he could a good man who practiced any other profession. Doubtless, if I were elected to fill some very important public position, I would be prompted to seek as assistants and associates the most capable men I knew of. Beyond doubt I would be better able to recognize talent in journalists than in any other class of men. There are not so many opportunities for journalists to obtain great distinction as there are for lawyers. As a rule, they talk little and their writings are anonymous, and hence I would have had no such army to select from as Taft had.

Taft, being elected president, chose his lawyer cabinet, and he chose to win over by policy rather than the "big stick" the support of Congress. It was natural and proper for him, in pursuing this course, to give his attention to those men in Congress who had established their leadership. Now developed another condition of affairs which might have been expected. First, the Roosevelt element in the party [was] surprised, shocked, and made indignant. Next, the anti-Roosevelt element was surprised and rejoiced.

Wrongly, I presume, these anti-Roosevelt people presumed that Taft had always been at heart with them, and that he had always been at heart opposed to his predecessor, and they gave Taft credit for nothing more than hypocrisy in all his previous course, and assumed that Taft had at last thrown off his mask and openly joined them. They did not give Taft credit for being an honest man (which after all he may be). While Taft thought he was capturing the reactionaries in Congress and in the country, the reactionaries thought that they had captured Taft.

The Payne-Aldrich tariff bill went through. Taft at first moderately and delicately remonstrated. Then he made his speech at some college meeting where he spoke in more certain language, declaring, while the tariff bill was still before Congress, that if the Republican party did not live up to their promises they would be destroyed and should be destroyed.

Both his gentle remonstrances and his more vigorous protest failed. Finally the bill was passed by both houses and was in the committee of conferees, and Taft made a final, and it is presumed too late an, effort to get his party in Congress to redeem their pledges. All he could get out of them were some small concessions on hides, oil, and, I believe, lumber.

Perhaps in his own mind he was greatly chagrined. He was in an embarrassing position. At this time the smart men in Congress, taking advantage of Taft's considerable ignorance in commercial matters, and of their great ability to juggle figures and statistics, sought to and succeeded in convincing

Taft that the Payne-Aldrich bill was a tariff revision downward. We all know how it has been possible for able advocates on both sides of the question to present in each case apparently unanswerable arguments. I have had experiences with bookkeepers and accountants myself. I have found that these men could furnish almost indubitable evidence that a balance was a deficit or a deficit a balance. I have found, perhaps because of a lack of knowledge as an accountant, that in judging of the condition of any business I could place no reliance whatever on so-called bookkeeping. I have had to depend upon my own knowledge of business and my own system. Depending upon these things, it has been impossible for figure-jugglers to fool me.

But I do not know enough about tariff (nor presumably does Taft) to make it possible for me to declare on the basis of my own knowledge, even now after as much as I have read, that the recent tariff revision was up or down. However, I know and Taft probably now knows that nearly all of the really able men who are capable of analyzing this tariff, who are not interested personally or employed by persons interested, have decided that the revision was not downward, but that it was upward.

Doubt, suspicion, and perhaps even final conviction [have] percolated into Taft's mind, until he has become convinced that he was made a fool of by the very men in Congress on whom he was relying to act in good faith, and in a friendly manner toward him. Perhaps he is very uneasy in his own mind today on this account and somewhat resentful at having been fooled.

Then came the Ballinger incident. Taft was a friend and admirer of Pinchot. But Ballinger was a shrewd fellow. He succeeded in leading Taft on step by step, and [in] maneuvering Pinchot into one position after another until finally Pinchot was driven to taking a certain course which compelled Taft to take the action he did.

Perhaps Taft feels resentment against Pinchot for having forced his own dismissal. It is quite likely, however, that Taft recognizes the Iago of his cabinet in Ballinger. It is certain that Taft fully recognizes that public sentiment of the best sort in the United States is on Pinchot's side, and is against Ballinger. Taft is the kind of man who would better enjoy the friendship of the Pinchot class than of the Ballinger class. Perhaps Taft today suspects that he has been betrayed in Congress and in his cabinet, and forced into a position before the public that is most distressing to him.

McRae tells me that he met Charlie Taft in Washington recently and that he was told by him that the President was living in a perfect hell.

It appears that early in the administration Taft imbibed the idea that the "insurgents" in Congress were really making warfare upon the administration, and even as late as after the present session of Congress he was led to make indiscreet remarks about withholding patronage from the "insurgents." It really looked for a time that Taft had become the most important member of the "reactionary" party in Washington. It seemed to only require the Pinchot incident to convince the public at large that Taft had taken the final step in severing all relations with the Progressives.

But just at this time began to appear some evidence that Taft had really waked up and discovered: (1) that he had not and never had had any personal glory — that all the fame he enjoyed was reflected — in other words, that the people had trusted him because Roosevelt had trusted him; (2) that his confidence had been imposed upon by the great financiers, by leaders in Congress, and by some of his cabinet advisers.

About this time, Taft began sending messages to Congress that had the true ring of Roosevelt in them. He began submitting bills as administration measures, such as even Pinchot and the most radical pro-Rooseveltians approved of. He began to show a bold and independent front with the financial magnates. His appointment of [Henry S.] Graves to take Pinchot's place indicated that, either from purposes of policy or from conviction, he had no idea of surrendering the government to corporate and individual looters of the public domain.

The so-called "regulars," the old opponents of Roosevelt, at the same time began to show a certain amount of lukewarmness toward the President, or a disposition not to hurrah and rush through Taft measures.

Has Taft all along been only an honest man, and only been fooled? Has he begun to suspect, or is he convinced that he has made a mistake in supposing that he could get by diplomacy more than Roosevelt had been able to accomplish by pugnacity? Is Taft really a bad man, or has he only been a very simple one?

It is said that Taft is slothful, that he will not read any publications that criticize him, and that he has even turned his back upon and been deeply offended personally by those of his intimate friends who have had the hardihood and daring to tell him what the real sentiment of the people was.

McRae tells me of having met Captain, or Colonel, Clarence Edwards (the son of the once famous Billy Edwards of Cleveland, Ohio, the business partner of an old-time politician and congressman, [Amos] Townsend). Edwards is apparently high in the favor of Taft, and is a warm personal friend of the President. Edwards spoke to McRae of the latter's former acquaintance with Taft and asked him, McRae, to go to the President himself, and tell him personally his own views on the subject. McRae said he declined to do so: first, because his acquaintance with Taft was not close and intimate; and second, because he knew the experience of other men who had tried to speak plainly to Taft. Edwards seemed to be very anxious because Taft was in no position to learn, or because he would not take the trouble to learn, the trend of public opinion.

The *Outlook*, much to the disgust of many of its old friends and readers, has to a considerable extent made itself Taft's apologist. But even the *Outlook* has been saying things which, just because of its general attitude, must have struck Taft in a disagreeable way, considering the known attitude of that publication.

Albert Shaw, editor of the *Review of Reviews*, has persisted in a loyal and friendly attitude toward the President, and yet has published some articles, notably the one on the "make believe" tariff and some editorials which, if Taft has read, must have convinced him that there were loyal friends of his whose judgment was good but who had to recognize public opinion and voice sentiments adverse to his administration's expressed views.

Taft well knew that he had given serious offense to his old friend, Roosevelt, in naming his cabinet, and that, too, before Roosevelt had left the country. He must have heard and read much of the pother about "the back from Elba" cry. Undoubtedly, scheming politicians of the Hitchcock [37] type have felt it necessary to warn him against a possible Roosevelt party defection. Altogether in one way or another, it seems that Taft must have discovered now that he is no longer an object of universal admiration and public confidence. He must have discovered that he has been viewed with resentment by many, black suspicion by others, and doubt even by the most conservative of his old partisans.

I have always considered Taft as a perfectly honest and sincere man (until a few weeks ago some things occurred which made me fear that he was more of a rascal than weakling). For the most part I have felt that his unfitness for the presidency arose mainly from his breeding, training, and association, which was such as to make it impossible for him to understand and hence sympathize with the great majority of his fellow citizens. Only such men as were socially, intellectually, and financially the superior people in this country could possibly be congenial with a man like Taft, and hence only these would make his environment and mold the character of his administration.

But recent events indicate that for some cause or causes unknown to me, Taft may yet surprise and disgust his recent friends, and surprise and rejoice the friends of his campaign days.

Today, while I am dictating this, I feel that it is just possible that before Taft's administration is much older, I may retract all of my criticisms, written and spoken, and be as glad to support Taft as I ever was to support Roosevelt.

Taft is certainly physically a heavyweight.[38] Mentally he may have the same characteristics. It takes a good deal of force and a great deal of irritation sometimes to move such men to activity, even in the performance of

[37] Presumably a reference to Postmaster General Frank H. Hitchcock.
[38] Taft weighed 350 pounds.

their ordinary duties. Perhaps Taft's first ten months of office may have aroused him.

Taft is the kind of man who would rather sit still than exert himself. He is the kind of man who perhaps will not perform any kind of labor which he does not have to perform. He may be slothful and lacking in keen political insight, but nothing that I have ever heard of him indicates that he lacks courage in the least. His various mistakes — the very faults that he has committed — have indicated that he has no timidity. He might have been fooled into whitewashing Ballinger. He might have had no idea that it took courage to do this thing, but he could not have been fool enough not to fully recognize all the penalties which would result from his dismissal of Pinchot.

I recall a certain experience of my own, which had relation to Taft's character. Several years ago Boss Cox, a most corrupt and villainous man, after having for years dominated, corrupted, and pillaged Cincinnati, had embarked upon an adventure to capture the boss-ship of the whole state of Ohio. Being in Ohio several years ago, some things occurred which called themselves very forcibly to my attention. Certain things occurred which humiliated and finally angered me. I determined to begin the fight myself against Cox, and I began the fight.

In Cincinnati I began to look around for friends and associates. I heard much of individuals and associations who were grumbling and even bitterly complaining of the situation. The *Times-Star*, the paper owned by C. P. Taft, brother of W. H. Taft, a very wealthy man, that had some years before opposed Cox, finally completely surrendered to Cox and became his most servile organ.

I was told that I should not judge W. H. Taft by his brother, C. P. Taft, as in fact the two men were politically as far apart as the poles. I was told what W. H. Taft had said in private conversation both about his brother's political course and about Cox. Then I asked: "If W. H. Taft so despised Cox, why did he not say aloud, publicly, these things instead of confining his remarks to a few persons in confidence?"

About that time the state convention of the Republican party was to be held. The then governor of Ohio, Myron Herrick, was completely under the domination of Cox, and was using his office to build up the Cox machine. Herrick was seeking renomination. Cox was seeking control of the Republican party in the state. It was very desirable for both of these men that they should have the recognition of the national administration, and the endorsement of Ohio's favorite political son, W. H. Taft. To further this plan W. H. Taft was called from Washington to act as chairman of the state convention which was to nominate Herrick. The convention was held. Taft acted as chairman. Herrick was nominated and the great and good W. H. Taft appointed Boss George B. Cox and someone else to escort to the convention and the platform the successful candidate, for the purpose of the latter thanking the convention, etc.

I was in Cincinnati at the time and caused to be published in the *Post* a cartoon representing George B. Cox on a bootblack's throne and W. H. Taft and Governor Herrick acting as bootblacks, blacking the boss's shoes. The caricature was perhaps the most offensive that could have been conceived. It was bitterly resented by that large respectable element in the state who were Taft followers.

Mr. McRae and my counsel, J. C. Harper, had been in St. Louis during the day or two previous and only returned on the evening that the caricature was published. Both of these gentlemen regarded Taft as almost a demigod. They came to my room at the hotel greatly perturbed. Not only were they deeply moved on account of the offense given to Taft, but on account of the effect that they felt certain would be produced as to the prosperity of the *Post*. They both pronounced it a terrible business mistake, if nothing worse. McRae went so far as to prophesy that the cartoon would yet prove to be the ruin of the *Post* as a property.

However, offensive as was the publication of the caricature, the public only too well realized its justice and the mistake of Taft himself. From that moment a most bitter campaign, both in the state of Ohio and the city of Cincinnati, was inaugurated against Cox and his machine candidates. Mr. Harper, deeply as he had been wounded personally in the Taft matter by the cartoon, had been more deeply wounded by Taft himself. He entered so heartily and so vigorously into the spirit of the campaign that I was inaugurating as to prove the perfect sincerity of all his political motives. Then we began in earnest to organize a party.

A few, a very few men were brought to me to discuss the matter. Those who came were very, very timid. They were willing to fight Cox, but wanted to do so anonymously. The whole community was terrorized. We wanted a campaign fund. Only a few would subscribe to it and, these too, only in very small amounts. They regarded the case as hopeless. In fact, I found only two men in Cincinnati whom I considered capable and who were willing to cooperate with me. They were J. C. Harper and Elliott Pendleton. There was an association called the "Honest Election League," or something of that sort, composed of men of no great standing in the community. The only two real prominent citizens connected with it were Harper and Pendleton. But it was difficult to get funds. I gave Mr. Harper authority to draw on me to an amount up to ten thousand dollars, and indicated that I was willing to spend more under certain conditions.

The campaign was organized, though it was principally a Scripps newspaper campaign. Our papers made a good campaign, and in time it began to dawn on the public that the campaign might be successful. Later it began to look as though the campaign would be successful.

About this time it was deemed advisable to interest President Roosevelt himself. Roosevelt was interviewed on the subject. I do not think that anyone knows just what took place as the result of this consultation with the President. It has been said that Roosevelt called W. H. Taft to him, and advised him that neither the Republican party nor Taft himself could afford to have a Republican victory in Ohio which would have to be considered as only a Boss Cox victory. It was said that Roosevelt advised or instructed Taft to go into Ohio and make a speech which would make this clear.

The battle, it must be understood, was almost won, or supposed to be almost won, before Taft appeared in Ohio, and in a little city in northern Ohio, Akron, he made a speech in which he said that there were reasons why he could not or would not cast a vote in Cincinnati, his home, but that if he were in Cincinnati on election day and had a right to vote, he would cast his vote against the Cox machine candidates.

The election took place. Cox's candidate for governor, Herrick, and his candidate for mayor of the city of Cincinnati, were defeated. The Democratic nominees for governor and mayor were elected.

I recall this incident only because it appears to me that it may throw some sidelight on W. H. Taft's character and may help to determine Taft's future actions as President. In the Ohio campaign Taft held back, said nothing, and did nothing until it was made clear to him that there was a tremendous amount of public antagonism to the rule of the Cox machine. Now, is not the general national political situation somewhat similar to what it was in Ohio several years ago? Taft let Cox have his own way until he learned of the public sentiment.

Taft has been letting Ballinger, Hitchcock, [Senator Nelson W.] Aldrich, [Speaker of the House Joseph G.] Cannon, *et al.*, have their own way in Washington until the public outcry and clamor has risen to a high pitch and until the "insurgents" in Congress have shown in their defeat of Cannon on the Ballinger-Pinchot investigating committee matter that if the power of the bosses has not been broken, it has been greatly weakened.

Are not the President's recent messages to Congress, the bills that he has sent to Congress and some of his recent public utterances to be compared with the Akron speech aforementioned?

While it takes only a little switch to make a thoroughbred horse spring into activity, it takes a knotty club to induce a camel to quicken its pace, and a sharp iron-pointed goad to give a hint to an elephant. Roosevelt might be compared to a thoroughbred horse, and Taft to a leather-skinned elephant.

I would not advise those good men who are pounding with clubs and punching with iron-shod goads to relinquish their labors just yet, but I would advise them, while continuing their efforts, to do so with not too great animosity toward the beast they are encouraging. I would advise them to watch hopefully and be prepared for the possibility of their victim yet arousing himself and going to work effectively for good.

I have been accused of not only expressing but actually feeling great pleasure in being able to say "I told you so" with regard to Taft. Yet I believe I can conscientiously say that I have been unfairly judged. I have had my hopes and my misgivings as to my judgment from the first.

There is nothing in the world that I hope for more than that Taft will, by his future conduct, prove that I and his other critics have been as blind and unjust as Lincoln, in the end, proved that the Greeleys and Garrisons were too zealous to be clear-sighted.

The National and California Political Situation

[*March 18, 1910*]

"Miramar," Calif., March 18, 1910

Mr. W. B. Colver
410 American Trust Building
Cleveland, Ohio

My dear Colver:

Your letter of the 10th addressed to Jim, I have read.

It seems to me that the announcement of Roosevelt's determination has cleared up and settled the whole line of policy for our newspapers for some time to come. Our attitude toward the immediate future political situation is this:

1. We regard as inevitable a completely new political cleavage.

2. In the old Democratic party there are two elements — reactionary and radical; the radicals being in the majority in the northern and western parts of the country.

3. The Republican party is composed of the same two elements. But while the radicals or progressives are perhaps a great majority, it is probable that only a minority would openly and continuously oppose the old machine organization.

4. We have never had any patience with the Republican party, and have finally despaired of the Democratic party organization being able to accomplish anything.

5. We have espoused the cause of the "insurgents" as against the "regulars" in the Republican party and our efforts have been, and will continue to be, rather to beat the regular Republican organization for the benefit of the "insurgents" than to attempt to serve the Democratic party only, by splitting the Republicans.

6. We should be as much opposed to those representatives of democracy who are reactionary as we are opposed to Aldrich, Cannon, *et al.*

7. We are anxious to have Roosevelt a candidate in 1912. We prefer to have him an independent candidate, or rather a candidate who would be bolted by the reactionaries in the Republican party, as Bryan was bolted by the reactionaries in the Democratic party.

8. With Taft as candidate for the "regulars" and some such man as Judge Parker [Alton B. Parker, the 1904 candidate] as candidate of the Democrats, and a Roosevelt, a LaFollette, or a [Senator A. B.] Cummins as the candidate of the progressives of both parties, the situation would be ideal. It requires no alteration of our general newspaper policies to aid and bring about this condition.

What I wanted to write you about was on a particular subject. Hiram Johnson, Heney's legal lieutenant in the San Francisco graft fight, has been chosen as the leader of the anti-Southern Pacific element in the Republican party in this state, as a candidate for governor. We all tried to get Heney to take the leadership, but he could not, or would not, and Heney himself nominated Johnson to take his place.

The only thing that I dislike about the Johnson candidacy is that the public recognizes him as a Lincoln-Roosevelt League candidate for governor.

The Lincoln-Roosevelt League of California is composed of all the men who are opposed to the Southern Pacific machine. It includes the "sore heads" who would have been "regulars" if they had been allowed to hold office, as well as the radicals of the Republican party. Its representatives in the late legislature voted for [Senator George C.] Perkins, and a number of its staunchest men are still Taft "regulars."

Johnson himself is really an "insurgent," and has very little sympathy with, or interest in, that large element of the Lincoln-Roosevelt League who are only "sore headed" or ambitious. He frankly and publicly denounces Taft and his cabinet. He goes further than most of the men that I have heard speak on the subject. He says that Taft is not honest and could not be honest and have men in his cabinet like Ballinger, [George W.] Wickersham, Knox, and Hitchcock.

Hiram Johnson has just started his campaign for the gubernatorial nomination. He came to the extreme south of the state to open his campaign. He has spoken in San Diego and several of the smaller towns in San Diego County. He tells me that he proposes to go on clear through the state, going into every county and into every community in the state, speaking. The new primary election law of this state requires just such a campaign.

At Mr. Heney's request, I invited Johnson to "Miramar," and at the same request Johnson came to see me.

I had two conferences with him while here. He was very eager to learn from me what he could about the probability of Roosevelt's course. Gilson Gardner's first cablegram appeared in the San Diego *Sun* on the evening that Johnson arrived at my house. I told Johnson that I interpreted this cablegram to mean that Roosevelt would come back a thoroughgoing "insurgent." This information pleased him greatly. He said that he considered that his success as a gubernatorial candidate would be assured if Roosevelt took that course, which would encourage the "insurgents" of California and convince the Republicans of this state that they did not have to give up their republicanism in supporting him, Johnson.

If by any chance Roosevelt, after he arrives in America, could be induced, for any purpose whatever, to make a trip clear across the country through the middle-western "insurgent" states and the Northwest and arrive at California, I believe that his mere presence in these territories would greatly strengthen the "insurgent" movement all through the country, and further I believe that it would make Johnson's election in California assured.

With Johnson governor of California and a safe "insurgent" legislature to elect a senator to take [Senator Frank P.] Flint's place, great impetus would be given to the forward movement of the Progressives.

I would like to have my ideas, or some of them, brought to the attention of Mr. Roosevelt's friends and advisers. Doubtless Heney, who is in the East now, has already vouched for Johnson in such a way as to secure him the confidence of his eastern friends.

Yours sincerely,

E. W. Scripps

Statesmanship and Poverty

[*April 17, 1910*]

I have had more or less personal acquaintance with, and knowledge of, some prominent persons in political life today — some popular idols of democracy. I know of the cases, for instance, of Senator LaFollette, the graft prosecutor Francis J. Heney, Judge Ben B. Lindsey of Denver, Governor [Joseph W.] Folk of Missouri, and Theodore Roosevelt.

When Mr. Roosevelt gave up the presidency, he took the position of associate editor of the *Outlook* publication.

A few months ago when Gilson Gardner, the chief political writer for my newspapers, was with me at "Miramar," we were discussing the editorial attitude of the *Outlook*. Gardner is a warm personal and political friend of Roosevelt. I consider Roosevelt as the main hope of present-day democracy. The *Outlook*, from the time Roosevelt left this country, had been a pro-administration organ. I expressed my regret to Gardner that Roosevelt was being committed by that paper. I said that it was a mistake for Roosevelt, as a politician, to be connected with any publication.

When, a few weeks ago, Gardner met Roosevelt in Egypt, he told the ex-President what my idea was on the subject of his being a journalist. To this Roosevelt replied: "But what can I do? I am not a rich man, I must have an income, and I must earn it."

The other day I received a letter from the famous ex-Mayor Tom L. Johnson of Cleveland. In this letter he urged me to make up a purse by subscribing myself, and getting Rudolph Spreckels, Joseph Fels, and some other people to join, and proposed that we should raise twenty-five thousand dollars to help LaFollette in the coming senatorial campaign.

I have had Judge Lindsey as my guest at "Miramar," and I met him at Denver. I have also had some considerable correspondence with him. Lincoln Steffens, who is a great friend of the judge, once urged me to make a better use of the money I was giving away by endowing Lindsey with an

481

income which would permit him to be a free man in the prosecution of his political plans and the upholding of his political ideas. Lindsey is in a state of chronic financial debility. He has to go into debt in every campaign that he makes, and it takes all of his earnings as a judge and as a platform speaker, between campaigns, to pay these debts.

Several months ago Francis J. Heney visited me at "Miramar." At that time there was a very strong movement on foot to get Heney to contest for the gubernatorial nomination. I told Heney that I would support him in my papers and contribute ten thousand dollars to his campaign fund. Heney told me he could not afford to be governor, that he was fifty years old, that he was "strapped," and that it was necessary for him to resume his profession and earn enough money to support himself and wife in their old age.

Joseph Folk of Missouri has to make a living by being a platform lecturer.

James R. Garfield [Roosevelt's Secretary of the Interior] who, on account of his connection with Roosevelt and Pinchot, and perhaps largely on account of his own high moral principles, has a national reputation which, if it does not make him an idol, at least makes him a man of great reputability. And Garfield is a poor man.

Gifford Pinchot is the only one of this set of men, concerning whom I have much personal knowledge, who is not only a well-to-do but a rich man. Pinchot, notwithstanding his wealth, is a man of the very highest moral and political ideas — perhaps he is the superior of all the others whom I have named. While the exception may only prove the rule, Pinchot furnishes evidence that the possession of wealth is not absolutely and necessarily a corrupting condition.

Rudolph Spreckels is a rich man. He has spent a great deal of money and made great sacrifices in the way of time and social status, to a good cause, but it is quite evident that his enthusiasm is fighting an unequal battle with his selfish interests.

I wonder what would have happened to such men as LaFollette, Lindsey, Heney, and Roosevelt if they had been possessors of great wealth — would they have been of the character of Pinchot or Spreckels? I can be pretty certain of Lindsey. Of the others I would have my doubts. The great men of the world have been both rich men and poor men, very rich and very poor. I believe that civilization, morals, and culture have been advanced more by the very poor than by the very rich. I doubt if the Carnegies' and Rockefellers' work ever has been, or ever will be, anything else but injurious to morality, culture, and the advance of civilization. A Roosevelt, a Lindsey, a LaFollette, and a Folk, from the very necessity of their positions, must have far greater capacity for sympathy with the great masses of the people than can be possessed by men of the Pinchot and of the Rudolph Spreckels types.

Scripps Tries to Energize
a Reform Party

[*September 20–27, 1910*]

Sensing that the time had come to enter a new party in the field, taking advantage of the progressive movement within both the older parties, Scripps attempted to encourage the formation of a third party. The genesis of his effort is to be found in the September 22 letter to Colver of the NEA, discussing a conference with Gifford Pinchot which began on September 20.

His next move, on September 25, was to draft the planks of a proposed party platform — what he called "A New Platform" — which he forwarded to Colver and Pinchot under date of September 27, 1910. Copies of those letters and the platform went to all group editors-in-chief, Paine, and Gardner.

All three letters and the new platform were included among his disquisitions under separate titles, but have been grouped here under one heading to achieve greater unity.

The letter to Pinchot appears to have been edited in Scripps' hand.

"Miramar," Calif., September 22, 1910

Mr. W. B. Colver
Cleveland, Ohio

My dear Colver:

I spent two or three hours with [Gifford] Pinchot at San Clemente Island yesterday morning and the evening previous.

I believed that Pinchot was in a position to know exactly Roosevelt's privately announced intentions for 1912.

Billy [William] Kent was at the island and we two had a short personal talk. Kent had not any too-exalted idea of Roosevelt. He thinks he is too busy, and always has been too busy to be well and definitely informed, and to ever

483

have time to think out anything. He said our man for 1912 would, he believed, be either Roosevelt, LaFollette, or Pinchot.

I believe that we both agreed that LaFollette would be the most consistent leader.

However, I took my clue from Kent's remark and went for Pinchot on the subject of his training independently for his candidacy.

We thrashed this matter out in two hours spent in my own boat alone, and quite incidentally Mr. Pinchot told me that Roosevelt was fully decided that he was under no obligations to refrain from running for a third term, and that he would cordially accept a nomination.

I know that this has been assumed by others who are intimate with Roosevelt, but I believe that no one could possibly be better and more intimately informed of Roosevelt's intentions than Pinchot.

Whatever else I may say, it is only incidental, as my main object was to discover Roosevelt's position.

I told Pinchot that I would rather see LaFollette the candidate than either himself or Roosevelt, and I told him that I believed LaFollette could poll a bigger vote than Roosevelt because LaFollette knew now and always had known what he was after, while Roosevelt was being formed by conditions concerning things that LaFollette and I and many other people had known a long time and that was that the people were really mad clear through. I also said that I thought LaFollette would have a better chance than Pinchot to get a big vote.

Pinchot asked why. I said LaFollette was a plebian, while he, Pinchot, was a man "who might grace any court." Pinchot replied with spirit that he believed he was a gentleman, and that he thanked God for it.

"Yes," I said, "you may congratulate yourself, but just now the people would have more use for an Andrew Jackson kind of a man than any other type — in fact, even a strong taint of vulgarity would be relished."

Pinchot said that about March 1st, next, he wanted to leave the country and be alone by himself where he could have time to think more, digest his information, and assimilate into his mental constitution the facts and knowledge which he had been acquiring during the past strenuous year.

In his previous visit to me [1909] and in this talk much had been said about Australia, of whose politics I know something.

I urged him to stay in this country and keep in sight and let his views constantly be heard, but if he was going abroad that he should by all means live and think in the atmosphere of the new kind of democracy prevailing in Australia and New Zealand.

I pointed out to Pinchot that he had one vast advantage over Roosevelt as a candidate.

Roosevelt had a political past that was well marked with many of the ordinary mistakes of a climbing young politician, and also by some excesses due to the intoxication of great power. Kent and Pinchot and Pinchot's brother [Amos] asked me what I was after, or rather what I wanted. I told them I was going to do all in my power to have Taft nominated by the Republicans and a man like [Governor Judson] Harmon [of Ohio] by the Democrats in order to force the radicals to form a new camp in which to organize the new army from which should be eliminated as nearly as possible everything reactionary. Kent protested against eliminating any votes from the Republican party if the Progressives controlled it. I protested against any sort of association or partnership or cooperation with those strong and crafty men in the two old organizations, since the latter would be a constant source of danger — being traitors in the camp.

On the whole, I left the island feeling rather depressed and discouraged and with a very distinct impression that the Roosevelt group was more anxious for the temporary advantage of the immediate future than they were deeply imbued with the necessity of organizing for the future.

In fact, they desire a good president, a majority of good men in Congress, and a better personnel on the bench more than they do to change the general system of government and politics which has always in the past tended to bring about conditions the evils of which are similar to those of the present, and which in the future can be depended upon — no matter what temporary betterment may be made — to revert into the same evil conditions.

It was on account of these feelings that I suddenly cut short my visit and returned Pinchot to his own boat and steamed for home, not staying over for another day or two as I had rather expected. Pinchot saw that I was disgruntled and tried to get me to explain the cause of my feelings. He seemed to think that he was in some way personally responsible. I could not explain and I did not try. He asked me to write to him and I told him I would if the spirit moved me to do so.

It is this damned party fetish that has got in its grip all of our insurgents, and the worst of it is they don't know to what extent they are victims of superstition.

They still believe that the temple of republicanism is a holy place and that it has not been forever contaminated and put beyond the condition of possible purification.

Mr. Pinchot promised me a two or three days visit next spring.

Sincerely yours,
E. W. Scripps

"Miramar," Calif., September 27, 1910

Mr. W. B. Colver
410 American Trust Bldg.
Cleveland, Ohio

My dear Colver:

As I was about to leave Pinchot the other day, he several times urged me to write him and suggest "planks" for a political platform. I told him that I would do so if the spirit moved me.

The other day I did feel like trying to formulate some of my own ideas, and some of the principles that formed the underlying foundation of our journalistic course.

I have made two essays at this task, and have at least produced a document which I can understand, and which I believe fairly well represents the collective views of the Scripps concern.

I have also written Pinchot a letter.

It occurs to me that during my talk with Pinchot at San Clemente, he recalled and repeated the substance of all that was most important in our last summer's confab. Amongst other things he said that he had constantly in mind, while he was writing his letter to Senator [Jonathan P.] Dolliver, the substance of my two letters to him and our conversations.

For various other reasons I suspect that he put some weight on my views.

I forgot to ask Pinchot his address, and I do not know it.

I remember that he was particular to ask me if I wrote at all to get my letter to him before October 15th.

Therefore I send you in an envelope my letter to Pinchot and my platform, and ask you to forward the same to him so that he may get it within the time he mentioned.

I am sending to you and others copies of my platform and of my letter to Pinchot, as I believe all of you should know what is going on in my mind. I also want to have all of you give these ideas of mine some consideration, to discuss them when you have occasion, and to make criticisms and suggestions both to me and among yourselves.

While modesty is a very commendable virtue, I think that we would all be very foolish indeed if we did not recognize the full extent of our power in creating and formulating public opinion and directing it toward organization.

I am confident that we owe more of our power to our peculiar strategic position than to the magnitude of our institution.

It is because we have our newspapers, little and big, scattered all over the country, and because through the United Press and the Newspaper Enterprise Association we are able to find our way into the editorial sanctums of many other newspapers, that we are really able to force upon the attention of the whole people every important news fact and very many of our ideas.

I have no particular care for, or interest in, any particular political campaign. I don't care very much for the winning or losing of any particular election.

The great thing that I think we have to strive for is "by laying one brick at a time" to get one voter after another all over the country to recognize not only existing evils but the practicability of remedying them.

Providing that we ourselves have practical ideas and statesman-like ability, time will only be required for us to produce, if not a universal, at least a majority public opinion that will result in progressive steps being taken that would not otherwise have been taken.

So far, however, from our desiring to seek notoriety or glory or credit for our accomplishments, I believe that we should prefer for strategic purposes to remain unrecognized as a moving spirit in the body politic. It is the results in the way of public improvement that we want to accomplish, and we will be more apt to succeed, perhaps, if we leave to others the position of being "shining marks" to be attacked by the arrows of those who envy and those who hate.

Sincerely yours,
E. W. Scripps

"Miramar," Calif., September 27, 1910

My dear Mr. Pinchot:

You asked me in our recent talk to suggest to you some planks of a platform.

You know that I admit (I don't claim) that I am so radical and so progressive and so impatient that I have few fellows among the people of your class — that is to say, the class of men who are today furnishing the great majority of the men who fill official positions.

On the other hand, my views are exceedingly conservative as compared with those of the great 95 per cent of the inarticulate, unorganized masses of the country.

While you and Kent and others know that the people are angry, you have no idea just how very angry these people are. I fear that you are yet, sooner or later, to be surprised and shocked by some great demonstration of the people led by a man or men governed more by passion than by reason.

When such a blatant braggart as a Hearst [39] can command an army of

---

[39] Having political ambitions for himself, Hearst entered the Independence League in the presidential lists in 1904 and 1908. He served in Congress from 1903 to 1907, but was defeated in races for governor of New York and mayor of New York City, and did not run for president.

from 100,000 to 150,000 personal followers in conservative old New York, what an army there must exist in this whole country ready to receive orders from a real and sincere though perhaps passionate and mistaken leader!

I told you that we men who are rich are hated — that is to say, feared. We are hated and feared, not as individuals always, and not because we are all bad men doing evil deeds, but because collectively we are oppressing the people, and because individually it is known that we may, if the whim moves us, severely injure, each of us, the many of our neighbors.

I have heartily thrown in my lot with you men who were Republicans — not long ago satisfied with that party, but who are now insurgents seeking either in the Republican party or outside of it to ameliorate some of the evils from which the country suffers.

I have only chosen the association with you because you have a strong organization and have aims that are higher and better than those of any other large and powerful political organization in this country.

I recognize in Mr. Roosevelt a man skilled in leadership who can, if he will, do a greater work for the world than Napoleon did, and do an infinitely better work for the world than did Napoleon.

Roosevelt can do for this country at this time as great a work as did Washington. Washington succeeded in establishing an independent nation. Roosevelt can succeed in establishing a real democracy. Lincoln preserved the union of our country by striking down the institution of African slavery, and incidentally a powerful oligarchy of wealthy and intellectual men. Roosevelt may save this country from eventually drifting into an ineffective, unscientific form of socialism and save the principle of individualism largely shorn of its present evils.

A great new condition of society has developed. Some radical changes in governmental systems are needed. These changes have got to come. A century or more ago the only possible change would have been reversion to monarchy and aristocracy, but now the only change that can be made is toward a more perfect democracy, and the Socialists are offering us a form of democracy that, even if it were a scientific possibility of the future (something I cannot believe), is premature.

Louis XIV destroyed the enemies of his state by ruining his most dangerous rivals, the great nobles, but he did not save his state. Roosevelt or you or some other man must do what Louis XIV did, and more.

I told you that if the spirit moved me I would try to formulate a platform. I have done so and enclose it.

Do not think for a moment that I am so foolish as to believe that any national convention of the Republican party or any smaller conference or committee of practical politicians would for a moment give it consideration.

However, I have the ear, or perhaps I should say the eye, of more than a million voters in this country and if I live I will have many more, and in my peculiar way and by my own peculiar methods I shall continue such a propaganda as will, I hope and even expect, result in there being leaders of the people who will be prepared someday to venture a platform not one whit less radical than this one I am sending you.

I have learned how effective is the instrument I have in my possession.

You stated the other day that, considering our previous talk at "Miramar," you had been surprised at the attitude of the Republican press in this country during the past year. I do not claim to have intentionally promoted that attitude, but newspapermen are human. I cannot pick up a newspaper today and read it without recognizing that there is much in it that is a result of imitation — perhaps imitation of imitation of imitation, of what my own associates have done.

In the last several years the Scripps papers have been printing things and the Scripps United Press Association has been reporting things and the Newspaper Enterprise Association has been sending out copy. As it was impossible to altogether suppress certain facts, it was necessary that *all* the newspapers had to disseminate them. Because the Scripps papers printed certain things that made them popular and successful, the others papers had to print the same or similar things or suffer.

If I am right in reading the public character and understanding the public attitude, I have only got to appeal to that public sentiment in order that all over the country every other newspaper has got to do the same thing or suffer.

From what you told me of Mr. Roosevelt's tour it appears that during that trip he learned for the first time, or to the full extent, much of the condition of the public mindedness that I have before known and perhaps that I have contributed to.

Please do not think that I am boasting. If you only knew how humble I was and how mortified I am because of the smallness of my work as compared with my opportunities you might listen to me more patiently.

Sincerely yours,
E. W. Scripps

A NEW PLATFORM

Plank I. — We believe that the time is come when the people should have an opportunity to give expression to their views untrammeled by any checks and formalities hitherto existing on the subject of the basic principles of their government. We believe that a new constitutional convention should be convened, the members of which should be named by free and secret balloting.

Plank II. — We assert that this government has ceased to some extent to be a government of the people, by the people, and *for* the people, and that it has become largely a government of the people by a few of the people for the people who possess large property and privileges, and that unless this evil condition ceases at an early date by lawful and orderly methods, the time will sooner or later come when the very existence of the nation as a free people may cease or at least when the nation will be involved in a revolutionary struggle greatly destructive to both life and property.

Plank III. — We assert that the judiciary has from the beginning of our government been encroaching upon the province of the two coordinate branches of government, viz., the legislative and executive, until at the present time neither Congress nor the executive are in full possession of their constitutional prerogatives which our present Constitution was intended to guarantee. We assert that the courts have not now nor should they ever have any constitutional right to pass upon the legality of any act of Congress that has been approved by the executive or that has been passed by that body over the veto of the executive by a two-thirds vote. The judiciary department has no more right to pass upon the constitutionality of acts of the legislature and the executive than have the legislative and executive departments to pass upon the constitutionality of the acts of the judiciary. All constitutional questions should be determined by votes cast by each of the departments of the government, that act being deemed constitutional and legal that secures the approval of two of the three governmental departments.

Plank IV. — We believe that not until the people shall have through a new constitutional convention, and until the whole people have ratified these proposals [*sic*], should the courts be permitted to initiate or affirm the existence of any law or rule of procedure not sanctioned by the legislature. Government by injunction and punishment for contempt other than contemptuous interference in a courtroom during trial should be prohibited.

Plank V. — We believe that the time has come when it is necessary to form a new compact of union and national organization. The people should have an opportunity to pass upon the organic form of their government. The people should have an opportunity to readjust the representation of the various sections and populations of the nation as a whole in our national Congress. At present in the Senate an undue proportion of power is held by representatives from small states having small populations to the injury and detriment of other sections and populations whose present representation is far inferior proportionately to their contribution to the government support and their ability and duty to defend the nation in time of war.

Plank VI. — We believe that written constitutions are not only valuable but absolutely necessary as a foundation of a democratic government, but that such constitutions can only be made tolerable working instruments by means of their containing within themselves facilities for changes and amendments to be easily made by the whole people whenever a majority of the whole people desire to make such amendments and changes.

Plank VII. — We believe that the common law principle governing the validity of title to property that applies as between any two citizens should apply as between the state and a citizen or corporation. No title to any property should be considered valid that does not originate in some legal, honorable, and equitable transaction. The man who buys from a thief a stolen horse has no title to the possession of the horse. No individual or corporation who has obtained land grants or any sort of franchise or privilege from the government by means of corruption, false pretenses, or any sort of chicanery should become possessed of assignable title to such land, franchise, or privilege. The rule of *caveat emptor* should be enforced against the victims of dishonest men rather than that the government alone should suffer all of the penalty of a crime committed; provided that the government may for reasons of state, with or without consideration, grant to any citizen or the victim of crime against the state good title to stolen property if such citizen shall prove that he is innocent of any collusion in the original crime and that he has exercised reasonable care to protect himself and the state against deception, but no principle of "vested interest" or so-called "statute of limitation" should be permitted to stand between the guilty man and the forfeiture of his dishonest gains.

Plank VIII. — We believe that the possession of extraordinarily large fortunes by individuals or small combinations of individuals and that the control even of large fortunes by individuals or small combinations of individuals must be a public menace, unless the actions of the owners and controllers of such large fortunes shall be strictly and constantly regulated by the government to the extent that the public shall always gain and never lose by the conduct and management of the property which constitutes the fortune; and further that the government shall not and cannot enter into any contract, such as a charter or franchise, with any individual or corporation that will limit forever or for any part of time the powers and rights of the government to alter at any time its own method of regulation.

Plank IX. — We assert and emphasize the historical principle that the government is the actual owner of all property and all forms of wealth in the state and that the individual occupant or controller of any such property or wealth has no other rights than those of steward or agent for the government and that it is the government's right and duty to dismiss from agency or trusteeship any person who is deemed not to be making the best possible use for his own and the public's benefit of any such property; providing only that the person as agent or trustee dismissed shall be equitably remunerated for such services as he has performed and such improvements as he has made either personally or by the hands of some other from whom he has received, as gift or inheritance or any other form of assignment, the property in question.

Plank X. — We believe in the greatest freedom of trade between the people of our nation and the peoples of all other nations consistent with the protection of the high standard of living for the least fortunate of our citizens, and we believe that all customs duties levied in excess of the amount required for such protection have no other result than the establishment and maintenance of unjust monopolies.

Scripps Views Wilson

[September 6, 1917]

Scripps wrote this letter to his sons after he had moved to Washington "for the duration," which proved to be of short duration because of his stroke. The letter came from his Letterbooks, not from among his disquisitions.[40]

Messrs. James G. and Robert P. Scripps:

Mr. Wilson owed his nomination to the office of the presidency some five years ago to a condition of affairs which would never have existed except for the Scripps newspapers.

Even in the Baltimore convention [1912], at a critical period, the effect of the Scripps papers was evident.

We could not have prevented Wilson's renomination for the presidency had we tried.

However, we know perfectly well that he would not have been re-elected president excepting for the activity of the Scripps newspapers and other organizations during and at the time of the last campaign.

We are responsible to the people of the United States, then, for Mr. Wilson's holding his present position.

The President had striven successfully for more than two and one-half years to keep this country out of the war. It is true that in our campaign we especially recommended Wilson to the voters of this country on the ground that "he had kept us out of the war."

However, our papers had been more or less vigorous advocates of preparedness and, during this advocacy, we indicated that conditions might arise where the President could be expected to declare war and when we would support such a move on his part.

Later, our papers took the lead amongst the newspapers of the United

[40] Title of this disquisition supplied by editor.

States in demanding that war should be declared against Germany, and carried on such a vigorous propaganda that I believe that we organized anywhere from 5 per cent to 25 per cent of that public opinion which finally induced the President to declare war.

In this matter, no one of us three took any active part. The editorial leaders in our concern acted on their own volition largely. So far as I know, Jim was not responsible for this campaign in any other way than by acts of omission. I am not so free from responsibility, however. At the time the submarine boat U-53 attacked and sank a number of ships off our coast a short time prior to the November election, I sent a personal wire to President Wilson urging him to take a more vigorous course. I recall that I sent a copy of this telegram and the President's reply to Messrs. Rickey [Ohio] and Canfield [Northwest] and some others. Rickey and these others were fully justified in believing that I personally was belligerent. How much effect this copy of my telegram to the President had on Rickey and the others, I do not know. It possibly had a material effect on them.

Then, we are not only responsible for the existence of the present administration, but also, to a very large extent, responsible for the condition of war between the United States and Germany. On the whole, since Mr. Wilson has been elected president, he has — more than any other president we have ever had, and more than any other man who could probably be made president — acted in a way consistent with the principles advocated by our institution for nearly forty years. Remarkable instances of this disposition on his part are: the Federal Reserve law; the farmers loan bank [Farm Land Banks]; the Adamson eight-hour law; and the general personal income tax law (Mr. Taft and the Republican Congress had previously been responsible for the corporation income tax law and the adoption of an amendment to the federal Constitution permitting such income taxes).

Since Mr. Wilson has become president, he has, more than any other man who has been president during my life, been amenable to public opinion. He has, on a number of occasions, entirely reversed his opinion on important political matters as a result of his "keeping his ear to the ground" and being responsive to the public wish.

I believe that we have indirectly had great influence on the activities of Congress and of the President himself since Mr. Wilson was first inaugurated as president. I believe that in the immediate future, so far as we are willing to mold public opinion and give it expression, we will not only have a great influence on the acts of the President but upon Congress.

Our institution has grown to be one of tremendous political influence in this country. This places upon us great responsibility. Our acts of omission and commission during the next few years, and especially during the progress of this war will, I am sure, seriously affect the country's welfare for good or evil.

Mr. Wilson, in declaring war, and in his acts since, has not in a single instance that I can recall seriously diverged from a line of policy publicly and urgently advocated by the responsible editors of our institution. If in some particulars his acts have been other than such as we three approve of personally, they have not been inconsistent with the utterances of our newspapers in any single important case.

He has not complimented us by calling us personally into his counsels or conferring with us on any matters. So far as I can learn, he has not distinguished any other individuals by such a course.

It is my conviction that the President and our constituency have a right to expect us to "stand by the President"; and, in a large and general way at least, to support the government's general war schemes.

After nine years or more of retirement from the actual control of the Scripps papers, coming to Washington I resumed contact with the editorial organization of our institution. I found but little change had taken place during these nine years in the personnel of the organization.

I found that there had been no other change in the editorial spirit of our institution than the natural growth and development that accompanied the growth of the power and influence of the institution itself.

In fact, during his whole term of occupancy of the position of control of the Scripps institution, Jim has made few changes in the editorial personnel, and none in the editorial principles.

Abraham Lincoln said, "It's a bad time to swap horses when you are crossing a stream."

This whole country now is in the midst of a stream of very deep water. Our institution is one of the most important elements, politically speaking, in the country. I believe that it is a bad time to make radical changes in the personnel of the editorial, and that to make a change in the spirit of the institution or its aims at this time might and probably would seriously affect the welfare of our people, and even the prospect of our victory in the war.

I have no desire to take any part in controlling or directing our newspapers in the institution.

More than ever, I feel inefficient on account of my age and on account of my long retirement.

It is my conviction that neither one of us differs seriously in the aims and objects that we would pursue in our dealings with the public.

If we differ at all, it will be on the minor details of persons and of *how* to do things, distinguished from *what* to do.

Concerning myself:

It is my personal desire that when the present editorial organization which now controls the editorial policy of the papers has changed, it should be only in the way of my eldest son's becoming *de facto* as well as *de jure* editor-in-chief.

Since Jim has other great responsibilities, he should, I think, have a chief assistant in this department.

It would be easier and temporarily more convenient for him to have as his chief assistant and his right-hand man someone of large experiences and whom he knows to be personally amenable to his will. On the other hand, the appointment of such a man would only be or should only be a temporary "stopgap."

As soon as possible, Bob ought to be editor-in-chief of the whole institution, subject, for a number of years at least, to the absolute control and direction of Jim.

I believe that Bob is as well qualified today to take this position as I was to take the editorship of the *Press* when I was twenty-four, and as Jim was to take the control of the whole institution in his twenty-second year.

The only way for a man to learn how to be an editor is to be an editor. Bob has the natural qualifications. Only responsibility and experience will develop these qualifications and make him efficient.

The last act that I wish to perform for the benefit of the institution which I founded, and for the benefit of my sons, is to obtain their pledge that they will loyally support the present administration during the war; to do all in their power to avert discontent, revolt, or any kind of internal struggles in the country; and, in this way and others, to bend their whole energy, regardless of purely selfish and financial interests, to the prosecution of the war to a successful end.

It will be consistent with the welfare and interest of our institution for me to continue to live in Washington for a considerable time, and to have free access to and be in close and confidential relations with my sons, and to have free access to the persons employed by them in Washington.

I am sure that no injury will result if you and they shall receive and consider such written and verbal communications as I can make — my purpose being more to serve the interests of the country itself than the business interests of our institution.

> Affectionately,
> E. W. Scripps

Two Presidents

[*November 5, 1921*]

Wardman Park Hotel, Washington, D.C.
November 5, 1921

Miss E. B. Scripps
La Jolla, Calif.

Dear Ellen:

HARDING

I had not expected to see Mr. Harding while in Washington, nor did I really want to see Mr. Wilson.

However, I have been aware for a number of years of the tendency on the part of some person or persons to have me press-agented, or perhaps I had better say, to exploit my personality for purposes not wholly comprehensible by me.

Some one of our men had told me that I ought to go and see the President.

One day I was told that I was to call on the President at four o'clock the next afternoon. Though I assented, I couldn't think of anything that I wanted to say to Mr. Harding nor anything that he could possibly want to say to me.

I arrived at the White House almost on the minute of my appointment, going to the Executive Offices. It appeared to me that there had been considerable change in the rooms since I had been there before.

As usual I was met at the entrance and shown to the anteroom of the President's office. There was the usual youngish-looking man seated at a big table, the usual colored men coming and going, an occasional newspaperman dropping in, while I was seated awaiting my summons.

Presently the youngish man at the big desk, who wore very round and very thick-framed spectacles, arose from his seat and came over to me, holding

497

498 Scripps • POLITICS

out his hand, saying, "I am Mr. Christian." I didn't know who the devil "Mr. Christian" was, but still I extended my hand and said, "I am Mr. Scripps."

I think my thoughts were woolgathering at the time, but they came back to me in time to see a tall, young fellow in black clothes stalking over to his desk. I had never heard the name but it eventually occurred to me that he might be the President's private secretary.

After about five minutes of waiting, or ten, I was shown into Mr. Harding's room. He came forward to meet me, recognizing me and calling to memory the time he met me while I was at "Airlie" [41] four years ago.

Now I recall the first time I met President Wilson was also the first time that I had met a President during his term of office and I recall that I was somewhat awed for a few minutes.

The case was entirely different with Harding. I cannot conceive that anyone would be awed by him.

The President gave me a good seat with the light on his face rather than on my own.

I told him that I was uncertain whether I was with him by his consent or request. I forget his reply. Then I began talking and, as usual, taking the lead.

I wanted to know about that Anglo-Japanese treaty and what they were going to do with it — that is to say, whether we were going to consent to any arrangement with Great Britain so long as she retained her alliance with Japan.

About every time the President told me anything or spoke of anything in particular, he impressed upon me that it was really confidential. But it really seemed to me that he said nothing that might not have been published in all the newspapers and very little but what had been published. However, I construed what he meant by confidential was only that I was expected not to print and publish it.

One of his confidential communications was that the English government considered itself very fortunate indeed that this disarmament conference was going to give them the opportunity of withdrawing from the Japanese alliance without giving unnecessary offense or appearing to be too ungrateful.

He said the Japanese, he felt pretty certain, had come fully prepared to meet all the terms that our government could reasonably make.

I spoke of this matter of the "reasonableness" of our requests. I told him it seemed to me that our position so far appeared to be altogether too modest and deferential and that it seemed to me quite likely that Japan and England would go away with a good deal more than they would have been perfectly willing to concede. In fact, I held that the attitude of both Japan and England

[41] Scripps' home in Washington.

was in the nature of diplomatic bluffing and that our government was in a position to wave aside all serious consideration of the assumed attitude of the two parties.

Mr. Harding said he thought that the word "bluffing" might be considered too harsh a word and went on to assure me that he felt almost certain that the outcome of the conference would be fully satisfactory to myself and everyone else who was not an outspoken and avowed Anglophobe.

I am pretty sure that Mr. Harding is leaving all this matter of the conference to the State Department and receives far more information than he gives out orders. I told him that Mr. [Charles Evans] Hughes had greatly surprised and pleased me since he had been Secretary of State and that I had come to have a very great amount of respect for him.

While I was speaking of this, I told Mr. Harding that, only a day or two before, I had had a meeting of some thirty or forty of my editors and somewhat surprised my audience by telling them that I thought the present administration was doing very well indeed and I told him that this opinion especially referred to Mr. Hughes' and Mr. Mellon's [Secretary of the Treasury Andrew Mellon] departments.

I went on to say that my only justification for taking up his time and using my own energies in this visit was that as a publisher and wide disseminator of news and, perhaps somewhat, a large molder of public opinion, I would give myself the opportunity of being impressed and that he ought to take the opportunity of impressing upon me as much as possible his ideas and plans.

I recognized in speaking this way I was showing some conceit, but it didn't appear to me that Mr. Harding had the same view. His face lighted up and he said, "I know all about you, Mr. Scripps, and your concern and what it implies, and I will always be glad to meet you and give you personally any information you request," and he added that he hoped I would come often to see him.

I then took up with him the subject of the tax revision bill and told him frankly that I believed the country at large was even far more impatient than I was personally at the dilatory methods of Congress and implied, rather than stated, the opinion that he was somewhat responsible.

At this he dropped the subject of the tax business for a time and struck out on a new line. He said, "I have always been a partisan and a party man. I believe in the caucus. I believe that when a congressman or senator is elected by either party, or any party, and comes to Washington he is bound or should be bound to submit to the party conferences."

I interjected, "You mean the caucus."

"Well," he said, "I think that all the members of a party ought to get together and thrash out all these public matters and that each member should be ruled in his conduct by the majority."

He continued, "I believe that such a course is absolutely necessary for the successful conduct of a democracy."

"But," he said, "what a condition Congress has gradually assumed during the past decade or so! Congress is now utterly unregulated. Each individual congressman and senator is thinking only of his own re-election and is utterly indifferent to the interests of the party as a whole and hence to the interests of the government, the people."

"Why," he said, "here are men that have appealed to their constituents as Republicans or as Democrats for their votes and, after having been elected, come here to Washington and immediately throw off all party obligations. They form blocs like the agricultural bloc, larger or smaller cliques, allegiance to which is absolute while party allegiance is entirely neglected."

In speaking, his tone of voice, the expression of his face, and the whole attitude of his body was that of distinct depression. He said something like this: "I don't know what we are coming to and it seems to me that disastrous results must follow a development or scheme of things [*sic*]."

Then we went back to the tax revision bill. He said he believed he could assure me with considerable confidence that before Thanksgiving Day the tax revision bill would be passed and that at least the country thereafter would know what to count upon and plan in the way of meeting taxes.

He said, "You will see that after every one of these little fellows, and some big ones, has had his say and made his speeches and made his appeal to his own constituents, these men will come to their senses and realize the necessity for action."

I told Mr. Harding of my recent conversation with Mr. King [42] and Mr. [David F.] Houston, the ex-Secretary of Agriculture and the Treasury. I said that King was recognized by both practical and theoretical economists as one of the ablest men in the country and that he and a number of men associated with him had been engaged for the last year and a half in making computations as to what the gross income of the United States, the value of all products, for the year 1919 was, and that they had decided it was very nearly 66 billion dollars. I told him that I had left King to speak to Houston on the same matter and that Mr. Houston had told me that his department had estimated that the gross output of agricultural products at the farm was 26 billion dollars.

"Now," I said, "the farmers in the United States produced 26/66 of all the products in the United States during the year 1919." I went on to say that Houston and I estimated that while 48 per cent of the people in the United States was reckoned by the Census Department as being rural, this

42 Possibly he referred to Willford Isbell King, who worked as an economist for the National Bureau of Economic Research from 1920 to 1927 and was interested in gross income. However, Scripps usually referred to Willford Isbell King as "Professor King."

included all people in towns of less than 2,500 and it could easily enough be determined that not over 25 per cent of all the people in the country were actually engaged in agriculture.

"Now," I said, "here are 25 per cent of the people, the farmers, enjoying 40 per cent of the income of the country and yet they have formed an agricultural bloc for the purpose of compelling Congress to give them even a larger share."

Mr. Harding listened to this with apparent great interest and in telling him that Congress and congressmen individually should be informed of this, I tried to leave the inference that he was the one to inform them, that he ought to speak plainly.

I told him that I was myself in a position to be able to recognize that there was something absurd in the inequities of the present tax system in this country, because, although the expenses of running the government were now only four times as great as they were in 1914, my taxes had increased almost sixtyfold. I admitted that my wealth since that time had probably doubled; still, even making allowances for this, an increase of thirtyfold in my taxes was unreasonable.

I said I had every reason to suppose that there were thousands and probably tens of thousands of cases similar to my own, though perhaps none so startling. I said that I knew that one of the Republican senators had just told me a few days before that the Republican party had not agreed formally in so many words to repeal the excess profits taxes of 1920, still the opinion of the country was universal that the party was bound to do this very thing. I asked Mr. Harding what was the difference, at least politically speaking if not morally, between violating an actual pledge made in so many words and disappointing an expectation which the Republicans had caused to exist.

The President tried to soothe me by explanations — not excuses.

"Oh," I said, "I am not complaining of any personal hardship." I said that in fact neither I nor any of the other large taxpayers were suffering much from the condition, but I said, "I do believe a large part of the business troubles in the United States is due to a system of taxation for which I feel that I was largely responsible, as I had taken the lead through my papers in a campaign to make the rich men pay."

But I told him that I felt that my estate, as an estate, something that my heirs will inherit, is going to be a great deal larger than it would have been had there been no such system of taxation. That the result had been in my case, as it had in many other cases, that we had not exactly evaded taxes, but that we had avoided taxes by keeping our money in our business and in the development of it to be invested in new enterprises and new developments, rather than turning it out in profits.

I reminded him that he must have known of many instances where new enterprises had been held back by reason of the owners of real estate not being willing to sell their property to would-be founders of new businesses on account of the income taxes.

It seemed to me that the President was either uninclined or unable to follow me into too deep water.

Two or three times while I was talking, Mr. Harding coughed. Finally, he had a rather hard spell of coughing and impatiently broke out, "Why, here, I've had this cold now for a week and it don't get any better." [43]

I had been with the President the best part of an hour, so, not waiting to be dismissed, as is supposed to be the etiquette, I got up and told the President that I felt I had taken too much of his time, so I was going.

I had noticed that while we were talking together his secretary had come in two or three times to make certain announcements, I suppose of visitors, and that the President was apparently directing where to place the visitors while waiting. On two of these occasions I suggested that I had better get out but he urged me to stay longer. When I did get up and turned to leave, Mr. Harding rose and followed me to the door still speaking, saying amongst other things, "I thank you for coming to see me and hope you will come again and often." He was actually speaking when I opened the door and went out.

I found the anteroom chockfull and I imagine that there were several other parties waiting.

When I left the White House I drove immediately to my dentist who was working on my teeth at the time and told him to disinfect me thoroughly and he did so.

Before leaving, I did take up the subject of banking conditions in the United States with Mr. Harding. I told him that it was my opinion that the banking condition in this country was as bad as it possibly could be, that it seemed to me incomprehensible how we were going to get through without very extensive banking trouble. Harding replied that he agreed with me to a large extent but he said, "That is what this administration is doing and has been doing. We are saving the banking situation."

He indicated that through the Federal Reserve Banks and through the offices of the Comptroller of the Currency, the administration was straining every nerve to prevent catastrophe. He stated one case where, by the activities of the administration, a bank crash was prevented which would have shaken the country and caused the ruin of a very large number of respectable banking institutions.

---

[43] This carries an amusing undertone, suggesting that Harding had been briefed on Scripps' obsession about avoiding contact with persons who had colds, and used it to rid himself of a garrulous visitor.

He admitted that conditions were very critical and he said nothing to indicate that he was even approximately sure that the crash would not yet ensue.

Now as to Mr. Harding — I will try to give a personal description of my judgment of the man.

He appeared to be perfectly at home in his position and spoke rather slightingly of it. I think that for the moment, perhaps on account of his troubles with the Senate, he was feeling as though he would like to be out of the job. He said so, anyway.

Harding is a tall man, I think an inch or two taller than I am. He probably weighs ten or twenty pounds more than I do. His published portraits are good portraits of him. He is one of the kind of men who can stand the camera and the printing press.

You are, of course, familiar with what is often said as to the ruling British officials in India and outlying provinces. They are large in stature, good natured, not superlatively intelligent, possessed of just ordinary common sense. I think there are really many hundreds of thousands of men of the Harding type in these United States and perhaps as many more in England.

They are not intellectual; they are not possessed of that finesse of mind such as, for instance, the Wilson mind or the Latin mind.

They are simple, natural, and the worst that can be said of them is that they are rather unmoral than immoral. They can look wise and avoid revealing their lack of wisdom, or rather, of great knowledge.

I think that Mr. Harding will pass four years in office in a way that will give general satisfaction and I am rather inclined to think that he will be re-elected if he chooses to be re-elected and I am rather inclined further to think that he will choose to be.

I enjoyed my two interviews with President Wilson more than I have this interview with Harding, only it is much harder work to keep up with Wilson's mind than it is to trot alongside the Harding mind.

WILSON

Before I came to Washington, Mr. Crane and Mr. Houston and Mr. Colver and some others told me that they hoped when I came here that I would see Mr. Wilson. I replied that I saw no reason for intruding on Mr. Wilson and that I didn't believe that he would really care to see me.

In fact, as I think you have heard me say, I felt a sort of grudge against Mr. Wilson for not pardoning Debs and issuing a general amnesty.

I had been here perhaps about a week when Colver told me that Mr. Wilson wanted to see me before I left and later he fixed a date, Sunday afternoon last, at 2:30 P.M., and I promised to go to see him. In Saturday morning's paper I saw a notice that General Foch called on Mr. Wilson, but had been met with the word that Mr. Wilson had suffered a severe stomach attack and that his physician refused to allow him to see anyone. Sunday morning Mr. Wilson's secretary called Mr. [Frank] Westberg [Scripps' secretary] by phone and told him that Mr. Wilson was too ill to keep the appointment with me but asked how long I was to be in town.

Thursday Mr. Colver called me up to tell me that Mr. Wilson would like to have me call on him for a fifteen-minute visit on Friday at three o'clock. I was at the Wilson house promptly at that time. His secretary, who is also his brother-in-law, met me and chatted with me for a few minutes until the ex-President was able to see me. His secretary told me that Mr. Wilson was steadily improving in health. I asked him if he thought it would be possible for Mr. Wilson to prepare a memoir — something that he could leave behind him to be published after his death, which would be a valuable document. The secretary spoke very definitely to the effect that Mr. Wilson would never write anything.

I have been told that Mr. Wilson bought a fine home and even that he had paid as much as $250,000 for it. While the Wilson home is in rather an aristocratic neighborhood, it is a very unpretentious building. On the outside it looks even a little run-down. As I entered the house it seemed to be particularly gloomy and dark and uninviting. I had occasion to pass through several of the rooms. There was an air of worn-outness and a lack of something or other or some or all of those things which might be described as homey.

After several minutes wait, I was taken up to the second floor by a small electric lift, passing through a part of the kitchen or pantry — a sort of back part of the house place — and finally entered Mr. Wilson's library.

The library was a fine large room — perhaps as large or maybe larger than your sun parlor. It was well lighted and better furnished than the downstairs rooms. Mr. Wilson was seated by the fireplace, a shawl over his shoulders and a robe over his knees.

As I came up he recognized me and called me by name (of course he was expecting me). He excused himself for not rising, saying that he was unable to do so without help. I shook hands with him and took a chair facing and near him. Whatever little feeling of resentment that I had previously harbored against the man disappeared instantly. It was a pitiable sight. I certainly would not have recognized him had I seen him anywhere else. There is more flesh on his face than when he was in good health, but the skin is a very unhealthy color, not too white but quite the reverse — it seemed sort of a bluish tinge. One corner of his mouth was hanging down considerably and it appeared as though the jaw hung awry. His large eyes had lost nearly all of their lustre. I think they might be described as sad looking.

I had been asked not to condole with Mr. Wilson or remind him of any of his misfortunes in any way. In speaking to me Mr. Wilson's voice rather quivered as it was not clear. His whole attitude was that of a broken, old man. At first glance and at first sound of his voice one might have thought that he was verging on senility.

I saw it was difficult for him to talk so I took the lead. I told him that I had had a slight stroke of paralysis and that it was at almost identically the same age as that at which he had suffered and told him the course of treatment that I had submitted to. I spoke especially of the vast advantage I gained by being on the water and that I felt that I owed my recovery largely, perhaps, not so much to being afloat, as being out of sight and hearing and all reminding of this "damned human race." At this he smiled and said, "Well, there is something in that."

I told him of my trip around the coast through the canal and the good accommodations that I had had in traveling — my special apartments on an upper deck, with a private deck where I could be outside and out of reach of anyone.

When I spoke of Mr. [Newton D.] Baker his eyes lighted up. He said Baker was one of the finest fellows he ever knew, and I was rather surprised at his also mentioning [Thomas] Sidlo, who he understood had been with me for some time. He spoke a good deal about Colver, expressing admiration for him and confidence in him.

He told me that he had learned of my intention of starting a paper in Washington and that he was greatly gratified by it because he said at present there was not a paper in Washington that could tell the truth about anything, and that he felt sure if Colver was going to be the head of the new paper it could do a great work.

And then he gave me a start. He said, "I have got a brother-in-law downstairs, the man who met you. Now he has been in the advertising business for a good many years and he would be a good man for you to have."

I sidestepped this.

On one and perhaps both of my previous visits to Wilson I had had occasion to speak to him about you and our relations and attitude with regard to journalism. He recalled what I had said and he remembered that you were quite along in years and asked about your health and asked particularly to convey to you his feelings of high respect and goodwill.

He had heard of James' death and spoke to me about that and also had a few kind words to say about Bob.

I didn't want to tire or bore him and watched him closely. I am sure he was really pleased to have me call on him. On several occasions he thanked me for having called on him. (In this one particular it seemed to me that his mind was not acute or his memory strong — that, in fact, he would forget that he had already been gracious enough.)

Finally I told him that I had better go, but that before doing so I would like to know if I could do anything that would add to his happiness or contribute to his interest. He responded in such a way that I saw that I had taken the wrong track. His lips quivered and his voice was quite husky in thanking me. He held me back for a few minutes by referring to his own condition with a peculiar sadness because he was unable to do anything. I think I had elicited this by what I had just said before.

I then arose to go. As I shook hands with him he held me back for a moment or two longer to express his hope for the success of the new paper and to wish me success in all of my endeavors.

It has been more than two years since Mr. Wilson has been stricken. I have read in the papers and have been told by his brother-in-law that he has been steadily improving in health, especially since he left the White House. If he has been steadily improving all this time I feel that he must have been a terribly sick man during the whole period of his remainder in the White House.

Colonel House and others have remarked, in something of a complaining way, of their having been debarred from seeing Wilson, after he became sick, by Mr. Wilson's personal entourage.

If I had ever been as sick as Mr. Wilson is now, I would have considered it an outrage if my family had permitted anybody to come into my room.

Still, Mr. Wilson may not have a temperament at all like mine. In fact, I remember that one of his friends, I forget which one, in urging me to call on Mr. Wilson, stated that my visit to him would cause him great pleasure because, since his illness and since his departure from the White House, he has had a feeling that he has been neglected by that portion of his old circle of friends whom he, Mr. Wilson, regarded as his intellectual equals. You can imagine how this idea tickled my vanity — to think of my being regarded as intellectual by an ex-university president, an author, and a scholar!

It is rather refreshing to find even one man who regards me as anything else but a rich man or a powerful political personage.

A COMPARISON

Intellectually, there can be no comparison between Harding and Wilson. In fact, Harding does not exist in the field where Wilson shone.

Still, Harding is of tougher fibre. As an animal he stands as greatly superior to Wilson as the Wilson intellect is superior to the Harding intellect.

Affectionately,

E. W. Scripps

FOREIGN AFFAIRS

A clear perception of long-range trends distinguished Scripps' discussion of foreign affairs, and enabled him to make a series of predictions, of which several have been borne out by time. This is not to suggest he was some sort of latter-day Nostradamus, for some of his prophecies coincided with contemporary thought, such as that of an inevitable war between America and Japan. Usually, he based his analyses — and hence his prophecies when he made them — on historical antecedents, what he perceived as trends as through time, population pressures, and national resources.

Thus, he predicted in 1915 — when many Americans abhorred the very thought of military power and involvement in world politics — that the United States would be the most powerful military nation in the world by 1935 or 1945, intervening in international affairs and enforcing the peace. If he could thus come within months of hitting the bull's-eye of an over-the-horizon target, with 1945 as the latest date, what is one then to make of a related prediction — that the United States would disintegrate ultimately before the combined attack of all the other nations of the world?

Scripps' career coincided with the growth of America as a world power, resulting in changes as he saw them as of 1909 in "How Things Change!" In common with a restless imperialism which gripped other Western nations, America embarked on overseas expansion — the Spanish-American War adventure, hegemony in the Caribbean, ownership of Hawaii, control of the Philippines, construction of the Panama Canal. When some feared Germany would penetrate the Caribbean, after Great Britain withdrew her heavier naval units from the area, Scripps would have deflected such a German threat — and the possibility of a European war — by having Germany colonize the southern half of South America. His reasons were quite sound: Germany would thus obtain the elbow room it needed, and the Western Hemisphere thus would have a Teutonic nation which could help to defend

509

the hemisphere better than the Latin-Americans could against an attack from Asia, which Scripps was convinced would someday come; he discussed these views in "The Heir to England." President Roosevelt intervened in both European and Far Eastern affairs, encouraging the Algeciras conference of 1906, which averted the threat of a general war over Morocco, and arranging the peace conference of Portsmouth, N.H., which ended the Russo-Japanese War in 1905. In 1908, the United States and Japan agreed, through the Root-Takahira agreement, to help preserve the status quo in the Pacific and the open door policy in China. Thus, by the time Scripps started writing his disquisitions, America indeed had long since become a world power, however reluctant her people may have been about assuming the role.

Scripps wrote sixty-six disquisitions that can be classed as dealing predominately with foreign affairs. In them, incidentally, his usual contradictions melt away, because his point of view was the strength and welfare of America. Throughout all of them, and even through the several included here, one finds considerable repetition, because Scripps paced back and forth over much of the same ground — particularly with regard to population and natural resources — in trying to understand the meaning of his times and the portent of the future. The repetition may be bothersome, but to eliminate it through editing could bowdlerize that which should be left intact.

In the beginning, Scripps approached foreign affairs in a manner true to the nature of his English heritage — a strong navy and a weak standing army. A navy would defend the nation from foreign aggression, but soldiers might be used for civil oppression. His earliest, clearly stated advocacy of American naval supremacy has already been presented in "Principles That the N.E.A. Should Stand For," in the Journalism section.

By the spring of 1908, Scripps undertook almost a missionary crusade in behalf of a powerful navy. In December of 1907 Roosevelt had sent the Atlantic fleet of sixteen battleships on an around-the-world cruise. Leaving Hampton Roads, the fleet under command of Rear Admiral Robley D. Evans sailed around the Horn and up the west coast of South America, arriving in San Diego in April, 1908. At San Diego Rear Admiral Charles Sperry replaced Evans in command, the latter being down with the gout, and Scripps served as chairman of the San Diego welcoming committee and entertained Sperry at "Miramar."

But Scripps' more significant action was in giving detailed instructions to H. L. Clotworthy, who was replacing Norman Rose as the NEA correspondent with the fleet for the rest of the trip around the world. During an evening and part of a day at "Miramar," Clotworthy received an intensive indoctrination in Scripps' views and what Scripps expected of him in the way of making the American people realize "the fact that they have got to fight for a century or more on the Pacific, and it is only a question of whether they lick or whether they get licked." [1] To be sure, Clotworthy must provide a reasonable amount of copy for NEA, but Scripps had a much broader role in mind for him. He told his editors-in-chief:

Being the person most interested in journalism, in a financial way, in all these newspapers, which are represented, I proposed to give him a special commission and through him to exercise my right of authority over these newspapers and cause them to perform, as well as possible, what I consider a great national service without regard to their financial profit, or journalistic fame and prestige.

Being personally impressed with the necessity of a great military navy and being particularly well-situated and well-fitted myself to judge affairs on the Pacific Ocean, I proposed through him to exercise all the influence I could on the people of the country to get them to share my views, in general and particular.

While I felt particularly incompetent to judge the present existing frame of mind of the people at large in regard to naval affairs, I felt that, such was the general militant character of the Americans, . . . it would be possible for the right man, using the right methods, to at least plant seeds that in time would grow to be a large naval sentiment.

Holding these views, I advised Mr. Clotworthy that the most essential part of his duties during his trip around the world was rather to fit himself for effective journalistic and literary work in the future than to produce immediate effects by his correspondence.

He should study as best he could conditions in our own as well as other national fleets.

He should, so far as possible, absorb the spirit of the American Navy, or rather to permit himself to be absorbed by the spirit of that Navy, the members of which were by temperament, training, rules of the service, if not dumb, at least taciturn.

He should fit himself to speak of those things which his temporary associates of the voyage should only feel and think.

I told Clotworthy that he should practice by his immediate writings and their publication in our papers, and by learning by experience what writings were effective and what were not, to develop an individual and special power as a publicist.

To impress upon him the real significance of the mission that I gave him, and the fact that I was not setting him to work simply for glory and fame, or the financial success of the papers in which I was interested, I told him that at any time he should find better avenue to the public than our publications, he should not only be at liberty but duty-bound to make use of the same. Furthermore, I

[1] EWS to W. B. Colver, Apr. 17, 1908.

told him that he should take advantage of his association with other journalists with the fleet, with journalists at home, and such as he should meet abroad, to obtain [*sic*] that they should be missionaries in our common cause.

In fact, our object was not at all to obtain for himself or for our newspapers any prominence, but the whole object and aim of his labor should be to secure a great and powerful navy for the United States, and the proper recognition, on the part of the people of the United States, of the necessity of activity on the Pacific Ocean.

There are two things that I desire of you in this connection, and only two: (1) I desire that a very extensive and complete use of Mr. Clotworthy's special articles should be made; and (2) I desire that Mr. Clotworthy's name and personality shall be made as prominent as possible, in order that later on, as time goes on, he will be sufficiently recognized as an authority to be listened to respectfully by the public and by officialdom.

What I do not want is that, in this case at least, you and your editorial staff in general, should decide such questions as to whether a large naval policy was the right general policy for the government or whether such a naval policy was immoral or not.

I know very well that, unless orders are given to the contrary, the different editors on our papers and the present NEA rules will be able to suppress Clotworthy entirely, and thus defeat my purpose.[2]

To help prepare the ground for Clotworthy's future contributions to magazines, Scripps included the above excerpt in letters to S. S. McClure of *McClure's* and Norman Hapgood, then editor of *Collier's National Weekly*.

Within three or four years, Scripps became an equally strong advocate of a strong land force, discarding his former antipathy toward a standing army in view of the developing world situation. He dated his change in view from the revolution of Francisco Madero in Mexico in 1911, which led to several years of civil war and generally unstable conditions which in turn led to American occupation of Vera Cruz briefly in 1914 and invasion of Mexico by a punitive expedition in 1916–17. The Mexican turmoil convinced Scripps that the United States should have an army powerful enough to dominate Mexico. He also concluded that America should have an army powerful enough to resist invasion by Japan. His thinking along this line was preconditioned by his talk with Sperry in 1908 and the visit of General Arthur MacArthur to "Miramar" upon the latter's return to the United States after completing his term as military governor of the Philippines in 1901. Sperry and Scripps discussed the situation in the Orient at length, but Sperry told Scripps that America's first naval contest would be with Germany — that the United States and Germany would determine at sea whether the Monroe Doctrine should be maintained. Scripps quoted MacArthur as predicting that Japan would attack the United States, in

[2] EWS to Harry N. Rickey, B. H. Canfield, J. C. Harper, W. B. Colver, Dec. 4, 1908.

which case the Philippines would be vital either for negotiations or for bases in the Pacific. It should be noted that Scripps wrote his recollection of the two conversations several years after they took place.[3] Indeed, Scripps became so much a militarist that he advocated universal military training as a permanent part of the American system in "Why Should We Fear to Be Strong?"

From about 1909 on, Scripps foresaw that the military and population pressures building up in Germany would erupt in war, ultimately, a view that he may have absorbed from contemporary discussions. He discussed the probability of such an eruption in several disquisitions, including "The Heir to England" and "Industrialism and Decay." But it was all very far away, and it had been so long since there had been an important war in Europe that he could talk about the prospects with the detachment of a scholar.

The crash of German artillery in August, 1914, re-echoed as an intellectual thunderclap at "Miramar." Scripps became preoccupied with the war and what it would mean in the long run, groping and grasping his way through the maze, sometimes in response to urgent requests from associates who wanted his assessments, but mostly in response to his own concern. Gradually, he stabilized his thinking along the lines of "The War and the Business Outlook." The immediate effect of the outbreak of the war was to produce a temporary depression in America, but by early 1915 a period of prosperity set in, partly due to increased orders from Europe.

When America entered the war in April, 1917, Scripps was just as perceptive to its meaning for the future, as shown in "Predictions," as was the British Foreign Secretary, Sir Edward Grey, who said in 1914, "The lamps are going out all over Europe. We shall not see them lit again in our lifetime."

On April 2, the day President Wilson asked Congress to declare war, Scripps telegraphed a strong appeal for a pay-as-we-go policy in financing the war, urging that all incomes above $100,000 a year be conscripted and that all soldiers and sailors be paid at least $3.00 a day, saying that such legislation would cost him personally more than half his present income. While strongly advocating substantial increases in the income tax — which were brought about by the War Revenue Act of October, 1917 — and having NEA campaign to bring about full publication of all income taxes paid, Scripps ultimately came to realize that the tremendous cost of the war could not possibly be placed on a pay-as-we-go basis. In June, before action had been taken on higher income taxes, Scripps said that, since "Congress refuses to lay on us half the taxes that we should pay," the Concern should

[3] "An Uncomfortable Situation," Sept. 7, 1917, EWS Writings, 6:298–99.

spend large sums "for the public welfare" in expanding the work of NEA. Urging his son Jim to double the number of NEA clients, Scripps said, "We have the biggest kind of a job on our hands in the matter of educating and molding public opinion, and no one can do this work so well as we can, and I believe that no one else can do the work that has to be done. . . ." [4]

Scripps moved to Washington in June, 1917, assuming a position as "a sort of unofficial head of the Scripps concern in Washington," a staff of about twenty men.[5]

In spite of his militarism and advocacy of a strong standing army, Scripps was shocked when he learned that the President planned to send a conscript army to France. Men registered for the draft in June; in July, Scripps seriously considered financing an appeal to the Supreme Court to block the sending of conscripts abroad; send regulars and volunteers abroad, yes, but not draftees. However, by September he had changed his mind, and was confirmed in his new view — that is, to not question constitutionality of sending draftees overseas — during a long conference with Brandeis, who had by then been appointed to the Supreme Court.[6]

His thinking and attitudes during the war are typified by several of the following selections, including "Taking Stock," which is the closest he came to describing the way in which World War I changed his whole outlook and thinking.

After the war he continued his interest in foreign affairs on a lesser scale. As he cruised about the world in his yacht, he paid close attention to the government and economy of the countries and colonies where he put into port, and thought about them in the larger context of the course of civilization. His ruminations along this line, however, usually found expression in letters to his sister Ellen, rather than in disquisitions.

And as he cruised the Pacific in the early 1920's he became more convinced than ever that the United States indubitably would fight a major war with Japan, and soon.

[4] EWS to James G. Scripps, June 7, 1917.
[5] EWS to Mrs. Nackey Scripps Meanley, July 12, 1917.
[6] EWS to Mrs. E. W. Scripps, July 24, Sept. 9, 1917; EWS to EBS, Sept. 1, 1917.

How Things Change!

[*May 26, 1909*]

In 1870 I was a sixteen-year-old boy on the farm. The first time that I can remember when I was interested in the news of the daily papers and other periodicals was at the time of the breaking out of the Franco-Prussian War. I know that I must at that time have had some little acquaintance with the geography and history of modern nations, for I recall that I was an anti-Napoleonist and that I regarded the French as a great and powerful nation and that I considered Germany her inferior. I recall that my sympathies were at first with the Germans and that this sympathy was based solely upon my considering them the "underdog" in the fight.

Up to the event of this war I believe that the commonly accepted idea was that France was the superior military nation of the world; if she had a rival at all her equal, I believe it would have been considered England.

I remember, too, that I had been taught in my schoolbooks that Russia was a semibarbarous nation. Of course I, in common with all other American boys, believed that the United States of America could, if it wanted to, lick any nation in the world.

In those days, Japan was considered no more of a world power, or of having any such possibilities, than Persia, for instance.

All of this was less than forty years ago. From those days Germany began to loom up.

I do recall something earlier than the Franco-Prussian War; I remember reading about Garibaldi, and especially of seeing pictures of him in his red shirt. So it seems that even my memory covers the whole period of existence of the Italian nation.

While Germany and France had places in my mind as being great military nations, the United Kingdom of Great Britain loomed an enormous figure of a nation, on account of her great wealth and her superior position as a manufacturing and trading nation, and largely also on account of her great

515

commercial navy. England was the bugaboo of the people of the United States, and it seems like only a few days ago when John Sherman [7] made himself glorious in the eyes of his countrymen by his habit of twisting the British lion's tail.

In those days the United States was considered, and was practically, only a nation of agriculturalists; the manufactures of this country were insignificant; we got money from England to build our railroads, and we got the old-fashioned iron rails for these railroads from England. The United States' foreign trade consisted of outward shipments of agricultural products and other raw material, and its inward shipments of manufactured stuff. We almost felt that we were owned by our English creditors.

Germany's manufactures and trade were also small.

For a long period of time, in fact up to only five or six years ago, I believe the Hapsburg Empire was considered to be a mere bundle of sticks held together by an old and rotten withe — the very aged emperor, Francis Joseph. Not infrequently there appeared in magazines articles seriously written by supposedly very intelligent publicists on the coming breakup of the Austrian Empire; in these articles was depicted a most discouraging condition of government. The nation was composed, it is said, of some twenty-four different nationalities, each of which was a faction warring against all the others. Hungary, the so-far dominant party in the dual monarchy, it is said, was aching for freedom from the yoke. Pan-Germanism was rampant and it is said that the present German Emperor was only waiting for the death of his aged kinsman in order to proceed to annex not only all of the two Austrias but the more eastern provinces of the Balkans, in order to push his frontier down to the Mediterranean and make Salonika a German port. Now Austria appears on the scene as almost the equal partner of her great ally, Germany, and as a military power equal to if not superior to any other European nation except the German Empire. The German-Austrian alliance (Italy is supposed to be, if not detached from the triple alliance, at least unnecessary to it) threatens Europe and, beyond all question of doubt, today dominates it.

It was only eleven years ago, at the breaking out of the Spanish-American War, that I was talking with a young officer, at my club [the Cuyamaca Club in San Diego] about the prospects of the war; he was as confident of our ultimate success as were the rest of the American people, but he bemoaned the condition of our Navy, even as compared with that of Spain. He said it was an outrage that the American people had so neglected their Navy that it was only a poor sixth amongst the navies of the world. It was

[7] Sherman served in the House of Representatives from Ohio, 1855–61, and in the Senate, 1861–77 and 1881–97; was Secretary of the Treasury, 1877–81, and Secretary of State, 1897–98; author of Sherman Anti-Trust Act and Sherman Silver Purchase Act.

only two or three years ago that, owing to the naval program of the United States, it turned out that the American Navy was the second in the world. I am not sure [but] that it is still holding on, by its eyebrows, to this position. But the Germans are forging ahead with such rapidity, while our own government is so conservative, that it seems quite probable that in a few brief years the German Navy will far outmatch our own.

For some time there have been appearing in English magazines articles by Ellis Barker, a man who seems to be both an expert on national finances and naval matters, warning the English people that it will not only be impossible for the English nation to longer maintain what is called the two-power navy, but that it will be impossible for the English taxpayers to keep up such a navy-building program as to prevent the Germans from very shortly overmatching her alone with a navy. He explained that while the English taxpayer was already paying a per capita tax far greater than the German taxpayer, the former is constantly losing his wealth and hence his capacity to pay taxes, while the latter has not yet begun to pay taxes up to one-half of his ability while he is growing richer by leaps and bounds.

It seems to be only a question now of a short time when the Germans alone, or at least Germany and Austria, will have a land army greater and more efficient than that possessed by any possible combination of nations that may be made against them, and a navy that would only have to fear the coalition of two or three of the other greatest naval powers in the world.

Of Japan's startling rise to the position of a world power it is unnecessary to speak further.

The United States has taken England's place as the wealthiest nation in the world; it has also taken its place as the nation with the greatest trade and manufacture; and, as has been said before, it has attained the second position as a world naval power. The only possible rival of Germany for the future on the seas, as it appears now, will be the United States; we alone amongst the nations are wealthy enough to outbuild, in ships, Germany, as is Germany able to outbuild England.

While it may be conceded that it takes time to build navies and train officers and men to handle them, still the history of the past ten years has shown that the race for naval supremacy may be easily won by the nation with the longest purse.

There is only one thing that may cause the United States to become the greatest nation on earth, including a greater population than any other nation and a far greater area of territory. All that is necessary to accomplish this is that Germany shall not move too swiftly, or that England shall keep up the struggle for parity long enough in order that when the time comes that Germany shall completely overmatch the power of the Briton — a power that national stupidity cripples by the continuation of its obsolete, impractical, non-imperial organization — then the American nation will be in a position to take over to itself not alone hegemony of Anglo-Saxondom but, through annexation, the majority if not all of what was once the British Empire.

Either the Anglo-Saxon of the United States must make himself forcibly the heir of the Briton or else see his patrimony filched by the Teuton. The time has not yet come when the Briton at home or in the colonies is able to conceive of such a condition, nor does it appear that any American statesman has taken a serious view of an early impending event.

There is only at present existing one sign that Anglo-Saxon statesmen are comparatively sane: It is now considered in Washington and in the principal capitals that warfare or even serious differences between the two great Anglo-Saxon peoples are not to be thought of. Perhaps it requires only the growing significance of the increase of the German nation's military power in order to make the Balkan people more active and the people of the British Empire more disposed to rely on the eldest child of the nation.

It is only a few years ago when, whatever the opinion was in the chancellories of Europe, the great mass of the people of all civilized nations regarded Russia as the one great power to be feared; it was this fear and hence hatred of Russia that caused American people to so sympathize with Japan. We wanted Japan to curb Russia, but it never entered our heads — or the heads of but few of us, and I was not one of these — that a Japanese victory would produce for the American people an enemy far more to be dreaded than ever Russia could have become.

Poor Russia! At the present moment she seems to be completely prostrated.

Every year sees France growing rapidly weaker, relative to Germany.

There are today five powers that may be considered great; they are Germany, Austria, England, United States, and Japan. Germany and Japan are rising rapidly; England is decadent; whether the United States is to be a great military nation or not is still to be learned by events. But it seems inevitable that the United States must be a great military nation, and perhaps for a time the greatest.

It would seem that even in these brief forty years covered by my memory there has been a whole chapter of the rise and fall of nations.

The prick of the little brown man's bayonet exploded the bladder of Russian prestige. It is presumed that England has far more prestige now, even, than virtue. One blow at the heart of England, that might be easily struck in the next five or ten years, would burst the English bladder.

There might well occur still such a catastrophe in the land of the Hapsburgs as would reduce that whole empire within a generation to a worse state, comparatively, than has Turkey been reduced during the reign of Abdul-Hamid.[8]

Russia is impregnable. The vast area of her territory, populated by a race that breeds doubly as rapidly as any other white people, gives her a unique position. A short generation of good luck or good statesmanship may see her rise to a position far superior in Europe to what it was even supposed to be a decade ago.

They say that China is awakening. If Japan has done what she has done why cannot China do still more?

Historical events come quickly in these latter days; their pace may be even enormously accelerated, so that changes of the forty years past may be more than matched by the changes of the next twenty years. One thing is quite probable, I believe, and that is that my children will look out on a very, very different world than that I have seen, or even than that which I am now imagining.

It may well be that forty years hence there will be but one great Anglo-Saxon nation; that a single German power may rule all of western Europe, and that Russia will divide Europe with its German government and Asia with one or more governments of Asiatic peoples, and that all of the world will practically be divided between four governments. The territory of the world and the people of the world may be either directly and completely absorbed and governed by the several nations, or parts may be in a condition which is now called "spheres of influence."

[8] Abdul-Hamid was sultan of Turkey from 1876 until deposed in 1909.

The Heir to England

[*July 22, 1909*]

It would be more than rash to say that the British Empire is on the eve of breaking up.

On the other hand, not even the most sanguine Briton fails to recognize the possibility of a great catastrophe such as a well-aimed blow at the Empire's heart by some single great power or combination of powers. Apparently, perfectly sane British writers, and level-headed ones too, are coming to admit the fact that a military struggle between England and Germany is all but inevitable.

The organization of the British Empire, as a whole, is very crude and ineffective. The English colonies, which are now occupied by peoples making an aggregate population of upwards of 12 millions, are so far from being elements of strength, from a military point of view, to the British Empire, [as] the reverse.

For many years there has been an attempt made to get all the countries of the British Empire to first recognize the necessity of and then to organize the Empire into a centrally and homogeneously governed nation.

Face to face with a possible great military emergency in the next ten years, it seems impossible that an effective organization of the British Empire can be effected.

England is embarrassed with tremendous territorial possessions whose extent are so great as to require more than a century for populations to so increase as to make any one outlying section of the present Empire formidable in opposing an attack made by any of the first- or second-rate powers of Europe; on the other hand, for practical purposes, Germany has no other territory than that little fragment of Europe which is only geographically 50 per cent larger than the state of California. In fact, the English have too much land for their people and the Germans have not nearly enough for the Germans.

The Anglo-Saxon nation in the Western Hemisphere holds a somewhat similar relation to the rest of the world as does England. The United States' territory is not excessively large, considering its population, though it is perhaps twenty or thirty times larger in proportion to its population than is Germany. By reason of the Monroe Doctrine, however, the government of the United States has included in its sphere of influence all the Western Hemisphere.

Germany, like the old woman who lived in a shoe, has so many children she does not know what to do, unless she enlarges her dominion by fighting. There is no territory fit or desirable for the German people to emigrate to except such as is owned by one or other of the two Anglo-Saxon nations.

There is not such a vast difference between the civilization of the Germans, the Britons, and the Americans as to make it impossible for whole large sections of peoples now included in these three governments to transfer or have transferred their allegiance from one of these governments to another without any perceptible loss of material and spiritual comfort. If Australia, South Africa, or Canada were to pass under the German rule and be rapidly populated by vast numbers of German immigrants, the individual citizens of these colonies would never feel the change for the worse, save in the matter of sentiment.

Were it not for purely sentimental reasons, the people of the United States should welcome, rather than antagonize, the occupancy and control of the south half of South America by Germans. The Monroe Doctrine served its purpose last century; doubtless it is useful to the American Republic today in defending its frontiers on the Gulf of Mexico, the Caribbean, and the great isthmus. I am one of those who believe that a long-distance national view should prompt the American people to make the equator the southern boundary of the Monroe Doctrine's sphere of influence. Here are my reasons:

Germany's growing population, wealth, and military power will inevitably cause that nation to make a successful extension of her territory. Germany must help herself at the expense of the British Empire or the South American republics. It is perfect folly to suppose that the strongest military nation on earth, one of the second wealthiest and the first in point of equipment in scientific knowledge, can be successfully resisted in the attempt to extend her territory and preserve from suffocation and starvation her growing millions.

Germany has a right to live and to grow, and when this right is backed by her army, her navy, and her growing wealth, history must inevitably record her success in upholding this right.

In the course of nature the great world-embracing empire of Britain, that is composed of fragments, must disintegrate. The little islands that compose the United Kingdom are even now overpopulated, but are populated with only the leavings or the residue of a great people, whose greatest sons have left the old home. Man for man the population of the United Kingdom today is, in fighting qualities, perhaps inferior to any other nation of Caucasians.

The strong men of the British Empire are largely citizens, and even natives, of the colonies now called dominions,[9] and have no voice in the government of the Empire as a whole and no sufficiently great interest in the integrity of the Empire to make them constitute themselves its main defenders.

Such has been the effect of pioneering, colony, dominion, and nation-building that all the people who have left England have de-Anglicized themselves in just such a way as to make them each more like the other than any of them are like the people remaining in the mother country of the United Kingdom. The American, the Canadian, the Australian, and the South African have all tastes, aspirations, political ideals, and practices more similar each to the other than any of them are similar to those of the people of England.

It appears that the world's progress and civilization are along lines of race. Even geographical location has less to do, perhaps, with the formation of a nation than has language. The English-speaking people of the world perhaps double the German-speaking people. In point of wealth, both acquired and of natural resources, and in inherited military strength, the English-speaking people would be more than a match for the Germans if the latter were doubly as numerous as they are.

It is altogether probable that the few great nations of the future will be composed of those vast sections of men who speak a common tongue. The English-speaking people or nation will occupy all that part of the earth's territory where the English language dominates.

Now, if Germany is moved to and is able to strike a blow at the heart of the British Empire, she will doubtless take as a spoil of victory some such vast territory as Australia or South Africa, together with many other small territories of importance strategically for military and commercial purposes; incidentally, this would result in these acquired territories becoming flooded with Germans and becoming Germanized in speech as well as in all other ways. If, for instance, Australia becomes a prize of victory to the German Empire, it would be forever lost to [the] future English-speaking nation.

If, on the other hand, Germany is given an outlet into South America there will grow up in that country a mighty Teutonic nation; perhaps a na-

[9] By this time the British Empire included crown colonies in which English rule was supreme, colonies which had representative government, and self-governing dominions such as Canada and Australia.

tion that not many generations hence would hold the hegemony of the German-speaking world nation.

The present occupants of southern South America are reported to be a people of great natural ability. Free from the competition of neighboring nations of Teutonic, Scandinavian, or Slavonic blood, they are thriving well enough. However, these peoples of South America are, after all, members of decadent races — the European Latins and American aborigines — and the best that they could do for their country would not be a quarter of what the German people would do with the same. The kinship and mutual helpfulness and sympathy between German-speaking and English-speaking peoples [are] greater than [they are] between either of them and the Latins.

A great German nation in southern South America would, in future ages, be more effective in repelling the attack of Asiatics on the American shore than would be the most powerful possible Latin-Indian nation. By giving Germany the South American field to exploit, all her attention and all her growing peoples would be occupied for many generations. In the meantime, the British Empire would have time to find itself, or to gently and in orderly fashion dissipate and disappear by absorption into a greater empire or nation of English-speaking people whose greatest mass, and hence whose real government, would be located on the North American continent.

The days of little England as a world power must pass quickly away; her royal scepter must pass into the hands of a stronger government, or people of her own race, and that government is that of the United States of America. If England is not yet moribund, in the course of nature she soon must be defunct as a great power. Her eldest daughter-nation must succeed to the domain of the mother-nation.

Therefore, the American people, as heirs of this old lady living in a little house on the outskirts of Europe, who feel that it is their business and to their interests to defend her fortunes against robbery will, in defending England's present possessions, only be saving for themselves their future inheritance.

The natural alliance between Germany [undoubtedly Scripps meant the United States] and Great Britain is not one of sentiment purely, or of blood relationship.

Perhaps, by reason of the breaking up of the British Empire by Germany's strong blow at her heart, an immediate advantage would be gained for the United States. The British Empire being destroyed, Canada would be compelled to join the United States and become an integral part of it; there would also be other fragments of the old lady's estate that would undoubtedly fall into its hands. By letting the robber kill our grandmother and steal a portion of her possessions we, as heirs, would get what was left. By defending this old lady and allowing her to die peacefully we can get all her estate.

There is one sure and certain way by which we can defend our British inheritance, and perhaps without striking a blow or shedding a drop of blood. We are able, financially, to far outbuild Germany in battleships and outfight her on the seas, and if we keep ourselves constantly prepared and equal, or more than equal, to Germany in our Navy we may effectually keep the peace between Germany and England for reasons following:

Allow that Germany, having a great army, shall also in time build up a navy equal to or superior to that of Great Britain, and allow at the same time that the American Navy is always somewhat superior to that of Germany; when the time comes for Germany to make her attack upon England for the purpose of helping herself to English colonial territory and world trade, her statesmen will be confronted not with an American naval alliance with England but by an American aloofness.

Let us suppose further that these German statesmen are foolish enough to attack England and be successful in their conquest, Germany will come out of the struggle with crippled resources, a navy battle-worn and depleted, and with her government financial strength in even worse condition. At that time the American government, with its superior fleet of warships and its financial resources untouched, will come onto the scene and, taking to itself such parts of the British Empire as prefer an American alliance to the rule of a conqueror, will assure to the remaining self-governing dominions of the old empire protection, and leave to Germany only a barren, unfruitful victory.

Under such conditions as I have described, however, the German Navy would never fire even the first shot nor embark the first regiment on a transport for the invasion of the English islands.

There is really no occasion for an Anglo-American alliance; there is really no occasion for any display or even feeling of friendly, brotherly, or cousinly relations between the English and the American people. Nature has ordained that America shall be the heir of Britain, and America has only to wait to come into its inheritance. This inheritance will be sure and inevitable, even if the most disagreeable relations existed between the heir and his benefactor, voluntarily or involuntarily.

There is only one possible contingency that could occur by which Germany might profit at the expense of either America or England: If these two latter countries should involve themselves in an imbecile war and so weaken themselves materially and so embitter their mutual relations that there could be no combination of the two parties for defense, then and then only could Germany rob Great Britain of her immediate possessions and the American people of their rightful inheritance.

Industrialism and Decay

[*October 23, 1909*]

Germany has a population of some 60 millions of people; the land area of the German Empire is, I believe, slightly greater than that of France, and it may be a little larger or smaller than the territory of the United Kingdom; it is, perhaps, 50 per cent larger than the state of California and considerably less in size than the state of Texas.

In soil productiveness and other natural resources the territory of the German Empire is supposed to be inferior to France, and very much inferior to England. All things considered, it is perhaps not much superior to that of California and is far inferior to that of Texas.

Germany's population is 50 per cent greater than that of France, and 40 per cent greater than that of the British Isles; it is, perhaps, 30 times greater than the population of the state of California and 20 times greater than that of Texas. Population is practically stationary in France. The rate of increase of the British population is perhaps not one-half that of Germany. The increase of the German population is what we would call the natural increase — that is to say, the increase caused by births being greater than deaths.

At the present rate of growth or increase in the population of Germany, the population of this country might more than double in fifty years.

Up to forty years ago the peoples that now compose the German Empire were mainly engaged in agriculture; manufacturing in Germany was insignificant in proportion as compared with England. The German people were poor people.

For a hundred years or more — for more than three generations — the English people have been a manufacturing people; prior to the beginning of the nineteenth century the English were mainly engaged in agriculture.

The English people engaged in large industrial pursuits — that is to say, labored in large factories situated in the cities — some two generations or more before the German peasant turned from agriculture to factory tools; they left the pure air of the fields and began breathing in the poison of the city factory. English industry is now decadent. German industry has not, perhaps, reached its zenith.

The physique of the English working classes is, I believe, supposed to be tremendously inferior to that of the same classes one hundred years ago. There appears to have been no such deterioration among the Germans.

I have been speculating on some of the above facts, and I believe there have been two causes contributing to the deterioration of the inhabitants of England; one of these causes has been the enormous emigration of the best type of Englishman to English colonies and to other lands.[10] A very large proportion of the most vigorous, in mind and body, of Englishmen have deserted their native land, and only the residue — the inferior class — have been left at home to breed. Another cause has been industrialism itself.

The healthy, strong, and vigorous peasantry of the English fields and villages have been tempted into the large manufacturing cities; there the men have been employed in unsanitary work and lived in a most unsanitary environment. Their wages being increased enormously more rapidly than their culture, these men have, to a large extent at least, devoted their increase of earnings to the gratification of their sensual proclivities, excessive drinking, and have indulged in other vices. This manner of life has undermined their physical and spiritual constitution, and these men have become the fathers of the succeeding generation.

The women — the wives and daughters of these men — have also been removed from the more healthful surroundings and pursuits of their forefathers, and as a consequence have deteriorated.

Opportunities being presented, parents have been tempted to employ their children in factory and other unhealthful work with the result that, being not only handicapped by lessened vitality of their parents, they have been further stunted and injured physically before they arrive at manhood and womanhood, fatherhood and motherhood.

The sum total of all these causes has been the effect of a vast number of inefficient, unfit men and women, all that class that is called in England "the unemployed." As England has grown richer, pauperism has grown in extent.

Almost the whole body of human material on which industrialism must rest has, in England, become deteriorated. Industrialism in Germany is new yet; it has barely passed through one generation. What will be the effect of three generations of industrialism in Germany?

[10] Between 1870 and 1900, approximately 6,000,000 persons emigrated from the United Kingdom; between 1901 and 1914, emigration averaged 200,000 a year.

Germany has ceased to be an emigration country and has become an immigration country. The German peasants are rapidly leaving the farm and are as rapidly being replaced there by laborers from alien lands — Poles, Russians, various peoples from the Balkans, and large numbers from Italy. The German population has already outgrown the capacity of German lands to feed them.

Germany has become a great exporter of factory-made goods, and is rapidly growing greater in this direction; at the same time, Germany has become a great importer of foodstuffs, and it is inevitable that she will grow much more rapidly in this direction, since all her new population must be fed on provisions produced outside of Germany. Every year, it is estimated that Germany has a million more mouths to feed than she had the year before.

Agricultural lands in Germany must, of necessity, decrease in area to make room for growing cities, factories, and all sorts of transportation and other industrial facilities. The area of productive agricultural lands will also be cut down by increasing numbers of wealthy families who, while maintaining their old landed estates and securing other landed estates, will not depend upon the small returns of agriculture but rather on profits from manufacture and trade, and thus they will neglect either altogether or partly the economic cultivation of the lands.

It may be expected that Germany will avoid the mistakes of the English people, mistakes that were the result of pure ignorance; Germany will have had its object lesson in England's experience. Germany is more careful and will continue to be more careful of the health and vitality of her people. But, on the other hand, progress is so much more rapid in this century than it was in the nineteenth century that the development of industry, and hence its demands upon the vitality of the people, will be probably more than doubly as rapid in the twentieth century as it was in the nineteenth.

Is there any reason, then, to expect that Germany will not be in a far worse plight in the year 2009 than England is today?

But how long will Germany continue to increase its population at the present high rate? It is well known that city life is race suicide; there are few of the third and hardly any of the fourth generations of city dwellers. It is as yet unknown what the exact effect will be of intensive and universal school life amongst the young. German scientists and investigators have already for some time been sounding a warning and declaring that the intense work of the German public schools is undermining the health and constitution of attendants.

School life and child labor, factory work and city dwelling may be all set down as physically injurious to the human family.

England sent her best sons abroad to found empires and nations, and, though England may die as a nation, there will remain mighty empires of English. Germany has in past times eliminated from her people vast numbers of the best kind of Germans to the advantage of other lands, and yet has founded no colonies. But, for the most part, Germany has kept her people at home and is overcrowding if not overworking her people to such an extent that the end of German glory may well be not a century hence.

English statesmanship is not to be credited with the glory and success of the English people; individually [efficient] Englishmen saved the English people by individual enterprise. German statesmanship may save Germany.

It is a well-known fact that plant and animal life is often and always [*sic*] greatly improved by transplanting into other soils and other climates and other conditions than those of origin. There is no reason to suppose that the human animal is not benefited by the same process.

Germany is today one of the richest of nations; she is overwhelmingly the superior of any other nation in land military strength; she is erecting a navy with startling rapidity. Such are her human resources that there can be no question but that if she willed it her navy would surpass that of England before a half-century is over, maybe before a quarter-century is past.

Either the crucial moment has arrived, or is about to arrive, when Germany may choose that her people shall long endure and enjoy a masterful position in the world or consent to become decadent.

Nearly all of the world's spaces have been occupied — that is, nearly all of those spaces that will permit Europeans to thrive have been occupied — but the peoples occupying these vast areas are very unequal in the scale of national force and civilization. There is, in particular, one vast area of land in a temperate climate which is occupied by a very inferior and mongrel race of people whose governments are tremendously weak, as compared with any government that the country could maintain. The south half of South America may be left for an indefinite time in the possession of the incapable mongrels of native, African, and Iberian stocks, or it may be seized by some superior race or nation.

The English people have pre-empted a territory that will require centuries for it to fill by natural increase. The Americans have a whole continent to cover, and from Alaska to the southernmost border of the Republic of Mexico, excepting the hot lands of the Gulf and the two seas, all over this continent there is a living place for peoples of European stock.

The French and all other Latin peoples are decadent. The Slavs with their various branches already occupy mighty areas in northern Asia and all of eastern Europe. Slav civilization lags and although the Slav population grows more rapidly in numbers than that of all other European peoples, there are sufficiently good reasons why we should expect that several generations should pass before the nation would have either ability or desire to go overseas.

Germany needs more space. South America is uneconomically occupied and used. German statesmanship and German power can and should possess and occupy and people all of South America.

Such is the condition of Europe today that there must be an explosion and a German eruption soon. Shall this explosion disrupt Europe and develop into a mighty war of German conquest of Europe, or shall it take the direction of the least resistance and perform a great world's service in a German conquest of South America?

It is true Australia might be lost to the English Empire, and the empire of Anglo-Saxondom not be crippled; it might be benefited. But Australia is not so good a field for the Germans as is South America; Australia is farther away from Germany than South America, and Australia is defended not only by a great naval nation but by a citizenship of native-born Anglo-Saxons far more capable of defending their home than are the South Americans. Perhaps it would be easy for England [Germany] to conquer 30 million South Americans as against 3 million Australians, even if the Australians were unprotected. The United States of America alone stands in the way and bars the road from Germany to South America, but the opposition of the United States to German conquest of the South American continent is purely sentimental. No matter how strong this sentiment is, sentimentality has never been strong enough to overcome the onrush of practicality.

There can be no lasting world peace so long as Europe contains such a powerfully expensive [expansive?] body as the German people on a small area of land from which there is no escape valve through which the nation can pass as a nation for further national expansion.

The War and the Business Outlook

[*August 7, 1914*]

This disquisition appears to have been edited in Scripps' hand.

One of my business associates has asked me to formulate my opinion on the probable effect of the present war on business conditions in the United States.

To begin with I am pretty sure that, after all the fighting is done, history will have to record that the war resulted in practically a drawn battle.

I mean that Germany will not only fail in conquering Europe but even if she is nominally victorious her position, of the immediate past, of European hegemony will be greatly lessened.

Neither will the Russian colossus extend her border westward by a mile. Even if Russia should be nominally victorious she will possibly lose territory, as the Polish nation may be re-established. If Russia is not victorious she will, in the final settlement, probably lose to Germany the Baltic provinces and to a, yet to be born, Scandinavian federation, Finland.

If the central powers, Germany and Austria, are defeated, a great part of the territory that is now Austria will become Italian and the greater part of the Slavic people that are now included in the Austrian Empire will become a part of the Slavonic Empire or Kingdom, of which Serbia will be the nucleus. It is almost certain, also, that Romania will extend her territory northward to include a great Romanian population now living within the Hungarian lines. Austria may be disintegrated entirely and Hungary and Bohemia become antonomous and independent nations while the German territories will be added to the German nation.

If Germany and Austria are defeated, Alsace and Lorraine and (possibly) Luxemburg will probably be reunited with the French nation. Schleswig-Holstein will probably be returned to Denmark. France will also recover the

Congo territory ceded to Germany recently, while England may attempt to obtain the remainder of the German territory in Africa.

It is almost inconceivable that England will fail, no matter how successful Germany may be on land, to destroy the sea power of both Germany and Austria. Under these conditions the conquest of England would become impossible.

The conquest of Russia is equally impossible. However successful Germany and Austria may be in the war, it would be impossible for them to overrun Russia or anything but a small part of Russian territory. Even if the Russian government should sue for peace, she could not possibly lose more territory to Germany than the German Baltic provinces. Germany's past experience with her part of the Poles has been such as would cause her to refuse to take any more territory that included Slavic peoples. To Germany's experience has been added that of Austria. The fundamental weakness of Austria has been the inclusion in a German monarchy of so many Slavs and so much Slavonic territory. Russia might ransom her capital and some other of her large cities by paying a money indemnity and surrender to Germany the Baltic provinces and to the Scandinavian federation, Finland.

If Russia were entirely successful, it is inconceivable that she would consent to a large new Slavonic power rising in the Balkans. Russia would be willing to make considerable sacrifices in order to prevent the substitution of the polyglot Austrian Empire by a great homogeneous Slavic power.

Italy has nothing to gain now by joining Germany and Austria. A defeat of these two powers, as a result of Italy's neutrality or cooperation with a western power, would cause a great accession of territory to Italy. It would only be in case of Germany and Austria completely overwhelming all other enemies that Italy could be punished by her former allies and that punishment could only take the form of a money indemnity. Austria would certainly want no more Italians, and there would be nothing excepting Tunis and some Mediterranean islands that the German Empire would possibly covet. The most that could befall Italy would be a fine in the way of war indemnity. This could hardly be any greater than the cost a war would be to Italy if Italy stood by her old allies.

Allowing the central powers greatest possible success on land, without equal success on sea Germany and Austria could get no English territory in the way of colonies or any money indemnity.

Allowing that England, France, and Russia should completely overwhelm Germany and Austria, it would be inevitable that in the final settlement of European affairs France, England, and Italy would have common interests with Germany and Austria, or with all those smaller nations that now exist or would be brought into existence by the crumbling of the Austrian Empire, in opposing Russia's ambition to extend her territory to the Mediterranean. It must be remembered that the more than century-old antagonism between the Muscovite and the Anglo-Saxon has been based upon a real conflict of interest between the two peoples. England is the last nation in the world that could afford to have a greater and stronger Russia.

In ancient times statesmen and war lords recognized no practical objection to an empire being composed of peoples of different races and religions. But during the past century nothing has been more apparent to statesmen than that a nation is weakened by having its different sections composed of peoples of different nations and different religions.

Austria is weak because it is a German monarchy, while the majority of the monarch's subjects are not only non-German but anti-Germanic in instinct and prejudice. The only part of the English Empire that is really troublesome to England is non-Anglo-Saxon India. [Scripps seems to have overlooked South Africa in this regard.]

England and France both rule over tremendous African domains with large populations that are not Anglo-Saxon, but these populations are composed of ignorant, barbarous, or at best semicivilized peoples — peoples who are on the average no farther advanced than the inhabitants of the Philippine Islands.

I have said that after the war was over, historians would have to record practically a drawn battle, because when it is all over conquerers and conquered will in the main retain their same relative positions and almost identically their same home territories and the same governmental independence.

A real conquest of Europe by any one people must be slow. It cannot be accomplished by force of arms. It must be accomplished by a process of breeding. Some years ago, the [English] journalist, William T. Stead, called attention to the fact that the Slavic population of Russia and the Balkan states was increasing at the rate of two million per year. The increase of the German people and of the Germans in Austria was rated about one million per year. The French population stands stationary. England's population is increasing at a rate that doubles in a little less than one-half century.

But while Russia already owns territory enough to accommodate ten times its present population, while England, through her colonies, is even better provided for the future, the Germans and the Scandinavians occupy geographical areas that are already more than comfortably saturated.

Perhaps the real and only cause of the present great war is the territorial situation of the German people. On the west she is bounded by nations whose populations are tremendously dense. On her northern border there are only fragments and fringes of habitable lands occupied by people whose fecundity is as great or greater than that of the Germans. To the east, excepting the Baltic provinces of Russia, the whole territory is occupied by Poles, Russians, and Slavs of other names. And Russia, who holds all this territory, is a mighty and powerful nation. In the south and southwest, Austrian and Swiss territory is already fully occupied. And yet the German population, in this limited territory, is growing faster than that of any other European nation except Russia. Sooner or later Germany has to conquer more lands for her people over the sea or reach a point of absolute suffocation. The war that is now raging was inevitable sooner or later.

Of course, Germany is the cause of the war. She must win the war, or the German nation, as a nation, must cease in the course of a century to be a great power.

When the war is over then we may expect some slight changes in the European map in the north. In southern Europe there may be great changes. Unless Germany conquers at sea it seems to be impossible, no matter how successful she may be elsewhere, that she can gain any colonial acquisitions without the consent of England.

England's statesmanship may be such as to cause that country to seek to insure future peace by giving Germany, as a colony, a large part of Asia Minor. If the whole of the present Turkish Empire were made a German colony, England would, for a century or more, fence her great rival Russia off from the south — from access to the Mediterranean. France and Italy, the first easily and the other more reluctantly, could be persuaded to consent to such an arrangement.

After Russia has helped France, England, and Italy to crush the German peril, it is more than probable that she will be forced to retire without any fruits of victory. France and England might take a lesson from Russia's textbook. When Russia was assailing Turkey in 1878 and was in danger of defeat, she called Romania to her aid and Romania responded and made a Russian victory possible. But at the conclusion of the war Russia only rewarded Romania by taking to herself a large part of Romania, namely the province of Bessarabia. England and France might placate their once mighty foe and turn enmity into friendship by giving Turkey over to Germany.

But my correspondent has not asked me for a political prophecy. He is a man whose capital is almost wholly invested in properties largely dominated by me and what he wants to know is, what will be the effects of the war on the business of these properties. Before seeing his letter I had dictated a short disquisition, "The War and American Business."

The business in which I and my correspondent are interested is going to grow or decay without regard to the fortunes of any nation now warring in Europe. Its growth and decay will depend entirely upon the business skill and force of character of the men who control it.

Neither does the growth or decay of this business depend at all on the average or general prosperity of America as a whole. While the force of character of the managers of our business is the main element in it, intelligence is of nearly equal importance. In order for us to be very successful it is necessary for us to be able to foresee conditions that are imminent.

I think my correspondent really wanted me to endeavor to make a forecast.

In my essay on "The War and American Business," I indicated roughly what I considered to be the order of events in the business world for the immediate future.

I anticipated a more or less short-lived period of considerable activity in America as a result of the war in Europe. Because I have hardly any doubt that the English and French navies will soon sweep the seas clear of German and Austrian war vessels, I believe that our export trade to all European countries excepting Germany and Austria (and possibly Russia) will soon be enormous. Europe will not only need foodstuff but all manner of other products that are not contraband of war such as a neutral nation is bound not to export. It may be that after transportation has ceased to be dangerous, our own government will become very liberal in the interpretation as to what is contraband of war and consequently non-exportable. [Neither side had developed the offensive use of the submarine prior to World War I; hence, even a man as well informed as Scripps could not take the U-boat into consideration at this point.]

Because Europe will be too busy with war to produce anything that is merchantable, it is probable that American goods of all sorts will soon be exported to other parts of the world than Europe, where formerly European goods alone supplied the market. If this war should continue for a year, American manufacturers might capture the world's markets and, once having them captured, retain them indefinitely. Under such conditions it is probable that, although Europe might become too poor to buy and pay for much that we could produce, other parts of the world might more than compensate for this loss of European customers.

I recall the explanation (that has always been given by writers on economics) of England's tremendous lead over the rest of the world during the nineteenth century.

During the Napoleonic reign, which lasted over a period of many years, continental Europe was so constantly engaged in war and political re-adjustments consequent upon war that manufacture of goods almost ceased.

What manufacture there was was in countries dominated by Napoleon. England's war vessels made it impossible for these countries to export.

During all the time that Europe was in this turmoil, the island of England had to supply only large sums of money in the way of subsidies to her fighting allies and small armies to continental Europe and a comparatively few men to man her war vessels. English manufacture went on and thoroughly developed itself, and English trade overseas grew enormously.

Although England incurred tremendous indebtedness and suffered in other ways from the war, her position relative to the continental nations was one of tremendous advantage, so that after the close of the Napoleonic Wars England was found with her manufacture and trading industries thoroughly organized and developed, while that of all continental Europe was thoroughly demoralized and largely annihilated.

Even in the present war, England's advantage in a trading and manufacturing way over continental Europe is tremendous, because, at most, she will not have more than 5 per cent of her male population engaged either in war or the manufacture of war material, while her business rivals will have all their men engaged in warlike enterprises.

Were it not for America, and to a smaller degree Japan, England would be in about the same situation today as she was during the Napoleonic Wars. But with all England's industry fully employed, such is the condition of her trade and manufacturing organization, she would be unable to supply to overseas markets the immense amounts of products formerly exported by continental Europe.

If our American businessmen, manufacturers, and traders recognize their opportunity they may wonderfully profit by this war, and I have no doubt but that the American businessmen will recognize the opportunity.

However, while we have been rapidly growing to be an exporting nation, we are not organized as was England in the beginning of the nineteenth century to take full advantage of the opportunity presented.

Europe has been, by far, our largest customer and for the things that we have been manufacturing for export to Europe, other parts of the world have no great need.

Then, too, in the beginning of the nineteenth century England not only dominated the seas with her warships but hers was the only mercantile navy that amounted to anything in Europe. Unfortunately, America has no mercantile navy to speak of, and even if our exports become tremendously large, England will, for some time at least, have a monopoly on transportation of such exports. In fact, it will be seen that our position is not entirely identical with that of England after the Napoleonic Wars.

How long it will take the Americans to adjust themselves so as to take full advantage of their opportunity I have no idea, but it seems quite likely that the war will have ceased long before this readjustment has taken place. But the effects of the war, perhaps, will not have ceased for many years.

In my disquisition on "The War and American Business" I was almost entirely pessimistic. In fact, I wrote the latter disquisition at the time when I was dazed and confounded by the great explosion. Something had happened — something horrible had happened and I was only thinking of immediate and present safety. I was only thinking of preparing for the worst that might happen.

Today the reaction has set in. The pendulum of my spirits has swung from pessimism to optimism.

All changes are costly because of their being disorganizing. If there is to be a change in the world's trade conditions with respect to America this change must be costly and disorganizing.

Those businessmen who can the soonest adjust themselves to the change will be those who will profit most. But our (my correspondent's and mine) business is mainly with that order or class of men who are not the most able and alert, who are not manufacturers and foreign traders. It is probable that 99 per cent of these customers of ours will take months to pass through the same mental phases that I have done in days. It is not until they become optimistic that they will become good customers.

It will take a long time for the wise businessmen to conceive the business projects that the new condition will invite them to and to carry them out by employment and begin that chain of business which will gradually have its effect on the prosperity of the country as a whole.

My two disquisitions, taken together, may be considered as two opposing arguments on the same subject.

In the course of several weeks or several months I may amuse myself and furnish some amusement for others by another disquisition.

It has only been a week now since the European war was considered anything like a certainty, and I have been, like I suppose everybody else, far more interested as a sportsman than as a businessman.

European financiers prophesied, immediately after the passage of the [Federal] Reserve Bank bill [in 1913], that one result would be enormous exports of gold from this country to Europe. When we had so much currency as we were going to have under this bill, it was natural to assume that American holders of gold could make a profit by selling it to Europe.

Then came the war scare and the demand for gold in Europe was enormous and its export would have been great had there been no change in our financial system. It is conceivable that as the war proceeds the demand for American gold will increase. Our debts to Europe are so great and the profits that can be made by gold shipments are, and will continue to be, so great that nothing but governmental action can prevent an enormous out-flow of gold.

And is there any occasion for the government to act?

It is probable that our export trade is going to grow tremendously and that our imports from Europe will tremendously diminish, but our exports will be to countries who may pay on a gold basis but cannot pay in gold.

I have found out that bankers are fully alive to the gold condition. [Julius] Wangenheim, the president of my little bank here in San Diego, who is a bigger man, in finances a great deal, than San Diego is as a city, tells me he recently made a wager with a banker in Los Angeles that there will be a premium paid on gold in six months, and expressed to me the belief that the United States will be on a paper basis within a year and that practically all the gold in the world will go into hiding, that is not held in government re-serves. It may be that I am an ignoramous in such matters, but from the standpoint of my experience in the newspaper business I cannot see how any suffering is to come to us as the result of gold being at a premium. As a speculator, I think, if I had a large sum of gold, I would hold onto it for the premium and hence the profit that might result, but I do not think I would keep my gold for the purpose of safeguarding or even improving the business prospects of our newspapers.

Of course, paper money and anything like elastic currency must, of ne-cessity, produce inflation, and therefore I consider it almost certain that prices of all commodities will rise and that prices of real estate will not fall so much as [they] otherwise would.

It stands to reason that inflation of currency must of necessity result in a reduction in wages.

It is probable that those businesses like ours (the price at which we sell our papers being fixed while the cost of white paper may increase) and such industries as railroad transportation (passenger and freight rates being fixed) may suffer some temporary loss, until readjustments have been made.

America First

(A SECRET PROPHECY)

[*October 19, 1915*]

With the by-line, "By a Famous American Editor," this disquisition appeared in Harper's Weekly *of April 8, 1916. Norman Hapgood, the editor, had specifically requested Scripps to write an article about the war.*

At the outbreak of the present European war the aggregate wealth of the United States was approximately equal to the combined wealth of the three most powerful of the twelve belligerent nations.

At about the same time, the value of the annual products of the people of the United States was but little less than the value of the combined products of all the European belligerents. The foreign trade of the United States was inferior only to that of England and to that of Germany.

At the beginning of the war practically one-quarter of the gold of the world was in the United States — in the banks of the United States or in the hands of American citizens.

In 1914 the leadership of the United States, in relation to all the other nations of the world, economically speaking, had become absolute and even startling in its conspicuousness.

Early in the year 1915, if not in the latter part of the year 1914, the population of continental United States reached 100 million. Only two other civilized nations had much more than one-half of this population.

Owing to the Negroes in the United States, the effective white population in the United States was not over 90 million.

Perhaps the population of Germany, which is something short of 70 million, is more effective, man for man, than is that of the United States. considering its whole 100 million. However, even with fair allowance being

538

made on account of our colored population, the strength of Germany, based upon effective population, is much less than that of the United States.

The population of all the territory of the Russian Empire is perhaps 50 per cent greater than the present population of the United States. But the strength of this Russian population is, man for man, so much less than that of the United States, by reason of the race inferiority of a large section of that population, as to make it possible for the Russian people to be inferior in strength to the United States people, even if the institutions of civilization were as general in Russia as they are in the United States. But, conditions being such as they are, it is doubtful if the man-force of Russia today is as great as that of England, which is less than half as great as that of the United States. Beyond this the Russian state is greatly weakened because, instead of its population being homogeneous or even a well-mingled and mixed heterogeneous population, it is composed of a great number of separate nations welded together by force — nations, each of which is composed of a distinct race, some of which have not only different religions from the Russians but antagonistic religions.

The annual increase of the population of Russia has been estimated by W. T. Stead at 2 million, which is practically the same as has latterly been the increase of the population of the United States.

The population of Germany has been increasing latterly at the rate of something less than 1 million per annum.

The present white population of not only Great Britain but the whole of her colonies combined is something less than 60 million. The native colored populations of England's colonies are rather a source of military and financial weakness than of strength to Great Britain.

Germany has no white man's territory outside of her European boundaries, and this European territory of hers is now supersaturated.

While France has territories in northern Africa capable of sustaining a large white population, the increase of the French people, both at home and in her African colonies, is negligible and will probably continue to be negligible.

The territory of the home country of the United Kingdom is more supersaturated than that of Germany. The population of Great Britain can, in future, only grow to any considerable extent through her dominion colonies; and it is doubtful as to how long these self-governing dominions will remain a part of the British Empire.

Lack of home territory and other conditions make it impossible for other of the European nations than those mentioned to compete with the United States in the matter of population.

By means of conquest some of the colonies or colonial territories of France or Great Britain might change hands politically.

Were Germany to obtain French territory in northern Africa she might build up a great population there with her home surplus. But German rule of the present Anglo-Saxon self-governing dominions would not change the Anglo-Saxon character of their peoples.

Now that the European white races have (having passed over the full width of North America) reached the Pacific Ocean, it is inevitable that sooner or later — sooner rather than later — the Asiatics and Europeans will be at warfare in a military way as they are now in [an] economic way.

It was not necessary that there should have been a great war in Europe (and that the international conflagration in Europe should have destroyed the best part of the European people and have worked vast injury to the economic condition of Europe) in order that the United States should have rapidly forged ahead, not only of individual European states, but of all Europe together. During the nearly half-century of peace or comparative peace in Europe, the United States overtook and passed, one after another, each of the great European nations in the matter of population and wealth, and hence in force, until, as it has been said before, she had actually gained the hegemony of all the world's nations long before the present European war broke out. Still, there can be no question whatever but that the relative position of the United States, as compared with each of the European states, is rapidly changing in favor of the United States as a result of the war.

The United States is not only progressing relatively to Europe, but intrinsically, both in population and general economics. In the latter respect, though not in the former, its progress is being made more rapid by reason of this war.

The reason underlying Great Britain's supremacy in the financial world for so long has been that, until the emergence of the United States, Great Britain has been the wealthiest nation in the world. Just as the money center of any country is bound to be in the city of the greatest wealth, so is the money center of the world bound to be in the territory of the wealthiest nation. Financial supremacy was bound, sooner or later, to be transferred from England to America, war or no war. Universal human conservatism — that is to say, habit and custom — is a great force, and to this force alone is due the fact that for a decade or more London rather than New York has been the money center.

For over a century Britain has ruled the waves.

For a generation or more Prussia has dominated continental Europe.

The conflict between Germany and England today has perhaps points of similarity to the Roman-Carthage conflict, and the conflict between the Athenians and Spartans. But in those other two great conflicts the contestants were the two most powerful nations of the then civilized world. At present the contest between England and Germany lies between two nations who, had they been united, would have been unequal in a contest, either military or economic, with the United States, had the latter recognized in time and prepared for a conflict.

Either [Even, in *Harper's Weekly*] in case of victory by either Germany or England, the victor can, at most, only obtain as a prize the second place in the community of nations. To the extent that both are injured by this war, to just that extent, and perhaps more, will the nation of the United States be raised to a higher level as compared with either or both of these two belligerent nations.

Politically speaking, then, the war in Europe today is a war to hasten the progress of the United States to the position of world domination.

To one who is not a scientist [Socialist, in *Harper's Weekly*] it must be considered a fact, though lamentable, that the hierarchic system must prevail amongst private individuals. There can be no doubt but that for long ages yet to come the individuals amongst the family of nations must be governed by a similar system. There must be an almost all-powerful if not an all-powerful nation that can, if it wills, control the political actions of the other states.

There was a Pax Romana.

There is just passing a Pax Britannica.

Hereafter, the peace of the world must depend upon the American people, and much else must depend upon them — leadership, direction, and control.

The American nation might be compared with England as one would compare a son with his father.

Long after the son has obtained his full maturity and perfect, at least potential, independence of his father, the son retains the habit acquired in childhood of obedience to and respect for his father. In like manner the father continues to require such obedience and respect from the son. Often enough these two sets of habits result in an anomalous, absurd, and even laughable situation.

Notwithstanding the fact that the American son of the British father revolted and established independence in a political way over a hundred years ago, the American people have, in spite of all their braggadocio, regarded the British father as a father instead of just another individual.

It has been these two sets of habits — the English and the American habit — that have so long bolstered up the English credit, financial and other.

The keen-minded American, while his heart bleeds at seeing the pain and suffering of the parent country, cannot now refrain from some exultation, or at least some resignation, such as the son and heir of a wealthy man must feel when his father lies suffering on his deathbed.

It needs not that England should be crushed and ruined in order that the American heir should become possessed of the better part of what would be coming through his heirship.

Within two, three, or four decades, of necessity, the American people will be intervening in all international and world affairs, settling disputes between nations and suppressing such international conflicts as may, by disturbing the world's peace, disturb the serenity of the American people.

At this writing there seems to be an almost universal acquiescence on the part of the American people to the project of a great naval expansion.

Of course, we are pretending that our budding naval policy is dictated by caution — by a sense of necessity for self-defense in an emergency. But, consciously or unconsciously, the people as a whole are adapting themselves to a situation that is more or less recognized to be inevitable.

Whatever may be the final outcome of the present movement against militarism, there can be no doubt but that, in an early future, whatever may be the military establishments of other nations on land and sea, the military strength of the United States, as compared with the rest of the world's nations, will be dominant.

Taking Stock

[*March 15, 1916*]

This disquisition appears to have been unfinished, but was not so marked as other unfinished ones were.

Lately an impression has been gaining ground with me to the effect that there have been considerable changes in my opinions on various subjects.

During the whole period of the war in Europe, I have had little inclination to read about anything else or to think about anything else.

I recognize that, under the stress and pressure of these European events, my mind is not in its ordinary condition. I think it is quite possible that some of my recently formed convictions may, in the end, turn out to be no convictions at all, but only temporary attitudes of mind.

I have always been a thoroughgoing theoretic democrat. I have believed in democracy, that people living under a democratic form of government were more effective, not only individually but collectively, than were people living under any other form of government. However patent to my eyes were the evils and vices of democracy, until recently I was never able to believe that any other thus-far-tried system of government could be so effective and so comparatively virtuous as democracy.

For a number of years of my life I devoted all of my spare time to reading history and the philosophy of government. I was fairly familiar, too, with contemporary conditions existing in various nations of the world. I had traveled considerably, and, in reading, kept up with current events of various countries.

I had no faith whatever in the German governmental system. Though the German economic system had been much lauded, and especially by those writers whom in a general way I most esteem, I still felt that there was abundant evidence to prove that not only in the long run would the German

543

economic system prove a failure but that even in the present it was not so effective as the system prevailing in the more democratic countries.

Then the war began. And then began a series of shocks and surprises. This series has continued up to the present time. The result has been to cause me to think that all of my previous reasoning has been faulty and that my convictions were based on no better foundations than prejudice, perhaps patriotism. The things that had been taught me were by people who were ignorant of facts, prejudiced, and indolent of mind.

My faith in democracy began to disintegrate. My mental attitude began to take on a reactionary form. All of the vices and errors that I had previously noted in democracy began to appear far more significant. I began also to perceive that my own whole life's career had been that of an autocrat, and that this career in itself had proved the vast advantage of the autocratic system over the democratic system.

I had always been intensely anti-militaristic. I detested not only the national army but the state militia, and even the organized municipal police system. I had no objection to a large and powerful navy, but felt that such a navy was an absolute necessity. To my mind the navy was bound to be, under a democratic government, an instrument only of defense, an instrument to defend all of the people, rich and poor alike. On the other hand, the army, it appeared to me, was an instrument of oppression, an instrument controlled and directed by a few of the rich and powerful of the nation, to be used by them only to oppress the poor — the wage slave.

Today, I am resigned to the calling into existence of a great army, thinking perhaps that, as between the evils of the country as a whole — that of being defenseless, and that of the common people of the country being oppressed — the latter is the lesser evil.

Until lately my own desire has been that this nation should stand aloof from all other nations of the world and that it should never attempt by either force or persuasion to influence other peoples or other nations. I have felt that the only business of a government should be that of taking care of the domestic affairs of its people.

Today, I am desirous of seeing the United States the most powerful military nation on the earth, and I am not only willing but anxious that the United States should be the "big policeman" of the world.

Heretofore, I have felt that every man, and every woman perhaps, should have an equal voice in the government of the nation.

Today, I am not only ready to consent to the existence of a ruling class, small in number, but feel that the future of the nation depends exclusively upon the effectiveness of the members of this class.

I expect, in fact I am convinced, that the Germans, in the end, will be defeated in this great war. Her defeat, also, will be accomplished by the democratic element in the nations against whom she is contending.

However, such a defeat of Germany can in no way be considered evidence of the inferiority of the autocratic monarchial system.

Germany has had to fight nations whose combined populations outnumbered 2.5:1 the population of Germany and her allies; she had had to contend with a combination of nations whose wealth was three or four times greater than the combined wealth of Germany and her allies. Not only has Germany to face on the battlefield these superior numbers, but she is contending against the ill will of all the rest of the world — the so-called neutral nations.

The fact that it is requiring such overwhelming numbers to wear out and finally defeat the German Empire must be considered evidence of the superiority not only of the German military system but Germany's economic system.

Germany has also had to contend with even a more serious obstacle than the armies and navies of her antagonists; she has had to contend with a peculiar vice and weakness such as afflicts no other nation on earth; this vice is the overweening vanity and conceit of every individual German.

Overconfidence in herself will sooner or later be recognized by historians as the principal cause of Germany's final failure.

What Germany — with a population of not more than 75 per cent as great as that of the United States and whose wealth is not greater than 25 per cent of that of the United States — might fail in accomplishing, this people might well succeed in.

The fact that this nation is composed of people of many races safeguards it against the weaknesses of race egotism, of race conceit.

Whereas the Germans were almost all Germanic in their origin, and hence possessed of a race psychology all [their] own, and hence, also, incapable of fully comprehending the spirit governing other nations and even the material forces of the same, the American nation is composed of all races, a large percentage of which even are Germans. This being the case, in matters of diplomacy as well as military foresight, it would be certain that this, as a military nation, would be far better equipped to encounter the intelligence of other enemy nations than Germany has been.

I am unable to say how far my mind has been influenced [in] dealing with other subjects by my consideration of military proceedings in Europe. However, that there has been a change in the attitude of my mind toward other subjects is quite apparent.

Whereas I once considered the existence of poverty as being indubitable evidence of the wickedness of the wealthy few, I am now inclined to believe that poverty is criminal. I am beginning to think that, barring a few exceptional cases, a poor man is poor because he wills to be poor, just as a thief is a criminal because he wills to be a thief. I am thinking that the poor man is poor because he refuses to make those sacrifices and exercise that self-restraint which he knows would, if exercised, inevitably result in his possession of at least sufficient wealth to make him independent and free from even the danger of oppression. I think that there are few men with such defective minds as to make it impossible for them to foresee the inevitable results of improvidence. A poor man is one who chooses to sell his birthright of independence for a mess of pottage in the way of some desirable but insignificant present pleasure.

Whereas I formerly detested wealth and wealthy men, I have developed a mental condition which enables me to see the possibility and even the probability that men of wealth and great power, political or otherwise, are moved by the spirit of self-sacrifice for public service. Just as it is impossible for me to believe that even the thoughtless, ignorant poor are unable to foresee the consequences of improvidence, so it is even more impossible for me to believe that men of great wealth and great activities are ignorant of the burdens they necessarily bear. From the earliest beginnings of a man's acquisition of material things he begins to learn the cost and labor and anxiety of maintaining his possessions. As progress is made in the accumulation of wealth, these lessons become more instructive as the burdens of the possessions increase.

Why should any man sacrifice all or nearly all of the pleasures of life in order to accumulate a great fortune or to perform the difficult services of some great and honorable office? While there may be many answers to this question, I myself believe that at least one, on the occasion of such a great service, is a natural inborn spirit of altruism. This spirit may be unconscious for much of the time and always to a large extent, but that it is in existence sometimes and to some considerable extent always, I have no doubt.

However much I may hate and condemn the German Kaiser, I cannot fail to recognize that the Kaiser, during this war, is laboring harder and suffering more things and in more ways, perhaps, than any of his subjects. The chances of his eventual death, as a result of this war, from sickness or overstrain or other causes are perhaps greater than those incurred by any young recruit in his army.

Can anyone doubt that the Kaiser is not fighting for his people — for what he thinks is the people's good? Only prejudice and bitterness of feeling on the part of anyone of his and his country's enemies can cause that person to believe that the Kaiser is carrying on this great war and suffering all that he does suffer for his own personal gratification.

The Inevitable

[*August 28, 1916*]

This disquisition appears to have been edited in Scripps' hand.

Some months ago I wrote a disquisition which I first captioned "A Secret Prophecy." As I wished to submit copies of this disquisition to various critics, I changed the heading, making it "America First."

A rather badly edited, or I might say garbled, copy of this disquisition appeared in the N.E.A. sheets.

In one of the latest numbers before the demise of that publication, appeared the article in *Harper's Weekly*.

This disquisition is intended to be partly a summary and partly an extension of the train of thought which evolved "[A] Secret Prophecy," or "America First."

The caption of this disquisition indicates that it is a prophecy, and that it is the prophecy of a man who has no doubt to his authority to prophesy. The present world war is only an incident, and not even a causative incident, in the procession of events that are to culminate in that thing that I maintain is inevitable. It will be seen that the fundamental basis of my conviction lies far deeper than the present world-shaking catastrophe.

This world is a small piece of territory at most. But small as it is, that part of it which is inhabited by people that have in the past and will in the future, perhaps for centuries to come, govern and shape society, is very small as compared with the total habitable part of the globe.

While map-makers amuse us by light and shade effects, showing how large a proportion of the world's territory is involved in this war, there are only two small specks of world territory inhabited by the real combatants of the present European conflict. These two specks of territory consist of the island of Great Britain (not including Ireland) and that small portion of the German Empire that was the Prussian state of perhaps not over a hundred years ago. All the other belligerents, quasi-belligerents, and pseudo-belligerents — the latter not belligerents at all — are merely in the state of excitement induced by the conflict of two little peoples inhabiting two little lands.

The island of England does not rule the British Empire any more than does the King of England rule England. The King of England reigns over, but does not rule, England. The British island presides over the British Empire, but does not govern it.

The British Empire is even far less an empire in fact than was the Roman Empire. Prussia has ambition for an empire, perhaps more Roman than British in likeness.

The Romans could not Romanize all of their empire, and they only partially Romanized a very small portion of it. Prussia has not even Prussianized the, territorially speaking, little state of Germany.

England has colonized, partially it is true, vast territory in the world — territories, however, in which alien or un-English populations are insignificant. Time and the fertility of the colonies will thickly populate with Englishmen all of these territories.

At the present time, there are Englishmen, Irishmen, Scotchmen, and Welshmen — about 60 million white men — in the British Empire. Three-quarters of this population inhabit the islands of Great Britain.

But the United Kingdom is more than saturated with population. It has not raw material enough, including food, within its island territory sufficient to support one-half of its present population.

The at present thinly populated territories of the British Empire — territories where, however, there are no rival races to speak of — are sufficiently large to accommodate a population of from 50 to 100 times greater than can be supported by the natural products of the United Kingdom [*sic*].

The territory of not only Prussia but of all the present German Empire, including the German part of Austria, is so small that already the population of Germany cannot subsist on the natural products from her own territory.

The German land is completely surrounded by land at present occupied by dense populations of people, who in the average are more fertile and who are little or no less natively virile than are the Germans. Forever, these surrounding populations must press upon Germany and the Germans. It is impossible for them to be annihilated by the Germans so that their territory can be taken from them.

It is conceivable that Germany may in this war, or some future war, conquer with the sword vast territories in the world at present thickly or thinly occupied. But she cannot do more than conquer these lands with the sword and rule them with the sword. She cannot populate them with her children. In all historical times, Germany has been losing her children by emigration. The children of past dead and gone Germans are Frenchmen, Russians, Northern Italians, Hollanders, Belgians, Englishmen, Americans, and South Africans. I think that there is no question of doubt but that there is today more German blood flowing in the veins of un-German nations than is flowing in the veins of the present inhabitants of the fatherland. The German people of today are but the residue — the organized national residue of the great German people that inhabit the earth. German organism, German culture, all of these things and every one of them which are used to define and classify that which we call Germany today, are but partly and in a minor degree the result of inheritance.

Germany's position in the world is unique. Those conditions that are a necessity to the existence of the German people and that have made the organism of the German state such as it is exist nowhere else. Hence, German institutions, German government have always been and still are impractical of exercise in other lands and under other conditions than those existent in the present territory of the German Empire in Europe.

The Germans might conquer a mighty empire, but it could never be a homogeneous German Empire; it could never be peopled by Germans to anything like the extent which would make the Germanism the dominating ethnical, ethical influence.

At most, it requires only a few generations before England, the United Kingdom, will cease to hold even the position of hegemony in the empire bearing her name.

There are not in Europe today over 80 millions of people in the empire of Germany, plus the German people of Austria.

Granting that the Germans and the German part of Austria be united in a single empire, we have a population, then, 25 per cent less than the population of the United States.

The population of the United States is 66 per cent greater than the total white population of the British Empire today.

The natural resources and the territory of the United States are many times greater — perhaps more than twenty times greater — than are the natural resources of all the territory in Europe occupied by the Germans and of all the territory of Great Britain and Ireland combined.

While the land of the Germans and the island of Great Britain, together with their resources, have been worked to the point where complete exhaustion is within a computable distance of time, the natural resources of the United States have hardly yet been surveyed, much less noticeably consumed.

Yet even in this comparatively populated territory of the United States, where so little has yet been done to employ and use the natural advantages, the existing wealth is fully double that of the combined existing wealth of Great Britain and Germany. Beyond this it is now known that the value of the annual products of the people of the United States is treble and even quadruple the value of the combined products of Germany and the United Kingdom.

Although the people of the United States are numerically 15 per cent less than the combined populations of Great Britain and Germany, the per capita productivity in the United States is so great as to produce the results outlined in the last paragraph.

Perhaps it is not too much to say that the per capita productivity of America is three times greater than that of the German or the Englishman, or the average of both.

As an economic machine, then, an American is far superior to a German or an Englishman. But what of him as a fighting machine? The American is so much English, so much German, and so much of all the best fighting blood of Europe that it stands to reason that he is capable of organizing himself into a fighting machine no less effective than the German or English machine. It is not quite possible that on account of his environment, on account of his governmental and social institutions that the American can, relative to his European competitor, be as superior a fighting machine as he is an economic machine.

A man can only learn to fight, however, by fighting. Of all the people in Europe today, the German has had the most practice to make himself practicable at being a soldier.

Is it possible that conditions could so develop in America as to train the fighting man of America to the high pitch that the German has been trained?

I hold that it is possible. I hold that it is probable. I hold also that it is almost certain. Man is a fighting animal, and the fact that he changes his residence from one country to another does not change his mental or physical constitution. Americans must fight, because they are fighting animals.

Whom will they fight?

The Americans will fight any or all other nations in the world. They will fight individual nations and alliances of nations, and before they are done, they will have to fight the world in alliance against America. In this last great fight, or before the last great fight, the Americans will suffer terrible defeat, and in probability suffer disintegration not long after defeat.

Before the days of the great wars, the people of the United States will occupy a whole continent, perhaps two of them — not as conquerors and rulers over alien people but as the dominant and majority populations in all those parts of the Americas that are inhabitable by men of European origin.

It is inevitable that that part of the British Empire which is now American territory will be in some form, either a federation *en bloc*, or in provinces or states, a part of the United States in the future age.

Long before this time of uniting comes, the nations of the United States will hold the same position of hegemony in the Anglo-Saxon world that England now holds in the British Empire. The first great training that the American people, people of the United States, will have as an organized fighting unit will be in conflicts with the people or peoples of Asia. Either Europe collectively, or some state or states of Europe, will have to try conclusions of war with the United States during the twentieth century before the giant of the West is fully grown, or there can be no such war, as after that, or at least a longer period of time, the United States relative to any European state or coalition of states, will be invulnerable to attack, and perhaps engage in an offensive war against European nations or Europe on the whole.

I am not prophesying for this or the next generation as I did in "America First." I am prophesying for the first, second, third, and perhaps fourth centuries after the present century.

Wars will never cease amongst men until men cease to exist. Man must fight man, because man is man.

Predictions

[*April 16, 1917*]

This letter to his two surviving sons, James and Robert, was written ten days after the United States declared war on Germany.

"Miramar," Calif., April 16, 1917

James and Robert

My Sons:

This is the end of old times. The new times are beginning. What is before us, I do not know. I will now attempt to predict some things.

I think that the old European world and the new American are about to change places.

Political democracy will entirely displace aristocracy.

Political democracy is to be reinforced by economic democracy.

The political revolution in Europe will be paralleled by economic revolution in America.

Socialism is not impending. Individualism will be more dominant than ever before.

There will be great changes, however, in the personnel of the ruling powers in the economic world.

There will also be great changes in the manner of succession in the matter of property. Wealth and power will pass from hand to hand, and generation to generation, by reason of the inherent fitness of men rather than by reason of blood relationship.

As there will be a better selection of captains of wealth and power, these new captains will be more effective.

In America this revolution will not probably be one of violence and bloodshed, but will take a more practical form, and, hence, be more effective.

I believe it is inevitable that the territory of the United States will be

552

extended far to the south within one or two generations; that is to say, that the greater part of Mexico will soon enough be a part of the territory of the United States. There is no use in giving thought or consideration to the ethics of such a happening.

The Anglo-Saxon world will be united politically and economically either by confederation or by some sort of conquest — probably economical conquest of the leadership of this portion of the world's population by the United States.

The three great powers of the world in the early future will be the Slavs of Europe and Asia, the Anglo-Saxons led by the United States, and the Japanese-Chinese confederation of Asia.

I believe to a certainty that the United States will in a generation be the leading military, naval, and commercial power of the world. Henceforth, the United States is to be a military nation. It is useless to regret and contend against the inevitable.

While this country is to become more democratic than ever before and the rest of the world is to be democratized, pure democracy, which is socialism, is not to be forthcoming. The rulers will always be few in number. These rulers, however, must be more efficient than have been all rulers political or economic in any past time.

There will be a great war, perhaps many great wars, between America and Asia. The first of these, between the United States and Japan, is not long to be delayed. One people will rule the Pacific, as this rule cannot be divided between two peoples.

Such is the nature and solidarity of humanity that the ruling class of the world at large, or a nation in particular, depends for its growth, development, and progress upon the growth, development, and progress of all those whom they rule.

The comfort, happiness, and welfare of the ruled-over depend upon the competence and vigor of the ruling class.

Class warfare must be perpetual.

The ruled-over class will be critical of their rulers, and will depose and punish those of the ruling class who are incompetent to serve the ruled.

Your enemies, or those against whom you should contend, should never be the subordinates or ruled-over class. Those against whom you should contend should be the ineffective and stupid members of the ruling class, who are not only jeopardizing their own interests but yours by their own inefficiency or incapacity to recognize the rights and powers of the subordinate class.

You are in a position which will enable you to, for good or ill, greatly influence the direction of the impending revolution in this country.

Your effectiveness for public good, and hence for private gain, will depend largely upon your success in ignoring petty and selfish things, and concentrating your minds and labors on the great essentials of the future — the large and greatly important problems of your time.

The petty interests that will intrude themselves upon you are, beginning from the bottom and proceeding upward, purely family bickerings and contentions; the little internal politics of your own institution; and the selfish ambitions and stupidities of the few score of men in public life who have the opportunity to come in personal contact with you.

This is to be a military nation; then do your best to make it an effective military nation.

If there is to be an economic revolution, don't spend your energies in opposing it, but adapt yourself to the new order of things, and always endeavor to make the new order better than it might have been without your efforts.

In other words, don't quarrel with the inevitable. Forever be on the alert to make the most of what is, and is to be.

The only reason that you can possibly have for increasing your wealth is that thereby you may increase your power.

You both know that the larger your payroll is, the greater your wealth is. It should be equally evident to you that the greater amount of taxes you pay, the greater is your wealth. A large tax not only indicates that your wealth is great, but it seems clear to me that the direct and indirect influence of paying large and larger taxes will be of such character as to directly be the cause of increasing your wealth.

The future belongs to those men who will be ever vigilant and on the alert, and always ready to adapt themselves to conditions whatever they shall turn out to be. This attitude is contemptuously called "opportunism," but only those are condemned as "opportunists" who try and fail to make use of opportunity. Those opportunists who succeed in profiting by opportunity are praised as being wise men and patriots.

E. W. Scripps

Why Should We Fear to Be Strong?

[*May 28, 1917*]

This disquisition was reviewed and revised by Scripps.

"Quit yourselves like men: be strong!"

Sir Thomas Runton, the great English physician, who died only a year ago in England, heartbroken because of the distress of his country, for more than a score of years made this vain appeal to the deaf ears of his countrymen. It was as a physician, even more than as a patriot, that he appealed to Englishmen to give that military training to her youth that was essential, he thought, not only to their physical well-being but to their intellectual and moral development.

Dogs delight to bark and bite, because it is their nature to. Men delight to love and fight, for the same reason.

Civilization is a process of man's conflict with nature; in large part, a conflict with his own nature.

Man is a fighting animal by nature. Society can only exist by reason of man's being more or less successful in suppressing his bellicose instincts and activities.

There is, however, no law of nature that can be successfully and wholly opposed. The forces of nature can be harnessed, but they cannot be annihilated. They can be used by man, but they cannot be destroyed by him.

Man's natural instinct to fight may be so directed as to be of great service to society, but the instinct cannot be suppressed.

The instinct of the individual is also the instinct of groups of individuals and hence of a nation.

Were it possible for the fighting instinct of any one nation to be entirely suppressed, it would not be possible to suppress the fighting instinct of all nations; so that any nation that might denature itself would certainly become the victim and the prey of the nation next to it.

555

This nation of ours, because it is composed of human beings, must be a fighting nation. It must fight — successfully or unsuccessfully. It must defeat, or be defeated. It must fight with its muscles and with its mind. It must fight with its brawn, and with the tools that are the joint output of its brawn and mind.

Every nation is a potential enemy of every other nation. The ally of one time must be the enemy of another time.

The United States must be strong to encounter its enemy of today, and it must be no less strong to defend itself at some future moment against its allies of this day.

In fact it appears, at least to the writer of these lines, that the enemies of the United States of tomorrow are to be more dangerous to these states than is the enemy of today.

Once two Negroes, one old and one young, were watching a fight between two opossums. The opossum is not naturally, I suppose, a fighting animal. The younger Negro expressed surprise at the persistency of the two antagonists. The old Negro explained, in reply to the younger one, that he supposed "those two 'possums are brothers."

The United States has brother nations.

But away back — so far back in time that there are no historical records of the event — the ancestors of the people who now occupy Europe and most of North America and who dominate all the Western Hemisphere left the cradle of their race, somewhere in the Far East.

Westward the course of empire took its way. Always westward the white man has traveled.

From Asia he invaded Europe, to its western shores and its utmost confines of what was the then-known world.

After centuries and milleniums in Europe, the white man found the New World. He swarmed into it, and across it. He had increased and multiplied until Europe was crowded, and by tens of millions he invaded the New World, and swept across it until every mile of these two great western continents between the Atlantic and the Pacific has been occupied by him.

Has the white man completely run his race?

Is the Pacific shore the utmost boundary of his western march?

We know that this cannot be so.

Having swept almost clear around the world, the white man still looks westward, over a very wide ocean, to a comparatively thin strip of land that divides him from his ancient cradle land — the land of his birth. Successfully, or unsuccessfully, the white man will try to bridge that wide ocean (even now he has long been building his bridge). He will then, moving westward still, attempt and almost certainly succeed in the effort of completing his circuit of the world.

The white man that occupies, as a nation or as nations, the American continent will, sooner or later, be arrayed in battle against the Asiatics.

Will the Asiatics first attack the American continent, or will the Americans first attack the Asiatics?

It matters not. The conflict is inevitable.

Therefore, the American people must be a military people.

What are the ethics of the case?

Millions of years before Christianity was, and before there was born any of the religions of today's world, man was; and the white man had evolved the white man's character and habits.

There is an older ethics, and a more controlling ethics, in humanity than any that religion codifies.

Warfare was once almost wholly a matter of brute force, though there never could have been a time, since man became man, when warfare was not, partly at least, a matter of wits, craft, cunning.

However, whatever were conditions in the past, warfare today is mainly a matter of a battle of minds.

While the successful military nation of today must be possessed of much brawn, it is even more important that it must possess a high degree of mental development.

In order that a nation may be strong in a military way, its men must be wise men — men who can think clearly and see far with their minds.

Up to the present time, wars have been fought by a few men of great mind, and large armies composed of men who have been trained to obey, and who have also, perhaps, been trained not to think. Under these conditions, victory has gone, and must go, to the nation whose directing few are superior in mentality to the directing few of the antagonist nation.

The tendency of autocracies, monarchies, and aristocracies is to limit to the smallest possible number the ruling and directing class.

The tendencies of democracy are to create the largest possible number of men who are potentially strong in mind.

At the present period of the world's history, there is a conflict between the two systems of political and social organization — the monarchial and the democratic.

Long before the great wars between the East and the West shall begin must be settled the question as to whether or not the white man of the world is to follow the democratic or monarchial system.

The European war, in which are now involved all of the nations of the white man, as well as some other nations, is probably going to settle this question.

America — the United States — must and will be a great military nation. Its power in a military sense must become consistently strong, relative to the economic force of this nation.

What shall be the form of our military organization?

It cannot be absolutely democratic, for reasons that must be patent to all who are intelligent.

It cannot be monarchial or aristocratic in form, since a nation can be no more half-democratic and half-monarchial than it can be half-free and half-slave.

Our military organization must be something in the way of a compromise. It must be partly democratic, partly autocratic; or, rather, it will be a mingling of the two.

Our military organization should be like our political organization in that, instead of its containing and being constructed so as to only produce a few men capable of directing and ruling, it shall throw up the greatest possible number of men who are potentially strong as rulers.

Our military organization, then, should be of such a character as will not by training — too much training (too much training to obedience) — disqualify all the great mass of the army for anything but to obey and to fight and die by orders.

Our soldiers, from the lowest ranks to the highest, must be respectable and respected.

The commonest of common soldiers should socially be the equal at least — and preferably the superior — of his fellows in the ranks of the class from which he has been called to military service.

There must be assured him a wage and salary sufficiently large to enable him to easily secure and enjoy intellectual culture.

Now follows the suggestion of a layman who has at least tried hard to make of himself a philosopher.

The suggestion is that there should be a national policy of universal, obligatory military service. That is, that every young man who is to become a citizen should be subject to a call to service in the army, service to begin not earlier than the first of his eighteenth year and not later than the first of his nineteenth year. Each year there should be not less than a half-million young men called to the colors.

These young men, during their legal minority, should be clothed, lodged, and fed by the government, as is the rule in all armies, and should, during the period of their minority, receive but a portion of their soldier's wages — a fourth or a third or a half.

Upon the occasion of their honorable dismissal from active training service and their transfer into the reserve, they should receive, in a lump sum, the residue of their wages.

The wages of these soldier-pupils should be larger, rather than less, than the average wage of industrial employees.

The two or three years spent by the pupil-soldier would be years that, if he were not in the army, would be devoted to school or college education, apprenticeship in some trade, or to training for some business pursuit. As his military employment would preclude the possibility of his making any advance in either of these last two directions, his compensation for serving in the army should be larger than the compensation that would be granted to him were he an apprentice of the trades or business.

It is not good, either, for young men or for the country as a whole that the date of marriage of these young men should be too long postponed. The lump sum which each of these pupil-soldiers would receive when leaving the army would go far toward making it practical and advisable for him to contract an early marriage.

I believe that three dollars a day, during the period of their active training and service, should not be considered too great.

It should be considered a badge of honor for a young man to be selected by draft to enter the army. Why not? He would, naturally, be selected only by reason of investigation proving that he was physically, intellectually, and morally superior to others who would compete for him for the honor of entering the army.

The population of the United States is now increasing at the rate of about two million per annum. By reason of deaths, in order to keep up this increase it is probable that there are three or four million young men and women coming to the age of nineteen each year, and hence one and one-half to two million boys coming to that age.

Then a draft of half a million boys a year would only include from a third to a fourth of those who, at that time, would be considered as candidates by reason of their age.

Under these conditions, it will be evident that by the selective draft only the best third, or best fourth, or possibly even the best fifth, of the whole young male population would be selected. Then would not any young man feel that he had been honored by reason of being selected as the best of three or four or five candidates?

Further, the very fact that the financial compensation he would receive would be so much greater than that of the rejected candidates would add greatly to his satisfaction and to his self-respect, and to the respect of others, especially including those very people whose good opinion and goodwill he most esteems, namely, the young girls from whom he would be expected to select a wife.

One of the greatest evils, perhaps, of military or barracks life, during peace times, is the necessary idleness of the soldiers which, under ordinary conditions, is only mitigated by harsh, frequently useless, training and discipline and labor imposed upon the soldiers by their officers.

Barracks life or camp life of these young soldiers should be, in some respects at least, similar to that of boarding school or any other school life, or life in industrial trades.

Only necessary hours should be devoted to military training. Other hours should be devoted to military study. But after both of these demands have been made upon the time of the young soldier and have been met, there remain daily many hours that could be devoted to study and instruction, and even to industrial and business training, never forgetting that the boy's physical, mental, and moral needs require considerable recreation and sports.

Every pupil-soldier should be, because he is a pupil-soldier, a candidate for promotion to military office. According to their merits, these young soldiers should be promoted, so that all of the officers of the army should be recruited from the conscripts.

In almost every other trade, profession, and business in America today, men are selected or promoted for merit rather than by reason of seniority.

Unfortunate as it may be to individuals that they should be retired from positions of great remuneration or honors at a comparatively early age, any and every organization is strong and effective just in proportion as it is officered and controlled by younger, rather than older, men.

With such an institution and organization as the army, upon whose effectiveness the very life and existence of a nation may depend, no mawkish sentimentality should be allowed to stand in the way of the army having the most vigorous and most effective men in command. Age, and aged men, have their uses. Often enough old men are wise executives, and their experience and training are of high value. But that organization is the most effective in which the best balance exists — where there are not too few young men in command, and where there are enough older men to do the work that old men can do, but where there are no old men who are doing the work that younger men can do as well and, on account of their youth and vigor, even better.

Washington, the Capital—And Me

[*June 1, 1917*]

I remember seeing a cartoon in one of our comic papers a number of years ago, illustrating the relative status of a man in his own hometown as compared with that of his status in the national capital.

The figure in one part of the picture was that of a portly, well-dressed man, carrying a valise. He was walking down the street of his hometown. He was depicted as of Brobdingnagian stature, while his neighbors and townspeople, who were gathered to see him off on his journey to Washington, were represented as veritable Lilliputians. The latter were bestirring themselves around the mammoth figure of their townsman, waving salutes to him, while he strode on with level eyes, seeing none of the little ones who were worshipping him.

This was Mr. Great-Man of the village, who was just departing for Washington to solicit some government office. The other part of the picture represented another Brobdingnagian figure: the congressman of Mr. Great-Man's district or the senator of Great-Man's state. This Brobdingnag had also a level gaze, seeing out so far above the little figure standing at his feet that there was no possibility of the latter's being observed. In this part of the picture there was only one Lilliputian. He wore the same hat and clothes, and carried the same piece of hand baggage, and was, in fact, a miniature replica of the other Mr. Great-Man.

When I left my home in California some two weeks ago, with Washington as my destination, I was on a mission entirely different from that of Mr. Great-Man. I wanted no office; I wanted no honorable distinction. I felt that no congressman of the lower house nor any senator nor even any member of the Cabinet, and not even the President himself, could bestow on me any mark of distinction, or any honor, since I felt that the whole government at Washington would be unable to add anything to the importance of my

561

own personality or to contribute anything to my authority or my own responsibilities.

Still, while I was on my California ranch, I did nurse the idea that in Washington, the capital of the nation, I would be an effective and an important factor.

A very candid and very old and experienced friend of mine told me that it would take me only about two weeks after I had come to Washington to become thoroughly disgusted with myself and with all the individual members of the government with whom I came in contact. On only three other occasions have I ever been in Washington, but on those occasions I had seen enough and learned enough to fully comprehend what my friendly adviser meant.

Still, I nursed the idea that, being something of a superman myself, I would, by patience, by persistence, and by shrewd tactics, find a way to accomplish, and to succeed in accomplishment.

I knew that nothing in the way of disillusionment was coming to me on account of my finding that the possessors of names that fill the newspaper columns were, on the average, only very small and unimportant human units.

I had long known some of these men; I had longer known most of them. Nearly half a century of journalism had taught me that only men of a certain caliber could find places in the legislative halls or government offices. It was on account of my knowledge of these things that I was most hopeful — and even more or less confident.

Owing to events that occurred during the recent presidential and congressional election, and owing to a very general knowledge which was possessed by the great leaders in the capital city concerning my own life's activities, I felt sure of not only being able to gain audience with any man I chose, even from those highest placed, but that from not a few I could expect solicitation of counsel, or at least of conferences.

I am a diffident man and, for this reason, contact with those who are, or feel themselves to be, superior men is extremely distasteful to me.

I do not like "hobnobbing" with either great men or little men. The first sort embarrass me, the second sort bore me.

Therefore, I did not contemplate, and do not contemplate, becoming at all conspicuous or to be recognized personally as a power in the land.

There are some things that I want to do. I have more or less at my command more facile men, men possessing more of the *savoir faire*, who can speak and act more effectively than I can, and who are willing and able to speak and act as I would have them speak and act in order to accomplish the results that I want accomplished.

However, having discounted myself to the farthest extreme that I was capable of, before reaching Washington, I am bound to acknowledge a sense of depression, of incapacity, and of my own comparative futility, now that I have been in the city of Washington for more than a week.

I am constantly asking myself if it is worthwhile for me to make any sort of an effort — whether or not, in fact, I can accomplish anything commensurate with the effort and self-sacrifice that I am bound to make if I continue here and continue to prosecute my plans.

There is only one thing to fortify my resolution — or I should say my persistence — and that is the feeling on my part that there is nothing else for me to do that is worthwhile.

Life in Washington for me will be a lonely life, but life for me has always been lonely. I detest the society of men, but I have never yet succeeded in overcoming the regret that companionship is so little enjoyable to me.

I know that I will not have a pleasant time here, but I am certain that I never have pleasant times anywhere. I have never succeeded in securing, and perhaps have never tried hard to secure, happiness. The greatest degree of contentment that I ever have had, or that I ever expected to have, has been of a negative sort. Whenever I am free from physical or mental pain of some sort, I count myself lucky.

I have always found the greatest freedom from any sort of pain when work, or care for others, or even when anxiety distracted my mind to such an extent that I was incapable of recognizing pain in any of its forms even when it had taken hold of me.

If I can find work here interesting, and if by work I lose consciousness of self, whether I am successful or unsuccessful in my endeavors, I shall count my coming to Washington as a piece of good fortune.

In fact, this is an adventure of mine where I have all to gain and nothing to lose.

What are my objects in coming to Washington? They are, I think, only two. First, I want the United States to become the strongest military power on earth.

Second, I want to increase the comfort, well-being, and intellectual development of what is called "the lower class" — the 95 per cent of the people of this country who are doing the country's work and who are, under present conditions, illy compensated in every way for the work they do.

I have had no illusions concerning the matter of bringing about my proposed reforms by means of personal intervention, by discussions and arguments with, or by pleadings and petitions to the ruling class in this country —either that class or its representatives in the government.

I know that in the great journalistic enterprise that I have founded and organized and developed lies my weapon.

Through it, and only by its means, will I and my successors, my colleagues and the colleagues of my successors, be able to compel both the ruling class and its official representatives to adopt the course that I want them to adopt.

It is only to be through the voters who elect officials, and the laborers who support industrial captains and money lords, that I will be able to compel my country's rulers to act more justly, and hence more wisely, than they are naturally inclined to do.

Only by force — by the force that I can exert through my influence upon millions of men who trust me or my institution, some more and some less — can I accomplish anything.

My visit and my stay in Washington will be informative to me. I will learn better how to do some things than I could elsewhere learn.

The city of Washington is the capital of the nation. Here are assembled the lawmakers, the law interpreters, and the executive officers of the nation.

For a long time, I have been taking stock of myself, or, rather, of my institution. By analysis, I have discovered that my institution represents one ten-thousandth of all of the wealth of the United States. By analysis, I have found that I am one of the thousand richest men in the United States.

I have learned the political power and the something-more-than-political power — let us call it social power — of my institution.

By reason of its good repute and, I venture to say, wise conduct, it has won such a position of power in this country that if there were ninety-nine other men placed as I am — that is to say, holding an equal amount of power — each of these men holding other stations, say, on the bench, or as great political leaders, or as great financial magnates, as religious teachers or leaders, as scientific men, or what not, with the whole hundred of us acting together, we could and would rule this country, absolutely.

My conceit has gone so far as to cut this number in half.

This being the case, and I claim it to be the case, I count that I am at least 2 per cent responsible for all that is good or ill in the management of this great nation.

Having in myself so great a power for good or evil, I have not been able to disabuse my mind, much as I have sought to do so, of the idea that a very grave responsibility is at present resting upon my shoulders, and soon enough it is to be resting upon the shoulders of my successor or successors.

I have no right to any of these things that I possess, either wealth or political influence, unless I am both able and anxious to bear full responsibility.

My conceit does not weigh me down oppressively. It causes me no loss of sleep, and perhaps not enough of heart-burning and anxiety.

This much I have learned from the school of my life's experience, and that is that society as a whole is wise. As a whole, it selects wisely — for positions of great trust, power, and authority — men who are capable of discharging the duties of their positions.

I would not have been selected for the job I hold unless I had the capacity to perform the tasks imposed upon me, and that, too, without great strain and effort.

Perhaps, during this late period of my life that has already grown so long, my chief cause for anxiety is as to whether or not my heirs of the flesh, and my heirs by institutional inheritance, sufficiently realize their own responsibility, and are as willing as they are capable, to perform the duties which are the major portion of their inheritance.

A Short Visit with the President

[June 29, 1917]

It was with extreme reluctance that I carried out the pledge that I had made to one of my friends to seek an interview with the President.[11]

On my arrival in Washington, having come with the feeling of considerable pessimism regarding the general war situation, and especially with regard to conditions in this country, I encountered a large amount of evidence to confirm my pessimism.

I have seen Secretary Baker, sized him up, and have been greatly depressed, because he did not seem to me big enough for his job.[12]

I have heard considerable from members of my staff, concerning the character and activities of other Cabinet members, which was unsatisfactory.

I was told that the President was, in fact, his own Secretary of State, Secretary of War, and Secretary of all the other departments where anything much was doing.

It was said to me that the President looked tired and worn and anxious, if not actually depressed.

I heard much of the apathy of the people of the country at large concerning the war and the rising tide of discontent throughout the working population, both on account of the rising cost of living, and their general impression that Washington was full of and that the government was being overwhelmed by a crowd of self-seeking representatives of industry, and especially those representatives who had become famous, or infamous, as "labor-baiters."

First, Mr. [Herbert] Hoover succeeded in throwing a terrible scare into me (and I am sure that I and many other people needed that scare). Then, Billy [W. B.] Colver had been telling me much of the machinations of indus-

---

[11] Part of this disquisition appears in Cochran, *E. W. Scripps*, p. 179 f.

[12] Obviously he changed his mind about Baker, in view of his enthusiasm about having Baker draft the will that established the E. W. Scripps Trust.

trial captains, and their success in thwarting the activities of his Commission — the Federal Trade Commission — as well as all the other government officials. [Lord] Northcliffe's repetition to me of the story that I had learned by my own reading of English publications of the bungling, muddling stupidity of his own Anglo-Saxon democracy, followed by his diagnosis of the present situation in the United States being so similar to what the situation had long been in England, disheartened me.

Frank Walsh, Amos Pinchot, and some of Neg Cochran's labor-leader friends all repeated the cry of "Woe, woe!"

I had been told and believed, and I still believe, that the President and his Cabinet have had too few opportunities to learn from the people, and the people's representatives, the story of the country's general discontent and suspicion of Washington affairs. All the time of these gentlemen has been consumed either by the performance of their necessary governmental duties, or by the obtrusive self-seeking and very intelligent representatives of Big Business.

I felt that the only excuse for my own intrusion upon the President or any of his Secretaries would be to give testimony for the inarticulate or unrepresented or improperly represented masses.

But from the time that I made my promise to seek an interview with the President, there began unrolling before my view greater and more intelligent activity in Congress itself, and more and more an increasing evidence that the President and his Cabinet better realized the real situation than I had thought they did. Parallel with all this was a growing lessening of the pessimism of my own immediate associates and staff. Further, there was evidence that the registration for conscription and the campaigns for the bond issue and Red Cross funds were having the effect of waking up the people at large to the realities of the war situation.

By the time that my application for an interview with the President had resulted in an appointment for me to meet the President, a great deal of my past anxiety had oozed out.

So, on the eve of my conference, I regretted the appointment, feeling that my message to the President was not nearly so important as I had thought it might be.

However, the appointment had to be kept, and I arrived at the White House a little before three o'clock, Wednesday afternoon, June 27. I first drove to the White House executive offices, and was there told that the President would meet me at his rooms in the White House. There, my auto door was opened by a Negro; at the door, my hat was taken by another Negro; and I was met by a young man who showed me into a waiting room.

Promptly at three o'clock this young man came to me and led me into the room where the President was. A storm was about to break outside, and the

room was quite dusky. I saw what appeared to me quite a small man crossing the room to greet me. I had seen the President before, and had had the
impression that he was quite a tall man and somewhat imposing in appearance. When I saw the President before, he was sleek and groomed to perfection, as though he had been prepared to face the camera.

But this rather smallish gentleman appeared with his hair somewhat tou-
sled; he was tanned, if not even sunburned.

I think I was more interested in observing the man, his manners, his general mental attitude, than I was in anything that Mr. Wilson said.

Although it was three o'clock in the afternoon, and although the President had had an unusually large number of visitors during the day, he seemed
not in the least fatigued. His face was anything but careworn. The expression of his eyes and face was calm; he laughed outright on several occasions;
and his smile seemed anything but perfunctory or "put on."

He did not appear as one bearing a great weight of care and responsibility. He could hardly have looked more at his ease had he been acting as the
president of a university during routine times. Neither by effort nor unconsciously was his attitude and manner "official" or anything approaching dignified.

At times he spoke earnestly; he indulged in a few swear words, especially
when he was making reference to many of the people who have been gathering in Washington for the purpose of making profit off of the government's
difficulties.

During the half hour that I was with him, I experienced a sense of growing
content and assurance, on account of my feeling that we had a President
who had learned the President's job thoroughly, and who had entire confidence in himself and in his plans. He seemed to have no doubt of his ability
to cope with any problem that he would have to face.

I had a sort of a realization of the "why" of the membership of the President's Cabinet. This kind of a man wanted, it seemed to me, a lot of good,
executive clerks — men whom he could rely on to do what he told them to do;
men who could do their work well enough, but wouldn't show themselves
too brilliant or too spectacular. He evidently had sense enough not to work
and worry himself into ill health or a condition of overwrought nerves.

Any other person, as well as I can, can form an estimate of Mr. Wilson's
ability by his public record. There will, of course, be differences of opinion
on this subject.

I left Mr. Wilson with the feeling that, in all probability, our President of
the United States today is perhaps as good a man for his job as any other
man who could have been selected.

I think that, barring accident, or some assassin crank, or some attack of
disease, he will live through the war and for long afterward; and that he will

come out of the wartimes as vigorous and as strong as if he had lived through the same period without any great responsibilities.

I feel that a report of my conference with the President is of small significance.

Perhaps what I said to the President may have some slight effect — but very slight effect — on the immediate future actions of Mr. Wilson.

I found that the President had very similar views to my own, and that he had come to similar conclusions. It is just possible that what I said might have added a little by way of confirming his views, and of increasing the vigor of his decisions and his actions.

I recall that during my first visit to the President, I was somewhat awed not by the man perhaps but by the consciousness of the great office that he filled. On this occasion I felt no such awe.

I went to talk, and not to listen. I wanted to deliver my little message and get out; and so I think I did most of the talking. I am almost sure that I was somewhat rude on several occasions, by "cutting in" when the President was talking, instead of listening respectfully to what he had to say. However, the President showed no impatience with me, nor any feeling of offended dignity.

I began my interview by telling him that, although I had called for the purpose of delivering him something that I called a message, and by way of adding my testimony to what I felt sure he had heard from many other sources, still I felt I had earned the right to come in and say "How do you do" and shake hands with him, even if I had nothing to say. To this he beamed on me with the greatest good nature, and laughingly stated that I surely had the right to as much of his time and attention as I chose to demand.

In speaking of my part, or alleged part, in the recent campaign that caused his re-election, I said that I had not been moved to such activity on the score of personal friendship, or even personal admiration for him, but solely because . . . during the four years he had been in office before the last election, his record had been such as to convince me that he, better than any other probable or possible candidate, was more to be relied upon by the people who formed my constituency.

I referred to several pieces of legislation that he had secured, or that he had been charged with securing, and stated that the position he had taken in the railroad controversy, and which had resulted in the Adamson law,[13] was what had made it possible for us to cause his re-election.

[13] The railroad brotherhoods threatened to strike for shorter working hours in 1916, and Wilson pushed through Congress the Adamson Act which set an eight-hour day for railroad workers. The threat of the strike, incidentally, kept him from actively campaigning until September.

I apologized to him for our having resorted to the plea of "He kept us out of the war" in order to secure him votes. I stated that I had only reluctantly consented to this part or feature of the campaign, and that I had only been willing to use this argument to get votes for a man who had shown other qualities that I admired much more. In fact, I told him, I had been very impatient with him because he had kept us out of the war so long.

To this he laughed aloud.

I spoke a little about the California incident and, with a sly smile, he indicated that he understood what had happened. But I protested that in this case I had not been moved by partisan zeal in his behalf, but wholly by a desire to try a little experiment in psychology.[14] At this he laughed outright.

Then he took up the subject of his Reserve Bank bill, saying that the very men who most opposed him in that matter now were fully agreed that his action was beneficial to the country at large. But I shut him off on this line of talk by saying that it was my opinion that he had gotten a thousand votes from the Adamson bill case to one from the Reserve Bank legislation.

I told him that what I wanted to urge on him was that, as he had won the people's confidence, their respect, and their affection, on account of his attitude toward the common people, he should, in all fairness, if for no other reason, continue to more vigorously than ever champion the cause of the unpossessed.

In a most vigorous and earnest tone of voice, he assured me that that was just what he was going to do, whatever else he did.

I told him that while the people had confidence in him personally, I believed that they were very suspicious of, and very resentful toward, the great gathering in Washington of capitalists and capitalist representatives, of labor-baiters, and of the use that he was making of them in his various voluntary committees and commissions. I said that the people were probably, and rightly, becoming alarmed that these people would overwhelm him and, by sheer force of numbers and weightiness of their interests, would wield altogether too much influence over the administration. He told me that he was well aware of this attitude on the part of the public, and that he recognized that the suspicion aroused was thoroughly justified, and that it would not be long before this cause of suspicion would disappear.

---

[14] It is difficult to tell exactly what Scripps was talking about here, but he may have referred to the difficulty he had had within his own organization when the Los Angeles *Record* under James G.'s direction severely criticized the administration during the spring of 1917, deviating from the Scripps policy of supporting the administration. Scripps had then required that James G. either have an editor-in-chief who would, or give his father his personal pledge that he would, support the administration loyally so long as Wilson made no extreme departure in economic affairs from the course pursued since his first inauguration; this may have been what Scripps meant by "a little experiment in psychology." Scripps and his son continued to spar over the same issue for the next few months.

I mentioned three men whose presence and whose activities had become quite prominent: namely, Rosenwald, Peabody, and Barney [Bernard] Baruch.

He said, "Referring to the three men that you have mentioned, I have already determined to eliminate two of them entirely. I recognize their character, their attitude, and what they are here for. But, as to the third, Barney Baruch, I intend to use him. I think that Baruch has seen the light."

"You think that he has ceased to be Saul and become Paul," I said.

"Yes, I think so," he replied, "but I will find out soon enough; and if not, I will send him to join the other two" — the other two being Rosenwald and Peabody. He said, "Barney Baruch knows the inside of all these things probably better than anyone else who is accessible to me. He can give me information and assist me as perhaps no one else can."

I interjected: "Is it your idea to set a thief to catch a thief?"

"Now! now!" he replied, "I don't want you to regard Mr. Baruch in that light. He's really a nice fellow, and I feel very friendly toward him. I wouldn't like to call him a thief."

"Oh!" I said, "some of the most genial and agreeable fellows one can ever meet are these men who, in common parlance, are called thieves — I mean such as these captains of industry, etc., etc., for instance, like myself, for I am something of a captain of industry, also."

He laughed and said, "Oh, well, if that is what you mean, it's all right; but I think Baruch is going to come out all right, and that he is going to be of great assistance to us. But time and events will show that, and, if he doesn't — well, we can get along without him."

I asked him if he had not already contemplated the possibility of its sooner or later becoming necessary to have something like a wages board; in fact, if it wouldn't be necessary for the government to intervene in the matter of fixing a minimum wage. He said that this was a matter that he had on his mind.

At this point we took up the subject of a possible economic revolution taking place during the war, as a result of the long-standing discontent of the people on account of their comparatively low wages and on account of the rapid growth of the wealth of employers. He spoke on the subject as though it had been thought of and probably discussed by him a good deal.

"In fact," he said, "I recognize that there is really a great danger of an economic revolution in this country during or following the war."

I think that I had been the first to mention revolution. In doing so, he asked me what my idea was about the revolution. I told him that he, of course, recognized that revolution was a very contagious disease, and that revolutions started in one country were almost sure to be followed by revolutions in other countries. "Now," I said, "while in Europe the people may revolt against their political government, they cannot in this country revolt against the government which they themselves control, but when the spirit of revolt gets abroad, it has got to find expression somewhere, and here in this country the most natural object against which revolt would be directed would be capitalism — in fact, I fear that it is almost inevitable that in this country we will have some sort of an economic revolution sooner or later."

It was with reference to this that he stated that he contemplated the possibility, and even the probability, of such a revolution as that of which I spoke.

At this point, I reminded him of my effort on behalf of the income tax, and especially of publicity in the matter. I reminded him of a visit that Mr. [H. N.] Rickey had paid to him on my account sometime prior to the late election. He recalled the visit, and the subject matter discussed. I did not remind him of his tacit promise to Rickey that, if he were re-elected, he would take up and act on the matter of publicity of the income tax. I only hoped that my reference to Rickey would recall to his mind this pledge.

I told him that I had all along differed with [Secretary of the Treasury William Gibbs] McAdoo, both as to the matter of the gross amount of the income of this country, and also as to the matter of the advisability of publicity. I told him that I believed that, by reason of my own study and thought in the matter, I was as well qualified to give an expert opinion on this subject as perhaps any other man that he could come in contact with. I told him that I was sure that Mr. McAdoo had never had the same reason, and never had had the time, to give this matter the same study as I had. McAdoo had stated that the gross income of this country, at the time the law was put into operation, was 32 billion dollars. I reminded him that the Census Department [*sic*], had, several years before, placed it at 50 billions, and I stated that there were good reasons, which I would not have the time to give, that the income of the United States was more like 60 billion dollars now.

But, I said, supposing we would take the lowest possible figure that Mr. McAdoo has now set, namely, 40 billion dollars.

I suggested to the President that he was doubtless aware of what the average professional man's income was in the United States. He said he was. I said, of course we have had the reports of all these labor commissioners of the nation and of the different states, and that it must be evident to him that very few families in the United States had incomes of over $1,000 a year. He said that he judged that $1,000 would be a liberal estimate of the income of all of those, excepting a very few.

I said, "Now, with 100 million people, there should be 20 million families, and 20 million families would account for not over 20 billion dollars of income a year. Who is getting the other 20 or 30 or 40 billion dollars?"

He repeated my words almost exactly, "Yes, who *is* getting that remaining 20 or 30 or 40 billion dollars?"

I had the impression at the time that only in this matter did I suggest to the President an idea that he had not before considered.

I said that I knew the handicap under which the [Secretary of the Treasury] is laboring in the matter of collecting the income tax, from my own personal knowledge. I told him that I had in my family and among my acquaintances a number of people who had very large incomes, and that I knew that none of us had been investigated or had our incomes examined into, to any extent worth considering at all. I told him that I had never been called on personally by any of the revenue agents, and that I knew from a report from my agents that such investigation as had been made into my affairs was so trivial and so inadequate that, had I chosen to pay not more than half of what I had paid as income tax, I would have gotten off without being discovered, or without any real danger of exposure. I said that I knew, from talks I had had with other people of comparatively large income, that it had been the same case with them. I told him that I believed that, practically, all the income-tax payers of the United States were making returns according to their own conscience, or according to their own selfish bias.

I told him that I urged publicity in the matter of income taxes not only for the purpose of the government's securing the aid of informers but for the purpose of inducing rich men, in their own interest, to make a fair return.

"Why," I said, "if all of us rich men had our incomes published, along with the amount of income tax we were paying, there would grow up amongst us a spirit of rivalry, or at least emulation; our pride, and the vanity of our wives and family, would impel us to pay the biggest income tax we could charge ourselves with, and thereby lift ourselves to the highest possible rank in 'the peerage of plutocracy.' Mrs. Blank would not permit her husband to pay a lower income tax than was paid by the husband of her social rival, Mrs. Dash, if she has the influence over her husband that most wives do have.

"Then, as to the smaller income-tax payers, lots of these women would rather forego the ownership of an automobile or the purchase of a new dress than submit to the humiliation of their husband's name not appearing as one of the income-tax payers."

This was all near the conclusion of my brief visit.

I had noticed, when I first got a good light on the President's face, that his large nose seemed a little red, and there was a suspicion of wateriness about his eyes. One of the windows was open, and a brisk breeze was blowing in. The President sneezed once — a mild little sneeze — but I was fearful. I had just concluded one of my perorations on the income-tax subject when the President sneezed again, and sneezed violently.

I was pretty sure that the President would have been willing to have had me stay longer, but I had said all that I wanted to say, and there was that sneeze! So, without waiting to be dismissed, I arose and told him that I would not further trespass on his time.

The President also arose and accompanied me to the door, and, with a hearty handshake from a firm and warm hand, bade me good-day.

What Changes in the Amount and Ownership of Wealth Are to Result from the War?

[*August 5, 1917*]

In the first place, I dismiss as an absurd proposition the idea that war destroys more wealth than it incidentally creates.

Some very shrewd thinkers and students have expressed the opinion that not more than 5 per cent of the potential productivity of any civilized people is made effective during ordinary times. In peacetimes, only a few people work to produce, and these people work in a most leisurely fashion. There are vast numbers of people who idle away more or less of their time. A large class of women in America do not even have a chance to produce anything. Few children, male or female, are at all productive up to the age of fourteen and, with few exceptions (male and female alike) produce, prior to the age of, say, eighteen, one-half as much as men and women of somewhat more advanced age, yet of no greater capacity, produce in the same time. Even the moderately aged have ceased to produce as much, in proportion to their strength and ability, as they produced when they were a few years younger. In America, the men and women past forty (or at least forty-five) generally are considered undesirable as employees. There are few men and women past fifty who produce enough even to furnish their own individual subsistence.

All of these conditions are changed under the stress of war. Almost every man and woman works harder and produces more during such a period of excitement — periods when excitement is great, inducements are large, and necessities pressing. Amongst all of the usually productive classes, production is increased by a considerable percentage. During wartimes, the age of children entering into full employment in productive work is decreased by

575

several years; in wartimes, for instance, a boy of eighteen will be employed at an occupation that he would not have been called upon to fill in peacetimes before his twentieth or twenty-first year. The opportunities and needs to work, for men and women past forty-five, are greatly increased. Even the very aged are employed in some productive work.

It is certain that the aggregate increase of production by a given population, as a result of war, is far greater than the aggregate of all the losses that are occasioned by war.

Then, too, there is great exaggeration in the minds of men as to the destruction, waste, and other costs of war. In peacetimes, many goods are produced that are not produced in wartimes. These goods are used up and destroyed by reason of petty peace activities. Some examples: In peacetimes, there are many pleasure automobiles that are produced and worn out; in wartimes, there are fewer pleasure automobiles and more trucks produced. In peacetimes, there is much fine fabric made and worn out by women; in wartimes, there is less of this kind of fabric and more of cloth material for soldiers. In peacetimes, pleasure yachts are built and worn out; in wartimes there are more fighting vessels. The sportsman's gun and ammunition are displaced by the soldier's rifle. In thousands and hundreds of thousands of ways, peacetime products are displaced by wartime products, and peacetime wear and tear are displaced by wartime wear and tear.

But such is the effect of war in speeding up labor and increasing energy that the total products of wartimes are so much greater than the total products of peacetimes that the increase far more than offsets war's destructions.

History has proved that, with few exceptions, the wealth of a nation increases more rapidly during wartimes than during peacetimes.

So, I confidently expect that there will be a great increase in the wealth of the United States during the period of the present war.

Now, what individuals or what class of individuals are to become the owners of this new wealth?

Over and beyond the consideration of this new-made wealth, we must consider a vast amount of relocation or redistribution of present-existing wealth.

While the nation as a whole will increase in wealth, there are reasons why some individuals or classes of individuals will not only get the whole of this increase of wealth, but will have transferred to them a large part of the wealth already existing.

For example, here is one man who is deriving an income of, say, $10,000 a year from fixed investments — property perhaps received as an inheritance from his father. A direct war tax is levied in the way of an income tax. A certain portion of this man's $10,000 a year is taken out each year by the government, and is employed in producing war material. If the man originally spent the whole of his income in living expenses, and if he should continue, notwithstanding the income tax, to spend $10,000 a year, he would be constantly depleting his capital by transmitting a portion of it to the government. The government takes this money and pays it to someone else, in turn, for war material or other services.

Take the case of an ordinary wage-earner who may be obtaining a wage of five dollars a day in peacetimes. If the cost of commodities, including provisions, should increase 50 per cent, and this man's wage should only increase 25 per cent, then this wage-worker would really be giving to the government, as a sort of indirect tax, a considerable portion of his real wages. The government passes this money on to some other man, in exchange for material or services.

Perhaps there are scores, and perhaps there are hundreds, of ways by which actual existing property or income is being taken from one man or set of men and transferred to another man or set of men.

It is estimated that this government may, during wartime, expend as much as 20 billion dollars a year, in the purchase of war material and in the payment for services. In part, this money will be raised by current taxes and, in part, it will be raised by bonds — that is to say, by mortgages on the country as a whole.

The wealth of the country as a whole is neither increased nor decreased by the taxes, since the money derived from the taxes is but transferred from one citizen to another. The wealth of the country as a whole is neither increased nor decreased by the bonds issued by the government; these bonds, while they are a liability on the country as a whole, become immediately the assets of certain individuals.

It is true that in this war the government will spend a certain small portion of money derived by taxes and bonds in foreign countries, so that people who are not citizens of this country would have transferred to them this money. But such are the conditions of trade that it is probable that foreign countries will send to the United States, to make purchases here, many times as much money as this government spends abroad.

The wealth of this country will not only increase by reason of the greater activity of the American citizens' production, but also by reason of the increasingly high prices the citizens of this country will get from foreign buyers as a result of the war.

Every bushel of wheat and every ton of iron commands a higher price in the foreign market, due to the war, than the same would command during peacetimes.

But who, then, is going to pay not the cost of the war, because there will be no costs, but rather profits? Who are going to lose money or other property as a result of the war, and who are going to gain from the same cause?

There is to be, of course, a vast disturbance in the flow of the medium of exchange in this country. Its volume and velocity, it seems to me, must be greatly increased by reason of government purchases and employments at a cost of approximately 20 billion dollars a year. This condition of affairs is going to vastly improve the opportunities for obtaining wealth — both the new wealth and that old wealth which is to be lost by the old holders.

Men of fixed incomes (whether derived from salaries or interest) and wage-workers will, almost without exception, suffer a reduction in their income, and hence in the real — that is to say, comparative — value of their fortunes.

The class of people who will have the opportunity — whether these people make use of it or not — to gain by this new condition in the circulation of money is very large in number, perhaps not less than 25 per cent of the whole number in the country, and perhaps even a larger percentage. Almost every individual who is producing salable goods on his own account (for himself and not for some employer) will have a chance to dip up from the flowing current of commerce, and save and retain for his own use a portion of the same. Among these are the owners of farms, mines, factories, ships, and perhaps many other enterprises.

All such men will have the opportunity to increase their wealth. But the volume of flow that offers itself to be taken up by those who will is to be enormous.

There will be perhaps millions of men who will have their real income greatly increased as a result of the war, but of all of these (excepting a few hundreds of thousands, and perhaps even but tens of thousands) there will be no savers. The great majority of these will increase their expenditures in exact proportion to the increase of their incomes. Through their hands will flow larger or smaller streams of money. The money will flow through their hands, but not remain in them. These people will not be enriched, at least in the way of accumulating capital. They may live more abundantly, more pleasantly, more healthfully, and in a way to increase their intellectual development. But they will not dip up or take up and store away for themselves any part of this flow of wealth. They will take in and throw out money, just as they take air into their lungs and throw it out again. Vast bulks of water pass through the gills of comparatively small fishes, but the water adds nothing to the bulk of the fishes themselves.

To conclude: I have shown that a great deal of wealth is to be pried loose by this war from the possession of present holders, and that vastly larger sums of new wealth are to be produced by the greater activity of the people of the country.

The natural law of physics is nearly directly applicable to economics. The law of nature has reference to the indestructibility of matter and the conservation of force.

Wealth is not indestructible, exactly, but it is very persistent. Old wealth continues, at least in bulk, and new wealth grows, so that the bulk of wealth is increasing. In the present order of affairs of human society, wealth must have individual owners. Who are going to be the owners of this new wealth, and this old wealth that has been dislodged from its old moorings?

The answer to this question is self-evident. The owners of this wealth are to consist of those few who increase not at all, or but very little, their expenditures, while their incomes continue to grow larger and larger.

There will be, of course, an entirely new crop of millionaires in this country. There will be a larger crop for the next decade, numerically speaking, than that produced by any previous 10 decades; and the aggregate wealth of the richest 1,000 people in the United States 10 years hence, in all probability, will be many times — perhaps 10 or 20 times — greater than the aggregate wealth of the richest 1,000 in this country today.

Bringing Down to Date
Some of My Views
Regarding the Administration

[*August 17, 1917*]

This disquisition appears to have been edited in Scripps' hand.

This morning I arose feeling greatly discontented with myself. Here I am, living in Washington during the most momentous period of the world's history, and at a time when my own country is taking over unto itself the leadership of all those nations that are forward-looking to the greatest liberty and progress.

I have been spending a great deal of my time pitying myself and nursing grouches, both idle and useless occupations.

I am an onlooker of events that are transpiring, and though not by any means a sharer of the confidence of the "inner circle" of the government, I still enjoy a very favorable position to view the scenes and to see more than the majority of the people.

I ought to be spending more of my time diarizing and disquisitioning and writing documents that should be of vast interest to my children, and my children's children, and perhaps the children of many other men in years to come. I ought to be preparing matter that should be of great value to future historians.

Instead of all this, I have been sulking. I have been feeling that I am a much-abused man and thoroughly unappreciated by the members of my family, and by both the rank and file of that fairly large and respectable organization which I created.

Notwithstanding all of my philosophy, all the preparations that I made, and all the resolutions that I had come to, for my retirement while still in

580

vigorous manhood, I cannot help but feel resentment because I am being pushed and crowded out of the field of activity — not only by the young-sters in the institution, but by men who have grown so old in my service as to be but by a few years my juniors.

While it has been my own choice that I am living alone, separated from every member of my family for the most part, and refraining from taking an active part in the movements that are going on within the organism of which I am the father, I nevertheless feel oppressed by my loneliness and distressed by my own unhelpfulness.

There is a peculiar irony in my own position relative to the government. Not only do I know that, but for me, the present administration of the gov-ernment would not have been, but the personnel of this government's ad-ministration know this also, as do many, if not most, of all of the persons well informed in political affairs.

The President was polite to me when he met me; the two members of the Cabinet whom I know personally were equally polite and perhaps a little more deferential. Leading members of both houses of Congress, I have every reason to believe, if I sought their society, would treat me cordially or re-spectfully enough.

But all of these people are quite willing to let me rest on my laurels and to impose no further burdens on me.

I have good reason, too, to believe that any counsel or advice that I would offer them would be entirely unwelcome and entirely ineffective.

If anything should occur which would prompt me to come out of my se-clusion and to express myself publicly and to use my own personal influence, I am sure that all of those who owe their present position of distinction, di-rectly or indirectly, to me, would treat me as an enemy and, more likely still, with contempt.

My philosophy teaches me all of this, and it enables me to tolerate the situation.

There is nothing in all the above that will ever be of any value to a his-torian, or which will add anything to the pride that my progeny may feel for their forebear.

What of my present view concerning the man who now holds the high of-fice of chief magistrate of the most powerful nation of the world — the man who only holds this position because a few months ago, holding the political balance of power in this country, I threw it to him, and thus secured the posi-tion for him?

A few weeks ago, I met the governor of one of our great states, in his pri-vate office at the state's capitol.[15] This governor asked me, then, what I

15 Governor James M. Cox of Ohio.

thought of the President, and whether or not I believed that his name was to occupy a high position in the history of the country, as to whether or not his fame would go rolling on through generations?

I replied that that would all depend upon whether this country won the war on which it was just entering.

Whether or not the governor understood just what I meant by this, I do not know. What I meant was that, whether Mr. Wilson was a great man or a small man, whether or not our victory or our defeat was to depend upon the President's capacity and power, or lack of the same — or whether one or the other should result from the capacity or lack of capacity of the President — the mere fact that Mr. Wilson was President at this important epoch would, if the country is victorious, make him a famous man whose name would be glorified.

I have elsewhere stated that, on leaving the White House on the occasion of a recent visit with the President, I had a distinct feeling of satisfaction on account of the impression the President made upon me. That impression was that the country was fortunate in having as President such a man as Mr. Wilson during these trying times.

I knew but little of the Cabinet members, personally. I considered Mr. Lane [Secretary of the Interior Franklin K. Lane] a man of average abilities, well-enough qualified to discharge the duties of his office. I had far less confidence in Secretary of War Baker. I considered him a man distinctly out of place in the position he fills.

From what I had learned of the Attorney General [Thomas W. Gregory] and Mr. [Robert] Lansing, Secretary of State, I had and still have the opinion that they are something worse than mediocrities. Owing to personal experiences that I had had with the Secretary of the Treasury, Mr. McAdoo, and my own hardly acquired knowledge of all of those subjects with which such an officer would have to deal, I had, concerning this man, a feeling of mixed discontent and distrust. Of the Postmaster General [Albert S. Burleson], the Secretary of Agriculture [David F. Houston], the Secretary of the Navy [Josephus Daniels], and of Mr. [William C.] Redfield, [Secretary of Commerce], I had — and have — a low opinion. But of these latter gentlemen, I knew but little personally, and I have been and have always been indifferent on the subject of their departments.

At about the time when I was feeling pleased with the President for the kind of man he was, I was, at the same time, nursing the view that there must be and should be very important changes made in the Cabinet.

It would seem that at one and the same time, therefore, I was approving the President and disapproving of him. If he was a good enough man to be President, he should have been a good enough man to make a wise selection of his Cabinet.

I have always believed that I was a pretty fair judge of men. This belief is founded upon my own success in choosing capable men to assist me in my own enterprises.

I know, both by experience and by observation, that there are two kinds of successful executives. There are those successful executives who are strong, able, straight-thinking, who choose to do all of the important work in the affairs over which they rule, using only tractable, second-rate (in point of intelligence) men as their lieutenants, their instruments. Then there is the other sort of capable executive. A man of this sort has certain "all-round" capacities, some little knowledge of all of the things with which he has to deal, who is not an expert in any particular field, and not a man much given to detail. A rule of conduct for such men is to do nothing himself that another person can do nearly as well. Such a man will have strong, able men, each expert in some particular field, all of them loyal and industrious, these men to be not his instruments, not even his lieutenants, but his field marshals. To these men, the executive assigns each his department to rule over, while the chief executive confines his activities to merely coordinating the work of the whole group and, acting as an umpire, to settle disputes that may arise between his subordinates as a result of the impossibility of laying down strict lines of division between different fields of operation.

Wilson is a powerful and successful man, as was shown during four years of occupancy of his high office. Therefore, he must be such a man as I have first described above — the first of the two sorts of men that I have described as successful executives.

It seems to me that Mr. Wilson is not only ruling Congress but the country at large rather by the strength of his own personality than by reason of his being the representative of the opinion of the majority of either — either the members of Congress or the people of the country at large.

I have the impression that a very large majority of the congressmen in the capitol would, were there a less powerful man in the office of president, be pursuing a diametrically opposite course than that which they are pursuing under the President's influence.

I believe that the people of the country as a whole were surprised by the President's leading them into war, and I believe that a good, large majority of these people — even those who voted for Wilson — are more or less dissatisfied with the present situation. I think there is a very large minority (and even possibly a majority) who are more than discontented and who are really angry with their government on account of what that government has done and is now doing.

Hysteria Raised to the Nth Power

[December 26, 1918]

During the past four years, nearly all the people of Europe have been keeping themselves worked up to a high pitch of hysteria, and during the past year and a half, the people of the United States have been trying to do in days what it took the Europeans months to do. Amongst other things, they have been trying to get just as excited as the Europeans were. Apparently, they have succeeded.

Some years ago, a small band of pacifists in America began the work of reforming the United States and the world in general by a series of peace propaganda. It first took official form, I think, during the Taft administration, in the way of negotiating international arbitration treaties.

Later, some enthusiast crystallized an idea of a "League of Nations to Enforce Peace." If my memory serves me rightly, this scheme was proposed before the great war broke out.

Of course, antedating all of this American movement was the Hague Peace Conference idea.

The real, Simon-pure pacifist party was not nearly so numerous as the Prohibition party, and it was perhaps no more effective. But the great war gave the pacifists their great opportunity. Ex-President Taft, as president of the "League of Nations Peace Association," had had much to do with creating for it prestige.

Then came President Wilson, at the zenith of his popularity and power, who not only sanctioned the scheme, but made it one — in reality the chief — of his own personal policies.

The "League of Nations" people have become so very vociferous that their clamor and shouting fill the air. Perhaps not one person in ten thousand would care to run the risk of being howled down by expressing opposition to the idea.

584

But, on the other hand, I do not believe that there is one man in a thousand, who expresses approval of the League of Nations plan, who really believes in it and, at the same time, wants it adopted.

The United States is peopled by ordinary human beings. The ordinary human being is a fighting animal. The ordinary human being is selfish on his own account and, collectively, nationally, he is no less selfish.

All thoughtful men know that the era that is just dawning is the era during which the United States will be the most powerful nation on earth.

Men love power, and so do nations. If such a thing as a League of Nations, in a lasting and effective form, should come into being, the Americans will have surrendered, even before they have grasped it, the power to dominate the world.

I have often enough expressed the idea that neither the people of the United States nor of Europe have really waked up to and realized the relative position of the United States among the nations. But notwithstanding this, the people of this country do sense, to a certain extent, something approaching the realities.

Of course, love of power is an unreasonable mental attitude. Perhaps it isn't a mental attitude at all — that is to say, a rational attitude. Perhaps it's only an instinct.

Instinct and reason are seldom, perhaps never, good companions.

Men, singly and collectively, function by instinct. They only use reason to excuse or account for actions prompted by instinct.

Every man in possession of much personal power — whether it be of wealth, political office, or social standing — knows that this possession costs more pain than it attains him pleasure; yet if at rare intervals a man turns up who abdicates, or even refuses to take over power, he is reckoned insane — that is, if he is not so old and decrepit and physically weak as to be considered no longer capable of the enjoyment of anything.

It is barely probable that there will be some sort of League of Nations formed. But I hold that it isn't possible that such a league will be able to function in the way of keeping peace.

Perhaps such a League of Nations might exist 10, 20, 30, or even 50 years during which peace would prevail — that is to say, during which there would be no great war.

But for 44 years after 1870, there were no great wars.

Such little scraps as our Spanish-American War, and the South African war, and the Balkan wars even, could hardly be dignified by the name "war" — especially at this period, after the great war. But whether the League of Nations be formed or not, wars, and great wars — little wars and pretty big wars — will succeed one another.

Wars have their origin in instinct. The only foundation for a League of Nations would be in reasonableness; and sweet reasonableness only exists in the minds of poets and other dreamers.

A few days ago, I read in the papers a statement by one of the members of the new Japanese Cabinet to the effect that the next great war would be between the white races and the colored races, or between some white race and some colored race.

This statement struck me forcibly, perhaps only because I have been, for a long time, predicting that the white races, in their westward pilgrimage of ages duration, having reached the eastern shores of the Pacific, were bound to continue their course westward and to at least attempt the conquest by arms of Asia.

I wonder if this Japanese statesman's mind has not been traveling over pretty nearly the same path that my mind has been pursuing.

During the last three decades, Japan has been demonstrating that she is a good fighting nation.

The Japanese are not ethnically identical with the Chinese. They are supposed, I believe, to be a sort of bastard or hybrid race, partly Malay and partly Mongol. But whatever their origin, judging them by the scores of individual Japanese I have known, I consider them, man for man, the equal of any of the white nationals that I have known.

There are about 500 million white people in Europe. There are on the continent of North America something like 100 million pure whites, and perhaps 10 million more people of mixed blood, partly white. There are a great many mulattoes in the United States, and a great many Mexicans have white, Spanish blood in their veins.

England's experience in India has been such as to teach us that there will be no Indian nation capable of and willing, individually or in alliance, to successfully meet on the battlefield white men.

China may be only a "sleeping dog," as Napoleon called her, and she may be potentially what William II called her, "The Yellow Peril." But many decades must pass by before Japan will succeed in militarizing China to any effective degree.

But it will require a century, or several centuries, for China and Japan to develop industrially, as well as in a military way, to such an extent as to make those two powers very formidable antagonists, even against the one American nation. Then there are Australia and Canada who, in any conflict with Asia, would be most effective allies to the United States.

Long before "The Yellow Peril" can be a real peril, that war which the Japanese statesman prophesied will have taken place.

The people of France, Italy, and Spain are all of kindred race and institutions. There can be no strong bonds of sympathy between these Latin European peoples and the Anglo-Saxon peoples, either the British Empire or the United States.

The people of Germany and Scandinavia are very closely akin to the Anglo-Saxons.

The passing of one, or at least two, generations will be accompanied by the entire forgetfulness of all of the animosities of the war just closed. We must not forget that England had for centuries been the traditional enemy of France, and that up to a short seven years before the world's war broke out, Russia and England had been for half a century at swords' points. Japan and Russia, who became war allies in 1914, were, hardly a decade before, fighting mighty battles as antagonists.

I am old enough to remember the days of the Civil War. I remember the bitterness of feeling between the people of the North and South that lasted for years after that war closed. I know that the feeling of English and Americans against Germans today is no more bitter than was the feeling between northern people and southern people when I had grown to be nearly middle-aged.

In every age, history proves that amongst civilized or European peoples there has been one nation that has attempted and sometimes succeeded in dominating the rest of the civilized peoples of Europe. Of course, there was the Roman era, but that was a long time ago.

From the time of the Emperor Charles V and his son Phillip, Spain was lording it over a large part of Europe.

France was a powerful nation and threatened the peace of Europe long before Napoleon's time.

Since the France of Napoleon suffered eclipse, England has been the most powerful European nation. Germany, under Emperor William II, challenged her position, and Germany fell, conquered by an alliance of nations which existed because England formed that alliance and successfully maneuvered the success of the Allies.

The British Empire is a great nation, rich and powerful today. But her one-time federation of colonies — the oldest son of her family, the United States of America — has grown more populous (whites alone being considered) by more than 50 per cent than Great Britain, while the wealth of the United States and its industrial capacity is at least three times as great as that of all of the white populated part of Great Britain.

If the sole object of a League of Nations is to keep the peace of the world, then there is no occasion of having a great, cumbersome federation of nations, including big and little, forward- and backward-looking peoples. A League of Nations composed of the United States, England, and her colonies and dominions can so far dominate the world as to permit of no other wars than such as the Anglo-Saxon nations deem beneficial.

Ambitious Germany attempted to thwart the further growth and developments of Anglo-Saxondom. But long before Germany can possibly recuperate from the effects of her defeat in the war, Great Britain will have grown so strong as to be able to defy Germany, alone and without allies. And during this period of time, while Germany, cramped in her territorial area, will not only be unable to increase her population but probably will see it diminish, the great American Republic will increase more rapidly than ever in population and wealth and strength.

Russia (or the Russian people, or the Slavs) have possibly, and probably, at last entered on a career that will, a century from this time, eventuate into a highly civilized, effective, and tremendously populous nation.

The three great nations or peoples of the world at the beginning of the twenty-first century will be the two Anglo-Saxon nations and the Russian.

Before the beginning of the twenty-first century, the Asiatic question will have been settled. There will be great and powerful Japan, and great and prosperous China, and perhaps even an autonomous India. But one hundred years from now, all Asia will be no more capable of threatening the peace of the world than India is today.

But what, in all this, is there in the way of an argument against the League of Nations that Messrs. Wilson and Taft want to establish?

Why, a League of Nations, if it is effective, would prevent such a development or such an evolution of nations as to bring about the condition of affairs that I have been here predicting.

There have got to be wars in order to bring about the changes in the way of international relations that I consider to be inevitable.

But I am not worrying about the matter much, because I do not fear that there will be an effective and enduring League of Nations.

The President of the United States might be the father and the real organizer and creator of a League of Nations. He is, or is supposed to be, a very powerful man. He was able to suspend the Constitution of the United States, or to so bend or interpret it as to be unrecognizable, in order to successfully take part in this war. The tradition of over a hundred years standing, that this government should not indulge in any European warlike adventures, vanished, not because Wilson desired it to vanish but because the people of the United States found that tradition standing in the way of the course they wanted to take.

But the people of the United States fifty years hence, or one hundred years hence — or maybe only ten to twenty years hence — might find a League of Nations inconvenient. At that time, there will probably be another president whose ear will be as close to the ground as ever was Mr. Wilson's ear, and the Constitution of the League of Nations will be no more effective in turning the people aside from their desired course than has been the Constitution of the United States.

Today it appears that the pacifists — the world pacifists (not the little Norman Angell or Socialist kind of pacifists) — are on top and are dictating affairs.

Ten, twenty, fifty, or a hundred years hence, an entirely different party, with entirely different views, will be playing the part of bellwether to the people of this country.

The Americans of today and of the future will be human, and they will permit no document, bearing signatures and sealed, to obstruct a course which they greatly desire to take.

How can I or you write and sign a contract which our children, after we are gone, or our grandchildren after we have been long gone, will respect?

Why should the people in America one hundred years hence consider themselves bound by contracts made by statesmen who were dead before their fathers were born?

If the League of Nations be formed and lasts that long, and if the American people at that time consider the league a good thing, they will continue in it and continue it because it is a good thing, and not because some bygone president has signed a paper and thereby attempted to bind his nation.

Oh, yes, the League of Nations may be formed, and its text may be the subject of hundreds and thousands of oratorical efforts. But because human beings are human beings, the constitution of a world state can never be other than "a scrap of paper."

Disorganization

[*January 30, 1920*]

This disquisition appears to have been edited in Scripps' hand.

They are having mighty bad times of it over there in Europe. We are not exactly comfortable here in the United States.

Not only are all the belligerent nations in trouble, but even the nations that remained neutral during the great war are suffering from the high cost of living because some of the nationals have suddenly grown rich and don't know how to behave themselves and because great majorities of the people have been made poor because their incomes have not been so elastic as their outgo.

Actually millions of people are dying annually from want and real starvation — lack of sufficient food. The under-nurtured human animal is subject to disease and is far more apt to succumb when attacked than is the well-nurtured animal.

There is not nearly enough food in Europe, even if it were fairly and equitably distributed, to meet the actual needs of the populations of the various countries. There is not enough clothing to decently clothe all the people and protect them against the inclemencies of the weather.

There are far too few houses in almost every European country at the present time to shelter all the people and at the same time secure decency and morality and even freedom from exposure to infection. For that matter, Europe has never had enough houseroom to accommodate all of the people in such a way that none of them would have to submit to unsanitary home living conditions.

But today, notwithstanding that millions of people were killed in battle in the war and that many more millions have died from the indirect effects of

590

the war, housing conditions in nearly all the European countries are now far worse than they were before the war — that is to say, only five years ago.

Houses, like clothes, wear out. I think it is estimated that in America the period of complete usefulness of a house as a home is not over twenty years on the average. In Europe if they do not build better, they at least build more durably. It is probable that the average period of usefulness of a building as a home in Europe is from two to three times what it is in this country.

Still, there are 450 millions of people in Europe. That is to say, there are probably approximately 90 or 100 million families. This number calls, then, for approximately 100 million homes. Even if the average period of usefulness of a home building was fifty years, there would be required for a stationary population not less than 2 million new homes every year.

During the four and a half years of war and the subsequent year and a half of demoralization, there was no time, no money, and no labor that could be spared for home building.

Not only did railways, canals, boats, and ships wear out or fall into disrepair during and after the war period, but the farms from which food for the millions of people had to be secured wore out. The soil lacked that fertilization and cultivation which was necessary to maintain it up to the same standard of productiveness that it had before the war. Farm implements and farm stock wore out, died of old age, or were consumed by war necessities.

Factories and all sorts of industrial plants wore out, were destroyed, or became obsolete, so that they could not employ so many work people as they formerly did. And on this account those work people who were employed were not individually so productive as they were formerly.

Trade and commerce, both of the big and the little sort, became disorganized. [Vice-Chancellor Karl] Helfferich, the German financier and statesman, made the statement some five or six years ago that 28 per cent of the people of Germany won their livelihood by manufacturing for export and by foreign trade of export and import.

For five years foreign trade for Germany did not exist, and only a small fraction of the former business in this line has yet been recovered. England, France, and Italy did not suffer so badly in respect to foreign trade as Germany, Austria, and Belgium.

Spain and the Scandinavian countries and even Holland gained considerably in percentage in the matter of foreign trade. But owing to the smallness of the aggregate populations of these countries and their former comparatively small productiveness, the benefit accruing to these countries was infinitely small as compared to the aggregate of foreign trade of the whole of Europe.

Perhaps, notwithstanding the comparative anarchy that has existed in Russia during the past three years, Russia has suffered less from war conditions, plus its anarchy, than has any other of the belligerent nations. This is because 80 per cent of the Russian people are engaged in agriculture, while in all of the other belligerent countries a very much smaller percentage are so employed. Not much more than 10 per cent of the English population are engaged in agriculture.

In the case of an industrial nation, the great preponderance of the population dwells in cities and is composed of men and women who have acquired only one trade or one profession or skill in one kind of work. Very few such people, even if they were inclined to do so and there was landroom enough for them, could engage in agriculture and produce enough to maintain themselves and their families.

However, it is not only the actual physical and mental disabilities of these city dwellers that stand in the way of their being self-supporting in other employments than those which they are accustomed to, but they are rendered even more helpless for psychological reasons. Even in this country in the building trades a carpenter objects to doing a mason's work, even though he might gain more. A doctor, a lawyer, or an engineer would submit almost to starvation rather than engage in the work of a mechanic, a salesman, a farm laborer, or any other manual or intellectual employment that he considered inferior to his profession.

In America, where not much more than one-quarter of the possible agricultural lands are cultivated, and where there are scarcely any farms at all which could not, with profit to the workman and the farm-owner, give employment to many fold more workmen than are usually employed, during periods of what are called "hard times" there are millions of unemployed men and women who remain idle and suffer great privations simply because no employment can be found in the trades and industries to which they are accustomed. These men and women, it would seem, would almost rather starve to death than "demean" themselves by resorting to farm labor.

There are many millions less people in Europe today than there would be had it not been for the war. But notwithstanding this great reduction in the number of hands, working people are suffering because there is no work for them to do that they are willing to do, or that they think they know how to do or are strong enough to do. Had there been no war, not only would there be millions more people working in Europe today, but most of these people would be producing more and living more comfortably than is the smaller number today.

Europe is not hard up because so many people were killed, so many died, and so many were crippled. Perhaps, had the mortality been several times as great, those who were left living would have been better situated, individually, than are those at present living.

No, I do not think that any part of the suffering on account of lack of material things in Europe is owing to the mortality of the past five years. After the great plague of the fourteenth century (I think it was the fourteenth century), which destroyed, I think, half or more than half of the people of England, the money wage and the real wage of the working people of England increased tremendously.

Nor do I think that the actual destruction of material property by the war, or even the wearing out and becoming obsolete of such property, has seriously affected the economic condition in Europe. The replacement of all this destroyed and worn-out property merely requires more work, rather than less. As there is more work to do and fewer men and women to do it, employment should be more general and wages higher.

It is doubtful if that nation which suffered the greatest devastation of material property of all the belligerents has suffered a 1 per cent decrease in actual material wealth, relative to the conditions existing in the country just prior to the war. If much valuable material property were destroyed, a vast number of things were destroyed which were not only worthless but more than worthless. Houses, buildings, and factories of all sorts were in existence before the war, the use of which was unprofitable. Old machines were being used in factories which could have been profitably scrapped in order to make way for more modern and productive machinery. A tremendous proportion of all the buildings used in Europe, in the cities and in the countryside, for homes, have become unsanitary and, for that and various other reasons, costly to the occupants. Any one of the European nations might gain tremendously, economically as well as in the comfort and happiness and health of its people, by having all of these old structures destroyed and replaced by modern buildings.

I would be willing to venture the prediction that those portions of northern France and Belgium which were the battlefields of Europe during the great war will, in a few years time, be found to be the most prosperous parts of Europe.

The governments of Europe have paid out 250 billion dollars or more in prosecuting this war. But to whom did they pay this money? For the most part they paid it to their own nationals — that is to say, to themselves.

There is as much land in Europe today as there was before the war. This land is potentially as valuable today as it was before the war. The war consumed an infinitesimal fraction of the natural resources of Europe. There is probably as much coal and iron under the surface of Europe today as there would have been had there been no war.

It is not probable that more than 0.5 per cent, or anything like that amount, of the buildings and machinery of all sorts that existed in Europe before the war were destroyed by the war. Perhaps Europe is poorer today on account of the cessation of maintenance of all kinds of material that resulted from the war than she is on account of the actual destruction of such things.

Few of the nations of Europe lost much property by reason of their nationals having to sell securities. Debts incurred in foreign countries by European states form, as an aggregate, a very small percentage of the cost of the war.

Perhaps not less than 90 per cent, perhaps even more, of all the debts of all the European countries are due to the nationals of each country. Even if Germany should be compelled to pay enormous indemnities to her victors, still Europe as a whole will be none the poorer on account of these payments. What the German has to pay, the Frenchman, the Englishman, the Belgian, the Italian, and the Serbian will receive.

Europe as a going concern, then — Europe taken as a whole — can properly enough be inventoried today as having only a fractional percentage less intrinsic value or wealth than would have been the case had there been no war, considering only material things.

And yet Europe is poverty stricken. People are dying at the rate of millions a year on account of starvation and lack of sufficient nutrition (which of course means the accompaniment of disease) on account of the lack of proper homes and medical care.

Europe is in material things as well off or nearly as well off today as it was five years ago, and yet is in fact in a condition of pauperdom. What is the matter?

The only answer that I can give is "disorganization." The war threw everything out of adjustment. It separated the job and the man. It broke up the machinery of credit and banking. It destroyed mutual confidence between man and man and between the men of one nation and the men of another.

It is a hobby of mine to maintain that wealth is not a thing, that it is not a material thing, that it is not even a condition of mind. Wealth is an ordered process. It not only exists because of human activity, but it is a proper name for all that group of human activities which include such things as mining, manufacturing, buying and selling, lending and borrowing — in fact, all sorts of employment or activity which might be classified under some such head as economics.

Man is not a chemical compound or a physical body. Neither is man a mind or a soul. Man is a condition of certain sorts of activity.

The wealth of a nation is not computed by the number of citizens to the square mile of its territory or by its possessions of forests, mines, rivers, and harbors. The wealth of a nation is not so much evidenced by things as it is by the ordered activities of the citizens acting individually or collectively.

The wealth of a nation does not consist either of the muscular power exerted by its citizens or the amount or quality of the thinking of its citizens. The wealth of a nation consists of or is the living activities of its citizens ordered with a view to economic production.

A few years hence Europe as a whole will be not only as wealthy as she was in 1913, but probably far more wealthy. Disorganization, disorder, discoordination, and misdirection of individuals and the group will slowly disappear and in place of these will appear order and cooperation, and unity of direction.

A pot of gold hidden on a desert island, or a power loom or a great steam engine similarly located, have equal value and equal valuelessness. And even if all of these things were located in the midst of a great and thriving community and not used by any man, they would be equally valuable and equally useless.

A single individual living on an otherwise deserted island on which were to be found the means of producing food and clothing and shelter would be worth, capitalized, a sum of money which, put out at interest, would bring sufficient to feed and clothe and keep housed a single individual enjoying no other benefits than could the island occupant. This man might have all the qualities, characteristics, and abilities of a mighty industrial captain, a great general, a great legislator, or a great teacher, or he might have only the wits and capacities of a clod of a farm laborer. But whether he is one or the other of these kinds of men, his capital value would be neither greater nor less than that of desert island man.

In Europe today there are far too many men whose actual intrinsic capital value is little more than that of the desert island occupant, simply because there is more disorganization than organization. Instead of there being full integration in each of the nations, there is, for the most part, only disintegration.

In time these men will find useful places in society, and society will make full use of them. And this integration and coordination will be a condition which will be entitled to a name. My name for this condition is Wealth.

I do not say that many other names might not be given to the same condition, each one indicating a different attribute or qualification to the condition. The name might be simply Happiness. It might even be Wisdom. To it might even be applied the name God.

Wanted—A Tyrant

[*September 4, 1921*]

Concerning existing chaos in the economic world, I am trying to recognize conditions that exist and to learn if possible the cause of these conditions — all this for the purpose of endeavoring to improve conditions.

I am weary of reading and hearing declarations, criminations, and recriminations. What's the use of trying to fix the blame for unfortunate conditions on any individual, class, race, or nation?

Sometimes I am led to believe also that the world as a whole (or its people) is no more unhappy in its present state of economic anarchy than it ever has been before when order, comparatively speaking, prevailed in the field of production and consumption.

I might have the very worst sort of a toothache and if some hoodlum came along and insulted me and made me very angry, I would forget all about my toothache, that is to say, I would cease to suffer from it, and the emotion of anger would at least be relatively a feeling of pleasure as compared with that of the toothache pain.

It is no more painful to die of starvation than it is from any other cause. We have all got to die anyway.

Viewing conditions in England from the distance that I do and having to depend for information concerning conditions there upon writers on the scene, all of whom are biased, I can only be aware of the fact that the people of England are not producing as much as they consume and that their stock of provisions or material which they can exchange for other provisions must soon run out.

The miners of coal by a prolonged strike succeeded in greatly reducing the products of the people as a whole, such production as they would necessarily exchange for food.

Industrialists in all other occupations in England are demanding wages, none too great for the support of themselves and their families comfortably, according to the standard of living in that country, but so great as to make it impossible for those whom the working men desire to furnish employment to pay and produce goods that can be sold at home or abroad for prices equaling the cost of production.

The government is levying taxes in order to obtain money to take and dole out to the unemployed and use in the way of subsidies for food and other life essentials at prices below cost. The government is employing hundreds of thousands of servants at a cost which is far greater than the taxpayers can afford to pay.

It might be said that the government is incompetent. It might be said that the class of Englishmen which is composed of capitalists and employers are incompetent. It might be said that the working people of England by reason of their ignorance are vainly striving to squeeze blood out of a turnip. But at the present time there is only one fact worthy of consideration and that is the people of England are living beyond their means.

Like conditions prevail all over the continent of Europe. All of Europe is living beyond its means. It is producing less than it consumes and its consumers are clamoring for even still more material for consumption.

The peoples, as peoples, are lacking in intelligence. Individual is combating individual; class is arrayed against class.

Everybody is fighting for something that is not in existence, viz., a sufficiency of all sorts of material and spiritual things desired.

Because some individuals and some classes of individuals have more of these things than other individuals in other classes, the "have nots" think that the "haves" have got more than enough for themselves and everybody else.

Perhaps the workingmen should gladly accept lower wages than they are now clamoring for. Perhaps their employers should gladly relinquish all but a fraction of their desired profits. Perhaps vast communities of the people should cease to produce unessentials and bend all their energies to producing those things essential for life alone.

Perhaps in these overcrowded countries the baby-makers should take a vacation for a sufficient number of years to allow population to decline to such an extent that the land would produce food and other things for all that remain.

Damn the "perhaps"! Damn the "shoulds"! Damn the "ought-to-be's"!

No man or woman can do the disagreeable thing until absolutely compelled to do so.

There is a science called the science of economics. The professors of this science have built up a whole house of cards, of theories, names of things, of systems that don't work and can't work. The science of economics is like the modern church in that both preach dogmas and assert that to be true which is false.

Neither the world of science nor the association of theologists have any message for the people. Nothing that either of them preach is applicable to real life.

The world is irreligious and the people of the world are hungry. All of Europe is really in revolution and the revolution is progressing quite as effectively as if it were carried on by gunfire and bayonets.

The whole organization of society is being torn to pieces fragment by fragment.

What is occurring in Europe today violently is occurring in other parts of the world where European civilization exists less violently, but progressively more and more violently.

Are the people of Europe and of European descent destroying their own civilization and themselves in order that they shall become so weak as not to be able to resist the onslaught of other peoples — unable, even, to escape annihilation?

There are so many ignorant people in the world and so few who are wise! Unless the wise rule the unwise, the instructed direct the ignorant, the unwise and the ignorant will rule themselves and also the wise and the instructed.

The world, the European at least, has become a world of democracy, while the fear of Hell and the hope of Heaven, viz., the influence of the church, has ceased to exist.

What is going on in this world of ours? Are we dying by nations and individuals while yet remaining ignorant of the nature of our malady?

Gustav LeBon covertly but bitterly insinuates that the destruction of the hegemony in Europe of Germany has resulted in the hegemony of England — that little island whose intrinsic weakness is visible to all who care to observe.

And these big United States! What are we doing? At present we are destroying ourselves economically and morally. We are not effectively organized.

Our government is not composed of great men of great vision and of great force. Had all of our officials of the executive and legislative and judicial classes been selected by lot, rather than election by ballots, it is not likely that our government, as a government, would have been much less, if any less, efficient than is our present government.

Our President [Harding] — I only met him once and that was before I had any idea of his being a possibility as a presidential candidate. [This was written before "Two Presidents" in the Politics section.]

I have had much to do with men, have known men in all stations of life. I have had occasion, that is to say, the necessity, of studying men for the purpose of understanding their character and of appraising their worth in the way of net ability.

My own estimate of our President is that he has qualities in no way superior to those of many hundreds of thousands of other Americans whose names and personalities would not make them particularly conspicuous even in any small community of mediocrity.

It is absurd, then, to think of looking to America as an able physician to be called in to treat the malady of a sick world.

The big war didn't make all this trouble. The world war was a symptom of the world's disease. The war was an effect, not a cause.

Perhaps the world's disease is overpopulation. Perhaps it was caused by the atrophy of that organ of the body politic which might be called organized religion or church. Perhaps the disease is nothing but overgrown machinism.

But more likely it was caused, according to my views, more than anything else by the brutish instincts of the animal, man, too long allowed freedom from the lash of its trainer or strong men who alone in all the history of the world have ever been able to compel obedience and order — autocracy in fact — great autocracy, ruling autocracy, not the simulant of autocracy like the late German Emperor and the late Czar of Russia.

As Caesar grasped the imperial crown when the Roman republic had become decadent, as Napoleon seized power in France at a given time, and as Lenin has striven and is still striving to seize and hold power of dictator in Russia, so may we have to depend on some coming strong man to reorganize the family of nations called European to save the white race from destruction either at its own hands or at the hands of some other nations or races submissive to and ruled by some strong man picked from their numbers.

AMERICAN BUSINESS
AND LABOR

In writing about economics, Scripps repeatedly directed his attention to five questions above all others: What is wealth, really? What is the mainspring of man's economic behavior? Why are some men rich and others poor? How can a more equitable distribution of property be effected? What *is* a dollar?

Scripps' foremost qualification to speak with some authority about American business and economic theory is at once obvious: he made of himself a multimillionaire within the American business system. Consequently, much of what he has to say is based on personal experience and observation — empiricism of a sort, if you prefer — and sometimes a testing of general propositions against specific instances in his experience. Yet he also could approach his subject from the theoretical as well as the pragmatic.

He enlarged his observations into stimulating discussions by adding to the practical experience the ideas produced by the constant questioning of a mind in ferment, stored with the fruit of long years of unremitting and eclectic reading. Around 1908, for instance, he subscribed to about forty or fifty magazines, and constantly added books to his library. The periodicals included the better American magazines of the day, scholarly quarterlies in economics and political science, and British as well as some French periodicals. And he read widely, not just about economics, for Scripps regarded himself as an anthropologist, sociologist, practical economist, journalist, political thinker, iconoclast, and reformer.

As a generalist, then, he brought to bear on economic questions — because man "as an economic animal" interested him more than any other single subject — the full extent of what he knew, or thought he knew, about biology, sociology, psychology, economics, political science, agriculture, and anything else he happened to think of. Naturally, his thought, as his reading, was eclectic. In this connection, note his evaluation of authors in various fields:

> I have been reading books and books, by the hundreds and thousands, all my life. . . . I have small quarrel with the writers on biology, because these men know all that I know, and a great deal more. The psychologists and sociologists, I recognize, know some things that I do not know, but naturally I have learned some things that some of them have not learned.
>
> But when it comes to writers on economic subjects, I am always in a condition of greater or less exasperation. The writers on these subjects seem to me to know hardly anything at all about the subject on which they are writing.[1]

Scripps' writing and thinking accorded with the spirit of the times, for both the economic face of America and economic thought underwent a transformation during the years in which he wrote. The principal change that occurred in American business was the decline of laissez faire in the face of stricter and increasing governmental controls which, however, did not damage the essential element of free enterprise. Government regulation came increasingly from Theodore Roosevelt's Square Deal through Woodrow Wilson's New Freedom. Beginning with more effective control of railroads through a broadening of the powers of the Interstate Commerce Commission, the regulation continued on through the creation of the Federal Reserve System as a means of giving the United States a centralized and a more elastic currency, as well as the creation of the Federal Trade Commission to regulate certain aspects of interstate trade. Merely illustrative, the federal regulations thus mentioned also were part of a spirit that manifested itself at the state and municipal levels with public utility regulation and workmen's compensation laws, for instance, and municipal ownership of waterworks.

Within the economy itself, other major changes occurred. Through increasing mass production of consumer goods, American industry helped to standardize Americans, American communities, and American goods. One effect of mass production was to narrow the once painfully visible gap between workmen and employer, although the full effect did not come into operation until later decades. Whereas American industry had been built originally — and America thus made the premier industrial nation of the world — by individual entrepreneurs who owned and ran their own businesses, investment bankers took control of more and more industries as the twentieth century progressed. Indeed, the transfer of authority from entrepreneur to finance capitalist was perhaps the major internal change within the economy between 1900 and 1914. At the same time, American prosper-

[1] EWS to Scott Nearing, unsent letter of Jan. 24, 1917. For a short time, Scripps wrote frequently to Nearing, an economist of socialist leanings. At one point, Scripps suggested that Nearing might be retained to make a study of the economic history of the Scripps concern, but the study wasn't made.

ity burgeoned in terms of total wealth, gross national product, wages, and population increases.

Simultaneously, a group of new thinkers re-adjusted economic thought, among them Thorstein Veblen. The iconoclastic Scripps reacted to Veblen like one who had had a glimpse of Glory, as in "Force and Fraud." For Veblen's thinking accorded with Scripps' own. Scripps read Veblen as saying that wealth really consisted of technology, which Scripps equated with his own laboriously-arrived-at definition of wealth — knowing how to do things. Veblen first appeared on the scene with *Theory of the Leisure Class* in 1899 and *Theory of Business Enterprise* in 1904. Caustically analyzing contemporary business and industry as being directed by men seeking only monetary gain rather than the pride of accomplishment found in the old handicraft economy, Veblen ripped deep, but did not win full appreciation until the depression of the 1930's turned many thinkers in search of new ideas. Thus, Scripps was one of the few contemporaries to recognize, appreciate, and, perhaps more importantly, agree with Veblen.

His delight at finding Veblen he expressed again a few years later, remarking that his definition of wealth as consisting of "knowing how to do things" had been considered "a pure absurdity by everyone" to whom he had submitted his conclusions. Thus, on reading Veblen, he said jocularly, he "was delighted to find that another man with great mental capacity had arrived at a similar conclusion." [2]

Continuing his consideration of the nature of wealth, in "A Question" he advances the thesis that a natural law of some sort fixes the upper limit of a nation's wealth. The nation's total wealth may fluctuate at various levels below that maximum level but never rises above. Likewise, he suggested, natural law may be such that the aggregate wealth of a nation cannot be more, because of deterioration, than the total amount of wealth that can be produced by two years of labor. Thus, even though he defined wealth as knowledge, he frequently used the word "wealth" in its material sense. He carries his argument a bit farther in "Why Some Men Are Rich and Others Poor" by saying there is a strong indication that a natural law governs property distribution among men.

Consider, too, his formulation of the concept of the dollar as a symbol of relativity. If his contemporaries of the early twentieth century — businessmen, economists, and the general public — did not regard the gold dollar as something fixed, stable, and having a worth in and of itself, Scripps was convinced that they did. But he was not sure that was the nature of the dollar at all. By degrees, he formulated his concept that a gold dollar, in and of itself, is of little worth, but is of considerable worth as a measuring stick for determining the relative values of other things.

[2] "Simple Truths and Absurdities," EWS Writings, 5:116.

Scripps first adumbrated his concept in 1910 in "The Increasing Gold Supply and Its Relation to My Business," and finally stated it positively in 1919 in "One Aspect of Money." In 1921, he read an article by Irving Fisher, an economist at Yale University; Fisher became one of the most forceful advocates of a stable money, arguing that a dollar was a dollar in name only, and ultimately proposing a compensated dollar, or "goods dollar," the value of which would be determined by the price index of a selected list of commodities. Upon reading one of Fisher's articles, Scripps wrote him, continuing a correspondence that had begun about three years earlier:

> I have just concluded reading your article in the July *Review of Reviews.* I do not expect you to consider it a compliment when I tell you that your idea of what a dollar is (under present conditions) is identical with my own.
>
> .   .   .   .
>
> It is my opinion that the chief reason why some men are rich and some are poor and that there are very few rich men is that the generality of men believe the dollar really is stable — that it is a thing of substance rather than a symbol of relativity.[3]

The difficulty Scripps had in communicating his idea of the dollar, even to one trained to distinguish between subtleties, is shown in an exchange with his scientist friend W. E. Ritter. Noting that he "had not even made a dent in your mind in the matter of my definition of 'what a dollar is,'" Scripps told Ritter he had recognized that he did not know the words, or lacked the skill in using words, that would be necessary to make his idea clear. But it so happened that he had just read Alfred Korzybski's *Manhood of Humanity,* upon Ritter's recommendation, and found in Korzybski identically the same idea but with a different word. Scripps quoted Korzybski as saying an inch of wood or iron represents nothing but the piece of wood or iron, but the mental value of an inch, as a measurement of space, can be used in determining the location of a planet, and that an inch has no value of itself but is precious as a measurement of length. If Ritter were to substitute "dollar" for "inch," Scripps said, he would have "identically the idea that I tried to express in my writing and talk about 'what is a dollar?' "[4]

Scripps had his own, practical explanation of cyclical depressions, too. Contemporary economists offered various explanations, such as overproduction. Scripps held that the occurrence of depressions about every twenty years could be attributed in part to the turnover in executive personnel. That is, each chief executive would experience one severe depression during his business life, and would be out of the picture and his experience thus lost when younger successors faced the conditions that brought on the next de-

[3] EWS to Irving Fisher, Aug. 8, 1921, in EWS Writings, 9:218.
[4] EWS to W. E. Ritter, Sept. 12, 1921.

pression. Without experience in handling a depression, then, businessmen could not take the appropriate measures to head it off, or to soften its blow upon them. See "The Next Business Panic."

In several places in the succeeding selections, Scripps again protested on behalf of workingmen, but he also protested on behalf of capitalists. Although he never ceased to flail those capitalists who let greed and power blind them to their own self-interests, Scripps argued that most people had no conception at all of what a capitalist had to go through before he controlled any amount of wealth. Certainly, he said, the general public recognized that a skilled workman in any trade must go through an apprenticeship before becoming a journeyman. But they did not realize that a capitalist had to put in many, many more years of apprenticeship. Business failures, he said, showed that of the thousands of apprentice capitalists only a few score became journeymen.[5]

As between capital and labor, in a day when class consciousness was sharp and many the predictions of ultimate class warfare, Scripps considered industrial peace both impossible and undesirable, as being against what he saw as nature's law of conflict.

Part of the reform movement during prewar years had been aimed at establishment of a minimum wage, which was accomplished at the state level in several instances, and for which Scripps worked actively. Through computations of his own, he said in 1912 that the minimum wage should be $3.00 a day for men and women in non-agricultural callings; $2.00 a day in agriculture; half the adult wage for minors; and $1.00 a day for domestic servants who received room, board, and clothing from their employers.[6] In 1917, he said the wage scale should be doubled, holding that a minimum wage of $1,000 or $1,200 a year would not be "overgenerous."[7] Also in 1917 he wrote that workingmen, to increase their wages, must produce more, because an employer's wages could not exceed the total amount of production. "Marx's cry was 'Workingmen of the world unite.' I would repeat this cry and add the words — 'to increase your efforts in producing.'" The first step toward higher wages, he said, should be greater production; the second, to exact "by force if need be" from employers "a fair and just proportion" of the product thus increased.[8]

But after the war, when he saw the storm cloud of an economic disaster approaching, he concluded that one reason for the storm would be that wages were too high. Thus, he could reason academically, wages should be reduced. But he well knew the dynamite such a proposal would contain. In-

---

[5] "Work or Starve," EWS Writings, 8:62.
[6] "The Minimum Wage," EWS Writings, 4:2–3.
[7] "One of a Hundred Million," *ibid.*, 6:5 f.
[8] "The ABC of Wages," *ibid.*, 6:294.

deed, he said, the person who advocated such a course, bringing tidings of an approaching depression, would be in the position of bearers of bad tidings who were killed on the spot at the order of Oriental despots.[9]

Before the war, politicians and economists expressed concern at the growing population shift from farm to city, a concern which Scripps shared. One who paradoxically despised cities, which were the source of his wealth through newspapers, Scripps remained a constant advocate of country life. Indeed, in spite of his city-based enterprises, he lived most of his life in the country — on the home farm, at West Chester, and at "Miramar."

Among several writings in which he urged young people to stay on the farm, he once said that cities are the graveyards of families, which die out in a city within two or three generations. It is unreasonable, he maintained, for anyone to take pride in being one of a large crowd in a city, but most people do. Even on the West Coast where for nine years out of ten the working people opposed immigration of Asiatics, he said, that opposition melted away in the tenth or census year, for the inhabitants of all cities took pride in growing population. Naturally, he conceded, property owners desired a larger city population, because it increased the value of their holdings. He reckoned that every man, woman, and child added to the population of a city added a minimum of $4.00 to the intrinsic value of his newspaper in that city, perhaps as much as $8.00 in San Diego. In the shift from country to city, Scripps saw a denial of hedonism as the moving spirit of man, for, he said, the man on the land is the one who lives the longest and happiest life, and agricultural nations are those that endure the longest.[10]

The most novel of the ideas expressed in his disquisitions on economics was the suggestion that a National Industrial Congress be created to represent all segments of American economic life, and that it sit in Washington as sort of a third house. He predicted that in time such an economic congress would make Congress its mere instrument. He advanced the idea in "The Real Thing in the Way of an Industrial Democracy."

[9] "The World Is in Need of Truth-Tellers," EWS Writings, 9:65 f.
[10] "Back to the Land," EWS Writings, 3:286 f.

Force and Fraud

[*May 7, 1909*]

Whenever one man hears another express opinions similar to his own, the party of the first part is pretty sure to consider the party of the second part a wise man. This feeling of admiration and respect is even aroused when words are lightly spoken and the subject spoken of is common-place, and even when the opinion expressed is well-nigh universal.

But when the hearer is himself a man of either exceptional intelligence, or possessed of peculiarly advanced views, his delight at hearing another give expression to the same views is increased a hundredfold, and his respect for and admiration of his colleague in opinion is unbounded.

This explains why I am so great an admirer of Professor Thorstein Veblen. I know nothing more of the man's personality than the fact that he was a professor at Chicago University and that latterly he has been a professor at Palo Alto. He certainly is not a man who has made much noise in the world.

My reading covers a large field of scientific subjects. Whether Veblen is a professor of sociology or some form of economics I know not; that he has found publishers for two remarkable books would indicate that he has a high standing. I have read two of his articles in the *Quarterly Journal of Economics*, and my first attention was directed to him some years ago by a brief review in a journal of similar standing. But I do not recall ever having seen his name elsewhere mentioned in the hundreds and perhaps thousands of books and magazine articles that I have read. In none of the daily papers nor in the high-class weekly journals have I ever seen any reference to Veblen.

For some reason he seems to be almost completely ignored. The names of scores of other literary college professors are familiar to me and to the public, made so by the public prints.

Yet, of all the publicists, great and small, in this country and in Eu-

609

rope, it seems to me there is not one superior and few equal to Veblen, in brilliancy of intellect, in great perception and in lucidity, and in pleasing and agreeableness of literary style. That which makes this situation is the more remarkable since Veblen is giving expression to so many views that are extremely sensational in character — views that the cynical critics of the press would delight to exploit and controvert by ridicule and argument.

To my mind Veblen is a modern Machiavelli, but he is as far advanced over the old Machiavelli as is the modern science of astronomy above and beyond the astrology of the days of Machiavelli, or immediately preceding those days.

It has been many days since I have [read] Machiavelli's *Prince* but from what I can remember of that book it would seem that Veblen's mind has traveled along the same line with Machiavelli, only farther along in it. I remember that when I read Machiavelli's *Prince* I could not feel that intense sense of loathing or repugnance toward the man and his ideas which it was commonly supposed that every good and virtuous man should feel.

I felt that Machiavelli was telling the truth to his Prince, and that he was not teaching immorals, but that he was calling his attention to real facts concerning human nature. He was not telling his "Prince" any lies about the world and man; he was not telling him how to rule an ideal non-existent body of human beings, or impressing upon him the duty of creating himself an ideal community by pretending to play the role of an ideal ruler of an ideal people.

Thorstein Veblen has studied and largely discovered man — his mind, his character, his motives, his institutions, his individuality, and his social habits. He has placed man and man's society under a sort of mental microscope, and studied his subjects as unfailingly and perhaps with less bias of mind than the biological investigator has, with his actual microscope in his laboratory, studied material life organisms. In his writings Veblen tells us what he sees, and shows great freedom, perhaps too much freedom, in making his deductions. But in this matter he has not, perhaps, been any more free than the ordinary investigator.

Of course, no religionist could for an instant tolerate any of Veblen's deductions, and for this reason, perhaps, no religionist could consent to the existence even of the facts as Veblen has presented them.

No man who can see things as Veblen sees them can at the same time be possessed of the convictions of those who believe revealed religion of any sort. (I suppose all real scientists are in the same condition.)

In the various of my disquisitions I have more or less indefinitely hinted at, or crudely stated, my own idea, but without regard to any sentimentalities, that the two fundamental, necessary virtues of a human being were those two characteristics which were denounced as the worst of all vices, namely the use of physical force for purposes of oppression, and of craft or cunning for the purposes of deceiving and cheating. The public expression of this doctrine might, and probably would, bring upon me the condemnation and hatred of society. If any person interested in me should attempt to defend me at all it would be by pleading insanity, and it would not be difficult either to establish such a defense, since none but an insane man would dare to give expression to such views to the commonalty of people.

Veblen himself finds it necessary all through his writings to keep explaining again and again to the reader that his use of words and of terms does not indicate anything invidious or deprecatory. He keeps trying to make his reader believe that the author is only unfortunate in that the human language, as it at present exists, does not contain the right words to fully and clearly express his meaning. I believe that one-half of the text of one of the books, *Theory of the Leisure Class*, is taken up with this protest against the possibility of his books being read and interpreted according to the vulgar and common meaning of words.

Veblen certainly is determined to do all in his power to avoid the fateful reputation of his great Florentine predecessor. Perhaps it is because he has so consistently and thoroughly blunted the point of all of his arguments that the sensational journalists have been warded off from him.

Still, Veblen knows well enough that the few, the intellectual and hence the sympathetic, readers of his books will not fail to see all of his points, and will not fail to brush away the thick veil of words which he has hung over his creation in order that vulgar minds shall not be able to perceive all that the author has revealed.

Here is a good enough place to state an idea of my own, and that is that modern science is greatly hindered by its lack of esoteric conditions. Scientific investigators and writers in modern times are compelled to use vulgar languages, and are compelled to resort to print, so that all they report of their discoveries and all that they relate in the way of deductions is not only liable to but almost certain to come under the eye of the vulgar, not only the uninformed but the great mass of the misinformed public — men and women who only know one definition for a word and who are only capable of making false deductions by reason of the great mass of false, often religious, ideas that have been impressed upon them, false deductions from words, phrases, sentences, and whole books.

While writing for the learned and the illumined, the scientific writer must ever be on his guard against the ignorant fury of the mob. He is fearful, and rightfully fearful, both of being misunderstood and of being understood by the great popular masses, who are led and controlled by chiefs — political, religious, and industrial — whose greatest self-interest lies in keeping the mass of the people not only in ignorance but misinformed and believing things the reverse of truth. Perhaps it would be impossible for any profound student of and thinker on scientific subjects to express all he knows on one of these subjects, and to make deductions from same, either in speech or in writing, and be able to maintain a position as college or university professor, or even be tolerated as a member of any society or as a citizen of any state.

But still these scientific men are gradually discovering previously unknown facts, and are gradually insinuating into the public mind the knowledge of the same, together with consistent deductions to be drawn from them.

Veblen's theory that force and fraud are the two greatest of human virtues is, perhaps, not so novel as is the fact that he has dared even to insinuate the idea in writing. I do not recall that he has succinctly and definitely made the statement that force and fraud were virtues; to the extent, however, that he has even insinuated this idea, he has been careful and politic, in that he has also insinuated that these characteristics are mainly those of the very few of the wealthy and ruling class — the very small class of democracy in all its forms and in all parts of the world.

As a matter of fact, I believe that the moral disposition, the desire, or in a way the willingness, to commit acts of rapine and chicanery is no greater in one class of men than in another, and that these characteristics are only detested by the commonalty of mankind because they do not possess sufficient of either fraud or cunning to themselves become members of the wealthy and ruling class. I more than suspect that Veblen has identically the same views as my own, and that the only reason for his being less candid than I is that he writes for publication and speaks before audiences, while I am content to bury my thoughts out of sight and out of reach.

It is easy enough not only for the common mind to realize as virtues force and fraud, and even for the most biased religious fanatic to take the same view, and [to consider] man as a savage when he lives in a condition little better than that of the beasts and when all of his fellowmen are in the same condition of lack of social organization. The savage man's warfare was first against the savage beasts of the field and the forest; his existence depended upon both his ability to procure food by killing other animals and by preventing himself being made the food of these other animals. Some of these animals are so small as to be no match for the man, in power, so that man has to but lay his hand upon them in order to devour them. But nearly all such animals are man's superior in land locomotion, and the others escape to the air, where man cannot go, and into the water, where man cannot live. Hence, man's only chance to lay hands on these animals is to resort to cunning. There are other larger animals, good for

food, but too huge in bulk and too great in muscular strength to be captured and slaughtered by bodily assault; the man must therefore resort to
cunning traps and other devices. There are other larger animals, savage
carnivora, which delight to feast on man's flesh, against which man's force
is inadequate as protection, so he must again depend upon his cunning
and his craft.

This savage man has also to encounter other savage men; he must defend his body against these other savage men, who may be cannibals or
who may only desire to rob him of his booty of the chase. There are times
when this man would die of starvation himself were he not able by force to
overcome and by fraud to cheat other savage men of their lives and of their
booty of the chase.

It would seem that all men would agree with Veblen and myself that there
have been, perhaps for ninety-nine hundredths of the whole term of existence of humanity on earth, times when force and fraud were, if not virtues
as virtues are defined by the vulgar and modern, at least characteristics
absolutely necessary for human existence.

Right here let me ask, Is it any more a vice for a man to decoy a fish
onto his hook, with a tempting bait, and to decoy a partridge into a net
than it is for the same man to obtain food that is necessary for him by deceiving some other man?

Biologists teach us and our own common sense indicates to us that mankind is a species of animal, that he is a part of the animal kingdom, and
that he is governed by all the laws of that kingdom. Man as he exists today is the heir to all the ages, and whether he be virtuous or not he is the
image of his ancestors in mind and body in all his characteristics, and his
ancestors have been nine hundred ninety-nine savages, at least, to one civilized man. He is by right, and must be, the heir to all the instincts of all
his progenitors; he cannot be otherwise. He can only live and react to the
same stimuli as his ancient forefathers lived and reacted to.

Man is a predatory animal. He is gregarious now and has been for ages,
but before he was gregarious he was solitary, and for perhaps a hundred
times longer was he a solitary animal than he has been a gregarious one.
It was in solitariness that man acquired all of his physical attributes and
perhaps even the brain and nerve cells that he is possessed of today. Man
is carnivorous; naturally he must be cannibalistic.

All of man was formed before society, but long ages of social experience
have developed in him the social instinct to a certain extent. But it will
require millions of generations yet to come for the old and original individual instinct to be entirely and completely subordinated to the social instinct.

Not to so great an extent today as formerly are oppressive force and fraud human virtues. The social institutions make it possible for man to live without robbery or cheating. But present conditions will not permit the passive and non-resisting to rise to positions of personal freedom and of great material possessions, nor once having either of these things to retain them. A whole community of such passive, non-resisting men would not be permitted to exist, either by savage beasts or by less peaceable men.

Even a nation, numerically very great and very wealthy in a material way, could not exist on earth today except by resort to force and fraud. Poor old China is being compelled to adopt Western military methods in these days, in order to defend herself from the depredations of great Christian nations composed of men in whom civilization is a thousand years in advance of that of China.

There are men, and many of them, in this and other civilized countries who believe that the time has come when international peace is possible. Perhaps there is a larger number of men who believe, or think they believe, that the oppressive use of force and fraud by individuals is wrong. But the men who believe in this latter principle are not men of profound learning or thought, nor do they in their own minds place the same definitions on the words force and fraud as do learned and profound men; these men regard as fraudulent only those acts and schemes which are specifically mentioned and prohibited by statute law, by religious rule, and conventions. When they cry out against the use of fraud and force they only mean to denounce that use of force which they had no need to use, and that use of fraud which law and convention denounces.

Yet fraud and deceit, in numerous ways, is practiced by every father and mother in dealing with their children, by every husband and wife in dealing with his or her spouse, by every citizen and voter, and by every democratically elected or monarchially appointed officer. White lies are told in the family, in the society, and in the pulpit. Even the landscape gardener who, with a few trees and shrubs, succeeds in creating the impression on the beholder in the middle of an acre of land that he is in the midst of a forest or a mountain wilderness is a fraud before he is an artist. No self-respecting lady, who is a credit to her family and to her society, is free from the virtuous duty of making her personal appearance more naturally beautiful in form than it really is.

As for business (Professor Veblen's work on *Theory of* [*Business Enterprise*], full and illuminating as it is, will teach no businessman any new tricks in his own business; it is only remarkably interesting because of the unexpected revelations it makes to one businessman concerning the practices of another) there is only one word to describe it fully and completely and that is "fraud." The whole practice and method of business is that of one man, at least, trying to cheat the other.

I think that this statement would appear very trite to every businessman, and I also think that no really good businessman could ever be induced, under any circumstances, to admit to any other human being that he believes this statement to be anything less than an outrageous slander. If, by chance, some other man than myself should make this statement in the public print he would find it very easy to prove his thesis when the idea should be applied to any business transaction that takes place between two men.

Now, as I myself come to the point where I dare to formally express my convictions — facts that I will not say that I have discovered but that I will say I have confirmed, and know them to be facts — what deduction shall I make from them in order to govern my life and in order that I should give the very best possible assistance, in the way of training, to the men of my family and to the men who are my associates in business?

Some time I may take up this subject.

The Unimportance of Waste

[*January 8, 1910*]

Some days ago, I discussed some of my ideas on the subject of the waste of human efforts [not included among these selections] — waste by useless destruction of products, waste by energy devoted in producing useless material, and waste by abstention from effort on the part of a large part, perhaps the major part, of humanity. At the same time, in my conclusions, I pointed out how quickly universal and intelligent effort would overcome all those social economic evils which are the most berated by the most energetic would-be reformers.

Several months ago [September, 1909] I was honored by a visit from a man who was not only eminent, but deservedly so, on account of his great ability and his great activity as a national economist. This man was Gifford Pinchot. The object of a lifetime of most energetic effort on his part has been to save from waste the forests of this country. He has also added to his laurels, recently, by undertaking a further movement — that of saving for the public rather than for private use the national resources in coal, petroleum, phosphate rocks, waterpower sites, etc. [See Politics section.]

At least the ostensible object of his visit to me was to observe the results and to encourage further efforts on my part to redeem from uselessness lands in southern California, by employing these same lands for forest growth. One subject of our conference resulted in a practical controversy. It pleases me to think that the result of this controversy will be that a great leader and recognized authority in a very important field of economics will somewhat amend his views and somewhat alter the direction of his future thoughts and teachings.

I was able to show Mr. Pinchot some tree plantations of my own, which he declared samples worthy of remark and future consideration.

In fact, in this neighborhood, southern California, where there exists what is called semiaridity, there are millions of acres of land, the soil of which is too poor to be of much value for ordinary cropping purposes. The land is also too rough, hilly, mountainous, and generally broken up to make it arable even if the soil were good and there was plenty of water for irrigation. Perhaps in other portions of the country there are other areas of land the aggregate of which may be hundreds of times, if not thousands of times, greater than the area in this section, which are of small value for other purposes than timber culture and grazing.

I showed him that I had demonstrated that this land could be planted to forests at very small acreage cost. In fact, a large portion of it might be roughly planted at a cost of not greater than $5.00 per acre. Any of the land is capable of being forested in the most perfect imaginable form at a cost of not to exceed $40.00 per acre. This $40.00 per acre cost includes clearing the land of all of the brush now covering it, plowing it, planting it out in trees, irrigating the trees for the first two or three years, and cultivating the same.

These lands are capable of producing ripe trees in a period of not to exceed 40 years — trees large enough to give the best form of sawed lumber, and the largest kind of sticks needed for any purpose, at an acreage rate of from 1 to 300 trees according to the quality of soil and other conditions.

At the present rates of transportation, it could be figured that the cost of transporting to this section the amount of lumber that would be furnished by one tree would be not less than $2.00. As there is no natural timber in this section, all lumber needed here has to be imported from forests remote from this locality. To the transportation rate must be added the intrinsic value of the timber wherever it is grown.

There is to be added, too, to the present prices of the timber, that increase in price which must result through the depletion of the present wild forests in the country, and the rapidly increasing demand, on account of the growing population, for timber.

While Mr. Pinchot was with me, he was visited by one of the chiefs of his staff in the Bureau of Forestry [Forest Service] at Washington, part of whose duties was to make calculations, based on statistics, of the future value of lumber. I asked this man what estimate he would put on the value of a eucalyptus tree 40 years old, 40 years hence. He said he had figured on this subject, and he estimated that the value would be about $5.00 per tree. This figure does not seem excessive, considering what I had previously said about the cost of transportation and the intrinsic value of growing timber, and the probable rapid appreciation in prices.

According to the above it would appear, then, that the money value of the timber yield of this land would range between $500 and $1,500 per acre per 40 years.

I have already indicated that the land has no value for agriculture. For grazing purposes it will hardly ever be worth more than $1.00 per acre. For this reason, the first cost or intrinsic value of the land itself, in considering forestry, becomes a negligible quantity.

If the foresting cost but $5.00 per acre, then in 40 years the value of the product would be one hundredfold greater. But even if the cost were $50.00 per acre and the minimum yield in lumber was obtained, the investment would result in a tenfold return for 40 years. Even the last figure given would indicate that money invested in forestry would be doubly as profitable as would the same money invested in any interest bearing obligation.

Now Mr. Pinchot's greatest effort has been to save the natural forests of the land from wasteful methods of lumbering and from fires, etc. I raised this question with Mr. Pinchot: Is it profitable to maintain natural forests when the same amount of labor could produce artificial forests that would be much more valuable in the acre yield and in the annual growth?

Nature is wasteful in her processes, regarded from a standpoint of the usefulness of her product to civilized man. Nature did not set out to produce, in her forests, material for man's exclusive use, namely for housebuilding, ship-building, furniture-making, piles, railroad ties, telegraph poles, or even fuel.

The tree growing in a natural forest expends by far the greatest amount of its vital energy not in self-development but in its struggle for existence, in overcoming and destroying its competitor for soil nutriment, for water, for air, and for sunshine. Owing to this excessive competition, the great majority of trees in a natural forest are so stunted and so malformed as to be of but little worth to the lumberman. Considering all the trees in any forest from the year-old seedling up through the sapling to the giant timber-producer, perhaps not one tree in one thousand, in any given area of land, is of any value.

However, the sum total or the aggregate of all of the wood material on an acre of forest land may be, and probably is, several times greater than that part of it which is useful to man because of its size.

The aggregate vital effort of any forest put forth in a lifetime of a single mature tree has been many thousand times greater than that necessary to have produced the lumber which could have been produced on the same area had the trees been systematically planted and had competition been artificially eliminated by the destruction or the non-appearance of trees which were incapable of maturing into lumber-producing trees.

I cited the case of the buffalo, the deer, the turkey, the quail, and other game. These animals, living in a state of nature, required many hundred times more acreage than would be required by domestic animals and fowls capable of producing, as food, meat in as great quantity, and producing meat of better quality, more palatable, and more nourishing. I cited the case of the western prairie where Nature, prior to the coming of man, had been laboring to produce rough grasses only fit for forage, and only a part of which was fit for forage for wild animals. The vegetation of these prairies was of such poor quality that it was rarely profitable for man to harvest it in order to feed [his] stock on it.

The acre value of such prairies, even for grazing of domestic animals well cared for, rarely exceeded $1.00. By stripping the ground of Nature's products and devoting it to man-controlled agriculture, these wild lands have been increased in productivity, and hence in value, from one hundred- to one thousandfold.

Now in this matter of forestry, where we have bare unwooded lands, we can plant trees and so equably distribute these trees that none of their vital growing energy will be exhausted in cut-throat competition between the trees themselves. On account of planting in this way, the labor, or effort, to safeguard these forests against fires and other enemies, is infinitely small compared to that which is necessary to save natural wild forests from destruction.

In fact, I suggested to Mr. Pinchot that if the people desired to retain as forest land the land at present covered by forests, the wise and economical thing to do might be to entirely cut down all of the present forests and replant the lands in such a way as to save the tree-growing energy from waste of competition between the trees and conserve all of this energy for the growth of the tree itself. In fact, I intimated, by inference, that perhaps Mr. Pinchot's life of labor had been wasted in a vain effort to secure the survival of unfit forests at the expense of preventing the creation of the most fit and many more times economical artificial forests.

Although I made no such clear statement to this effect, the inference was clear, and I believe perceived from Mr. Pinchot's countenance that he recognized it, and that the recognition caused him to wince.

After all, is it not a fact that this great philanthropist, thinker, and student is himself the victim of that spirit which is called conservatism — that spirit which is the dead-weight drag that is holding back and preventing the fulfillment of the desires of progressive humanity?

The economics of Mr. Pinchot may be and probably are the economics not of the progressive, not even of the mediocre, but of the most ignorant, stolid, and stupid of humanity.

In the matter of housing, there are two classes of men engaged. A member of the most intelligent classes, if he has need for a building in which to locate his family, his factory, or his mercantile business, and if he has a given piece of land on which there already exists some old structure inadequate for his purpose, will utterly destroy and remove the old structure at considerable expense and at further considerable expense erect an entirely new building perfectly adapted to his requirements.

A member of the other class will attempt to repair the old structure, make additions to it, and remove only a few of the formerly existing disabilities. While the first cost of such repairs and additions would not equal the cost of removal and rebuilding, still such cost would be very large indeed, and the cost, as compared with the usefulness, would be far greater. As to the relative wisdom of these two types of men, we have only one means of making a test, and that is by observing and weighing the evidence of mental superiority. The result of such a test invariably results in finding that the man who has destroyed and rebuilt, and not the man who has repaired and made additions, is the man whose sum total of productivity, in his life, is by far the greatest.

I cannot but smile when I remember reading in my youth the ignorant diatribes of short-sighted sentimentalists against the so-called ruthlessness and alleged wicked slaughter and destruction of the buffalo herds, on our middle-western prairies, during the third quarter of the last century.

Today I have but small patience with those legislators and societies who put so much effort, vain effort, to preserve the wild game of the land. Sometimes it seems to me that race instinct prompts mankind to pursue a course far wiser than any scheme propounded by individuals possessed of the greatest learning and the greatest capacity for scientific thought.

Is Nature blind? Is she wasteful? Has she any vices that individual man can recognize? The individual man is, of course, a member of the human race, and a part and a whole of the human race, and a part of the scheme of Nature.

What the human race does collectively is to obey natural laws, and in its obedience is wise beyond the conception of any peculiar individual member of the race.

While Pinchot may be wasting his life energy in combating human instincts in the matter of forests, I feel that I may be equally rebellious and foolish in persuading others to pursue a course antagonistic to that social evolution that is going on among the people of this country, and the peoples of all other civilized lands.

I must be an exceptional and peculiar man, and hence that which appears right to me, cannot be right for the whole body of society, because society as a whole is obedient to Nature and must do right.

The subject cause of this disquisition has been my reading this morning of a part of an article appearing in the *Political Science* [*Quarterly*] on the subject of "Eugenics." The writers on this subject of eugenics appear to be in rebellion and warfare against past and present social institutions. The question arises in my mind, however, as to whether it is not possible that the new science of eugenics is but simply the appearance in another field of an idea or of a method which, compared with accepted formulas, holds the same relative position as do my ideas on artificial forestry compared with Pinchot's idea of preserving the old haphazard — so far as man is concerned — natural method of producing timber.

The eugenicists, with their plan of artificial lethal selection, might be compared to the old American pioneers of the West who destroyed the buffalo herds and dispossessed the ancient redman of his land.

I have frequently complained of waste, complained of Nature's waste and man's waste. Like others, I have been moved by a feeling of great concern, and even of indignation against society, for what has appeared to me to be wanton destruction and irreparable loss of things formerly existing. I have been hugely moved with the contemplation of the enormous loss of life as a result of man's wars, as a result of the so-called mad dollar-hunting, life-destroying course of modern industry. I have looked aghast at the figures relative to the enormous loss of life occasioned by preventable diseases.

Yet, notwithstanding all this so-called waste, the world is full of humanity, almost as full as it can hold. The human family is increasing in numbers at such a rate at the present time that unless the growth is checked, standing room will, in a few centuries, be inadequate for the human race, leaving out of consideration not only comfortable existence but sustenance.

There is recalled to my mind the bitter saying of a certain French journalist concerning the Iron Chancellor Bismarck. Doubtless the saying was a libel so far as concerning its literal truth, but perhaps it was most truthful in characterizing the mental attitude of Bismarck and men like Bismarck. The French journalist stated that, upon Bismarck's being told of the mortality in the German army resulting from one great battle, he said in effect: "Oh, that don't matter, one night in Berlin alone will make good to the fatherland all the lives that have been lost in this battle."

Let the forests be destroyed by the ignorant and dishonest lumberman, and let millions and millions of little children and grown men and women be put to death by the criminal ignorance and rapacity of the indolent neglect of the ruling classes, and in the end we will have more and better forests, and a larger and much better population as a result.

There is a power, there is a cause that moves and rules all things, and whether we understand or do not understand the course of direction, and whether we rail against or applaud the result of this ruling energy, the supreme law must be obeyed, and that which will be, will be, and that which will be, will be good.

The Increasing Gold Supply
and Its Relation to My Business

[February 19, 1910]

This disquisition appears to have been edited in Scripps' hand.

Gold production had doubled since 1896, as a result of new discoveries in Alaska and Australia, and increased production in South Africa. The increase in gold, which then was the sole basis of the value of the American dollar, resulted in inflation.

In the American *Review of Reviews* for February, 1910, there is an article by Professor Walter Clark of the College [of the City] of New York, entitled "Why the Cost of Living Increases." In the same review is an article by Professor Irving Fisher of Yale University entitled "Gold in Relation to the Cost of Living."

It is something over a year ago, now, since I began thinking and writing on the subject of the Increasing Gold Supply.

There are good reasons for believing that the actual value of gold, as measured by that of other commodities — for instance wheat, copper, iron, lumber, and physical labor — is decreasing at a rate more than equal to 4 per cent per annum. Thus, it has appeared to me that all capital kept in the form of money — coin in vaults, certificates of loans, such as bonds and mortgages, etc., and other investments like life insurance policies — was deteriorating at the expense of the owner.

Now that there is great agitation in this country on the subject of [the] high cost of living — that is to say, the high price of provisions, food, clothing, and shelter — I find that the opportunity is presenting itself to bring to public attention this whole subject.

It has only been lately that I have been giving some sort of consideration to the subject of the increasing supply and diminishing value of gold as it relates to my business.

622

Recently some advocates of the railroad interests have been calling the public's attention to the fact that by charters and special laws railroad passenger rates almost universally, and to some extent freight traffic rates, are limited. Even where there is no legal restriction, there have been other reasons why the mile rate in dollars and cents of carrying human and other freight constantly diminishes instead of increases. While invention, increase in the volume of business, and improved management are working on one side to reduce the cost to the railroads of carrying traffic, on the other side there is going on a rapid rate of increase to the cost of such traffic, in the rising money price of labor and all sorts of commodities used by the railroads.

The point has not been reached where the rise, from one source, of cost has overcome the lowering of cost from other sources; however, it is recognized that in some instances, that is, in the case of some roads, the cost increases have been greater than cost reductions. It has also been recognized that it is extremely probable that in a very short time, the rising cost of commodities and labor will gain such a momentum as to make the railroad business unprofitable, until after there has been a change in the laws and customs now governing the traffic rates charged by the railroads.

Gold being the standard of value, it measures both the value received by the railroad for services to the public and the value of all those things which the railroad has to purchase in order to render public service. In nearly all states, either by charter or general law, the railroads are forbidden to charge passenger rates beyond a certain fixed amount per mile. In some states both law and custom [have] fixed a maximum passenger traffic rate of two cents per mile. Now this two cents is received in gold. If the value of gold is falling at the rate of 4 per cent per annum, the rate that the railroad is receiving for carrying passengers is actually falling by 4 per cent per year. Gold has been depreciating at the rate of over 4 per cent for the past ten or twelve years. It is estimated, I believe, that the fall has been even over 5 per cent. If this should be continued for ten years, after the minimum rate of two cents per mile had been fixed, while the different railroad companies would receive as many cents as the law provided for, the purchasing power of these gold cents will have fallen one-half. As a fact, the railroad's return for its services to the public will have decreased one-half.

Now the falling price of gold is constantly and consistently raising the market price of nearly all the commodities purchased by the road. Yet there are some items of the railroad's expense which are not rising constantly and consistently with the falling prices of gold — for instance, the amount of money paid for interest on bonds does not increase at all. There is but slight rise in the salaries of most of the higher class employees. The great bulk of the payroll, however, is cheaper labor, and in this case it has been found that during the past ten years while gold has fallen 50 per cent in value — most commodities having increased proportionately — the laborer's wages have only increased 22 per cent. I have not the figures before me of the labor cost of railroading, but I imagine that if the price of labor had raised proportionately with the cost of material commodities, and had railroad charges been kept at their present level, the whole railroad business of the United States today would be done at a loss.

In our business we have two sources of income, one from advertising and the other from sales of newspapers. While the advertising rate may be fluctuating, that is to say, steadily increasing even at a higher percentage than the fall in the value of gold with which we are paid for this advertising space, the wholesale and retail price of our newspapers remains fixed.

The exigencies of our business at the same time are calling for increase in the size of our newspapers, that is to say, for an increase in the volume of white paper for each customer. For many years the price per pound of white paper was steadily falling. It finally reached a point below which invention and improved management could not permit the reduction of price, of making paper, by the pound. Now, it seems to me inevitable that from this time on the cost of print paper will steadily increase.

If all the time the selling price of our newspapers remains fixed, our revenues will be reduced in two ways: first, by the increased size of our newspapers; and second, by the increasing cost per pound of the white paper used. It seems to me that it is absolutely necessary for us to keep this situation constantly in view in making all of our plans. We have got to face a diminishing profit or an increasing loss in the matter of sales if we maintain our present prices of subscription.

Advance in business, then, in order that it shall be accompanied by a proportionate advance in our profits, must be accompanied by one of three things: (1) we must either reduce the size of our papers; (2) or increase our retail and wholesale selling price of paper; (3) or very largely increase the advertising space rate.

Present tendencies of the business are making us depend entirely on advertising receipts for all the profits and most of the expense of the business.

It seems to me that the time is not far distant when we cannot look for profit from mere increase of the size of our papers and the accommodation of larger amounts of advertising at comparatively low rates. Growing circulation and the growing price of white paper will soon make the white paper bill so large as to cause actual loss on all advertising which can only be accommodated by increasing the size of the paper.

Already, in the past, our concern has devoted too much thought and too much energy to the mere increase in volume of our business.

It seems to me that the only safe course for us to pursue is to demand immediate and present profits, and to take care never to increase to any extent, whatever, our volume of business, without the certainty that every dollar will yield its proper amount of profit. It seems to me that it would be foolish to build up a large volume of business based upon such circulation and advertising rates as in the future would be inadequate to meet the future rise in the cost of labor and material.

We can depend upon it that, by reason of the falling price of gold, ten years hence the cost of white paper, ink, composition, rent, salary of management, and all other things will be from 30 to 50 per cent larger for each square inch of advertising than at present.

From what we know of business, it seems quite practicable to look forward to even a higher percentage of increase in the rate of advertising than 30 to 50 per cent in ten years. Still, in making our calculations for the future, our young men are too apt not to anticipate as a certainty this great percentage in the increase of cost.

I have already called attention to three sources of probable and almost certain gain to us in the future. Our interest cost will rise very slightly. It is probable that the cost increase in larger salaries will be nothing like in proportion to the cost of material commodities. The general labor bill, namely, the ordinary wage scale, while it will probably rise more rapidly in rate than the first-class salary account, will probably not rise at a rate of more than one-half that of material commodities. In this case I am not considering simply justice and morality. I am neither pleading the cause of labor nor advocating oppressive measures. I am only indicating the probable conditions of business.

Now there is another thing which I want to consider in this matter of relation in the increase of gold supply to our business.

During the past ten years the average price of commodities has risen 50 per cent; that is to say, that $1.50 will not buy as much today as $1.00 would have bought ten years ago; that is, it can be said further that $1.50 is only worth what $1.00 was ten years ago. The man whose property would have been appraised at 1 million dollars ten years ago and whose property would be appraised at 1.5 million dollars today has not increased in actual wealth 50 per cent. In fact, he is worth no more today than he was ten years ago. Along with his capital we may assume that his income is increasing proportionately, measured by dollars; but on account of the rising prices this income, increased by 50 per cent, today has no greater purchasing value than the smaller income of ten years ago.

Now let us suppose that exactly the same rate of progression continues for ten years as obtained for the past ten years. For our purposes we may adopt any figure as representing the present value and, hence, wealth of our concern. We will, for the purposes of this calculation, adopt the rule of three. According to this rule, the concern is worth 12 million dollars and does 4 million dollars of business per year. If we should double our business each five years, five years hence we would be doing 8 million dollars of business, and the concern in value would be considered worth 24 million dollars, and at the end of ten years we would be doing 16 million dollars in business, and the concern would be valued at 48 million dollars.

But ten years hence each dollar will be worth only two-thirds of what a present dollar is worth — dollars in gold (and the gold standard makes it necessary for us to figure on gold values). Our concern ten years hence, then, instead of being worth four times what it is at present, namely, 48 million dollars, will be worth in gold at its present value only two-thirds of 48 million dollars, or 32 million dollars. It would appear, then, that instead of the value of our concern having quadrupled, it would have only increased 266⅔ per cent.

My son James, being conservatively inclined, has stated that he would be satisfied if the concern doubled its value in ten years. Now this would mean that ten years hence we would be doing 8 million dollars of business, and by the rule of three we would be worth 24 million dollars, measured in gold value. But ten years hence the actual value of a dollar will only be two-thirds of what it is now, and so compared with present prices and conditions, the concern ten years hence would be worth only 16 million dollars. So it will be seen that the actual increase in the value of the property would be only 4 million dollars or 33 per cent. Considering the compounding of interest, this would indicate only about a 2 per cent per annum growth to our estate.

Providing the hypothesis is correct that gold is depreciating at the rate of 5 per cent, money loaned at 7 per cent would give 2 per cent growth per annum to an estate. There are other matters which I recognize are to be considered in this, one of the principal ones being the living expenses of the stockholders.

If our money was loaned at 7 per cent, the living expenses of the owners might fully equal the 2 per cent margin of profit, whereas in our business, such as I have figured, the increased value of the estate is reckoned to be 2 per cent above the living expenses and some of the incidental investments made outside of the newspaper business. I think we ought to take all of these matters, however, into full consideration, and that we should take particular care not to deceive ourselves by making any calculation on a wrong basis.

The fact of the matter is that the world is doing business on a financial and monetary platform which instead of being fixed, as the solid earth, is not so much fluctuating as steadily and progressively changing its position in one direction relative to all other things.

In order to make correct measurements and hence correct estimates, it is necessary for us to always keep in mind the fact that our measuring stick, which is gold value, is constantly diminishing in length.

From what we have learned in the recent past, it seems to me that it would be safe for us to charge off of each year's profits, by cash, and appreciation, 5 per cent in order to rectify the changing length of our gold measuring stick.

For instance, if from our books it should appear that during the year 1910 the capital value of our concern had increased by appreciation 1 million dollars, we should recognize the diminishing value of gold, by charging off 5 per cent, or $50,000, of this profit.

It occurs to me, here, that perhaps not only should this $50,000 be charged off, but $50,000 of every other 1 million dollars. One year hence a million dollars worth of gold will only buy what can now be bought for $950,000. If this concern is worth 12 million dollars today and if it is estimated to be worth 13 million dollars one year from today, then instead of it being worth $12,950,000, it might be reckoned to be worth only 13 million dollars less (13 × $50,000) or $650,000, or $12,350,000, and therefore the actual increase in value would have only been $350,000 instead of 1 million dollars.

I am going to give more attention to this idea.

It does seem to me that a man of my business experience and habit of analyzation should be able to instantly determine the existence or nonexistence of a profit and loss item equaling $650,000. However, if I am so weak in this matter, what must be the mental attitude of the vast majority of my fellow businessmen who have neither the time, inclination, nor ability to consider such problems. Under these conditions it is no wonder that the world at large considers all business transactions as mere gambling and guesswork.

I can well imagine how an innumerable host of men would laugh at my cogitations and accuse me of unprofitable theories, and as being thoroughly impracticable. Perhaps 999,999 men out of every million regard a gold dollar as a fixed and invariable quantity. These men speak of dollars as measures of wealth and income, as though dollars were as substantial and permanent as geometrical figures. They have been educated to believe that the gold standard was in reality a standard, a thing as fixed and to be depended upon as a pound, a yard, a foot, an inch, a ton, or an ounce. The ordinary man takes his position on standardized money much as the savage holds his position on the moving earth. The savage sees the sun rise and set and he imagines that the sun is moving from east to west over him, occupying a fixed position. He never dreams that the sun is relatively to himself fixed, and that the motion of the earth carries him under the sun rather than the sun over him.

The ordinary civilized man stands on his gold dollar and sees the prices of things which he buys rise or fall — in these days generally rise — and never dreams that relatively these things are stationary. He does not recognize that the apparent rise of prices of commodities is only apparent and that at present, at least, prices remain stationary and that gold is falling.

It is said, and I believe that statistics will prove it, that at least 98 men out of 100 who attempt business fail. It is probable that the 2 per cent of businessmen who do not fail are composed of two sets of men — one an infinitely small number who really know and understand the laws of business and obey the laws, and the other the numerically larger set who simply watch and imitate the actions of the knowing few.

There are very good reasons why not only the whole civilized world but the business world is confused and distracted by present conditions.

I believe that there is double as much gold in the world today as there was thirty or forty years ago. It is stated that more gold has been produced in the last ten years than was produced in the hundred years preceding this decade.

Human history is over four thousand years old. During the whole of this period, history has been made and set down in books, and is crystallized into a general understanding of world conditions.

Nearly all of the knowledge that civilization has today is based upon the history of the experience of the race prior to forty years ago. Yet during this period of forty years, gold — the basis of all of our business transactions — has doubled in quantity. In ten years the gold output has been equal to from 20 to 50 per cent of the total gold previously existing.

Gold is being produced today at the rate of 435 million dollars per annum. Only ten years ago the annual production was some 200 million dollars. The value of the annual gold production today is greater than was the aggregate value of the annual production of both gold and silver when fourteen years ago the famous Bryan free silver campaign was made in this country.

The gold-standard men who fought Bryan at that time believed and asserted that only financial catastrophe could follow the continuation of a system which would introduce new money metal as rapidly as it was presumed would follow the success of the Bryan idea of silver money. And yet, as a matter of fact, business is having to be conducted in the face of a larger inflow of monetary metal than was anticipated as a result of free silver legislation in 1896.

All of those business principles and maxims which held good for thousands of years, when money metals were being worn out more rapidly than they were mined, and even during the whole of last century when the production of money metal was slow in comparison with the growth of the use of money metal, have been annihilated by present conditions.

I am convinced that cataclysms, panics, and financial chaos must continue until after all the business public and a large part of the world shall have adjusted themselves to the present conditions. The capitalist and money-lender must change their methods. It seems to me that the whole banking system which is founded on customs and practices more than a century old is obsolescent. We are well advanced into an entirely new business era. The businessman of today must no longer read history to learn how to govern himself. He must take it for granted that most things that were good business up to ten or twenty years ago are now bad business.

It is a good thing for the shrewd and knowing young businessman to recognize and make a profit from the almost universal lack of wisdom and knowledge that surrounds him. He knows and should profit by the knowledge that a gold dollar borrowed today can be paid back at the end of ten years with 66 cents. He should recognize, however, that the vast majority of these dollars are held by men who have no true conception of this condition of affairs — men who are glad to lend their money at 4, 5, and 6 per cent interest, because they have no idea that even at 4 per cent they are actually presenting to the borrower 1 per cent of their capital; at 5 per cent they are actually lending money at no real interest; and at 6 per cent they are actually obtaining an income of not over 1 per cent.

This remarkable change in business conditions is going to have one effect. It is going to wipe out of existence the fortunes of those indolent inheritors of wealth, whose wealth is composed of bonds and other interest-bearing securities.

Per contra, it is going to give to the active and intelligent young masters of business of this generation the opportunity to sweep up and convert to their own ownership, control, and use that vast area of capital that has been accumulated by the great savers of previous generations.

Up to half a century ago, during most of the time when such economists as David A. Wells were writing and governing the actions of the business world, the only safe and absolutely certain way of growing wealthy was saving money and lending it at interest, and saving the interest and lending it again. I remember that David A. Wells in one of his famous essays stated that, as the average profit of all business transactions in the United States did not exceed 2 per cent, every man who borrowed money at 6 per cent stood to be an average loser of 4 per cent per annum.

During those times and for many years previous to those times, the dollar, instead of being a diminishing quantity, was an increasing quantity. Each year found it capable of purchasing commodities that were of more value than those commodities which could be purchased for the same value the year previous. All that is changed now. The one possession which can be counted on more than any other to depreciate in value is money. The one business that for ages was the most sure and profitable, namely, that of money lending, has become no longer profitable, but dependable as a loser.

Before this existing young generation has passed from the world, there will be an entire change in the personnel of plutocracy. The rich of today will not, perhaps, have become poor absolutely, but they, represented by their families, will have become relatively poor. The great financiers, the owners of great wealth in 1950, will be those who have not only borrowed money liberally, but who have been able to borrow on such safe terms as to enable them easily to repay when the time comes, and who have further made a wise investment of the money.

While gold and other forms of liquid capital are depreciating in value, it must be remembered that money — gold or other forms of liquid capital — exists in the aggregate in a very small proportion relative to other property.

For instance, I believe that there are only some 11 billion dollars of gold-flowing money in the whole world. The sum may be less, and yet the actual bank deposits in the United States alone today amount to over 14 billion dollars. Like conditions exist all over the world. Beyond these 14 billions of deposits in this country, which are the basis of credit capital, there is a vast quantity of other liquid capital in the shape of easily negotiable bonds and other certificates of debt.

But thinking of the gold and all of the bank and other credits, still the aggregate is perhaps not 20 per cent of the total property value of the world. No man, therefore, can afford to be in debt to such an amount that he cannot, when the money debt falls due, easily repay the same in money.

It is needless to say that the demand loans from banks, or even time loans from commercial banks, are the worst possible form of borrowing money.

Gold is constantly decreasing in value. Land is constantly increasing in value. The numerical increase in population is perhaps pretty near[ly] equal in proportion to that of the increase in gold output. Land cannot be increased in quantity or volume. Population demands land. Land in all countries has always been considered the very best possible basis of credit. It has simply got to increase in value, as the demand for food and shelter grows. However, land values have a peculiarity. While on the average they are constantly and steadily increasing, individual blocks of land only increase by jumps. There are long periods of stationary value, and even periods of retrogression in value, but sooner or later, inevitably, prices rise.

During my early business career I felt it was not economical for me to invest any of my small capital in real estate. Of late years I have become sufficiently well-to-do and my business has extended to such an amount that reserve capital is necessary. Recognizing, as I have done, the fall in the value of money and the increasing value of property (and I have recognized this merely as a matter of observation, long before I discovered or even thought of the causes), I have been willing to accumulate real estate. I have felt that reserve capital in this form was more profitable than reserve capital in bank deposits or bonds. It is always possible to borrow money on real estate by means of mortgages. It seems to me that it would be good policy for our concern to own real estate which, in this country, is increasing at an average rate of much more than 6 per cent, and in case of need to borrow money by mortgaging this real estate.

Our concern, as a whole perhaps, owns several hundred thousand dollars worth of unencumbered real estate. This unencumbered real estate is really a reservoir of capital that can be tapped in ordinary times, but never in times of panic. It is my intention to try and impress upon my sons, and perhaps partnership and other business associates, some of the views I have hereinbefore expressed.

But I recognize fully the danger of too strongly urging a one-sided view of the situation, namely, the view of the advisability of borrowing money. Never, under any circumstances, would I advise my sons or business associates to borrow money, except on long-time loans, and even then I would not advise them to borrow money to any considerable extent except to extend their business and other holdings in an almost absolutely sure profit-paying way. I should advise them always to have a certain part of their possessions in such a form as would enable them, without too great sacrifice, to obtain all the money that would be needed to meet falling-due obligations.

Let us take an example — the Cleveland *Press*. Supposing we set its value at 3 million dollars. Newspaper property, for reasons easily recognizable, is the least practical basis for credit. If the Cleveland *Press* was worth 3 million dollars, and if it owned $500,000 worth of real estate, it is probable that a larger sum could be borrowed on the real estate than on the whole credit of the newspaper aside from the real estate.

The concern should always have, then, a sufficient amount of real estate on which money could be borrowed so that the aggregate money received from this real estate loan added to the bank deposits and ordinary bank credit, in time of extreme panic or depression, would equal any possible falling-due financial obligation. So long as this condition can be kept in existence, I think I would advise the most progressive and aggressive conduct of business extension possible.

No opportunity should be lost to acquire capital when the same can be acquired on such terms as will insure safety in the matter of repayment.

It has always been my desire to make corporation dividends as small as would be consented to by the stockholders, in order that as much capital as possible could be kept in the hands of the skillful managers of the corporations.

It is inevitable that all the money distributed in the way of dividends will be dissipated in one way or another by those receiving it, so that in times of stress it can never be recalled in any considerable amount to meet the exigencies of business.

No hardship is ever suffered either by the stockholders, for, while some economy is enforced on them, the money that is withheld from them is ninety-nine times out of a hundred more profitably employed by the corporation managers acting for a corporation than it could be by the stockholders acting individually. The history of this concern of ours furnishes the indubitable evidence of what I have said in this disquisition.

A Question

[*October 3, 1910*]

A year or two ago in one of my disquisitions I tried to define wealth. My conclusions were at that time that wealth was mainly composed of "knowing how to do."

Two of the tenets of modern science are: (1) matter is indestructible; (2) that forces and energies, while convertible, are indestructible. These two ideas are referred to as "conservation of matter" and "conservation of energy." The adjective "material" derives from the noun "matter." As distinguished from things spiritual or intellectual, the word "matter" stands for substance, something tangible.

When we speak of material wealth we mean the existence of substance in some form or another — something that can be touched by the hand, seen by the eye, tasted, and smelled under certain conditions, and under certain conditions capable of making its presence known through the ear. Material wealth is some form of matter that is useful to man — is valuable to him, and hence is desired.

The word "materialism" is used often enough as a term of reproach. The man who overmuch desires, or is supposed to overmuch desire, the possession of material things is the object of scorn to him who desires knowledge and spiritual refinement more than he desires material possessions.

We speak of a man being spiritually rich, and we can speak of a man having a wealth of knowledge.

But riches spiritual and wealth consisting of knowledge only are held in contempt by those men calling themselves practical. In fact, the word "wealth" as used by economists generally, and as vulgarly understood, applies only to things whose existence is proved by one or more of the five senses. It applies to valuable substances generally.

It is admitted that there are intangible forms of wealth, such for instance as a franchise granted by a government, the right to manufacture certain

633

things in certain ways granted by government patent, the "goodwill" attaching to a name or trademark as a result of the long use of the same in a successful business or the extensive advertisement of the same. There are other forms of intangible wealth.

However, in all of these cases of wealth that may be described as intangible, the value of the same rests upon the ability of the possessor to produce something that has substance, and a substance that is valuable, material, and tangible, without anything more than ordinary intelligence in the directing of the operation. For instance, the owner of a patent right to manufacture some special kind of machine does not require to have — and having, to make use of — such intellectual force or capacity as was necessary to discover or invent the machine that he manufactures.

The man who owns a patent right owns a property, the capital value of which can be appraised and which is appraised, and the government taxes it in proportion to its value. But the man whose brain conceived of and invented the machine in question and who has the ability to invent other machines of great value is not considered the owner of any property which can be appraised and valued and taxed.

A lawyer or other professional man who is possessed of knowledge and expertness in the use of same is capable of selling his services for a large price. There are such men who can and do sell their services at such a rate as produces $100,000 a year or more. The knowledge and expertness of such a man has a productive value greater than a million dollars worth of other property in material form. Yet this man's possession of faculties is not reckoned as property, something that can be appraised and a value set on it, or to be used for the purpose of taxation.

For the most part, then, wealth consists of some sort of substance.

All the wealth of the people of the United States has been appraised at an aggregate of 120 billion dollars. I have assumed that fully one-half of this 120 billion dollars consists of natural resources — of something toward the existence of which man has contributed nothing by his works. Then 60 billion dollars represents the value of all the material things in this country that [have] been produced in part or wholly by man's manipulation.

When it is considered that this country has been occupied by civilized white men for three hundred years, and that these men are in point of physical and intellectual strength and energy the pick of the whole world's population, it is remarkable that all the savings of material wealth in three hundred years only equals the product of two years labor of the present population.

All the savings of three centuries, then, amount to a per capita possession of $600, more or less, for every person in the country. When it is considered that any fairly intelligent and physically strong man can at common labor earn $600 a year, this small savings account seems to be absurdly small.

Taking the whole capital wealth of the United States of 120 billion dollars, and allow for it a rate of interest higher than the normal — viz., 5 per cent — it will be seen that the interest income from all this wealth would be only 6 billion dollars.

The value of the annual product of the country is something like 30 billion dollars. Therefore, labor and intelligence are producing in this country an income four times as great as that that could be produced by interest at 5 per cent on the aggregate savings of three centuries of intelligent labor.

These people of the United States are a new people. This nation is the youngest of all the great nations. It has had to contend with no great cataclysms of nature or eruptions of human passions. Among all the nations it has been the most fortunate in having been able to save nearly all of its products.

The wealth of this nation is fully double that of any other civilized nation. Therefore, in three hundred years the people of this nation have saved twice as much as have the people of any other nation, three, four, six, and ten times as old.

What has become of the wealth — the savings — of Italy, of Spain, of Germany, France and England, of Russia, of the Austrian Empire, and of the numerous other small European nations, and large nations of other continents?

Is it not quite evident that the material possessions of any people must be limited by natural laws? There is a point beyond which the level of wealth cannot rise, and below which it constantly fluctuates, falling at times, sometimes falling very low, sometimes rising, but never rising above the high point designated.

I have in mind something analogous to this law limiting wealth.

In this country (southern California) the annual evaporation of water in an exposed reservoir is five feet per annum. In this particular section of the country where I am living the average rainfall is, say, twelve inches. The rainfall, then, is only one-fifth of the evaporation.

In about ten weeks on the average, the air is capable of absorbing, and does absorb, as much water as is precipitated in rain in a year. This condition of relative rainfall and evaporation limits the possibility of water storage in this country. At any ordinary reservoir site in this section, the holding capacity of a dam increases so as to double approximately for every five feet of increase in the height of the dam. This means that half of all the water stored in any local reservoir is lost by evaporation each year, since evaporation equals five feet per year.

Now, as the dam or reservoir rises, so also increases proportionately the superficial area of the water behind the dam. As the amount of rainfall is not only less, but much less, than the evaporation, it matters not how high the dam is built, the water impounded in the dam can never rise higher than the point where the surface of the dam is so large that the watershed is only sufficient to raise the dam [water] five feet in a year.

Of course, it can be seen that at any place where the rainfall is greater or equal to the evaporation, the contents of the reservoir would go on rising continuously from year to year if not drawn out.

It would seem that there is a natural law which prevents the growth of a nation's wealth beyond a certain point. The highest level of wealth can only be at some point where climate and other causes destroy existing material wealth as fast as man can produce other material wealth.

Now we know that all sorts of grain have, after being harvested and stored, a life of but a short period, from one to, say, five or six years. Nuts as a rule continue edible not much longer than a year after they are gathered. Fruits and even most of the vegetables from the truck garden can be kept in edible form for only a very short time unless preserved in some way or another.

The life of the most of the meat-producing animals is very short. A cow, unless it is killed and eaten in twelve or fourteen years after its birth, has lost its food value. The meat of an animal after being slaughtered cannot be preserved in its fresh form for more than a comparatively few weeks even by the most modern methods of refrigeration. In other forms it may be preserved in a fairly edible state two or three years.

Therefore, all that kind of material property which consists of foodstuff, if not soon consumed by man, is destroyed in a comparatively short time by the elements, and kept at a comparatively low value in the aggregate, just as the water in my reservoir is evaporated.

There are other forms of property. Perhaps the most durable of these are represented by some form of house-building. Now, if the house is composed of wood, its protection beyond a certain period of years will only result from such considerable care as to make it financially impracticable to preserve it for a long period of time. Houses of brick and stone are both soon enough destroyed by the action of the elements, but their value is destroyed much more quickly by reason of their becoming obsolete, and hence valueless as possessions of a people whose civilization is rapidly advancing.

It is doubtful if in all the world there exists today more than a few million dollars worth of buildings that existed half a millennium ago. I mean by this that there do not exist such buildings which have any considerable value on account of their being usable. Such value as they have is entirely

on account of certain sentiments (relics, perhaps, of past glories, or cu-
riosities).

Material wealth, therefore, must be considered something as very perishable.

By reason of two things — (1) wear and tear by use or by climate and
other forces of nature, and (2) growing obsoleteness — it is reasonable to
expect that within a generation all but an infinitesimal small percentage of the
60 billion dollars of man-made wealth in existence today will have disappeared.

By reason of the fact that such a large proportion of this existing wealth
is of such short life, it is conceivable and probable that the average longevity
of material wealth does not much exceed two years. I have heretofore
pointed out [that] the product of this people annually now equals half the
value of all existing man-made wealth in the country.

It is possible, then, that natural law is such that under present conditions
of the highest forms of civilizations the level of aggregate wealth cannot
rise above a two-years product. As civilization advances, and as man learns
better and better how to do, man is learning amongst other things not only
to produce more material but produce material which on the average will
last longer as a useful possession.

For instance, our railroads are using steel for rails instead of iron, the
former being capable of standing wear and tear longer than the latter; and
where the railroads, the nation, the state, and county and municipal corporations were formerly building in this country wooden bridges, they are now
replacing these with structures of reinforced concrete and stone.

Doubtless there are many other instances of the increase of production
of longer-lived material wealth.

I maintain that by far the greater proportion of the wealth of any nation
and any man consists not in existing things but in man's knowledge of how
to produce other and new things.

The ratio of the value of knowledge of how to do, and of things done,
has been indicated above, where it is shown that the men of this country
produce every year four times as much as would be produced by a high
rate of interest on the value of all things previously produced by man and
nature combined.

If our wealth, then, consists of 80 per cent of knowledge of how to do
things, and only 20 per cent of existing material things, and if only half
of material things have been man-made, it stands to reason that it is absurd
for great civilized nations to engage in internecine warfare and striving for
the possession of this small fragment of 10 per cent of the total of the people's wealth when there are so much greater prizes to be contended for.

The great political struggle of the present day in this country is that of the people as a whole trying to "conserve" for the whole peoples' use the as yet undistributed natural resources.

The whole natural resources are set down at a value of 60 billion dollars. The undistributed portion of these resources is comparatively small. Then all this struggle and bother is being made about something of so little value as not to equal perhaps what can be, and what is being produced, by a few months or perhaps only a few weeks of national effort.

The one great prize that is worth being contended for is that of the possession of knowledge. The field of knowledge, then, is the great common in which not only do the people have an equal right but it is a field that can be monopolized by no one.

Poverty does not shut the door or close the gate on this field. Ignorance and supine weakness of purpose, or rather supine weakness of purpose alone, can be said to bar any man in this country or any other country from entering into possession of all that can be desired for the welfare and happiness of any human being.

Much is being said in these days of inequality of opportunity. It is presumed that certain few men have such control over opportunities that they can debar all but their favorites from enjoying opportunity. Notwithstanding the specious arguments which are used to uphold this proposition, I regard the whole proposition of there being any inequality of opportunity as almost axiomatically absurd.

There is far more truth in the old saying "that you cannot keep a good man down."

Willful sloth and cowardice — unwillingness to incur the danger and the effort necessary to enjoy full freedom, economically and politically — are alone the occasions for any man failing to obtain his birthright of opportunity.

A Theory of Waste

HAVING REGARD TO ITS EFFECT IN ADVANCING
HUMAN MATERIAL WELFARE
AND INTELLECTUAL DEVELOPMENT—
IN FACT, CIVILIZATION

[*November 4, 1910*]

Although the first paragraph makes clear that this disquisition is speculative, it should be noted that the internal structure indicates that Scripps was theorizing on the basis of assumed facts which he did not ordinarily accept as such.

I do not intend to here develop an argument. I only propose to formulate, in the shape of notes, some ideas and suggestions that have lately occurred to my mind. It is possible that this subject will seize upon me and compel me to give it further and long consideration, so that at some future time I may treat it more fully.

Is waste an evil or a good? Can a natural law be an evil?

Is not the collective mind of the whole human race far more liable to arrive at wise conclusions than the mind of any individual of the race?

What would occur if every human being should suddenly, or even by degrees, become possessed of that intellectual faculty or peculiarity which now marks only a very infinitesimal number of the whole family of man?

At the present time there are only a few people out of every million who practice to any considerable extent what is called economy — that is to say, who do not consume, immediately after having become possessed of it, any natural or artificial product however come by.

These few accumulate possessions such as land, buildings, all sorts of manufacturing implements and organs of trade, money in the form of coined

639

metal or government certificates of the same, of obligations of other persons such as notes and mortgages, etc.

On two previous occasions in my attempts to define what wealth is, I have tried to show that the amount of material wealth in existence is not only very small but that it cannot be increased beyond a very limited extent.

Property in foodstuffs of all sorts and descriptions is so perishable that on the average perhaps not over three months of existence in useful form can be attributed to the aggregate of food provision.

The life of wearing material, while many times longer than that of food provision, is yet so brief that even without use, with the greatest care, no article of wearing apparel can exist in useful form longer than a period of one lifetime.

Wooden buildings decay rapidly. Even stone, brick, and cement buildings cannot withstand the elements for more than a fraction of the period of historical times. The most substantial products of engineering conception can endure but little longer than the most substantial dwelling-house. And even these two most substantial forms of man-made products can have a life of usefulness far shorter than their mere material endurance on account of obsolescence.

I have shown elsewhere that all of the existing property or man-made wealth in this country is only equal in the aggregate of what might be, and could be, reproduced in six months if all the people in this country were to devote themselves to productive labor for six months.

Now let us imagine that all the men, women, and children of this country should be set to work, or should set themselves to work, as producers, even under our present very crude and wasteful methods, and that at the same time they should not be allowed by themselves or others to consume anything more than is required for their material subsistence and for a perfectly rational enjoyment of life. (Beyond question these two great needs could be supplied by consumption of not more than one-quarter of the total product.)

In that case the material wealth of the country, as present existing, would be doubled in 8 months, something more than trebled in 16 months, something more than quadrupled in 2 years, and at the end of 30 years — providing there were no laws of nature that worked to destroy the product of human labor — the material wealth of this country would be forty or fifty times as great as at present.

To provide as far as possible against the natural destruction of the products of labor, our society should produce annually in food provisions no more than our people could consume, plus what we could transport and sell to other peoples for consumption. The amount of labor, then, devoted to the production of food provisions would be but an infinitesimal fraction of the whole potential productivity of the whole people.

As wearing apparel has a longer life than food provisions by some twenty or thirty times, the value of wearing apparel capable of being manufactured and stored up might be far greater than that of stored foodstuffs. But what service would this saving of clothing be? Each day and each month and each year the whole people, by devoting a very small fragment of their total labor to the producing of clothing, could supply the current needs and in advancing usefulness of form and quality. The making, then, of clothing in advance of needs and storing it up for future use would be only making for a condition of future idleness in this department.

To what other fields of production could the labor of all the people be devoted? Having found that only a fragment of from 1 to, say, 5 per cent of human labor could be devoted profitably and intelligently to the two first greatest needs of a man, viz., food and clothing, there would remain from 99 to 95 per cent of productive labor to be devoted to other things.

Next in importance to food, perhaps, are the two other necessities — clothing and housing.

Of the whole 120 billion dollars of property in this country, I have estimated that perhaps one-half, say, 60 billion dollars, is represented by some form of natural resources. Of the remaining 60 billion dollars it is not to be supposed that over one-third is represented by housing — say, 20 billion dollars.

Now elsewhere I have indicated that the product of human labor in this country amounts to some 24 billion dollars a year. In the same way, I have estimated that not more than one-fourth of the whole potential energy of the country is employed in producing; therefore, our people might by labor produce property at the rate of 100 billion dollars a year. If all of the 95 per cent of productive labor not employed in producing food and clothing was devoted to house-building, at the end of one year we would have our people living in five times as many houses or five times as good houses as at present. Assuming that the race would be advantaged if its housing improvement was increased tenfold it would require only two years of the total producing labor of the country, over and above that devoted to food and clothing, to supply this kind of housing.

Assuming that such improved houses would not have a useful life of more than thirty years, it would appear that only two years in thirty would be required by the people to furnish their housing, while at the same time that they were doing this work of building houses they would be supplying all their needs for food and clothing; therefore, not over $6\frac{2}{3}$ per cent of the total human labor would be required for housing, perhaps not over

6 per cent, and that, too, in furnishing houses of such a character and such a number that the poorest inhabitant of this country could have a dwelling equal to that possessed now by the most fortunate of our citizens outside of the ranks of the few millionaires.

Now, then, let us allow that food and clothing would require 5 per cent of the total labor, and that housing will require 7 per cent, we have only disposed of 12 per cent of the aggregate of potential produce. That leaves 88 per cent of productive labor of the country to be employed.

Into what fields of production can we turn this 88 per cent of labor? There is the field of improved highways, steam railroads and their equipment, improved waterways and boats, greater harbors and better harbors. We have allowed that 88 billion dollars worth of labor per annum can be called upon for these uses.

I believe that the total present value of the railroads — including such natural resources as their real estate and an infinite quantity of what the public calls "water" — amounts to only 16 billion dollars. It is probable that 10 billion dollars would be a large sum to assess as the value of what human labor has put into our railroads. Then, providing that the whole of the left-over 88 billion dollars of productive labor of the country is devoted to railroads, in one year's time we would have ten times as many or ten times better railroad equipment.

Another year's labor would give us rivers and harbors and boat equipment probably twenty or more times superior to our present possessions.

Let me put all these above propositions in another way:

We have a productive labor capacity of 100 billion dollars a year.

Five billion dollars worth of labor a year would furnish us all our food and clothing.

That would leave us a margin of 95 billion dollars a year.

Our housing, we will say, may now be worth 20 billion dollars, it being remembered that real estate and all natural resources are left out of consideration in this particular argument.

Our railroads, less real estate and "water," are worth, say, 10 billion dollars. Our water and harbor possessions, aside from natural resources, probably will not exceed in value an amount over 2 billion dollars.

Then our present possessions in these three departments amount to about 32 billion dollars. If all our productive labor, over and above that employed in the food and clothing field, was devoted to these three departments, we would produce each year three times as much as we have got, to be added to that which we already possess. At the end of the first year, then, our possessions of this character would be four times what they are at present. At the end of two years they would be seven times as great, and at the end of three years they would be ten times as great.

Our civilization — our intellectual capacity for using (that is to say, en-joying) such possessions — is not yet developed to anything like the extent that would make such a vast increase of possessions worthwhile.

But after we have arranged to supply all of our necessities of food and clothing and shelter and transportation, in three years we will have noth-ing on which to employ thereafter for the next twenty-seven or more years the 95 per cent of the labor not required for food and clothing production, unless we devote it exclusively or almost exclusively to purely aesthetic pursuits.

I doubt if as much even as 10 per cent of the total productive labor of all the people in this country could be profitably and usefully employed in the production of food, clothing, shelter, transportation, and every other product in material form that could be useful or even enjoyable to and by the people.

According to this view, 90 per cent of the potential productive energies of the people must either remain idle, or else a large part of the population must devote themselves not only to consuming products but to wasting and destroying them. The larger the number of people that are not working productively, the more labor there will be for others to perform. Those that are wasting — that is to say, consuming uselessly — labor products are adding still more to the amount that must be produced by the producers, and those that are actually employed in tearing down and destroying that which others are producing will add a further quantity of work for the producers.

I don't say that it is good for the human race that a large part of its members shall be non-productive, and that another large part shall be wasteful, and still another large part shall be destructive. I only recognize that man is subject to universal law and that the race of man as a whole cannot be in the least disobedient to nature's laws.

Therefore, I cannot believe that there is anything illegal or vicious in social conditions that have existed in the past and are existing now.

All that has been, has been right. All that is, is right. All that has been that has been changed, has been rightly changed. All that is now that is to be changed, will be rightly changed.

The intellectual and physical development of man has been the result of man's contention with natural forces, and civilization is the outcome of the struggle. Civilization is a term that defines not man's overcoming of nat-ural laws but his growing understanding and use of the same.

Infinitely far away is the period when the race of man will cease to exist, and during all this period, or at least during a large part of this period, man may be expected to progress in knowledge and civilization — that is to say, in the understanding and use of natural laws and resources.

Whether or not the time shall ever come when man shall become so well instructed in, and have so great an understanding of, the laws of nature that every individual living man shall enjoy equally, one with another, in any society, or in the world's society, the best conceivable life, I do not know.

However, I am inclined to believe in the doctrine that I think was taught by the German philosopher Fichte, viz., the doctrine of opposition — of the necessity of contention and of struggle — that this or these are the very principles of life itself.

Is not waste and so-called willful destruction a part of the natural law of opposition?

Has not man really discovered without knowing it the principle of life as being that of opposition, and that he is employing it in a way of waste and destruction to advance himself the more rapidly in his intellectual and physical development?

Now imagine this kind of an Utopia: In three, or five, or a hundred years, let society accumulate every possible material object that can be useful to man, including transportation facilities, housing, clothing, and food. Let us imagine that aside from food, all other forms of possessions at a given time have a lifetime of thirty years. Then let us set aside 2 per cent of our population to produce the current supply of food, or let each one devote 2 per cent of his time — say, seven or eight days per year — to food production. Now then, the world has everything else it needs for thirty years, and suppose the race as a whole should decide to rest for that thirty years, what would the 100 to 300 or 400 million people now or then in this country be doing? If they all lived in peace and all refrained from every sort of productive employment what would happen, what could happen?

Socialism, Individualism, Etc.

[*December 20, 1910*]

"Miramar," Calif., December 20, 1910

Mr. R. F. Paine
Mr. W. B. Colver

Gentlemen:

I have been interested in trying to find out the point of your controversy on the subject of socialism. I am afraid I have not been successful. So far as I have been able to judge from all both of you have written and said, and from your actions, you are both so fully agreed with the other that no outsider — even supposing I am an outsider — would be able to discover the point of your differences.

It has been said that nearly all of our wars and other contentions have been the result of pure misunderstanding — perhaps in the use or meaning of a single word.

I believe that if all humanity equally well understood the proper definition of the word "wealth," humanity would not quit fighting but it would save a lot of time and energy that is now wasted, and work more effectively.

John Ruskin has said that "wealth is life." Veblen infers that it is technology.

I have tried to formulate a definition myself, using English words, and I have said that wealth is only "knowing how to do things."

If Ruskin and Veblen and myself are right in our various definitions, there is no cause for quarrel between a Socialist and an individualist. In fact, the thing over which individualists and Socialists quarrel is found not to exist.

Physicists are finally determined that matter is not substance — that is to say, it is not what the mind usually conceives as substance. Matter is a condition. It is energy.

Wealth should not be considered by economists, then, as being any more

645

a substantial substance than is matter a substance to the eye and the mind of physicists. Nothing that exists on earth is of any intrinsic value except to the individual who knows how to do things with it for his own service.

If, then, there is no wealth-substance no one can possess wealth or have a legal title to that which does not exist.

Don't pooh-pooh me or laugh at me. Ruskin and Veblen and some scores of other people are no more entitled to be laughed at and jeered at than were their few forebears of only a few centuries ago when they declared that the earth was round instead of flat, and that instead of the sun moving around the earth the earth moved around the sun.

That wealth is not material and is not a substance to which any man individually can have or claim to have a title to as his own is easily proven.

Even the dullest and least logical of minds can easily grasp a part of the idea when he is asked to account for and point out in substantial form the material possessions of a single nation like our own.

What have we to show in a material way for all of the products of labor during the three centuries or more that our white race has been in this country? Aside from our natural resources — the largest element of which has an appraised valuation as land surface — this nation does not possess over 30 billion dollars worth of things which owe their shape and value to man's handling.

That is to say, the totality of existing things thus produced has not an appraised valuation greater than the appraised value of the product of one year of our labor. Where has gone all the products of the year before last, and of the centuries of years before that? They have gone nowhere. They did not exist in material form.

Such wealth as did exist consisted of human life, as Ruskin says; of technology, as Veblen says; of the knowing how to do of the men of those times, as I would say.

The whole wealth of the United States today is appraised at 120 billions. The interest or rent product of this wealth is less than 5 per cent annually; less, then, than 6 billions.

The annual product of life energy and so-called accumulated wealth together is some 30 billions. Then at least four-fifths of the total productivity remains uncapitalized in any form to which a legal property title such as a court could consider.

This wealth, then, is in the hands and in the possession of what you may call a form of socialism or individual possession.

A square rod of land being dealt with by a man who knows how to deal with it as well as an ordinary citizen is more productive than many square miles of the earth's surface to a man who knows no more how to deal with it than a savage Indian.

All of our quarrel between capitalists and proletariat and between two parts, respectively, individualists and Socialists, is about a fifth of our whole domain, and nobody in particular has given any attention to the other four-fifths.

The most that any landlord can own of any piece of land is not over a quarter and perhaps not a tenth of its intrinsic value reckoned by its productivity.

There is not an acre of farmland owned, as it is alleged, by the holder of its title deed but can and does produce four or five or ten or twenty times as much annually as the share that goes in rent to the alleged landlord — the man who is not lord of the land at all, the man who really has no control over the land's productivity.

The man who does not own the land that he works is not the man who cannot own it, but the man who will not take the little necessary trouble and exercise the little necessary self-restraint which would be required to dissolve the existing partnership between himself and his landlord.

No man can own and keep in possession today for a day an acre of land, or . . . any other piece of property which can be defined by title deed, who does not himself know how to make use of it, unless the party who does not know how to make use of it himself consents to and really elects to have a landlord or an employer over him or with him or under him.

I do not own a dollars worth of newspaper property which you men and your associates and possible successors could not take away from me at an hour's notice or on an instant.

You men have elected me to my position of authority and responsibility just as clearly and regularly as you and your fellows have ever elected a man to hold the office of mayor in your city or governor of your state.

All my wealth consists in knowing how to govern and direct an organization of men who have voluntarily formed the organization.

The agriculturists of this country produced this year 9 billions worth of product — practically one-third of the whole national product. As you know, gentlemen, farming does not pay. As I pointed out, the man who does not conduct his own farm cannot get more than a quarter of its actual production nor more than a tenth of its actual product. For such reasons as these, agriculture could not be profitable under universal landlordship. (Socialism would be universal landlordship.) For these reasons and others the farmers of this country possess not only four-fifths of the product and the means of product of agriculture, but — in small holdings — nearly all of the other fifth.

Then, in the agricultural department of the industry, which possesses one-third of the whole, the capitalist, so called, has not only a small interest, but for the best of reasons never can have a much larger interest.

Agriculture is capitalized at something like 30 billions, or one-fourth of the nation's wealth. The savings banks of this country hold some 4 billions of property of the common people. Building societies and other associations of this character represent not less than 6 billion more dollars — the two together not less than 10 billions. Add the 30 billions of agricultural wealth to this and you have 40 billions, or one-third of the national wealth. The homes and the home furnishings owned by the people away from the farms in value aggregate some billions more. Not less perhaps than one-half of the nation's total wealth to which legal title can be given is now in the hands of the commonalty.

The people, as I have said before, own — in their capacity for labor — four-fifths of the productivity aside from that which is represented by so-called capital or wealth, and they own one-half of that, that is to say, the property to which title can be given and courts can consider.

Thus, at the very least, the people now have possession of nine-tenths of the real wealth of the country, the wealth that can be defined in title deeds and the wealth that can be described as the "knowing how to do."

That leaves us in the condition of the whole nation rowing and "squabbling" over a measly one-tenth of the nation's possession.

If by socialism or any other form we should seize this and divide this one-tenth up equally amongst ourselves, we would only have property which would yield 3 billions a year to our 100 million people, or $30.00 a year to each individual. You would say that adding $150 a year to the average family of five persons would be a whole lot, but it would not be as much as any average laboring man could save from his waste or [add] to his income by very slight exercise of mental or physical effort, whether it should be by exercising his productive capacities or simple passive self-restraint.

I fully recognize and believe in the principle that the wage system is a slave system, and that the wage-taker is himself a slave. But I maintain that all slaves are either voluntary slaves, men who prefer to be slaves rather than free men, or else men who do not possess that which Ruskin, Veblen, and myself maintain is the only thing that is really wealth — the knowing how to do things.

The big thing that we men have to do, that we men who yearn for justice and a square deal, is to try to get our fellows to know what wealth is, to know that they possess most of it now, and to know how to individually keep possession of and make use of their possessions rather than [turn] over their capital savings, so called, to other men to keep and manage — to savings-bank directors, to insurance company officials, to railroad magnates who accept the public's money by the way of bond issue and watered stock.

Sometimes I reproach myself for allowing the newspapers which I control to teach the people that there is a possibility of their getting relief from suffering by sending millionaires to jail or depending upon legislatures and governors and congresses and presidents to watch over and control capitalists.

Every man should learn that his own material welfare depends 99 per cent on his individually "knowing how to do things" and what to do, and 1 per cent upon his fellows in the government knowing how to act collectively in securing the management of community affairs.

Sincerely yours,

E. W. Scripps

Arguments in Favor of the Closed Shop

[*February 3, 1911*]

Man is a gregarious animal. He, like other such animals, instinctively herds and organizes a herd government. This instinct to herd and organize is, I consider, the foundation principle upon which has been built organized society.[11]

I will not attempt to trace, as others may, the evidence of this herding instinct from the first primitive groups of mankind up to the point where there are great communities living in cities and great organizations evidenced by the state and nation.

While all men are attracted each to the other and into large groups, it is but natural that these larger groups should crystallize into almost innumerable subgroups of men. These smaller groups are attracted together by race affinities or by similarity of mental development, but they are more naturally formed by reason of common interest and desires.

Lawyers gather themselves together in communities in bar associations. The medical fraternity organize into local and larger societies. Merchants and manufacturers in every community form local associations. Even such small groups of men as are engaged in the banking business instinctively associate and organize. We have artists clubs and literary societies. In fact, wherever in any community there are a number of men engaged in the same calling, the herding instinct causes them to form associations and organize for mutual benefit.

Even agriculturists, who by reason of their occupation are scattered over wide territories and thus find it difficult to come in touch one with the other, submit to the herding instinct and sooner or later organize. The American Grange [is] an example.

Now, as a matter of course, laborers have the common herding instinct, and as a matter of course among them are formed groups and eventually

[11] An edited version of this disquisition appears in Cochran, *E. W. Scripps*, p. 259 f.

650

associations or unions composed of those laborers who have an identical trade or an almost identical trade.

It is natural and beneficial to society and the advance of civilization that all of these various organizations should attempt the task of mutual benefit and protection.

Therefore I consider it proof that labor not only has the right to organize, but that society benefits by its organization. But whether such a right exists or such a benefit exists, still primitive instincts are such that even if such combinations were harmful, they would have to be. If in society all the other units congregate and combine defensively and offensively, then it would be manifestly unjust to deny the right of labor to organize.

But the purpose of this disquisition is not primarily to defend the rights of labor to organize, but to set forth arguments favoring the closed shop.

If the principle of closed shop did not practically exist in every other organization, it would be unfair if only one of such organizations — viz., labor unions — should attempt to enforce it in their attitude toward the public. But it would be easy for anyone to demonstrate that the principle of the closed shop is a governing principle in every other association.

If we admit that labor has a right to, and ought to, organize for mutual benefit and mutual protection, since we know that there can be no such benefit or protection without the practice of offensive and defensive action, we cannot deny unions the right to so act.

Now it happens that the principle of the open shop would rob organized labor of all its offensive weapons and most of its defensive. Labor unions then have the moral right to strive strenuously for the closed shop, just as the employers who organize for their own benefit have the moral right to oppose any movement that they consider disadvantageous to themselves.

Some years ago Carroll D. Wright, who then held the position of Commissioner of Labor at Washington [under Roosevelt], made an official report to the government concerning the organization and development of labor unions in this country. It has been a number of years since I read this report, but as I remember, it furnished perfectly clear evidence that not only had all the laboring people in the United States, organized and unorganized, been greatly benefited by the development of union labor, but that the material welfare of the whole country had gained even more greatly from the same cause. The reading of this report will prove helpful to anyone seeking confirmation of the statements made herein.

Because of our democratic institutions and our comparatively free government, labor unions have been far more effective in this country than they have been in any other country.

Labor unionism is older in England and has been more completely organized there than here. England is the most democratic country in Europe, and hence labor unionism has been more effective there than in any other European country.

Labor unionism in France, which is now a democracy, has on account of racial peculiarities and historical national development taken a somewhat different form than it has in England.

I know less of the development of union labor in Germany than I do of it in the other countries mentioned. However, the German government has never been democratic, and the lack of freedom in that country has doubtlessly served to make unionism in Germany less efficient than in the more democratic countries.

Now, as I recall from my reading some comparatively recent statistics, the labor wage scale in the United States is three or four times what it is in England, and in England I believe it is twice what it is in Germany, and in Germany the wage scale is double or more than double the average wage scale in countries where labor unionism has not been developed at all or but slightly.

In fact, there seems there is a prima facie case established that the prosperity of a nation at large and of the employer and employee classes is in direct proportion to the wage scale. If, then, we can consider it proved that organized labor, the main principle of which is the closed shop, results in increased wages, it is at least possible to consider that the employing class and the capitalistic class benefit as much as if not more than the laboring class as a result of organized labor.

Parenthetically, we would have to admit there are opponents who raise the question, "Which is cause and which is effect?" and that they will also raise the question as to how much wages depend upon other conditions than social organization and customs.

I am myself a man of means and a large employer of labor. Naturally enough, my associates have been largely composed of other capitalists and employers. Often enough I have been held by my associates to be entirely inconsistent and foolishly blind to my own interests when I have advocated the cause of union labor and the closed shop.

It is useless, I have found, to attempt to discuss with these men the subject on moral grounds or even from a very large and general view of the subject. However, there is one argument that I generally use which generally nonplusses my contestant in an argument on this subject.

These men usually regard a common workingman as being a fool and incapable of knowing what his own best interest is and of gaining any real advantage from either large wages or assured employment.

They will always admit readily enough that the workingmen gain little or nothing at all from a big wage, because no matter how large the workingman's wage is, he will squander it.

I can easily then come to an agreement as to premises with my opponent in the argument on this subject. Having come to this agreement I then say: What difference does it make to us employers, capitalists, and businessmen as a class what wage we give our men so long as all of us give the same and no one of us has the advantage over the other by paying a lower wage, since all that we do is to lend, for a day or two or a week or a month at most, to our workingmen the money we are supposed to give them as wages? They no sooner get their wages than they come back to some of us and give us their wages in return for commodities or services which we sell at a large profit. We as a class get all our money back again anyway. We know this must be so because, as a rule, while the rich are growing richer very rapidly, only a few of the poor are becoming comparatively less poorer [*sic*]. If the wage-worker got and kept his money, then only could the moral question arise as to whether the union laboring man through the closed shop got more than his share of the joint product of capital and labor. But we cannot admit this so long as we hold to our first premise, viz., that the wage-earner is such a fool that he will not keep his wage when he gets it.

Now there is a doctrine that every active businessman and capitalist and employer maintains, and that is the "survival of the fittest." He believes in the doctrine that "might makes right." He believes it wrong for society to protect by organization the weaker units of the laboring class and hence he must admit that it is equally wrong for society to protect any other weakling.

In fact, the active businessman detests more than anything else the useless ward of a trustee — the ward whose property is protected by another and who has the benefit of its income and who labors not either with his hands or his brains.

Now, there exists no better means of transferring from the hands of the unfit ward to the fit, the active businessman and the man of financial power, than that of paying and causing others to pay to the laborer large wages which have to be paid by the inefficient ward of a trustee for all he obtains, just the same as it has to be paid by the capable man of affairs. All the money that this drone is compelled to disgorge to the laboring-man, the active businessman will sooner or later receive from the wage-worker and keep.

In fact, every businessman will admit that civilization and society advances in the direct proportion to the mobility of wealth, and if he admits that money moves more rapidly through the hands of the workingman and wage-earner than through any other hands, then he should admit that any system which permits the laboring-man to increase his wages is a good thing for society at large.

On Knowing How to Spend Money

[*April 7, 1914*]

This letter to McKee, a Fresno attorney, was not mailed, but was filed with the disquisitions.

"Miramar," Calif., April 7, 1914

Mr. Harry McKee
314 Forsyth Building
Fresno, Calif.

My dear Harry:

Yours of the 3d instant at hand. I think that this may be more a disquisition than a letter.

You wrote this from a former communication of mine: "The most skillful handler of money for good or for ill is he who has become possessed of it by his own acts." To disprove my contention, you refer to my expenditures of money on "Miramar" and Fanita [12] ranches. You not only assume that money has been spent on these ranches unskillfully, but you accurately voice the opinion of nearly everyone else that I know on the same subject. The few exceptions in this regard are men of great wealth or other great attainments. Not all men of this character have differed from your point of view.

The best explanation of this case of extremely divergent views can perhaps be formulated by repeating the previous quotation, namely, "The most skillful handler of money for good or for ill is he who has become possessed of it by his own acts."

If the average man was able to appraise the actual intrinsic value of the investments made in Fanita and "Miramar," then socialism would be an accomplished fact, because if all men (the average man) were capable

[12] Fanita Ranch was in El Cajon Valley, east of "Miramar."

654

of exercising judgment in economic affairs as well as the most skillful, there could not possibly be any large disparity between the fortunes — possessions — of the whole community of men.

When, several years ago, Joe Fels was visiting me, he said to me once, "Isn't it easy to make money when one knows how?"

I replied, "Yes, but, Joe, have you ever yet met a poor devil who didn't think that you were only a fool for luck?"

We finally both decided that the poor devils were always right. We both knew we were fools, and we both knew we were lucky. Our luck consisted in having learned how to make money.

Most of the great individual fortunes, as you well know yourself, are either inherited or possessions of old men. Why is this?

The answer is that the really great and profitable investments are those that take many years for a turnover. Most men are in such immediate need, or think that they are in such immediate need, of returns on their investments that they will only invest their money or their efforts in things that produce the quickest turnover. The laborer wants his day's wage at night, consents to take it at the end of six days, grumbles if he has to wait for two weeks, and will not tolerate a longer period than thirty days. Most farmers are only willing to wait till the end of the season. The average tradesman thinks he cannot wait for returns for a period longer than a few months or at most a year. Big businessmen who build railroads, factories, and develop mines, waterpower, and such things are willing to wait from three to a dozen years for a turnover. Men of very big business invest from the beginning of their young life's activities with the view of getting their final and full returns at the edge of the grave. There are some who actually make investments, no returns on which can be expected during their lifetime.

Judged from your standard of necessity, it being always assumed that cash divisible profits were the sole object of investment, my expenditure on "Miramar" and Fanita was something more than a joke; it was a social crime.

One reason why it has been so easy for such an all-around chump as I am to make money has been that all my investments have been in noncompetitive fields. As I never have, as yet, invested any money in anything that my neighbors and acquaintances didn't judge to be fool ventures, I have had all the advantages of being able to get a good start before imitators began to compete with me.

I have always been a joke and a butt of ridicule, and I am today.

Give a man a reputation for being a first-class fool and then even with second- or third- or fourth-rate abilities you will have easy sailing.

Harry McKee's letter is only one of innumerable evidences that I have of my great success in keeping up a most valuable reputation.

If such a simple, good-hearted, kind friend of mine as Harry McKee is were able to see anything but a joke in "Miramar" and Fanita, I might have to go to work for a living.

While I am not famous or even notorious in this country, there are thousands of newspapermen who know me or know of me, and up to the present moment there are not as many men as I have fingers on one hand, who are not as sure of the Chicago *Day Book*'s being a joke as you are sure of Fanita and "Miramar" being a joke. If I were ten years younger than I am, I am sure that I could turn the *Day Book* idea into a much larger fortune than my present one before I died seventy years of age, and before imitators would offer me dangerous competition.

Now, Harry, you have judged me and are ready and able to prove to the satisfaction of 999,999 men out of every 1 million that your judgment is correct.

I know how impossible it is for any man to correctly judge another. I know that I cannot correctly judge you, but I am going to make a guess. You are incompetent to be a successful lawyer. No honest man can be a successful lawyer. You are unfit to be a leader in socialism because you are utterly incapable of judging the character and quality and resources of those who combat socialism on account of selfish interest. Whereas you could convince all but one in a million that you are right in your judgment of me, I know that I would be very lucky if I, on the other hand, could convince even one out of a million that I was right in my judgment of you.

You have a good mind; you are capable of thinking logically. You are honest and industrious. All your motives are good.

But many of your premises are wrong, and more of your premises that are right in the main are not visualized by you wholly, and hence deductions made from a part of each of these premises, instead of the whole, leads you astray. If I could place money in your hands which you could use one-half as profitably in the way of obtaining the common end that both of us desire as I could, I would be glad to share the burden of my responsibilities with you.

Even in the social state, you would have to be employed in order that you should produce as much as you consume. In some employment where you could make the best use of your capacities, you could make a sufficient use to provide as much to the common purse or receptacle of commodities as you withdrew. Someone or some collection of persons would have to find that place for you. In the then-existing condition of affairs, socialism, in order to be successful, would have to be as competent to direct the activities of the individual as it would be to distribute the general product. Perhaps this person or these persons would not be so well able, then, to gauge your qualifications under that system as I am now to gauge your qualifications under the present system.

How far the world must advance, then, before there can be harmony between all individuals, when it is so impossible for two men, such as you and I are, who hold each other in such mutual esteem, who have common ends and who are personally friendly, to agree upon so fundamental and simple a question as the fitness of each for his respective job.

You would be a lawyer yourself, and a member of a profession acknowledged by all of us as most inimical to everything progressive. You would make of your daughter a nurse, a member of the profession that is unequally divided between the propagation of pauperism and the relieving from responsibility and labor and care of men and women who prefer to enjoy leisure rather than minister to the sick and unfortunate of their own families.

Another daughter you will make a schoolteacher, who will be unable to gain and retain employment unless she teaches young children those things which the rulers of society, the plutocrats, big and little, desire to have them taught.

I know, I believe, all of the splendid and convincing (to the 999,999 out of 1 million) arguments that you can make in all of these three cases.

To me they will be as convincing, and no more convincing, as was your argument proving that men who had obtained possession of wealth by their own activities were incapable of wisely using the same.

Yours sincerely,
E. W. Scripps

Wages, Management, Capital

[*April, 1914*]

This disquisition appears to have been edited in Scripps' hand.

Why is it that there is such inequality between individuals in respect to material possessions? There are two main sources from which are drawn these possessions.

One of these are so-called natural resources, those resources which have not been produced by laboring men, but which existed before the advent of man and which would be in existence even if there were no man — fish in the water and animals inhabiting the dry lands, minerals of all sorts and air itself, harnessable natural forces such as those of running water and moving currents of air, wild plant life, and many other forms.

The other source of supply is the effect of man's labor in so altering and transforming natural objects as to make them useful to man.

There are two kinds of labor — physical and mental. No two men are born exactly equal in respect to physical strength and mental energy, nor in respect to special adaptability or capacity for any particular class of labor, physical or mental. Therefore, it is consistent with nature's laws that no two individuals should have or can have exactly equal proportions in the way of material possessions.

Is there any natural law which can limit the extent of the variation or divergence in amount of the possessions of any two men? Yes. No man can have a proportion less than an amount equal to the necessities of subsistence of life, and hence life. For when a man has less than this amount he ceases to live; he dies; he does not exist.

What are the natural limitations in the other direction? No man can possess more than the difference between all that exists and what is necessary for the subsistence of all other living men.

658

Theoretically it would be possible, according to natural law, that one man in the world could be possessed of the whole of this difference.

Practically, however, it is not possible for any one man to possess more than an infinitely small percentage of the totality of all of the things, or even that part of the totality which is left over after all of his fellows have had sufficient for subsistence.

But so far as can be observed from the reality of things at present and during ordinary times, it appears there is a natural law requiring the possession by a comparatively few of all existing things which are not required for the sustenance of the many.

The fact that religion exists and always has existed — considering the fundamental foundation of all religions — is evidence that in respect to economics as in respect to every other natural law, man's effort is to combat nature, overcome her laws, and adapt nature to man's use. This combat with nature, if it cannot be described as civilization itself, is an evidence of civilization, or rather the sole cause of that condition which we describe as civilization; whether we consider as existent a Divinity whose law is a natural law or not, man's effort has always been to overcome this law, and this effort has always been to a certain degree successful.

To revert: One thing is certain, and that is, there is a most marked difference between the possessions of those whose labor is physical and those whose labor is mental.

Sometimes I doubt the existence of one of the elements named in the caption of this essay. I doubt the existence of capital. I am rather inclined to believe that capital is nothing more than one of the elements of management, that is to say, of intelligent labor. Sometimes I think, instead of its being a fixed quantity, it is nothing more than a mental attribute or a mental attitude. Capital may be only a word defining one of the forms of mental activity. It may be likened to a statute law or a rule of the game, which only exists so long as the ruling majority or ruling minority of men can maintain it as a rule. One thing is certain, that under the most favorable conditions, capital must dissolve into thin air the instant constant and tremendous effort to maintain it is removed. Such things as running water, veins of coal, fertile soil, etc., which by the rule of the game are capital, would remain were civilization to disappear and mankind itself. But all man-made things are bound to decay and revert to elemental conditions in a brief period of time, even despite the most strenuous efforts of man to maintain them. But little of these man-made things can be made to exist for a small fraction of the life of a generation.

Labor, physical and mental, not only are required to produce capital, but even to keep it in existence for even the briefest period of time.

For these reasons it seems to me reasonable to regard the ordinary view of mankind, with regard to capital, as being a pure illusion and also to consider it Bergsonianly as the condition of continuing.

There are certain political economists, both orthodox and heterodox, who maintain that all wealth is produced by labor. This idea has been adopted by large numbers of men who have no other idea of the meaning of the word labor than that it means physical exertion.

Psychologists have demonstrated that mental labor is in many respects identical with physical labor; for example, that a severe exercise of mental faculties produces the same bodily physical conditions produced by those of muscular or physical labor.

All forms of physical or mental labor are more or less distasteful and against the inclinations of all men. Perhaps there does not exist a single individual, even one of the most highly developed intellectually than one who could produce the greatest results by his greatest activities, but who would not prefer, if the rewards were equal, to perform a year's work, a day's work, or an hour's work with his muscles to an equal amount of work measured by time [*sic*].

Perhaps the only inducement for men to indulge in the most distasteful labor is that its rewards are so much greater than are the rewards of physical labor.

How many men are there who would perform any sort of physical labor if they could have this labor done for them? A man must labor to live. Man should perform physical labor and obtain enough such labor to keep him in existence. No man could leave to another to do his mental labor without giving to that other person, as a reward for such labor, all that he produces.

But a laborer, one who only labors physically, can shirk nearly all mental labor and still have an existence. If the so-called capitalist doesn't labor with his mind to maintain his capital, he ceases to have capital, and, therefore, in order to exist, must resort to physical labor. So many so-called capitalists do shirk the labor necessary to maintain their capital, and hence revert to the condition of being a physical laborer. It is notorious that the so-called capitalist class or ruling class is a constantly revolving and renewing body. This condition has often been described by the saying that, "there are only three generations between shirt sleeves and shirt sleeves."

Eight Hours—Enough

[*October 23, 1914*]

"All work and no play makes Jack a dull boy."

"All work and no play makes Jack's father a stupid, inefficient citizen."

"A man learns only by experience."

"Man, collectively, learns only by experience." Primitive man had few experiences, and, hence, learned little. In a state of civilization, man collectively has been learning a great deal.

It was not so many decades ago that our fathers had no other idea than that a laboring man could produce 12 times as much by working 12 hours a day as he could produce by working 1 hour a day, and that he could even produce 16 times as much by working 16 hours a day as he could by working 1 hour a day. At that time the Sabbath Day was set aside as a day of rest for the laborer, because of an ancient religious commandment, and not at all because the employer of the laborer believed that he could get more work out of a man by allowing him to work only six days in the week than he could by allowing him to work seven days.

It has not been because of altruism that gradually, as civilization has developed, the hours of daily labor have been shortened, and that it has become customary to add to the rest day of the Sabbath other holidays and also to give annual vacations to large numbers of certain classes of employees.

Experience has taught employers of labor, and laborers themselves, that a gain of product is made by a reasonable reduction in the hours of daily labor, and a reasonable reduction in the number of days in the year to be devoted to labor.

It is true that the laborers who are most favored in the matter of short hours and holidays with full pay are those who are (as they are called) brain-workers. Doubtless, the reason for this class being the most favored is that their work is similar to that of the employers — namely, brain work. The hard brain-working employer soon enough discovers, for his own bene-

661

fit, that he can accomplish more work in a day of a few hours than he can by devoting many hours to his work, and he also discovers that his average efficiency is greater and the period of years, during which he can efficiently work, is increased by more or less frequent vacations. Having discovered for himself the cause of the increase in his own efficiency, he naturally argues that his own selfish interests will be served by shortening the working hours of his brain-workers, and by giving them holidays in which to recuperate. But by the time a man has become an extensive employer of labor, he has long ceased to have (if he ever had) any experience as a manual laborer, and, hence, he is unable to deduce, from his own experience, the idea that the output of manual labor can be increased by shortening the hours and giving holidays. Still, most employers can and do recognize enough similarity in the matter of brain and manual labor to enable them to grant at least a possibility that increase in production may result from reducing working hours.

By degrees, there has been going on for many years a shortening of the hours of labor, until now, in all those trades and employments in which skilled labor is involved, the 10-hour day has become as much the custom as was ever the 12-hour day. The more than 10-hour labor day is now abandoned, excepting in the cases of farmers, sailors, domestic employees, and a few other occupations of almost purely menial character. Hardly anywhere in this country today, even on the farm, does a man work from sunrise to sunset; a generation ago, the labor day of from "sun to sun" was almost universal on farms in this country.

The change from the 12-hour day to the 10-hour day, and, in a good many trades, from the 10-hour to the 8-hour day, has been attended by many inconveniences and many individual losses, by reason of the inevitable demoralizing conditions that must attend every change and every readjustment, but the employers of that class of laborers who only work 8 hours a day are no less prosperous now than they were when their laborers were working 10 hours each day; nor are they any less prosperous than were their predecessors whose workmen of the same trades worked 12 hours a day. I think that statistics would prove that, as a rule, both the percentage and the volume of profits made by employers of 8-hour-day workers are greater than that [sic] of those employers who work people 10 and 12 hours a day; and, yet, on every occasion when there was a change, first from the 12-hour to the 11-hour day, next from the 11-hour to the 10-hour, then from the 10-hour to the 9-hour, and finally, when the change was made from the 9-hour to the 8-hour day, those businessmen whose employees were reducing their hours of labor regarded the change not only with disfavor but with despair. "How (they would say) can we afford to pay the same for an 8-hour-day's work as we have been paying for a 10-hour-day's work? If our profits, now, in our business, are only 10 per cent, how can anything but bankruptcy occur to us if our workmen reduce their hours of labor 20 per cent?" But these employers have not only continued to be as prosperous as formerly, but, as we have indicated, have become more prosperous. There must have been some reason for this continuing, or increasing, prosperity. Very naturally it would be said that the employers merely passed the burden of increased expense along to their customers, and that in the end someone would have to pay what was practically an additional wage.

There are no satisfactory statistics on the subject, and it could not be possible under the circumstances (labor-saving inventions, etc.) to prove conclusively, by any statistics, that the product of 8 hours' labor is less or more than that of 10 hours'. However, it is my opinion, and the opinion of many other experienced and observing men, that the actual product of the average man working 8 hours a day has been greater than that of the average man working 10 hours a day; and that, therefore, instead of there being an increase in price for a piece of work, there has been a decrease in the price which the consumer has had to pay.

Now, while it is impossible to make an absolute and particular analysis in this case, it is possible to make a general analysis: that the average working-man produces more in 8 hours and 10 hours and 12 hours than he does in 10 hours and 12 hours and 14 hours, is a thing proven by the fact that, while the average American workman labors from 3 to 4 hours less per day than does the average English workman, he produces from three to four times as much per day as does the English workman, and is paid from three to four times the Englishman's wages.

Statistics prepared by Ellis Barker, Leroi Beaulieu, and many other competent statisticians have shown that the money value of the average American workman's daily product is from three to four times greater than the money value of the average European workman's daily product. That the employers of these high-wage, short-hours laborers are the gainers by this situation is self-evident. For instance, take the case of an English mechanic who may work 10 hours a day, and compare his case with that of an American mechanic: We will set, as the value of the Englishman's daily product, 100, and the value of his compensation we will set down as 80. We will next take the case of the American mechanic, the value of whose product is 400; now we pay the American mechanic four times as much as we do the English mechanic — that is 4 × 80, or 320. It will be seen that the employer of the American mechanic makes 80 on each of the mechanic's day's work, while the employer of the English mechanic only makes 20. But it takes too much statistical matter to make this demonstration perfectly satisfactory, and statistics are, rightfully enough, universally considered to be unreliable. Let us then take, or rather make, some general analyses: In the year 1910 the population of the United States was almost exactly double that of Great

Britain. The actual product of wealth in England at that time, including interest on capital already acquired, is known to have been about 10 billion dollars annually; the actual annual product of the United States at the same time was not less than 32 billion dollars. It is known that fully 2 billion dollars per annum accrues to the citizens of England from interest on liquid capital. So far as the United States is concerned, it is known that its citizens as a whole, instead of receiving interest from saved capital, are actually borrowing and paying interest on capital at a rate of not less than 300 million dollars per annum. Deduct the 2 billion dollars capital income from the total product of England, and you have, accruing from industries, 8 billion dollars per annum. If the United States, with only double the number of laborers that England has, is producing four times the product, it would appear that the per capita product of American workmen must be greater than that of the overworked and underpaid Englishman.

But then, even in the above statement, I have had to give some statistics. Let us depend upon no statistics other than such well-known facts as that the Europeans work longer hours and get less pay than the Americans. We know that fortunes accumulate much more rapidly in this country than in England; yet, all of this has been accomplished, notwithstanding the fact that we have worked all of our employees fewer hours each day, and paid all of them more wages for each day's work, than the English have worked their employees and paid them. With these facts known, can there be any doubt that, so far, the American people have been greatly the gainers, both by reducing the working hours of their workmen and giving them such large wages as to enable them to be well fed, well clothed, well housed, well educated, and well supplied with opportunities and necessities of developing mental capacity, and, hence, the manual efficiency of all of our working people — men, women, and children?

The people of California this year are called upon to vote on a constitutional amendment, making it illegal for any man or woman to perform more than 8 hours work in a day. Of all the reasons that are urged against the adoption of this law, I have not heard expressed the best of reasons; which is, that the universal 8-hour labor day is coming rapidly enough, without legislation, and at the same time is coming in such a way as to permit the readjustment to take place so gradually as to cause no great shock and serious loss to both employers and employees in those industries where such a change is most difficult — among others, agriculture.

But there are so many other and better reasons in favor of this legislation that — now that the question has once been raised — it had better be disposed of, once and forever, by putting in statute form, as a commandment, a rule, with regard to labor, that is economical for the state at large, to employer and employee alike.

"Back to the land" is a popular slogan in these days. It is recognized that most of the ills that this and every other civilized country are experiencing today originate from the lack of proper culture of their lands. Young and old people alike are flowing from the farms to the cities, abandoning wholesome, health-giving, out-of-door employment, in order to take up employment in trade and manufacturing. The high cost of living is caused by this migration in two ways; first, the supply of food is cut off to the extent of agricultural labor being cut off; and second, the demand for such food that is produced by the farmers is increased by every non-agricultural stomach that has to be filled.

No matter how great the business depression may be, nor how large becomes the army of unemployed, there never is a time when it is not hard to get able and willing domestic help.

Now the principal outcry against the 8-hour law comes from the very people who employ farm and domestic labor. Of all of the many reasons given for the national suicidal policy, of the abandonment of the farm by the young and capable men and women of the country, there is perhaps not one that can so well account for the exodus from the farm as that of the long hours of labor of employer and employees — of the sons and daughters of farmers as well as the sons and daughters of farm-laborers.

If it is a fact that the factory hand, the carpenter, the machinist, and the blacksmith can produce more in a 10-hour day's work than he can in a 12, and if, as it seems quite, or at least almost, proven, any of these laborers can produce more in 8 hours than he can in 10, why should it be believed that the farmer or his hired man cannot produce more of farm products in 10 hours, or even 8 hours' work than he can in 12 or more?

There are various employments where the peculiarity of conditions are such that work must be done when the seasons or other conditions permit, and considering the present organization of farm life, it would appear that such emergencies as harvests should be taken into consideration. But, still, there is no reason why any one man should be required to work on a farm more than 48 hours a week, or $4\frac{1}{3} \times 48$ hours in a month.

But why not the 8-hour day on the farm? There have been times in some countries when the day's work on the farm, in summer, was 16 hours long; and in all countries today there are some farmers who work themselves, and have their laborers work, during some part of the season, 16 hours a day. In California, however, a day of more than 12 hours' labor on the farm is almost unknown. The 10-hour day on a California farm is more common than the longer day, even now. If there is any reason why a farmer should work more than 8 hours a day, there is as just as good a reason why he should work 16 or 24 hours a day.

Notwithstanding all the outcry by the farmers against the legislation for the short day, I have no doubt at all but that the 8-hour day is coming to the farm sooner or later, law or no law; and that when it comes, even if it comes as a result of the November elections, the gross yield to the farmers of California will be no less next year than it has been this year; and I believe also, that both the gross yield, and the yield of net profits from the farms will be much larger within a year or two, after the adoption of the 8-hour day, than it is now, or even could be under the present system.

Supposing that the first result of this shortening of the agricultural labor day is the increase in the price of agricultural commodities. What of good or what of bad would result from this? One good thing would be that life in the city and city wages would be so much less attractive, on account of increased living expenses there, that fewer and fewer farmers' boys would go to the city, and more and more men would leave their city employments to go to work on the farm. This would result in an increase of farm products, and a decrease in consumers, until a level had been reached at which the advantages of city work and life would become exactly equal to the advantages of farm work and life. A shorter farm labor day would result in not only furthering inventions and a greater use of inventions, so as to make farming by machinery much more the rule than it is now, but the necessities of the case would stimulate intensive farming, and cause more and more the abandonment of purely extensive farming. When it costs as much for labor to reap 8 acres of grain as it does now to reap 12 acres, it will become absolutely necessary for the farmers to become more enterprising in fertilizing, selecting of seed, and cultivating. But perhaps the chief gain will be that, as farms must be profitable in order to be run, the men who work the farms — owners or employees — will be compelled to work much harder during the hours they are at work than they need work now, when they have 50 per cent more time in which to accomplish their task than they will have under the 8-hour rule.

All three of the arguments that I have presented above in favor of the 8-hour farmer work day apply only to the commercial side of the question. When the farmer's boy, and his grown son, and the farmer grown to manhood, has had, for a few years time, only enough hard manual labor to do in order to keep himself in a good physical condition, he will have become a very different sort of boy, young man, and adult man than the farmer of today; he will have enjoyed health-giving, pleasurable sports; he will have heard lectures and concerts; he will have had theatres or at least picture shows furnished him; he will have learned to read books; in a word, he will have become as much a man of culture as any of his city cousins. It is the "all work and no play" of the farmer boy and man that makes the farmer a clodhopper and a jay, and the butt of the city man's ridicule.

What good effect would the 8-hour day have on domestic labor?

I only wish that one effect might be that the house mother and the house daughter would, by being compelled to do their own work, learn to feel that joy of life which only people who work can feel. The only people who enjoy life are those who do enough work and not too much work. When the cook, and the housemaid, the waiter or waitress, the man-of-all-work, the stable-boy, and the chauffeur, have, each, only 8 hours' work to perform every day, there will be no such great difficulty, as now exists, in the way of getting competent men and women to fill these places. As everyone is familiar with domestic help of various kinds, in house, stable, garage, and garden, everyone knows that the principal occupation of all of these domestics is marking time between those infrequent and not long periods when their services are really required; in fact, all of our servants, so called, might better be described as men and women in waiting. We only employ them and keep them standing around to perform only occasional services. For the most part, we only bother our heads about keeping them at work because of our feeling that, as we are paying them for their time, they are swindling us when they are not working. In order to give an example of what I mean, let us compare the work done by an ordinary housemaid in a private home with that done by a chambermaid in a large hotel: So far as sweeping, bed-making, furniture-polishing, dusting up, etc., is concerned, there are few hotel chambermaids who do not accomplish from four to ten times as much work in a day as any maid in a private house. In like manner, one might compare the actual work done by a chauffeur in a private family with that done by a chauffeur in a public garage. The actual number of meals cooked and dishes prepared by a cook in a private house is, perhaps, on the average not one-fifth as much, in the way of output, as that given by a cook in a large restaurant or hotel. Give the general housemaid, the cook, and the chauffeur each 8 hours' work a day, and full freedom to dispose, as he or she will, of the other 16 hours, and it is almost certain that fewer servants will be required, instead of more, as a result. Of course, there will have to be a number of new adjustments made; perhaps there can only be two full meals a day served; perhaps the breakfast will have to be prepared by one of the women of the household — which would be a good thing for her; perhaps the evening meal would be changed from its present rather common form of a heavy dinner to the form not uncommon a generation ago in many families — a light and simple meal — there being nothing hot on the table excepting the tea in the urn. One thing is certain, and that is that if we are not allowed to keep a cook at work for more than 8 hours a day in any of our households, the incomes of our doctors will be diminished and all of us will enjoy better health. The people who only eat twice a day, instead of being unhealthy, are generally those who are the best nourished and who enjoy the best of health. Were it not for the present custom of three hot meals a day in America, there would not be the least difficulty in the world in readjusting any household to the 8-hour rule for servant's work. Those women who are rich enough and smart enough (or who think they are) to give evening parties should be either rich enough or smart enough, in one case, to employ and pay extra for help, and in the other, to, themselves, supply the guests with refreshments.

But let us take up the whole subject of the 8-hour day; I mean the subject as referred to the whole wage-earning population. Let us suppose that it is a fact — notwithstanding all the evidence to the contrary — that a reduction of the hours of labor from 10 hours to 8 is going to reduce the product of all labor 20 per cent. What of it? What proportion of the labor performed by all men, women, and children in the United States, who are engaged in so-called gainful pursuits, produce anything that is really valuable? Suppose we should have to call upon all those who are performing unnecessary and even positively injurious work today, in order to get that work done which is really necessary and helpful. Amongst the various fields from which we could recruit this necessary labor might be the men's clubs; we could take from them the stewards, the barkeepers, and the boys and young men who carry drinks to the members. There are hundreds and thousands, young and old men and women, who are now employed in making foolish and extravagantly costly, fashionable female apparel, and jewels, and all sorts of knick-knacks which women use to clutter up their husbands' houses, much to the latter's discomfort. There are tens of thousands of able-bodied men, many of them with fine artistic minds and great mentalities, who are employed in the new trade of automobile manufacture — employed in making, upholstering, and decorating machines whose cost is, in proportion, of from 50 to 80 per cent of show, to from 50 to 20 per cent of usefulness as vehicles of carriage. Anywhere from 60 to 40 per cent of all the things that are manufactured in the United States have no other reason for their existence than to furnish visible signs that some of our men and women have more money than some of the others. The production of luxuries, so called, has grown to such an extent that the greater part of those *choses de luxe* are infernal nuisances to their owners. For a dollar, I could get a shirt, in every way as serviceable as an article of clothing, and far more comfortable, than the shirt I am wearing now, which cost me $6.50 — this shirt, with its infernal stiff collar and stiff bosom front, that causes me to instinctively swear every time I have to put it on and button it.

Some years ago, being at the time possessed of a certain amount of data obtained from census reports and elsewhere, I made a calculation and wrote a disquisition on the subject of waste. I recall that the result of my analyses was that . . . all those things useful in a material way, and all those things that are valuable from an ethical or esthetic point of view, which would be needed by all the people in this country, could and would be produced, if every adult man and woman in good health would work for less than one hour a day or an average of one hour a day.

Perhaps, too, if it were really a fact that a workingman or workingwoman could not, and would not, produce as much in 8 hours as in 10, there would be another vast advantage to the community, as a whole: Those rich people who cannot and do not spend their whole incomes because of the present low level of wages would be compelled, in order to secure for themselves all the things they want — useful, luxurious, and wasteful — would have to distribute more of their surplus, and give their poorer neighbors something in the manner of wages nearer the requirements of the wage-workers.

Any law or any custom that can be introduced that will make it harder for the rich man to grow richer and easier for the poor to keep from growing poorer is a good law and good custom, and should have the support of every good and patriotic citizen, without regard to its immediate effect upon his own personal comfort or convenience.

Wealth of Nations

[*May 5, 1916*]

The term "wealth" has a significance determined by its application. I do not refer to such applications as are made when we speak of wealth of wisdom, wealth of beauty, or wealth of sentiment. I am considering wealth in the sense of material things as measured by money terms. Still, from this point of view wealth signifies many different things.

I remember that once a niece of mine was boasting of the splendid catch in the matrimonial market that her uncle had made. "Why," she told me, "Jim married the only daughter of the richest man in the city of ————!" An afterthought on her part: "That is to say, he was the richest man before he became bankrupt." Clearly, what she meant was that the father of her uncle's wife had lived in a big house, kept many servants, and spent large sums of money ostentatiously.

I suppose the vast majority of people would coincide with my necessary definition of what wealth is.

Perhaps the term wealth has as many significances as there are living individuals. We certainly know that what one man may consider wealth another may consider poverty.

Several years ago I read a statement made by a certain man to the effect that he had just read himself two items from a newspaper. One item referred to a suicide in Baltimore, and the suicide was a man who had held several millions of dollars worth of stock in one of the express companies at the time of the adoption by Congress of the parcels-post law [1912]. The man's stockholding was very largely of express-company stocks. By reason of the passage of the parcels-post law these stocks fell tremendously on the market, so that the man's fortune fell from a value of several millions to a value of only a few hundred thousands of dollars. So chagrined was the man by this misfortune that he took his life. In the same paper was another item concerning a young laboring man in one of the middle-western cities who

670

had unexpectedly inherited $30,000 from a relative. The article gave an account of a big dinner that the heir had given his fellow workmen in celebration of the sudden acquirement of great wealth.

There is the wealth of earned income, the wealth of unearned increment, and then there is the wealth of capital that produces an income in the way of interest, rents, or dividends — capital previously earned by its owner or inherited by him or partly earned and partly gained by social increment.

The net results in the way of income from these three sources may be identical in all three cases. So far as the recipient of the income is concerned, he has the same opportunity and privilege of obtaining necessities and luxuries from its expenditure. Three men deriving income from these three separate sources, during the time of the receipt of same, are, so far as the public can see, on identically the same level. The difference between these three kinds of wealth is only apparent to the public at death or, in one of the cases, the disability to work. In one case the income cannot be passed on to an heir, and in the other two cases at least a large portion of the income can be passed on to the heirs.

But there is another distinction to be made in the significance of the term wealth — one that has no relation whatever to amounts either of capital or income: That man is wealthy — no matter how small his income may be, no matter how it is derived, whether from labor, physical or mental, or from interest, dividends, or rents — whose income is more than enough to supply his necessities and all of his desires for luxuries.

That man is a poor man, no matter how large his income is or from what source it is derived, if his income is insufficient to procure for him all of those things which he greatly desires.

The term wealth has perhaps a peculiar significance when it is applied to nations — not entirely peculiar, because it may have the same significance when applied to communities, corporations, or individuals, but its significance is more apparent when applied to nations and very large aggregates of people.

Political economists generally classify nations as "creditor" nations and "debtor" nations.

Among the creditor nations of the world are England, France, Holland, Belgium, and Germany, and their relative positions are about in the order named. Little, conquered, oppressed, and exploited Belgium is, in a certain sense, richer even than her conqueror; she is, in this sense, richer far even now than the United States.

A creditor nation is one whose government or people owe nothing or but little to other governments or people of other countries and to whom much is owed by other countries and people of other countries.

A debtor nation is one whose government and whose people owe to other governments and the people of other governments much more than is owed to it by other governments and the people of other governments.

In this sense the United States is the poorest nation on earth.

In this sense wealth consists not in quantity but in surplus capital or capital that is not required as a foundation of industries of its own or its own people and much less for the subsistence of either government or individual citizens.

The man, or the collection of men in the form of a nation, who has surplus capital to lend out at interest, who has more capital than he can profitably employ in his own business, is wealthy in an entirely different sense from that of the man whose capital is only equal or somewhat less than he can employ in his own affairs, that is to say, in some form of production.

That nation whose people, to any considerable extent, have considerable funds to lend out at interest, invest in rent-paying property, or to invest in corporation shares of corporations in foreign countries, is not only considered wealthy by political economists, but is considered to have great trade advantages and many other privileges that are not enjoyed by the nation or the people of the nation that is in the debtor class, that has no capital to so invest.

The most palpable evidence, according to the economists, of the wealth of a nation is the comparatively low rate of interest its capitalists will let out their money for. There is just as much competition between money-lenders as there is between the individuals of any other class of businessmen and workers, either in the physical or intellectual sense. Interest rates are fixed by the law of supply and demand. He who is able and willing to lend his money at the lowest rate will get not only the most customers but the best customers amongst borrowers — a good customer being the one who can give the best security for his loan.

It has been found that the foreign trade of a nation depends to only a very small extent upon that nation's ability to sell cheap. It depends far more upon the ability of that nation or its people to lend money at a low rate of interest or a lower rate than the people of any other nation.

When a Belgian lends money to a Brazilian, for instance, the Brazilian does not, because he cannot, pay the interest and repay the capital with money. He must, perforce, pay his interest and repay his capital with products from his country. The Brazilian, then, must pay his interest to the Belgian with Brazilian products; and it is the Belgian who determines the amount of product he will take in lieu of money; in fact, the Belgian fixes the price. Of course, it is possible in individual cases for the Brazilian to sell his product in some other country and remit the money to the Belgian, but this roundabout and complicated method of paying debts does not permit such large transactions as are necessary in balancing accounts between great debtor and great creditor nations. And even to the extent that this method is adopted, it is at so much greater expense that direct payment in the way of products can be made to the Belgian money-lender at a lower cost for the product than would otherwise be the case. The roundabout method requires, amongst other things, transportation on ships that carry cargo only one way, which is expensive. It also involves the expense of bankers' and brokers' charges, and the more hands through which such a transaction passes the greater is the risk. It results in the Belgian money-lender getting coffee from Brazil at a lower price than the American coffee-buyer gets it, so that the Belgian can sell his coffee to the citizens of another nation at a lower price than can the American and yet make the same or a larger profit.

It is claimed by these political economists, therefore, that the people of the United States could never compete with some of the people of the European nations in foreign trade until the time comes when capital in the United States shall so far outstrip the demands of the people of the United States for capital that capitalists shall be able to lend money to the governments and the people of other governments at a higher rate than they can get from borrowers in the United States. When that time comes, citizens of the United States will make great investments in foreign countries and receive their pay in the products of those countries and, to the extent of their investments, will have advantages in the way of foreign trade.

Foreign trade in the United States is handicapped in various ways. First, capital receives a higher rate of interest in the United States than elsewhere; second, on account of the cost of labor and material, ships cannot be built so cheaply in the United States as in some other countries, nor can they be operated as cheaply after they are built; third, so great is the demand for labor in the United States that the cost in this country is far greater than it is in the overcrowded, overpopulated European countries. While this cost of labor and material in the United States is to a great extent offset by the advantages of quantity production — labor-saving appliances, etc. — still, up to the present time, it has not been possible for the manufacturers in the United States to produce for foreign export goods that can be sold at a profit to foreign countries as cheaply as can this country's competitors in Europe, at least not sufficiently cheaper to overcome the advantage of direct payments over indirect payments.

It will be said that, if domestic trade is more profitable than foreign trade, then why should our American manufacturers seek foreign customers?

They should not, and only a limited number do so. But foreign and national shipping facilities have a value to a country other than net financial profits. Amongst others, values of such trade can be easily recognized, not only as a military value direct, but an indirect military value, in that commercial intercourse and social intercourse go together along with diplomacy to produce such social relations as will minimize the necessity for military preparedness.

If all the above contentions are based upon sound premises, logic would indicate that two things or two conditions are necessary before the United States can take a really prominent and effective place in the community of nations. First, free capital, the result of individual savings, must be accumulated in this country beyond the needs of the country and its people. Second, the population must grow to such an extent that the demand for labor in this country will be so much less than the supply necessary to produce for America what Americans want that there will be so great a lowering of the wages paid American workmen as to permit American manufacturers and tradesmen to compete in foreign markets, in the way of prices, with the manufacturers and tradesmen of other countries.

I have, a number of times in my writings, had occasion to quote Professor [William] James, the elder, who made the statement that "it was the tendency of every organism, animate and inanimate, to overspend its income." It is a universally recognized fact that the individual man has this propensity. That is the reason why it is found in all countries, even the highest civilized, that 65 per cent of all of its populace live from hand to mouth, never saving from present income for future needs; that 15 per cent of the people in all of these countries possess no more property than that represented by household or domestic effects and the tools that individual workmen must possess themselves; and further, that 18 per cent of all of these people never, as a result of their savings, acquire a capital greater than is sufficient to return, in the way of income from rents, interest, and dividends, an amount equal to what its owner could earn at a salary or wage; and lastly, there are a number of people, not greater than 2 per cent of the whole population of all of these countries, who possess capital large enough to produce an income even great enough to supply ordinary necessities and luxuries. Not 0.1 per cent of the people of these countries have incomes from their capital so much in excess of their necessities and the luxuries they indulge in as to permit, without some form of sacrifice, the accumulation of income that would eventually take the form of capital.

It has been determined by students of this subject that all of the world's capital wealth, that is to say, its savings, does not today and never has at any time equaled in amount of value or value of amount more than the value of the total product of three or four years resulting from the labor of men, women, and children.

It is a natural law that man, like other organisms, always consumes or destroys or wastefully applies all he produces.

Civilization, in the economic sense as well as perhaps in all other senses, can be defined as the successful effort of man to overcome to a certain extent natural law. By damming the mountain torrent, man gets what is called waterpower. By opposing the wind's current by a certain contrivance, man gets power from a windmill and as in the sailing ship. Man attacks nature's law or nature's conditions in thousands and hundreds of thousands of ways to draw advantages to himself.

The individual who restrains his natural propensity, not only to expend all of his income but to spend more, derives benefit to himself in the way of capital goods.

First the conception and later the acquirement of capital seems to be the starting point of civilization — that is to say, all forms of intellectual and some forms of physical development.

I have sometimes compared capital to fat goose liver, from the latter of which we derive the delicacy of *pâté de foie gras*. The goose from which the fat liver is obtained has its natural instincts opposed. It is not only fed like other animals with enough, but additional food is forced down its gullet so that its liver becomes diseased and overdeveloped.

A capitalist is a man on whom society has put such pressure as to compel him to produce, not only enough for his support, but much more than his nature requires — to produce of his own efforts, directly or by his efforts in compelling others to produce, more than he will consume himself and more than he will allow others to consume.

Some Frenchman once described the harlot as "a high priestess serving at the altar of society." Victim as she herself was, this Frenchman considered her a great benefactress of the people.

What is it that makes a capitalist? In what way is a capitalist benefited by his proceedings in becoming a capitalist? Is he more fortunate than the goose that has extra food thrust down its gullet or the prostitute who protects the virgins who are to be wives and mothers? Is not the capitalist, whether he be willful or only willing, society's servant and savior and its most valuable member? Does not the capitalist suffer all of the ills that a common man is subject to and more? Does he not labor harder and are not his risks of life and comfort greater than that of the ordinary man? Is he not socially ostracized, perhaps by the necessity of his employment, perhaps by the necessity of his peculiar situation, perhaps by his own vanity and conceit, and perhaps and far more likely by reason of his own mental acquirements making him no longer congenial to the mass of men or the mass of men congenial to himself? Is not the capitalist, then, as much a high priest to society as the prostitute is a high priestess? Are they not both, the man capitalist and the woman harlot, essential and unhappy victims of the only kind of social order that man has thus far been able to invent and develop?

All of the immediately foregoing is but a diversion from my main argument. If universal social intercourse all over the world is desirable, if commerce amongst all of the nations is desirable in order to secure this universal intercourse, and if commerce depends upon capital, cheap and abundant, and if it is almost the universal tendency to refuse to acquire, and if acquired, to destroy, capital, is it not necessary, for the future well-being of the United States and the whole world itself, that there should exist and should be further developed and enlarged in this country a class of abnormal men who, resisting their instincts and their natural propensities, become accumulators of, guarders of, and administrators of capital?

Why Some Men Are Rich
and Others Poor

[June 25, 1916]

When Scripps finished this disquisition, he observed that he was tending to become more conservative in his views. Asking for "caustic comments," Scripps sent a copy of this disquisition to Gardner, with a letter of June 28, 1916, saying he had observed "evidences in myself of mental decay — senility in fact," in the recent past. Although he was losing faith in democracy, he said, he was not yet ready to be classed as a reactionary, but it did seem to him that the trend of his disquisitions was toward the arguments of the reactionaries, who had been his opponents of old.

Anticipating that Gardner might say Scripps had grown so rich he had lost touch with the people, Scripps said that would be unjust, that it would be "kinder to me if you attribute my backsliding to senile decay."

Although Mallock's comments on King's book had been the immediate occasion of this disquisition, Scripps told Gardner the foundation of the disquisition lay in a series of books he had read recently on biology, psychology, and economics, by Edwin Grant Conklin, Charles Benedict Davenport, Gustav LeBon, Charles Minot, and Raymond Pearl.

He observed, too, that his former belief in heredity was fading, and that he still was enough of a democrat to believe that all men are born equal but become unequal through environment.

Scripps told Gardner, also, that he once had found "considerable encouragement" in the work of Herbert Spencer (an English philosopher who applied to society the evolution theory of Darwin and thus gave a strong ground for survival of the fittest as a tenet of laissez faire economic thinking), but now realized he either had misread Spencer at that time or could not understand him now. Scripps then said that Spencer was not the author but was "a preacher" of the idea that human society should be likened to a human organism.

"You will note the same idea in my disquisition, and the lamentable result of my deductions from it."

Upon reading this disquisition, it will be seen at once that King's book furnished some of the ideas that went into the immediately preceding selection, "Wealth of Nations."

677

Professor W. I. King, of Wisconsin University, in his recent book *Wealth and Income of the People of the United States* [13] seems to have unconsciously made a great sociological discovery. At least in reading the book I was startled in some things that he revealed, and was even more startled at the fact that the text of the book did not show that its author recognized the significance of the facts related.

I thought it was possible that, although I have for many years been reading the productions of some of our greatest economists and sociologists, it might be that while I have been in utter ignorance of the situation as revealed by King, King and others had not been so ignorant.

However, when I find W. H. Mallock, an Englishman who is recognized as being one of the leaders in the science of economics, has devoted no less than three articles recently to Professor King's book, and had been struck by the same two points in the same that struck me, namely, that first King had made a great discovery, and second, that he had not himself realized it, I am impressed with the idea that King's discovery is a new one after all.

Professor King undertook to discover something about the distribution of property in his own state of Wisconsin. He carefully studied the records of the probate courts of five counties in Wisconsin, one of them including the large city of Milwaukee. It is well known that whenever a man dies, if he leaves an estate of an even inconsiderable value, its distribution is passed upon by the probate court of the county in which he lived.

Therefore the county records of these five counties had to reveal the possessions of the men who died in the counties. The study of these records was for a period of years, I believe 20, thus revealing the average distribution of wealth in the county. These records showed that 65 men out of every 100 of those who died in those counties during the period over which the investigation extended left no property at all. Out of every 100 persons who died, 15 left an estate valued at from $1,000 to $2,000. Eighteen out of every 100 who died left estates of from $2,000 to $40,000, and 2 out of every 100 who died left estates of from $40,000 upwards.

It is well known that the state of Massachusetts is the premier state of the Union in the matter of keeping vital statistics, and many other records, including those concerning wages and incomes and property possessions.

After investigating the five Wisconsin counties, King undertook to compare the records of these counties with regard to estates to those of Massachusetts. He found that during a similar period of time, the wealth of the people of the whole state of Massachusetts was distributed in almost identically the same proportion as he had found to be the case in Wisconsin: that is, he found that 2 per cent of the people left fortunes of $40,000 and

[13] Willford Isbell King, *Wealth and Income of the People of the United States.* Macmillan, New York, 1915.

upwards; 18 per cent left fortunes between $2,000 and $40,000; 15 per cent left estates valued from $1,000 to $2,000; and 65 per cent left no estates at all.

King, being aware of the very common public opinion to the effect that the rich were growing richer and the poor were growing poorer, undertook to prove the soundness or unsoundness of this public view. Conditions were such in the comparatively new state of Wisconsin as to make it impossible to get accurate data for the past periods of time there, hence he turned to the Massachusetts records. He took up a period of time some years in the past, perhaps twenty or thirty or forty years, I forget. An analysis of these old records of Massachusetts showed that identically the same conditions existed in that state in the past generation as now [exist]. That is to say, 2 per cent were wealthy; 18 per cent moderately well-to-do; 15 per cent owned small estates; while 65 per cent of the people were not possessed of any property.

Further, he discovered that in Wisconsin, as in present and past times in Massachusetts, the 2 per cent of rich people owned from 57 per cent to 60 per cent of the total property.

In all three cases the 18 per cent of moderately well-to-do people owned upwards of 30 per cent of the total property. Eighteen per cent of the population (which he described as the "lower middle class") owned the remainder of the property.

Having discovered the condition of property distribution in the state of Massachusetts at the present time and in the past generation, and the property distribution in the five counties of Wisconsin at the present time, King next turned his attention to England, Germany, and France.

He found that almost identically the same conditions in the matter of distribution of property prevailed in Germany and France and the United States. In England he discovered a slight difference. For instance, in England 0.5 per cent only of the whole population owned a little larger proportion of the whole property of the people than did the upper 2 per cent of the whole population own in France, Germany, and the United States. A further investigation indicated that what had been gained in England by the richer class had been lost by the class immediately below them, the class that King called the "upper middle class." However, in England, as in the United States, France, and Germany, it appears that 65 per cent of the population were propertyless.

Now extremely different political and race conditions exist in these four countries, and it would naturally be supposed that other different conditions, political and otherwise, would exist between an old state like Massachusetts and a new state like Wisconsin.

France and the United States are real democracies. England, while a monarchy, is supposed to be politically a democracy. In Germany the government is practically an absolute monarchy tempered with bureaucracy. The German Reichstag, as a governing power, is hardly to be compared at all with the English Parliament, or the American national Congress, or the state legislatures.

Besides the different political conditions existing in the four countries, there is at least commonly supposed to be great race differences. The French are a Latin people; the English are a mixed Teuton and Celtic; the German are supposed to be almost pure Teuton; in America there is a conglomeration of all the races.

If we could obtain economic statistics of all the other great and little countries of the world, we could possibly discover whether or not race, religion, and political systems could, under conceivable situations, have any effect in the matter of property distribution.

So far as the investigation has been made by Professor King, it would seem that there are strong indications that there is an absolute natural law governing property distribution among mankind.

Man is a gregarious animal. He is a social animal. By inherited instinct he organizes himself socially. Both history and observation seem to teach that he can only organize himself in a hierarchical form.

Wherever three or four, or a dozen, or a hundred, or a thousand, or a million or a hundred million human beings become members of an association — little or big, political, economic, or religious — they tend to divide labor. They place one man at the top and call him "king," "dictator," "pope," or designate him by some other name. Below this chief they create another small class that is sometimes termed "aristocracy." In the field of religion they are the members of the higher priesthood. Below this upper class (which is generally quite small in number) there are other larger and larger classes of lower grades, the lower the grade, the larger the number of people composing the class, and at the bottom of all are the so-called "masses" — the common people — the proletariat of the Romans.

We can all easily enough distinguish the universality and the persistence of this hierarchic system in political and religious communities.

Of course we can all observe in the economic field all of the classes found in the other two fields with the slight difference that, while there is the equivalent of the "king" and "pope" in small economic organizations, there is no all-embracing economic organization headed by a "supreme chief."

Perhaps this peculiarity, the absence of the king of an all-including economic organization, is to be accounted for by the fact that while political and religious government can be presumed to be as old as mankind itself, economic man is comparatively a new thing in the world.

For perhaps thousands of generations man organized for war and for religious purposes before the idea of personal property and individual possessions came into existence. Therefore, up to the present there has not been time sufficient for an economic organization to develop to the same extent that political and religious organizations have developed.

All modern nations are composed of great numbers of economic organizations, large and small. There are thousands of petty economic kingdoms, and principalities and baronies, and there are great numbers of independent free lances. The economic world of today, with reference to government and political conditions, is in practically the same condition that Europe was a thousand years ago.

Perhaps there were more kings and kinglets and robber barons in Europe in the year 1000 than there are respectable business organizations today.

Why was there one man made a king, and another a pope, and another a great lord, while there are infinite numbers of serfs, soldiers, and laborers? Why should one man be rich and another man poor?

Why should mankind in four great modern nations divide itself into four classes, the overwhelming larger of the four propertyless, the smallest [having] possessions far greater than the sum total of all of the other classes?

Biologists and psychologists do not find physical and mental attributes distributed among mankind in anything like the proportion that would be indicated by the possession or non-possession of political powers, of religious authority, or wealth possession.

There is no such great difference between the absolute physical and mental possessions of the king and commoner as there is between the official rank of the same. In all of the priesthood of Rome, perhaps there never was a pope who was endowed to an extent much above the average of the whole priesthood. The kings of the world have but rarely been men of mental and physical attributes much superior to their subjects. Perhaps the United States has never had a president who was not inferior in some if not all of the qualities that would fit a man for this high office, inferior to hundreds and thousands of his constituents.

Aside from inheritance, the possession of wealth by a man is a better indication of his relative superiority than his possession of political or ecclesiastical office as an indication of relative superiority.

Yet it will be almost universally acknowledged by men who have great wealth, first, that accident (some call it "luck") has played a large part in the attainment of their possessions, and second (and in this naturally all are emphatic in their outspoken convictions), that nearly every one of their fellowmen could obtain, or could have obtained, similar possessions of wealth had they submitted or would they submit themselves to the same hard discipline of labor, mental and physical, of self-restraint, aye, even self-sacrifice. It is your rich man who always tells the pauper that he is himself most to blame for his poverty, and if such a rich man is sincere, he is sincere in saying this.

For my own part, I have the profound conviction that hundreds of the men who have served me in various capacities, high or low, have originally possessed native qualities superior to my own. I am sure for my own part that I did not personally seize the wealth I am possessed of, nor have I played more than a minor part in acquiring it. I know that by a sort of perpetual election I have been chosen by one voter after another to the office of his superior in economic work. I have also been chosen to a large extent as "purse-holder" by men and women who preferred to shift on me the responsibility and danger of becoming the treasurer.

What is it that causes 65 per cent of all the people that are born in this country, Germany, France, and England to surrender their right of personal self-control to another? Why do these men work for wages, salary, or for some other share of their own personal product while turning over to their self-elected chief by far the largest proportion of the products of their own labor?

Society organized has been likened to the body of an animal or a plant. It has been likened to a man's body. All of the cells of the human body have a common origin, the oosperm, the product of the conjunction of the ovum and sperm. In order that there may be a man there must be all the organs of a man. The multiplying cells, by instinct and law, divide their labor. One cell becomes a nerve cell; another, a cell in the bony skeleton. One cell takes its place as part of the organ of sight; another, that of hearing. One becomes part of the liver; another, part of a man's beard. One cell takes its place with its colleagues in the tongue, while another chooses companions in the rectal region. I know that biologists, most of them, and I think psychologists, scoff at this analogy of society and the living body.

Perhaps the theory has been overworked.

However, just as the cells of identical origin in the human body must distribute themselves in order that the body shall exist, so, in order that society may exist, must identical members of society so distribute themselves as to perform all the functions of society.

In order that society shall exist, there is a vast amount of humble hard work to be done, manual labor. In order that society shall continue to exist, it must be directed, and, therefore, there must be directors — a very few high officers, and larger and larger numbers of inferior officers, the number increasing as the rank falls.

There have been successful political states existing even in historic times, the total population of which did not exceed 250,000.

There are in the United States today no less than 250,000 people who do no manual labor, people whose incomes we will say are over $3,000 per year. Now let us imagine what would happen if we would gather together this quarter-million of the extreme upper class (economically speaking) in the United States, and segregate them, making a state of them in the center of an otherwise unpopulated continent. This new state would have to organize. How could it organize and exist unless more than one-half of its people performed menial and manual labor? Neither could it organize unless it had all of the other social, or political, or religious classes.

Organization would be absolutely necessary; hence, is it not almost certain that before this new state was a generation old there would be identically the same distribution of property, the same political, religious, and other offices as now exist in Wisconsin, Massachusetts, England, France, and Germany?

In more than one American city there are no less than 250,000 absolutely propertyless human beings. To a large extent they are denizens of so-called slums.

Let us suppose that we should take 250,000 of these people and locate them in the center of an otherwise unpopulated continent. Man being what he is, these people would have to socially organize. They could not exist without more than half of the people laboring, or without all the people being directed and in some way governed by a few. Is it not certain that at the end of a generation this new state would be organized economically exactly as Professor King has found that other communities organize today? There would certainly be one man playing the part of "king," and perhaps another that of "pope." There would be judges, doctors, and captains of industry. There would be caterers, story-writers, poets; there would be inventors. There would be 2 per cent of the people owning 60 per cent of the whole property, and there would exist the upper middle class, and the lower middle class, and the propertyless class.

All this would have to be because man is what man is.

When the queen bee of a hive meets with an accident, and the hive has no queen, the working bees choose an egg that under ordinary conditions, if the queen bee were still alive, [would] develop into another working bee. This egg is so nurtured and so treated that it develops into a new queen bee, an animal that is as fertile as the working bee is infertile. (Perhaps this is a myth.)

Why not compare human society to a bee hive? In the hive are the working bees, the drones, and the queen. There are only three classes in the bee community, but the human community has a large number of classes.

If a community of human beings loses its king and all the royal family, or if it loses its president or governor, or if it loses its pope, or cardinal or archbishops or its priests, if it loses its doctors or lawyers or captains of industry, or if it loses too many of the large number composing these classes, that human community immediately sets to work to develop out of its material persons with the desired qualities to fill the vacancies.

It might seem easy enough, considering the vast numbers to select from, to find in any community a man fit to be king or pope. It might not be so difficult to select a number of men to make aristocrats of, or captains of industry, or judges, or doctors.

It is not so easy to conceive how a whole working class of proletariat could be developed from the upper strata of society. Yet, given necessary conditions, that this problem not only could, but would, take place, must be evident to anyone who considers the subject.

Perhaps there are few men existing today, no matter how exalted their position may be, who have not at times had to perform for themselves, there being no one else to do so, the most menial and most laborious of tasks. What man of high station would be a bootblack or a barber? Yet how many men are there who have never shined their own boots or shaved themselves?

I venture to say that if 10 million of the richest, most intellectual, highly developed human beings on earth today were gathered together in one community, from which was excluded everyone else, it would not require a longer time than even a few months to find 6,500,000 of these doing the drudgery of the new nation, with little, if any, better comparative compensation for their work than is received by 65 per cent of the propertyless people of Wisconsin and Massachusetts.

Letter to the Editor of the New Statesman

[September 26, 1916]

Scripps thought this letter [14] too long to be published, and was much pleased when it was printed, although he knew that "for the most part, my name should never appear in print larger than agate." [15]

He said he knew it was "sound to the core as a disquisition on economics, but when I had finished it, I felt that I had only uttered another vain cry of protest against the fate that dooms me and all of my kind." [16]

"Miramar," Calif., September 26, 1916

Editor of the New Statesman
10 Gt. Queen Street
Kingsway
London, W.C., England

Sir:

I am an American — a hyphenated American. My father was born an Englishman, and my mother an American. I am what we Americans call "a newspaperman," as was my grandfather, who more than a century ago, began his career in the office of the *True Briton*. Later, I believe, he was with the London *Daily Sun*, and, still later, the London *Literary Gazette*.

The *Illustrated London News* was my favorite publication at the time I was emerging from infancy. For years I was familiar with the London *Times*, as I was with any American publication. Such English publications as the *Fortnightly*, the *Contemporary Review*, the *Nineteenth Century*, the *Edinburgh Review* — and the, to me lamented, *Westminster Review* — *National Re-*

[14] Appeared in the correspondence section of the Nov. 4, 1916, issue under the heading, "The Future of British Industry."
[15] EWS to Robert F. Paine, Nov. 30, 1916.
[16] EWS to Countess of Warwick, Dec. 2, 1916.

view, the *Statist* and the London *Economist* and the *New Statesman*, have been read by me regularly for many years.

I have several times visited England and have numerous relatives there. (Over a score of these are fighting in the British Army and on the ships of the English Navy.)

I have personal business interests in London and an office there.

I cite all of these facts only to indicate that I have a sort of familiarity with England and the English institutions, and especially English politics and English economic affairs.

Several years ago, Mr. J. Ellis Barker published an article, or a series of articles, in the *Fortnightly*, comparing English industrial affairs with those of America. As I recall these, Mr. Barker showed by figures that the per capita product of the American workingmen in two score industries averaged from two to four times that of the English workingmen. He accounted for this superiority on the part of the Americans by citing the fact that in America steam power and labor-saving machinery was in far greater use than in England.

For my part, I am convinced that while American superiority in steam power and labor-saving machinery was, and is, an important factor, Mr. Barker did not put his finger on the weakest part of the English system.

I am sure that there is another and better reason for the greater productiveness of American workingmen as compared with that of the English, French, German, and in fact all other European and Asiatic workingmen.

The average wage of the American workingman is several times greater than that of the English workingman. The average hours of daily labor of the American workingman are from 20 to 40 per cent less than those of the English workingman.

There are slums in American cities; there is sweating in American shops. There are many poor, underpaid and undernurtured men, women, and children in America, but I know enough of the average conditions in England and her cities to know that on the average the American workingman is not only far better nurtured and nourished, but that he is far better housed and clothed, and that his children are far more generally, and perhaps far better, educated than those of the English working class.

I have learned, by my own experience and actual experiments, that the products of all kinds of human labor are greatly increased by plentiful nourishment, good housing, good clothing, and abundant time for recreation.

Located now as I am on a ranch in southern California, from which I can look over into Mexico, I have lately had splendid opportunities for observing the good effects of intelligent care of human animals. There is crossing the international border a constant stream of Mexican ex-peons. They come over here poor, emaciated, half-starved, ignorant, stupid, energyless men. The paucity of white labor is such as to compel us here to employ these Mexicans. Such are our state laws and customs that we are bound to treat all laborers alike. These Mexicans are paid the same wages as white men. They are fed in our ranch boarding houses as plentifully and generously as are the white men. They work the same number of hours. The result of this treatment of the Mexicans is that in one, two, or three years they become almost as strong, able, and efficient workingmen as are their fellows of the American stock.

To get the full value in the way of product from a fine high-priced workhorse, one must feed him well, stable him properly, and work him only a limited number of hours a day and limited number of days a year. In order to get full value in the way of returns in product from the two-legged animal, one must give him the same care and attention he gives his four-footed brother. [This paragraph was deleted in the printed version.]

Mr. Barker and other English writers, in dealing with the subject of wages, state that the English employer cannot increase the wages of his employee and shorten his hours, since the margin of profit on the English workingman's labor is already so small that even a slight increase in wage or a slight reduction in the hours of labor would wipe out all this little margin of profit.

I say, and American employers by reason of the necessities of the laws and customs of this country have proved, that by increasing the wages and shortening the hours of labor, the product of labor is increased to such an extent that the profits per man employed is, instead of being decreased, greatly increased.

As the employer of some thousands of men, and as the purchaser of millions of dollars annually of material that would be affected for good or for bad by the increase in the wage and the shortening of hours of labor, I am an enthusiastic supporter of the eight-hour labor day system, and I use all my political influence to secure legislation favorable to shorter hours of labor, higher wages, workingmen's indemnities, and similar favorable conditions for the working people.

If I do not deny any altruistic motive, I at least assert and believe that my selfish interests as an employer and as a capitalist of a sort is served by such legislation.

Your George Bernard Shaw has stated, in effect, that wartimes are the best of times for the working people of England.

It is my hope that these wartimes will teach the English people such a lesson as will cause this war to be an unending blessing, not only to the working people of England but to all of the people of England.

The fruits of such a lesson persuaded may be so great as to a hundredfold offset all the material costs of the war, and all of the physical and mental agony that the English people have been suffering, and will continue to suffer, on account of the war.

If the English people will, when peacetimes come, continue to keep up anything like the present scale of energy and productiveness and wholesale employment of all of her people, the increased value of the productiveness will, in a few years, wipe out all of the present great English debt, increase their capital many fold, and, far better than all of this, increase the health, and happiness, and vigor, and manliness, and womanliness of the whole people to an extent inconceivable to the most enlightened present-day economists.

I have just concluded reading Percy Alden's article on "The Dilution of Labor" and A. C. Pigou's article "Labor Problem after the War," both appearing in the September number of the *Contemporary Review*.

What all you Englishmen are asking yourselves, it appears to me, is "What are we going to do with all of our working people after the war ends when millions of soldiers come back to work?"

To me, it seems that no question could be asked — or rather which could be more easily answered [" — or rather" deleted in printed version].

Why keep all of your present workingmen and women at work? [Printed version reads, Keep all of your present workingmen and women at work.] Increase their wages and shorten their hours, and give every one of these brave soldiers that have been fighting for you a job at better wages and at shorter hours than they ever had before or ever hoped to have.

God knows that there is more work, and profitable work, to be done in England today than England has men and women enough to do. You have vast acreages of lands that are now practically unproductive, and vaster acreages that can be made many times more productive than at present.

Fully two-thirds of each of your cities need rebuilding. The generality of farm and village houses that I have seen in my travels in England are nothing like as fit for human habitation as they should be. It would take many more men than there are now in the English Army a lifetime to do well only these two things that I have mentioned.

England needs, in the way of foodstuffs and many other things, far more than she can produce. She should produce in her factories many more times the amount of products than she has ever produced before, and produce them much cheaper than she has ever produced them before, and send them abroad to pay for her imports, and to pay off her debts that have accumulated during the war.

England will need more factory space after the war, far more than she is using now to produce war material and goods for home consumption. She needs new factories, and she needs not only all of the labor-saving machinery used in America but more of it, and better than the Americans now have. England needs to feed her people better, to clothe them better, and to house them better, and to give them better facilities and better opportunities for recreation than they now have.

You Englishmen are constantly creating royal commissions and parliamentary committees galore. Why not create one more commission, composed of the ablest men that England can produce, and send them here to America, not to criticize and scoff but to learn how it is, and why it is, that the value of American manufactured products alone are nearly double the total product or income of England — including that of shipping, foreign investments, and foreign trade.

Although I have not data at hand, I am inclined to think that the total number of men employed in manufacturing in the United States is not so great as the men employed in manufacturing in England.

You Englishmen should stop explaining American prosperity — or trying to explain it — by referring to America's great natural resources. It is true that America's natural resources are one hundred times more; she has more power to use. But England has at least many times more natural resources than she is now using.

The really great natural resource of England and America, and in fact of all countries, consists of human beings.

That this greatest of England's resources is being misused and wastefully used — and has been misused and wastefully used for decades — is my firm conviction.

WAKE UP, ENGLAND!

Respectfully,
E. W. Scripps

The Fourth Element in Production

[*November 25, 1916*]

For the past month my most serious occupation has been the reading of, and trying to thoroughly understand, Professor John Bates Clark's book *Distribution of Wealth*.[17] In a way it summarizes and coordinates about all that I have gathered from other writers on pure economics.

Only one writer of distinction, who, however, is, I believe, not recognized as a full-fledged political economist, has dealt with the subject of capital in a way that nearly approximates those views and opinions of mine that have been gained from much reading and a long life of experience in the business world. This man is Professor Thorstein Veblen.

However, if Clark and men of his ilk diverge from the realities of business or, to speak more correctly, cover only a very small part of the field of realities on one side, Professor Veblen rather, I think, ostentatiously ignores on another side an equally large part of the field of realities.

Clark and his confreres deal only with material things — the physical and almost tangible elements in business affairs. On the other hand, Veblen, by his pronouncement that capital is only technology (knowing how to do things) overstates the unimportance of the material.

Although Clark defines capital generally in two ways — as pure capital (values) and capital goods (things that have value) — whenever he speaks of capital, he speaks of something material.

When Clark refers to labor, he refers to muscular effort or the mental effort of directing muscular labor.

Even Veblen's term, technology, infers only intellectual effort, or the possession of intelligence of a character applicable to the direction of muscular labor.

If my memory serves me well, Veblen did not deny the existence of ma-

[17] John Bates Clark, *Distribution of Wealth*. Macmillan, New York, 1899.

690

terial capital so much as by inference he minimized its importance as compared with technology (meaning how to do things).

Clark does not anywhere in his book assert that there is no such thing as immaterial capital, but in his argument he proceeds as though this immaterial capital was not important or even necessary.

All of the other writings on political economy that I have read are, according to my opinion, defective in the same way that I consider Clark's arguments are defective.

I can well enough understand that Clark and all his confreres would assert, in answer to such criticism as I make, that their statements concerning capital and labor include, by presumption or inference, the existence of capital in intellect and of labor in intellectual processes.

The most that they would concede would be that if there was anything in my criticism at all, it would be that their accent of material things was disproportionately great as compared with that that was placed on the material [*sic*].

In other of my own writings, I have tried to make a very marked distinction between intelligence and force. Knowledge is one thing, force is another. Knowledge is a tool, force is a driving power behind the tool.

The carpenter's saw is just as much a saw when reposing in the carpenter's kit box as it is when in the carpenter's hand it is cutting wood. A man's muscle is just as much muscle in repose as when it is performing labor. A man's knowledge of how to do things is just as real when a man is doing nothing as it is when a man is making effective use of his knowledge.

One carpenter will cut deeper into a block of wood with a saw in a given time than another, according as his intelligence and the muscular effort he puts forth are greater than that of the other man. A strong carpenter with a saw will, in a given time, cut through more or less wood according as his muscle works to full power or to part power. The productivity of a man's knowledge will be in direct proportion to the amount of force applied to driving his mental machine.

There are good, sharp saws, and poor, dull ones. There are strong muscles and weak ones. There are minds richly stored with knowledge and others poorly equipped. Some men possess great spiritual or intellectual force, and others poor, weak wills.

A good tool, like a saw, possesses more value when in the hands of a strong industrious workman than it does when in the hands of a weak, indolent workman. A given quantity of knowledge (technology) is a larger part of social capital when it is backed by great spiritual force than when it is backed by a lesser amount of spiritual force. A jackknife, in the hands of a workman possessed of strong muscles, who is industrious and who possesses intelligence and ingenuity — technology, in fact — backed by a great force of character, represents a far larger proportion of what Clark calls capital goods (valuable things) than does a whole kit of wood-carving tools in the control of a weak-muscled, unintelligent, unforceful man.

Clark, like the classical political economists whom he derides, puts almost all of his accent on material capital and capital goods (producing instruments).

Veblen puts most of his accent on technology — on the knowledge of the workman.

On the other hand, while I still recognize that material tools (capital goods), muscular strength and knowledge (technology) are necessary, I maintain that by far the largest element in productivity is the spiritual force possessed by the possessor and user of these other things.

Clark, and nearly all of the other writers on political economy, measure the wealth of peoples by their possession of capital as represented by material things.

Veblen would apparently measure the wealth of a people by its technology, by its knowing how to do the things that produce wealth.

I maintain that by far the largest proportion of the actual, the real capital of individual men, and of whole peoples, is represented by something that might be nearly accurately defined as force of character.

There does not exist, and never did exist, a material tool that, during the period of its existence, has been used or will be used up to the full limit of its potential utility.

There was never a man, and perhaps never will be one, who has put forth and will put forth all the potential muscular energy of a human body.

No man ever makes use of more than a small fraction of the knowledge he possesses during his life. Rarely, except in what might be called life and death emergencies, does any man exert to the full the spiritual or intellectual force that is in him.

A large part of the usefulness of every material tool is wasted by workmen who do not exercise all the care possible.

Some recent investigations have demonstrated that a large part of physical energy of every workman is wasted by unnecessary and profitless motions and muscular strains in wrong use of muscles and tools.

Similar investigation has shown how ill-trained workers in the purely intellectual field are wasting large parts of their mental energy by lack of care in coordinating and methodizing their thoughts.

But by far the greatest waste of all results from men not using anything more than a small part of that spiritual force which is native to them.

In order for any man to accomplish the greatest possible results in the way of productivity of any kind, he must first think hard, and second, think straight. If he does these two things, he will make the fullest possible use of his knowledge, of his muscles, and of the tools he has in hand.

Capital, or wealth, is, according to my scheme of things, composed of four parts, important in inverse proportion to the sequence here given: (1) material things, capital goods, or pure capital; (2) muscular energy; (3) technology; (4) spiritual force.

(It has been with reluctance that I have always in the foregoing qualified "force" with an adjective or in other manner.)

Having defined wealth as in the above, I will go farther and say that all the wealth existing in the world today, or rather all that wealth that is recognized either by political economists or even the commonalty of men, is infinitesimally small. Such wealth, as compared with what we might call the potential wealth of the world, is as a pail of water dipped from all the oceans.

To go back a little, to some point before the above final conclusion — I have in previous essays attempted to demonstrate the enormous wastefulness of human energy in even this, the most enterprising of all the nations of the earth.

In those essays I tried to prove that if all men, and women, and children of this country worked as hard with mind and muscle as do an infinitely small proportion of the whole population, the aggregate of the products of the people of this country would be increased twentyfold. I tried to show that everything that is now produced could in quantity be increased twentyfold, or in quality be made twenty times better.

I am satisfied that I have demonstrated that, by such universal activity, the people of the United States could replace every material thing, other than natural resources, now existing in the United States, in six months, and during that six months, consume things on the present average scale.

In fact, I maintained that, if all the people in this country worked as hard as some of them do, that the surplus product, the savings, of six months, would equal in value the total savings of all the white people who have been in this country during a period of three hundred years.

Subsequent to the writing of these essays, I discovered that other students [of] this subject have confirmed my judgment, at least to the extent of saying that not over 5 per cent of the energy of any whole civilized people has, up to the present, been employed in producing the things that political economists call "consumers' goods" — the things that men place monetary value on.

Mankind as a whole lives from hand to mouth. It has been said that, if for three months, all men and women would cease producing foodstuffs, and if during that time all people continued to consume food in the same proportion that they did at other times, everybody on earth would die of starvation.

Man has only made a slight advance beyond the beasts of the field in the way of foresight and providence, since man, as a whole, provides and creates for rainy days for only a few months. Ordinarily, beasts provide for not one day. Some rodents, perhaps, store up food; the bees store honey. Such hibernating animals as bears and serpents store up food supply in their own bodies to carry them through the period of hibernation. Man is as yet so low in the scale of intelligence that, on the whole, he submits to no other force than that of daily necessity. He will not exert more than 5 per cent of his energies to the production of consumable supplies, because such small use of his energies is sufficient to supply his barest necessities, or what he as an individual considers to be his necessities.

No better proof of the wastefulness of human kind under ordinary conditions can be found than by observing what is now occurring in Europe. Notwithstanding the diversion from fields of productive labor of more than 20 million of the best workmen of Europe, and the employment of more than another 20 million of people in providing, directly and indirectly, the tools and other expenses of war, the peoples of Europe are making only slight draft on their previously unused energies. They are living now, on the whole, and on the average perhaps, better than they have ever lived before. Capital is being shifted from person to person, but it is doubtful if any part of it is being consumed. Inconvenience and discomfort are being caused more as a result of readjustments and changes in organized life than as a result of the diminution of the products of consumers' goods.

If in ordinary times not more than 5 per cent of the energies of any people are used productively, it is conceivable that 95 per cent of the total energy of any European people could be devoted to war purposes, and so long as a residue of 5 per cent were left unused by war, there need not necessarily be any lack of consumers' goods.

If all the men of Europe would engage on the battlefront, then, properly directed, the labor of half the women could be more than sufficient to produce not only all the munitions of war but an aggregate of other products greater than was formerly produced by society in Europe as a whole.

Lending to the Poor

[*June 15, 1917*]

"Lending to the poor": it is the common jest at the gambling table. The tyro at the game, or the usually unlucky player, wins several large stakes. At the table are one or more experts of the game, who have just paid losses. The "greenhorn" is chuckling and boasting. Says the expert: "Oh, well, young fellow, I have just loaned it to you for awhile; I'll soon have it back, with interest." And, sure enough, nine times out of ten, that is just what happens.

One of the great New York bankers recently, in writing or speech, divided the mass of people into two classes: "the spenders," who are many, and "the savers," who are few.

Statistics gathered by practical men of affairs and theoretical economists prove that in this country and elsewhere in the civilized world, 2 per cent of the people own about 65 per cent of the wealth, each individual of which class in the United States possesses from $40,000 to hundreds of millions of dollars of property; and that some 33 per cent of the people own all other property, save the clothing, food, and the minor inexpensive tools necessary for maintaining a mere existence such as [is] held by the remaining 65 per cent.

Perhaps not less than three-fourths of existing property is held as a result of inheritance or gift from wealth-making kindred or friends. This three-fourths is gradually melting away from and dribbling through the fingers of the more or less inexpert beneficiaries of the bounty of others, falling into the general stream of circulating capital, which is soon enough to be taken up and appropriated by the master savers.

It is probable, then, that the real savers among all the people will not represent more than 0.5 per cent of their total number. These real savers pass

695

on, partly during life and principally at death, their hoards to the parasitic friends and kin.

So wealth, as far as ownership is concerned, is a constantly circulating, constantly moving stream. Wealth may be likened to the blood of an animal, as, proceeding from the heart, [it] goes out through the arteries, is distributed throughout the body, and returns through the veins to the heart.

The real savers may be likened to that organ which is called the heart in the living animal. This element of society, this economic heart, this class of savers, is a pump that keeps the moving flood of wealth in more or less active circulation. Like the muscle tissue of the heart which is constantly, by the force of metabolism, changing its material through the decay of old cells and the building up of new cells, so is this heart organ of the economic body constantly losing its individuals (individual cells) and adding to itself new individuals.

The economic heart is constantly lending the blood of wealth to the body politic, and constantly pumping back into itself the capital that is loaned.

The circulating flood of wealth keeps the body politic alive and healthy. That body would as quickly die, were its heart to cease to act, as would the animal body die if the heart pump ceased to function.

The animal body's heart cannot appropriate and keep for itself all the blood that passes through its valves. It is physically incompetent, by way of capacity, to hold such an amount of blood.

The economic heart, like the animal heart, can only live by functioning. Neither heart can live except by constantly giving and constantly taking.

Wealth unloaned and not in use ceases to be wealth.

If the inlet valve of the heart should be open and active, and the outlet valve clogged and inactive, both the body as a whole and the heart organ itself becomes sick. If the outlet valve is normal and the inlet valve weak, the heart races to its early destruction.

No man can really be said to keep his wealth, because wealth kept and unused ceases to be wealth. In order that wealth should be wealth, a man must give or lend his wealth, for wealth must always be circulating, in order that it shall be wealth.

The more wealth the savers give or lend to the body politic, the more wealth will return to the economic heart — the saving class.

Anyone who has tried to analyze and to thoroughly understand what wealth is soon finds himself involved in an unescapable labyrinth of metaphysics. Perhaps it is no more necessary to my argument to define the true nature of wealth than it is necessary for the physician to understand the chemical and all the other thousand attributes of the animal bloodstream.

We will think of wealth in common terms, as we think of blood in common terms.

Having reached the conclusion that wealth is only wealth when it circulates, and that the wealth of the body politic as a whole as well as its economic heart depends upon the free and normal circulation of wealth, it appears to me that any legal or conventional effort to restrain the free flow and circulation of wealth is injurious alike to rich and poor, employer and employee, to the capitalist and to the dispossessed.

Why, then, should there be any effort on the part of the capitalist and employer to reduce the wages of workmen, or even to set up any obstacle to the increase of wages?

It matters not at all how much wages we employers give to our workmen, since we only lend them to them, and since they are sure to return. The more wages we give, the more profits we must receive.

There is one limit to wages, and only one: and that is the volume of wealth in circulation. *Wealth can consist only in production.* The employer can give, in the form of wages, no more than his workman produces. If the workman demands as wages more than he produces, he simply demands that which it is impossible for his employer to give.

There is only one cause for workmen being deceived in this matter. Their employer may have in the past accumulated, in savings, capital; so that for a more or less brief time, so long as his capital lasts, it is possible for him to give as wages more than the value of the product of his employees. But bankruptcy comes soon. The reservoir of wealth, being exhausted, ceases to flow, and economic life must be replaced by death.

The wealth of a whole people consists hardly at all in material things that remain in existence for more than a brief time. Wealth consists of two processes: production and consumption. Stop either one of these processes, and there is no wealth.

The body politic, being an organism, so long as it is producing and consuming, functions and lives.

Wealth is a process. It consists not only of the things made by physical and mental labor but the activities or processes of the economic heart of the populace's functioning and pumping, into itself at one door its wealth, and out of another door this same wealth.

The interests, then, of capitalists and employers, of workmen and employees, must be identical.

But my heart and body metaphor is not completely descriptive. In order to make the definition intelligible, we must attribute to the economic heart of the economic world all the functions of the brain. The economic heart is not a blind muscle depending for its governance upon the medulla oblongata, but upon its governor, the brain; or rather, it is both brain tissue and heart muscle.

What wages should be paid to the workmen in order that the body politic should be in the most healthy condition, and in order that its heart — the class defined by the banker as the saving class — shall be most prosperous?

The wages paid to the worker should be such as will enable him — and, if possible, compel him — to be highly developed physically and mentally, to be developed to the highest point possible. The wealthier and the more intelligent a workman is, the more he can produce; and the more he produces, the more wealth there will be passing through the hands of his employer; and, hence, the more prosperous the employer will be.

It is a law of business that the greatest prosperity obtains where the profits are small and the volume of business large.

Then, the wage-payer should "loan" to his employee, in the way of wages, the largest possible amount of his, the employee's, product. The amount should be such a large portion of the laborer's product as will leave the employer the smallest amount of profit consistent with his capital and credit necessities, considering the present system of business.

The unintelligent, the penurious, the overgrasping employer who starves, mentally or physically, the employment of his operations — that is to say, the men in his service — may, in individual cases, set at naught natural law, and yet personally thrive and prosper. This is because the flood of wealth created by others than himself is so great that he can purloin a certain part of it without doing the body politic any great or fatal injury. However, if the whole class — all the individuals of the employing class — should attempt to emulate the example and follow the practices of such an individual as I have mentioned, the whole economic system must break down, just because wealth, in such a situation, would not be freely circulating; and the economic body and the economic heart organ would instantly begin to sicken and soon die.

Our workmen in this country, as a whole, do not receive wages to keep them up to anything like the full standard of physical and mental health or development, and, because of this, the economic growth and development of the country as a whole is vastly retarded.

Still, poorly as our American wage-workers are paid, and overworked as they are with regard to time and effort, they are far better paid and far less severely strained to hard work than are the workingmen in any other country on earth. The result of this slight advantage — that might be many times multiplied — is that the per capita production of the American workingman is from two to four times greater than that of any other workman in the European countries; the per capita wealth of this country is from two to twelve times greater than that of any European nation; there are more capitalists in this country than anywhere else on earth; and the capitalists are wealthier and, as a whole, enjoy comforts and luxuries such as no capitalist of the same grade in any other country can possibly enjoy.

If the little more sensible treatment of the American workman has produced such great results, how is it possible that our people should be so blind as not vastly to increase the wealth, the comforts and luxuries, and the pleasant and wholesome living of all of our people, rich and poor alike, by giving — "lending" would be the better term — to our workmen more wages, fewer hours of labor, less straining and health-undermining pressure than we have hitherto given them?

Another metaphor —

I propose to consider the circulation of wealth from another standpoint, and I propose to indulge in another metaphor.

Potential wealth may be likened to all the oceans and other bodies of water on the earth's surface.

The sun in the heavens represents human intelligence.

The physical sun radiates vast stores of heat that strike these oceans and other bodies of water, setting up kinetic motion that results in part of the waters turning into vapors, which rise above the ocean and above the land, and is finally precipitated. That portion which falls upon the land performs a function of bringing into existence, first, vegetable and then, animal organisms. Having performed this function, the larger part, if not the whole, of the water drains off, trickles off, flows off into streams, rivers, lakes, and the seas, and renews the latter's great body.

There it is again subject to the sun's rays; it is again transported to the skies; again it is precipitated to the earth; again it causes more life; and returns to the sea. Thus, the waters are performing their unending cycles, and life is.

In our economic world, the ocean consists of the vast reservoir of potential human energy. The sun of intelligence strikes its beams on this ocean, and transforms potential into actual energy. This energy is transformed into human products. These products go to feed the ocean of potential human energy; this energy again transfers itself into production, so that cycle succeeds cycle, and economic life is.

If the sun of intelligence ceases to function, there is death; if the sea of potential energy should be unmoved by the beams of intelligence, it would lie stagnant and cease to be. It would not only be stagnant and dead, but it would not be.

Life is movement, activity, energy. The greater movement, activity and energy let loose, the greater life is itself.

Man is something more than an animal. To live, he must not only feed his body and develop it, but he must feed his mind and develop it. In order to do this latter, man must take the form of society; society connotes organization; organization is human effort; human effort must be fed.

Organization is government, amongst other things, and government must function. In order to function, it must labor. The more complex the organization is, the greater amount of labor, physical and mental, that must be devoted to the functioning. Those who perform this labor must be fed, and clothed, and housed, and nourished, and all this costs money. The more complete and complex the organization, the larger the productions of society as a whole that must be devoted to government expense.

The money to meet this expense is obtained by a process called taxation.

The better the government is, the more costly it is; but the better a government is, the more is production facilitated; so that if any government is profitable, the better a government is (that is to say, the more a government does), the more profitable it is to all the elements that form the government — the vast body of which elements is constituted by the people who are governed and who have little part in the governing.

The functions of government are various. One of the most costly functions is warfare.

While warfare is, or is supposed to be, destructive and non-productive, warfare that is successful is less destructive, and possibly is even productive. That nation is the most prosperous that is successful in war, and hence no nation can afford to be unsuccessful in war.

But in matters of warfare, as well as in all other government functions, no man is so ignorant as not to understand that government processes, if the government is good and pure, are far more profitable to the individual than individual processes are. Hence, we see a constant straining on the part of the government to increase the proportion of universal products which shall be used and expended by the government itself.

That country, everything else being equal, is the most prosperous whose government levies the largest taxes in proportion to the whole production of the country, and expends the money it derives in a governmental way.

For reasons that are easily intelligible to all of those who have given consideration to the subject, large-scale operations are more economical and more fruitful than small-scale production.

Wealth, I have declared (and most economists agree with me), consists of the flow of things through production and consumption. Prosperity is in direct proportion to the rapidity of this flow. Everything else being equal, the government is a master "entrepreneur" in any nation. It is the superentrepreneur.

Society, in the form of a nation, then, may be likened to the ocean reservoir of potential energy. Its government should, and really does, take the place of the sun in the physical world, and of the sun of intelligence in the economic world.

The stronger are its beams, the more rapidly does it turn potential energy into active energy, and the more rapid and the more immense is the flow of the economic stream.

I will play with my metaphor a little more.

We will call the workers of the nation the reservoir or sea of energy. We will call the capitalist class (the saving class) the clouds.

The sea is excited into energy, and this energy throws up the vapor that gathers into the clouds. The capitalist clouds hold for a brief time the vapors, and precipitate them on the earth in the form of increasing prosperity.

It is the government's function, having indirectly produced the clouds, to cause them to precipitate, partly in the way of government works, and partly in the way of nourishment of the individual workers.

The capitalist class, then, is a part — and a necessary part — of the cycle of the constant flow of that which we define as wealth.

The cloud that remained a cloud in the sky would be useless to the cloud itself and to the earth beneath it. It is only useful because of its constant forming and its constant disintegration.

That is the best government that produces the most or largest clouds, and hence the greatest precipitation, and, hence, the greatest and most rapid flow of wealth, and greatest and most rapid production, and the greatest and most rapid consumption.

It appears from all the evidence at hand today (it at least is the belief of the large majority of the most intelligent persons on earth today) that the democratic form of government is the most successful form of government, and there is no lack of evidence, or knowledge even, that the democratic form of government takes to itself the largest proportion of society's production, and expends the same as a government.

This proposition would go to prove that the chief benefits of government are not good order nor any of those other things that appear to be the merits of the monarchial system.

The chief benefit of government is to be found in the rapidity and magnitude of the economic current it sets up and continues.

The Real Thing in the Way of an Industrial Democracy

A SUGGESTION OR A PROPHECY

[*January 1, 1919*]

Even though he did not review or revise this disquisition, Scripps sent a copy of it to several of his editorial lieutenants and influential men in various fields, including Irving Fisher, the Yale economist; Benjamin Ide Wheeler, president of the University of California; Hiram Johnson, by then United States senator from California; Senator Robert M. LaFollette; Justice Louis Brandeis; Judge Ben B. Lindsey; Clarence Darrow; Max Eastman; Amos Pinchot; Charles R. Crane; Roger Babson; Professor W. E. Ritter; Frank P. Walsh, who had been cochairman with former President Taft of the War Labor Board; Arthur C. Townley, who had organized the Non-Partisan League; Samuel Gompers; Theodore Roosevelt; Basil Manley; and William E. Kent.

Agricultural cooperation — cooperative association of agriculturists — has been well developed amongst fruit-growers and dairying people in this country. The economic condition of the people of Ireland has been vastly improved by the work of Sir Horace Plunkett in the way of forming cooperative associations of Irish farmers. Cooperative dairying and other farming enterprises are successfully conducted in all the Scandinavian countries, especially in Denmark. Banks for farm loans, which also assist the farmers in other ways, have been long established in Germany, and have been greatly beneficial to the agriculture of Germany.

A national system of farm loan banks has been inaugurated in this country. The Farmers Alliance in our northwestern states, both as a political party and as an economic institution, is in a flourishing condition and bids fair to spread. The Grange movement, inaugurated in this country a generation ago, exists still; it has, at times, exercised a good deal of influence in a political way.

I know something about the fruit-growers' exchanges in California. These exchanges are associations of fruit-growers. They have a central organization whose officers and employees undertake to receive and pack and ship and market the fruit for the individual members. They also purchase at wholesale prices all sorts of fruit-growers' supplies, such as fertilizers and all sorts of implements, which the members buy at a cost just sufficient to pay the expense of maintaining their staff.

Why should not all, or nearly all, of the wheat-growers of the United States form one great organization, which should own its own elevators and which would receive and market all the wheat raised, and thus keep within the hands of the grain-producers all the profits of the "middlemen" and the brokers of the wheat exchange? This organization could gather and always have on hand data which would enable each of the members to know what the prospects were for future demands of wheat and the price of the same.

In this way, remunerative prices could be maintained and there could be prevented the carrying over of a supply from one season into another. In scores of ways, such an organization of wheat-growers could be vastly beneficial to the wheat-growers themselves and to the public at large.

The organization of this wheat-growers' exchange or association could be quite democratic in form. There could be annual conventions in each county and each state of wheat-growers. The county conventions could, by vote, elect a committee of one or more men to represent that county. The vote of each wheat-grower in the county would be proportioned to the number of acres of his previous year's planting.

Following very closely after the annual county convention of wheat-growers should be a state convention to elect a state committee of one or more men. Following these state conventions, there could be a national convention in which all of the states would be represented by their committeemen.

The national congress of wheat-growers, through its agents, would have charge of the marketing of the whole country's wheat product. It could be authorized to assess on each bushel of wheat sold a certain charge to meet the expenses of the general wheat-growers' congress, and also to buy in or build elevators.

Proper officials of this congress, cooperating with the Agricultural Department of the United States, could disseminate more thoroughly and more authoritatively (because these representatives of the wheat congress would be more practical men) all sorts of valuable information to all of the wheat-growers of the whole country.

Having sketched the organization of the wheat-growers, it might be suggested that identically similar organizations should be formed by the corn-growers, by the hay-growers, fruit-growers, poultrymen, dairymen, cattle-raisers, sheepmen, swine-raisers — in fact, by the producers of all the most important of the agricultural products of the United States.

We have had in existence for a long time a system of trades unions which has developed into a tolerably effective national federation of labor.

There are now in all of the industries national associations of employ-ers. The lumber-producers are organized nationally. There are associations of operators in anthracite and bituminous coal. There are bankers' asso-ciations. There are national newspaper associations.

All of these associations, and others, could be more effectively organ-ized, and more thoroughly organized.

There is in nearly every city a Chamber of Commerce that includes in its membership all sorts of businessmen. There is now a rather large and loosely knit organization called the United States Chamber of Commerce. But these Chambers of Commerce, both local and national, are too in-clusive at present, and hence their memberships cannot be sufficiently homo-geneous and centralized in their efforts.

Perhaps the best organized and most effective national organization in the United States is that of the bankers.

The lawyers have their local, state, and national associations, but these are not very effective, so far as caring for the interests of the membership.

All of the churches, or nearly all of them, have national organizations.

All of the trades, all of the professions, all the various kinds of manu-facturers, all the various kinds of mining enterprises, all farmers, all the different kinds of labor, could, and perhaps should, have their city, county, state, and national organizations.

Annually, at the national capital, at the same time, all of these con-gresses could hold their sessions.

Each of these economic congresses could elect one or more members to a single NATIONAL INDUSTRIAL CONGRESS, the representation in this single national congress to be somewhat nearly proportioned to the number of people represented by each national congress of specialists, and somewhat proportioned, perhaps, by the public interest that is represented by each special body.

This congress of the congresses could sit at the national capital and be in session during the whole time of the session of the political Congress. The economic congress would naturally exercise so great an influence over the political congress as to make the latter body really its instrument in the way of legislation. In the course of generations, the importance of the po-litical Congress would atrophy, and probably, in time, it might die out al-together, leaving the government of these United States in the hands of a more representative and a far more efficient body of men than could be any congress, selected as our present national Congress is selected.

I imagine that all of this is "syndicalism," carried to its logical conclusion.

I take it for granted that this idea of mine, or something like it, has been hitherto formulated.

It would take perhaps a revolution, and a bloody revolution, to bring about this change of political government suddenly, or even in a few decades.

My idea, of course, is to avoid such a revolution. In fact, the aim of my suggestion is not to bring about such a revolution or such a government at all.

The aim of my suggestion is to bring into immediate existence, or comparatively immediately, a group of county, state, and national, effective organizations, each one of which will, at each step in its progress, be of immediate benefit to every member of every organization.

IF this be bolshevism, then I am willing to be called a bolshevist.

The Next Business Panic

[*April 26, 1919*]

By "panic," of course, I mean a period of business depression.

I have experienced three panics: that of 1873, that of 1893, and that of 1907.

I have read of a panic occurring in this country in 1837 or thereabouts. This date is well fixed in my mind.

I have a very strong impression that there was a panic in 1857 or thereabouts. Concerning this panic, I have no recollections — no recollection of reading about it.

There exists in the business world a general idea that panics are periodic, and that they occur about every 20 years.

I have a slight remembrance of reading somewhere that there were panics prior to 1837, separated by periods approximating 20 years.

There are plenty of people who argue and believe that each individual panic and each individual period of business depression has been caused by some particular event or general condition, and that the 20-year periodicity has only been because of accidental coincidences that do not prove a rule.

The three panics that I have spoken of as being in my own experience were major panics — "world-shakers," to use a seismological term.

But about midway between two of these panics there have been what might be called minor business depressions. For example, in 1884, almost midway between the panic of 1875 and 1893, there was quite a noticeable period of business depression in this country. Just 10 years after the great crisis of 1893, in 1903, there was a "bankers' panic."

In 1907 there was a severe business depression.

All of these three latter periods of depression that were so noticeable in the United States were also noticeable, to a greater or lesser extent, in Europe.

The panic of 1907 preceded by six years the 20-year point. The panic of

1873 also came three or four years too soon. It was argued by the periodicitists that the panic of 1873 was rushed forward somewhat by reason of the American Civil War and the Franco-Prussian War in Europe. I do not remember having heard any explanation of the 1907 panic coming in that year rather than in 1913.

There are good reasons, considering the matter psychologically, why great panics should be periodic and why they should be approximately 20 years apart.

It is usual to assume that a generation of the ordinary population has an extent of about 30 years. Until lately, the average longevity of the people in Europe and America was 30 years.

Biologists reckon as a generation the period of parenthood in the lives of men and women. Perhaps not less than 99 per cent of all children born are those in families in which not more than 25 years separate the birth of the first-born and the last-born child. The generations of businessmen, measured by years, are perhaps on the average 25 per cent shorter than 25 years. Taking all the businessmen in a country like ours, as a whole, it is probable that the average period of actual business activity of any man is not over 20 years. (I reckon this period from the time when a man ceases to be an apprentice or an employee and sets up in business for himself, up to the time when, although he continues nominally in control of his property, he has turned its management and actual control over to some younger man.)

Thus it would appear that there is, on the average, one major business panic to each active businessman's life experience.

It takes the experience of a severe business depression to make a businessman conservative and cautious. Any businessman who has experienced a severe panic and has weathered the storm will never be one of those overconfident, exuberant persons who contribute, through business excesses, to another panic.

I began my business career just a few months before the panic of 1873 broke. But I was in no condition to personally suffer much in the way of financial loss or personal discomfort on account of this panic. Still, I was old enough (I was in my nineteenth year) to observe its effects on others. Within a year or two after the panic of 1873, I launched out in a larger enterprise. I was successful and became very confident, not only in myself but in the business institutions of the country as a whole.

I had just fairly entered into a comparatively large further extension of my business ventures when the minor business depression of 1884 appeared. My experiences in, or rather observations of, the panic of 1873 were of advantage to me, so I became cautious and I easily weathered the minor depression of 1884.

At the time of the panic of 1893, I was in full swing in my business career. My recollections and my observations of 1873, reinforced by my experiences of 1884, were the cause of my encountering and passing through the panic of 1893 not only scatheless but something quite the reverse. I actually profited, and profited handsomely, from the panic of 1893 because I was one of only a comparatively few men then in active business who had learned what panics meant and how to handle them. I recall that it was about this time that I first began to make the statement that any fool in business could make money during good times, but that a really wise man could make more money in bad times than he could in good times.

The cry in 1893 was that the country was suffering from "want of confidence." This term was so universally used that we newspapermen fell into the habit of using as a symbol for these words the capital letters W.O.C. The "jokesmiths" on the newspapers made much use of this symbol.

My business career continued. I recall that I had become such a confirmed periodicitist and was so convinced that we would not have another panic until 1913 that I was actually reckless in my ventures so late as 1906. During that year, I undertook five or six or seven new enterprises and made extensive real estate purchases.

It was only late in the year 1906 and the very early part of 1907 that I became skeptical of the periodic theory.

I recalled something of what I had heard during the panic of 1873. In those old days, the wiseacres in journalism and elsewhere accounted for the panic of '73 by saying it had been preceded by a period of overproduction. Railroads had been building at the rate of 10,000 miles a year in this country. Old industries had been extended and their productions much increased, and many new industries had been initiated. Also there had been a great rise in real estate prices.

The minor panic of 1884 had been preceded by a somewhat similar condition, and even in 1884 the wiseacres were talking about overproduction.

It was late in 1906 or early 1907 that I began to take notes of general business conditions. Prosperity was general and excessive. Real estate prices had been mounting with great rapidity and there were general conditions similar to those I had heard of prior to the '73 panic and that I had known of prior to the '93 panic. I became obsessed with the idea that there was a panic coming, and that it could not be held off to the end of the 20-year period.

Now, at the time when I met the '93 panic, all of my then business associates were much younger men than I. None of them had any memory of the 1873 panic or perhaps had ever even heard much about it. These young men simply could not understand how there could be a panic and wouldn't believe that there was going to be one. The drastic measures I adopted at the beginning of the '93 panic caused a sensation of disgust

and even contempt at myself amongst my associates. Had I been no better equipped with acquired knowledge and personal experience than my
associates, I have no doubt that I would have gone down to ruin in the
panic of 1893, just as thousands and tens of thousands of other businessmen
did in 1893.

In 1907, nearly all of my active business associates — my captains and
lieutenants — were either young men or else men who in 1893 had not
been in a position to learn from their own experience what a panic meant.
I was comparatively old and worn out. The youngsters were virile and ambitious and confident. It required every bit of my energy and my force of
character and resolution to so far restrain the youngsters as to prevent the
whole crowd of them rushing pell-mell into destruction.

This, then, is the reason I have to give for the existence of the 20-year
cycle (approximately) of depression: namely, that at periods approximately
20 years apart there are in command of the great majority of the business
enterprises of the country young men who have not "had their fingers
burned" — who have not learned that there is a limit to human endeavor
in the way of propagating and developing business.

When too many controlling men of the business world are so young as
to be lacking in the personal experiences of a business depression, there
is a time when overconfidence prevails and when business disaster is at the
open door ready to enter in.

Such disturbing causes as the Civil War in America and the Franco-Prussian War in Europe may, by first exhilarating business too much, hasten a
period of depression.

The late tremendous war in Europe wonderfully excited and exhilarated
enterprise in all the civilized nations. The cessation of this war and the
condition in which things were left bid fair, for a time at least, rather to increase the exhilaration of the activities of the people of many nations.

The last major panic or business depression was in 1907. Under ordinary conditions, the next panic might be looked for in 1927. However,
conditions are not ordinary. They are quite the reverse, and therefore I
shall not be surprised if the next great world-shaking business panic and
depression should set in not later than four years hence. It may occur a
year or two sooner, or a year or two later. But it seems to me that it is
inevitable that we shall have a great business depression years before 1927.

If the panic of 1907 was not nearly so disastrous as was that of 1893,
perhaps this can be accounted for by the fact that, coming earlier, it found
more old and seasoned and experienced men in the saddle.

If this conclusion is right, then we should feel that the sooner the next
panic comes the better, as the more certain it will be that there will be in

the places of business control a very large number of men who had the training of the 1907 panic.

Now, assuming that this panic (this great business depression) is due to arrive in a period approximately four years hence, what immediate steps should be taken by an individual in control of a large business now?

First, I would have him read in Genesis the story of Joseph who, during a period of seven fat years in Egypt, saved all the surplus grain produced and put it in granaries, with which to feed the people during the seven lean years that his wisdom taught him were about to come.

The businessman of today, then, *while business is very good, should be more than ever careful and cautious in obtaining the largest possible profit and in building up his reserve funds.*

He should have his reserve funds consist of the most liquid capital possible short of actual gold or money in bank. His reserves should consist of many securities usually called "gilt-edged" — securities that can at any time, even in the worst of panics, be transmuted into money.

While in ordinary times I hold that actual money is the least profitable kind of property that anyone can hold, I am inclined to think that in these times that are not ordinary, money or securities that can be turned into real gold money at any time might be the best sort of property to hold.

Today we have a great inflation of currency. We have a tremendous amount of paper money that cannot be redeemed in coin even by our government. This inflation of the currency has caused the inflation of prices of all sorts of things — perhaps even of land itself, though land seems to have been the least affected.

If there is to be deflation (according to the present consensus of opinion of practical financiers and economic theorists, it appears that this deflation is going to be made as slow a process as possible), then there is going to be a great decrease in the valuation of almost everything except money. It is said, for instance, that a dollar today will not buy more than half a dollar would have bought five years ago. If deflation were to be made instantaneously, or almost instantaneously, the result might be that the price of all sorts of commodities will fall to nearly half their present level. In that case (in the case of an instantaneous deflation), then the man who had turned all of his paper dollars into gold coin securities, and would sell almost all sorts of property he owned today on a present valuation — selling for paper money and turning the same into gold money — he could, after a year or two or three, buy back with his gold money twice as much property as he had sold, and buy with the paper money that he had turned into gold money twice as much property then as he could now.

There were great fortunes made during the war just closed by businessmen who were fortunately situated or who were shrewd enough to see opportunities and take advantage of them. I am inclined to think that far more money will change hands in the next five or six years than has changed hands during the last five or six years, and I am also inclined to believe that a large portion of the wealthy and well-to-do people (or those who consider themselves wealthy and well-to-do today) will have lost all or nearly all of their fortune to the advantage of their shrewder neighbors and business colleagues.

Many of the war financiers who made their money easily will lose it even more easily. These of all people will be the least competent readers of the signs in the business world.

Indolent, old, and conservative men who are no longer able to be alert in reading the signs or anxious to take advantage of them will suffer, to the advantage of younger and more alert men.

I would say that these are days in which to sell, just as a few years ago I said that those were days in which to buy.

One Aspect of Money

[*May 3, 1919*]

For years I have been trying to find out what really is the thing I call a dollar. I sometimes tried to define the thing by calling it a condition or a relation or a process. Of course, a gold dollar is a piece of gold and a silver dollar is a piece of silver. Then, dollars can be made up of collections of nickel coin or copper coin. I think it was Lycurgus who gave his Grecian city an iron dollar — perhaps not a dollar, but something very much like a dollar.

There is the idea of a dollar being a measuring stick — something like a foot rule.

A dollar might be made out of wheat or diamonds or coal, of a kilowatt of electricity, of a singing woman's voice, of a scientist's thought, or a poet's dream.

Dollars are money. A dollar is a symbol. It can stand for a part of anything or a part of everything. The symbol is never the same thing as viewed by any two or more men.

A great peculiarity about the dollar is that everybody thinks he knows what it is and, although his knowledge is ignorance absolute, it is just as usable as if it was wisdom absolute.

Just today I caught a fleeting glimpse of what I think may be a whole definition and description of a dollar — namely, its attribute.

Every living thing, every inert organic mass, every thought — each and all of these things — have many attributes, perhaps an infinity of attributes. Perhaps a dollar has only one attribute. (Maybe I should use the word money now instead of dollar.)

The attribute of money is that it is a relation between two things that men value. It is not a thing at all, either in the way of material or thought. Mentally, the relation between two things can be conceived, but the relation is not a thing. I wonder if it can be defined as a condition.

Money is used as a means of exchange. In terms of quantity of money is expressed the relative values of two things or of many things.

The words "more" or "less" do not indicate things; they indicate relations. There is only one attribute to "more" and only one to "less" and only one to "many."

A man is a material body; a man is also what they call a mind or spirit or soul. But is a man a material body at all? Is not that thing which we call mind or spirit or soul — that thing which is no thing — the man?

Like a human being, money has material form. It can be counted and weighed and otherwise measured. But is this material substance which we call money, money at all? That element which makes money money at all is not a material thing or even an idea; it is only a relation.

Well, all this may be metaphysical and probably is intolerable to the reader as it is to the writer.

Water is a solvent of many things. It is a solvent of a number of minerals. Some of these minerals are plant food. A plant cannot ingest its mineral food unless it be dissolved in water.

Tom Smith has a pair of shoes. John Jones has a horse. Richard Roe has a bushel of potatoes. Anna Moore has a gallon of milk. And an infinite number of other people have an infinite number of other things. All of these people need for their sustenance some of these things owned by all those people. Before any of these people can obtain the use of any of these things, they must all be subjected to the solvent properties of money — that is, their relativity must be established. How much of each thing is to be exchanged for how much of another thing? The relativity of any of these things is conceived in the mind, and the conception of this relativity is not the cause, but the existence, of money. Gold, silver, nickel, copper, and other things may be made to constitute dollars, or money, or perhaps be made to contain the element which is called money. The element that is called money is imbedded in a material thing — gold, silver, copper, etc. — just as the soul is imbedded in the body of a man. Not the gold nor the silver nor the copper is money, although they each have a relativity to wheat, potatoes, milk, and boots.

Suppose one man has a house and another man has a steamboat. The two men contemplate exchanging property. The relative values of the two things are considered by both to be identical. The house is exchanged for the boat. The former owner of the house now owns the boat and the former owner of the boat now owns the house.

In this transaction it may be that the word money has not been used. Even the conception of dollars and cents related to the transaction may not have occurred to either mind. But the condition of relativity exists and, had that condition been expressed as a part of the process of exchange, it would have been expressed in terms of money.

The house might have been valued at $10,000 and the boat also at $10,-000. That is to say, both of these objects could have been exchanged for other things the values of which would have been measured by dollars — for things the aggregate value of which would have been $10,000.

It would have been perfectly correct to say, then, that the man sold his house for $10,000 worth of something and that the man sold his ship for $10,000 worth of something.

Money is relativity; it symbolizes relation; it is a term expressing relation; money is not a thing; it is one attribute of everything that has value; it is not a number of attributes; it is only one attribute. In reality, men do not want money, no matter what appearances indicate. They want valuable things — things whose relative value to other things is expressed in money. Gold and silver and copper and nickel, etc., are things, but they are no more money than are wheat, potatoes, shoes, or musical notes.

In the primitive times of barter and exchange they had no pieces of metal called money. In those days it was only possible to exchange one whole thing for another whole thing. At best one whole thing might be divided into several parts, each of which would be a whole thing. These parts of one thing could be exchanged by barter for the parts of another thing. But the division of things into parts was difficult and cumbersome and there was a limit to the diminutiveness in the size of parts. A part of a thing might be too small for practical use. For instance, a savage could not exchange a half of his hut for a half or a quarter or a whole deer.

The recognition and naming of the conception of money and the attaching to different objects, such as pieces of gold, the attribute of relativity (which is money) permitted the growth and development of an infinite amount of exchange of commodities between different people.

As I go blundering along with these words, words, words, I am wondering how many other people have caught a glimpse of the meaning of money, as I have just done, and have found it just as impossible as I have found it to describe that thing which they have glimpsed.

The Wisdom of Gotrox

[*May 22, 1925*]

Scripps thought this one was "quite good."

My young friends, you have come to me for advice as to how to become rich.[18]

If you had wanted to know how to become an alderman, a legislator, a congressman, a governor, a member of the president's cabinet, you should have gone to a politician.

If you had wanted to know how to become a favorite with the ladies, you should have sought advice of Lothario.

If you had wanted to become wise in philosophy and science, you should have gone to a college professor.

There are many ways in which a man can become distinguished and there are as many kinds of men who can assist you in each of these ways as there are ways themselves.

But you want to get rich. Very well, let's get down to brass tacks.

First. — Never spend as much money as you earn. The smaller your expenditures are in proportion to your earnings the sooner you will become rich.

Second. — It is more blessed to give wages than to accept them, or at least, it is more profitable.

Third. — Never do anything yourself that you can get someone else to do for you. The more things that someone else does for you the more time and energy you have to do those things which no one else can do for you.

Fourth. — Never do anything today that you can put off till tomorrow. There is always so much to do today that you should not waste your time

---

[18] Combined with other material, an edited version of this disquisition appears in McCabe, *Damned Old Crank*, p. 109 f.

715

and energy in doing anything today that can be put off until tomorrow. Most things that you do not have to do today are not worth doing at all.

Fifth. — Always buy, never sell. If you've got enough horse sense to become rich, you know that it is better to run only one risk than two risks. You also know that just as likely as not the other fellow is smarter than you are and that whether you buy or sell, in each case you run the risk of getting the worst of the bargain. By adopting my rule you will diminish by one-half your chances of loss.

Sixth. — Never do anything if you can help it that someone else is doing. Why compete with one person or many other persons in any occupation or line of business so long as it is possible for you to have a monopoly in some other field?

Seventh. — If circumstances compel you to pursue some occupation or to follow some line of business, which occupation or line of business is being pursued by some other person or persons, then do you do your work in some other way than that in which it is done by others. There is always a good, better, and best way. If you take the best way, then the other fellow has no chance in competing with you.

Eighth. — Whatever you do once, whatever way you undertake to do a thing once, don't do the same thing again or don't do the thing in the same way, because knowing one way of doing a thing you must know that there is a better way of doing the same thing.

Ninth. — If you're succeeding in anything you are doing, don't let anyone else know of your success, because if you do some other person or persons will try to do the same thing that you are doing and be your competitor.

Tenth. — When you become rich, as you will become rich if you follow my advice, don't let anyone know it. General knowledge of your wealth will only attract the tax-gatherer, and other hungry people will try to get away from you something they want and something you want to keep.

Eleventh. — One of the greatest assets any man can secure is a reputation for eccentricity. If you have a reputation for eccentricity you can do a lot of things, you can even do the things you want to do without attaching to yourself the enmity of others. Many an act performed by an ordinary person which would arouse indignation, animosity, and antagonism can be performed by a man with a reputation of eccentricity with no other result than that of exciting mirth and perhaps pity and sympathy. It is better to have the goodwill than the bad will, even of a dog.

Twelfth. — Never hate anybody. Hatred is a useless expenditure of mental and nervous energy. Revenge costs much of energy and gains nothing. Carlyle once said of the English people that there were so and so many millions of English people, mostly fools. When you find many people applauding you for what you do, and a few condemning, you can be certain that you are on the wrong course, because you're doing the things that fools approve of. When the crowd ridicules you and scorns you, you can know at least one thing, and that is that it is at least possible that you are acting wisely. It is one of the instincts of man to covet applause. The wise man regulates his conduct rather by reason than by instinct.

Thirteenth. — It is far more important to learn what not to do than what to do. You can learn this invaluable lesson in two ways, the first of which and the most important is by your own mistakes, the second is by observing the mistakes of others. Any man that learns all the things that he ought not to do cannot help doing the things that he ought to do.

Fourteenth. — Posterity never can do anything for you. Therefore, you should invest nothing in posterity. Of course, your heirs will quarrel over your estate, but that will be after you're dead, and why should you trouble your mind over things which you will never know anything about?

Fifteenth. — A man can do anything he wants to do in this world, at least if he wants to do it bad enough. Therefore, I say that any of you who want to become rich can become rich if you live long enough.

Sixteenth. — After what I have said, it goes without further saying that you should save money, but no man can save himself rich, he can only make himself rich. Savings are capital. It is only by doing things that one learns how to do things. It is only the capitalist who handles capital that learns how to handle capital profitably. The more capital you have the more skillful you become as a capitalist.

Seventeenth. — Fools say that money makes money. I say that money does not make money, it is only men who make money.

Eighteenth. — There are two cardinal sins in the economic world, one is giving something for nothing, and the other is getting something for nothing, and the greater sin of those two is that of getting something for nothing — or trying to do so. Really, I doubt if anyone ever does get something for nothing.

Don't marry a rich wife. Women are what they are. At best they are hard enough to get along with. They are always trying to make a man do something that he doesn't want to do, and generally succeeding, but when a woman is conscious of the fact that she has furnished all or any part of your capital, her influence over you will be so great as to be the worst handicap that you can carry.

Nineteenth. — If you're a prospective heir of your father or some other relative, you should also consider that a handicap. I would advise you to refuse to be an heir.

Twentieth. — Despise not the day of small things, but rather respect the small things. It is far easier to make a profit on a very small capital invested in any business than it is to make the same proportion of profit off of large capital. It is true that after you have learned how to make a profit on a business that has small capital, and after successively as your capital grows you learn how to handle it profitably, the time may come, aye, I would say that the greater your capital becomes in this way the greater your proportion of profits on it should be. And, for an additional reason, as your wealth and skill grow rapidly, your so-called necessary expenses grow much slower and in time cease to grow at all so that beyond a certain limit all your income and added income becomes a surplus, constantly to be added to your capital.

Twenty-first. — It is far easier to make money than it is to spend money. As it becomes more and more difficult to spend money, you will spend less and less of it, and hence there will be more money to accumulate.

Twenty-second. — The hardest of all labor performed by man is that of thinking. One can think hard and even think straight, and yet, without financial reward. If you have become rich, train your mind to hard thinking and hold it well in leash so that your thinking will all be with but one object in view, that of accumulating more wealth.

It is true that a man cannot serve both God and Mammon. If your only aim is to obtain wealth, then you should devote all of your services to Mammon.

It has been said that that is the happiest nation which has the least history. I will say that it is the most successful wealth-getter whose wealth is the least known of by the public or even his most intimate associates.

Some fool has said that as nothing succeeds like success, then a reputation for being successful is equally good with the fact of success. I once knew a man who was so obsessed with this folly that I felt certain that he would rather have a real income of $10,000 a year, with the reputation of having $100,000 a year, than to have a real income of $100,000 a year with the reputation of having $10,000 a year. This man was an easy mark for his associates who gave him offices and positions of distinction in return for great services which he performed for small pay.

The investments of capital that make the greatest profit are those on which the returns are longest delayed. The greatest fortunes in the United States today are those on which the income returns were longest delayed. The reason for this is that most of us live practically a hand-to-mouth existence, and only those whose capital, compared with their daily expense account, is large can wait 10, 20, 30, 40, 50, or 100 years for their returns as investors. The longer the prospective time to elapse between investments and dividends, the fewer are those who can either afford to wait or have intelligence enough to wait. I'll make an exception in this case of giving an example which is an explanation.

A man has one piece of land. If he plants it with garden truck he can expect returns from it in three to four months. If the piece of land is large enough he can plant it to a crop which will give him no returns for six or eight months. He can plant it to corn, for instance. If he is both wise and forehanded he will not sell his corn, he will feed it to pigs and sell pork, perhaps a year or more after he has made his first investment in planting his field. If the same man has both intelligence enough and a large enough income, he may plant it to timber. If at the end of 40 years he cuts and sells this timber he will sell it at such a profit as to be far greater than would have been the total profits of 40 years of annual crops. If he is still intelligent and at the same time regards his heirs as being but an extension of himself, he will allow his timber to grow for 80 or 90 years, and then when the timber is cut and sold, it will be found that the profits will be greater than would have been the total profits had he cut and sold his timber when it was 40 years grown.

It has been truly said that he who can take good advice doesn't need it. This is the large class [sic]. I doubt if there are more than two or three among you who can benefit by what I have said. I consider it more than probable that none of you will profit by what I have said.

I know I have said a number of things that most of you think are paradoxes and that an equal number consider it to be downright foolishness. I know that if I permitted you to do so you would deluge me with questions asking me to give you a logical explanation of my brief statements.

However, I am convinced that if there are any among you who are yet to become wealthy those will be able to answer for themselves all the questions that any of you could ask.

MAN AND UNIVERSE

"What is this damned human animal, anyway?"

Scripps' blunt question — which, variously and more esoterically put, has engaged philosophers for centuries — comes from, and goes to, the heart of his interest in science. In approaching and encouraging scientific investigation, Scripps was concerned first and foremost with Man, his nature, his problems, and his place in the universe. A generalist here as in other areas (and on much less sure but equally critical grounds), he had little sympathy with the artificial separateness of the social, physical, and natural sciences, holding that all should be coordinated toward the common end of learning more about and understanding Man.

Scripps' interest in science was aroused about 1904 and continued until his death in 1926 — roughly, the period in which American science came of age. During those years, science became dominant in and central to American culture, making its impress on life, thought, and faith. During most of the preceding century, Americans had been, comparatively, an uneducated people who used a practical approach in conquering a wilderness and unlocking the wealth of a continent. But as wealth increased through industrialization, itself developing with a scientific impetus, more and more Americans became able to afford the expensive luxury of university training. Beginning especially in the 1870's, an increasing number of young Americans trooped to European universities, where they were trained in various disciplines, bringing home to America new theories and new knowledge which they transferred to an increasing number of universities. As the century advanced, more and more Americans were trained in American universities. By the early 1900's, scientific research in America was vigorous and mature, for its time. Most of the research was being done in university and corporation laboratories. Increasingly, the government became involved in and contributed to research, first through state universities and later through laboratories maintained by various federal agencies.

At the apex of the changes wrought by science stood a new direction of thought. The rationalism by which older philosophers and theologians had sought truth through logical deduction gave way grudgingly to the positivism of scientific thought — scientific fact-finding through experimentation. The new trend resulted in a massive conflict between science and theology. Gradually, the systematic approach of science became imbedded in American thinking, and "scientific" became something of a talisman. In place of blind faith, science substituted scientific determinism and materialism. The growing importance of science was shown in the curricula of high schools, most of which required at least one science course by 1910.

Both basic and applied research produced constantly widening areas of knowledge which contributed to human welfare and re-adjusted philosophical conceptions. In medicine, researchers identified the source of and means of controlling yellow fever and malaria; they developed serums to immunize people against the dread typhoid and child-killing diphtheria; they found novocaine as a local anesthetic; they identified and found means of controlling the hookworm. Closely related to medical research, chemistry reached in these years what has been called a harvest time. By developing chemicals that would kill bacteria, chemists helped to cure and prevent disease. By examining food chemistry, scientists discovered vitamins and means of preventing diseases caused by diet deficiency.

Psychology moved out of philosophy and established itself as a science, just as other social sciences, especially sociology, adopted the terminology and approach of science. Along with psychology rose what is now its medical senior, psychiatry. Psychoanalysis proceeded from Sigmund Freud's conclusions in Vienna that nervous and mental disorders proceeded from sexual repressions, and Freudianism — promising release from the sham of Victorian ethics — became a cult in America after 1910.

Of greatest importance within the frame of reference here, biological research was particularly intense. Mendel's law of heredity, based upon botanical research, became known about 1900. Thomas Hunt Morgan of Columbia and Edwin Grant Conklin of Princeton added to knowledge of heredity through research dealing with chromosomes. Proceeding from the same general impetus came the school of eugenics, begun in England by Charles Darwin's cousin, Francis Galton, and his son, Leonard Darwin, which initially was aimed only at segregation or sterilization of defectives. But extremists carried the idea much farther in developing notions of racial superiority which placed the Aryan at the top of the human heap.

In the thought currents generated by the research, there arose the old question of free will in a new guise: Could man direct his evolution for his own welfare? And a new school of philosophy developed through the thought of John Dewey and William James — pragmatism, which, in essence, held that something was good if it worked well.

In short, science introduced a whole new thought stream into American culture in the early 1900's, of which Scripps made himself part and left a mark which, as with almost everything else he touched, has endured to this day. He made his most important tangible contributions to science through aiding in establishment of and giving initial direction to what is now the Scripps Institution of Oceanography at the San Diego suburb of La Jolla, and the Foundation for Population Research at Miami University, Ohio. He made his most important intangible contribution in conceiving, originating, and placing in operation the present Science Service, which has been disseminating reliable scientific information to the general public through newspapers for almost half a century now.

However, Scripps did not initiate his interest in science; he was drawn into it. Beginning in 1892 the department of zoology of the University of California had begun a series of summer field investigations of the animal life of the Pacific Ocean, under the direction of Professor William Emerson Ritter. Having been conducted at different sites along the coast, the research was being carried out at San Diego in 1903. At that point, Dr. Fred Baker — a San Diego physician who studied mollusca — took the lead in making the research station in San Diego permanent. Baker brought Scripps into the picture by inviting him to visit the station, probably Scripps' first glimpse of a laboratory. Scripps became interested to the extent of contributing some money, getting Ellen B. to contribute more, and finding a permanent site for the station by inducing the city of San Diego to deed a 170-acre pueblo which it held from an old Mexican land grant. Along with those who were taking the lead, Scripps participated in forming the Marine Biological Association of San Diego in 1903, which helped provide financial support for the summer research. Ritter took up permanent residence there in 1906 and, permanent buildings having been erected, directed year-round research. In 1912 the University of California assimilated the station as the Scripps Institution for Biological Research.

Scripps had been much taken by Ritter on his visit to the research station in 1903, and had invited Ritter to visit him at "Miramar" where he became ever more interested in the scientist, who was about his own age. Indeed, he said several times that he threw his support, and later his enthusiasm, to the infant institution simply because he wanted to see what Ritter could do. If true, it was his old technique of betting on a man, the same reason that prompted him to engage the sculptor Arthur Putnam when he did not care a dime for sculpture itself. He did not endow the institution so much as he endowed Ritter, he said.

Ritter became his closest personal friend of a lifetime, and the two men interacted upon each other in a way that was of great consequence to each of them as individuals.

Born in 1856 on a Wisconsin farm where he spent his boyhood, Ritter was graduated from the Oshkosh Normal School in 1884, obtained a Bachelor of Science degree from the University of California in 1888, and a Ph.D. from Harvard in 1893. He joined the California faculty in 1891.

Ritter was a tall, straight, large-boned man with twinkling blue eyes. In conversation, he gave full attention to his companion, leaning forward to listen, and then leaning back and gazing off into the distance as he spoke in a strong, deliberately paced voice. His associates remembered him as a lovable man and a scientist of force and originality.[1]

Their friendship — that of a man of the world and of a man from the academic cloister — rested upon an intellectual attachment, a common idealism, and a common role of inquirers seeking the truth wherever it might be found.[2] At least two or three times a week, and often daily, Scripps dropped in on Ritter unannounced. Poking his head in the door, Scripps would remove his cigar, and throw a question at Ritter. Often, he prodded Ritter with the question, "What is this damned human animal, anyway?" The conversation that ensued when Scripps visited the institution, which he called "Bugville," could embrace anything in the heavens, on the earth, or in the ocean. The two men became so close during the years that Mrs. Ritter and Scripps' secretary, unbeknownst to each other, dubbed them David and Jonathan.[3]

The change that took place in Ritter's outlook through the influence of Scripps' broader, humanistic interest can be seen in Ritter's work. Until about 1910 Ritter confined himself to discrete researches in the classification of and study of the form and structure of plants and animals. But increasingly he broadened his view until more and more he wrote in a philosophical and interpretive vein, becoming what one biographer called a biological philosopher. Both Ritter and his wife attributed this change to Scripps' influence. In 1927, a year after Scripps' death, Ritter retired to Berkeley and spent the last sixteen years of his life carrying out what he regarded as Scripps' last assignment to him, as couched many times in the question: "Ritter, you are a zoologist. Why can't you tell us what kind of a thing this damned human animal is?" Not until after Scripps' death did Ritter realize the sincerity of the question, having regarded it when asked

[1] Dr. Denis L. Fox, Scripps Institution of Oceanography, interview with editor, July 19, 1961; Francis B. Sumner, "William Emerson Ritter: Naturalist and Philosopher," *Contrib. Scripps Inst. Oceanography*, No. 223 (Vol. 10, Pt. 1, 1944), reprint from *Science*, Apr. 28, 1944, pp. 335–38.

[2] Mary Bennett (Mrs. W. E.) Ritter, *More Than Gold in California* (Berkeley, 1933), p. 306.

[3] *Ibid.*

as an expression of a hopelessly complex problem. But in looking back, Ritter realized Scripps had hoped the scientist could "throw some light on this appalling and terrifying problem. . . ."[4]

Ritter no less affected Scripps, opening to him the world of scientific inquiry. As Scripps' interest in science ripened, his letters and disquisitions showed that he was reading and thinking deeply. Through Ritter and others, Scripps became personally acquainted with several eminent scientists.

Ritter had started out with the idea as early as 1901 that the biological station should be involved in physical, chemical, hydrographic, and biological research, but Scripps conceived a broader role for it. Scripps stated his ideal in 1909:

> The ideal institution that I had in view was not a school of instruction but a school of research and compilation, and (to make a bad use of the word commonly made) of generalization.
>
> .   .   .   .
>
> I am convinced that modern civilization is the outgrowth of philosophy, religion, and of codes of ethics, of customs and institutions that were founded upon known data far inferior in quantity and in quality to what science can furnish today. This data is not only inferior in quantity and quality but much of it, perhaps the greater part, is false data. As a result of this condition of affairs, the lives of most human beings are unhappy.
>
> .   .   .   .
>
> I would have a school for the study of life — and perhaps life extends far and away beyond the borders of that field which the term biology is supposed to cover.
>
> I would have a school of life the organization of which would be divided into three departments, the lowest, the elementary department, of which would be engaged in what is called research. The second department would consist of one or more men who would record, correlate, assemble, and segregate into groups the facts gathered by the first department. The third department would consist of men who would generalize all the information gathered and recorded and therefrom make deductions which would be passed out to the world as authoritative and as the last word so far uttered concerning what is actually known, in order that the people might govern their conduct individually and as social organisms according to so much of nature's law as had been discerned.[5]

He had tried to impose originality upon the institution three years earlier in advising Ritter against buying a library which had been offered for sale. Following the same rule that he adopted with his newspapers, Scripps urged putting money into men rather than equipment, and starting on a modest scale in order to make future financing easier. But his most important point

[4] William E. Ritter, *Charles Darwin and the Golden Rule*, comp. and ed. Edna Watson Bailey (Washington, 1954), pp. xiv–xvii.

[5] "The Biological Station Begins to Be a Disappointment," EWS Writings, 2:194–96.

was that Ritter did not yet know where the idea behind the institution would take him, that adoption of "conventional and traditional" equipment would force him into a rut, that old books and old ideas were fine for young students but that Ritter and his associates should be projecting themselves into the unknown instead of falling back on the known, and that "the library you should covet should be the one that is yet unwritten and uncatalogued." [6]

Because Scripps' whole idea from the beginning was that the institution should be directed to the study of man, he envisioned it as containing an important sociological research function. But the university, deciding about 1915 that such scope did not accord with its plans, held the Scripps Institution to biological research. Scripps blamed "a bunch of wooden-headed, visionless, university men" for tearing up his and Ritter's plans, and accused them of having "burned down our temple to roast a little pig." [7]

As time went on, the institution focused more and more upon study of the sea, and was renamed the Scripps Institution of Oceanography in 1925. Scripps was not particularly happy about but accepted the change.

With the original dream smashed, Scripps in concert with Ritter turned his attention in another direction. While recovering from his stroke, Scripps had said in 1918, "I have a tremendous ambition to at least make the beginning of an entire new system of investigations of sociology, economics, and psychology, and to at least make a start in a new way, considering the effects of environment." [8] He did not elaborate that idea at the time, and did nothing more along that line. But in 1919 he began drawing plans for the "American Society for the Dissemination of Science." He planned to endow such an organization, place at its head one editor and one business manager (the old formula), and through it channel to the people, via newspaper, articles written by scientists. In 1921, the organization became Science News Service and later Science Service. Using George H.'s estate, Scripps endowed Science Service with $500,000, allocating to it $30,000 a year until it should become self-supporting. It was, and has since been, directed by trustees nominated by the National Academy of Sciences, National Research Council, American Association for the Advancement of Science, the E. W. Scripps Estate, and newspaper groups. Science Service has developed into a specialized news service that has been in the forefront of popularizing scientific knowledge, a movement that began after World War I. Previously, a complete lack of rapport between scientists and newspapermen had cheapened and even falsified what information a newspaper reader usually received about science, particularly in the sensation-

[6] EWS to W. E. Ritter, Oct. 22, 1906.
[7] "Intended to Be Vitriolic," EWS Writings, 6:168.
[8] EWS to EBS, Apr. 25, 1918.

alized, pseudoscience accounts in Sunday supplements earlier in the century.

Also working in concert with Ritter, Scripps endowed the Foundation for Population Research at Miami University in 1921, and placed at its head Professor Warren Thompson. That he foresaw an urgent problem is demonstrated by the great concern over the "population explosion" being shown in the 1960's.

The editor of Ritter's posthumous book concluded that Ritter and Scripps viewed the three institutions — oceanography, Science Service, population foundation — as one foundation for the study of man and dissemination of the results of the research.[9]

Because of Scripps' dedication to humanism, he was a close student of social, political, and economic subjects, but nothing more than what Ritter politely called a "dabbler" in the physical and natural sciences, yet even in those fields his spirit of protest manifested itself. For instance, Scripps noted that scientists said at one and the same time that man was the most perfectly developed animal and that he was the last of the life-forms to inhabit the earth. If man is the highest form of life and if the theory of evolution is valid, Scripps reasoned, why the view that man is the youngest and not the oldest of life-forms? The mere fact that archeologists and paleontologists had not uncovered the remains of a civilization superior to our own did not at all satisfy Scripps that such a superior civilization had existed.

He said science's view of man as the youngest life-form may have no better basis than the story of the Garden of Eden. Indeed, on another occasion, he said Sir William Ramsay, the English scientist, and Thorstein Veblen were the only two authors he had ever read "who have never shocked me by frequent revelations of their being biased by superstition and tradition. . . ."[10]

Noting the various fields and theories of science, Scripps wondered whether scientists in all fields might not be benefited by adopting and testing a common hypothesis. This undoubtedly would have given much impetus toward the solution of the problem in which he was most interested — the nature of man — but he did nothing to help formulate such a common hypothesis.

Scripps read and mulled over the writings of the eugenicists, flipped their ideas to the underside and considered the question from what he knew of horse-breeding, flipped it back up and decided it was not for him. However, the Aryanism that came from eugenics did infect some of his thinking, as indicated in the Foreign Affairs section.

To the rising school of psychoanalysis, which he called the "nasty sci-

[9] Ritter, *Charles Darwin and the Golden Rule*, p. xi.
[10] EWS to W. B. Colver, Apr. 11, 1909.

ence," Scripps reacted violently, even with deep revulsion. He simply could not conceive that repressed sexual desires could account for so much human behavior. Falling back on a faith in goodness and beauty, he refused to believe that a baby at his mother's breast was engaged in a sex act.[11]

Before approaching the study of science, Scripps had formed two points of view which he had not previously regarded as contradictory. One was that a man inherited about 90 per cent of his characteristics; the other was his oft-repeated dictum, "the job makes the man." Becoming better versed in the current discussions of heredity versus environment, Scripps fought the question out within himself, finally concluding that he was an environmentalist.

Through his reading of biology he became acquainted with the various theories of heredity, almost always bringing his discussion of biology back to himself, thus demonstrating anew the magnitude of his egocentrism. The biologists astonished him, too, when they informed him that the biological process of transmitting characteristics was such that it was possible some of his descendants would have none of his characteristics. See "When an Ancestor Is Not an Ancestor."

At that time, important work in biology was being done by Morgan and Conklin, with whom Scripps chanced to have a three-way conversation. His description of the conversation may be illustrative of his manner in dealing with men who were leagues in advance of him. The conference occurred when Scripps visited the Woods Hole, Massachusetts, oceanographic laboratory in 1922.

I had the good fortune of meeting Professor Edwin Conklin of Princeton University who had spent a couple of days with me on my yacht in the Pacific last summer. I have been greatly interested in his books and in his theories, and, personally, he is one of the most agreeable of men I have ever known. We were just in the midst of a discussion on his last book when the still more famous and more eminent biologist, Professor Morgan of Columbia, came to the door, and seeing me, started away, but having told Conklin that I wanted to see Morgan, Conklin ran after him and brought him back, and for an hour or more we had a three-cornered controversy (Conklin and Morgan have diametrically opposite views concerning the merging of the microsomes). I knew not enough of the subject to contribute much to their discussion on this point, but I led them off by way of Stoddard Lathrop's *Rising Tide of Color* into a discussion of the subject of the rapidly crowding world. I soon had Morgan going fast. He declared that human beings had been on earth at least several million years and that so far they had never overcrowded, although by the law of geometrical increases and by the simple process of unrestrained breeding of the human race the whole earth might have been at any time during the past overcrowded be-

[11] "Nasty Nature," EWS Writings, 8:81 f.

yond standing room had there not been reliable checks. "So," said he, "what's the good of our worrying about that matter?" Mr. Conklin agreed with my contention that populations were now growing more rapidly than ever before and, whatever the check was and whenever it came, the sum total of human misery was to be incomprehensibly great. That brought up the subject of neo-Malthusianism or birth control and then it got into and out of eugenics and finally into self-regardedness and other-regardedness. Morgan surprised me by declaring that we were all pure egoists, having no regard for others but each for himself.

Conklin assured me that Morgan was lying to me and that he was only pursuing a propensity of his to contradict everybody.

. . . .

I was a little flattered when both my antagonist and protagonist in the discussion seemed to hesitate and to question themselves when I put forth my argument and my evidence that, entirely without any reason, men were compelled by their nature not to cooperate but to actually sacrifice self for others.

Of course I take it for granted that, being regarded an old gentleman with some tendencies sympathetic with their own, both Conklin and Morgan chose to be polite.

. . . .

While I enjoyed my visit very much, after I had gotten back on the boat I felt, if not exactly tired, at least a certain feeling of relief in getting away from men who made me talk and think.

I don't know whether I would not suffer more than I would find pleasure in the constant companionship of men of high intellect.

The ordinary damn fool human being at worst only bores me, but those men who are not damn fools and who do not bore me have another way of tiring me out.[12]

In addition to toying with the ideas of biologists, Scripps amused himself with his calculations that showed his increasing concern with population, such as "Arithmetic and Humanity" in Search for Self.

The breadth of Scripps' view in considering science inevitably involved him in questions of ethics, typified here by "Morals." And it is in this regard that the question of his religion comes out. Many times he protested that he was an atheist or an agnostic, but the whole tenor of all he did and wrote strongly suggests that he was a deeply religious person but without a formulated belief. Organized religion he brushed aside as superstition. But on the question of God, he said privately that he neither believed nor disbelieved in God. "I just don't know," he said.[13] At any rate, he placed great store in the wisdom of the Ten Commandments, making them part of the guideline, as you recall, for his editors to follow when he retired in 1908. All

[12] EWS to EBS, Aug. 4, 1922.
[13] Harry L. Smithton, "Notes . . . on Gilson Gardner's . . . *Lusty Scripps*."

his writings — disquisitions and correspondence — are also sprinkled with quotations from the New Testament, not ostentatiously, not in quantity, but in a number and a way to show that he knew and had thought much about Christianity.

Ritter undoubtedly was the person best qualified to evaluate Scripps in relation to science. His evaluation, taken from three sources, follows:

The problem of the nature of man always had a dominant place with Scripps. Several of his disquisitions and letters throw a sometimes glaring light on his efforts at solving this problem through thinking of his very own. No more striking example of thinking in disregard of prescribed patterns is known to me than is furnished by some of these essays. These incursions into the problem of man were closely connected with his original induction into the natural sciences, the biological division particularly. "From the very earliest days of my connection with the Institution, I have been developing and formulating a scheme of my own relative to it." Looking back now over the records and my recollections, I find evidence a-plenty of his developing a scheme of his own. I must confess that at the time I failed to perceive either the magnitude or the scientific and philosophic soundness of his scheme. He soon reached the conception that "Biology, as a science, might be considered the parent stem of all the social sciences." He decided that since here was the germ of an institution for research in the science of biology, not only would he help us financially but advise his sister Ellen to help also.

.   .   .   .

. . . his learning, though shamefully unconventional, was almost unparalleled in area and depth.

.   .   .   .

. . . had the phrase "scientific humanist" become current in his day, it would have fitted him well.

.   .   .   .

Nothing stands out more sharply from Scripps' writing and sayings than his concern with the moral problem and with evidence that the moral problem is really part of the greater problem of the nature of man himself. In this he allied himself with those few of the greatest thinkers, from Aristotle and Confucius to Shaftesbury, Voltaire, Dewey, and Santayana, who recognize the problem of morals as an aspect of the problem of human nature and hence of all Nature. . . .[14]

Objectively realistic to the very root-tips of his nature, his attempts at self-analysis brought out conclusions that were striking, to say the least.[15]

His curiosity touching everything and everybody round about him was insatiable. His native ability for assimilating facts and principles was astonishing,

[14] Ritter, *Charles Darwin and the Golden Rule*, pp. xi–xvii, *passim*.
[15] W. E. Ritter, "Science Service and E. W. Scripps' Philosophy of Life," *General Science*, Dec. 25, 1927, p. 201.

and the objectiveness of his thinking was naive almost to childishness. I doubt whether any kind or measure of training could have begot in his mind either a trace of doubt as to the reality of sensory experience or of surmise that he ever had experiences which did not contain sensory elements. In that sense metaphysics simply could not exist for him. Add to these characteristics of him the fact that of formal schooling he had almost none, and that by natural bent he was humanistic to the core, and you have the background of his views as to what science is. . . . So far as concerns humans as objects of knowledge, it always seemed to me that for Scripps human beings were no more separate from the rest of nature than are stars, mountains and horses. . . .

A phase of his identification of man with nature and his concomitant assumption that man, like the rest of nature, is a subject for scientific study and treatment, was his own common practice of treating human problems quantitatively. . . . His calculations were typically of the roughest sort, hardly better than second or third approximations. But they served the purpose of bringing his problems into broad and general, but, insofar, entirely trustworthy view. When greater accuracy became necessary for the practical working out of the problems, somebody could be called in who had more learning, more skill, more time and more patience, for such details.

One consequence of these ideas of his about man and nature and science was his enormous belief in science as an instrument for human welfare. I have often said that I never knew a professional scientist whose faith of this sort was more alive and confiding than was that of Mr. Scripps. . . .[16]

Because of Scripps' greater role as a social thinker, the better of his disquisitions which were written after he came under the influence of scientific thought have been presented in preceding sections. Yet he wrote about sixty disquisitions dealing with physical and natural science. Most of them are flatulent. Some are simple regurgitations of something he had recently read; some, schoolboyish book review sort of things; some, fanciful wanderings as he let a scientific idea carry him into the construction of a romance. But the six presented here show, for the most part, a critical faculty at work.

[16] W. E. Ritter, "The Relation of E. W. Scripps to Science," *Science*, Mar. 25, 1926, p. 291.

Morals

[*May 20, 1908*]

This is to be one man's effort to formulate in his mind and put into some sort of words his own views as to his moral relations toward his kind.

I find myself, whenever I stop to think seriously about the things I am going to do, about the things that I wish to do, and about the things that I think other people should do or should wish to do, arriving at an understanding of the cause of my mental attitude.

I find that my motives, my aspirations, are entirely contrary to all of the convictions that are based upon such powers of reasoning as I have.

I consider that instinctively I am a moral man, and I consider that I am extremely moral, and very often and for the most part of the time, I am quite vain of my distinction in this regard.

Now, I begin to recognize the absurdity of my position when I begin to consider and define the meaning of morality.

I believe that the word and idea of morals is derived from a Latin word meaning custom. That which it is customary for men to do, hence, is always the moral thing to do. A man gets his morals as a result of training, and if there is any rational basis for these morals, it is very difficult to discover. A man's morals — that is to say, his training — are almost wholly originated during the extreme youth of the individual, during the time when the childish mind is so plastic and so unformed as to be practically only embryonic. A man's morals — that is to say, a man's habit of regarding some things as right and some things as wrong — are never self-originated. It is but the result of the handiwork of someone who has lived before the child was born; it is a mental condition that has been shaped and formed by the hands of another being, or other beings, much as a bit of clay has been shaped and formed by the potter's hand.

At least, I sometimes, and for the most part, so regard this question.

734

There are other times, however, when I am prompted to doubt this condition. Why is it that a man, a member of society, not only exercises ordinary common sense in assisting his neighbor, that is to say, the community of which he is a part — and hence in the end assisting himself — why is it he not only does these things, but actually feels all through him a sense of real sympathy for his fellow: grief and pain at the sight of another's misfortune, and joy and pleasure at another's happiness?

There are perhaps a few monstrosities in the world, but I have never yet known a man or woman who could for longer than a brief period of time feel any sensations of pleasure or exultations over the pain and misery of another human being.

I believe that no man or woman exists who is not capable of making at least some sort of personal sacrifice for the benefit of another without regard to any possible selfish benefit, without regard even to the idea of the community's being benefited. The most cruel and selfish of men, the most pugnacious, those who will fight the hardest for their own part, will seldom, and perhaps never, inflict any personal injury on another from pure wantonness. I do not believe that there exists a man who will not forego some part of his possible advantage in favor of his enemy, not only after the latter has been vanquished but before. I do not believe that this condition of mind could ever have been impressed on the infant or childish, plastic mentality.

I do consider, then, that it is not only possible but probable that altruism, so called, has its origin in something far deeper and remote from view than ordinary morals — that is to say, transmitted customs.

I am able to conceive the whole of a race, say, the Aryans, as being one body, physically and spiritually or mentally.

I can conceive the whole human race as such a single body, the whole animal kingdom, and even the whole aggregate of living things as being one body.

I can go farther and conceive that the whole world, animate and inanimate, and even the whole universe, as one creature, having one existence, material and spiritual [sic].

If one hand or one finger on the hand of a man is wounded, the other hand is not indifferent — perhaps temporarily it is to the pain, but not to the effect of the wound, since the wounded one hand may result in the death and destruction of the whole body, including the other hand.

We know that every individual cell in the body of an animal or a vegetable is really a separate, distinct, living organism — as separate and distinct from all the other cells of the body as is one total animal organism separate and distinct from another. Yet all the cells of an individual body originate from one cell, the so-called germ plasm, so that while all of the cells have a separate and distinct existence, they are all the same in origin, and only separate developments of the same thing.

But just as all the cells of one body are of the same cell in origin, and are only different in development, so are all the members of one family (the sons and daughters of a man) the same in origin, being developments of the germ-plasm cell of the father. Each and every member of the family is the same thing, then, separately developed.

Doubtless, each separate race of mankind had its origin in the germ plasm of an ancestor, or the two germ plasms of the ancestors, male and female. Perhaps all the races of mankind originated in a similar way — perhaps all animal and vegetable life.

Let us suppose we have a common earthworm: an individual. We cut this worm in half. Both of the halves live and become apparently fully developed individuals. Are these two worms, then, one animal or two?

When a new, individual human comes into existence, it is caused by a practically similar division of the original individual. In the case of man, the original individual is not cut in half, so that each part develops into two individuals, but a small segment of the germ plasm is in some form cut off, either as a sperm or an ovum, and begins a new life.

This is not exactly a parallel case to the worm's division, but the difference may be more apparent than real. The simple fact that in the case of the worm there is a division of only one individual into two may not mean much if we consider that in the animal kingdom generally there is an individual made up of two parts, the female and the male element. If the man and woman are really one organism, then [in] the cutting off of this organism of the two extremities of their dual body, the male and the female germ plasm, to join to become another individual, we have the same life phenomenon that is exhibited in the division of the worm.

What constitutes, then, the difference between the earthworm as one individual and two individuals? Perhaps the only difference is that the material, the physical, nerve filaments have been separated by space, so that the communication from one part of the worm body by means of the nerve filaments is not carried to the other. The communication between the two parts of the worm body has become at least partially cut off, but is it entirely severed? Is the only means of communication between different parts of any living body confined to the string of nerve cells alone?

We know that in the case of highly organized animals this is not a fact. The father and mother animal can communicate with their offspring by voice, by physical touch, and most all of the higher animals are able to communicate in some form or another with each other.

May there not be even another line or other lines of communication than those that are palpable and visible?

There is the fact of telepathy, of hypnotism. Even some of the most learned scientists admit that there is something in so-called spiritualism.

I believe that, consciously or unconsciously, most human beings have a communicating sense one with another, or some ones with some others. I know that there is a great degree of difference in the power of this sort of sensing. For my own part, I have always been aware of a very strongly developed sense of this kind. Without the aid of speech, of sight, or hearing, I have always felt a disturbing communication between myself and other human beings in my immediate neighborhood.

It has never been necessary for me to depend upon my sight, my hearing, and my touch to become aware of the presence in my immediate vicinity of other human beings. When I am in a house alone, I know it. I am just as well aware of the presence of others of my kind in the house that I am occupying, whether I see or hear or feel them or not.

If I were rendered insensible by anaesthetics or otherwise while I was in the midst of a completely deserted place and were removed in that condition to the heart of a great city, and there became again conscious, I would know of the fact, even if every telltale sight and sound were suppressed.

That I have what may be called telepathic sense I am constantly reminded of by the fact that I am just as much disturbed in my mental equilibrium by the presence in my room of a strange man of mind inharmonious with my own, when he remains speechless and out of sight, as though he were speaking and acting.

I have felt as keenly, through other senses than sight, hearing, and touch, the different kinds of individuals that I come in contact with, as I have been able to recognize by any of my material senses. I can respond as quickly to the unspoken, unexpressed mentality of my vis-à-vis as to any word or action of his.

Every individual adapts himself to his surroundings more or less quickly — that is to say, instinctively — and more in respect to that part of his environment which is human. This is natural with all men, I believe. I have to have direct contact communication with a variety of people; to some I can at almost any time adapt myself easily and quickly; to some it requires a considerable effort; to some I can at one time be entirely sympathetic and harmonious with them, while at other times it may be difficult or even impossible to have any kind of communication or contact without more or less mental pain and discomfort. It is true that the spoken word tremendously magnifies the sense of harmony and disharmony. But that there is communication going on all the time between myself and my immediate neighbor I know from internal evidence. While one person is in my room, my mind quickly adapts itself to trains of thought which are harmonious with my visitor, and even this is the case when for any reason that person is not speaking or not intruding his personality on my observation.

Although I am, or am supposed to be, almost devoid of what is called a religious sense, I have always felt myself very susceptible to this influence. I have come in contact with persons of various sorts of religion. I have incidentally been present at various kinds of religious worship. The two most notable impressions on my memory are attendance at Roman Catholic worship in Italy, and of Mohammedan worship in North Africa (perhaps an equal or almost equal impression was made by some camp meeting revival experiences in my youth).

In a Roman cathedral I felt all of the religious sentiment, or the desire to give expression to such sentiment, as would a most devout Catholic.

With the half-wild followers of Mohammed, during the time of their celebration of religious rites in the Atlas Mountains, I felt subject to the same frenzy of religious excitement as my neighbors.

In the presence of a businessman of large affairs, even if he be sitting still and alone in the lobby of a hotel, reading his daily paper or sitting abstractedly musing, my own thoughts invariably revert to counter ones: my own business affairs.

In the presence of the parson, the professor, the journalist, and the lawyer, my mind has been shaped and directed largely by the thoughts, spoken or unspoken, of these men.

But the mere fact that I can think and feel in more or less harmony with a vast number of individuals and classes of individuals convinces me that my organism is but a part of a very large and common organism.

When I said in the beginning that man's moral sentiments, his ideas of right and wrong, were not original and self-developed, but entirely the result of some other molding hand, I said what I believe is true, so far as concerns the great mass of the practices and customs that are evident in everyday life with all classes of people and all individual units of any community. But the hand that first began molding must have had a sense, an object greatly desired. It is possible that this sense was a recognition, that is, oneness, with its family, its race, its species, with its earth life, its world, and its universe. Perhaps there is, after all, only one common origin for religion and morality in men, and that is the undefined and undefinable sense that all men have that each is but a part of the whole; and that, being a part of the whole, all of its efforts are common efforts.

Long before Christ bade men to conform to the Golden Rule of loving one's neighbor as one's self, man knew that loving one's neighbor was loving one's self, and that all one's neighbors were, in fact, only another part of the self of which he was one part.

But morals and customs are, to use the term in its highest form, selfish.

The morals and customs of one period of race development might [be] and generally are vicious and injurious to another period. The customs that are wholesome and necessary to life in the tropics are, in many details, entirely destructive to life in the humid and temperate, and much more so in the frigid, zones.

The morals and customs of the people living under despotic monarchy would be and are destructive to the people living in a democracy.

Civilized man so far outgrew the customs, that is to say, the morals, of primitive times, that these same customs had to be reformed, and they were reformed under either the leadership or supposed leadership of men like Buddha, Christ, and Mohammed, to a very large degree.

But these customs and morals that were good for their time have, I believe, to a large extent grown obsolete and injurious. Perhaps there was nothing fundamental and perhaps there could be nothing fundamentally injurious in the idea that lay behind the spoken or written rule or law.

For instance, perhaps the spirit of the Golden Rule, which requires us to love our neighbor as ourselves, has been lost sight of, or overlooked, or even was never known, and perhaps the necessarily crude and awkward formulation in words of this rule caused a misinterpretation.

The rule has been so interpreted by modern society as to include among those who should be loved, and hence cherished, the insane, the imbecile, the physical and mental degenerate, and the criminal, and all of the unfit.

It has been carried so far that it includes the dead, useless, and even injurious physical remains of once-living men and women. In a thousand ways, civilized man has extended in the way of laws and social functions, fundamentally correct moral principles into such details and practices as are really paradoxical. These extensions and formulations of fundamental morals have gradually, insidiously, turned farther and farther away from the line of original direction and curved again and again until their direction is absolutely the opposite of the primary and beneficial custom or moral.

Great confusion has ensued; every intelligent man, and even men of ordinary intelligence — men whose morals are sound, directly descended from the original, beneficial custom or moral — are finding themselves all the time most embarrassingly situated in society. That which is commonly and literally construed the morals of any community, they consider absolutely immoral from the viewpoint that has regard only to the interests of their kind and those laws that are called natural laws or the laws of nature.

It is not only dangerous to their peace of mind, but dangerous to their lives, for them openly to oppose and refuse to comply with customs and practices — that is to say, the morals — of the people of which they are part.

The first law of nature is self-preservation, and man being the weakest and most defenseless of all created beings, in a physical way — defenseless not only against other species of animals, but the overgrown sickness and corruption of the body of which he is a part, civilized mankind — he is always and must always evade danger by craft [*sic*].

On the subject of morals, he is a hypocrite. To some degree and in regard to some subjects, perhaps every man is a hypocrite. At least, most men profess with their mouths and their pens acquiescence with the morals and the customs — that is to say, the laws and conventions — of society while they have no such personal convictions, and while they constantly practice evasion.

No physician would dare to declare that it was right to terminate any human life except in punishment for crime, or community, that is to say, national, defense (war). Any physician who would declare that he had terminated a human life by an act of his own would be punished. But if the physician loves his neighbor as himself, and if he could do so without personal danger to himself, he would terminate at the earliest possible moment the life of a suffering, hopelessly irrecoverable, brother human being. There is no doubt but that many physicians do, by acts of omission and commission, perform this most humane of deeds.

It would be difficult indeed to find any moral principle that has been formulated in words, which, if literally and to its logical end be practiced, would not become a vice — so serious a vice as to threaten even the very existence of humanity. Every so-called virtue becomes a vice, by process of time, and by change of conditions. In our language there are two words, one commendatory and the other condemnatory, of every human practice. A virtue in one man and at one time becomes a vice with another man or with the same man at another time.

Thrift and providence, which are virtues with some people at some period of their lives, become the vices of miserliness and selfishness; they become follies and become of national menace.

Charity, defined by Christ the greatest of all virtues, extended in whatever direction or whatever form it may be to a sufficient extent, becomes a positive menace.

Morality is not righteousness, just because customs are not always good customs.

The word "fashion" is synonymous of the word "moral." Applied to many things, it has the same meaning. A man wears a certain kind of clothes because it is the fashion to do so, because it is common to do so, because it is customary to do so.

He goes to church because it is the fashion to do so, or the custom of the people of his class to go to church.

He becomes a Democrat, a Republican, a Socialist, or an Anarchist far more as a result of fashion than as a result of any inward conviction.

It is immoral for a woman to wear man's clothes; the practice is prohibited by law in obedience to public sentiment. It is immoral, simply because it is not customary.

In this era, when all womenkind amongst the most cultivated and intellectual classes wear corsets, it is immoral not to wear corsets, because it isn't the custom. The words "custom" and "moral" and "fashion," and many other words, are practically identical in meaning. It has become in this country almost immoral for a man to wear a full beard.

Every man who antagonizes public morals, customs, and fashions is punished by society, but there are various degrees of punishment, according to the degree of ancientness of custom.

If I wear a full, unkempt beard, and old and unfashionable clothing, society resents this and to a certain extent punishes me.

If I appear on the streets dressed in the clothes that my father wore eighty years ago, I would be punished by ridicule.

If I should appear on the streets of San Diego clothed in the costume of a people that number 400 millions, I would be more severely punished.

If I should appear dressed in the clothes that are customarily only worn by the military section of our country, I would be punished severely by imprisonment and would be fined.

If I believe that my child would suffer in health, even if I knew that his life would be terminated ten or twenty years sooner by reason of my putting him in school, or even by reason of my making him learn the alphabet and to read and instruct himself by books, and if I knew of a better way of conducting and training him to be a good citizen and an efficient man, because it is the custom of the society in which I live to give all children a certain school training, and that, too, with printed books, I would be deemed an immoral man by my fellows, my associates, and I would be punished by public condemnation and by the authorities of the community in which I live.

Christ was an immoral man, because he did not conform entirely to the customs and practice and belief of the other people who lived in Palestine, and he was punished with death.

There is no proof, I believe, that morals are essentially right, and that immorality is essentially wrong, from the viewpoint as far back as we can conceive that God himself could occupy, unless we sanction and are really convinced of the truth of that system of philosophy which requires that "whatever is, is right."

The moral law is nothing other perhaps than "the rules of the game" which modern civilization, in this country, has adopted. In Africa, they have other rules; in India, still other rules; in China, another set of rules. The disciples of Mrs. [Mary Baker] Eddy are trying to establish another set of rules. The founder of the Mormon Church had some rules that were peculiar and were adopted by that church; these rules were so peculiar that in order to live morally as a Latter-Day Saint, the disciples of Joe Smith had to live immorally, according to the views of the great majority of the people of the United States.

Cannibalism has probably been practiced when it was not only moral, because it was customary, but because it was moral as a natural law.

The Causes of Things Human

[*September 23, 1916*]

Why does a man want wealth? Why political office? Why ecclesiastic dignity? Why a prominent position in society or in a community? Why many friends?

Why do men throw themselves so wholeheartedly into business? Why, after a man has obtained a complete competence, does he continue to struggle in business and continually, time after time, jeopardize all the enough that he has for the chance of gaining more than the enough which he considers possible? Why do young men run footraces, and in groups struggle one group against another, on the diamond in a game of baseball, and on the gridiron in a game of football? Why do boys box with bare fists or with gloves, and why is it that one nation wars against another? Why do clergymen preach, and professors teach?

Why are all men active gainfully or wastefully, viciously inclining to excesses, or nobly resisting bad instincts, striving to serve, and serving their fellows?

It has suggested itself to my mind that there may be one all-sufficient answer to each and every one of the above questions, and thousands of more questions.

Why does the sun shine, giving light and radiating heat? Why does the apple fall to the ground? Why does the vapor arise from the lake?

To these few questions and many thousands more, one answer might be sufficient. One answer might be sufficient to answer both series of questions.

The answer?

Force!

So far as we know, force is everywhere in existence, and is as infinite as space and time. From both the religious, or supernatural, and the materialist point of view the soul or the mind of man can be defined as force, whatever other definitions are applicable to the same thing.

743

The mind of man can only exist in a condition of expressing itself in force, and the body of man is either a dead body, or in every one of its parts expressing itself in force, and existing only and because of this expression in all of its multitudinous forms of activity.

The mind of man is force, expressing itself in DIRECTION, and perhaps in many other ways.

That part of force which is man's mind or soul, whether it be a collection of many forces, or is one indivisible and eternal force, must continue and must have DIRECTION. The desires for wealth, political office, ecclesiastical dignity, or social pre-eminence are each of them directions of the force of the mind. Force cannot be annihilated; it can only be diverted from one path by collision with another force.

Men strive for wealth, for position — they strive on the market and on the battlefield — because men are forces. Only things that are dead and inert can be directionless and devoid of force. If force is ubiquitous and eternal, there can be nothing dead and nothing inert. A granite boulder may only differ from a human being in the direction of its force expression.

It is only because force is, or forces are, eternal that those elements of force that are expressing themselves in the human mind or soul, that men seek wealth and distinction, seek victory on the battlefield [*sic*].

Peace.

What condition does the word peace signify?

Peace is a definition of something that is not existing. Peace signifies an absence of conflicting forces or directions in men's minds or souls.

But mind or soul is only force, and force must have direction. Can all force — for example, the forces that are represented by human mind, bodies — exist and have direction, and not be in conflict? The physicist might with reason declare that, theoretically, such might be the condition, but at the same time, he would have to declare that nothing discernible in the universe, material or spiritual, indicated that forces ever took parallel lines in the same direction. On the other hand, both physicists and metaphysicians might go so far as to argue that if force did not express itself by encountering other force, it would not be force at all. Such an imaginable force might be equal to and equivalent to that other figment of imagination, deadness or inertness.

Eternal peace indicates the absence of conflict or friction, struggle, and that imaginary thing called death, or inertness.

Even if the minds of some men yearn for death, for annihilation, for the Buddhist Nirvana, their yearning is no more effective than is the child's desire to grasp the moon.

Life and peace are antitheses.

Men will war one against another, many against another many, so long as men live, for exactly the same reason that the sun radiates heat and light.

A dead sun will not radiate heat and light, but the sun we recognize is the antithesis of a dead sun. In fact, a dead sun is not a sun.

Nor would a peace-keeping, non-struggling entity be a man. Such an entity would be something "never seen on land or sea," something that would be impossible to both imagine and logically explain.

Fatalism? Of a sort, perhaps.

Is This Ritter's Thesis?

[*May 15,1919*]

At some point in a line extending, in one direction, toward infinity in the metaphysical and, in the other, through the physical on into infinitude, the individual becomes cognizable. The individual has two attributes only: (1) will to activate; and (2) possession of substance capable of being activated by will. The general definition of this entity is that it is a living organism.

The will of this entity activates the substance, which is first recognized in two forms — the sperm and the ovum — which, on becoming joined by fusion, constitute the first cell of the organism. This cell is directed or compelled by the will to divide into two cells, which the will increases in size by adding to the original substance more substance, so that these two cells each become as large as the original parent cell. The will, continuing to activate, causes a long but limited series of cell divisions and cell increases — a united mass of substance. The will, continuing, causes this mass of substance to differentiate into a large but limited number of organs and tissues and a skeleton-supporting frame: organs functioning dissimilarly but mutually supporting; tissues that perform the function of binding together individual parts of the mass; a skeleton framework supporting the whole mass; channels (veins and arteries) through which is transported cell-building material; lines of communication (nerves), by means of which direction is given by the will to individual cells and to collections of cells (bodily organs).

The will builds up its body to a certain size and in a certain form — the will being limited in the construction of the substance under its control, both as to quantity and as to form.

When the will has completed its task — that is to say, when it has reached the limit of its ability to control substance — the bodily size and form of the living organism have been completed. Thereafter the will, for a limited time, controls and directs all of the activities of the organism until, for one reason or another, the will, gradually or instantaneously, exhausts its power to hold together in working form the substance of its organism, when death ensues.

Does not Ritter maintain that the substance — the cells of which the body is composed, the so-called organs of the body, the skeleton frame, and other material of the body — is in itself inert substance, having no part in its own direction or control or the control of the organism as a whole?

Query. — Is not this will the same thing that metaphysicians and theologians attempt to define as the soul? Granting the correctness of Ritter's thesis on the infinitude of Nature, would it not be perfectly evident that the entity called the will is infinite, never having had a beginning and never to have an ending?

Physics and Metaphysics. — The mental as well as the physical vision of man is limited, both as regards duration and extension. Perhaps physics begins and ends at the farthest points to which the physical and mental vision of the human being can be extended. Beyond the circle of these visions lies the infinite realm of the metaphysical.

How Science Is Disseminated

[*July 8, 1919*]

This disquisition appears to have been edited in Scripps' hand.

In the preface to his translation of *The Philosophy of the Practical,* [17] by Benedetto Croce, Douglas Ainslie congratulates himself and the world on the fact that in time Croce's philosophy will be in the possession of the common people of the world.

He designates the route that will be pursued by the philosophical ideas of Croce down from the mountaintop of aristocratic intellectualism to the plains below where dwells the common herd. First, Croce's gospel will be discovered by book reviewers and critics, and passed on by them to the writers of fiction. From the latter the writing journalists will absorb the new message and consciously and intentionally, or perhaps more often without consciousness of will or intention, will color or modify the productions of their pens (or perhaps rather have the productions of their pens colored and modified) by those thoughts and convictions the author of which was Croce.

These journalistic disseminators and propagators of the Crocian theories may not and probably will not, in the long run, know that there ever was such a man as Croce or that he was the first to discover and enunciate the new philosophy. Even the writers of fiction, who are the bearers of the message to the journalists, will not owe to their own reading of Croce's books the possession of the message. For the most part they will have absorbed the Crocian doctrine from some fellow writer of fiction or perhaps from some philosopher who has had his own views molded by direct contact with Croce's writings.

[17] Benedetto Croce, *The Philosophy of the Practical,* trans. Douglas Ainslie. Macmillan, London, 1913.

748

The path pursued by all great new ideas from individual discoverers down into the sea of commonalty has generally been the same as Ainslie has indicated.

It is a fact that the great mass of humanity is far better informed in matters of science than it is supposed to be by the usual run of intellectual aristocrats. The cause of this misapprehension is easily to be discovered. It is because it takes from one to two generations for scientific knowledge to percolate through the masses of the people that those who esteem themselves intellectual and who are intellectual are always a generation or two ahead of the commonalty in becoming possessed of knowledge — the latest developments of science — and it appears to them that the common crowd is not only ignorant of new scientific truths but of all science.

Except those men and women who are more or less imbecile, there is no one whose mind cannot grasp and is not compelled to grasp, sooner or later, all the wisdom and all the knowledge that has ever become existent.

It ought to be comparatively easy for any man who has reached an age equal to my own to demonstrate for himself the truth of the contention I have made. It is only necessary for him to recall to memory the teachers he had in school and out of school, the elderly people who instructed and advised him in his youth, to recognize that the most ignorant of the present day are wiser and possessed of more knowledge than were the most instructed men of his youth.

Let us take, for example, the Darwinian theory of evolution or natural selection. A general knowledge of this theory is now almost universal, even among the least educated, and even among men who have had no education, so called, at all — perhaps even men who do not know how to read.

I had grown to young manhood before I even heard of the existence of such a theory. I had never heard or seen in print the name of Darwin.[18] And yet from childhood I had been a voracious reader and, hence, a reader of serious books as well as trash. I had read the daily and weekly press and such periodicals as the *North American Review* and the *Atlantic Monthly* and other current literature of a similar type. I had had frequent opportunities to listen to older people who were at least reckoned to be far above the average in intellectual attainments. I had heard political, theological, historical, and scientific subjects discussed frequently.

I can picture to myself a return to this earth of some of those old people I knew in my youth, and I can see how their mentality would compare with that of a number of the present-day so-called proletariat. Why, my old friends would appear, in the matter of their simplicity and lack of knowledge, no better than children, as compared to the lineal, physical, and intellectual de-

[18] Charles Darwin's *Origin of Species* appeared in 1859, five years after Scripps was born.

scendants of that class which my old friends, in their day, regarded as inferior in intellect and in ethics.

In the intellectual world there is a law similar to what might be called diffusion to equilibrium in the physical world. If in the great ocean there is a single gallon of water that, at a given instant, has a greater degree of salinity than any other similar quantity of water, then action begins and persists until the salinity of this original gallon of water is no more and no less than that of every other gallon of water in the ocean.

So it is that that thing which we call knowledge, or even something else than knowledge — that intellectual force or activity which prompts the growth of knowledge, which is the potential possession or attribute of every human brain — cannot rest content in one bony envelope. It must disseminate. It must penetrate all surrounding brains and, penetrating one brain, must pass onto another — a constantly widening circle — until all humanity at least tends to possess that which was first only possessed by one human. (There is this difference between physical diffusion and intellectual diffusion: In the former case, the salinity gained by one gallon of water is at the expense of another. In the case of knowledge, that which is gained by one person is not at the expense of any other.)

I take it that what is called philosophy is something distinct from what is called knowledge. Knowledge consists of facts, more or less concrete. On the other hand, philosophy, among other things, is a capacity to absorb knowledge and correlate facts.

Not only does all knowledge persist in disseminating itself, tending always to equalize in amount or degree amongst men, but in like manner does philosophy — what might be called mental energy — tend to establish universal equilibrium.

I have given much time and effort, by reading and observation, to the study of the laws of economics. I have concluded that, like the salt in the gallon of water, like the bit of knowledge gained by one man, so does that something we call wealth tend ever to disseminate and seek a condition of equilibrium throughout the whole mass.

Not only is the wife of the common laborer possessed of more knowledge than Queen Elizabeth had, but on the whole she possesses more wealth, or its equivalent, than had Queen Bess.

The rank and file of humanity today are not poor intrinsically. They individually possess less wealth than some of their fellows. This condition is the real cause of the discontent of the masses.

It is not that the common herd is today altogether ignorant and unphilosophical, but that they are more ignorant and less philosophical than some of their fellows that is the cause of the discontent on the part of those who have more knowledge and a higher degree of philosophy. (Perhaps no man was ever yet so ignorant and stupid but that he believed his mental endowments were equal to those of any other.)

This discontent (noble discontent) on the part of those best equipped intellectually is revealed in every book, every magazine, every newspaper one reads, every sermon from the pulpit, every lecture from the rostrum. All these writers and talkers seem to exclaim, "Oh, why are the people so ignorant, so unreasonable?" The employer of labor is no less eager in teaching his employees the doctrines of sweet reasonableness than is the clergyman in the pulpit, in addressing his congregation.

No man can rest content so long as he has knowledge of any fact that another man has not, or so long as he has a capacity for reasoning that another has not, until that other and every other man has the same knowledge and at least as high a degree of philosophy as he himself possesses.

Thus it appears that in the nature of things, that quality which is called altruism has to exist in, or be a part of, every unit of humanity.

When an Ancestor Is Not an Ancestor

[*May 17, 1921*]

Recently I had the opportunity of entertaining on my boat an eminent scientist, Edwin Grant Conklin, professor of biology, Princeton University.

Some years ago I had read with great interest a volume published by him on the subject of heredity.

Although my reading in biology has been large enough, I was considerably surprised by one of Conklin's declarations. This declaration was to the effect that no human being could have more than 48 real ancestors at any particular period of time in the past.

This statement was so much at variance from what I and I suppose almost the universality of men believed that I was startled, especially considering the standing Conklin had in science.

David Starr Jordan, in one of his lectures, told his audience that every person present who had any Anglo-Saxon blood in his veins must certainly have had as an ancestor some man or woman who lived in the time of King Alfred in England.

A statement that I had read in one of Conklin's books had been to the effect that during the period of a thousand years, if there had been positively no inbreeding among a man's ancestors, a man would have to have at least a billion ancestors.

Anyone can figure this out in the following manner. Every individual has 2 parents, 4 grandparents, 8 great-grandparents, 16 great-great-grandparents, and so on.

I also remember a statement by Galton, the originator of the eugenic school. It was to the effect that half the heredity of any person came from the immediate parents, a quarter from the grandparents, an eighth from the preceding generation, a sixteenth, a thirty-second, a sixty-fourth, and so on, so that every living human being had in him a part of all of his millions and millions of ancestors.

752

Now this man, Professor Conklin, declares that no man, no matter how many ancestors he may have, could have contributed to him characteristics by more than 48 ancestors at some particular point of time or any period of time measured by generations.

To make clear his statement he began with the Mendelian theory, a theory that is well understood by all biologists and highly educated men and women. It was unnecessary for the professor to more than touch on this subject in his talk with me, but I will try to explain the Mendelian theory as I understand it:

Any male and female of any one species can conjugate and produce offspring. Some of these offspring are fertile, but others are infertile. These infertile hybrids are called mules.

Mendel made this discovery through experiment with peas. In his garden he grew some tall peas and some dwarf peas. He crossed by artificial pollenization the tall peas and the short peas which resulted in a hybrid. As I remember it, this tall pea had a green fruit; the short pea had a yellow fruit. His hybrids were all tall and all, I believe, had yellow fruit.

Then the next season he planted his peas from the hybrid plants with the result that practically one-quarter of the new generation of peas were tall, having green fruit, a quarter of them were short, having yellow fruit, and half of them had the characteristics of the immediate parent, i.e., hybrid tall plants and yellow fruit.

After that he planted, in a separate bed for each, seeds from all three of the different plants. The seeds from the short dwarf peas produced short plants and yellow fruit. The seeds from the tall, green-fruited plants produced other peas of the identical strain.

In planting the seeds of the tall plants with the yellow fruit he found that there again appeared the three different sorts of peas, the hybrid tall plants with yellow seeds, the short plant with yellow seeds, the tall plants with green seeds.

Similar experiments have been tried with many other plants, with mammals, and with birds, most of which experiments produced similar results to those of the original pea experiments.

Now our biologists have been at work for the last thirty or forty years with their microscopes. The reproductive cell of the female is called an ovum. The reproductive cell of the male is called a sperm. Under the microscope it is discovered that the ovum is many times larger (I think a thousand times as large) than the sperm. If I remember rightly, the female of the human species ejaculates only some 3,000 ovums or eggs, while the male ejaculates several million.

The ovum and the sperm are both true cells. Both are composed mainly of protoplasm, a transparent jelly-like substance, contained by a membrane, but floating in this liquid protoplasm is a substance called the nucleus, and this nucleus contains or is made up of separate particles or threads.

These last-mentioned particles are called chromosomes by the biologists. The reason for their being given this name is that when the egg cell is brought into contact with some coloring matter these cell particles take on the color while the rest of the cell remains colorless. Were it not for this characteristic of these particles to take color they could not be distinguished by the user of the microscope.

But the cells of every different species contain a different number of chromosomes. The number of chromosomes in a cell has no relation to the size of the ovum or the sperm or the size of the animal that has ejaculated them. (For instance, I remember reading once that the ovum and sperm of the little rose bug or louse has a vastly greater number of chromosomes than does that of the elephant.)

But in the case of the human ovum cell and the human sperm cell, each cell originally has 48 chromosomes. As the human cell cannot have more than 48 chromosomes, in order for the male sperm and the female ovum to join together, as they do to produce the beginning of a human individual, each of these cells must first throw off and eliminate from its body one-half, or 24, of its chromosomes, so that when the two fuse together to form oosperm there are only left 48 chromosomes.

Experimentation and observation have proved that while the male and female cells fuse together to form one cell, the chromosomes do not fuse, and, hence, half of them have to be thrown out.

Conklin and in fact all other biologists, I think, now believe that all of the hereditary principles, all those things that pass from one generation of living beings to another, are carried through the chromosomes. Conklin calls these chromosomes transmitters. When the female ovum discards half its chromosomes, it at the same time discards half the transmitters of characteristics. The sperm cell does the same.

In this process, Conklin argues, half of the inheritances from the woman and half the inheritances from the man are eliminated. The result is that the offspring of a man and a woman does not retain all of the characteristics of the mother and all of the characteristics of the father, but only half the characteristics of the mother and half the characteristics of the father.

Now, when my son's sperm cell fuses with the ovum cell of his wife, it is possible, but according to the law of chances extremely improbable, that all of the chromosomes eliminated from his sperm cell may be those derived from me and that the cell retains only the chromosomes which he has received from his mother.

Therefore, it is possible that a man may be the grandfather of a child that has not in his or her composition and characteristics a single characteristic or attribute derived from this grandfather.

According to the law of chances, however, half of the transmitter chromosomes of the father and half of the transmitter chromosomes of the mother will pass into the new being.

But as it is believed to be proven that chromosomes are individual particles, not divisible or not fusable, Conklin holds that no human being can be transmitted characteristics from more than 48 progenitors.

No child of a man or a woman can be identical with either parent. Individual characteristics, then, depend entirely upon the presence of the chromosomes in the particular ovum and sperm which fuse to form the oosperm.

Apparently a great deal depends upon the relative position of the chromosomes in a cell. Conklin estimated that the mere arrangement of these chromosomes in a cell might account for some 2 billion different characteristics in the children of two parents.

But the idea that struck me most forcibly was that such was the law of chances that it would be next to impossible for one of my descendants of 50 or 100 generations hence to have in his cells even one of the 48 character factors of myself.

DEDUCTIONS

The first law of nature is self-preservation.

The second law is reproduction.

It has been commonly enough argued that the second law is in reality an extension of the first law.

It is the instinct of nature common to every living organism to retain life as long as possible. If our children are in part ourselves, the process of procreation might be considered an instinctive effort to keep on living.

Maternal instinct at least and, probably to a smaller extent, paternal instinct is to protect offspring.

From the time my first child was born to me I became conscious of a feeling that the life of my child was as much a matter of concern to me as my own life. A similar feeling accompanied the birth of each of my children.

When my first grandchild was born I included him as a matter of supreme concern to myself.

I have sometimes wondered whether or not we do not have two separate and distinct relations to our children and grandchildren. The feeling of affection is not necessarily the only feeling of interest we have in our children. A man's affections may attach themselves to numerous human beings and even animals without regard to relation.

Paternal or grandfatherly affection may exercise great influence. It would seem to me that I have recognized, especially in myself, another link attaching the father or grandfather to a child other than that of affection.

It is often said that mother love is different from father love and that generally the interest of a parent or grandparent in a child or grandchild is rather personal pride or vanity. I thought it just possible that a father's feelings toward his children and a grandfather's feelings toward his grandchildren had the same motive as that which prompts a man to preserve his own life, his own comfort, his own reputation.

When the son of a worthy father behaves badly the father feels himself humiliated perhaps to the same extent, or nearly to the same extent, as he would feel if he had been discovered in some unworthy action himself.

I think it is usually the case that a father is more interested in his sons than his daughters, and that he is far more interested in the children of his sons than he is in the children of his daughters.

This attitude of the father or the grandfather is not biological. I imagine it is owing to personal pride. His son's succeeding in life, succeeding in obtaining the admiration of others, will redound more to the credit of the father whose name he bears than will that of the daughter who may bear the name of another man. Those of his grandsons who bear his own name and who become distinguished will add something to his own credit.

If, however, all the world becomes instructed, and if Conklin's hypothesis is universally accepted as the truth, then half a man's satisfaction and his love for his son's achievements are lost and three-fourths of his enjoyment of his grandson's achievements are lost.

The veriest nincompoop might well be the grandfather or great-grandfather of the ablest of men. The most worthy and eminent of men frequently have grandchildren who bring shame on the name. Such a grandson is described as a degenerate.

The probability is that such a young scapegrace has not degenerated at all and that he is fully up to the standard of those of his ancestors who in their time were no better than he.

One of the greatest promptings to energetic and honorable living that a man can have is that of family pride. If his immediate forebears have been eminent and numbers of other members of his family have been eminent, he is driven to strive energetically to become of equally good repute.

Now, if the children or grandchildren of great men or individuals of a prominent family begin life with a realization that society expects no more of them than of any other member of the same society, they will be deprived of this urge.

For myself, I am planning to do all I can to secure the prosperity and high position in the community not only of my children and grandchildren but of other descendants, just as thousands of other fathers of families are doing. But when Conklin convinces me, if he does convince me, that there is a possibility of my grandchildren being in no part myself and that the probabilities are great that many of my great-grandchildren will inherit nothing from me excepting my name and my fortune, my motive will be weakened if not entirely destroyed.

These confounded scientists have taken away too much from us, a good deal more perhaps than they have given us in the way of knowledge.

That man Freud has pretty nearly completely disgusted me with humanity as a whole.

Mental Standards

[*May 24, 1921*]

In Chapter III, headed "The Biological Bases of Democracy," Edwin Grant Conklin's book, *The Direction of Human Evolution,*[19] appear the following paragraphs:

The mental tests used in our army revealed a surprising amount of illiteracy, and, what is much worse, an alarmingly low level of average intelligence. These tests were devised to measure intellectual capacity or inherited ability rather than acquired information or education, and for the first time they give us a means of estimating the approximate number of persons in this country of low, mean, or high intelligence. The tests were of two sorts, the Alpha test for those who could read and write, the Beta test for all others. These tests were taken by about one million and seven hundred thousand drafted men, who may be assumed to have been somewhat above the average intelligence of the entire population since none who were evidently feeble-minded were drafted. Seven grades were recognized, ranging from A to D–, these grades being designated as follows: A "very superior intelligence," B "superior," C+ "high average," C "average," C– "low average," D "inferior," D– "very inferior." The "mental ages" of these different grades and the relative numbers in each are shown in the following table:

GRADE	MENTAL AGE	PER CENT OF WHOLE
A	18–19	4½
B	16–17	9
C+	15	16½
C	13–14	25
C–	12	20
D	11	15
D–	10	10

[19] Edwin Grant Conklin, *The Direction of Human Evolution*. Scribner's, New York, 1921.

Assuming that these drafted men are a fair sample of the entire population of approximately 100 millions, this means that 45 millions, or nearly one-half of the whole population, will never develop mental capacity beyond the stage represented by a normal twelve-year-old child, and that only 13½ millions will ever ever show superior intelligence.

When it is remembered that mental capacity is inherited, that parents of low intelligence generally produce children of low intelligence and that on the average they have more children than persons of high intelligence, and, furthermore, when we consider that the intellectual capacity or "mental age" can be changed very little by education we are in a position to appreciate the very serious condition which confronts us as a nation.

Note what is called the "mental ages" in the tables.

Now, what is meant in this case by "mental age"?

Hitherto, in reading sections of similar subjects I have presumed that when they would say, for instance, that a person was of a mental age of 12, that what was meant was that this person had the intelligence of the *average* 12-year-old boy (or girl).

But from the foregoing table it would appear that the age standard used is not the average, but is some arbitrarily adopted standard.

The author plainly states that the 1,700,000 American conscripts were really about the average of all of the men of similar age in the country.

When the psychiatrist says of this or that person that he has a mentality of a 12-year or 14- or 16- or 18-year-old youth, what particular youth does he refer to?

It seems probable to me that the standard adopted in this case is the intelligence of those youths or men who are very superior and who represent only 4½ per cent of the men examined. That would be equivalent to saying that all the men included below "C–" in the table had only about two-thirds of the intelligence of the "A" class.

It appears that in the case of the tests made of the members of the Army the object was to measure intellectual capacity and inherited ability rather than acquired education or information.

Granting this, what standard was adopted as the basis from which to measure intellectual capacity or inherited ability? Was the standard a purely biological one, viz., that intellectual capacity which would enable its owner to maintain life and succeed in procreating under any and all conditions to which a human being might be exposed?

Such a standard might be, and I think certainly would be, an entirely different standard than that which would be adopted by a purely military man — a man who would value other men according to their ability in warfare to kill enemies and preserve their own and associates' lives.

But both the biological and the military standards would be entirely different from such a standard as would be adopted by, say, an educator. The educator would value men according to their ability to acquire skill as gatherers and disseminators of knowledge and in training other men's minds to think correctly, say, in philosophy of mathematics or any other science.

But all of these foregoing mental standards would be entirely different from the standard that would be selected by what is called the businessman. The latter would choose as his standard a capacity to make money, a capacity to correctly value from a monetary point of view things that he would buy and sell or things that he would make to sell, and in making things to sell, capacity to make things cheaply and sell dearly.

All human activities are directed by the intelligence (not only the knowledge) — by the capacity to use knowledge so as to make activity more or less effective. From the ditch-digger to the chief executive of a great nation, the same rule applies.

Observe any two laborers excavating a trench and you will find that their effectiveness is only to a small extent dependent upon their respective muscular strength. One man will use his pick to loosen a larger quantity of earth than the other man and that, too, as a result of his mental processes: his calculations as to the nature of the earth he is dealing with, as to the weight of his tool, as to the sharpness of its cutting edge or penetrating point. Then observe these two men handling their shovels or spades. With approximately equal muscular effort the two men will lift from the trench different quantities of earth. One man, by reason of taking a certain bodily posture, will be able to take more advantage of the principle of the lever than the other. One man will so judge of the character of the earth he is removing, its physical shape, as to get more earth on his implement than the other.

It has happened that I have had personal intercourse with a number of men who are called psychologists or psychiatrists — men who are supposed by themselves and others to be skilled in appraising intelligence. Several of these acquaintances of mine happened to be among those who were engaged in prosecuting these tests of the intellect or intelligence of the American Army.

In truth, we are all psychologists, although many of us do not really know what the word psychology means, and still more of us who do not know the Greek root word on which has been built our own word, psychology.

I am one of these psychologists, of course.

I have had the opportunity (and have made use of it) of testing the mental capacity of my psychologist friends. I can truthfully say that, according to my standards of mental capacity, nearly all of these men are mentally so defective that I could not honestly place them as high as grade C plus. As specialists some of them might be given the grade of A.

Usually I have found that, as all men are specialists, all men not congenitally or by reason of accident possessed of an incomplete nervous organism, can, according to the standard adopted, be graded in all the classifications from A to D minus. From a purely biological standard nearly the whole of that 4½ per cent that have been ranked as Class A by the examiners of the American Army intellect are not entitled to a grade much if any above C minus.

Biologically speaking, the highest grade of men are those who can subsist under the most adverse circumstances and propagate. (The first law of nature is self-preservation; the second, propagate the species.)

I have had a comparatively wide acquaintance with college and university professors, with lawyers, with doctors, with clergymen, with artists and with literary men — the so-called intelligentsia. Regarded as a class, I know no other term so descriptive than that of economic imbeciles.

The first law of nature is self-preservation. Economics is a highbrow description of the science of keeping alive.

Yet it is among the members of the intelligentsia that we find the greatest number of those whose whole mode of living tends to shorten their lives. Those amongst them who live to ripe old age owe their good fortune in this respect to two causes — one, inherited longevity; and the other, to the protection and care given to them by their fellowmen.

The second law of nature is the propagation of the species and yet the most barren of all of our men and women are those who are supposed to know and claim to know more than their fellows, and who believe themselves and are believed by others to be able to think the straightest — the most correctly.

I remember in my reading of Herbert Spencer a statement of his to the effect that if the ability to play chess was rewarded more highly than any other ability, then everyone would endeavor to play chess well. If the ability to play chess was made the standard of excellence, our Army would have had a different grade.

For centuries in China the means of obtaining political and hence economic success has been the learning by rote of the Chinese classics.

My own personal observation, coupled with a fair amount of reading of a number of scientific books, has been continually impressing upon me the conviction that there is but slight difference in the inherited nature and potential intellectual capacity between any two human beings, male or female.

The effects of environment begin perhaps in the instance of conjugation of ovum and sperm. The mother in one case, by reason of the influence of environment, may be more or less capable of nourishing the embryo, the foetus, the developing child. From the moment of birth no two children are subject to the same environment, that is to say, extraneous influences, during the whole course of their life. This environment affects the physical body slightly as compared with its effect upon the psychic, the mentality. Just as each of the eggs of the queen bee that are not male is susceptible of being developed into a queen bee, so are all eggs of the female of the human species — after being vitalized by the sperm — susceptible of being developed mentally into adolescent individuals of any of the grades used by the Army classifications from A to D minus.

A pin prick, a slight overpressure of the obstetrical forceps, or an infinitely small disease germ might have made of Benjamin Franklin a common ditch-digger. Any one of millions of occurrences might have so influenced the mentality of Ben Franklin as a child in such a way as to have caused him to have been one of the humblest and least effective men of his time.

REFERENCE MATTER

Appendix A

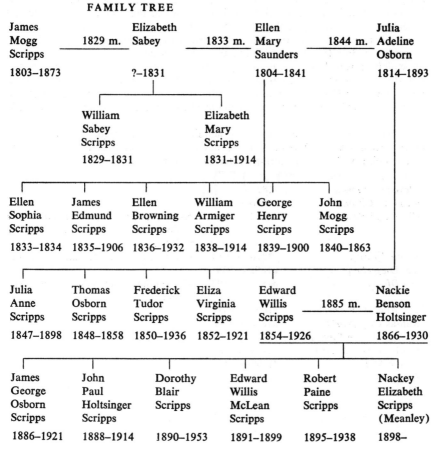

FAMILY TREE

James Mogg Scripps 1803–1873	1829 m.	Elizabeth Sabey ?–1831	1833 m.	Ellen Mary Saunders 1804–1841	1844 m.	Julia Adeline Osborn 1814–1893

William
Sabey
Scripps
1829–1831

Elizabeth
Mary
Scripps
1831–1914

Ellen Sophia Scripps 1833–1834	James Edmund Scripps 1835–1906	Ellen Browning Scripps 1836–1932	William Armiger Scripps 1838–1914	George Henry Scripps 1839–1900	John Mogg Scripps 1840–1863

Julia Anne Scripps 1847–1898	Thomas Osborn Scripps 1848–1858	Frederick Tudor Scripps 1850–1936	Eliza Virginia Scripps 1852–1921	Edward Willis Scripps 1854–1926	1885 m.	Nackie Benson Holtsinger 1866–1930

James George Osborn Scripps 1886–1921	John Paul Holtsinger Scripps 1888–1914	Dorothy Blair Scripps 1890–1953	Edward Willis McLean Scripps 1891–1899	Robert Paine Scripps 1895–1938	Nackey Elizabeth Scripps (Meanley) 1898–

Appendix B

THE E. W. SCRIPPS NEWSPAPERS

The following table lists only those newspapers and services owned by E. W. Scripps and his associates during his lifetime, beginning with the Cleveland *Penny Press* in 1878. To avoid confusion because of the sometimes complicated genealogy of a newspaper, the table shows only the date of founding or acquisition of a newspaper and the date and method of disposition for those that no longer exist. For the sake of simplicity, each newspaper is listed by the name by which it was last known during Scripps' lifetime, with notations in the right-hand column as to changes in name since that time. The Scripps-Howard additions after Scripps' death in March, 1926, are not shown here, but the Scripps-Howard Newspapers as of 1965 are listed in the introduction to Journalism.

Abbreviations: *f* — founded; *a* — acquired; *m* — merged; *s* — sold; *k* — killed. An asterisk (*) denotes those newspapers the control of which passed to the heirs of James G. Scripps after his death in 1921.

Cleveland *Press*	*f*1878–	
St. Louis *Chronicle*	*f*1880–*s*1908	
Cincinnati *Post*	*a*1881–	Known as the *Post and Times-Star* since absorption of *Times-Star* in 1958.
Kentucky *Post*	*f*1890–*m*1914	Combined with Cincinnati *Post*, 1914.
San Diego *Sun*	*a*1892–*s*1939	
San *Diegan*	*a*1892–*m*1892	Merged immediately with San Diego *Sun*.
*Los Angeles *Record*	*f*1895–*s*1933	
Kansas City *World*	*a*1896–*k*1908	
Scripps-McRae Press Assoc.	*f*1897–*m*1907	See United Press.
San Francisco *Report*	*a*1899–*k*1900	
*Seattle *Star*	*f*1899–*s*1942	
Akron *Press*	*f*1899–*m*1925	
Akron *Times*	*a*1925–*m*1925	
Akron *Times-Press*	*m*1925–*s*1938	
Scripps News Assoc.	*f*1899–*m*1907	See United Press.
Chicago *Press*	*f*1900–*k*1900	

Newspaper Enterprise Assoc. *f*1902–
Des Moines *News*   *a*1902–*s*1924
*Spokane *Press*   *f*1902–*s*1939
San Francisco *News*   *f*1903–*s*1962   The *News* was merged with Hearst's
                                                  Call-Bulletin in 1959, and Scripps-
                                                  Howard disposed of its interest in
                                                  the *News-Call-Bulletin* in 1962.
Toledo *News-Bee*   *a*1903–*s*1938   The *News* and *Bee* were acquired sep-
                                                  arately on the same date and
                                                  merged immediately.
*Tacoma *Times*   *f*1903–*s*1949
Columbus *Citizen*   *a*1904–*m*1959   Merged with the *Journal* in 1959 to
                                                  form the morning *Citizen-Journal*.
Sacramento *Star*   *f*1904–*k*1925
Fresno *Tribune*   *f*1905–*k*1912
Denver *Express*   *f*1906–*m*1926   In November, 1926, Scripps-Howard
                                                  bought the morning *Rocky Moun-
                                                  tain News* and afternoon *Times*,
                                                  which had been under a single own-
                                                  ership; the *Express* and *Times* were
                                                  merged to form the *Evening News*,
                                                  which was published from 1926 un-
                                                  til its sale to Denver *Post* in 1928.
Evansville *Press*   *f*1906–
Publishers Press   *a*1906–*m*1907   See United Press.
Pueblo *Sun*   *f*1906–*k*1910
Terre Haute *Post*   *f*1906–*s*1929
*Dallas *Dispatch*   *f*1906–*s*1938
*Portland *News*   *f*1906–*s*1939
Oklahoma *News*   *f*1906–*k*1939
Memphis *Press*   *f*1907–*m*1926   Scripps-Howard acquired the Memphis
                                                  News-Scimitar in November, 1926,
                                                  and merged it with the *Press* to form
                                                  the present *Press-Scimitar*
Nashville *Times*   *f*1906–*k*1907
Berkeley *Independent*   *a*1907–*k*1913
United Press Assoc.   *f*1907–   Formed by merging SMPA, SNA, and
                                                  Publishers Press; became United
                                                  Press International upon absorption
                                                  of International News Service in
                                                  1958.
Newspaper Supply Co.   *f*1907–   Renamed Scripps-Howard Supply Co.,
                                                  1929.
Oakland *Mail*   *f*1909–*k*1910
Chicago *Day Book*   *f*1911–*k*1917
Houston *Press*   *f*1911–*s*1964
Philadelphia *News-Post*   *f*1912–*k*1914
Birmingham *Post*   *f*1921–*k*1950   Published as morning *Post-Herald*
                                                  since 1950.
Norfolk *Post*   *f*1921–*k*1924

Fort Worth *Press*	*f*1921–	
Washington *Daily News*	*f*1921–	
Knoxville *News*	*f*1921–*m*1926	Scripps-Howard bought the Knoxville *Sentinel* in November, 1926, and merged it with the *News* to form the present *News-Sentinel*.
E. W. Scripps Co.	*f*1922–	
Newspaper Information Serv.	*f*1922–*k*1944	
Youngstown *Telegram*	*a*1922–*s*1936	
Indianapolis *Times*	*a*1922–*k*1965	
El Paso *Post*	*f*1922–*m*1931	Scripps-Howard acquired the *Herald* in 1931, and merged it with the *Post* to form the present *Herald-Post*.
Baltimore *Post*	*f*1922–*s*1934	
United Features Syndciate	*f*1923–	
Pittsburgh *Press*	*a*1922–	
New Mexico State Tribune	*a*1923–	Merged with Albuquerque *Journal* in 1933 and since published as Albuquerque *Tribune*.
United News Pictures	*f*1924–	Name changed to Acme Newspictures, Inc. in 1926; Acme was merged into NEA Service, Inc. in 1946 and then sold to United Press in 1951.

Bibliography

PRIMARY SOURCES

Scripps v. *Sweeney, Record,* Wayne County Circuit Court, Docket No. 28,906, Mich., 1905; *Scripps* v. *Sweeney* 160 Mich. 148, 125 N.W. 72 (1910). This material consists of 2 volumes printed by the Record Printing Co., Detroit, 1909. The volumes contain testimony and documents introduced in the Circuit Court of Wayne County in a suit (William A. Scripps *v.* John S. Sweeney) over disposition of the interests in the Quadripartite, occasioned by the death of George H. Scripps. The trial was first heard in 1905, and appealed to the Michigan Supreme Court in 1910.

Scripps, E W., to Ellen B. Scripps, 1873–1926. These letters — often long and profusely detailed — provide the best self-revelation of Scripps to be found anywhere. Because of his attachment and devotion to his half sister, as well as because of a certain emotional dependence upon her, Scripps kept her informed of every move, and, it seems, almost his every thought. Until 1900, the letters are in his broad-stroked scrawl; after 1900, the letters are typewritten and, as with his other writings, not revised or reviewed after dictation, nor signed. The number of letters declined considerably after 1900 when both were living in the same neighborhood — she at La Jolla, he at "Miramar" — with a Sunday visit a regular part of his routine. Consequently, the only time he wrote her after 1900 was during a trip by one or the other, or in connection with business matters. Beginning with his move to Washington in 1917, the steady flow of letters was resumed and was continued throughout his years on the yacht. Filling the better part of a file drawer at "Miramar" in California, these letters must be regarded as the most valuable personal documents that Scripps left.

Scripps, E. W., to Nackey Elizabeth Scripps, 1915. At her ranch adjoining "Miramar," Mrs. Thomas (Nackey Scripps) Meanley permitted the editor to use letters which she selected from among those received from her father while she was away at school in 1915. They provide additional insight into Scripps, inasmuch as he sought in some of the letters to convey his ideas and reasoning to his daughter. Additional letters to Mrs. Meanley were found in the Letterbooks and used from that source.

Scripps, E. W., "Autobiography." This is a 626-page typescript filed at "Miramar" in California. Dictated in 1915, it was read, and corrected at one place, by Ellen B. Scripps, but apparently was not reviewed or revised by Scripps. It pro-

769

vides a skeleton account of his life, lacking the additional details that would make it a genuine autobiography. It also includes the text of several autobiographical disquisitions which he had dictated previously. This version is *not* to be confused with the "Autobiographical Notes," which was prepared by Gilson Gardner. Indeed, the "Notes" should be disregarded by future researchers entirely, because of Scripps' conviction that Gardner had deleted what Gardner considered to be unfavorable observations in the "Autobiography" and retained only those portions which placed Scripps in a good light.

Scripps, E. W., "History of the Scripps League." Written in 1889 and filed in the E. W. Scripps Trust office in Cincinnati, this 170-page bound typescript is a curious document. Although it contains some apparently valuable data, and the editor made use of some of it, Scripps' motive in writing it remains obscure. He disclaimed any intention of justifying himself in the controversy with James E. Scripps in 1889–90, but it actually does represent a justification of Scripps and a criticism of James E. It should be borne in mind that Scripps wrote this account at a time of great emotional upset, because of the rupture with his elder half brother. The account sometimes is contradictory in itself, and does flatly contradict, or is contradicted by, other and later accounts. For instance, in comparing this account with the "Autobiography" and autobiographical disquisitions, one will find considerable variance in Scripps' accounts of how he happened to go to Detroit in 1872, how strong was his ambition to be a journalist, and just where the drugstore arrangement fitted into the general scheme of things at that time. Moreover, the letters from James E. which are included in this volume are not all transcribed fully or accurately. At that time, Scripps had employed his first secretary, and it may be that he merely told the secretary to transcribe this letter and that, thus possibly making the transcription errors the fault of the unidentified secretary. Nevertheless, the errors are there. For that reason and the others stated, this account must be used with circumspection.

Scripps, E. W., Letterbooks. At "Miramar," these 60 volumes, representing about 37,500 pages, contain letters written by Scripps from the late 1890's until 1926, with copies pasted into the books. Most of the volumes are numbered, but 5 are identified by letter, and 7 by a combination of number and letter. On microfilm, they fill 30 reels. Almost exclusively, the Letterbooks contain correspondence to business associates, friends, and men of kindred interests, although a few letters to family members show up here and there. The big missing gap in Scripps' correspondence file is his letters to James E. During the 1870's and 1880's, Scripps wrote longhand letters, without retaining copies. The editor made an effort to find his letters to James E. in Detroit, but was informed that no such file existed among the James E. Scripps papers. Some selected replies to Scripps' letters have been drawn from other files at "Miramar." Scripps spasmodically dictated diary entries, such as "Diary Notes," which are included in the Letterbooks; such entries are few and far between, and are titled variously.

Scripps, E. W., "Writings." These are the 12 bound volumes in typescript of Scripps' disquisitions, short stories, and plays, averaging about 400 pages per volume. Scripps' writings were kept in the E. W. Scripps Trust office in Cincinnati from Scripps' death in 1926 until 1947. In 1947 Robert F. Winkler, secretary-treasurer of the Trust, had the individual writings bound into four sets of 12 volumes each for distribution within the family. The originals are in the bound set in the Cincinnati office. For the other sets, some disquisitions had to be retyped from faded originals; consequently, page numbers of the bound originals and carbons do not always coincide; page numbers referred to in footnotes in this book are those of the original set. Scripps included some letters among his disquisitions, thus indicating the value he placed on the points of view expressed in those letters. In both the disquisitions and Letterbooks, some letters were marked "unsent"; the fact that they were thus retained and filed was interpreted to mean that Scripps placed some value on the comments made therein, but did not feel disposed to express those ideas to his correspondent at that time.

Scripps, Ellen B., to E. W. Scripps, 1873–1926. Only slightly smaller in bulk than his letters to her, the "Miramar" file of letters from Ellen B. provides an illuminating counterbalance to his letters. Her deep love for him did not obscure the clarity of her understanding, nor did she permit it to stand in the way of cutting candor when he needed a point of view beyond the rim of his egocentrism. Also, these letters help round out the picture of the early years when he was in Cleveland, St. Louis, or Cincinnati, by showing the thinking and plans of James E. and George H. in Detroit. Read by themselves, these letters give an incisive view of Scripps. Read in conjunction, the two groups of letters make Scripps emerge as a rounded figure in a manner that no other documents, or secondary works, have achieved.

Scripps, James E., to Ellen B. Scripps, 1865–1900. Most of these few letters on file at "Miramar" deal with family matters, but become of value occasionally with reference to Scripps.

Scripps, James E., to Ellen B. Scripps, George H. Scripps, Milton A. McRae, and Willis Osborn. Without any indication that it is a complete file of letters received, these letters are in two folders in the "Miramar" File House. They are of particular importance in regard to the family-business tensions of the late 1880's and early 1890's. Osborn was one of several relatives drawn into the family's enterprises, working on the business side of the Cleveland *Press* at the time these letters were written.

Smithton, Harry L., "Notes." The Notes are in a folder, in the possession of his widow, Mrs. Edna Smithton, of La Jolla, Calif. The folder is headed "Scripps Genealogy and Notes for Preparation of Trial. HLS's Copy." The trial referred to was the unsuccessful contest of E. W. Scripps' will by Mrs. Josephine Scripps, the widow of James G. Scripps, in 1928.

Smithton, Harry L., "Notes by H. L. Smithton on Gilson Gardner's Book Entitled *Lusty Scripps; Life of E. W. Scripps.*" This 15-page typescript in the Cincinnati office files is, in the main, an attack upon the accuracy of Gardner's book. Smithton makes at least one telling comment: "This book must be considered as but *one* biography of E. W. Scripps. No one story of the life of E. W. Scripps can be complete." Otherwise, the attack is generally unfair. For instance, Smithton denies as untrue statements which Gardner took directly from Scripps' "Autobiography." The conclusion which this document forces is that Smithton, long Scripps' secretary, is reliable for those aspects of Scripps' life that came under his observation, but that he was not sufficiently informed of the contents of documents in Scripps' files to make him a reliable witness or critic in regard to other aspects.

INTERVIEWS

Elfstrom, E. F., publisher of the Fullerton (Calif.) *News-Tribune*, who was Scripps' secretary (1922–24) and later "supercargo" aboard the yacht.

Fox, Dr. Denis L., Professor of Biochemistry, Scripps Institution of Oceanography, who knew Professor W. E. Ritter.

Hawkins, Mrs. Margaret C., the widow of Robert P. Scripps.

Howard, Roy W., former president of the Scripps-Howard Newspapers.

Meanley, Mrs. Nackey Scripps, the last survivor among Scripps' children.

BIOGRAPHIES

Cochran, Negley D., *E. W. Scripps*. Harcourt, Brace and Co., New York, 1933. The best-rounded of the three biographies, Cochran's book fails to make full use of the great amount of Scripps' primary materials, particularly the family correspondence. It is particularly weak when dealing with the early years of Scripps' career, and is entirely non-critical in dealing with the later years.

Gardner, Gilson, *Lusty Scripps; The Life of E. W. Scripps*. Vanguard Press, New York, 1932. Gardner's biography likewise fails to make use of anything other than the obvious "Autobiography," but is valuable for throwing light on some of his own activities, under Scripps' orders, and for his evaluation of Scripps.

McCabe, Charles R. (ed.), *Damned Old Crank; A Self-Portrait of E. W. Scripps Drawn from His Unpublished Writings*. Harper and Brothers, New York, 1951. Emphasizing mostly the flamboyant and sensational, this volume is a hodgepodge of disquisitions and selections from the "Autobiography," put together in such a way that the resulting product retains the integrity of unity of neither the disquisitions nor the "Autobiography."

BOOKS

Curti, Merle E., *The Growth of American Thought*, 2nd ed. Harper and Brothers, New York, 1951.

Faulkner, Harold U., *The Quest for Social Justice, 1898–1914*. Macmillan Co., New York, 1931.

Filler, Louis, *Crusaders for American Liberalism*. Antioch Press, Yellow Springs, Ohio, 1950.

Goldman, Eric F., *Rendezvous with Destiny; A History of Modern American Reform*. Alfred A. Knopf, New York, 1952 (Vintage Books, New York, 1956).

Harlow, Alvin F., *The Serene Cincinnatians*. Dutton and Co., New York, 1950.

Hofstadter, Richard, *The Age of Reform*. Alfred A. Knopf, New York, 1955 (Vintage Books, New York, 1960).

Kennedy, Charles E., *Fifty Years of Cleveland . . . 1875–1925*. Weidenthal Co., Cleveland, 1925.

McGeary, M. Nelson, *Gifford Pinchot, Forester-Politician*. Princeton Univ. Press, Princeton, 1960.

McRae, Milton A., *Forty Years in Newspaperdom; The Autobiography of a Newspaper Man*. Brentano's, New York, 1924. This is valuable in giving the other side of the picture, but Scripps thought McRae had claimed too much for himself in the book, although he conceded that any man probably would have taken the same kind of self-view. Ellen B. Scripps had the impression that W. H. Porterfield, editor-in-chief of Scripps' California papers, had edited the McRae book.

Pinchot, Amos R. E., *History of the Progressive Party, 1912–1916*, ed. with a biographical introduction by Helene Maxwell Hooker. New York Univ. Press, New York, 1958.

Pinchot, Gifford, *Breaking New Ground*. Harcourt, Brace and Co., New York, 1947.

Ritter, Mary Bennett (Mrs. W. E.), *More Than Gold in California, 1849–1933*. Professional Press, Berkeley, 1933.

Ritter, William E., *Charles Darwin and the Golden Rule*, comp. and ed. by Edna Watson Bailey. Science Service, Washington, 1954. The Preface is of particular value. Written by Miss Bailey, it contains excerpts from an unpublished essay written by Ritter about Scripps and his relationship with him.

Rose, William G., *Cleveland; The Making of a City*. World Pub. Co., New York and Cleveland, 1950.

Schroeder, Theodore A., *Free Speech for Radicals*. Free Speech League, New York, 1916.

Steffens, Lincoln, *The Autobiography of Lincoln Steffens*. Harcourt, Brace and Co., New York, 1931.

PERIODICALS

———, "Life and Death of Edward W. Scripps, Pioneer Genius of Free Press," *Editor and Publisher*, Mar. 20, 1926. A hurriedly assembled obituary, inaccurate in some details.

Eastman, Max, "My Friend E. W.," *The Freeman*, Jan. 11, 1954.

Irwin, Will, "The American Newspaper, a Study of Journalism in Its Relation to the Public," *Collier's National Weekly*, Jan. 21; Feb. 4, 18; Mar. 4, 18; Apr. 1, 22; May 6, 27; June 3, 17; July 1, 8, 22, 29, 1911.

Ritter, William E., "The Relation of E. W. Scripps to Science," *Science*, Mar. 25, 1927.

Ritter, William E., "Science Service and E. W. Scripps' Philosophy of Life," *General Science*, Dec. 25, 1926.

Sumner, Francis B. "William Emerson Ritter: Naturalist and Philosopher," *Contrib. Scripps Inst. Oceanography*, No. 223 (Vol. 10, Pt. 1, 1944), reprint from *Science*, Apr. 28, 1944.

Index

82, 194, 247, 251, 261; appraised, 12, 55–56, 81–82, 246–53 *passim*; and AP, 197; attacked by mob, 54; Cincinnati *Post*, 53–57 *passim*, 248; custody of John Paul Scripps, 86; dismissed, 82, 187, 210, 211; "McRaeism," 82, 207; power of attorney withdrawn, 212; reputation, 82; retirement, 83, 212, 246, 261; and EWS, 59, 62, 80, 188, 212, 330; and Taft, 440; mentioned, 222. *See also* Scripps-McRae League; Scripps-McRae Press Association; Scripps-McRae Telegram Co.

McVicar, John, 64

Madero, Francisco, 512

Mahan, Capt. Alfred Thayer: cited, 250, 290

Mallock, W. H., 677, 678

Malthus, Thomas Robert: cited, 433

Man: attributes, 263, 681, 731, 735; defined, 172, 176, 229, 550, 555, 585, 594, 613, 620, 650, 680, 699, 713, 723, 726, 729; human nature, 257; intelligence, 761; mental conflicts, 744–45; EWS and nature of, 723, 732; self-preservation, 372, 693–94; value, sense of, 714. *See also* Humanity

Manley, Basil, 702

Marine Biological Association, San Diego, 725

Marryat, Frederick, 145

Martin, Earle, 344

Martyrs, 319

Marx, Karl: quoted, 607; mentioned, 147

Massachusetts: wealth in, 678–84 *passim*

Masses. *See* Common people

Masses, The: EWS helps finance, 356–57, 358

Materialism, 633, 724

Matter, 633, 645

Meanley, Nackey Scripps (Mrs. Thomas M., daughter of EWS): birth, 74; business ability, 284; home, 136; marriage, 84–85, 209; mentioned, 104

Meanley, Thomas Meredith (son-in-law of EWS), 85, 136

Medicine: research, 724

Mediocrity: discussed, 150–55

Mellon, Andrew, 499

Memory, 121

Memphis *Commercial-Appeal*, 213

Memphis *Press*, 79, 203, 211

Memphis *Press-Scimitar*, 213

Mendel's law: analogy to, 155; promulgated, 724; summarized, 753

Merchant marine, 535. *See also* Ship subsidy

Meredith, George, 340

Metaphysicians: view of "force," 744

Metaphysics: province of, 747; and EWS, 733

Mexican farm laborers in U.S., 686–87

Mexico: annexation, domination by U.S., 512, 553; revolution in, 396–97

Militarism, 434–35

Military service: registration for, 567; universal, 513, 558–60

Milton, John, 122, 340

Mines: government inspection, 273

Minneapolis *Daily News*, 211

Minot, Charles S.: cited, 414; mentioned, 677

"Miramar": building of, 72–74; citrus cultivation, 74, 84, 222; dams, 74; development of, 166; expenditures for, 654, 655, 656; forestation, 74, 84, 442, 616–19; itinerants at, 447; maintenance of, 77, 105, 136, 221, 223, 262; vigilantes march on, 447; visitors, 5. *See also* Highway construction; Scripps, E. W., Family

Miscegenation: alternatives to, 433

Miserliness, 740

Missouri Press Association, 238

Mobs: attack EWS, 319, 321

Mohammed: as reformer, 739; mentioned, 286

Monarchy: hereditary, 389; nature of, 393; tendencies of, 557

Money: acquiring of, 262, 263, 409, 708, 717, 718; concept analyzed, 712–14; currency reform, 273; deflation, 710–11; inflation, 710; and property, 710; question settled in 1896, 460

Monogamy: origin of, 416

Monopoly: news, 80; opposition to, 260, 300, 492

Monroe Doctrine: southern boundary of, 521; German navy to test, 512

Montaigne, Michel E.: EWS compared with, 357

Morality, 740

Morals: analyzed, 734–42; EWS concern with, 732

CORRECTION

P. 213, for the last two lines before the break in the page, substitute the following:

Pittsburgh *Press,* Hollywood (Fla.) *Sun-Tattler,* Stuart (Fla.) *News,* and Washington *Daily News.* It also embraced UPI, NEA, United Features Syndicate, three radio and four television stations.